Instructor's Manual with Test Bank

Life-Span Human Development

SEVENTH EDITION

Carol K. Sigelman
The George Washington University

Elizabeth A. Rider
Elizabethtown College

Prepared by

Bradley J. Caskey
University of Wisconsin - River Falls

WADSWORTH
CENGAGE Learning™

Australia • Brazil • Japan • Korea • Mexico • Singapore • Spain • United Kingdom • United States

For product information and technology assistance, contact us at
**Cengage Learning Customer & Sales Support,
1-800-354-9706**

For permission to use material from this text or product, submit all requests online at **www.cengage.com/permissions**
Further permissions questions can be emailed to
permissionrequest@cengage.com

ISBN-13: 978-1-111-35138-0
ISBN-10: 1-111-35138-4

Wadsworth
20 Davis Drive
Belmont, CA 94002-3098
USA

Cengage Learning is a leading provider of customized learning solutions with office locations around the globe, including Singapore, the United Kingdom, Australia, Mexico, Brazil, and Japan. Locate your local office at: **www.cengage.com/global**

Cengage Learning products are represented in Canada by Nelson Education, Ltd.

To learn more about Wadsworth, visit
www.cengage.com/wadsworth

Purchase any of our products at your local college store or at our preferred online store
www.cengagebrain.com

READ IMPORTANT LICENSE INFORMATION

Printed in the United States of America
1 2 3 4 5 6 7 15 14 13 12 11

CONTENTS

Part II: Test Bank

INTRODUCTION

Those of you familiar with the instructor resource materials that accompanied the 6th edition of Carol Sigelman and Elizabeth Rider's *Life-Span Human Development*, will notice a few changes in this Instructor's Manual and Test Bank. Once again, Dr. Brad Caskey, Professor of Psychology at the University of Wisconsin – River Falls, is on board as the author for all of the instructor resource materials. In this edition, he has continued with the basic look and feel of the 6th edition material but has expanded material throughout the text. He has also added some new features that should assist you in your class preparation.

As in past editions, the **Instructor's Resource Manual** portion of this text contains helpful information for teaching and classroom projects broken down by chapter. Below is a description of the types of supplements for each chapter.

Learning Objectives: The learning objectives can be used to help focus lecture content or as discussion or essay questions.

Chapter Outline: The detailed outline of each chapter may be used to help prepare lecture notes or may be used as is as a quick reference in the classroom.

Suggestions for Class Discussions or Projects: At least six suggestions for classroom discussion or student projects are presented for each chapter. In most cases, special materials and excessive preparation are not required.

Suggested Films and Videos: This section lists relevant films and videos, and includes their source, year of publication, type (e.g., DVD), length, and a brief description. The films and videos are varied and can be used to supplement lecture topics and exemplify concepts discussed in class or in the text.

Suggested Web Sites: There are five suggested web sites for each chapter. Each web site contains information that will assist you and/or your students in gaining a greater understanding of topics discussed within the text.

Suggested Readings: A set of five suggested readings are listed for each chapter with the majority coming from journal articles. The suggested readings can be used to strengthen your background on a lecture topic, or may be assigned as additional readings for students.

A **Test Bank** follows the chapter-by-chapter materials described previously. The test bank contains several different types of items that should be of use to faculty. Below is a description of the types of test items for each chapter and the epilogue.

MULTIPLE-CHOICE Questions: Each chapter contains 140 to 160 multiple-choice items from the text. These items are designed to assess knowledge for both the key terms as well as the major conceptual points. About half of the items are factual and assess basic terminology. The remaining items are conceptual in nature and assess student's ability to comprehend and apply the text information. Each of these items is keyed to the page(s) in the text containing the correct answer, a reference to the Learning Objective (e.g., LO 1.4) addressed by each item, and a descriptor of the estimated level of difficulty of each item (e.g., Easy, Moderate, Difficult). You will also note that we have embedded 20 items into the text bank that will be available to students via the Wadsworth Study Center on the world wide web at: http://academic.cengage.com/psychology/sigelman . Each web item has a WWW designator.

TRUE-FALSE Questions: Each chapter contains 20 true-false items from the text (including 5 WWW items). Each question contains the correct answer, a key to the text page from which it was derived, the learning objective covered, and the level of difficulty.

COMPLETION Questions: Each chapter contains 20 fill-in-the-blank items from the text (including 5 WWW items). The majority of these items are linked to the bolded terms found within each chapter summary. Each question contains the correct answer, a key to the text page from which it was derived, the learning objective covered, and the level of difficulty.

ESSAY Questions: Each chapter contains 10 essay items from the text (including 3 WWW items). These suggested essay items that address the major points and concepts from each chapter. Each question contains a reference to the text page(s) from which it was derived and the learning objective(s) covered. Three WWW items comes with a brief description of the key elements that students should address when answering the question.

FILM AND VIDEO SOURCES

Text resource:
APA (2000). Videos in Psychology: A Resource Directory. Washington, D.C.: American Psychological Association.

Company sources:

Annenberg/CPB Multimedia Collection

PO Box 2345
S. Burlington, VT 05407-2345
www.learner.org/catalog/catalog.html

Films for the Humanities and Sciences

P.O. Box 2053
Princeton, NJ 08543-2053
www.films.com

Insight Media
2162 Broadway
New York, NY 10024
www.insight-media.com/IMHome.htm

Magna Systems Inc.
330 Tesler Road
Lake Zurich, IL 60047
www.magnasystems.co

ASSESSMENT AND COURSE OBJECTIVES

Every instructor is faced with the difficult task of evaluating students. Specification of course objectives can facilitate the evaluation process. Assignments designed to assess specific objectives will provide the material necessary for an informed evaluation. In addition, the provision of course objectives to students at the beginning of the course will allow them to be clear about expectations. It might also be helpful to the instructor and the students to have a mid-term review of these objectives (perhaps including a student self-assessment of progress).

There are many ways to think about course objectives. A number of years ago, Benjamin Bloom introduced a useful taxonomy for classifying *cognitive* objectives. The six levels of this taxonomy are summarized below, along with an example of the type of question that would assess each particular level.

1. Knowledge--The ability to identify, recall, or recognize information
    EX: Define "accommodation"
2. Comprehension--The ability to demonstrate, explain, and rephrase information.
    EX: Explain the concept of accommodation in your own words.
3. Application--The ability to apply or generalize; to use the principles.
    EX: Indicate how accommodation relates to the process of equilibration.
4. Analysis--The ability to break a principle into component parts and understand how the parts relate; to analyze or deduce knowledge.
    EX: Discuss how Piaget's notion of nurture differs from Freud's.
5. Synthesis--The ability to put old knowledge together in new ways; to formulate or modify knowledge.
    EX: In what way(s) would Piaget's description of the preoperational stage need to be modified in order to better "fit" recent research in this area?
6. Evaluation--The ability to make judgments *based on knowledge*; to argue or to assess knowledge.
    EX: Assess the usefulness of Piaget's concept of equilibration and justify your response.

Bloom's taxonomy is hierarchical, yet overlapping. For example, analysis of a concept requires more sophisticated understanding than knowledge of that concept, but it is not isolated from earlier levels of understanding. Two frequently used formats for assessing cognitive objectives are multiple choice and essay questions. We often think that multiple-choice questions only assess lower levels of knowledge, but carefully constructed multiple-choice questions can assess higher levels of knowledge than poorly constructed essay questions. As noted earlier, a large number of the test bank items are designed to assess students above the basic "knowledge" level.

Bloom's taxonomy is only one way of thinking about course objectives. Not all course objectives are strictly cognitive, and tests are not the only method of evaluation. A list of course objectives might also include, for example: research skills; experience as a practitioner in the field; critical thinking skills; writing skills; increase in self-awareness; and ability to work as a team player. Some objectives might not be best assessed by a test, while the course projects in this Manual might prove useful. As an instructor, you will want to confirm that your evaluation methods fit your course goals. After considering your course objectives, tailor assessment materials so that it is possible to assess the student on the outcomes that you deem important.

When many of us think of our college experiences, we often remember sitting in a class taking notes while the professor stood at the front of the room lecturing on the material. Although this does not characterize all modern classrooms, lecturing is incorporated in many college courses. Even when lecturing is not used, students still need to keep a record of what took place in class. Unfortunately, students are often poor note-takers (this should come as no surprise to anyone who has taught even a single class). It should be obvious that students tend to perform poorly when they are asked to respond to information that they failed to record in their notes.

Note taking during class has two functions that are related to academic achievement. First, note taking increases attention, which increases encoding of material into long-term memory. The second function is to facilitate the review of class material, which is positively correlated with performance. Listed below are some suggestions and points to consider in order helping facilitate more effective note-taking by students. The points are also intended to make you think about techniques that you use in the classroom and perhaps discover ways to stimulate more active learning and better record keeping by students in your class.

1. Make students aware of the relationship between note-taking and academic performance. Note that the act of recording notes as well as the act of reviewing notes is important. The importance of reviewing increases as the interval of time between note-taking and test-taking increases.

2. In recording notes, more seems to be better than less. More notes and more ideas contained in the notes are related to higher achievement levels. However, this does not mean that students should try to take verbatim notes. Some research suggests that the relevant factor is not quantity of notes, but terseness of notes (having many ideas in few words).

3. Following one of the first classes, provide students with a model of complete and organized notes from that class. Allow them to compare their notes to this model and encourage them to modify their note-taking strategies on the basis of this comparison. Or, if time and class size permit, collect student's class notes for one class and provide individual feedback. This not only benefits students, but the instructor also gets useful information about the kinds of information that students record during a class.

4. Emphasize important ideas, repeat them, show them on an overhead, or write them on the board. Research has found that students record the vast majority of the material written on the board but only about half of the important ideas that were not written on the board.

5. Lecture rate has an inverse effect on note-taking such that the faster the rate, the fewer notes. Provide enough pauses during the lecture for students to keep up with the lecture in their note-taking.

6. Consider providing an outline of the lectures. Outlines provide an organizational structure for note-taking and allows students to see where you are in a lecture and where you are going. Research indicates, however, that handing out complete notes can actually lead to decreased

performance. Headings only, or the "bare skeleton" of notes, seem to be most effective because they provide students with some organization but also require students to be actively involved in taking their own notes.

7. If you are using PowerPoint slides in your course keep in mind that research has shown that students tend to view PowerPoint slides, in classes in which PowerPoint slides are the main mean of information presentation, as the ONLY thing that they need to takes notes on. This can lead to two note taking problems; 1) if slides contain only a brief outline, faculty need to emphasize the fact that the material that they expand upon when referring to the PowerPoint slide is just as important to record as the information on the slide, 2) if you use highly detailed slides you need to realize that students will likely be focused on recording verbatim the slide information at the expense of listening to you when you discuss the material.

8. Students record notes differently depending on whether they are anticipating an essay test or a multiple-choice test. Thus, it may be important that students know how they will be evaluated before they record notes on that material.

9. Students can benefit from rewriting their notes, and as they do, reorganizing them and integrating them with material from other sources, such as their textbook.

10. Finally, there are a number of excellent videos that are available for psychology classes. When a video is turned on, students often take this as a sign that they can put down their pens and mentally relax for the duration of the video. Sometimes this is an appropriate response, but if you wish to encourage more active listening, you might try giving students a set of notes for one of the first video clips shown in the semester. This allows students to see what your expectations are for the amount of detail that they should be watching for in videos. Outlines may also be useful for videos because the audio accompanying the video often moves faster than students can reasonably take good notes. Having a framework in front of them while they watch may enable students to get more out of the video.

WRITING IN PSYCHOLOGY

Improvement of writing skills may be an implicit or explicit goal in many college courses. Fortunately, most colleges and universities have resources that instructors can draw on to help students with their writing. There are, however, specific issues that may arise in undergraduate science courses, especially psychology courses. Perhaps most important is the issue of voice. It might be useful to draw distinctions early in the term between scientific papers and more personal papers/projects. Scientific papers tend to be written in the third person and rely upon empirical evidence generated using the scientific method. Personal papers may have an intimate voice and rely on anecdotal evidence and autobiographical information to support important points.

Students should be aware of these different types of writing, and the types of evidence on which each style depends. A discussion about scientific evidence might also include a discussion of the uses and misuses of the Internet, where information is not submitted to scientific review before dissemination to the public. Some students, particularly those interested in pursuing graduate studies, might appreciate the opportunity to practice writing in a more scientific style.

Writing groups might be organized to help students understand these distinctions in voice (as well as help each other with the other challenges of writing). Students working in groups of about three exchange papers, and write short critiques designed to strengthen their classmates' papers. These critiques might include responses to the following basic questions:
- What was interesting?
- What were you confused about?
- What would you like to know more about?

In addition, students might also help each other assess the appropriateness of their supporting evidence, or their ability to use APA style. Each student then rewrites the paper based on peer input before handing it in for the instructor's review. Instructors might wish to assess both the student's papers, and their critiques of their peers' papers. Guidelines for writing in APA style may be found on the Internet. One place to check out is: http://www.apastyle.org/

SUGGESTIONS FOR COURSE PROJECTS

Below are several suggestions for semester-long projects. Some of them require advance preparation, but offer the promise of enriching the course as a whole. In addition to these ideas, shorter projects specific to the material are presented in each chapter of the Instructor's Manual.

1. Community service: A community service (service learning) component will require some advance work in setting up placements, as well as the monitoring of placements throughout the course. There is, however, no substitution for the kind of hands-on, real-world learning that occurs in the field. Service learning can be a win-win situation in which the students' education is enhanced, and human service agencies are better able to meet the needs of the people they serve. For more information, you may want to check out the resources listed below.

Levesque-Bristol, C. (2009). Examining self-determination in a service learning course. *Teaching of Psychology*, 26(4), 262-266.

Lundy, B. L. (2007). Service learning in life-span developmental psychology: Higher exam scores and increased empathy. *Teaching of Psychology, 34(1)*. 23-27.

Marchel, C.A. (2004). Evaluating reflection and sociocultural awareness in service learning classes. *Teaching of Psychology, 31(2)*. 120-123.

2. Interviews: Another means of getting students into the field would be to have them conduct interviews (relating to the chapter under study) at daycare centers, preschools, nursing homes, or other agencies. Again, some advance work will be necessary to establish collaborative relationships with community agencies and organize the visits.

An alternative to visiting community agencies as a group would be to have students use the social networks that exist in the classroom to identify people of different age groups who might be observed or interviewed. A written report describing the data collected and interpreting and evaluating them in light of developmental psychology themes might be due at the end of the observation period. Alternatively, students might discuss their findings in classroom groups.

Students will need some background information on conducting interviews before they start, and ethics should be discussed as well. Below are a few articles that provide additional ideas on the use of observations and interviews:

X

McManus, J. L. (1986). "Live" case study/journal record in adolescent psychology. *Teaching of Psychology, 13*, 70-74.

Students meet with an adolescent approximately once a week and keep a journal record of their observations and interviews with this individual.

Schwanenflugel, P. J. (1987). An interview method for teaching adolescent psychology. *Teaching of Psychology, 14*, 167-168.

Describes a project in which students interview individuals to learn about adolescent development. Students begin by using several instructor-provided questions as guidelines. Following the interview, they prepare a written report interpreting the interview in light of topics/ideas covered in class.

Walton, M. D. (1988). Interviewing across the lifespan: A project for an adult development course. *Teaching of Psychology, 15*, 198-200.

Describes a project in which students interview five individuals from different phases of life and then write a paper using these data to illustrate developmental theory and research discussed in the course. Two purposes of the project are to apply theory and research to understand "real" people, and to develop interviewing skills useful in a variety of contexts.

Schwarzmueller, A. (2006). Interviews with primary-caregiving fathers via e-mail. *Teaching of Psychology, 33(4)*, 258-261.

Describes a project in which fathers were queried about various child developmental issues via e-mail.

Klinzing, D.G. (2006). A parent interview course assignment. *Teaching of Psychology, 33(3)*, 202-204.

Describes an assignment designed to increase students' knowledge of child development through interviews conducted with parents.

When considering the use of interview or observation projects, please keep in mind the potential research ethics concerns associated with using such techniques (e.g., children cannot give their own permission to participate in a study, recording participants without their permission is illegal). Before taking on any of these assignments, be sure to check with your college's or university's Institutional Review Board, Human Subjects Committee or equivalent committee, to get permission to conduct this type of research. This will save you from a lot of headaches and a potential lawsuit.

3. Current Events Portfolio: This assignment based on Rider (1992) involves keeping a notebook or file of current events relevant to developmental psychology from newspapers, magazines, television, or the internet. For each current event, students provide a brief description or explanation of how it is related to the psychological concepts covered in class or in the textbook. Portfolios can be assessed based on relevancy of the event, the accuracy of

student's comments, breadth of coverage, and creativity. The best portfolios are often those that have shown multiple interpretations of current events based on more than one theory or research concept.

Rider, E. (1992). Understanding and applying psychology through use of news clippings, *Teaching of Psychology, 19*, 161-163.

4. <u>Developmental Psychology in the Media (Television and the Internet)</u>: Students are continuously bombarded with media information concerning topics related to human development. In some cases this information is accurate and in other cases the information is "sketchy" at best. One way to help students develop effective evaluation skills is to have them write a paper or papers in which they critique a media report (television or internet) concerning some claim concerning human development. Hall and Seery (2006) provide some basic information on the rules students should use when evaluating media sources. Articles by Madsen, Van Abbema, Allen, and Schmidt (2006) and Roberts, Gomez, Kim and Corbin (2006) provide some information television portrayals. Goolkasian, Van Wallendael, and Gaultney (2003) present some interesting information on how to help students evaluate psychology-related websites.

Hall, S. S., and Seery, B. L. (2006). Behind the facts: Helping students evaluate media reports of psychological research. *Teaching of Psychology, 33(2),* 101-104.

Madsen, S.D., Van Abbema, D. L., Allen, C. C., and Schmidt, R.E. (2006). Questioning claims of baby genius: Students evaluate advertisements of infant stimulation products. *Teaching of Psychology, 33(2),* 134-136.

Roberts, M.C., Gomez, M.D., Kim, K.L. and Corbin, S.R. (2006). Dr. Phil visits the classroom: "Getting real" with child behavior and development. *Teaching of Psychology, 33(4),* 262-264.

5. <u>Thought Papers/ Important Points Paper</u>: For each chapter, or periodically during the semester, have students discuss what they view as the most important point from the textbook, and their rationale for selecting these points. If you are going to use student analyses as a basis for class discussion, it helps to have students commit to their ideas in writing before the class discussion (otherwise, there may be a quick consensus about what the important points are). Better yet, have students write short papers that are copied and exchanged with other class members before the discussion. Depending on the size of the class, papers can be distributed to everyone, or within small groups, or different groups of students might write papers and distribute them to everyone on different days. The student papers then become required reading before class. Encourage students to share not only ideas from their own papers, but from the papers of their classmates as well. If students write "Thought Papers" for each chapter, it provides them with a nice summary of the course material, and their relationship to it, at the end of the semester.

6. <u>Developmental Psychology Through the Arts (Literature, Music, and Movies)</u>: Issues concerning human development are often the focus of arts-based presentation. The goal of this project would be to have students select one or more types of presentations and apply them to what they are learning in class. For example, Boyatzis (1992) discusses how literature can be used to accomplish this goal. In this case students read a novel and use character(s) to describe some aspect of development. The book needs to be chosen carefully so that it provides ample evidence of development for students to discuss. Another option would be to have students identify ways in which developmental ideas are depicted in music. Daehler and Miller (2004) describe an interesting in-class exercise in which musical selections are used to illustrate points concerning child development. A third option would be to have students select a movie that depicts some developmental concept. One obvious choice would be the 2005 documentary *49-Up*. This movie is the latest in the "Up" series (e.g., *7-UP*) that has followed a group of British children from age 7 in 1964 until the presence. It is an excellent film worthy of showing in class or assigning as an outside viewing. Harper (1999) discusses the use of feature films as a springboard of discussing mental health concepts. Kupfer (2007) discuss the use of the 1977 classic film *Saturday Night Fever* as forum for the exploration of moral personality development.

An alternative assignment involves having students watch a film with central characters from two different generations, one character from the students generation and the other character from the generation of the individual with whom the students watches the film (e.g., Indiana Jones and the Crystal Skull, 2008, includes a teenage Shia LaBeouf and a 60-something Harrison Ford). The two can then compare the "accuracy" of the portrayal of characters of their age. This project could be the basis for a class discussion or a short paper.

Boyatzis, C. J. (1992). Let the caged bird sing: Using literature to teach developmental psychology. *Teaching of Psychology, 19*, 221-222.

Daehler, M.W., and Milller, K. E. (2004). Themes and principles of child development illustrated in music. *Teaching of Psychology, 31(3)*, 195-197.

Harper, R. E. (1999). Using feature films to teach developmental concepts. Journal of Humanistic Counseling, Education, and Development, 38(2), 88-97.

Kupfer, J. (2007). "Stay in' Alive": Moral growth and personal narrative in "Saturday Night Fever." *Journal of Popular Film and Television*, 34(4), 170-178.

7. <u>Communicating Across the Generation</u>: Assignments that encourage students to communicate across different generations can help them to put their own experiences in context, including an historical context. One interesting project involves having students write "fictitious" letters. Junn (1989) describes a project in which students write two personal letters, the first to a future child on the child's 18th birthday and the second to the student's parents.

Junn, E. N. (1989). "Dear Mom and Dad": Using personal letters to enhance students' understanding of developmental issues. *Teaching of Psychology, 16*, 135-139.

8. <u>Autobiography</u>: Autobiographical writing allows students to make the materials covered in class more personally meaningful. Autobiographical writing might take several forms.

Students may provide a chronological description of their life and then discuss it in terms of concepts covered in the course. Students might begin by constructing the facts of their life starting at birth (or prenatally if this information is available). Good sources of information for this are parents, siblings, grandparents, family photo albums, baby books, video records, scrap books, report cards, height/weight records, and so on. Included in the description should be information about their physical growth and motor skills, cognitive-intellectual development, language development, and social-personality development. Once this has been done, students can begin analyzing the facts using concepts from the course. No fact is "correct" or "incorrect," but analysis of the facts should logically connect to research, theory, and concepts covered in the text.

You could also consider a more specific assignment on a student's life-history like that discussed in the Haglund (2004) article.

Haglund, K. (2004). Conducting life history research with adolescents. Qualitative Health Research, 14(9). 1309-1319.

9. <u>Research analysis paper</u>: Students are asked to read, summarize and analyze a research article that investigates some aspect of developmental psychology. Articles should come from one of the major developmental journals (e.g., *Child Development, Developmental Psychology, Journal of Adolescence, Journal of Aging and Heath, Journal of Experimental Child Psychology, Human Development, Psychology and Aging*, and others). Goals of this project include familiarizing students with reading the different components of a research article, and learning how to summarize the relevant points of research.

In the summary, students might be asked to address the following questions (and perhaps others, depending on the article and goals of the assignment):
- What were the researchers trying to do (i.e., what is their question/research hypothesis)?
- What type of study was conducted? For example, was it longitudinal, cross-sectional, sequential? Was it experimental or correlational?
- How did researchers test their question (i.e., what did the participants do?)?
- What were the important findings?
- How does this research relate to concepts from the text?
- How does it relate to an issue in "real" life?

10. <u>Advice Column</u>: An advice-column format could be used in a variety of ways. You could collect actual advice column questions and have students respond to these. Alternatively, you could write a question for each chapter, have students submit a question and answer for each chapter, or have students write questions that are then answered by other students (e.g., all students put their questions in a hat and then pick one to which they respond). Students would be responsible for answering questions using information from the text and class. These could be turned-in throughout the semester and could provide a useful springboard for class discussion.

11. <u>Evaluation of Child Care Manual</u>: Students could be asked to evaluate one of the many popular books on child development available to parents in local bookstores. The book should be one of the general books on child development or child rearing so that more of it relates to the course in general, rather than one specific aspect of the course. Here are some points that students could consider when evaluating the book; 1) author's credentials and experience, 2) accuracy of the description of child development, 3) reasonableness of the suggestions, 4) theoretical orientation of the author, 5) whether or not claims are adequately supported by research, 6) and contradictions between the book and the material in your textbook.

12. <u>Original research project</u>: If the course includes the teaching of even *basic* statistics and research methods, or if students have already taken such courses, they might conduct their own original research study. Although surveys using correlational techniques may be the method of choice, simple experiments are also possible. In addition, non-controversial research questions and study designs will be necessary to avoid delays in the Human Subjects Committee (Institutional Review Board). Although this can be an anxiety-filled project for students who, in order to complete the project in a single semester, must be continually pushed to the next phase of research (as many of us know, formulating a question can take years in and of itself, never mind data collection and analysis). Students will need to make decisions in ambiguous situations without much experience on which to draw. They can usually be pushed forward, however, if they are assured that evaluation of this project depends on the insights gained, not the numbers of subjects tested or the significance of the results.

Completing an original research project, no matter how flawed, is usually seen as an invaluable experience that allows students to approach research in general with greater appreciation and humility. In addition, the application of research design issues, ethical issues, and statistics to one's own research project allows students to learn about these topics in a much more profound way.

Students might present their results to the class at the end of the semester in a poster-session format. It might be useful for the final write-up to include not only the research paper, but also a paper on "What I Would do Differently Next Time" that allows students to show how much they learned from their mistakes, regardless of the quality of the final study.

13. <u>Annotated Bibliography</u>: Have students create an annotated bibliography to accompany the course. They might be asked to find one, two, or three articles or books for each chapter and for each one, write a brief description or summary. This might also include an explanation of how/why they chose their articles or books. The annotations could be collected throughout the course as chapters are covered, or they could all be turned in at the end of the semester (or some combination of the two). Bibliographies might also be made available to classmates, who might be interested in pursuing additional topics.

MEETING APA GOALS

How does Sigelman and Rider's *Life-Span Human Development* 7th edition (©2011) meet the American Psychological Association Goals for the undergraduate major?

APA Goal #1: Theory and Content of Psychology

Demonstrate familiarity with major concepts, theoretical perspectives, empirical findings, and historical trends.

Sigelman and Rider's Life-Span Human Development includes ten unifying themes that are reinforced throughout the text and which represent the major concepts and attitudes of modern developmental psychology. These themes are: (1) Nature and nurture truly interact in development (environment an biology interact reciprocally); (2) We are whole people throughout the life span (advances in one area have implications for other areas); (3) Development proceeds in multiple directions; (4) There is both continuity and discontinuity in development; (5) There is much plasticity in development; (6) We are individuals, becoming even more diverse with age; (7) We develop in a culture and historical context, (8) We are active in our own development; (9) Development is a lifelong process; (10) Development is best viewed from a multiple perspective. These themes are also summarized at the very end of Chapter 17.

Information on major developmental theoretical perspectives (e.g., cognitive developmental theory, contextual-systems theory) and theorists (e.g., Freud, Piaget, Vygotsky, Kohlberg, Sternberg, Erikson, Kübler-Ross) is found throughout the text with extended theoretical discussions contained in Chapter 2: *Theories of Human Development*, Chapter 7: *Cognition*, Chapter 9: *Intelligence and Creativity*, Chapter 11: *Self and Personality*, Chapter 12: *Gender Roles and Sexuality*, Chapter 13: *Social Cognition and Moral Development*, Chapter, and Chapter 17: *The Final Challenge: Death and Dying*.

Each chapter is grounded in empirical research that often involve a description of the methods, results and implications of scientific studies on human development. Historical trend information is also depicted throughout the text (e.g., Chapter 1: *Understanding Life-Span Human Development Explorations* section that describes historical changes in periods of the lifespan).

APA GOAL #2: Research Methods in Psychology

Understand and apply basic research methods in psychology, including design, data analysis, and interpretation.

Sigelman and Rider's Life-Span Human Development devotes significant portions of Chapter 1: *Understanding Life-Span Human Development* and Chapter 3: *Genes, Environment, and Development* to an in-depth look at the research methods used in developmental psychology. Included in these sections of the text is both information on specific research techniques (e.g., experimental methods, correlational methods, twin and adoption studies) and reviews of special challenges faced by developmental researchers (e.g., conducting culturally sensitive research, accounting for the heritability of different traits). Specific designs and interpretations are also contained in chapters throughout the rest of the text. For example, Chapter 6: *Perception* contains descriptions of various methods for assessing perceptual abilities (e.g., preferential looking, evoked potential). Chapter 9: *Intelligence and Creativity* contains a lengthy discussion of the various approaches to assessing intelligence.

Sigelman and Rider's Life-Span Human Development includes descriptions of classic research designs like the Chapter 7: *Cognition* discussion of Piagetian tasks of cognitive ability and the Chapter 14: *Attachment and Social Relationships* discussion of the strange situation test used to assess attachment styles.

The Sigelman and Rider text is known and respected for the way each edition presents classic and current research in the field. Every chapter in the 7th Edition has been updated with the latest research findings and topics.

APA GOAL #3: Critical Thinking Skills in Psychology
Respect and use critical and creative thinking, skeptical inquiry, and when possible the scientific approach to solve problems related to behavior and mental processes.

Sigelman and Rider's Life-Span Human Development actively encourages students to utilize critical thinking skills when considering developmental issues. It also encourages the use of a scientific/skeptical approach to addressing these issues. To reinforce this theme, each subsection of each chapter contains a *Making Connections* sections that includes both specific questions that students should consider when reviewing the information that they just read (e.g., Chapter 3 "A DNA sample taken by swabbing a person's cheek can now reveal the person's entire genome. What do you think will be the positive and negative consequences of this scientific breakthrough for society? On balance, should we be pleased of concerned about this development?).

The text also encourages the scientific solution of problems by describing ways which data can be used in such an endeavor. For example, Chapter 3: *Genes, Environment, and Development* includes a description of how gene therapy might be used to prevent or treat certain disorders. Chapter 5: *Health and Physical Development* contains a section on whether research on brain development can be used to explain risk-taking behavior in adolescents. Chapter 6: *Perception* describes the scientific methods used to assess infant's visual preferences. Chapter 11: *Self and Personality* uses scientific data to address the issue of the existence of a "midlife crisis."

APA GOAL #4: Applications of Psychology
Understand and apply psychological principles to personal, social, and organizational issues.

Each chapter in *Sigelman and Rider's Life-Span Human Development* contains examples of issues that apply the text content to everyday life. For example, see Chapter 9: *Intelligence and Creativity* coverage of on methods of fostering creativity across the life span. Each chapter also includes at least one *Explorations* section on a single, high-interest issue to reinforce the practical implications of theory and research. Chapters also contain an *Applications* box that addresses how knowledge has been used to optimize development in a specific domain of development. Though they cover applied topics, these sections continue to review studies and summarize data as the main body of the chapter does.

The Instructor's Resource Manual for *Life-Span Human Development* contains a variety of *Suggestions for Class Discussions or Projects*, many of which involve applying text-based psychological information to personal, social, and/or organizational issues. Chapter 4: *Prenatal Development and Birth* contains suggestions for a project on planning the perfect delivery. Chapter 8: *Memory and Information Processing* contains a great in-class method of demonstrating the impact of knowledge on memory. Chapter 10: *Language and Education* includes a suggested in-class activity designed to identify how age, sex, and grade status might impact achievement motivation and subsequent academic performance. Chapter 16: *Developmental Psychopathology* includes a suggestion for getting students to identify reasons for delinquent behaviors in adolescence.

APA GOAL #5: Values in Psychology
Weigh evidence, tolerate ambiguity, act ethically, and reflect other values underpinning psychology as a discipline.

Sigelman and Rider's Life-Span Human Development encourages the weighing of evidence and tolerance for ambiguity by presenting both the specific strengths and weakness of different methods of inquiry and different theoretical perspectives throughout the text. For example, in Chapter 1: *Understanding Life-Span Human Development* you will find sections on the strength and weakness of both the cross-sectional and longitudinal methods as well as a section on why sequential designs may represent the best of both worlds. Chapter 2: *Theories of Human Development* contains descriptions of all of the major theoretical perspectives as well as the strengths and weaknesses of each position.

The issue of ethics is addressed numerous times in the text. For example, a section of Chapter 1: *Understanding Life-Span Human Development* focuses on ways in which developmental psychology researchers protect the rights of research participants (e.g., informed consent, confidentiality). Chapter 12: *Gender Roles and Sexuality encourages* students to consider the relationship between sex and gender and includes an interesting *Explorations* box on the impact of social labeling versus biology as the determinate of behavior. Issues of moral thinking are addressed at many levels throughout Chapter 13: *Social Cognition and Moral Development*. In an *Explorations* box in Chapter 16: *Developmental Psychopathology*, students are asked to consider whether autism might best be explained as an extreme version of the male brain.

APA GOAL #6: Information and Technological Literacy
Demonstrate information competence and the ability to use computers and other technology for many purposes.

Sigelman and Rider's Life-Span Human Development has numerous opportunities for students to improve their technological competence. Each chapter ends with a *Media Resource Area* that includes a list of *Websites to Explore* and *Understanding the Data: Exercise on the Web* section which allows students to acquire additional information on data presented in the text, by visiting a linked website. Students can also access the book companion website for a rich selection of resources, such as chapter-by-chapter learning objectives, online tutorial quizzes, chapter-related web links, flash cards, and critical thinking lessons.

APA GOAL #7: Communication Skills
Communicate effectively in a variety of formats.

The most direct way that the *Sigelman and Rider's Life-Span Human Development* text deals with APA goal 7 is through it's attempt to improve the quantitative literacy skills of students (e.g., appropriate use of statistical analysis, interpretation of visually presented information).

Other key objectives of APA Goal 7 (i.e., improve student's professional writing skills, improve oral communication skills, and improve collaborative skills) are addressed in the supplemental materials that accompany the book. For example, page ix of the *Instructor's Resource Manual* for *Life-Span Human Development* contains a series of tips for enhancing writing in psychology. Pages x to xv of this work contain suggested semester-long course projects, the majority of which involve the production of some written work. Many of the *Suggestions for Class Discussion or Projects* found in the *Instructor's Resource Manual* also involve the generation of a written project. Other suggested discussion or project ideas focus on oral communication (e.g., project 8.1 on early memory, project 9.5 on fair testing practices, project 12.6 on appropriate sexual behavior across the lifespan) or small groups activity designed to enhance collaborative skills (e.g., project 3.3 on inheritance, project 8.3 on a constraint seeking question game).

APA GOAL #8: Socio-Cultural and International Awareness
Recognize, understand, and respect the complexity of socio-cultural and international diversity.

Sigelman and Rider's Life-Span Human Development recognizes and acknowledges the importance of diversity at many levels. As noted in APA Goal 1, one of the themes that permeates the text is that "We develop in a culture and historical context." To reinforce this idea, the importance of the impact of cultural factors is noted throughout the text. In addition to noting the impact of cultural on development, the text also contains a plethora of specific examples of cross-cultural research. For example, Chapter 4: *Prenatal Development and Birth* contains a description of cultural factors impacting both child-birth and early child-rearing practices. In Chapter 7: *Cognition* includes discussion of theorists like Vygotsky who emphasize the importance of cultural on development. In Chapter 10: *Language and Education*, the authors discuss cross-cultural research on mathematics and science education.

APA GOAL #9: Personal Development
Develop insight into their own and others' behavior and mental processes and apply effective strategies for self-management and self-improvement.

It should come as no surprise that a major focus of *Sigelman and Rider's Life-Span Human Development* involves helping students to gain insight into self-development as well as the development of others. For example, the main purpose of Chapter 6: *Perception*, Chapter 7: *Cognition*, Chapter 8: *Memory and Information Processing*, and Chapter 9: *Intelligence and Creativity* is to further students understanding of how information is acquired from the external world and methods of mentally processing this information. A main purpose of Chapter 11: *Self and Personality*, Chapter 12: *Gender Roles and Sexuality*, Chapter 13: *Social Cognition and Moral Development* is to further students understanding of how mental processing impact the development of self, gender, and morality. *Sigelman and Rider's Life-Span Human Development* also takes every opportunity to instruct students in ways of more effectively managing and improving their lives.

Examples of insight into understanding the behaviors of self and others are found in every chapter. Specific examples include the following. The *Explorations* box in Chapter 2: *Theories of Human Development* challenges students to determine where they stand on major developmental issues. An *Explorations* section in Chapter 11: *Self and Personality* allows students to complete a brief personality survey. Chapter 16: *Developmental Psychopathology* begins with a discussion of how psychologists define abnormal thought/behavior. Students are also actively encouraged to gain personal insight via the *Checking Mastery*, *Making Connections*, *Explorations Boxes*, and *Applications* sections found in each chapter.

APA GOAL #10: Career Planning and Development

Emerge from the major with realistic ideas about how to implement psychological knowledge, skills, and values in various occupations and in a variety of settings.

Sigelman and Rider's Life-Span Human Development contains numerous references to ways in which knowledge gained from developmental psychology research can be effectively applied in occupational setting. Some of the best examples include the Chapter 3: *Genes, Environment, and Development* discussion of how prenatal tests can be used to detect abnormalities and how this information is used by genetic counselors; the Chapter 9: *Intelligence and Creativity* and Chapter 10: *Language and Education* discussions of ways for school to more effectively intervene with students at all grade levels; and the Chapter 13: *Social Cognition and Moral Development* discussion of methods that schools could use to combat youth violence.

UNDERSTANDING LIFESPAN HUMAN DEVELOPMENT

LEARNING OBJECTIVES

After reading and studying the material in this chapter, you should be able to answer the following questions.

HOW SHOULD WE THINK OF DEVELOPMENT?

1. How do developmental scientists define development? What does the typical path of development look like across the lifespan?

2. How has our understanding of different periods of the lifespan changed historically? What cultural and subcultural differences exist in perspectives of the lifespan?

3. What are the main components of each side of the nature-nurture issue?

4. What are the features of the bioecological model, and why is this perspective important to our understanding of development?

WHAT IS THE SCIENCE OF LIFESPAN DEVELOPMENT?

5. What are the three goals of developmental psychology and the seven assumptions of the modern lifespan perspective on human development?

HOW IS DEVELOPMENT STUDIED?

6. What is the scientific method "mindset," and how is the scientific method used to study development?

7. What are the essential features of the experimental method? What sorts of information can be gathered from an experimental study, and what are its strengths and weaknesses?

8. What are the important features of the correlational method? What sorts of information can be gathered from this type of study, and what are its strengths and weaknesses?

9. What are the advantages and disadvantages of the cross-sectional and longitudinal designs, and how does the sequential design resolve the weaknesses of these designs?

WHAT SPECIAL CHALLENGES DO DEVELOPMENTAL SCIENTISTS FACE?

10. What challenges arise in studying development, and how can scientists address these issues?

Chapter 1

I How Should We Think about Development?

A. Defining Development

1. Development involves systematic continuities and changes from conception to death in three domains

a. Physical development—growth of body, physiological change

b. Cognitive development—changes in perception, language, learning, and memory

c. Psychosocial development—changes in personality, emotions

2. Growth—physical changes from conception to maturity

3. Biological aging—deterioration of organisms

4. Aging—positive and negative changes in maturing organism

5. Developmental change involves both gains and losses

B. Conceptualizing the Lifespan

1. Periods of the lifespan: prenatal, infancy, preschool, middle school, adolescence, early adulthood, middle adulthood, late adulthood

2. Age grade (age stratum)—status, roles, privileges, and responsibilities based on one's age group

3. Legal definitions of age boundaries (e.g., adolescence and adulthood) vary by state

4. Culture impacts the recognized periods of the lifespan

a. Eskimo simply distinguish between boy/girl and man/woman

b. !Kung define old in terms of functioning, not age

5. A rite of passage is a ritual marking passage from one status to another

a. Jewish bar or bat mitzvah

b. Hispanic-American girl *quinceañera* at age 15

6. Age norms—expectations based on age

a. Social clock—sense of timing for life transitions

b. "Off time" (socially age inappropriate) events have more negative impact

7. Subcultural differences exist in age grades, age norms, and social clocks

a. Society is diverse with respect to race, ethnicity, or socioeconomic status

b. Individuals from lower-income families tend to reach adulthood milestones earlier than those from middle- and upper-class families

8. Meaning of childhood, adolescence, and adulthood change with historic period

a. In Western society, during the 17th century, children came to be viewed as distinct from adults

b. In medieval times, children were expected to grow up as fast as possible

c. Adolescence was recognized as a separate period in the late 19th and early 20th centuries

d. The need for an educated workforce and compulsory schooling helped to lead to adolescence being viewed as a distinct period of life

e. Emerging adulthood is the time from age 18 to 29

f. Middle age emerged as a distinctive stage of life in the 20th century (Exploration Box on emerging adulthood)

      g. Some characterize middle age as a time of crisis, but it tends to be a time of good health, peak cognitive function, and high satisfaction

      h. Old age also became a unique time period in the 20th century

      i. In the past, relatively few individuals lived to old age, in part because so many people died in infancy

      j. The average life expectancy (average number of years a newborn is expected to live) is 81 for a white female, 77 for a black female, 76 for a white male, and 70 for a black male /

      k. Racial differences in life expectancy have been declining while differences based on socioeconomic status have been widening

      l. While today's elderly are healthier than in the past, many do have chronic diseases and disabilities and require support

      m. Development must be viewed in historical, cultural, and subcultural context

C. Framing the Nature/Nurture Issue

    1. The two sides of the debate

      a. Maturation (nature)—biological unfolding of plan contained in genes (hereditary material from parents)

      b. Genetically influenced maturation guide us through many of the same changes at about the same time

      c. Individual hereditary endowment makes each person unique

      d. Environment (nurture)—external physical and social conditions, stimuli, and events

      e. The nurture-side emphasizes learning (relatively permanent changes from experiential influences)

      f. Development is due to interplay between nature and nurture

          i. Both social (e.g., patrilineal cultures) and genetic factors both influence levels of aggression

D. Grasping the Ecology of Development

    1. Bronfenbrenner's bioecological model

      a. Stresses how biology and environment interact to produce development

      b. Four environmental systems influence and are influenced by the developing person

          i. Microsystem—immediate physical and social environment individual interacts with face-to-face, involves reciprocal influence

          ii. Mesosystem—linkages between two of more microsystems

          iii. Exosystem—linkages involving social settings that individuals do not directly experience (e.g., parent's work day) but still influence behavior

          iv. Macrosystem—larger culture (shared understanding and way of life of a people) in which other systems are embedded

          v. Chronosystem—people and environments occur in particular time frame and unfold in particular pattern

      c. Models suggests that study of development will not be easy

          i. Influence of factors like person, context, time, and processes difficult to separate

3

II What is the Science of Lifespan Human Development?

A. Goals of Study
   1. Description of human development
      a. Normal (typical) development
      b. Individual differences
   2. Explanation of human development
      a. Why humans develop as they do
      b. Why some humans develop differently
   3. Optimization of human development
      a. How can humans be helped to develop in a positive direction (i.e., how can capacities be enhanced?)?
      b. Applied research on optimizing development should be based on evidence-based practices (i.e., grounded in research and demonstrated to be effective)

B. Early Beginnings
   1. Baby biographies
      a. Late 19th century scholars who observed and recorded the development of their own children
      b. Charles Darwin perhaps the most influential baby biographer
         i. Darwin believed that infants share characteristics with nonhuman ancestors
         ii. Darwin's evolutionary perspective influences early theories of development (Exploration Box on Darwin's baby biography on the development of anger in his son)
      c. Methodology poor
         i. Biographers emphasized different aspects of development
         ii. Observers not objective
         iii. Observed only a single child
   2. G. Stanley Hall
      a. Cited as founder of developmental psychology
         i. First President of American Psychological Association
         ii. Collected data on the "content of children's minds"
         iii. Wrote *Adolescence* (1904) in which that time of life was viewed as one of "storm and stress"
         iv. Book led to modern inaccurate notion of teenagers as emotionally unstable
         v. Wrote *Senescence* (1922), which was an analysis of how society treats (mistreats) older members

C. The Modern Lifespan Perspective
   1. Gerontology—study of aging and old age
   2. Lifespan perspective—focus on infancy through old age
   3. Key text themes
      a. Development is a lifelong process
      b. Development is multidirectional (different aspects of functioning have different trajectories of change)
      c. Development involves both gain and loss
      d. Life-long plasticity in human development

       i.   Plasticity—capacity to change to positive and negative experiences

      ii. Plasticity continues into later life

    iii. Neuroplasticity—brain's capacity to change in response to environmental experiences throughout the lifespan

    iv. Physical exercise and mental stimulation can change neurochemistry, create new connections among neurons (even in the aging brain)

  e. Development is shaped by its historical/cultural context

       i.   Great Depression impacted parental behavior and the development of children and adolescents

      ii. As societies change, developmental experiences change (e.g., modern children hold more individualistic as opposed to communal values)

  f. Development is multiply influenced (biology and experience)

       i.   Now talk of developmental science rather than developmental psychology

      ii. Understanding development requires multiple disciplines (e.g., biology, history, economics)

III How Is Development Studied?

A. The Scientific Method

  1. Scientific method—an attitude of systematic observation

    a. Believe the data

    b. Helps to weed out flawed ideas

  2. Theory—set of concepts and propositions intended to describe and explain some experience

  3. Hypotheses—predictions generated to test theory

  4. Good theories should be

    a. Internally consistent (i.e., not generate contradictory hypotheses)

    b. Falsifiable (can be proven wrong)

    c. Supported by data (i.e., have predictions confirmed by research results)

B. Sample Selection

  1. Research sample—group being studied

  2. Population—larger defined group from which sample is drawn

  3. Random sample—a portion of the population to be studies

    a. Means of drawing random sample from population increases confidence in the representative nature of the sample and makes generalization possible

C. Data Collection

  1. Three major methods of collection are verbal reports, behavioral observations, and physiological measures

  2. Verbal reports

    a. Often standardized interviews, questionnaires, or tests

    b. Cannot be used on infants, those who cannot read

    c. Age differences in ability to comprehend questions may occur

    d. Respondents may falsely present themselves in positive manner

  3. Behavioral observations

    a. Naturalistic observation—behaviors observed in everyday life

   i. Greatest advantage is that techniques study everyday life

   ii. Three limitations: some behaviors occur infrequently to observe; difficult to pinpoint cause; presence of observer may influence behavior

  b. Structured observation—researcher creates conditions to elicit a behavior

   i. Can study behaviors rare in natural settings

   ii. Concern about ability to generalize to natural settings

 4. Physiological measures

  a. Assess physiological responses (e.g., hormone levels, heart rate)

  b. Functional magnetic resonance imaging (fMRI)—brain-scanning technique using magnetic forces and measuring blood flow

   i. Can determine which part of brain involved in cognitive activity

  c. Difficult to fake

  d. Sometimes unclear as to what is being assessed

  e. Multiple approaches used to study behavior (Exploration Box on three approaches to studying anger and aggression)

D. The Case Study, Experimental, and Correlational Methods

 1. The case study

  a. In-depth examination of an individual (or small group)

  b. Multiple sources of information (e.g., observation, interview, testing)

  c. Useful in studying people with rare conditions

  d. Can be a good source of hypotheses

  e. Conclusions cannot be generalized

 2. The experimental method (Friedrich and Stein study on television shows and violence used as an example)

  a. Independent variable—manipulated by experimenter (Friedrich and Stein, type of television show watched)

  b. Dependent variable—behavior affected by independent variable (Friedrich and Stein, aggressive behavior)

   i. Friedrich and Stein results: children who were already relatively aggressive and watched more violent television became more aggressive

  c. Three critical features of any true experiment

   i. Random assignment to experimental conditions ensures groups similar to each other

   ii. Manipulation of independent variable needed to establish cause

   iii. Experimental control—hold factors constant

  d. Experiments: strength

   i. Can be used to determine cause

  e. Experiments: limitation

   i. Do not hold true in real world

   ii. Ethical concerns (i.e., cannot conduct experiments on certain issues)

  f. Quasi-experiment—nonrandom assignment to treatment groups

 3. The correlational method

  a. Correlation coefficient assesses extent that individuals' scores on one variable are systematically related to scores on another

    i. Huesmann and colleagues correlational study on television viewing and aggression
  b. Involves calculation of correlation coefficient
    i. Correlation coefficient (r) score (extent to which scores on one variable are associated scores on another variable) with ranges from +1.0 to -1.0
    ii. High positive (+) correlation indicates the variables vary together in same direction (e.g., +0.9)
    iii. High negative (-) correlation indicates the variables vary together in opposite direction (e.g., -0.9)
    iv. Correlation near 0 indicates no relationship between variables
  c. Alternative explanation to positive correlation between aggression and watching violent television (i.e., violent television causes aggression)
    i. Direction of causality may be reversed (e.g., being aggressive may cause one to watch violent television)
    ii. Third variable may cause observed association (e.g., peer rejection causing violence and more television viewing)
    iii. Ambiguity means that a correlation cannot be used to establish cause
  d. Numerous studies with convergent findings best way to establish cause/effect relationships
  e. Meta-analysis—study in which results from multiple studies is synthesized
    i. Meta-analysis results indicate that watching violent programs is related to roughhousing and more serious violent displays
E. Developmental Research Designs
 1. Cross-sectional designs
  a. Cross-sectional designs study different age groups (cohorts) measured at same time
    i. Cohort is a group of individuals born at the same time (either the same year or within a span of years)
  b. Cross-sectional design—provides information about age differences
  c. Age and cohort effects and limitations to cross-sectional designs
    i. Age effect—relationship between age and a particular aspect of development
    ii. Cohort effect—effect of being born in one particular historical context
    iii. Age and cohort effects are confounded or entangled (Exploration Box on cohort effects and Baby Boomers)
    iv. Cross-sectional designs observe an individual at only one point so they do not measure development of the individual
  c. Advantages of cross-sectional designs
    i. Quick and easy
 2. Longitudinal design—studies same group (cohort) measured repeatedly
  a. Longitudinal design provides information on age changes versus age differences and the direction or path of change
  b. Limitations of longitudinal designs

    i. Time of measurement effects—historical events and trends' effects on
       development
    ii. In longitudinal designs, time of measurement effects and age effects are
        confounded
    iii. Unsure if change is due to aging or the result of sociocultural effects
    iv. Method is costly and time-consuming
    v. Measures may become dated
    vi. Loss of participants leads to smaller, less representative sample
    vii. Participants can be affected by repeated testing
    c. Although both cross-sectional and longitudinal designs have weaknesses,
       they
       are both valuable research tools
3. Sequential design: the best of both worlds
    a. Sequential designs combine cross-sectional and longitudinal approaches
    b. Advantages of sequential designs
       i. Can identify age-related trends regardless of cohort
       ii. Can identify cohort effects
       iii. Can identify time of measurement effects
    c. Limitations of sequential design
       i. Method extremely costly and complex

IV What Special Challenges Do Developmental Scientists Face?
  A. Conducting Culturally Sensitive Research
     1. Ecological setting can influence development
        a. Must consider socioeconomic status (SES)—status in society that includes
           occupational prestige, education, and income
           i. Growing up in poverty or affluence will influence development
        b. Must study individuals from different subcultures and cultures
        c. Researcher must keep own cultural values from biasing perceptions
           i. Ethnocentrism—belief that own group and culture are superior may
              creep
              into designs, procedures, and measures
           ii. Researchers may judge minority children and adults labeled as
               "deviant" versus "different"
           iii. Cannot assume that all members of a culture or subculture are alike
                psychologically
  B. Protect the Rights of Research Participants
     1. Research ethics—standards of research conduct that researchers are ethically
        bound to honor
        a. Study reviewed in Exploration Box 1.3 addressed several ethical issues
        b. Ethical issues often arise in developmental research
     2. Ethical guidelines established by different groups
        a. American Psychological Association and Society for Research in Child
           Development guidelines
        b. Human-subjects review committees (Institutional Review Boards)
     3. Investigator's ethical responsibilities
        a. Weigh potential benefit and potential risk

b. Respect rights of participants by
   i. Allowing participant to make informed and uncoerced decision about taking part in the study
   ii. Debriefing after completion of the study
   iii. Offering protection from harm
   iv. Treating information as confidential
c. Informed consent
   i. Informed about all aspects of research that might affect participation
   ii. Those studying "vulnerable" populations must obtain informed consent from participant and someone who can decide on their behalf
   iii. Age (young children = lack of language, old age = possible dementia) and culture should be considered when obtaining informed consent
d. Debriefing
   i. Tell participant about purpose of study in advance
   ii. In cases where knowledge of the study would impact response, debriefing may occur after the study
e. Protection from harm
   i. Researcher may not harm participant physically or psychologically
   ii. If harm likely, then another way of answering the question should be explored
   iii. If participant is harmed, researcher must take steps to undo harm
f. Confidentiality
   i. Keep collected information confidential
   ii. Medical records now particularly well protected
   iii. Participants must give explicit permission to have information about them shared

SUGGESTIONS FOR CLASS DISCUSSIONS OR PROJECTS

1. To introduce the issue of a "lifespan" perspective on developmental psychology and to illustrate that there are different views of the lifespan, students might be asked how they would break up the lifespan into eight distinct stages (e.g., infancy, middle age). Follow-up questions could include 1) What characteristics would you use to describe each of these age groups? (These descriptions can be somewhat depressing to instructors who find that students view them as being in an older age category than they view themselves.) 2) Into which group would you classify themselves? What are the best and worst stages of life? Some of these might be discussed on this day; others might be referred to when the appropriate section is reached during the semester. This project could be done as a class, in small groups, or as a take-home assignment.

2. Hershey and Jacobs-Lawson's (2001) article in the *Teaching of Psychology* provides a great demonstration on issues/stereotypes in aging. This exercise has students rate the quality of life in several areas from young adulthood through old age. This project can be done individually or in small groups and is guaranteed to generate discussion.

   Hershey, D.A., and Jacobs-Lawson, J.M. (2001). Developmental differences in the quality of life: A classroom teaching exercise. *Teaching of Psychology*, 28(2), 114-117.

3. Have students design a study to test a research question such as one of those listed below. Ask them to identify the specific independent and dependent variable(s) they would use and how they would actually collect the data. Also have them discuss the advantages/disadvantages of using a cross-sectional, longitudinal, or a sequential design.

- What impact does school have on moral development?
- Do racial attitudes vary across cultures and history?
- Do memory abilities change across the lifespan?
- Do men and women perceive their retirements differently?

4. A major hurdle in conducting research is obtaining a representative sample. Discuss or have students brainstorm ways to obtain study participants of different ages and abilities— perhaps specifically for the studies they designed in Exercise 4, above. This is more difficult than students usually think. They may say they would obtain participants from the local school district, not realizing that many schools have tight restrictions on research. Other recruitment techniques include soliciting participants from an after-school program, or going through newspaper birth announcements and calling parents. Older subjects might be obtained at a bingo night or an adult daycare program. Once students have generated ways of obtaining a sample, they might discuss whether these samples would be representative of the population. For example, is there something different about older adults who play bingo versus those who do not?

5. Another important research issue is that of informed consent. Discuss or hand out American Psychological Association (APA) or Society for Research in Child Development (SRCD) guidelines for use of humans in research. Have students, individually or in small groups, write permission letters for different populations (e.g., parent of a preschooler, parent of an adolescent, guardian of a retarded adult or elderly person). Again, the studies devised in the exercises above might be useful, as students will need to have a study in mind so they can provide the hypothetical research participant with enough information to make an informed decision. Have students exchange letters and decide a) if they received this letter, would they give permission; and b) does the letter meet APA/SRCD guidelines?

6. Present students with the following fictitious "research abstract":

> A first-grade teacher is informed that all of her students would have to participate in a study designed to assess the relationship between punishment and learning. Class members were randomly assigned to one of three experimental conditions (high shock, medium shock, low shock). Each child then read a list of 50 foreign words and was asked to recall the words in the correct order. Whenever a child made a correct response, the researcher said, "Correct." Whenever a child made an incorrect response they received the following negative feedback: high shock condition = 500 volts for 10 seconds, medium shock = 250 volts for 5 seconds, and low shock = 10 volts for 1 second. The task lasted until students got all 50 words correct. During the task, students were reminded that they had to participate ("no quitting") and that their responses were a measure of their overall intelligence.

Have students give their overall reaction to the study with particular focus on their perception of the treatment of the participants. Then review the current APA guidelines (see Sales &

Folkman, 2000) for ethical treatment of participants, and have students decide whether this study could be conducted ethically.

Sales, B.D., and Folkman, S. (2000). *Ethics in Research with Human Participants*. Washington, D.C.: American Psychological Association.

7. Belsky (1980) uses Bronfenbrenner's ecological model to examine the issue of child maltreatment. Choose another social problem (e.g., substance abuse, dropping out of school) and examine how factors at different levels of analysis (e.g., individual level, various microsystems, the macrosystem) contribute to this problem. You might also try to propose solutions for each of the identified contributing factors to demonstrate that interventions also occur at different levels, and the solutions we attempt may depend on the level at which we conceptualize the problem.

Belsky, J. (1980). Child maltreatment: An ecological model. *American Psychologist, 35,* 320-335.

SUGGESTED FILMS AND VIDEOS

49 Up (2005 Feature Film): A documentary film presenting interviews with individuals who have been interviewed every 7 years of their lives starting at age 7.

Past, Present, and Promise (Annenberg/CPB Multimedia Collection, VHS and film): This "Discovering Psychology" video series provides an introduction to the science of psychology.

Research Methods in Psychology (2001, Insight Media, VHS 30 minutes): Program provides a solid description of strengths and limitations of description, correlational, and experimental research including discussion of causal link between video games and teen violence.

Understanding Psychology: Experimental Methods in Psychology (2004, Insight Media, VHS 37 minutes): Program uses research on attractiveness as a backdrop for describing different experimental methods.

Understanding Psychology: Non-Experimental Methods in Psychology (2006, Insight Media, VHS 32 minutes): Program uses the topic of cell-phone use to illustrate several non-experimental methods.

American Psychological Association Division 7 (Developmental Psychology)
http://ecp.fiu.edu/APA/div7/

American Psychological Association Ethical Standards
http://www.apa.org/ethics/code/index.aspx

Psychology Research On the Net
http://psych.hanover.edu/research/exponnet.html

Society for Research in Child Development
http://www.srcd.org/

SUGGESTED READINGS

Brummel, B.J. (2010). Develop of role-playing scenarios for teaching responsible conduct of research. _Science and Engineering Ethics_, 16(3), 573-589.

Creswell, J.W. (2009). _Research Design: Qualitative, Quantitative, and Mixed Method Approaches (3rd ed.)._ London, England: Sage Publishing.

Green, S., and Hogan, D. (2005). _Researching Children's Experiences: Approaches and Methods_. London, England: Sage Publishing.

Ramcharan, P. (2006). Ethical challenges and complexities of including vulnerable people in research: Some pre-theoretical considerations. _Journal of Intellectual & Developmental Disability_, 31(3), pp. 183-185.

Rutter, M. (2006). _Genes and Behavior: Nature-Nurture Interplay Explained_. Malden, MA: Blackwell Publishing.

2
THEORIES OF HUMAN DEVELOPMENT

LEARNING OBJECTIVES

After reading and studying the material in this chapter, you should be able to answer the following questions.

DEVELOPMENTAL THEORIES AND THE ISSUES THEY RAISE
1. What are the five basic issues in human development? Where does each major theorist—Freud, Erikson, Skinner, Bandura, Piaget, and Gottlieb—stand on each of these issues?

FREUD: PSYCHOANALYTIC THEORY
2. What are the distinct features of Freud's psychoanalytic theory? What are the strengths and weaknesses of the theory?

ERIKSON: NEO-FREUDIAN PSYCHOANALYTIC THEORY
3. How does Erikson's psychoanalytic theory compare to Freud's theory? What crisis characterizes each of Erickson's psychosocial stages?

LEARNING THEORIES
4. What are the distinct features of the learning theories covered in this chapter: Watson's classical conditioning, Skinner's operant conditioning, and Bandura's social-cognitive theory? What are the strengths and weaknesses of the learning theories?

PIAGET: COGNITIVE DEVELOPMENTAL THEORY
5. What is Piaget's perspective on cognitive development? What are the strengths and weaknesses of Piaget's theory?

SYSTEMS THEORIES
6. How do systems theories, in general, conceptualize development?

7. What are the essential elements of Gottlieb's epigenetic psychobiological systems perspective of development? What are the strengths and weaknesses of the systems approaches to development?

THEORIES IN PERSPECTIVE
8. How can we characterize the theories in general?

I Developmental Theories and the Issues They Raise
A. Introduction to Main Theories
   1. Guides the collection of new information
      a. What is most important to study
      b. What can be hypothesized or predicted
      c. How it should be studied
   2. Four main theories
      a. Psychoanalytic (Freud, Erikson, and neo-Freudians)
      b. Learning (Pavlov, Watson, Skinner, Bandura)
      c. Cognitive (Piaget)
      d. Systems theory (Bronfenbrenner)
   Criteria of a Good Theory
   1. Internally consistent—its different parts are not contradictory
   2. Falsifiable—generates testable hypotheses
   3. Supported by data—describes, predicts, and explains human development
   4. Five key issues on which theorists disagree
      i. Goodness or badness of human nature
      ii. Nature or nurture
      iii. Activity or passivity
      iv. Continuity or discontinuity
      v. Universality or specificity
      vi. (Engagement Box on where you stand on major developmental issues)
B. The Goodness/Badness of Human Nature
   1. Hobbes—children are inherently selfish and bad, and society must teach them to behave in civilized way
   2. Rousseau—children are innately good, and society must not interfere with innate goodness
   3. Locke—child are born neither good nor bad, but are like a *tabula rasa* or "blank slate"
C. Nature vs. Nurture
   1. Development as product of nature (Rousseau champion of innate goodness in children)
      a. Individual genetic makeup
      b. Universal maturational processes guided by genes
      c. Biologically based predispositions
      d. Change driven by biology
      e. Individual differences due to genetic differences
   2. Development as product of nurture (Locke claim that experience shapes development)
      a. Emphasis on environment
         i. Physical environment (e.g., pollution)
         ii. Social environment (e.g., societal trends)

D. Activity vs. Passivity
  1. Activity—have control over one's development (Rousseau)
  2. Passive—shaped by forces beyond one's control (e.g., environmental or biological) (Locke)
E. Continuity vs. Discontinuity
  1. Continuity—gradual change (small steps)
  2. Discontinuity—abrupt change (a series of steps)
  3. Qualitative or quantitative change
     a. Quantitative—change in degree (continuity)
     b. Qualitative —change in kind (discontinuity)
     c. Discontinuity theorists propose the existence of developmental stages—distinct phase of the life cycle
F. Universality vs. Context-Specificity
  1. Universality—developmental change common to everyone
     a. Stage theorists typically believe that stages are universal
  2. Context-specific—developmental changes vary by individual, culture, subculture
  3. Are both universal and context-specific aspects to human development
     a. Poet Mark Van Doren: "Two statements about humans beings that are true: that all human beings are alike, and that all are different"

II **Freud: Psychoanalytic Theory**
A. Sigmund Freud: Viennese Physician and Founder of Psychoanalytic Theory
  1. Psychoanalytic theory—focus on development and dynamics of personality
  2. Emphasis on humans being driven by motive and emotions of which we are unaware
  3. Belief that we are shaped by earliest experiences in life
  4. Theory far less influential than in the past
B. Instincts and Unconscious Motives
  1. Instincts—inborn biological forces that motivate behavior
  2. Unconscious motivation—instinctive and inner force influences beyond our awareness/control
  3. Emphasis on nature (biological instincts)
C. Id, Ego, and Superego
  1. Id
     a. All psychic energy contained here
     b. Impulsive, irrational, selfish part of personality
     c. Seeks immediate gratification
  2. Ego
     a. Rational side of personality
        i. Realistic ways to gratify instincts
     b. Capable of postponing pleasure
  3. Superego
     a. Internalized moral standards (developed age 3 to 6)
     b. Superego insists that people find socially acceptable outlets for id's undesirable impulses

Chapter 2

4. Id, ego, and superego conflict common/inevitable
    a. Problems arise when level of psychic energy unevenly distributed
        i. Antisocial personality may have weak superego
        ii. Unable to undress in front of spouse may overly strong a superego
    b. Analysis of dynamics among three parts of personality used to describe and understand human behavior
D. Psychosexual Development
    1. Importance of libido—sex instinct's energy shifts body locations
        a. Five stages of psychosexual development (oral, anal, phallic, latency, genital)
        b. Oral and anal stage conflict of id and social demands leads to heightened psychic conflict and anxiety
            i. Fixation—development arrested at early stage
            ii. Chronic thumb sucker or chain smoker stuck (fixated) in oral stage
            iii. During anal stage of toilet training, parents who are punitive may create children who are anxious and who resist demands from authority figures
            iv. Parent's goal—allow some (but not too much) gratification of impulses while helping child achieve some (but not too much) control over impulses
        b. Phallic stage—Oedipus and Electra complexes (incestuous desire) resolve by identifying with same-sex parent and incorporating parent's values
            i. Oedipus complex—boy loves mother and fears castration by father
            ii. Oedipus complex resolved through identification with father—taking on or internalizing attitudes or behaviors
            iii. Electra complex—girl desires father (penis envy), views mother as rival, resolves conflict through identification with mother
        c. Latency stage—sexual urges are tamed (age 6 to 12)
        d. Genital stage—experienced during puberty
            i. Trouble accepting new sexuality
            ii. Reexperience conflict and distance self from parents
            iii. Greater capacity to love and have children in adulthood
E. Defense Mechanisms—Unconscious Coping Mechanisms of the Ego
    a. Repression—removing unacceptable or traumatic thoughts from consciousness
    b. Regression—retreating to an earlier stage
    c. Projection—seeing in others the motives we fear we possess
    d. Reaction formation—expressing motives the opposite of one's real motives
    e. Defense mechanisms can be healthy and function despite anxiety or they can distort reality
    f. School refusal result of separation anxiety (Exploration Box on Freudian explanation of school refusal)
F. Strengths and Weaknesses
    1. Difficult to test and ambiguous (not easily falsifiable)
    2. Weak support for specific aspects of the theory (e.g., rate of sexual fantasy and child sexual abuse)
    3. Greater support for broad ideas
        a. Unconscious processes underlying behavior
        b. Importance of early experience
        c. Important emphasis on the role of emotions in development

III Erikson: Neo-Freudian Psychoanalytic Theory

A. Neo-Freudians—Important Disciples of Psychoanalytic Theory
   1. Notable neo-Freudians: Adler (sibling rivalry), Jung (midlife crisis, expression of both masculine and feminine sides of personality), Horney (challenged ideas about sex differences), Sullivan (importance of close friendships in childhood for intimate relationships in later life), daughter Anna Freud (psychoanalysis of children)
   2. Erik Erikson is most important lifespan neo-Freudian theorist
      a. Like Freud, was concerned with inner dynamics of personality and saw development in stages
      b. Unlike Freud,
         i. Less emphasis on sexual urges as drivers of development
         ii. Less emphasis on unconscious, irrational, selfish id and more on rational ego
         iii. More positive view of human nature
         iv. More emphasis on development after adolescence
   3. Psychosocial stages
      a. Erikson saw resolution of eight major psychosocial crises as critical
         i. Trust vs. mistrust—key is general responsiveness of caregiver (healthy balance of trust with some skepticism is optimal)
         ii. Autonomy vs. shame—concerning ability to act independently
         iii. Initiative vs. guilt—preschool sense of autonomy
         iv. Industry versus inferiority—elementary age sense of mastery
         v. Identity vs. role confusion—adolescent acquisition of identity that may involve an "identity crisis"
         vi. Intimacy vs. isolation—young adult commitment to a long-term relationship
         vii. Generativity vs. stagnation—middle-age sense of having produced something meaningful (family, work, or volunteer related)
         viii. Integrity vs. despair—elderly sense of life meaning and success
      b. Did not agree with Freud that personality "set in stone" during first five years
      c. Stage development due to biological maturation and environmental demands
      d. School refusal explained by Freud as due to separation anxiety (mother-child relationship from birth), and by Erikson as a crisis of industry vs. inferiority (Exploration Box on school refusal from Erikson's perspective)

B. Strengths and Weaknesses
   1. Strengths
      a. Its emphases on rational, adaptive nature, and social influences easier to accept that Freudian ideas
      b. Captures some central development issues within the eight stages
      c. Influenced thinking about adolescence and beyond
   2. Weaknesses
      a. Like Freud, vague and difficult to test
      b. Provides description, but not adequate explanation of development

IV Learning Theories

    A. Watson's Classical Conditioning

        1. Behaviorism—belief that only observed behavior should be studied

        2. Rejected psychoanalytic theory and explained Freud using learning principles

        3. Children have no inborn tendencies, as environment determines which way they grow up (like Locke)

        4. Classical conditioning—simple form of learning in which a stimulus that initially has no effects comes to elicit a response through association with something that already elicits the response

            a. First discovered by Russian physiologist Ivan Pavlov

                i. Accidently discovered while studying digestive system of dogs

                ii. Famous study in which Pavlov demonstrated that dogs could learn to salivate to a bell when bell was paired with meat powder that naturally elicits the reaction of salivation

            b. Key elements of classical conditioning

                i. Unconditioned stimulus (UCS)—unlearned stimulus (food)

                ii. Unconditioned response (UR)—unlearned response (salivation)

                iii. Conditioned stimulus (CS)—stimulus created by pairing UCS (meat power) with an new stimulus (bell ring) which becomes a learned stimulus

                iv. Conditioned response (CR)—learned response of salivation in response to CS of ringing bell

        5. Classical conditioning study with colleague Rosalie Rayners in which infant "Albert" was conditioned to fear a rat

                i. Loud noise created by banging steel rod with a hammer was unconditioned stimulus (UCS)—unlearned stimulus

                ii. Crying (fear) was unconditioned response (UR)

                iii. White rat became conditioned stimulus (CS)—learned stimulus producing conditioned response (CR)—learned response of crying after it was paired with loud noise

                iv. Study clearly demonstrated that emotional response of fear can be learned

                v. Fear generalized from white rat to other furry items like rabbit and Santa Claus mask

            b. Fear can be unlearned if fear stimulus is paired with UCS for happy emotions

        6. Classical conditioning involved when children learn to "love" caring parents

        7. Rejects stage conceptualization of development

        8. Learning is a behavioral change that is context specific and differs enormously from person to person

    B. Skinner: Operant Conditioning

        1. Operant conditioning—learning thought to become more or less probable depending on consequences it produces

        2. Reinforcement—consequences that strengthen a response (increase probability of future response)

        3. Positive—something added

            a. Positive reinforcement—something pleasant added in attempt to strengthen behavior

    i. Positive reinforcement best when continuous and when skill first being learned

    ii. Can shift to a "partial reinforcement schedule" once behavior is learned to maintain the behavior

  4. Negative—something removed

   a. Negative reinforcement—something unpleasant taken in attempt to strengthen behavior

    i. Fastening seatbelt to escape annoying noise illustrates negative reinforcement

    ii. Bad habits may develop because they allow person to avoid or escape unpleasant events (e.g., lying to avoid parental lecture)

  5. Punishment—consequences that decrease a future response (weaken a behavior)

   a. Positive punishment—something unpleasant added in attempt to weaken behavior

   b. Negative punishment—something pleasant taken in attempt to weaken behavior

  6. Extinction—no consequence given and behavior becomes less frequent

  7. Skinner emphasized positive reinforcement and generally discouraged the use of physical punishment in childrearing

   a. Many parents believe that spanking is necessary in raising children

  8. Physical punishment best used in specific circumstances

   a. Administered immediately following act

   b. Administered consistently following each offense

   c. Not overly harsh

   d. Accompanied by explanation

   e. Administered by otherwise affectionate person

   f. Used sparingly and combined with efforts to reinforce acceptable behaviors

  9. Carefully designed research indicates that physical punishment can have negative
effects on child development

   a. Berlin and colleagues found spanking associated with aggressive behavior and lower developmental scores

   b. Punishment may make children anxious and teach that hitting is an appropriate way to solve problems

  10. Skinner and Watson believed that development depends on learning experiences

  11. Skinner's operant conditioning principles help explain many aspects of development and is still applied in areas like cognitive-behavioral interventions in education and therapeutic settings

  12. Some psychologists believe that Skinner placed too little emphasis on the role of cognitive processes

 G. Bandura: Social Cognitive Theory

  1. Social cognitive theory formerly called "social learning theory"

   a. Humans are cognitive beings with active information processing skills

  2. Humans' sophisticated cognitive abilities distinguish them from other animals

  3. Agrees that Skinner's operant conditioning is an important type of learning but…

   a. Humans can think about behavior and anticipate consequences

   b. Humans engage in self-reinforcement and self-punishment

   c. Cognition affects behavior

4. Observational learning—(from models) most important mechanism for behavior change
   a. Imitating allows children to learn many behaviors
   b. Observational learning is a more cognitive form of learning in that it requires paying attention, constructing, and remembering mental representations
5. Classic Bandura experiment using "Bobo" doll showed that children could learn a behavior neither elicited by a conditioned stimulus (as in classical conditioning) nor performed and strengthened by a reinforcer (as in operant conditioning)
   a. Children shown movie of adult hitting Bobo doll with a mallet and harming it in other ways (e.g., with rubber balls)
   b. Children then saw adult in movie praised, punished, or receive no consequences
      i. Children seeing reward and no-consequence imitate models more
      ii. Children seeing punishment did not model but did demonstrate learning—process called latent learning
   c. Children displayed vicarious reinforcement—learner changes behaviors based on consequences observed being given to a model
6. Observation learning important in our society but more important in traditional societies
   a. Mayan children were more attentive to siblings playing with a new toy and learned more than European American children
7. Human agency—ways in which humans deliberately exercise control over environments and lives
8. Self-efficacy—sense of one's ability to control self or environment
9. Watson and Skinner believed people are passively shaped by environment, but Bandura disagreed
   a. Reciprocal determinism—mutual influence of individuals and social environments determines behavior
10. Like other learning theorists, Bandura doubts the existence of stages
    a. View cognitive capacities as maturing over time
    b. Learning experiences differentiate development of child of same age
    c. Learning theorists do not give a general description of the course of normal development
11. School refusal explained by learning theorists as learned through classical conditioning (traumatic fire drill), punishing or reinforcing consequences, or via observational learning (Exploration Box on learning theory explanations for school refusal)

D. Strengths and Weaknesses
   1. Learning theory strengths
      a. Precise and testable
      b. Controlled experiments show how people learn many things
      c. Principles operate across the lifespan
      d. Many important practical applications (e.g., optimizing development and treating developmental problems)

2. Learning theory weaknesses
    a. Doesn't show that learning actually causes observed developmental changes (just that it might)
    b. Oversimplifies development by focusing on experience and downplaying biological influences
    c. Today's learning theorists appreciate how factors like genetic endowment, previous learning history, personality, and social context affect learning experiences

V Piaget: Cognitive-Developmental Theory
A. Jean Piaget
    1. Swiss scholar; began studying children's intellectual development in the 1920s
    2. Greatly influenced study of intellectual development in children
    3. First scientific work (study of albino sparrows) at age 11
    4. Blended interest in zoology and philosophy
    5. Devoted life to study of how knowledge is acquired and used to adapt to the world
    6. Worked on IQ testing with Binet
        a. Emphasis on intelligence testing is on number of correct answers
    7. Piaget emphasized errors in thinking (wrong answers)
        a. Questions children to find out how they are trying to solve problems
        b. Argues that differences in cognitive development are qualitative in nature
B. Constructivism
    1. Constructivism—active construction of new knowledge based on experience
        a. Children are curious and active explorers of their environments
        b. Children use current knowledge to solve problems but also revise understanding to fit reality
    2. Stage progression due to interaction of biological maturation and environment
C. Stages of Cognitive Development
    1. Four major periods (stages) of cognitive development: sensorimotor (birth to age 2), preoperational (ages 2 to 7), concrete operational (ages 7 to 11), formal operations (ages 11 to 12 or older)
    2. Sensorimotor stage
        a. Deal with world directly through perceptions (senses) and actions (motor skills)
        b. Unable to use symbols to help solve problems mentally
    3. Preoperational stage
        a. Preschoolers
        b. Capacity for symbolic thought
        c. Egocentric thinkers who have difficulty adopting perspectives of others
        d. Fooled by appearance as demonstrated in conservation tasks
            i. Famous conservation liquid quantity task
            ii. Child shown two short, wide glasses with equal levels of water
            iii. Water from one glass poured into a taller, thinner glass
            iv. Tricked by height of tall glass into thinking that that glass now has more water (ignore width and focus on height)

v. Fail to appreciate the concept of reversibility and believe that if water poured from tall glass into short glass, it would overflow

4. Concrete operations stage
   a. School-aged children
   b. Use trial-and-error strategy
   c. Perform mental operations in their heads on concrete objects (thus the term "concrete operations")
   d. Can solve conservation tasks
   e. Difficulty with abstract and hypothetical concepts

5. Formal operations stage
   a. Adolescents
   b. Can think abstractly and define abstract terms (e.g., justice in terms of fairness versus the cop on the corner)
   c. Can formulate hypotheses in their head and will eventually adopt systematic and experimental ways to test these hypotheses
   d. Can devise "grand theories" about others

6. School refusal discussed in terms of thoughts concerning home life and school and an assessment of current stage of development (e.g., preoperational logic that murder on television may occur in school) (Exploration Box on Piaget's explanation of school refusal)

D. Strengths and Weaknesses
   1. Strengths of Piaget's approach
      a. Pioneer with long-lasting impact on thinking about human development
      b. Many of Piaget's concepts accepted (e.g., children active in own development, change in thinking can be qualitative, development occurs through an interaction between nature and nurture)
      c. Much of the description of intellectual development supported through research
      d. Very influential in education and childrearing practices
   2. Weaknesses of Piaget's approach
      a. Too little emphasis on motivation and emotion
      b. Questioning of stage model
      c. Underestimated children's cognitive skills
      d. Too little emphasis on role of others in influencing cognitive development

E. Other Perspectives on Cognitive Development
   1. Sociocultural perspective and information-processing approach challenged some of Piaget's ideas
   2. Lev Vygotsky's sociocultural perspective—development shaped by organism growing in culture
      a. Russian psychologist who took issue with Piaget's notion of universal stages of cognitive development
      b. Cognitive development shaped by sociocultural context that occurs and grows out of interactions with members of the culture
      c. Tools of thought in a culture, especially in the form of language, shapes behavior

   d. Cognitive development varies by social and historical context

   e. Children are social beings who develop through guided participation by others (e.g., parents, teacher) in culturally important activities

  3. Information-processing theory

   a. Dominant approach to cognitive development beginning in the 1980s

   b. Likens mind to computer software and hardware

   c. Focus on fundamental processes like memory, decision-making, and attention

   d. Developmental changes in capacity and speed of information processing and information in memory are important

VI Systems Theories

 A. Contextual, Systems, and Contextual Theories

  1. Some systems theories called contextual theories because they emphasize interaction between human and the contexts in which they develop

  2. Some systems theories called system/dynamic theories because they claim that develop arises from ongoing transactions in which changing organism and changing environment affect each other

  3. Changes over lifespan arise from ongoing transactions and mutual influences between organism and changing world

   a. Development takes a variety of paths

  4. Bronfenbrenner's bioecological model illustrates a systems perspective

   a. Individuals with biological characteristics interacts with four environmental systems

  5. Thelen's theory of motor development is an example of a dynamic theory

  6. Gottlieb's viewed in context of evolutionary history and interaction between individual and environment

   a. Bronfenbrenner began by focusing environment and realized the importance of biological factors

   b. Gottlieb began by focusing on biological factors (genetic influences) and realized the importance of environmental factors

 B. Evolutionary Theory and Ethology

  1. Gottlieb's perspective influenced by Darwin's work on animal and human development in the context of evolutionary theory

   a. Darwin maintained that genes aid in adapting to the environment and are passed on to future generations

    i. Evolutionary theory prompted research into how characteristics and behaviors may have helped our ancestors adapt

  2. Ethology—studies evolved behavior of species in natural environment

   a. Behavior adaptive in particular environments

   b. Must study behavior of animals in natural context

   c. Observe or experimentally study species-specific behavior

  3. Attachment theory is viewed in terms of psychoanalytic and ethological theory

  4. Evolutionary psychology—application of evolutionary theory to understanding the thinking and behavior of humans

C. Gottlieb's Epigenetic Psychobiological Systems Perspective
   1. Epigenetic Psychobiological Systems Perspective
      a. Development product of interacting between biological and environmental forces in a larger system
   2. Species change
      a. Starting point of epigenetic psychobiological systems perspective is recognition that evolution has endowed us with genetic makeup (not *tabula rasae*)
      b. Predisposition to develop in certain direction
      c. Genes and environments interact because humans actively and deliberately change their environments
         i. New environments make different genes more critical to survival
         ii. Genes associated with high tolerance for lactose milk have become more prevalent as dairy farming has become more common
   3. Epigenesis
      a. Genes do not dictate, just make some outcomes more probable
      b. Epigenesis—process through which genes and environment co-act to bring forth particular course of development
      c. Gottlieb's emphasized
         i. Activity of genes which turn on and off at different points in development
         ii. Activity of neurons
         iii. Organism's behavior
         iv. Environmental influences of all kinds
      d. Gottlieb accused biologists of wrongly claiming genes dictate what happens in development and genetic factors more important than environment
      e. Behavior cannot be explained by reducing it to simpler components (e.g., genes); need to appreciate that behavior and environment influence gene activity
         i. Stimulation from the environment, gained partly through an infant's exploratory behavior, not only produces neural activity and changes the brain but also affects the activity of the genes, which in turn influence the formation and function of the neural network necessary for further development and behavior
      f. Instinctive behaviors may not be expressed if environmental conditions do not exist
         i. Duckling vocalizations: if duckling embryos are exposed to chicken calls before they hatch and prevented from vocalizing at birth (having no experience with hearing ducklike calls), they come to prefer the call of a chicken to that of a duck
      g. Epigenetic psychobiological systems perspective helps us appreciate that development is driven by genetic, neural, behavioral, and environmental influences
      h. The nature-nurture issue vanishes in Gottlieb's perspective
      i. The developmental story cannot be predicted until we see what emerges from epigenesis

j. Bronfenbrenner and Gottlieb's models are in close agreement

k. School refusal could be the result of interaction between factors like genetic predisposition toward anxiety, the amount of neural activity in response to a noisy and chaotic classroom, the behavioral ability to cope, and an environmentally gruff teacher. (Exploration Box on Gottlieb's perspective on school refusal)

4. Strengths and Weaknesses

a. Strengths of systems theories
   i. Complex view of human development makes sense because human behavior is complex

b. Weaknesses of systems theories
   i. Fail to provide a picture of the course of development (and may never be able to do so)

c. Development may be more predictable than Gottlieb's theory implies
   i. May not be able to make exact predictions but can talk in terms of attainments that are more or less probable

VII Theories in Perspective

A. Theoretical Perspectives

1. Stage Theorists: Freud, Erikson, Piaget

a. Development guided in universal direction

b. Influenced by biological/maturational forces that unfold according to a master plan (assuming a normal environment), evolving through distinct or discontinuous stages

c. Parents subscribing to this theory would
   i. See selves as supporters of their child's development
   ii. Trust their child's tendencies to seek learning experiences
   iii. Not feel compelled to structure all their child's experiences (basic philosophy in Montessori schools)

2. Learning Theorists: Watson, Skinner, Bandura

a. Emphasis on influence of environment over biological factors

b. Parents subscribing to this theory would
   i. See themselves as "trainers" and take deliberate steps to shape their child's development

3. Systems Theorists: Vygotsky, Gottlieb

a. Focus on impact of both biology and environment with individual as an active agent

b. Potential exists for qualitative (stage) and quantitative change

c. Parents subscribing to Gottlieb's theory would
   i. See themselves as partners in the developmental process and appreciate the fact that as they influence their child, their child is also influencing them

4. Changing World Views

a. Our understanding of human development is ever changing

b. Systems theories more prevalent today
   i. Moved beyond black-and-white positions on nature and nurture influences

      ii. Understand potential to develop in good and bad directions

     iii. Understand that development is both continuous and discontinuous

     iv. Understand that there are both universal and cultural and time-specific aspects of human development

  c. Different theories make different assumptions and stimulate different research

  d. Theories guide practice (Application Box on different theories' take on ways of reducing teenage pregnancy)

SUGGESTIONS FOR CLASS DISCUSSIONS OR PROJECTS

1. Ask students to generate a list of observations concerning some question of development (e.g., Do males and females behave differently? Do people become more intelligent as they age?) Then ask them to develop a theory that ties these observations together and helps to explain them. Discuss the value of developing a theory in order to impose order on the vast number of seemingly diverse observations. Students may develop different theories that all have some value and can be used to discuss eclecticism. You might want to follow up on this suggestion by having students generate hypotheses from the theory they developed, and design a study to test at least one of the hypotheses.

2. Have students find and read excerpts from original writings of theorists such as Freud (1923), Piaget (1960), and Skinner (1982). Then have them compare these reading to the information presented in the text. Students could discuss advantages and disadvantages of using original source materials. You might also have them identify one key element found in the original material, but not in the text, and then have them write a new paragraph or two (on the material) that they would like to see added to the text.

    Freud, S. (1923). *The Ego and the Id* (J. Riviere translation). New York: W.W. Norton & Co., 1960.

    Piaget, J. (1960). *The Child's Conception of the World*. NJ: Littlefield, Adams & Co.

    Skinner, B. F. (1982). Baby in a box. In J. K. Gardner (Ed.) *Readings in Developmental Psychology*, 2nd ed. MA: Little, Brown & Co. Originally appeared in *Ladies' Home Journal*, 1946 (volume 62, pp. 30-31, 135-136, 138).

3. Obtain some older childrearing manuals (often available at flea markets, second-hand book stores, libraries, or from older parents) and have students discuss the theoretical underpinnings of the manuals. In many cases, it is possible to see the influence of theories such as behaviorism or psychoanalytic theory. In addition, students may be fascinated to read what parents were advised in previous generations. Early editions of Benjamin Spock (1945) can be found in most libraries. By comparing an early edition of Spock's book to a recent one, students might assess how thinking has changed over the years. Young (1990) reviewed nearly 30 years of *Infant Care* and *Parents* magazine to determine whether psychological theories and research were indeed accurately communicated to parents. She found that some advice reflected research findings, while other advice from experts reflected beliefs consistent with the larger social-cultural context, indicating that research itself is affected by culture (a Bronfenbrennarian notion).

Spock, B. (1945). *Baby and Child Care*. New York: Pocket Books.

Young, K.T. (1990). American conceptions of infant development from 1955 to 1984: What the experts are telling people. *Child Development, 61*, 17-28.

4. Choose a problem parents may have with their child (advice columns are a useful source) and discuss it from the different theoretical perspectives. For example, one mother wrote to an advice column that her 2-and-a-half-year-old daughter was sleeping in the parents' bed every night. This began soon after the child was born, and the mother found that it was easy to breast-feed in the bed while her husband worked the night shift. When his work schedule changed, they wanted the daughter to sleep in her own bed, but were unsuccessful in achieving this. Students can analyze this from several perspectives, including psychoanalytic (oral gratification, unconscious motivation), learning theory (reinforcement history of both child and mother), cognitive-developmental theory (cognitive schema for bedtime ritual, assimilation and accommodation of new behaviors into cognitive structures), and contextual/systems theory (change in the environment causes a change in the person, which in turn affects the environment). Other problems to explore might include bed-wetting, school phobia, or even ambivalence about an impending marriage. How would each theory (or selected theories) explain these problems?

5. The issue of adoption can be used to discuss the nature-nurture issue as well as the continuity-discontinuity issue. Some questions that adopting parents might ask are listed below. Divide students into small groups and have each group discuss these questions and formulate answers before discussing them as an entire class.
- How will early experiences affect the later development of this child?
- Can we provide an enriched environment that will overcome any adverse early experiences?
- What if some characteristics are genetically based and our environment have no effect?
- What traits might be lurking in this child's genotype?

6. Using the critical development issues of, 1) nature and nurture, 2) activity and passivity, 3) continuity and discontinuity, and 4) universality and context-specificity, have students develop their own theory of lifespan development. For extra interest and challenge, have them support their theory using examples from their own lives.

SUGGESTED FILMS AND VIDEOS

Bandura's Social Cognitive Theory: An Introduction (2003, Insight Media DVD, 30 minutes): Video featuring narration by Bandura concerning his early Bobo doll experiment and recent works.

History of Psychology 2: Freud, Jung, and Psychoanalysis (2006, Insight Media, DVD 30 minutes): Provides a great introduction to theories of adaptation and evolution that developed in the 1800s.

<u>Nature and Nurture: Heredity and Environment</u> (2003, Insight Media, VHS 30 minutes): Examines how environmental and biological factors combine to impact development. <u>The Developing Person</u> (2003, Insight Media, VHS 30 minutes): Traces study of human development from Lock/Rousseau to Piaget/Erikson/Bronfenbrenner.

<u>Theories of Human Development</u> (24 segments) (2002, Insight Media, VHS, 30 minutes each): Introduces six major theories (Freud, Erikson, Bowlby & Ainsworth, Bandura, Piaget, and Vygotsky).

SUGGESTED WEBSITES

Albert Bandura
http://www.ship.edu/~cgboeree/bandura.html

B.F. Skinner Foundation
http://www.bfskinner.org/

Erik Erikson
http://webspace.ship.edu/cgboer/genpsyerikson.html

Jean Piaget Society
http://www.piaget.org/

Sigmund Freud and the Freud Archives
http://users.rcn.com/brill/freudarc.html

SUGGESTED READINGS

Crain, W. (2005). *Theories of Development: Concepts and Applications* (5th ed). NJ: Prentice-Hall.

Guastello, S.J., and Koopmans, M. (2009). *Chaos and Complexity in Psychology: The Theory of Nonlinear Dynamical Systems*. Cambridge, MA: Cambridge University Press.

Newman, B.M., and Newman, P.R. (2007). *Theories of Human Development*. London: Psychology Press.

Salkind, N.J. (2004). *An Introduction to Theories of Human Development*. Thousand Oaks, CA: SAGE Publications.

Thomas, R.M. (2005). *Comparing Theories of Child Development (with InfoTrac®)*, (6th ed). Pacific Grove, CA: Brooks/Cole.

GENES, ENVIRONMENT, AND DEVELOPMENT

LEARNING OBJECTIVES

After reading and studying the material in this chapter, you should be able to answer the following questions.

EVOLUTION AND SPECIES HEREDITY
1. What do evolution and species heredity contribute to our understanding of universal patterns of development?

INDIVIDUAL HEREDITY
2. What are the basic workings of individual heredity, including the contributions of genes, chromosomes, the zygote, and the processes of mitosis and meiosis? Note the difference between genotype and phenotype.

3. How are traits passed from parents to offspring? What is an example of how a child could inherit a trait through each of the three mechanisms described in the text?

4. What methods are used to screen for genetic abnormalities? What are the advantages and disadvantages of using such techniques to test for prenatal problems? What are some abnormalities that can currently be detected with genetic screening?

STUDYING GENETIC AND ENVIRONMENTAL INFLUENCES
5. How do scientists study the contributions of heredity and environment to behavioral characteristics? Describe the logic of the methods, as well as strengths and weaknesses of each method.

6. How can concordance rates help researchers estimate the influences of heredity and environment? How do genes, shared environment, and nonshared environment contribute to individual differences in traits?

SELECTED FINDINGS
7. How do genes and environments contribute to individual differences in intellectual abilities, personality and temperament, and psychological disorders?

8. What do researchers mean when they talk about the heritability of traits? Which traits are more strongly heritable than others?

GENES AND ENVIRONMENT CONSPIRING
9. What is an example that illustrates the concept of a gene-environment interaction?

10. What are three ways that genes and environments correlate to influence behavior?

11.   What are the major controversies surrounding genetic research?

CHAPTER OUTLINE

I   Evolution and Species Heredity
  A. Main Points of Evolution and Species Heredity
   1. Virtually everyone develops in similar ways at similar ages
      a. Species heredity—genetic endowment members of a species have in common
         i.   Birds can fly and humans can feel guilty (but not vice versa)
         ii. Species heredity is one reason that certain patterns of development and aging are universal
         iii. Tied to Darwin's evolutionary theory
   2. Main arguments of Darwin's theory
      a. There is genetic variation in a species (members of a species do not share all of the same genes)
      b. Some genes aid in adaptation more than others do (e.g., how to find food)
      c. Genes that aid in adaptation to the environment will be passed on more often than genes that do not—the principle of natural selection
   3. Kettlewell's study of moths in England demonstrates natural selection principles
      a. Study of pollution and moth color
      b. Light-colored moths survived in rural areas with light-colored trees
      c. Changes in pollution led to changes in moth color
      d. Evolution not just about genes; rather, development is driven by interaction between genes and environment
   4. Cultural evolution—we "inherit" from pervious generations a characteristically human environment and tried and true ways of adapting to it, learning to adjust to it, and passing on what we know to the next generation
   5. Most significant biological evolutionary legacy is powerful and flexible brain that assists in learning

II   Individual Heredity
  A. The Genetic Code
   1. Early genetic materials
      a. Zygote—cell created at conception
      b. Chromosomes—46 threadlike bodies (23 pairs, one from father and one from mother) containing the genes
      c. Meiosis—reproductive cell division in which one 46-chromosome sperm or ova splits into two 46-chromosome cells, and these split into two more cells (each with 23 chromosomes), resulting in one viable egg (and three nonfunctional in females) or four viable sperm in males
      d. Mitosis—cell division producing two identical cells (e.g., 46-chromosome cell splits into two 46-chromosome cells) continues throughout life
         i.   Mitosis creates new cells that replace old cells

e. Deoxyribonucleic acid (DNA)—double helix molecule that comprises each chromosome
   i. Four types of molecules: A-adenine, C-cytosine, G-guanine, T-thymine
   ii. Gene—functional unit sequence of DNA
   iii. Humans likely have no more than 20,000-25,000 genes
   iv. Each gene has several variants called alleles
   v. Genes lead to production proteins that are the building block of bodily tissues and substances like hormones, neurotransmitters, and enzymes

2. The Human Genome Project
   a. Federally funded attempt to map out entire DNA sequence of all human chromosomes using supercomputers; completed in 2003
      i. 3.1 billion A, C, G, T molecules
      ii. Only about 2% of genome consists of traditionally defined genes (those that are transcribed into RNA and serve as templates for the production of certain proteins)
      iii. Remaining stretches of DNA consist of "junk genes" that regulate activity of genes
      iv. More emphasis being placed on that 98% of DNA
   b. Humans share majority of genes with primates
      i. Some gene alleles have evolved in recent centuries (e.g., variation that makes humans tolerate lactose in milk driven by rapid spread of dairy farming in Europe)

3. Genetic uniqueness and relatedness
   a. Each parent can produce more than 8 million genetically different sperm or ova, and any couple could produce 64 trillion babies without having two with identical genes
   b. Crossing over—exchanges in pairs of chromosomes before separating
   c. Identical twins (monozygotic)—one fertilized ovum splits to make two genetically identical individuals (1 in 250 births)
   d. Child shares average of about 50 percent of genes with each parent
   e. Non-identical twin siblings share about 50% of their genes
   f. Fraternal twins (dizygotic)—two eggs released and each fertilized by different sperm (1 in 125 births)
      i. Same genetic relationship as with any other sibling
      ii. Tend to run in families
      iii. More common today due to increased use of fertility drugs and in vitro fertilization
   g. Individuals share some genes with all kin members

4. Determination of sex
   a. 22 of 23 chromosomes (autosomes) are similar in males and females
   b. 23rd pair are the sex chromosomes
   c. Male has one X and one Y chromosome
      i. X is stubbier and has fewer genes than the Y chromosome
   d. XX is typical genetic code for female
   e. Karyotype—photograph of the arrangement of chromosomes

5. X vs. Y chromosome
   a. X has almost 1,100 genes
   b. Y has about 80 (many of which are involved in sperm production)
   c. Most of one X chromosome is normally inactive in females during early prenatal period, but the 15 percent that is active may contribute to sex differences
   d. Father's Y chromosome determines child's gender
   e. Women have been unfairly criticized for not bearing a male heir
B. Translation and Expression of the Genetic Code
   1. Genotype—genetic makeup one inherits
   2. Phenotype—actual characteristics based on genetics and environment
   3. Genes responsible for production of chemical substances (e.g., melanin, which impacts iris color)
   4. Genetically coded proteins guide formation of neurons, influencing potential intelligence and personality
   5. Genes influenced by biochemical environment surrounding genes and behavior of individual genetic "blueprint" written in erasable pencil (not indelible ink)
      a. Genetic expression—activation of particular genes in particular cells at particular times in the lifespan
         i. A gene is influential only if it is "turned on"
         ii. Genetic expression can be affected by environmental factors like diet, stress, toxins, and parenting
   6. Fraga and colleagues analyzed expression of genes in identical twins
      a. Older twin pair more genetically different from younger pairs
         i. Less time spent together was predictive of more genetic variation
         ii. Additional environmental factors (e.g., rat pup grooming by mothers) have been found to impact genetic expression (Exploration Box on early experience and gene expression)
   7. No one completely understands epigenetic process (transformation of a single cell into a living, behaving human)
C. Mechanisms of Inheritance
   1. Single gene-pair inheritance—characteristic influenced by only one pair of genes (one from mom and one from dad)
      a. Gregor Mendel (a 19th century monk) pioneer in inheritance research
         i. Noticed patterns in cross-bred strains of peas
         ii. Called one dominant, as it was likely to show up in later generations
      b. Dominant genes—if even only one gene inherited, will produce the effect
      c. Recessive genes—need one gene from both parents to produce effect
         i. Tongue curling dominant
         ii. Two tongue-curling parents could have a no-curling child if both pass on recessive gene (chances of this are 25%)
      d. Incomplete dominance—individual expresses a blend of dominant and recessive traits
         i. Child of one parent with dark skin and the other parent with light skin who has light brown skin
      e. Co-dominance—neither gene in pair is dominant or recessive
         i. AB blood type is mix of A and B blood types

2. Sex-linked inheritance—trait influenced by gene on sex chromosomes
   a. Most are X-linked (rather than sex-linked) as most attributes are associated with genes on only the X chromosome
   b. Color blindness (more common in males) is sex-linked
      i. Boy inherits defective X chromosome from mom and no color vision gene on Y will be color blind
      ii. Girl inherits defective X chromosome may inherit normal color vision gene on other X chromosome and will have normal color vision
   c. Hemophilia—genetic disorder resulting in deficiency in blood's ability to clot is sex-linked disorder
      i. More common in males as it is associated with a recessive gene on X chromosome
3. Polygenic inheritance—most human characteristics determined by multiple genes
4. Polygenic traits—characteristic influence by multiple pairs of genes
   a. The characteristic impacted by polygenetic traits (e.g., weight, intelligence, depression) tends to be distributed in the population in a bell-shaped or normal curve

D. Mutations
1. Change in structure or arrangement of one or more genes that produce new phenotype
   a. Hemophilia may have been introduced to royal families of Europe by Queen Victoria
   b. Environmental hazards (e.g., radiation) can increase odds of mutations
2. Some mutations beneficial
   a. Sickle-cell disease—sickle-shaped white blood cells protects from effects of malaria
   b. Does more harm than good in individuals living in non-malaria environments

E. Chromosome Abnormalities
1. Child receives too many or too few chromosomes (about 1 in 160 born with more or less than 46 chromosomes)
   a. Down syndrome
      i. Trisomy 21 (three 21st chromosomes)
      ii. Physical (e.g., distinctive eye folds, short, stubby limbs) and mental (some degree of mental retardation) impact
      iii. In some parts of the world, over half of these infants die due to heart defects, but in United States and other wealthy nations, many with Down syndrome are living into middle age (many show premature signs of aging including Alzheimer's disease)
      iv. Both mother and fathers can contribute to odds of having child with Down syndrome
      v. Odds 1 in 733 (but increase with parents' age, especially maternal age of 35 or higher)
      vi. As the result of more exposure to environmental hazards, aging ova and sperm more likely to be abnormal
      vii. Delaying parenthood until 30s or 40s increases risk of chromosomal abnormalities

2. Sex chromosome abnormalities
   a. Turner syndrome (about 1 on 3,000 females)
      i. Female with a single X chromosome (XO)
      ii. Physically small, cannot reproduce, stubby fingers, lower than average spatial and math skills
   b. Klinefelter's syndrome (about 1 in 200 males)
      i. Male with an extra X chromosome (XXY)
      ii. Tall but sterile and may have feminine sex characteristics
   c. Fragile X syndrome
      i. Most common hereditary cause of mental retardation
      ii. One arm of X chromosome nearly detached (thus the term fragile)
      iii. Results in mental retardation, some form of cognitive impairment, and autism in some
      iv. More common in males
      v. Too many repeated gene sequences leads to problem in formation of connections between neurons in brain
      vi. Those who carry the gene but do not have enough repeating sequences to have full-blown fragile X, may develop tremors or have problems with infertility or early menopause in middle age
F. Genetic Diagnosis and Counseling
   1. 97% of babies are born without major birth defects/disease/disorder
      a. Genetic counseling assesses risk concerning potential for genetic problems
      b. Human Genome Project results have increased access to information about genetic defects
   2. Examples of disorders that can be identified via genetic counseling: cystic fibrosis, hemophilia, phenylketonuria (PKU), Tay Sachs disease
      a. Counselors report percent probability of having a child with a disorder
      b. Genetic counseling for sickle-cell disease
         i. Disease causes the development of sickle-shaped blood cells that cluster together and result in less oxygen being distributed through the circulatory system
         ii. Impacts include breathing difficulty, joint swelling and pain, death from blood clots or that lead to heart or kidney failure
         iii. 9% of African Americans have Ss genotype (one dominant gene "S" and one recessive gene "s" for sickle cells)
         iv. These individuals are called carriers—have a recessive gene that can be transmitted to offspring but due to the presence of a normal dominant gene, they who do not show symptoms
         v. Carriers have two in four (50%) chance of having a child who is a carrier who has both round and sickle-shaped blood cells
   3. Common prenatal screening procedures used by counselors include ultrasound, amniocentesis, chorionic villus biopsy, maternal blood sampling, preimplantation genetic diagnosis (Exploration Box on prenatal detection of abnormalities)
      i. Ultrasound—visual image of fetus
      ii. Amniocentesis—sample of amniotic fluid analyzed for genetic material and other problems
      iii. Chorionic villus sampling—extract hair cells from chorion surrounding fetus and check for genetic defects

    iv. Maternal blood sampling—check fetal blood cells that entered mom via placenta

    v. Preimplantation genetic diagnosis—allow conception via in vitro fertilization, check DNA of first cells

  4. Huntington's disease

   a. Famous and terrifying disorder associated with a single dominant gene

   b. Typically strikes in middle age and deteriorates nervous system with numerous symptoms

    i. Slurred speech

    ii. Erratic walking, grimaces, jerking movements

    iii. Increased irritability and moodiness

    iv. Dementia and loss of cognitive ability

   c. Gusella discovered location for Huntington's gene on Chromosome 4

   d. Can be diagnosed post-birth or with preimplantation genetic diagnosis

III Studying Genetic and Environmental Influences

 A. Basics on genetics

  1. Behavioral genetics—study of the extent to which genetic and environmental differences are responsible for a given trait

  2. Impossible to give a specific percentage about how much the environment (or genetics) contributes to a specific trait

  3. Heritability—estimated proportion of trait variability attributable to genes

   a. To say that intelligence is heritable is to say that differences in intelligence between people are to some degree attributable to differences in genetic endowments

 B. Experimental Breeding

  1. Selective breeding—attempt to breed particular traits into animals

   a. Tyron bright and dull maze rats studies indicate that activity level, emotion, sex drive may have genetic basis

   b. Due to ethical reasons, selective breeding research cannot be done

 C. Twin, Adoption, and Family Studies

  1. Twins studies

   a. Compare identical twins (share 100% of genes) and fraternal twins (share an average of 50% of genes) raised together and reared apart

    i. Criticisms of this approach include problem of shared prenatal environment and more similar treatment of identical twins vs. fraternal twins

  2. Adoption study

   a. Similar environments and different genes

   b. If adopted children like adoptive parents, characteristic said to be due to experience, but if they are not like adoptive parents, characteristics said to be due to genetic factors

   c. Criticisms of the approach

    i. Maternal prenatal environment could also impact development

    ii. Must correct for tendency of adoption agencies to place children in above-average environments

3. Family studies
   a. Compare various members within family (e.g., half-siblings, unrelated siblings from step families)
D. Estimating Influences
   4. Concordance rates—percent of pairs if when one has trait, so does other
      a. Bailey and Pillard, homosexual concordance rate for identical twins 52 percent, fraternal twins 22 percent (indicates that genetic makeup contributes to sexual orientation, but so do environmental factors)
   5. Plomin and colleagues' behavioral geneticists estimated impact of three factors on emotionality
      a. Genes
         i. Some support for heritability of emotionality
      b. Shared environmental influences—common work or home experience
         i. Very weak support for influence on emotionality
      c. Nonshared environmental influences—unique experiences not shared by other family members (e.g., differential treatment by parents, different life crises)
         i. Support for the impact of unique experiences on emotionality
      d. Failure to find a strong shared environmental influence on a behavior does not mean family influences are unimportant
E. Molecular Genetics
   a. Analysis of particular genes and their effect
   b. Identify how much multiple genes contribute to polygenetic traits
      i. Many genes contribute to polygenetic effects
      ii. Goal is to identify the percent of contribution for each gene; results of this effort have been disappointing, with each gene making only a small contribution to the overall variation
      iii. Apolipoprotein E (ApoE4) gene linked to risk of Alzheimer's disease, but many with Alzheimer's do not have the gene
      iv. ApoE4 linked with greater memory deterioration but not Alzheimer's disease
      v. Having ApoE4 gene and experiencing specific environmental event (e.g., head injury) may increase risk

VI Selective Findings
A. Intellectual Abilities
   1. Bouchard Jr. and McGue correlated IQ scores of different pairs of relatives
      a. Correlation higher in more closely related individuals
      b. Overall heritability of IQ around .50
   2. Evidence for impact by genetics, shared, and nonshared environments
      a. Pairs of family members reared together have more similar IQ than those reared apart
      b. Fraternal twins, especially those with similar family experiences who grew up at the same time, tend to be more alike than siblings born at different times
      c. IQs of adopted children related to those of their adoptive parents
      d. Shared environment influences tend to make people more similar while unique nonshared experiences make them different

3. Influence of genes becomes greater with age until adulthood
   a. With age, IQ's estimated heritability increase for identical twins
   b. With age, IQ's estimated heritability decrease for fraternal twins
   c. Shared environmental influences become less significant with age
   d. IQs of adopted children more strongly correlated with biological and adoptive parents
   e. IQ levels of children (including adopted children) can be improved if they are raised in a stimulating home environment early in life
   f. Genes largely account for intellectual stability from early adulthood to late middle age
   g. Genetic influences on intelligence still strong in old age
   h. Heritability may diminish in old age as the result of disease and nonshared environmental experience

B. Temperament and Personality
  1. Temperament—set of tendencies concerning emotional reactivity, activity, and sociability
    a. Genes contribute to individual differences in temperament in infancy and to both continuity and change in later personality
    b. Average correlation between temperament score of identical twins is between .50 and .60, while the correlation between fraternal twins is around 0
    c. About 40% of variation in adult personality attributable to genetics, 5% from shared environmental experiences, and 55% from nonshared environmental influences
    d. Living in same home does not make children more similar in personality
    e. Family experience leads to more differences than similarities
  2. Personality
    a. About 40% of the variation on major personality dimensions is attributable to genetic differences
    b. Shared environmental influences can be important (e.g., children adopt attitudes and interests similar to parents).
      i. Parent conflict can cause multiple children in the same home to develop psychological problems
    c. Nonshared influences significant
      i. Little evidence that parents mold all children's personalities in similar directions
      ii. Parents often develop unique relationships with each of their children
      iii. Siblings grow up at different times and have different experiences
      iv. Brothers and sisters try to differentiate themselves and establish their own identities
      v. Children have different peer groups and teachers

C. Psychological Disorders
  1. Schizophrenia—serious mental disorder involving disturbed thinking, emotions, and social behavior
    a. Genes may contribute substantially to development of the disorder
      i. Average concordance rate for identical twins 48%, rate for fraternal twins is 17%
      ii. Adopted children with biological parent with schizophrenia are at risk for developing the disorder

b. 1% of people in general population have schizophrenia, 10% of children who have a schizophrenic parents will become schizophrenic, 90% of children with a schizophrenic parent do not develop schizophrenia

c. Do not inherit the disorder, but rather the predisposition to develop the disorder

d. Actual development combination of genetics and environmental stress (e.g., dysfunctional family)

    i. Genetically at-risk infants who came down with an infectious disease like the flu while mothers were pregnant are at increased risk to develop schizophrenia

    ii. Infants deprived of oxygen at birth are at risk to develop schizophrenia

    iii. Adopted children with biological parent who is schizophrenic are more likely to develop the disorder if they grow up in a dysfunctional adoptive home

D. The Heritability of Different Traits

  1. Some traits more influenced by genes than others

    a. Observable physical (e.g., eye color, height) and physiological traits (e.g., reactions to alcohol) strongly influenced by genetics

    b. Susceptibility to many diseases related to aging influenced by genes

    c. General intelligence moderately influenced by genetics (50% or more of variation attributed to genes)

    d. Genetic endowment contributes only modestly to attitudes and interests (e.g., vocational interest)

    e. Difficult to find a human characteristic that is not to some degree heritable

E. Influences on Heritability

  1. Heritability not fixed

  2. Heritability impact differs depending on the age of the individuals being sampled

    a. Genes explain more variation in eating disorders in girls during puberty vs. girls at age 11

  3. Heritability impact differs depending on environmental background

    a. One study found that genes explained IQ differences in children from wealthy families but not from poor families

    b. Understimulating environment negatively impacts children regardless of genetics

V Genes and Environment Conspiring

A. Basic trends in genes

  1. Genes are always turning on or off over the entire life span

  2. Environmental influences also impact from conception to death

  3. Unique genes exert themselves more as we become adults

  4. Shared environmental influences are stronger early in life

  5. Nonshared environmental influences remain important throughout the life span

  6. Don't ask "how much" of genes but rather how heredity and environment work together

B. Gene-Environment Interaction
   1. Genes do not determine anything but rather provide potential
   2. Caspi and colleagues described impact of genes and stressful life events on development of depression in New Zealanders
      i. Predisposition to depression results in somewhat higher probability of having depression
   3. Individuals with two high-risk variants for depression more vulnerable to depression than those with protective variant only if they experience multiple stressful events
   4. Multiple stressful events tend to not result in schizophrenia in those with protective genes
   5. Often takes combination of high-risk genes and a high-risk environment to trigger many psychological problems
C. Gene-Environment Correlations
   1. Gene-environment interactions tell us that people with different gene react differently to the experiences they have
   2. Gene-environment correlations say that people with different genes experience different environments
      a. Passive gene-environment correlations—parents' genes influence the environment they provide for children, as well as the genes the child receives
         i. Parents with "sociable genes" create a social home environment (combination of genes for sociability and social environment may make child more sociable than he or she would otherwise be)
         ii. Shy parents may receive genes for shyness and provide less social stimulation
      b. Evocative gene-environment correlation—child's genotype evokes certain reactions
         i. Sociable babies elicit more social reactions from others and provide more opportunities to build social skills
         ii. Sociable adolescents invited to more parties
      c. Active gene-environment correlation—child's genotype influences the environment that she or he seeks
         i. Extravert likely to go to every party in sight and build a "niche" that is highly socially simulating and strengthens social skills
      d. Scarr and McCartney suggest that the balance between the three types of genotype-environment correlations shifts with development
         i. Passive influences large in infancy
         ii. Evocative influences operate throughout life
         iii. Active become more important as we age
D. Genetic Influences on the Environment
   1. Measures of environment are heritable
   2. Genes affect similarity of environments we experience and perceptions of those environments
      a. Identical twins who are irritable could help create conflict-ridden families

3. Must constantly question assumptions about nature and nurture
   a. Aggression in children may be influenced by environment provided by parent and the parent's genes (possible that inherited gene that predisposed them to aggression also made parent hostile toward them)
4. Authors of book *The Relationship Code* argue that family processes are the mechanism through which the genetic code is expressed
   b. Genes and environment (especially unique experiences) conspire to shape development

B. Controversies Surrounding Genetic Research
1. While effective, genetic intervention has led to complex ethical concerns (Application Box on prevention and treatment of genetic conditions)
   a. Phenylkentonuria (PKU)—recessive genetic disorder that results in an inability to metabolize phenylalanine (found in types of food)
      i. Phenylalanine builds in body and causes mental retardation and hyperactivity
      ii. Test for PKU used to screen for disorder at birth
      iii. With proper life-long diet, impact of PKU minimal
   b. Gene therapy—substitute defective genes or alter genetic makeup
      i. Treatment for hemophilia and cystic fibrosis
      ii. May have deadly consequences
   c. Stem cells have the potential to become many types of different types of cells
      i. Can be transplanted to treat diseases and disorders
      ii. Use of embryonic stem cells highly controversial
      iii. Working on ways to convert adult cells back into undifferentiated stem cells
2. Behavioral genetics research has demonstrated that genes are important, unique experiences of siblings more influential than those that they share, children influence parents just as parents influence children
3. Criticisms of behavioral genetics
   a. Some behavioral geneticists overstate the importance of genes and underestimate the importance of family
   b. Techniques for calculating heritability may attribute too much importance to genes and not too little to environment
   c. May be impossible to cleanly separate influences of genes and environment
   d. Genetic explanations provide little information about epigenesis (the translation of genotypes into phenotypes)

SUGGESTIONS FOR CLASS DISCUSSIONS OR PROJECTS

1. Ask students to consider how they are similar to and different from their siblings. Have them speculate about the source of these similarities and differences (genetic factors or environmental factors). Point out that researchers argue that a shared family environment may actually contribute more to differences than similarities among siblings. To make this concrete for students, have them write down, or share with another student in class, an episode within their family that was interpreted one way by them and a different way by their sibling. For students who don't have a sibling, ask them to think of something that has happened within a group of

friends that was interpreted differently by each person present. Then ask students to speculate on how these different interpretations might lead to different developmental outcomes. An alternative (or additional) project would be to have students present evidence (including personal experiences) that suggests that shared environments actually result in increased similarity among siblings and others.

2. Ask students to provide examples of some behavioral traits that they believe are primarily genetically or primarily environmentally determined. What evidence do they have for their positions? Chances are that many will refer to media examples (e.g., talk shows, television shows, movies) as part of their "evidence." This could spark an interesting discussion of the role of the media in perpetuating beliefs concerning the "cause" of a behavior. One controversial issue that you might use to frame this discussion is the 2007 tragedy at Virginia Tech University in which a student shot classmates and teachers. Following that event, many sources reacted with reports as to the possible cause of this aggressive action. These reports included a letter from American Psychological Association President Pedro Ruiz asking the media to limit coverage of the event as it could lead to copycat killings. You may wish to have students read a brief comment of these remarks that can be found in Bond (2007).

Bond, M. (2007). The media make a killing. *New Scientist, 194*, 22.

3. Have students (possibly working in small groups) solve problems involving single gene-pair and sex-linked inheritance by drawing tables like those in the text (see Figure 3.2 in the text). For example, what are the odds that Arlo Guthrie will develop Huntington's disease (caused by a dominant gene) as his father Woody did? If a man and a woman are carriers of the gene for sickle-cell disease, what are their odds of having a child with sickle-cell disease? If a girl has hemophilia (sex-linked), what can we infer about her parents? If a boy has hemophilia, what can we infer about his parents?

4. To expand their knowledge of genetics, have students visit the Human Genome Project website:
http://www.ornl.gov/TechResources/Human_Genome/posters/chromosome/chooser.html
Have them select two chromosomes and create a list of 20 of the most important characteristics (e.g., disorders, physical traits) that have been linked to each chromosome.

5. In the movie *Spiderman*, a character states, "With great power, comes great responsibility." In Chapter 3, students are introduced to the Human Genome Project, a scientific endeavor that is destined to change the world as we know it (i.e., great power). Advances made by Human Genome Project researchers have also raised a variety of ethical concerns. For example, the development of tests to identify carriers of diseases and for prenatal detection of diseases such as cystic fibrosis and Huntington's disease has been met with mixed responses. Some applaud these tests as they could prevent many infants from being born with damaging or deadly illnesses. Others believe that the test has more drawbacks than benefits as they may lead to a world in which only "perfect" people will be allowed to be born. There is also growing concern over who should have access to the results of genetic tests.
The goal of this assignment is to help students consider what responsibility we have to protect

individuals from advancements made by the Human Genome Project and other studies of genetic influences on behavior. Have students consider the following issues as part of a class discussion on ethics and testing: 1) what is the value of genetic testing for someone who is not going to consider an abortion? 2) Should partners be obligated to inform each other of any genetic defects in their family? 3) Does a child or adolescent have the right to request (or refuse) to have genetic testing done to them? 4) Should insurance companies have the right to access the results of genetic tests so they can adjust the rates for an individual? 5) Should employers be able to screen potential employees based on genetic tests? 6) Should the government have the right to require genetic testing if it leads to healthier infants? 7) Should people have the right to purchase genetic tests for themselves? Students should read the Alsever (2009) article if you include question 7.

Alsever, J. (2009). Do-it-yourself DNA testing. *Prevention*, 61(4), 114-123.

SUGGESTED FILMS AND VIDEOS

Heredity and the Environment: Beginnings of a Baby (2005, Insight Media, DVD 29 minutes): This DVD discusses how both environmental and genetic factors combine to influence development. It also presents information on gene therapy.

Is There a Gene for Happiness? (2003, Insight Media, VHS, 29 minutes in three segments): Explores potential influence of genes and the environment on the development of characteristics like happiness.

Nature and Nurture: Heredity and Environment (2003, Insight Media, VHS 30 minutes): A top-selling video on factors shaping human development.

Personality: All about me (2004, Films for the Humanities and Sciences, DVD-R or VHS 60 minutes): Program from *The Human Mind: From Neurons to Knowledge* series exploring factors that shape personality across the lifespan.

The Biological Mind: Deeply Depressed (2006, Insight Media, DVD 46 minutes): This video provides a nice introduction to factors that influence vulnerability to depression.

SUGGESTED WEBSITES

Chromosomal Abnormalities: March of Dimes
http://www.marchofdimes.com/professionals/14332_1209.asp

Evolutionary Psychology: A Primer
http://www.psych.ucsb.edu/research/cep/primer.html

Gene Therapy
http://www.nature.com/gt/index.html

Human Genome Project
http://www.ornl.gov/sci/techresources/Human_Genome/home.shtml

MedlinePlus: Genetic Counseling
http://www.nlm.nih.gov/medlineplus/geneticcounseling.html

SUGGESTED READINGS

Hess, P.G. (2009). Diagnostic genetic testing for a fatal illness: The experience of patients with movements. *New Genetics & Society*, 28(1), 3-18.

Knafo, A., and Plomin, R. (2006). Prosocial behavior from early to middle childhood: Genetic and environmental influences on stability and change. *Developmental Psychology*, 42(5), 771-786.

Moffitt, T.E. (2005). The new look of behavioral genetics in developmental psychopathology: Gene-Environment interplay in antisocial behaviors. *Psychological Bulletin*, 131(4), 533-554.

Plomin, R. (2010). Genetics of learning abilities and disabilities: Recent developments from the UK and possible directions for research in China. *Behavioral Genetics*, 40(3), 297-305.

Rolland, J.S. (2006). Genetics, family systems, and multicultural influences. *Families, Systems, & Health,* 24(4), 425-441.

Chapter 3

PRENATAL DEVELOPMENT AND BIRTH

LEARNING OBJECTIVES

After reading and studying the material in this chapter, you should be able to answer the following questions.

PRENATAL DEVELOPMENT

1. How does development unfold during the prenatal period from conception until the time of birth?

2. How does prenatal behavior of the fetus relate to postnatal behavior of the infant?

THE PRENATAL ENVIRONMENT

3. How and when do various teratogens affect the developing fetus? How can you summarize the effects of teratogens during the prenatal period?

4. How do maternal age, emotional state, and nutrition affect prenatal and neonatal development? What about the father's state—can this influence development?

THE PERINATAL ENVIRONMENT

5. What is the typical perinatal environment like? What hazards can occur during the birth process?

6. What is the birth experience like from the mother's and father's perspectives, and from different cultural perspectives?

7. What are common sibling reactions to the birth of a child?

THE NEONATAL ENVIRONMENT

8. What are the advantages of breastfeeding? Are there disadvantages?

9. How can at-risk newborns be identified? What treatments are available to optimize development of at-risk babies?

10. To what extent are the effects of the prenatal and perinatal environments long lasting? What factors influence whether effects are lasting?

I Prenatal Development

A. Conception

1. Midway through menstrual cycle (every 28 days or so), ovum is released

a. Egg usually disintegrates and leaves in menstrual flow

b. If woman has intercourse, 300 million or so sperm enter body

i. 300 of the sperm survive the six-hour journey to fallopian tubes

ii. One sperm may enter the egg

iii. Biochemical reaction keeps other sperm from entering egg

iv. Conception has taken place

2. Infertility—not being able to get pregnant after a year of trying

a. Equally traced to men and women

b. Simple intervention methods

i. Man wears looser pants or underpants

ii. Woman takes temperature to determine ovulation

c. Assisted reproductive techniques used to increase fertility

i. Artificial insemination—injecting sperm of partner or donor into a woman

ii. In vitro fertilization (IVF)—eggs removed, manually combined with sperm, implanted into the uterus

iii. IVF might involve up to five parents: sperm donor, egg donor, surrogate mother to carry, caregiving mother, caregiving father

iv. IVF costly—$12,400 each attempt

v. Odds of birth for woman age 42 or older are 1 in 10

B. Prenatal Stages

1. Lasts for about 266 days (nine months)

a. Zygote to fetus—one cell to billions

b. Prenatal development occurs in three stages

i. Germinal period

ii. Period of embryo

iii. Period of fetus

2. The germinal period

a. Lasts about two weeks

b. Zygote divides to form blastocyst—hollow ball of 150 cells the size of head of pin

i. 15% of recognized pregnancies end in miscarriage

ii. As many as 50% terminate (often due to genetic defects)

3. The embryonic period

a. Lasts from the third to eighth week

b. Organogenesis—every major organ takes shape

c. Blastocyst layers differentiate forming new structures

i. Outer layer becomes amnion—watertight membrane surrounding chorion and chorion—membrane on outside of amnion containing villi, which attach to uterine lining

ii. Chorion eventually becomes the lining of the placenta—tissue fed by mother's blood vessels and connected to embryo by umbilical cord

   iii. Nutrients and wastes are exchanged through placenta and umbilical cord

   iv. Placental barrier—membrane through which the nutrient and small carbon dioxide molecules pass

 d. Interior cells of blastocyst give rise to ectoderm (e.g., brain and spinal cord), mesoderm (e.g., bone, heart, kidney), and endoderm (lungs, bladder) layers

 d. Brain development apparent after three to four weeks

   i. Neural plate forms neural tube (bottom is spinal cord)

   ii. Top of tube forms into forebrain, midbrain, hindbrain

   iii. Spina bifida—neural tube at bottom fails to become fully enclosed and spinal cord not fully encased

   iv. Anencephaly—tube at top fails to close, main portion of brain fails to develop

   v. Neural tube defects occur 25 to 29 days after conception

   vi. Level of folic acid in mothers critical for development of embryo

 e. Organs (e.g., heart, eyes) take shape

 f. Arms and legs appear

 g. Sexual differentiation

   i. Begin existence with undifferentiated sex tissue

   ii. About seventh to eighth prenatal week, sex genes impact formation of testes or ovaries

   iii. Embryo inheriting Y chromosome has gene for construction of testes

   iv. Embryo with two X chromosomes will form female ovaries

   v. Secretion of testosterone by male embryo stimulates male internal reproductive system and inhibits female system

   vi. Absence of these hormones results in developing the internal reproductive system of a female

4. The fetal period

 a. Ninth prenatal week to birth

 b. Significant brain development

   i. Proliferation of neurons (hundreds of thousands per minute throughout pregnancy)

   ii. Significant neural development between 10 and 20 weeks

   iii. Young infant has around 100 billion neurons

   iv. Increase in number of glial cells that support neural cells

   v. Neurons migrate into position traveling along surface of glial cells and detaching at programmed destinations

   vi. Differentiation—neurons begin to differentiate in function depending on where they have migrated

   vii. Stem cells—early "unspecialized" cells

 c. Organs formed in embryonic period continue to grow and function

   i. Harmful agents no longer cause major malformations as organs already formed

 d. Third month

   i. Distinguishable sex organs appear

   ii. Bones and muscle form

   iii. By end of third month (first trimester), movement of limbs

e. Second trimester (months four to six)
   i. Refined activities (e.g., thumb sucking)
   ii. Sensory organ functioning
   iii. Age of viability—around 23 weeks after conception, has possibility of surviving outside uterus
   iv. 2007 "most premature baby to survive" was born at 21 weeks and six days, weighing 10 ounces
f. Third trimester (months six to nine)
   i. Rapid growth in length and weight
   ii. Myelin—insulating cover on brain begins to develop (improving ability of neurons to transmit signals)
   iii. Infant states—organization of behavior in waking, heart rate, and sleeping patterns
   iv. DiPietro and colleges found increasing fetal heart response to stimuli, like vibrator placed on mom's abdomen
   v. End of prenatal periods tends to be in one distinct state (e.g., active sleep)
   vi. Late in pregnancy (32 weeks), spend more time in active, waking state
   vii. Beginning of continuity between prenatal and postnatal behavior (newborn behavior emerges long before birth)
   viii. Contractions of uterus typically begin birth process

II The Prenatal Environment
A. Mother's womb i "prenatal environment" for unborn child
   1. Fetus is impacted by physical environment
      a. A pregnant woman's use of cocaine may lead to extraordinarily fussy newborn
      b. Developing embryo-then-fetus is vulnerable
   2. Until the early1940s incorrect belief that placenta protected embryo and fetus from hazards
      a. Belief made it difficult to believe that alcohol consumption by pregnant mom
         could have negative impact on fetus
      b. First official acknowledgment of impact of alcohol on prenatal development
         came in the 1970s
   3. New focus on environmental factors that negatively impact prenatal development
B. Teratogens
   1. Teratogens—any disease, drug, or environmental agent that can harm prenatal organism
      a. Generalizations concerning teratogens
         i. Only 15% of newborns have minor problems, and perhaps 5% have more significant anomalies
         ii. Effects are worst during critical period when organ systems are forming
         iii. Effects determined by dosage and duration of exposure
         iv. Susceptibility is influenced by genetic makeup of mother and fetus, and the quality of the prenatal environment
         v. Prenatal and postnatal environments determine critical periods—times when organism is highly sensitive to damage (also called sensitive periods)

2. Drugs
   a. Thalidomide
      i. Widely used in Europe in the 1950s for relief of morning sickness (a type of tranquilizer)
      ii. Major impact (e.g., flipper limbs, deformed ears, missing thumbs) if taken between 20 and 35 days
      iii. Banned, but now being used to treat other disorders (e.g., leprosy, AIDS), with warning to not be used by pregnant women
   b. Tobacco
      i. Warnings labels have decreased number of pregnant women who smoke, but about 22% of women smoke during first trimester (when some may not know they are pregnant) with rates dropping to around 14% in the second and third trimesters
      ii. Inhibits prenatal growth, increases risk of miscarriage, retards growth of fetus, and may lead to central nervous system impairment
      iii. More than half of infants born to women smoking 20 or more cigarettes a day end up in neonatal intensive care units
      iv. Exposure to as few as five cigarettes a day can lead to damage
      v. Babies of smokers more susceptible to respiratory infections and breathing difficulties
      vi. Sudden infant death syndrome—sleeping baby suddenly stops breathing and dies; risk increases when mother smokes while pregnant
      vii. Maternal smoking linked to mild cognitive deficits that may last into childhood
      viii. Negative impacts are the result of nicotine and chemicals in cigarettes and toxic byproducts of smoking (e.g., carbon dioxide) (Exploration box on prenatal effects of smoking resulting from nature and nurture)
      ix. Outcome for babies can be improved if mothers quit smoking during pregnancy (greatest effects if this occurs in first trimester)
   c. Alcohol
      i. Alcohol consumed by mom crosses the placental barrier
      ii. Fetal alcohol syndrome (FAS)—more severe cluster of symptoms (e.g., small size, distinct facial features) associated with alcohol consumption by pregnant women
      iii. FAS increases risk for central nervous system damage, hyperactivity, seizures, below-average IQ scores, and attention deficit
      iv. Many FAS infants have mental health issues later in life
      v. FAS children more likely to get into trouble at school or to break the law
      vi. Most surveys indicate that about 15% of women drink some alcohol while pregnant
      vii. Incidence of FAS around 3 in 1,000 babies in the United States
      viii. Fetal alcohol effect or alcohol-related neurodevelopmental disorder—terms for children with milder alcohol effects than full FAS (estimated to be found in 35 of 1000 children)

Chapter 4

   ix. Binge drinking (four or more drinks during a single session) have larger negative impact than four drinks over four sessions

   x. Facial abnormalities occur in first trimester while stunted growth and brain development more common in second and third trimesters

   xi. One ounce drink a day still problematic

   xii. Impact depends on mother's physiology, other environmental issues (e.g., malnutrition, other drug use), embryo's genetic make-up

   xiii. Father's alcohol consumption may impact through indirect means (e.g., poor parenting)

  d. Cocaine

   i. No "cocaine syndrome"

   ii. Can cause spontaneous abortion, placenta detachment, or fetal strokes

   iii. Use can contribute to fetal malnutrition

   iv. Small proportion of infants may experience withdrawal-like symptoms after birth and experience sensory motor skill difficulties in their first year

  e. Parental behaviors (e.g., smoking, alcohol use, being less attentive to their babies) may also contribute to impact of cocaine

 3. Diseases

  a. Rubella—German measles

   i. In early 1940s, discovered prenatal impact that included blindness, deafness, heart defects, and retardation

   ii. Impact greatest during first trimester (nearly 15% of pregnant women with rubella miscarry)

   iii. 60 to 85% of babies exposed to rubella in first two months have birth defects

   iv. 50% of babies exposed to rubella in third month have birth defects

   v. 16% of those exposed to rubella in fifth and sixth month have birth defects

   vi. Immunizations of women before pregnancy critical

  b. Diabetes

   i. Gestational diabetes is a fairly common pregnancy complication

   ii. Controllable by diet

   iii. Poor control increases risk for negative impacts (e.g., miscarriage, large fetal size, immature lung development)

  c. Syphilis

   i. Sexually transmitted

   ii. Impact includes blindness, deafness, heart defects, and retardation

   iii. Impact greatest later in pregnancy—cannot cross placental barrier until 18th week

   iv. Early treatment (penicillin) can be effective but some infants still infected or die

  d. AIDS—acquired immune deficiency disorder

   i. Caused by human immunodeficiency virus (HIV)

   ii. Destroys immune system

   iii. Transmitted prenatally (through placenta), perinatally (exchange of blood during birth), postnatally (via breastfeeding)

   iv. Without treatment 15 to 35% of infants born to moms with HIV become infected

   v. Infants of mothers treated with AZT, zidovudine, or nevirapine have lower rate of developing AIDS

   vi. Bottle feeding reduces risk of transmittal from affected mom to infant

vii. Rate of mother-to-infant transmission lowering in U.S. but tremendous problem in other parts of the world (many in sub-Sahara Africa)

    4. Environmental hazards
      a. Radiation
        i. Mothers near Nagasaki and Hiroshima when nuclear bomb dropped tended to have still-born or seriously handicapped children
        ii. Leads to mutation
        iii. Take care with X-ray
      b. Pollutants
        i. Infants born to mothers near 9/11 World Trade Center site lighter, shorter, and slighter but impact may involve a combination of exposure to toxic pollutants from collapse of WTC and prenatal exposure to cigarette smoke
        ii. Heavy metals (e.g., lead) can have prenatal impact, especially lowered mental functioning
        iii. Mercury exposure (from fish or vaccines containing thimerosal) can result in problems with memory, attention, and language
        iv. Prenatal exposure to pesticides, dioxins, and PCBs associated with reflex and learning problems and lower IQs
        v. Chemistry of prenatal environment can have major impact on development

C. The Mother's State
    1. Parents can set stage for healthy pregnancy (Application Box on growing healthier babies)
      a. Better diet (good nutrition, avoiding alcohol, consuming less fish)
      b. Quit smoking
      c. Remaining physically active
      d. Avoid toxins like lead in paint or parasite in cat feces that causes toxoplasmosis
      e. Lamaze method
        i. 1940s technique for reducing fear and pain associated with childbirth
    2. Age and race/ethnicity
      a. Ages 20 to 40 are "safest" childbearing years
      b. Very younger mothers higher risk of complications including stillbirth— fetal death late in pregnancy
      c. Young woman's reproductive systems may be immature; more likely to live in poverty and drink alcohol
      d. Older women have trouble getting pregnant, miscarry, and have low-birth-weight babies
        i. Number of infants born to older mothers who die from genetic problems on decline due to extensive prenatal testing for women older than 35
        ii. Increased chance of fraternal twins in older mothers
      e. Non-Hispanic black women have highest rate of fetal mortality
    3. Emotional condition
      a. Damage may be due to stress hormones like adrenaline (also called epinephrine), which temporarily increase fetal motor activity
      b. Prolonged (chronic), severe maternal emotional stress may be damaging to fetus

i. Impacts include stunted prenatal growth and irregular heart rate
ii. May show delays in cognitive development and more fear as young children
c. Mild to moderate stress may be beneficial to fetal development
d. Maternal depression may negatively impact fetal development
4. Nutritional condition
a. Recommend additional 300 calories per day and 25 to 35 pound weight gain (for normal weight women)
b. Malnutrition can lead to birth defects
i. First trimester malnutrition impacts brain and spinal cord
ii. Third trimester malnutrition impact is smaller neurons, brain, and child
c. Prenatal malnutrition impact may lead to predisposition to adult diseases like hypertension and diabetes
d. Adequate levels of folic acid important as it decreases neural tube defects like spina bifida and anencephaly
i. Prenatal vitamins often prescribed to pregnant patients
e. Prenatal nutrition is important but so is diet and care after birth
B. The Father's State
1. Little research on father's contribution (beyond genetic)
a. Risk of miscarriage rate increases with paternal age
b. Elevated risk of heart defects, neural tube defects, kidney problems, and schizophrenia in children born to older dads
c. Risk of Down syndrome higher in infants of older men (especially if mom is older)
d. Father's exposure to environmental toxin (e.g., radiation, pesticides) can damage sperm and increase risk of defects

III The Perinatal Environment
A. Perinatal environment—social and medical environment surrounding birth
1. Major shift in birthing practices in Western cultures where birth has become more

medical, involving technology and doctors (1930, 80% of births at home; today 1%)
a. Many modern couples like security of medical technology but want comforts of home
b. Hospitals responded by restructuring delivery rooms and giving parents greater flexibility and control concerning delivery
c. New choices in delivery assistance including family physicians and midwives
d. Maternal-fetal specialists (perinatologist) recommended for high-risk pregnancies
e. Some countries (e.g., France, England) midwives commonly involved in delivery
f. Spouse, partner, mother, sister or friends more commonly allowed in the delivery room
i. Most women like the additional support
ii. Some have support of a doula—individual trained to provide continuous physical and emotional support throughout the pregnancy

       g. Support from others tends to shorten labor and result in reduction in use of pain medications and forceps and fewer cesarean sections

    2. Childbirth is Three-Stage Process

       a. Labor

          i. Begins with contractions of uterus and dilation of cervix

          ii. Duration average of 9 hours for first born and 4 to 6 hours for later-born children

          iii. Ends with dilation of cervix of 10 centimeters

       b. Delivery of baby

          i. Fetus passes out of uterus/cervix

          ii. Fetus emerges from woman's body via the vaginal opening

          iii. Mother told to "bear down" (push)

          iv. First deliveries about one hour in this stage, later deliveries short

       c. Delivery o placenta

          i. Lasts a few minutes

          ii. Participant(including fathers) often exhausted

B. Possible Hazards

    1. Anoxia—oxygen shortage (also called asphyxia)

       a. Due to umbilical cord pinched or tangled, sedatives given to mother, mucus in baby's throat, breech presentation—feet or buttocks first vaginal delivery

       b. Oxygen deprivation can cause death of brain cells and results in poor reflexes, seizures, breathing difficulties

       c. Severe anoxia can cause cerebral palsy—neurological disability inhibiting muscle movement or increased risk for learning, intellectual, and speech difficulties

       d. Mild anoxia typically does not lead to permanent problems

       e. Fetal monitoring during labor and delivery can avoid possibility of anoxia

       f. Fetus laying sideways in uterus may lead to cesarean section—surgical removal of baby through mother's abdomen

    2. Complicated delivery

       a. Forceps—salad tong-like instrument used to help extract baby

          i. Due to soft head, use of forceps may lead to cranial bleeding and brain damage

       b. Vacuum extraction—"suction-cup" device used to help extract baby

       c. Cesarean section (C-section) controversial form of birth

          i. Used if baby too large, fetus out of position, when placenta prematurely separates from the uterus, or when fetal monitoring indicates a problem

          ii. Process is safe, but mothers do take longer to recover and may be slightly less involved with their babies during the first few months after birth

          iii. Account for nearly 32% of U.S. births

          iv. Estimated that 11% of first and 65% of second-time C-sections are unnecessary

          v. Used to protect physician against malpractice suits

          vi. Women who have delivered via C-section tend to have subsequent children via C-section

          vii. Many are planned and elective

          viii. Optimal time to have C-section is 39 to 40 weeks after conception

3. Medications
   a. Medications used during birth to reduce pain (analgesics and anesthetics), to relax mothers (sedatives), and to induce or intensify contractions (stimulants)
   b. Sedatives can affect baby, making it sluggish or difficult to feed or cuddle during the first few days after birth
   c. Regional analgesics (epidural or spinal block) deaden pain in area of body and have less affect on baby, but use may increase labor time and need for forceps or vacuum assistance
   d. Oxytocin ("Pitocin") sometimes used to initiate or speed up contractions

C. The Mother's Experience
   1. Unique experience involving many psychological factors
      a. Attitude toward pregnancy, knowledge about birth process, sense of control over childbirth, social support from others (which is especially critical) all impact maternal birth experience
   2. Cultural factors
      a. Desirability to have children varies by culture
         i. China "one-child" policy resulted in fewer babies per family and slowed population growth
         ii. Average number of children dropped from five in 1970 to fewer that two today
         iii. Policy also results in abortion of female babies in favor of males, who would support parents in old age
      b. Birth practices differ by culture
         i. Kenyan families celebrate, dad stops hunting, baby given hot ash and herbs to vomit amniotic fluid, mom given time to recover
         ii. Uttar Pradesh (in Northern India) childbirth seen as polluting and treated as shameful act (due to blood)
            (i) Pradesh use poorly trained and hateful "day" to help deliver baby
            (ii) Mother kept in house for days as to not pollute others
            (iii) Baby's hair is shaved off because it is thought to be polluted
         iii. !Kung San of Namibia women labor by themselves as birthing alone seen as sign of strength
      c. Western societies have "medicalized" childbirth (done in hospitals hooked up to monitors)
         i. Infant and maternal mortality rates have dropped (50 years ago, 30 infants out of 1,000, now about 6 out of 1,000)
         ii. Rates are twice as high African American infants vs. European American infants
   3. Postpartum depression
      a. "Baby blues"—mild feelings of anxiety, irritability, and depression common for a few days after birth but typically fades
         i. Possibly the result of steep drop in hormone levels, stress associated with delivery, and new responsibility of parenting
      b. Postpartum depression—more serious postbirth feelings of anxiety, moodiness, and depression experienced by some women in months after birthing

i. Postnatal depression rare but serious; tends to be found in women with history of depression, who are experiencing other life stresses, or who have few social supports
ii. Influences mother-child interactions (e.g., children less attached)
iii. Children of postnatally depressed mothers may exhibit behavioral problems (e.g., violence) during late childhood and adolescence and show elevated levels of cortisol (associated with major depression)
iv. Depressed mothers tend to be unresponsive to babies and may feel hostility toward them
v. Most mothers recover from postnatal depression, but it may set the stage for ongoing problems affecting the child's behavior
vi. Problems exhibited may involve genes inherited from depression-prone mothers and/or stressful experiences

D. The Father's Experience
1. Western society fathers historically excluded from birth process
   a. Today, many men prepare for childbirth
      i. Take prenatal classes
      ii. Are present at birth
   b. Birth of their child tends to be a significant event in the life of most men
      i. Experience both positive and negative emotions in anticipation of becoming a parent
      ii. Are anxious during pregnancy and birth
      iii. Experience some of the same physiological symptoms as mothers
      iv. Couvades—physiological symptoms of pregnancy (e.g., weight gain, nausea, insomnia) that males experience along with their pregnant partner
      v. May be due to hormonal factors
   c. Many men find labor period to be more work than expected and feel scared or unprepared
      i. Prenatal classed increase knowledge but can increase anxiety
      ii. Stress levels highest during pregnancy
      iii. Negative emotions typically give way to positive emotions (e.g., joy, pride) following birth of child
   d. As many men as women experience symptoms of depression following the birth of a child
      i. Depressed fathers interact less with their children
      ii. Available supports help reduce problems
   e. Many first-time fathers experience sexual relations problems following birth
      i. Expect sex life to return to prepregnancy state and it doesn't
   f. Marital satisfaction declines for several years following the birth of a child.
      i. Planned pregnancies may diminish negative impact on satisfaction
   g. Some women unaware they are pregnant (Exploration Box on "I didn't know I was pregnant")
      i. Have irregular periods and/or infertility problems
      ii. Breakthrough bleeding during pregnancy
      iii. Home pregnancy tests not perfect

      iv. Birth control not 100% effective

      v. Strenuous exercise can result in lack of regular menstruation

      vi. Obese women may not notice weight gain

      vii. Some fetuses are not that active

E. Sibling Adjustment

  1. Quality of immediate environment (micro system) following birth of a new baby will affect older sibling's behaviors and sense of well-being

    a. Strong father-child relationship can insulate older siblings from decreased maternal attention

  2. Larger environment (exosystem) plays important role

    a. Older siblings who have strong social supports have more positive relationships with their siblings

  3. Mothers with one child tend to increase work hours within a few years after childbirth

    a. Children without siblings spend more time in group daycare outside the home

    b. Children with siblings spend more time at home

  4. Age affects adjustment to new sibling

    a. Very young children (under age 2) show less disrupted mother-child attachments than slightly older children (age 2 to 5)

IV The Neonatal Environment

A. Neonatal environment—emphasis on events in first months after birth

  1. Cross-cultural variation in beliefs concerning newborns

    a. The Beng (Ivory Coast)

      i. View newborn as not of this world until after umbilical cord falls off (achieve full inhabitance around age 4–5 years)

      ii. Give enemas twice a daily using a chili pepper solution

    b. The !Kung (southern Africa)

      i. Touched more than 7-% of daytime hours

      ii. Sleep in bed with mother

      iii. Infants are indulged well into life; breast-fed whenever they want and until age 4 years

    c. Industrialized nations

      i. Infants not touched as much (12-20% of time)

      ii. Often trained to feed on a schedule

      iii. Do not sleep in parents bed but in their own crib

  2. Brazelton Neonatal Behavioral Assessment—newborn assessment scale

    a. Assess reflexes and responses to 26 situations

    b. Test used to teach parents how to be responsive to infants

B. Breast or Bottle?

  1. Breastfeeding more natural form of nutrition

    a. Reached an all-time low in United States in early 1970s

      i. 1 in 4 mothers nursing

      ii. Bottle feeding the norm

    b. Research since then has shown advantages of breast milk over formula

    c. Now nearly 7 in 10 mothers attempt to nurse their newborns

         i.   Only 50% still breastfeeding at one month

        ii. Less than one-third still breastfeeding at six months

   d. Many health benefits of breastfeeding

         i.   Fewer ear infections and respiratory tract problems in children

        ii. Stronger lung function

       iii. Milk contains substances that provide nutrition and protection from infection

       iv. Helps premature babies with weight gain and positively impacts their immune system

   e. Failure to breast feed

         i.   Self-factors of mom (e.g., sore nipple)

        ii. Baby issues (e.g., concern that baby is not getting enough nutrition)

       iii. Younger moms, working moms, and African American moms less likely to breast feed

       iv. Hispanic moms high rate of breastfeeding

        v. Breastfeeding needs to be addressed as *the* option, not *an* option

       vi. Hospitals promote breastfeeding, but also support bottle feeding by sending home samples of formula

C. Identifying High-Risk Newborns

   1. At-risk status may be due to genetic, prenatal hazards, or perinatal damage

   2. Apgar test—used to assess newborn status

      a. Assesses factors of heart rate, color, muscle tone, respiration, and reflexes

      b. Simple five-minute test with score of 0, 1, or 2 for each factor

      c. Apgar score of 7 to 10 good, 6 to 5 ok, less than 4 low score and at-risk status

         i.   Low score symptoms include not breathing or limp

        ii. Low score infants immediately receive medical attention (different postnatal environment)

      d. Low-birth-weight (LBW) babies

         i.   About 8% of newborns are low birth weight—weigh less than 2,500 grams or 5 1/2 pounds at birth

        ii. Some are full term and some are preterm

       iii. Survival and health of major concern

       iv. Leading case of infant mortality; account for about 65% of all infant deaths

        v. Account for 60% of money spent on pregnancy and delivery

       vi. Very low birth weight mean even higher medical costs

      vii. Micropremies—those weighing less than 800 grams or 1.5 pounds

     viii. LWB strongly linked to socioeconomic status (poor women have worse nutrition and medical care)

      ix. African American women twice as likely as European American women to give birth to a LWB baby

       x. Associated with multiple births

      xi. Increase in multiple births in part due to greater use of ovulation-stimulating drugs

     xii. Higher-order multiple births (three or more children) have increased dramatically in past decades

     e.   With neonatal care, many low weight babies survive
          i.   LWB, especially extremely low birth weight (less that 1,000 grams or 2 lbs., 3 oz.) greater risk for numerous problems (e.g., deaf, autistic, cerebral palsy)
          ii. Health problems may persist into adulthood
          iii. Premature babies do not produced enough surfactant—substance that prevents air sacs in lungs from sticking together and allows for breathing
     f.   Several factors that can improve health and survival rates of preemies
          i.   Medical technology like surfactant therapy
          ii. Mother's breast milk can provide nutrients to boost immune system
          iii. Skin-to-skin contact like kangaroo care (resting on a parent's chest) can provide rhythmic sounds and body temperature that may be helpful
          iv. Massage therapy may help relax baby and assist in weight gain
     g.   Fate of low-birth-weight infants depends on biological condition and postnatal environment
          i.   Problems amplified by growing up in poverty with a single parent
          ii. More responsive mother leads to higher levels of cognitive achievement
     h.   Intervention programs like Infant Health and Development Program benefit low-birth-weight infants
          i.   Emphasis on growth-enhancing home environment (mother-provided childcare, education, and support)
          ii. Linked to increased IQ score in childhood in more at-risk infants
          iii. May not be as effective with infants weighting less than 2,000 grams (4 pounds, 6 oz.) at birth
     i.   Responsive and attentive parenting critical
  D. Risk and Resilience
    1. Werner and Smith longitudinal study of Hawaiian infants
     a.   Children classified into risk groups involving levels of exposure to prenatal or perinatal stress
     b.   Resilience—ability to get back on course of normal development
          i.   Effects of prenatal and perinatal complications decrease over time
          ii. Quality of postnatal environment determines outcome of early risk
    2. Protective factors help children overcome disadvantage
     a.   Personal resources—intellectual, social, and communication traits that help one cope
     b.   Supportive postnatal environment—social support from environment matters throughout life

SUGGESTIONS FOR CLASS DISCUSSIONS OR PROJECTS

1. Due to our reliance on chemicals to solve everyday problems, we live in a world in which potential teratogens are becoming more abundant. To help students appreciate the many potential dangers facing the unborn child, have them visit a grocery store and look at the warning labels found on the following types of items: vitamin supplements containing iron, cleaning agents, adhesives (e.g., glue), makeup products containing vitamin A, and alcoholic beverages. You

Chapter 4   58

could then have students share some of their more interesting findings. An alternative would be for students to write down the names of any five drugs that are advertised on a given night of television and then to search for the potential teratogenic effects for each drug.

2. Many students are familiar with prematurity but are not clear on its outcome. Medical technology is keeping more and more premature babies alive, although many of these children have serious complications. Discuss the medical and ethical issues involved in allotting significant resources to these infants who may have significant medical or psychological problems, and whose care can be extremely expensive. You may want to have students check out more information on premature infants at websites like those listed below:

http://www.marchofdimes.com/professionals/25079_1157.asp
http://kidshealth.org/parent/growth/growing/preemies.html
http://www.nlm.nih.gov/medlineplus/prematurebabies.html

3. Have students read and evaluate a current popular book on parenting and pregnancy. Many are available, and their focus ranges from general to quite specific. This project is most effective if you provide students with questions or issues to focus their reading. For example, you might ask students to verify the points in the parent or pregnancy manual by comparing them to research evidence presented in the text.

4. Have students plan the "perfect" delivery, considering preparation beforehand, setting, birth position, people present, use of drugs, and so on. Have them justify their choices. The websites listed below provide additional background on this topic. Many students are also fascinated by Frederick Leboyer's gentle birthing techniques, described in *Birth without Violence* (1975). Leboyer's methods include dim lights, gentle massage until the baby breathes, and a warm bath, all to make the transition from womb to world less traumatic. Research on the Leboyer technique suggests that infants born this way fare no better at birth or later in infancy than those who undergo standard obstetrical procedures. You might want to ask students to speculate on why there is any difference between the traditional and the Leboyer procedures. You may also wish to read the newest edition of this classic text.

http://www.webmd.com/baby/features/childbirth-options-whats-best
http://www.pregnancycorner.com/giving-birth/childbirth-options.html
http://ase.tufts.edu/cfw-test/?/category/medical/13/topic/childbirth-options/178/

Leboyer, F. (2002). *Birth without Violence*: *Revised Edition of the Classic*. London, UK: Pinter and Martin Publishers

5. In some cultures, the roles of men and women concerning childcare are very similar. In other cultures, men and women play significantly different roles in early childcare. Divide your students into two groups and have one group identify 10 strengths of having no role distinctions concerning early childcare. Have the other group identify 10 strengths of having specific sex roles concerning this topic. Then bring the groups together to from a consensus concerning "optimal" childcare.

6. Stem cell research is currently one of the hot-button issues in American politics and society. To gain a better appreciation of the pros and cons concerning the use of stem cells, have students search the Web for information on this topic using the search terms "stem cell and research" or "stem cell and controversy." Then, based on these readings, have them write a paper in which they identify and defend five reasons supporting stem cell research and five reasons opposing it.

SUGGESTED FILMS AND VIDEOS

A Joyous Labor (Filmmakers Library, VHS 30 minutes): Balanced presentation of birthing options available to women today. Also covers birthing customs in different cultures.

Childbirth Classes (Available at http://www.laughandlearn.com/home or DVD through the same site): Contains video options on the birth process and postnatal issues like breastfeeding and care of the newborn.

The Miracle of Life (1986, NOVA program available from NOVA as well as many video stores, VHS 60 minutes): Incredible photography inside the human body. This video shows male and female internal reproductive processes, conception, prenatal development, and birth. A classic.

Prenatal Development: A Life in the Making (1996, Magna Systems, VHS or DVD 29 minutes): Module 6 of *The Developing Child* series. Covers development from zygote to birth. Illustrates effects of cigarette smoking, and alcohol and drug use on a developing fetus. Shows how a fetus responds to various stimuli.

Modern Pregnancy Video Series (http://www.childbirthvideos.com, VHS or DVD): An extensive series of over 25 different videos covering virtually every aspect of childbirth (e.g., PREGNANCY *Maternal Body Changes & Stresses*, EMOTIONAL CHANGES & *Sexuality in Pregnancy & Postpartum*, PROCESS OF LABOR & DELIVERY: *Anatomy & Physiology*).

SUGGESTED WEBSITES

Birth Defects: Center for Disease Control
http://www.cdc.gov/ncbddd/bd/

Fetal Development: Westside Pregnancy Clinic
http://www.wpclinic.org/parenting/fetal-development/

Genetics and In Vitro Fertilization Institute
http://www.givf.com/

NOVA Online/Odyssey of Life
http://www.pbs.org/wgbh/nova/odyssey/

The Visible Embryo
http://www.visembryo.com/

SUGGESTED READINGS

Anhalt, K., Telzrow, C. F., and Brown, C. L. (2007). Maternal stress and emotional status during the perinatal period and childhood adjustment. *School Psychology Quarterly*, 22(1), 74-90.

Bi-Chin, K., Meei-Ling, G., Shian-Feng, W., Bih-Jaw, K., and Tsorng-Yeh, L. (2004). A comparative study of expectant parents' childbirth expectations. *Journal of Nursing Research*, 12(3), 191-201.

Godfrey, J.R., and Meyers, D. (2009). Toward optimal health: Maternal benefits of breastfeeding. *Journal of Women's Health*, 18(9), 1307-1310.

Jones, L., Rowe, J., and Becker, T. (2009). Appraisal, coping, and social supports are predictors of psychological distress and parenting efficacy in parents of premature infants. *Children's Health Care*, 38(4), 245-262.

Nava-Ocampo, A.A. and Koren, G. (2007). Human teratogens and evidence-based teratogen risk counseling: The Motherisk Approach. *Clinical Obstetrics & Gynecology*, 50(1), 123-131.

HEALTH AND PHYSICAL DEVELOPMENT

LEARNING OBJECTIVES

After reading and studying the material in this chapter, you should be able to answer the following questions.

BUILDING BLOCKS OF GROWTH AND DEVELOPMENT

1. How do the workings of the endocrine and nervous systems contribute to growth and development across the lifespan? To what extent are cells responsive to the effects of experience?

2. What is lateralization? How does it affect behavior?

3. How does the brain change with aging?

4. What principles underlie growth? What are examples of each principle?

5. How can we apply a lifespan developmental approach to our understanding of health?

THE INFANT

6. What is the difference between survival and primitive reflexes? What are examples of each type of reflex? What other capabilities do newborns have?

7. How do locomotion and manipulation of objects evolve during infancy? What factors influence the development of infants' motor skills?

8. What health issues should be considered during the first two years of life?

THE CHILD

9. How are children's motor skills advanced relative to those of infants?

10. What factors influence children's health? How can health be optimized during childhood?

THE ADOLESCENT

11. What physical changes occur during adolescence? What factors contribute to sexual maturity of males and females? What psychological reactions accompany variations in growth spurt
and the timing of puberty?

12. What health issues may confront adolescents?

THE ADULT

13. What physical changes occur during adulthood? What are the psychological implications of the physical changes that occur with aging?

14. What health concerns arise as adults age? How can health of older adults be preserved?

I Building Blocks of Growth and Development
  A. Growth and a Related Disorder
   1. Human growth is a complex process that occurs over many years and is influenced by genetic and environmental factors
    a. average U.S. female: 5' 4"; average U.S. male: 5' 10"; but great variability (tallest woman 7' 7", most women with Turner's syndrome 4' 8")
    b. Celiac disease
     i Inherited digestive problem in which gluten (protein found in all wheat) triggers immune response that can damage the small intestines
     ii. Cannot absorb nutrients from food, stunts growth and delays puberty
     iii. Treatment in form of gluten-free diet can lead to catch-up growth— body's struggle to get back to genetically programmed size
  B. The Endocrine System
   1. Endocrine glands secrete chemicals called hormones into bloodstream
   2. Pituitary gland —"master" endocrine gland located at base of brain
    a. Directly controlled by hypothalamus
    b. Triggers release of hormones from all other glands and produces growth hormone
    c. Growth hormones directly regulate growth
     i. Children lacking growth hormones unlikely to exceed 4 feet
     ii. If started before puberty, use of synthetic grow hormones can result in near-expected adult height in children lacking normal amount of growth hormones
     iii. Some children benefit from growth hormone therapy while other do not
     iv. Adults using growth hormones to improve athletic performance at risk for health issues like cardiac problems and insulin resistance
   3. Thyroid gland plays key role in growth and development and impact on nervous system
    a. Unnoticed deficiency of gland can lead to lower IQ in infants and slower growth
    b. Later thyroid deficiency results in slow growth but no brain damage
   4. Males and sex hormones
    a. Male fetus will not develop testes (a type of endocrine gland) unless gene on Y chromosome triggered
    b. Testes—endocrine glands that produce male hormones testosterone
     i. High quantities of hormones released during adolescence (time of "raging hormones")
     ii. Testosterone and other male hormones (androgens) stimulate growth
     iii. Androgens responsible for development of male sex organs and contribute to sexual motivation
   2. Ovaries—(female endocrine glands) that produce larger quantities of the primary female hormone estrogen and of progesterone
    a. Key female hormones released in high quantities during adolescence
     i. These hormones key trigger of female growth spurt during adolescence

        ii. Progesterone (sometimes called the "pregnancy hormone") because it allows for conception and supports pregnancy

    3. Adrenal gland secretes hormones that contribute to maturation of bones and muscles in both sexes

    4. In adulthood, endocrine glands continue to regulate bodily processes

        a. Hormones help body metabolize (break down) food

        b. Declines associated with menopause

C. The Nervous System

    1. The nervous system components—brain, spinal cord, and neural tissue

        a. Central nervous system—brain and spinal cord

        b. Peripheral nervous system—neural tissue extended outside central

    2. Neuron—basic cell unit of nervous system

        a. Dendrites—branches that receive signals from other neurons

        b. Axon—long segment of neuron in which signal is transmitted

        c. Synapse—gap between neurons

        d. Neurotransmitter—brain chemicals stored at end of the axons released across synapse

        e. Myelin—fatty sheath on axon that insulates and speeds neural transmission

        f. Myelination—process in which neurons encased in myelin

            i. Results in increase in speed of neural transmissions

            ii. Myelination may be responsible for the vocabulary spurt in toddlers

          iii. Increased myelination in prefrontal lobe corresponds to increase in hypothetical questions in adolescents

          iv. Differences in myelination may underlie attention and concentration limits in younger individuals

            v. Some have linked myelination to increase in risk-taking behavior during adolescence (Exploration Box on a brain development explanation of why adolescence take more risks than adults)

        g. Brain has as many as 100 billion neurons

    3. Brain development

        a. Birth brain weight: 25% of adult; age 2: 75%; age 5: 90%

        b. Development of early brain influenced by unfolding genetic plan and individual experiences

            i. Nelson argues that brain circuitry relies on experience to customize

            ii. Normal opportunities and experience leads to normal brain development

        c. Plasticity—neural responsiveness to environmental experience

            i. Early brain has great plasticity

            ii. Developing brain highly vulnerable to damage from sensory or motor deprivation

          iii. Young brain more adaptable and able to recover from injury

          iv. Greatest impact of stimulation in early development

            v. Synaptic organization continues to occur throughout lifespan

          vi. Critical (or sensitive) period for rapid development in late prenatal and early infancy

        d. Lateralization—asymmetry and specialization of functioning of two brain hemispheres of cerebral cortex

Chapter 5

       i. In most people, left hemisphere adept at sequential step-by-step processing needed for analytical reasoning and language

     ii. In most people, right hemisphere adept at simultaneous processing (including spatial skills and visual-motor ability)

   iii. Oversimplified as left side the thinking brain and right side the emotional brain

   iv. Sides of brain connected by corpus callosum, which allows for communication between hemispheres

    v. Left hemisphere considered seat of language, controlling word content and grammar, while right hemisphere processes melody, pitch, sound intensity, and affective content of language

   vi. If one hemisphere damaged, other may take over (ability may be limited or enhanced by age)

  vii. Lateralization evident at birth and may have genetic basis (other evidence for lateralization comes from handedness studies)

 viii. About 90% of people rely on right hand

   ix. Males somewhat more likely to be left-handed (odds of left-handedness greatest if have both parents are left-handed)

    x. Brain never completes development; continues to be responsive to experience and capable of neurogenesis, the process of generating new neurons (often in response to experience)

   xi. Neurogenesis once thought to be impossible in humans, but examples from brain-damaged individuals like Terry Wallis suggest that new cells can be generated

  xii. Researchers can demonstrate changes in brain blood flow in response to experience

  4. The aging brain

    a. Senility (e.g., Alzheimer's disease) not normal part of aging

    b. Gradual and mild degeneration common (e.g., loss of neurons that control sensory and motor activities)

    c. Brain weight and volume decrease in adult years

    d. With age, neurons atrophy or die, with loss greatest in brain areas that control sensory and motor activities

    e. Increased senile plaques (seen in abundance in people with Alzheimer's disease) and reduced blood flow to brain common with aging

       i. Older brain processes more slowly

    f. Brain change in response to activity continues throughout lifespan

       i. Greater integration of left and right hemispheres

      ii. Mental and aerobic exercise can enhance neural development; Cohen (*Mature Mind: The Positive Power of the Aging Brain*) argues that sophisticated thought like dualistic thinking, systematic thinking, and relativistic thinking only emerge during middle and older adulthood

    g. Key to enhanced intellectual functioning in older age is an "enhanced environment"

D. Principles of Growth

  1. Cephalocaudal principle—head to tail development

a. Head growth first, then trunk, then legs

b. Newborn head accounts for 25% of body; adult head accounts for 12% of body

c. During first year, trunk grows fastest

d. During second year, legs grow fastest

2. Proximodistal principle—center outward to extremities

a. Chest and internal organs before arms, then fingers

b. Trunk fills out before arms

3. Orthogenetic principle—global and undifferentiated to increased differentiation and hierarchical integration

a. Single cell to highly specialized cells (e.g., blood)

b. What begin as undifferentiated cells form functioning systems

E. A Lifespan Developmental Model of Health

1. Health is a life-long process (influenced by personal choice)

2. Health is determined by genetic and environmental influences

3. Health (and its study) is multidimensional

4. Changes in health involve both gains and losses

5. Health occurs in a sociohistorical context and can be enhanced or constrained by social and historical factors

II The Infant

A. Rapid Growth

1. Typical newborn 20 inches and 7 to 7 1/2 pounds

2. Early size related to prenatal experience

a. Ounce per day and inch per month gain

b. Age two, have attained half of adult height

c. Growth is in spurts (90-95% of days are growth free)

3. Soft bones ossify (harden) and become interconnected

4. Infants have all of their muscles, but they will grow and strengthen

B. Newborn Capabilities

1. Newborns use to be viewed as helpless and ill prepared to cope with world outside of womb

2. Reflexes—unlearned, involuntary response to stimuli

a. Survival reflexes—clear adaptive value

i. Breathing

ii. Eye-blink (protect eye from foreign object or bright light)

iii. Sucking (obtain food)

b. Primitive reflexes—some unclear value, others some adaptive value, at least in some cultures

i. Grasping reflex may help infants cling to caregivers

ii. Stepping reflex may be forerunner of later voluntary behavior

iii. Expression of primitive reflex (e.g., grasping) not related to later expression (strong voluntary grip)

iv. Primitive reflexes typically disappear in early infancy

v. Useful for diagnosing neurological problems

        vi. Disappearance of primitive indicator of normal nervous system development and that experience is influencing brain and behavior
    3. Behavioral states—organized, individual patterns of daily activity
        a. Predictable sleep-wake cycles within six months after birth
            i. Newborns spend half of time in active, rapid eye movement (REM) sleep
            ii. By six months, about 25-30% in sleep in REM, which more closely resembles 20% rate in adults
            iii. REM sleep associated with brain maturation and plasticity
            iv. Infants may sleep to regulate sensory stimulation as to not overload the immature nervous system
            v. To reduce stimulation, infants become less active and slip into sleep
            vi. Sleep important at all ages (Application Box on child and adult sleep deprivation)
C. Physical Behavior
    1. Toddlers show more mobility than infants
    2. Locomotor development
        a. Developmental norms—typical age of mastery
            i. Depend on group studied (e.g., children in some cultures walk earlier than in others)
            ii. Norms hide good deal of variation
            iii. Most early or late mastery is still in the normal range
        b. Principles of growth
            i. Cephalocaudal principle—lift head before trunk
            ii. Proximodistal principle—trunk activities mastered before leg or arm activities
            iii. Gross motor skills—large muscle, whole body, or limb movements (e.g., kicking) mastered prior to fine motor skills—precise movement of hands, fingers, feet, and toes (e.g., writing)
            iv. Orthogenetic principle—early use of whole body and later use of specific body parts
        c. Crawling
            i. Locomotion—movement from one place to another first accomplished in many ways (e.g., rolling, belly crawling, hands-and-knees crawling, cruising sideways along furniture)
            ii. Hands-and-knees crawling normally begins around 10 months
            iii. New ability allows for more exploration and interaction with others
            iv. "Back to Sleep" campaign to reduce SIDS caused some parents to be concerned that their children did not crawl at the correct age, but crawling appears to have no great developmental significance
        d. Walking
            i. Walking normally begins around one year
            ii. Thelen found that walking requires mature nervous system, muscle development, and need to be less top-heavy
            iii. Adolph and colleagues found that walking required an average of 13 starts and stops to show consistent performance of a motor skill (like taking one step forward and two steps back)

iv. By age 14 months, average infant taking 2,000 steps an hour and traveling a distance of seven football fields

 3. Grasping and reaching
  a. Innate grasping reflex weakens and is replaced by voluntary, coordinated behavior
  b. By middle of first year, infants grasp using clumsy clamp-like grasp (ulnar grasp—palm and outer fingers)
  c. By six months, able to bend elbow and movements become smoother
  d. With time (reliable by first birthday), the thumb to forefinger pincer grasp develops
  e. Key involves increased integration and differentiation of movement into coordinated actions

 4. Motor skills as dynamic action systems
  a. Rhythmic stereotypes—repetitive movement common in early infancy
   i. Infants move body in repetitive ways (e.g., swaying, bouncing)
   ii. Rhythmic stereotypes emerge shortly before a new skill emerges
  b. Dynamic systems approach—use feedback to gain control of motor skills
   i. Development takes place over time through "self-organizing" process (cumulative effect)
   ii. Development is highly individualistic
  c. Toddlers adjust walking to change in their body dimensions and the slope of a walkway
   i. Young toddlers can adjust walking in response to changing body shape
   ii. Can recognize when a walkway is too steep and will avoid the path or scoot down on their bottoms or on hands and knees
   iii. Through tumbles, infants learn which surfaces are safe and which are problematic
  d. Walking not just genetically programmed; feedback from sensory systems is critical, as is knowledge of own motor skills (fits with dynamic systems theory)
  e. Dynamic systems approach views motor development as an integration between action and thought

D. Health and Wellness
 1. Most babies under 750 grams (1 lb, 10 ½ ounces) die within first year
 2. Complications of premature birth second leading cause of death during first year
 3. Congenital malformations—genetic or prenatal event defects present at birth
  a. Leading cause of death during first year
  b. Examples include heart defects, spina bifida
 4. Use of vaccinations has led to significant improvement in infants' health
  a. In United States, immunization use is highly related to socioeconomic status

III The Child
A. Steady Growth
 a. Steady but slower (ages two through puberty)—2 to 3 inches and 5 to 6 pounds per year
 b. Growth and development continues to follow cephalocaudal and proximodistal principles

B. Physical Behavior
1. Unlike infants, children master ability to move in a changing environment (adaptation)
   a. Increased ball-throwing performance
   b. Improvement in throwing related to ability to integrate multiple body parts (e.g., raising arm, stepping forward)
2. Refinement of motor skills (initially awkward)
   a. Can run in a straight line
   b. Can integrate two motor skills (e.g., hopping on one foot and walking mature into skipping)
   c. Jump higher, run faster, throw farther
   d. Some gender differences (boys slightly better)
3. Improvements in eye/hand coordination often due to practice
   a. Age three, have hard time with buttons
   b. Age five, can copy letters
   c. Age six, can tie shoes
   d. Age eight, can use household tools (e.g. screwdriver)
4. Faster reaction times steady improvement across childhood
   a. Increased speed of neural processing leads to improvements in memory and other cognitive functions
C. Health and Wellness
1. Many factors impact health (e.g., parent's education, socioeconomic status)
2. Socio-historical context also plays role in the health and well-being of a child
3. Accidents a major negative influence on children's health
   a. Childhood marked by injuries
   b. Car crashes are leading cause of childhood fatalities
   c. Use of seat belts helps reduce possibility of injury
4. Nutrition important contributor to childhood health
   a. As appetite diminishes, children may become picky eaters
   b. Fast foods are often high in carbohydrates and low in nutrition
      i. School children often frequent convenience stores and consume many items with empty calories (e.g., sugary foods and beverages)
   c. Parents' impact
      i. Can model healthy eating and provide children with healthy food
      ii. Can steer children away from sugary sodas and popular sugar-sweetened beverages
      iii. Preschoolers who consume sugary soda between meals are more likely to become overweight
      iv. Children may eat more "comfort foods" in stressful environments, but only if they are available
5. Schools can have big impact
   a. Students in schools with breakfast programs have healthier weights as indicated by body mass index (BMI)—marker of body fat calculated from height and weight
   b. School lunches as health risk
      i. Lunches contain more fat than breakfasts and also have high levels of fat and sodium and low levels of fiber

Chapter 5
70

ii. Schools taking actions like removing fries and vending machine that offer fatty or sugary snacks

6. Physical activity fosters good health
   a. Children need 60 minutes of moderate or vigorous exercise a day
   b. Physical fitness may enhance cognitive functioning (including academic performance) and psychological functioning
   c. Participation in physical activities may positively influence self-esteem
   d. Contemporary lifestyles inadvertently promote inactivity
      i. Average child spends five to six hours per day watching television, playing video games, or working on the computer
      ii. Most kids are chauffeured everywhere

7. Increasing number of children meet criteria for obesity—being 20% or more above

   ideal weight for height, age, and sex
      i. Obesity rates have tripled in past 30 years
      ii. Children in neighborhoods with safe outdoor activities less likely to be overweight
      iii. Indoor sedentary behavior likely to being overweight
      iv. Playing active sports or video games beneficial
      v. Availability of portable sports equipment (in school) means more engagement in physical activity
      vi. Some children may be predisposed by temperament to be more sedentary and resist use of playground equipment

IV The Adolescent
   A. The Growth Spurt
      1. Puberty—biological change resulting in sexual maturity and capacity to produce children
      2. Adolescent growth spurt
         a. Triggered by hormones
         b. Boys and girls grow at different rates
            i. Female peak growth for height around age 12, male peak age 13.4
            ii. Female peak weight growth around age 12.5, male peak age 13.9
            iii. Both sexes return to slower grow rate after growth spurts
            iv. Girls adult height around 16 while boys may continue until age 20
            v. Both sexes gain muscle mass (boys slightly more)
            vi. Different distribution—girls gain extra fat primarily in hips, breast, and buttocks, while boys develop broader shoulders
   B. Sexual Maturation
      1. Sexual maturation due to adrenal gland activity and release of adrenal androgens (called adrenarche) and gonadal hormones
         a. Adrenarche primarily responsible for secondary sex characteristics (e.g., pubic hair)
         b. Obvious signs of sexual maturity emerge with increased production of gonadal hormones released by testes and ovaries
      2. Tanner scale used to measure progression through puberty and attainment of sexual maturity

a. Five stages from prepubertal—no evidence of secondary sexual characteristics to adult secondary sexual characteristics
b. Females
    i. Menarché—first menstruation
    ii. Normally between ages 11 and 14
    iii. Sexual maturation impacted by ethnicity (e.g., African American earlier)
    iv. Some breast development or pubic hair may be seen as early as age three
c. Males
    i. Process begins with enlargement of testes and scrotum around age 11
    ii. Semenarche—initial ejaculation (via "wet dream" or masturbation)
    iii. Production of sperm typically comes after semenarche at around age 13
    iv. Will sprout facial hair and experience the lowering of the voice (can result in embarrassment)

3. Variations in timing
    a. Genes help determine the rate of adolescent development
    b. Physical and sexual maturation triggered when hypothalamus of brain stimulates endocrine system
        i. Boys and girls have similar levels of "male" and "female" hormones during childhood
        ii. At sexual maturation, boys have larger quantities of male hormones (e.g., androgens)
        iii. At sexual maturation, girls have larger quantities of female hormones (e.g., estrogen)
    c. Secular trend—earlier maturation and greater body size in industrial societies
        i. Better medical care and nutrition
        ii. Taller and heavier girls tend to mature earlier
        iii. Anorexia nervosa—eating disorder involving severe dieting; can result in delayed maturation
    d. Stress may delay sexual maturation

4. Family situations affect timing of puberty
    a. Girls of depressed mothers tend to enter puberty earlier
    b. Girls in homes involving separation or divorce tend to enter puberty earlier
        i. Especially true if father was displaying dysfunctional behavior
    c. Harsh mothering at young age may trigger early puberty and menarche

C. Psychological Implications
1. Concern with body image
    a. Concern more prominent in females, with individual reactions varying widely
    b. Negative cultural view of menstruation lead to negative image
    c. Boys have more positive body images
        i. Welcome change in height and weight and related to athletic prowess; constitutional growth delay—characterized as being at or below fifth percentile on growth chart, later entering of puberty, but growing at near-normal pace
        ii. Eventually catch up with peers, but may have rocky experience being the smallest kid in class

  d. Boys often unaware of some of physical changes they are experiencing
    i. Notice first ejaculation but do not talk about it
    ii. While reaction to puberty is mixed for boys, tend to have more positive regarding semenarche than are girls to menarche
  e. Changes in relationships with parents
    i. Teens tend to distance themselves from family
    ii. Conflict due to increasing independence
    iii. Cultural beliefs impact parental relations (e.g., Hispanic boys closer to parents)
    iv. Relationships tend to become warmer after puberty

D. Early vs. Late Development
 1. Early maturation more advantageous for boys than for girls
  a. Early maturing boys
    i. More positive effects including social competence and self-assuredness
    ii. Increased risk for substance use, bullying, and delinquency
  b. Late maturing boys
    i. More negative effects, including anxiety, less sure of themselves, adjustment problems, scoring lower on school tests
    ii. Are less likely to drink alcohol that early maturing boys
  c. Early maturing girls
    i. Do not tend to gain status from increase in size (as boys do) and may be the subject of ridicule
    ii. Higher levels of body dissatisfaction
    iii. Tend to be more popular with older boys and socialize with older peers
    iv. More likely to date, smoke, drink, and engage in sexual behavior at an earlier age
    v. Report higher levels of depression (but unclear if depression or puberty comes first)
  d. Late maturation for girls
    i. Some anxiety but not as disadvantageous as for boys
    ii. Outperform others on school achievement tests
 2. Impact of time of maturity tends to fade with time
  a. May be some risk of long-term problems associated with early maturing girls who engage in risky behavior (e.g., sex) and with risk for mental health problems (e.g., anxiety and depression) in this group
  b. Early maturing males may be more conforming
 3. Psychological differences between late and early maturation becoming smaller
  a. Timing-of-puberty effect mediated by adolescent's perceptions
    i. Self-perception for reason of timing ("late bloomer" vs. athletic impact) important
    ii. Peer and family reactions can impact perception
    iii. Parents often more concerned about emerging sexuality of daughters

E. Physical Behavior
 1. Muscular strength and physical competence increases (e.g., ball throwing, jumping)
 2. Many adolescents not as active as they should be
 3. Boys outperform girls in activities involving strength

4. Gender-role socialization can help explain sex differences in physical performance
   a. Girls encouraged to be less "tomboyish" and more sedentary
5. Gap between male and female physical skills appears to be narrowing

F. Health and Wellness
1. Sedentary lifestyle of modern society undermining physical fitness of teens
   a. Adolescents drinking more nutrient-poor beverages gain weight and have higher systolic blood pressure, which increases risk for later health problems (e.g., kidney disease, arthritis)
   b. Rate of diabetes—high levels of blood sugar—significantly increased in recent years in teens
   c. Obesity product of nature (heredity) and nurture (e.g., inactivity, poor eating habits)
      i. Overweight parents provide sedentary models and often purchase higher calorie and less nutritious food
      ii. Overweight teens gravitate to each other, reduces stigma of being overweight
      iii. Overweight adolescents, even those who later slim down, run risk of health problems later in life
2. Unintentional injuries leading cause of death in teens
   a. Mostly vehicle accidents
   b. Homicides and suicide also common causes of death in teens
   c. Lifestyle choices can contribute to problems
      i. Alcohol (binge drinking), drug use, and smoking are bad
      ii. Teens under the influence of alcohol are more likely to smoke, engage in risky sexual behavior, get into car accidents, fight, and do poorly in school

V The Adult
A. Typical Changes
B. Appearance and Physical Functioning
1. Most changes after 40
   a. Wrinkles, graying and thinning hair, and weight gain
   b. "Middle-age spread" controllable by exercise, but adults often do not have the time
      i. Just 30% of adults engage in any physical activity during leisure time
      ii. 35% of African American and 25% of European American adults are obese
      iii. Obesity can carry health burdens like heart disease and Type 2 diabetes
      iv. U.S. Department of Health identified obesity as one of the most significant health problems facing Americans
   c. Weight loss common after age 60
   d. Loss often involves loss of muscle and bone
      i. Real culprit not age, but lack of activity (sedentary lifestyle) related to poor neighborhood characteristics and personal factors like caregiving responsibilities and lack of energy
   e. Aging involves gradual decline in efficiencies of body systems in later life
      i. Loss of heart and lung capacity

      ii. Loss of muscle strength

      iii. Decrease in ability to control body temperature and of immune system to fight disease

      iv. Women show small losses of muscle strength before age 55 and large decreases thereafter

      v. Men show steady loss of muscle strength

      vi. Aerobic capacity and physiological measurements vary more widely in those age 70 than those age 20

   2. Decrease in reserve capacity—ability of organs to respond to demand, lower maximal heart rate—is a fact of aging

     a. Older age decline related to decreased involvement in vigorous physical activities

C. Psychological Implications

     a. Negative stereotypes can lead to "ageism"—prejudice against elderly

      i. Some older adults bothered by physical appearance (women more so than men)

      ii. Many old individuals do not see themselves as old

      iii. Believed that they were not "old" because they avoided nursing home care

      iv. Remaining physically and socially active is often thought to be the key to avoid becoming old

     b. Most older individuals retain sense of well-being and function independently despite increased likelihood impairments like arthritis and diabetes

D. The Reproductive System

   1. Sex hormone levels fluctuate in both males and females

     a. Males fluctuate more annually

      i. High levels of testosterone related to aggression and sexual activity, but changes in hormone levels not clearly tied to changes in mood or behavior

     b. Females fluctuate more dramatically monthly

      i. Shifts have psychological impacts

      ii. Estrogen and progesterone levels peak at mid ovulation cycle

      iii. Premenstrual syndrome (PMS)—symptoms experienced just before menstrual flow including breast tenderness, bloating, headaches

      iv. Some question validity of PMS, may be impacted by expectation as much as hormones

      v. Severe PMS (experienced by less than 5% of women) may be due to changing hormone levels

      vi. Drugs like Prozac and vitamin D used to treat milder PMS symptoms

      vii. Genetic and social factors (e.g., stereotypes of what women should experience) influence premenstrual and menstrual distress

   2. Female menopause

     a. Menopause—ending of menstrual period in midlife (i.e., no ovulation or menstruation)

      i. Typical age range is from 45 to 54; due to drop in levels of estrogen and other female hormones creating a hormone mix more "masculine" and less "feminine" than that of premenopausal women

      ii. Age of menopause somewhat related to when a woman's mother reached menopause

    iii. Physical effects include hot flashes—sudden sensation of warmth and sweating—and vaginal dryness

    iv. Psychological symptoms (e.g., irritability and depression) vary greatly, and most women do not experience significant psychological problems

    v. Women who have experienced menopause tend to be more positive about it

    vi. Despite stereotype, menopause tends to be "no big deal" for most women

    vii. History of menstrual problems good predictor of menopause problems

    viii. Expectation of impact also predict reaction

  b. Hormone replacement therapy or HRT—replacement of estrogen/progestin—was thought to compensate for loss of hormones

    i. HRT often relieves physical symptoms of menopause (e.g., hot flashes, vaginal dryness)

    ii. HRT may increase risk of heart attack, stroke, or breast cancer

    iii. Risks of HRT may outweigh benefits of use

    iv. For those with severe symptoms, short-term HRT may be used

    v. Lifestyle changes like exercise and adequate sleep may be best options for menopausal women

 3. Male andropause

  a. Andropause—male loss of reproductive capacity ("male menopause")

    i. Decreased levels of testosterone

    ii. Slower and less dramatic progression than menopause

    iii. Symptoms include low libido, lack of energy, erection problems, memory problems

    iv. Less active sperm (but still capable of having children)

  b. Erectile dysfunction often the result of medical conditions and not loss of hormones

E. Slowing Down

 1. Older adults tend to perform motor actions more slowly and with less coordination

  a. Most trouble on novel and complex tasks

  b. Slowing in the result of slowing of brain and nervous system affecting motor and mental functioning

  c. Reaction times vary greatly in old age

    i. Fitness may impact speed (physically fit faster)

    ii. Health impacts speed (those without cardiovascular disease faster)

    iii. Aerobic exercise and playing video games can increase speed of reactions

F. Disease, Disuse, and Abuse

 1. Effects of aging confounded with effects of disease, disuse, or abuse

 2. Most older people have some chronic disease (e.g., arthritis, heart disease)

  a. Birren (1963) found one group of older men with no sign of disease compared with others with slight traces, but no clinically diagnosable diseases

    i. Healthier group of older men hardly differed from younger men

    ii. Aging in absence of disease little effect on physical and psychological functioning

          iii. Hard to separate out effects of aging and disease as most older people experience both
     b. Disuse contributes to steep declines in physical functioning ("use it or lose it" maxim)
          i. Body disuse (sedentary lifestyle) will result in muscle atrophy
          ii. Brain needs mental exercise to display plasticity
          iii. Abuse of body (high fat diet, smoking) contributes to aging
          iv. Increases in recreational drug use may be seen in older generation who came of age during the drug culture
          v. Drugs affect older more powerfully and interact with aging body's chemistry to impair functioning

G. Health and Wellness
1. Many 70-and-older adults have at least one chronic impairment
     a. About half have arthritis or hypertension (high blood pressure)
     b. About one-third have heart disease
     c. Tremendous variability in health and well-being in older adults, with some older adults more active than younger ones
2. Exercise very important to staying healthy
     a. Low-intensity exercise and weight lifting can increase strength
     b. Exercise can decrease stress and incidence of depression
     c. Exercise does not halt the inevitable aging process
     d. To beat aging, must become more active in old age
3. Osteoporosis—disease resulting in loss of bone mass due to loss of minerals, leaving bones more fragile and easier to fracture
     a. Nearly one-third of older adults with hip fracture die within one year
     b. Hip fracture leading cause of nursing home admissions
          i. Those who fall tend to restrict activity level
          ii. Restricting activity levels can lead to further loss of bone mass and muscle
     c. Females with light frames, who smoke, and have a family history of osteoporosis are at risk
     d. Calcium intake and weight-bearing exercise beneficial for reducing osteoporosis
     e. HRT can be used, but there are risks
4. Osteoarthritis—aging of the joints due to use that damages the cartilage resulting in pain and restricted movement

H. Successful Aging
1. Snowdon (2002) longitudinal study of nuns
     a. Underwent annual mental and physical testing
     b. Access to health records
     c. Level of education positively impacted longevity and health
2. Autobiographies written prior to study analyzed
     a. Healthier nuns used more complex vocabulary in autobiography
     b. Nuns with autobiographies with positive emotions lived longer

1. Ask students to report on the media's portrayal of physical characteristics across the lifespan. For example,

- Students might look through magazine articles and advertisements to determine the following: Are older people "less attractive"? Are physical changes more of a "liability" for women than men in our culture? What are psychological correlates of attractiveness at different ages?
- Students might watch television and answer the same questions listed above.
- Students might visit a greeting card shop and look at the types of cards available for various decade-marking birthdays. What do these cards tell us about popular notions of the various decades? Students might try to write alternative greeting cards for these birthdays.

2. Bring into class, or have the class collect, drawing samples from children of various ages. These can also be used to show children's early attempts at mastering this fine motor skill. Between the ages of 2 1/2 and 4, children tend to focus on the activity of drawing itself, and starting at about age 4, they try to actually represent something. They continue to refine their drawing and representation skills throughout childhood. Being able to represent depth in drawings typically doesn't emerge until about 9 or 10 years of age. For more information on developmental changes in drawing, see Nicholls & Kennedy (1992).

Nichols, A.L., & Kennedy, J.M. (1992). Drawing development: From similarity of features to direction. *Child Development*, 63, 227-241.

3. A number of sources have pointed to school lunches as a major contributor to the increased incidence of obesity in school children. In recent years, British celebrity chef Jamie Oliver (the "Naked Chef") has begun a one-man campaign to change the British school lunch system to include more healthy options and to ban junk food. This theme is making its way to the United States in the form of the ABC television show *The Food Revolution*. Have students check out some of his proposals at some of the websites listed below. Do they think he will be successful? What obstacles will he face? What are the benefits and liabilities if he is successful?

http://www.jamieoliver.com/school-dinners
http://abc.go.com/shows/jamie-olivers-food-revolution
http://www.webmd.com/diet/features/chef_jamie_oliver_makes_over_school_lunches?src=RSS_BLOGGER

4. Students can gain a better understanding of neonatal reflexes by seeing them in action. Have students with access to infants review the major reflexes identified in Table 5.2. Then have them attempt to identify whether these reflexes still exist (or have disappeared) in the infants they know.

5. In connection with the material on early and late maturation in adolescence, ask students of both sexes to describe their experiences about early versus late maturation and compare what they say to information in the text. Students may not want to talk about their own experiences,

but they would probably be comfortable describing the experiences of siblings or friends who were early or late maturing adolescents.

6. Have students interview adults between ages 20 and 100 on their current physical status and how that status has changed with time. Also, have students ask each person about their ideal age (i.e., the age they would most like to be). Get together in the group and discuss the response. Students may be surprised to learn that the "ideal" age is likely older then they imagine.

7. In order to get a hands-on experience concerning the impact of physical aging, have students interview four family members or friends from the following: 35-45 years old, 45-55 years old, 55-65 years old, and someone 66 or older, and ask them to respond to the following questions:

- On a scale from 1 (worst) to 10 (best), how would you rate your overall physical ability?

- Compared to your young adult years, in what area have you experienced the most significant physical decline?

- Compared to your young adult years, in what area have you experienced the least amount of physical decline?

- Is there any type of physical activity that you perform better now than when you were younger?

You could have a class discussion in which you aggregate the class data and see if any themes in physical aging occur. You could then see if the pattern of your students matches the information presented in the text.

SUGGESTED FILMS AND VIDEOS

Child Development Basics (2005, Insight Media, DVD 15 minutes): Program involves a visit to a daycare center where various aspects of infant and toddler behavior (including grasping) are highlighted.

Early Adulthood: Physical Development (1999, Magna Systems, VHS 28 minutes): Overview of physical changes during the young adult years.

Inside the Teenage Brain (2002, Insight Media, VHS or DVD 60 minutes): A PBS program examining brain growth and reorganization experienced during puberty.

Middle Adulthood: Physical Development (2000, Magna Systems, VHS or DVD 28 minutes): Overview of key physiological changes between age 40 and old age.

Older Brains, New Connections: A Conversation with Marian Diamond at 73 (2000, Davidson Films, VHS, 30 minutes): Dr. Diamond is one of the few individuals allowed to study Einstein's brain. This engaging video presents cutting edge research on the effects of aging on the brain.

<u>Playing and Growing: Physical Development</u> (2003, Insight Media, VHS 30 minutes): This video focuses on the development of growth and fine motor skills between ages 2 and 5.

<u>Women's Health: The Meaning of Menopause </u>(2003, Insight Media, DVD 29 minutes): This DVD provides an extensive look at perimenopausal and postmenopausal women's issues.

SUGGESTED WEBSITES

Early Physical Development Tracker
http://www.wholefamily.com/aboutyourkids/child/normal/physical_development.html

Menopause: MedlinePlus
http://www.nlm.nih.gov/medlineplus/menopause.html

PBS Whole Child
http://www.pbs.org/wholechild/abc/physical.html

Puberty 101
http://www.puberty101.com/

What Physical Changes Happen to the Brain?
http://websites.afar.org/site/PageServer?pagename=IA_b_neuro_2_physical

SUGGESTED READINGS

Adolph, K.E. and Berger, S.E. (2006). Motor Development. *Handbook of Child Psychology: Vol 2, Cognition, Perception, and Language (6th ed.).* D. Kuhn R. Siegler, W. Damon, and R. Lerner (Eds.). Hoboken, NJ: John Wiley & Sons Inc.

Garrity, J.M. (2010). A review of older, wiser, sexually smarter: 30 sex ed lessons for adults only. *American Journal of Sexuality Education*, 5(1), 88-95.

Green, C.S., and Bavelier, D. (2008). Exercising your brain: A review of human brain plasticity and training-induced learning. *Psychology of Aging*, 23(4), 692-701.

Kaminski, P.L. and Hayslip Jr., B. (2006). Gender differences in body esteem among older adults. *Journal of Women & Aging*, 18(3), 19-35.

Levy, B.R., Ashman, O., and Slade, M.D. (2009). Age attributes and aging health: Contrast between the United States and Japan. *Journals of Gerontology, Series B: Psychological Sciences and Social Sciences*, 64B(3), 335-338.

SENSATION, PERCEPTION, AND ATTENTION

LEARNING OBJECTIVES

After reading and studying the material in this chapter, you should be able to answer the following questions.

ISSUES OF NATURE AND NURTURE
1. What are the views of constructivists and nativists on the nature-nurture issue as it relates to sensation and perception?

THE INFANT
2. How are perceptual abilities of infants assessed?

3. What are infants' visual capabilities? What sorts of things do infants prefer to look at?

4. What are the auditory capabilities of infants? What do researchers know about infants' abilities to perceive speech?

5. What are the taste and smell capabilities of infants? To what extent are infants sensitive to touch, temperature, and pain?

6. To what extent can infants integrate their sensory experiences? What is an example of cross-modal perception?

7. What role do early experiences play in development of perceptions? What factors contribute to normal visual perception?

THE CHILD
8. What changes occur in attention throughout childhood?

9. What constitutes an attention deficit hyperactivity disorder? Can individuals with this disorder be effectively treated.

THE ADOLESCENT
10. How can hearing loss be minimized across the lifespan, beginning with adolescence?

THE ADULT
11. What changes occur in visual capabilities and visual perception during adulthood?

12. What changes in auditory capabilities and speech perception occur during adulthood?

13. What changes occur in taste and smell, and in sensitivity to touch, temperature, and pain during adulthood?

I Sensation and Perception
  A. Sensation and Perception Definitions
    1. Cytomegalovirus (CMV)—when contracted in utero can cause blindness in babies
    2. Sensation—process by which sensory information is detected and transmitted to brain
      a. From birth infants sense their environment (e.g., detect light, sound, odor molecules)
    3. Perception—interpretation/understanding of sensory input
      a. Know that an odor is a sizzling steak
    4. Sensation and perception are at the heart of human functioning
      a. Everything your do depends on your ability sense and perceive world
      b. Sensation and perception issues have been at the center of philosophical and developmental science debate

II Issues of Nature and Nurture
  A. Constructivists
    1. Perception constructed through learning over time (nurture side)
    2. At birth, equipped with sensory systems
    3. Need experiential interaction to infer meaning from sensations
      a. Must view objects from various distances to interpret different retinal images to create association between image and its meaning (e.g., a distant object)
  B. Nativist
    1. Born equipped with innate capacities and maturational processes, allowing us to perceive world in meaningful way (nature side)
    2. Infants equipped with sensory systems that are refined through innate plan
    3. Innate understanding of perceptual world (no need for experience to interpret sensory world)
      a. Brain automatically understands that different retinal images give insight into the distance of an object
  C. Current Debate on Nature-Nurture of Perception
    1. Constructionist view long popular
    2. New data caused shift toward more nativist perspective
    3. Some declines in sensory and perceptual abilities in later life

III The Infant
  A. Historical Perspective
    1. Williams James viewed infancy as a state of "blooming, buzzing confusion"
    2. Modern theorist believe that infants have greater perceptual skills than anyone suspected
  B. Assessing Sensory and Perceptual Abilities
    1. Habituation—learning to be bored (present same stimulus repeatedly)
      a. With repeated presentations, infants gets used to a stimulus
      b. Procedure can be use to test all senses
    2. Preferential looking—infants look longer at one of two stimuli
      a. Preference may indicate discrimination or liking one better

  b. May have a preference that is not displayed when looking but may come to light with use of an alternative method (e.g.. opportunity to interact with the object)
 3. Evoked potentials—measure electrical activity in response to stimuli
  a. Small metal discs (electrodes) attached to skin's surface
  b. Computer records skin activity while infant watches or listens to a stimulus
 4. Operant conditioning—learned behavior using reinforcement
  a. Can learn to suck faster if reinforced
  b. Infants can learn to turn head in response to stimuli
   i. Can be used to determine if sounds perceived as equivalent or different
C. Vision
 1. Basic capacities
  a. Newborn infants can detect brightness and can track slow-moving objects
  b. Visual acuity—ability to perceive detail
   i. Newborn visual acuity is poor (40 times worse than adult)
   ii. Improves quickly to about 20/120 on standard eye chart by age one month
   iii. Objects beyond 8 inches are blurry
  c. Limited visual accommodation—ability of lens to change shape to bring object into focus
  d. Infant color vision
   i. Very young infants do see in color
   ii. Use habituation task to determine color vision
   iii. Four-month-olds appear to be able to discriminate the basic color categories (red, green, blue, yellow)
   iv. Newborns have limited color vision due to immature receptors
   v. Are faster at detecting stimulus on a background of a different color
 2. Pattern perception
  a. Infants attracted to contour—amount of light/dark transitions
  b. Infants attracted to dynamic (moving) vs. static objects
  c. Infants prefer object of moderate complexity (e.g., checkerboard)
  d. Preference for faces seen in young infants
   i. Prefer mom's face to stranger's face
   ii. Prefer information in upper visual field ("top-heavy pattern")
   iii. Can pick out mom's face if they have also been exposed to her voice at the same time
  e. Infants like to look at what they can see well
  f. Around two to three months, infants begin to explore interior of stimulus (e.g., a face) and appreciate the "whole object" rather than just its contours
  g. Young infants visually fixate, while older infants can shift gaze
  h. By two to three months, infants truly perceive a meaningful face and not just an appealing pattern
 3. Depth perception
  a. Very young infants act defensively (blink) when objects move toward their face
  b. Size constancy—infant can recognize object remains same size even though the retinal size changes as object moves away (Exploration Box on infants' understanding of size constancy)

    c. Visual cliff—device used to assess depth perception (Gibson and Walk, 1960)
       i. One "shallow" side with checkerboard directly under glass and a "deep" cliff side
       ii. Young infants will cross both sides, but by seven months or so, many will no longer cross the deep side
       iii. Two-month-olds appear to perceive difference between deep and shallow sides (depth) but have not learned to fear drop-offs
       iv. Fear of drop-offs (and perhaps falling) due to experience in crawling

4. Organizing a world of objects
    a. Key ability is to be able to separate visual field into distinct objects, even when objects are partially or fully hidden
    b. Young infants notice irregularities in otherwise well-formed circles or squares
    c. Use common motion—movement of objects in same direction as a cue to "wholeness" of an object
    d. Use good form—logical continuation of a line to perceive object's wholeness

5. The infant as intuitive theorist
    a. Infants look longer at "impossible" events involving a ball's motion
       i. Ball drops behind a screen and appears to be suspended in midair
    b. Innately understand simple laws of physics (object entering right of screen should exit left of screen)
    c. Infants appear to be equipped with intuitive theories—naturally possess organized system of knowledge that allows them to make sense of the world
       i. Organize knowledge around domains of physics, biology, and psychology
       ii. Seem to understand causal forces
       iii. Have innate knowledge of the world and perceive and reason about it in ways similar to that of adults

D. Hearing
1. At least as important as vision, and we depend on it to communicate
2. Process of hearing begins when moving air molecules enter the ear and vibrate the eardrum; the vibrations then transmitted to cochlea in inner ear, where they are converted to signals that the brain interprets as sound
3. Basic capacities
    a. Newborns hear better than they see
       i. Are startled by loud noise and turn away
       ii. Turn toward softer sounds
    b. Ability to hear what is going on outside of womb develops as much as three months before birth
    c. Infants prefer relatively complex auditory stimuli
    d. Infants somewhat less sensitive to soft sounds
    e. Infants can discriminate loudness, direction, duration, and frequency of sound
4. Speech perception
    a. Can distinguish phonemes—basic speech sounds—very early in life
       i. Can distinguish similar consonant sounds (*pa* and *ba*)
       ii. Can detect difference between vowels *a* and *i* from second day after birth
       iii. Can distinguish normal from deviant (rare) sounds
       iv. By three months, can recognize phoneme spoken by different people

  b. Biologically prepared to learn and speak any language as infants
    i. By one year, begin to lose sensitivity to speech sounds irrelevant to native language and begin to show increased sensitivity to speech sounds relevant to native language
    ii. English speaking infants can differentiate between consonants *l* and *r*, but Japanese and Chinese infants whose languages do not contain *l* and *r*, lose that ability (as do adults in those populations)
    iii. Language experiences shape neural connections in the areas of the brain optimizing sensitivity to sounds that they have been listening to
  c. Infants especially attracted to female voices and can recognize mother's voice soon after birth
    i. Heart rate increases to mom's voice but not to that of stranger
    ii. No preference for father's voice
    iii. Ability to detect mom's voice related to exposure to her voice while still a fetus (as demonstrated in *Cat in the Hat* study)
    iv. Hearing problems can place at risk for language and communication problems and need to be treated as early as possible
 E. The Chemical Senses: Taste and Smell
  1. Taste buds mainly on tongue; sense not well understood but is the result of bud response to chemical molecules
    a. Are four basic tastes (sweet, bitter, sour, salt)
    b. Can distinguish tastes (sweet, bitter, sour) at birth, and like sweet
    c. Different taste sensations produce different facial expressions
      i. Smile when experiencing sweet
      ii. Purse lips when experiencing bitter
      iii. Will swallow more amniotic fluid if it contains higher concentrations of sugar
    d. Food preferences may be impacted by early tastes that we are exposed to during infancy (Mennella and colleagues research)
      i. Infants fed sour-tasting formula preferred sour-tasting items as children
      ii. Greater exposure to a variety of flavors during infancy may lead to more adventuresome eating habits
      iii. "Taste gene" may account for variation in taste perceptions
  2. Olfaction (sense of smell) result of receptors in nasal passage
    a. Well established at birth
      i. Newborns react unpleasantly to vinegar and ammonia
    b. Prefer smell of own amniotic fluid (indicates prenatal sense of smell)
    c. Breast-fed infants can recognize mother's milk odor and smell of mom
    d. Mothers can recognize their infant by smell and are less repulsed by the smell of their dirty diaper than that of other dirty diapers
 F. Touch, Temperature, and Pain
  1. All skin receptors (touch, hot-cold, pain) operating in some form at birth
  2. Reflexive touch apparent at birth
  3. Tactile sensitivity develops in a cephalocaudal direction
    a. Infants explore world via tactile receptors in the mouth
    b. Touch can stimulate growth in premature infants and may promote more regular sleep patterns

4. Newborns sensitive to warm and cold
5. Young babies respond to pain (e.g., needle prick)
   a. Ethical reasons restrict ability to test infants by inflicting severe pain
   b. Pain is responsive to learning
      i. Infants with history of heel pricks grimace when nurse preparing heel for pricking
   c. Controversy over infant's ability to sense pain and the use of anesthesia on infants during surgery
      i. American Academy of Pediatrics recommends giving local anesthesia to male newborns undergoing circumcisions
      ii. Breast feeding while experiencing a painful event (vaccination) reduces the behavior signs that an infant is experiencing pain

G. Integrating Sensory Information
1. Sensory systems like vision and hearing seem to be interrelated early in life
2. Cross-modal perception—recognize through one sense something known through another
   a. Needed for game in which someone sees an object that is then put in a bag and person is asked to reach in and pull out the object
   b. Infants have some ability to integrated multiple sensory inputs
      i. Oral-to-visual cross-modal transfer by three months (can identify by sight an object that they have previously mouthed)
   c. By four to seven months, can integrate vision and hearing to judge distance
3. Impressions from different senses "fused" in early life, thus infancy is not the "blooming, buzzing confusion" described by James

H. Influences on Early Perceptual Development
1. All senses are working to some extent by birth, and most perceptual abilities emerge in the first few months
2. Early experience and the brain
   a. Classic study by Hubel and Wiesel on kittens showed deprivation of vision early can lead to permanent loss of vision
   b. Better to discuss impact of early experience in terms of sensitive periods (rather than critical periods)
      i. Sensitive period—window of time during which one is more affected by experience and in which there is a higher level of plasticity than in later life
      ii. There may be multiple sensitive periods for vision (one for normal development, one for damage-period when absence of input leads to permanent deficit in some aspect of vision, one for recovery from damage)
   c. Infants born with congenital cataracts—clouding of the lens—at risk for later visual problems
      i. The earlier the cataract is surgically corrected or removed (by 10 weeks is optimal), the greater the chance for normal vision (delays can lead to blindness)
      ii. After corrective surgery, infants show normal development in some areas (e.g., recognition of shape of face), but may struggle with certain visual tasks like holistic face processing and recognition of face based on spacing of features

   iii. Maurer and colleagues (2007) suggest sleeper effect of early visual deficits (i.e., lingering effects of lack of early visual input)
  d. Normal hearing requires normal auditory experience
   i. Children with significant hearing loss who have cochlear implants struggle to understand signal input that is sent from implant to the brain
   ii. Brain must learn how to interpret information
  e. Maturation is not enough, as normal perceptual development requires normal perceptual experience
 3. The infant's active role
  a. Infants seek sensory experiences they need for development
  b. Gibson's (1988) three phases of exploratory behavior
   i. Birth to four months: explore by looking and listening
   ii. Five to seven months: voluntary grasping and closer attention
   iii. Eight or nine months: crawl, explore, examine
 4. Cultural variation
  a. Little difference in basic sensory ability
  b. Interpretation of sensory input can vary by culture
  c. Ability to perceive music changes with cultural experience
   i. U.S. infants noticed notes that violate Western and Javanese pelog scales, but American adults were less sensitive to unfamiliar Javanese notes
  d. Ability to draw the human form impacted by cultural experience
   i. Children in Papua New Guinea, a culture with no tradition of drawing and painting, draw humans like tadpoles or scribbles

III The Child
 A. The Development of Attention
  1. Attention—focusing of perception and cognition
   a. Attention of infant and young child often "caught" or "captured," while that of older child is directed
   b. Infants are attracted by novelty
   c. Orienting system reacts to events in the environment vs. having a focusing system that deliberately seeks out and maintains attention
  2. Longer attention span
   a. Young children have shorter attention spans
    i. Spend less time concentrating on a television program that they like
    ii. Brain myelination during childhood may positively impact ability to focus attention
  3. More selective attention—deliberate concentration on one thing while ignoring another
   a. Two-year-olds begin to show ability to focus
   b. Increase in focused attention ability between age 3½ and 4 years
   c. Kannass and Colombo (2007) study of attention
    i. Four-year-olds could work with intermittent distractions but were unable to complete tasks with constant distraction
    ii. Looking away without distraction not a problem but looking away with distraction impaired performance

iii. Keeping distractions at a minimum important when working with young children

4. More systematic attention
   a. With age, children better systematic perceptual searches (e.g., more detailed and exhaustive visual searches)
   b. Children's visual searches slower and less efficient than adults
   c. Six-year-olds more systematic searchers than four- and five-year-olds

B. Problems of Attention
   1. Attention deficit hyperactivity disorder (ADHD)
      a. Commonly diagnosed developmental disorder with combination of three key symptoms
         i. Inattention—child does not seem to listen, is easily distracted, has trouble following directions or finishing tasks, and tends to be forgetful and unorganized
         ii. Impulsivity—child thinks before acting and cannot inhibit urges
         iii. Hyperactivity—child is restless and perpetually fidgeting
      b. About 5 to 7% of school-age children meet criteria for ADHD diagnosis
      c. Boys twice as likely to be diagnosed (girls may be being underdiagnosed because they are not as hyperactive and do not act out as much)
      d. As symptoms are easier to spot, children with predominantly hyperactivity/impulsivity ADHD are diagnosed earlier (around age eight) than those with inattentive type
   2. Developmental course
      a. When symptoms are predominately hyperactivity/impulsivity condition may reveal itself in infancy
      b. Must take care to not mistake normal high levels of activity in preschoolers with ADHD
      c. By grade-school age, main problems are restlessness and inattention to schoolwork
      d. Most children outgrow overactive behavior, but may continue to be restless and have difficulty concentrating
         i. Often perform more poorly in school
         ii. May drop out
         iii. More prone to acts of delinquency
      e. By early adulthood, picture more positive but still more likely to have lapse of concentration, make impulsive choices, or procrastinate
         i. Hyperactive adults lower educational attainment
         ii. Become parents at a young age
         iii. Worst outcome involves those with both ADHD and conduct disorders
         iv. More severe the symptoms, the greater the probability that later life outcomes will be poor
         v. 20% of children with ADHD outgrow problem, 20% have severe problems in adulthood, and 60% have mild problems throughout their lives
   3. Suspected causes
      a. No consistent evidence of brain damage or structural defect in brain in most children with ADHD

    b. Barkely suggested that the problem may be the result of an improperly functioning frontal lobe that results in deficiencies in executive functioning (e.g., inhibition, self-regulation)

        i. Low levels of neurotransmitters dopamine and norepinephrine may be at root of executive impairments

    c. Genes predispose some to ADHD and may underlie physiological problems that underlie the disorder

        i. If identical twin or first-degree relative has ADHD, risk is increased by four or five times

        ii. No single gene causes ADHD

        iii. Some combinations may impact neurotransmitters levels

    d. Environmental influences

        i. Sugar consumption and food additives do not cause ADHD

        ii. Low birth weight, maternal smoking and alcohol consumption during pregnancy, and shortage of prenatal oxygen contribute to some cases

  4. Treatment

    a. Many children given stimulants like methylphenidate (Ritalin)

        i. Odd to give stimulant for overactivity but brains may be underaroused

        ii. Drugs increase levels of dopamine and other neurotransmitters in frontal lobe

    b. Controversy in drug as treatment

        i. Too many children who do not have ADHD given medication

        ii. Children who could benefit from drug may not be getting it

        iii. Has side effects like loss of appetite

        iv. Drugs do not cure ADHD, just improve functionality until effects wear off

        v. Drugs need to be part of the answer

    c. Behavioral treatment option

        i. Multimodal Treatment of Attention Deficit and Hyperactivity Disorder Study (MAT) found optimal intervention was a combination of medication and behavioral treatments including parent training, child training in summer program, and school intervention

        ii. The optimal treatment improved academic performance, school adjustment, and parent-child relationships

        iii. Need to carefully monitor prescriptions

IV The Adolescent

  A. Attention

    1. Adolescents vs. children

      a. Adolescents better able to sustain attention (longer attention spans)

        i. May be tied to brain myelination that speeds transmission of neural impulses

      b. Adolescents more efficient at ignoring irrelevant stimuli

        i. Learning likely to be thrown by distractors

      c. Adolescents better at dividing attention (switching between two stimuli)

B. Hearing
1. Loud music (above 75 decibels) may leave listener with hearing loss
2. Most common outcome of noise exposure involves tinnitus—ringing sounds in one or both ears
   a. As many as 85% of those attending concerts may experience tinnitus
   b. Hearing problems associated with both short-term exposure and regular exposure over time
3. Teens recognize awareness of potential hearing loss from exposure to loud sounds but do not view as a health concern for them
   a. Don't wear ear protection as it is not "cool"
   b. Those open to behavioral change more likely to use ear protection
   c. Higher socio-economic teens rate noise exposure more negatively and are more likely to use ear protection
4. Education programs
   a. Need to focus on danger of long-term exposure
   b. Need to address teens' perception that hearing not a health problem
   c. Reduce stigma of wearing ear protection
C. Another Look at the Chemical Senses
1. Taste
   a. Researchers may have found a new basic taste (in addition to sour, sweet, salty, bitter) called *umami*—Japanese word that roughly translates as "savory" or "brothy"
      i. Umami associated with amino acid glutamate found in proteins and in concentrated forms as MSG
      ii. Not tasty itself, but when combined with certain foods is said to be delicious
   b. Taste is mediated by smell and by "chemosensory irritation"—reaction of skin in nose and mouth to certain chemical compounds in food
      i. Burn of hot pepper or tingle of carbonated beverage examples of chemosensory irritation
   c. Taste influenced by cognition
      i. Taste what you expect to taste
      ii. Bright colored juices thought to taste better than pale counterparts
   d. Taste undergoes changes during adolescence
      i. Slight decline in preference for sweets and increased sensitivity to, and liking for, sour
      ii. More likely than school-age children to have an acquired taste for previously avoided or disliked food (e.g., snails)
      iii. More likely to enjoy foods with strong tastes (acquired through multiple exposures)
2. Smell
   a. Gender difference in adolescence with females more sensitive to a variety of odors
      i. Likely related to hormonal differences
      ii. Fertile women use odor as part of the criteria for selecting a desirable mate

iii. Men may also use odor as mate selection criteria

iv. Harder for males to hide their aroma from women, but woman can use perfume cover-ups to fool men

V The Adult

A. Vision

1. Sensory and Perceptual Change
   a. Usually gradual and minor, beginning in early adulthood
   b. Raised sensory thresholds—threshold for detection of stimuli (e.g., hearing a faint tone, detecting a slight odor)
   c. Declines in perceptual abilities
      i. Have more difficulty interpreting sensory information (e.g., trouble searching visual scene)
      ii. Perceptual declines vary by individual and may be compensated for

2. Basic pattern of change
   a. Most people will not lose sight with age
   b. Nine out of 10 will need corrective lenses
   c. One in four will have cataracts—clouding of lens

3. Process of vision
   a. Light enters through cornea and passes through the pupil and lens before being projected upside down on the retina
   b. Image is relayed via the optic nerve to the brain for processing
   c. Pupil of eye automatically adjusts to lighting conditions
   d. Lens automatically changes shape to keep image in focus
   e. Visual system normally at peak performance in adolescence and young adulthood

4. Changes in the pupil
   a. Pupil becomes smaller
      i. Transitions from dark to light tough
      ii. Reading low-contrast word in dim lighting is tough
      iii. Difficult to read menu in dimly-lit restaurant
      iv. Tougher to recover from glare (e.g., coming out of dark theater into bright sunlight)
   b. Slower to react, resulting in poor dark adaptation—process of eyes adapting to darkness

5. Changes in the lens
   a. Lens denser, less flexible, and yellows
   b. Thickening lens leads to presbyopia—difficulty seeing close objects clearly
      i. May compensate by moving newspaper further from eye
      ii. Middle-aged cope by getting reading glasses
   c. Distance vision fairly stable in adulthood
   d. Older females show greater visual decline than males
      i. More susceptible to falling
      ii. Loss may mean serious threat to independence
      iii. Uncorrected vision can lead to serious decrease in quality of life in old age

Chapter 6

e. Cataracts—clouding of the lens
   i. Leading cause of visual impairment in old age
   ii. Life-long heavy exposure to sunlight a risk
   iii. Can be removed surgically, improving vision and preventing blindness

6. Retinal changes
  a. Age-related macular degeneration—damage to cells responsible for central vision
    i. Vision blurry and fades from central of field of vision
    ii. Now leading cause of blindness in adulthood
    iii. No effective treatments
  b. Decrease in field of vision (loss of peripheral vision)
  c. Negative impact on tasks like driving (Exploration Box on aging drivers)
  d. Retinitis pigmentosa—loss of light-sensitive cells and peripheral vision
    i. Group of hereditary disorders
    ii. Can appear in childhood
    iii. Cannot be cured, but some promising new research indicating that vitamin A treatment might slow progress of the disease
  e. Glaucoma—increased fluid in eye damages optic nerve and peripheral vision
    i. More common after age 50
    ii. Key is to prevent before it occurs using eyedrops or surgery

7. Attention and visual search
  a. Adults are better able to control their attention (e.g., attend to angry face if told a threat may be present)
  b. Divided and selective attention tasks harder for older adults
  c. On visual search task, the more distractors, the harder the task
  d. More difficulty in inhibiting responses to irrelevant information
  e. Reduction in efficiency of visual search skills but can be improved with practice
  f. Greatest difficulty on novel and complex tasks
  g. Fewer problems when given clear explanations

B. Hearing
1. Hearing impairment and old age
  a. Hearing impairments three times as prevalent as visual impairments in older adults
  b. 90% of those over age 65 have at least mild hearing loss (which will become progressively worse)

2. Basic capacities
  a. Most age-related problems occur in inner ear
    i. Some degeneration of cochlear cells and neurons leading to the brain with age
  b. Prebycusis—noticeable loss of sensitivity to high-frequency sounds
    i. Trouble hearing child's high voice, flutes in an orchestra, and some high-frequency consonants
    ii. High-frequency sounds need to be louder to be heard
  c. Loss both age-related, due to experience (e.g., loud noise), and related to one's sex (males seem to show more detectable loss at earlier ages)

3. Speech perception
   a. Older adults have more difficulty understanding conversations
   b. Problems worse under poor listening conditions (e.g., loud background noise)
   c. Age-related declines in auditory sensitivity play a role, but so do cognitive declines (e.g., attention skills)
   d. Auditory perception more difficult if tasks are novel and complex

C. Aging of the Chemical Senses
   1. Taste
      a. General decline in taste sensitivity
         i. Some older adults report that food tastes bland
         ii. Ability to identify food by taste declines with old age
         iii. Some loss of taste may be side effect of taking medications
         iv. Less production of saliva also negatively impacts ability to taste
         v. "Sweet tooth" does not decline with age
   2. Smell
      a. Ability to detect odors declines in old age
      b. Difference between age groups small
      c. Greater decline in ability to detect pleasant vs. unpleasant odors
      d. Healthy adults maintain sense of smell better
   3. Taste loss related to loss of sense of smell and cognitive factors (e.g., ability to remember and name what was tasted)
   4. Use of flavor enhancers and related increase in food consumption may be a way to improve health in elderly

D. Touch, Temperature, and Pain
   1. Detection thresholds for touch increases and sensitivity is gradually lost from middle childhood
   2. Older people less sensitive to temperature change
   3. Older people less likely to report weak levels of stimulation as painful, yet are not more sensitive to stronger pain

E. The Adult in Perspective
   1. Declines in vision and hearing most important and nearly universal
   2. Some ability to compensate for loss, but loss cannot be eliminated
   3. Sensory impairments may impact basic tasks of living (e.g., walking)
   4. Most older adults with sensory impairments are living full quality lives

SUGGESTIONS FOR CLASS DISCUSSIONS OR PROJECTS

1. There are literally thousands of toys that claim to provide infants with stimulation and enjoyment. Many of these toys are marketed as being of educational value to developing children. Using the knowledge they have acquired concerning the sensory and perceptual capabilities of young children, have students go to any toy store and identify their top and bottom choices of infant-oriented toys. They could then share/defend their picks with the rest of the class. You could also have the class pick their top toy of the year!

2. Some people think older adults should not drive because of changes in perceptual abilities and reaction time. As a group, they are cited more than younger drivers for "failure to obey signs and signals," "failure to yield right of way," and "inattention." At the same time, 15- to 24-year-olds are more likely to die in a motor vehicle accident than 40- to 69-year-olds and 80+-year-olds. Discuss the implications of changes in sensory and perceptual abilities across the lifespan for road safety. Ask students how they might revise driving tests based on evidence presented in the chapter. Ideally, the discussion will end on a note of appreciation for older drivers who compensate for declines in visual perception and reaction time by driving slowly and cautiously.

3. Sensory changes across the lifespan often contribute to behavioral changes. Decreases in sensitivity to taste and smell may change cooking and eating habits. Decreases in hearing may lead to a reduction in the desire to attend movies or the theater. Have students write a paper describing 1) the most common age-related changes to the basic senses, 2) how these changes could negatively impact their quality of life in older age, and 3) ways in which they may be able to compensate to reduce the negative effect of the sensory loss.

4. Given the current fascination with music among teenagers, new technologies to deliver the music (e.g., iPods), and the propensity for students to play music at potentially dangerous levels, one interesting in-class activity would be to ask students about ways that they believe the message concerning potential hearing loss could best be delivered. Would advertisements on popular music programs or programs aimed at work? Would messages from rock stars be more effective? What type of message would be most effective? What type of message would be least effective?

5. In the past, old age meant significant loss of vision. As the result of modern medicine, many age-related vision problems are now easily treated. To increase students' knowledge concerning cutting-edge treatments for visual disorders, have then search the Web for articles using the search terms "cataract surgery," "lasik," "eye surgery," "presbyopia and treatment," and/or "glaucoma and treatment." Then, based on these readings, have students write a two- to three-page paper in which they describe the pros and cons of a two or more treatments for visual disorders.

SUGGESTED FILMS AND VIDEOS

Interpretations: Perception (2006, Insight Media, DVD, 30 minutes): Nice presentation on how the brain interprets sensations to form perceptions.

The Knowing Nose: Exploring the Science of Scent (Filmmakers Library, VHS, 46 minutes): This video traces the changes in sense of smell from infancy to older adulthood.

New Optics: Bringing the World into Focus (2004, Insight Media, DVD, 13 minutes): Short DVD investigating various perceptual issues including the interpretation of colors and shapes.

Sensation, Perception, and the Aging Process (2006, Insight Media, DVD, 24-segments: 30 minutes each): Great series of lectures on sensation and perception development.

<u>Sense of Hearing: Cochlear Implants</u> (2002, Insight Media, VHS, 60 minutes): Video identifies new developments in cochlear implant technology.

SUGGESTED WEBSITES

Attention Deficit Hyperactivity Disorder
http://www.nimh.nih.gov/health/publications/attention-deficit-hyperactivity-disorder/complete-index.shtml

Human Anatomy Online: The Ear
http://www.innerbody.com/anim/ear.html

Parent Tool Kit: Attention
http://www.allkindsofminds.org/ptk/attention.aspx

Postnatal Sensory Development
http://www.hon.ch/Dossier/MotherChild/postnatal/senses_percept.html

Seeing, Hearing, and Smelling Your World
http://www.hhmi.org/senses/

SUGGESTED READINGS

Curtindale, L., Laurie-Rose, C., and Bennett-Murphy, L. (2007). Sensory modality, temperament, and the development of sustained attention: a vigilance study in children and adults. *Developmental Psychology*, 43(3), 576-589.

Gerstorf, D., Lövdén, M., and Röcke, C. (2007). Well-being affects changes in perceptual speed in advanced old age: Longitudinal evidence for a dynamic link. *Developmental Psychology*, 43(3), 705-718.

Hwang, S., Gau, S.S., Hsu, W., and Wu, Y. (2010). Deficits in interval timing measured by dual-task paradigms among children and adolescents with attention deficit/hyperactivity disorder. *The Journal of Child Psychology and Psychiatry and Allied Disciplines*, 51(3), 223-232.

Örnkloo, H., and von Hofsten, C. (2007). Fitting objects into holes: On the development of spatial cognition skills. *Developmental Psychology*, 43(2), 404-416.

Stewart, R., and Wingfield, A. (2009). Hearing loss and cognitive effort in older adult's report accuracy for verbal materials. *Journal of the American Academy of Audiology*, 20(2), 147-154.

COGNITION

LEARNING OBJECTIVES

After reading and studying the material in this chapter, you should be able to answer the following questions.

PIAGET'S CONSTRUCTIVIST APPROACH
1. How do organization, adaptation, and disequilibrium impact intelligence and guide development?

THE INFANT
2. What are the major achievements of the sensorimotor stage, and how do infants progress toward these achievements?

THE CHILD
3. What are the characteristics and limitations of preoperational thought?

4. What are the major characteristics and limitations of concrete operational thought?

THE ADOLESCENT
5. What are the main features of formal operational thought?

THE ADULT
6. What are limitations of adult cognitive performance? In what ways might adult thought be more advanced than adolescent thought? How does old age impact cognition?

PIAGET IN PERSPECTIVE
7. What are the limitations and challenges to Piaget's theory of cognitive development?

VYGOTSKY'S SOCIOCULTURAL PERSPECTIVE
8. What is the main theme of Vygotsky's theory of cognitive development? How does social interaction contribute to cognitive development according to Vygotsky's theory? In what ways are Vygotsky and Piaget similar and different in their ideas about cognition?

I   Piaget's Constructivist Approach
  A. Cognition and Piaget's Start
      1. Example of 3-year old, 9-year-old, adolescent interacting with magnet
          a. 3-year-old amused, 9-year-old trial-and-error activities, adolescent abstract understanding of magnetism
      2. Cognition—activity of knowing and processing through which knowledge is acquired and problems are solved
      3. Piaget's interest
          a. Piaget noticed similarities in errors children make
          b. Devoted his life to studying how children think, not just what they know
          c. Clinical method—flexible question-and-answer technique—used by Piaget and sometimes criticized as not standardized (i.e., all children asked the same questions)
  B. What Is Intelligence?
      1. Piaget defined intelligence as basic life function that facilitates adaptation to environment
      2. Can be seen in children's interactions with the world
          a. Watching child figure out a jack-in-the-box
          b. Newborns are active agents in knowledge, observing, investigating, and experimenting
          c. Knowledge in form of schemes—cognitive structures (organized patterns of thought or action people construct to interpret experience) created in the brain
          d. Schemas are a set of rules for cognition
              i.   Infant's grasping an example of an early behavioral schema
              ii. Second year, children develop symbolic schemes including internal mental symbols
              iii. Older children able to manipulate symbols in their head
          e. Schema become more sophisticated with development
          f. More sophisticated schema allow for better adaptation
  C. How Does Intelligence Develop?
      1. Piaget took an interactionist position on nature-nurture issue
          a. Children actively create knowledge by building schemes from experiences (nurture) and using two inborn (nature) intellectual functions called organization and adaptation
      2. Organization—systematic combining of schema into new and complex cognitive structures
          a. Cognitive structures in older children grow out of reorganization of simpler structures
      3. Adaptation—process of adjusting to the demands of the environment (using complimentary processes of assimilation and accommodation)
      4. Assimilation—interpreting new experiences using existing schema
          a. Deal with environment in own terms
          b. Squeeze world into our existing schema

5. Accommodation—modifying existing schema to fit new experience
    a. Inventing new name or revising a concept
    b. Need to accommodate to advance understanding
    c. If we only assimilated information, understanding would never advance
6. When understanding is challenged by new events and our understanding is inadequate, we are in cognitive conflict or disequilibrium
    a. Motivated to achieve equilibration—mental state of stability
7. Four distinct stages resulting from interaction of biological maturation and experience
    a. Sensorimotor stage (0-2 years)
    b. Preoperational stage (2-7 years)
    c. Concrete operations (7-11 years)
    d. Formal operations (11 and beyond)
    e. Qualitatively different ways of thinking occurring in an invariant sequence
    f. Children may advance through stages at different rates

II **The Infant**
A. Sensorimotor Stage—spanning two years of infancy; coming to know world through senses and actions
    1. Dominant cognitive structures are behavioral schemes—action patterns that evolve in which infants coordinating sensory input and motor responses
B. Substages of the Sensorimotor Stage
    1. Substage 1: reflexive activity (birth to one month) based on innate reflexes
    2. Substage 2: primary circular reactions (one to four months) repeat interesting acts centered on own body
        a. Thus named because Piaget noticed that infants repeat (circular) actions related to own bodies (primary to themselves)
            i. Son Laurent accidently gets thumb in mouth and then begins to repeat this action, which brings him pleasure
            ii. Piaget bandaged thumb to end this habit
    3. Substage 3: secondary circular reactions (four to eight months)
        a. Repeat interesting acts centered on object in the environment (e.g., sucking on a toy) from which they derive pleasure
    4. Substage 4: coordination of secondary schema (8 to 12 months); combine actions to solve simple problems (e.g., push obstacle out of the way to grasp desired object)
    5. Substage 5: tertiary circular reactions (12 to 18 months)
        a. Experiment with new ways to solve problems (curiosity)
        b. "Interest in novelty for its own sake"
        c. Repeat an action with variation
    6. Substage 6: beginning of thought (18 months to 2 years); let one object represent another (e.g., cooking pot becomes a hat)
        a. Can imitate models no longer present
C. The Development of Object Permanence
    1. Object permanence (object concept)—understanding objects exist when they leave presence is lacking in newborns

a. Very young infants rely on senses, and objects only exist when perceived or being acted upon

2. Develops gradually over sensorimotor period
   a. Roughly through ages four to eight months it's "out of sight, out of mind"
   b. By Substage 4, they master basic understanding of hidden (out of sight) toy
   c. Still think that their behavior determines where a hidden object will appear

3. Commit A-not-B, error—looking for object where last seen, not new place
   a. Error may be influenced by task demand and physical limitations
   b. Infants do have a conceptual problem when it comes to object location

4. In Substage 5, continue to struggle with invisible displacements (e.g., put object in hand, place hand under pillow, remove hand while leaving object behind)

5. Object performance fully developed by 18 months or so
   a. Capable of representing invisible moves
   b. Object permanence mastered from this point on

6. Piaget may have underestimated timing of acquisition of object permanence
   a. Baillargeon and colleagues found early evidence of object permanence using looking task in which toy had disappeared behind one screen and reappeared behind a second screen without appearing on open space between screens)
   b. At 2½ months, infants on tracking task do not show object permanence
   c. At three months, have acquired the skill

7. Research on children with spinal muscular atrophy (SMA) provides insight into process of object permanence
   a. Infants with SMA have normal IQ but severe muscle problems
   b. SMA children are slower to reach for objects
      i. Slower reaching allows for longer thinking, and SMA kids do better on object permanence tasks
      ii. Results indicate that task conditions like interval between seeing and searching for hidden object may impact behavior

8. Data supports some of Piaget's ideas about object permanence
   a. Important to distinguish between looking and reaching
   b. Looking and reaching skills improve between 8 and 12 months
   c. By end of sensorimotor period, master very complex hide-and-seek games

D. The Emergence of Symbols
   1. Crowing acquisition during sensorimotor stage is acquisition of symbolic capacity—ability to use images/words to represent objects and experiences
      a. Piaget discussed example of his daughter Lucienne working to get a chain out of a matchbox
      b. She used the symbol of opening and closing her mouth to "think" through the problem
   2. By end of sensorimotor stage children have become deliberate and symbolic thinkers

III The Child

A. The Preoperational Stage (Roughly Age 2 to 7)
   1. More sophisticated symbolic capacity
      a. Imaginary companions—pretend friends created by young children (normal)

   i. Imaginative uses of symbolic capacity like imaginary companions associated with advanced cognitive and social development as well as higher levels of creativity

  b. Perceptual salience—focus on the obvious features of object or situation leads to children being fooled by appearance

2. Lack of conservation

  a. a. Conservation—certain properties of object do not always vary when appearance is altered in superficial way

   i. Problems of conservation-of-liquid-quantity task—lack understanding that volume of liquid is conserved despite changes in shape

   ii. (Exploration Box on can there be a real Santa Claus?)

  b. Decentration—ability to focus on two or more dimensions simultaneously (e.g., height and width of glass on conservation of liquid task)

  c. Centration—tendency to focus on single aspect of problem (e.g., either the height or width of the glasses on conservation of liquid task)

   i. Leads preoperational child to fail conservation of liquid task

  d. Reversibility—process of mental undoing or reversing an action

   i. Lack of reversibility leads to difficulty on conservation task

   ii. Irreversibility—cannot engage in reversibility

  e. Transformation thought—ability to conceptualize transformation (process of change from one state to another)

  f. Preoperational thinker engages in static thought—fixated on end state not transformation into another state

3. Egocentrism—tendency to view world solely from one's own perspective and difficulty recognizing the point of view of others

  a. When shown display of three mountains, children will assume that everyone sees the mountains from a vantage point similar to their own

  b. Often assume that if they know something, other people do too

  c. Assume others desire what they desire

4. Difficulty with classification

  a. Older preoperational children can group objects by color, shape, function

  b. Have trouble thinking about relationship between classes (e.g., pets) and subclasses (e.g., dogs, cats)

  c. Lack class inclusion—logical understanding that parts are included in the whole

5. Did Piaget underestimate the preschool child?

  a. Gelman (1972) used simplified conservation-of-number task with beads

   i. Reduced tasks to bare essentials, demonstrated that preschoolers not as egocentric as Piaget thought

   ii. Evidence that children can perform earlier than Piaget believed

  b. Classification skills are found in children younger than Piaget believed

   i. Three- and four-year-olds have a more advanced grasp of classification hierarchies than Piaget thought (e.g., dandelion is a flower)

  c. Simplified tasks allow children to focus attention on relevant aspects of a task and have shown that they have understanding of aspects of the physical world at a younger age than Piaget proposed

B. The Concrete Operations Stage
  1. Concrete operations stage—mastering many logical operations lacking in preoperational thinkers (roughly ages 7-11)
     a. Can perform mental actions on objects (e.g., adding and subtracting birthday candles, arranging objects from smallest to largest)
  2. Conservation
     a. Ability to solve conservation tasks improves
        i. Can decenter—mentally juggle two dimensions at once
        ii. Acquire reversibility of thought
        iii. Can engage in transformational thought (allowing a better understanding of the change involved in pouring the water on the conservation of liquid task)
     b. Some forms of conservation solved in earlier years than others (e.g., conservation of mass and number earlier; conservation of area or volume later)
        i. Piaget used concept of horizontal décalage—different skills within stage occur at different times—to explain this difference
  3. Seriation and transitivity
     a. Seriation—mentally order objects along quantifiable dimension
        i. Set of sticks arranged from biggest to smallest
     b. Transitivity—understand logical relationship of objects in a series
        i. Which of three children are taller than each other
        ii. Preoperational children need to have individuals stand next to each other in order to solve this problem
  4. Other advances
     a. Class inclusion—understand that two subclasses can be in a whole (e.g., brown and white beads are a subclass of the whole class of wooden beads)
     b. Can engage in mathematical operations in their head (e.g., keeping score of a game)
     c. Biggest limitations of concrete thinking is that it is applied only to objects, situations, or events that are real or readily imaginable (i.e., concrete) and not to hypothetical or abstract ideas

IV The Adolescent
  A. The Formal Operations Stage
     1. Formal operations—can perform mental actions on objects and ideas (age 11 or older)
     2. Hypothetical and abstract thinking
        a. Can invent ideas that are contrary to fact (e.g., the idea of having an eye in your palm) and can think logically about implications of such ideas
        b. More abstract thought
           i. School-age children define justice in terms of police and judges while adolescents think about abstract issues like balancing rights of different interests in a society
     3. Scientific reasoning
        a. Systematic and scientific (less trial-and-error) thinking

b. Concrete operational children will jump right into a problem, while formal operational thinkers will sit and think and plan a strategy for solving a problem

c. Good at drawing conclusions from observations

d. General problem-solving strategy is to generate and test all possible hypotheses

e. Hypothetical-deductive reasoning from general ideas to specific implications

   i.   If-then thinking

   ii. On string task, vary factors (e.g., length of string) while holding other constant (e.g., weight)

4. Progress toward mastery

a. Martorano (1977) study of girls on battery of Piagetian tasks found gradual transition into formal operations

b. Findings from Munich Longitudinal Study on Ontogenesis of Individual Competencies

   i.   10-year-olds showed an understanding of basic principles of scientific thinking

   ii. 12-year-olds could recognize good and bad experiments

   iii. Adolescents show an awareness of scientific reasoning, but may not be able to produce logical scientific reasoning until they are older

c. Piaget's claim that intuitive reasoning is replaced by scientific reasoning not supported

   i.   Two forms of reasoning—intuitive and scientific—coexist in older thinkers

   ii. Flexibility in problem-solving effective as long as appropriate strategy is selected

d. Ability to decontextualize—separate prior knowledge from task at hand

   i.   Can begin to separate personal beliefs (e.g., males are better at math) from demands of task at hand (e.g., reviewing a study in which females performed better than males)

   ii. Increases likelihood of using reasoning vs. intuition when analyzing a problem

e. Recent cohorts of teens show ability to solve formal-operations tasks at younger ages than in past generations

   i.   May be result of increasing incorporation of hands-on discovery learning in school curricula

f. Age and level of education influence performance on formal-operations tasks

g. Progress slow toward formal thinking; can be challenging to secondary-school teachers trying to teach abstract concepts

B. Implications of Formal Thought

1. Good news—formal thought may prepare person to gain greater sense of identity, to think in more complex ways about moral issues, and to understand others better

2. Bad news—while younger children tend to heed words of authority figures, formal thinkers tend to question authority and to raise questions about parents' decisions and the world in which they live

a. Can lead to confusion and sometimes rebellion

Chapter 7

b. Some teens may become idealists (inventing perfect worlds)
c. May flaunt their new-found schemes and irritate parents

3. Adolescent egocentrism (Elkind's proposal)—ignorance of perspective of others
   a. Imaginary audience—hypothesized audience (self-consciousness)
      i. Everyone is thinking about, or looking at, me
   b. Personal fable—tendency to think in terms of absolute uniqueness (no one understands me)
      i. If in love, may see themselves as first to be in such a state
      ii. No one can understand what they are going through or feeling
      iii. May feel that rules do not apply to them
      iv. High scores on measures of adolescent egocentrism associated with risky behavior
      v. Self-consciousness associated with imaginary audience most evident in early adolescence and declines by late high school
      vi. Adolescent egocentrism may persist when adolescents have insecure relationships with parents
      vii. (Exploration Box on humor and cognitive development)

2. Contrary to Piaget and Elkind, research unable to link onset of formal thought and adolescent egocentrism
   a. Imaginary audience fear may be due to real audience and consequences
   b. Adults also aware that actions and appearance judged by others

V The Adult
A. Limitations in Adult Cognitive Performance
   1. Half of college students and adults lack mastery of formal operations
   2. Many American adults do not solve scientific problems at the formal level
   3. Many reasons why more adults do not do well on Piagetian tasks
      a. Formal thought appears to require advanced schooling, which is lacking in many cultures and among many individuals
      b. Lack of expertise in a domain of knowledge hurts adult response
         i. Strongest performance in area of own expertise
         ii. Performance inconsistent across content areas
      c. Taking a contextual approach on cognitive development can lead to appreciation of role of individual experience and nature of task

B. Growth beyond Formal Operations?
   1. Piaget's own writing indicate that his thinking shifted from largely formal to something beyond formal operations
   2. Some argue that formal operations involve applying logic to a closed set of ideas and not an open set of ideas that characterize most adult issues
   3. Postformal thought—term for logic beyond formal thinking
   4. Relativistic thinking—realizing understanding in context and subjective to knower
      i. Absolutist thinkers assume truth lies in nature and there is only one truth
      ii. Relativist thinkers start with assumption that one's starting assumptions influence the "truth" and a problem can be viewed in multiple ways
      a. On real-life problems (e.g., John and wife Mary), adolescents tend not to realize that different assumptions may be in play

    i. Assumptions influence the "truth"
  b. Perry found changes in college students
    i. Students originally look for <u>the</u> answer to a question
    ii. Take position that any position is as good as another
    iii. Able to make commitments to positions
  c. Between adolescence and adulthood, many start as absolutists, become relativists (think unconventionally or "outside the box"), and then make commitments with more sophisticated awareness of nature
 5. Dialective thinking—detecting paradoxes and inconstancies among ideas and trying to reconcile them
  a. Mentally "wrestling" with multifaceted and difficult solution
  b. Repeatedly challenge and change their understanding of what constitutes the "truth"
  c. Common features of postformal ideas (proposed by Marchand)
    i. Understanding that knowledge is relative and not absolute (more shades of grey than clear dichotomies)
    ii. Accepting that world is filled with inconsistencies
    iii. Attempting to integrate contradictions into some larger understanding
 6. College students with greater diversity among their friendships exhibit more postformal characteristics
  a. Some suggests that there is no need for a fifth stage beyond formal thought as the evidence does not reflect a qualitatively different change in thinking that is universal and irreversible (that would be required for a fifth Piagetian stage)
C. Aging and Cognitive Skills
 1. Poorer performance on Piagetian tasks of older cohorts does not mean that there is a regression of cognitive abilities
  a. Brief training can improve performance (skills are not gone, just need to be reactivated)
  b. Piagetian tasks not relevant to everyday adult events—adults may lack motivation to solve the tasks
  c. Pearce and Denney (1984) research indicates that differences in elderly performance may reflect differences in problem-solving style
  d. Older adults do not perform concrete and formal-operational tasks as well as younger contemporaries
    i. Planner of adult education many need to bear this in mind
    ii. Differences between old and younger adults may be the result of education or motivation difference
    iii. Elderly who perform poorly on laboratory and unfamiliar tasks often are far more capable on everyday problems

VI Piaget in Perspective
 A. Piaget's Contributions
  1. Giant in the field of human development
  2. Stimulated research on cognitive development
  3. Showed infants active in own development using processes of assimilation and accommodation

4. Some logical processes of preschoolers explained
5. Accurate basic description of cognitive-developmental sequences
B. Challenges to Piaget
1. Some criticism mild while others very severe, suggesting that Piaget is fundamentally flawed and should be thrown out (i.e., Broughton)
2. Five common criticisms
   a. Underestimated young minds
      i. With more familiar problems, the hidden capacities of children, adolescents, and adults are sometimes revealed
   b. Failed to distinguish between competence and performance
      i. Failure does not necessarily mean lack of competence, could be result of lack of motivation, limited memory capacity, or familiarity with task
      ii. Overemphasized the idea that knowledge is all or nothing
   c. Wrongly claimed that broad stages of development exist
      i. Emphasized consistency of thinking within a stage and differences between stages
      ii. Ignored idea of domain-specific knowledge
      iii. Transition between stages not as swift as he proposed
   d. Failed to adequately explain development
      i. Vague description of how development comes about
      ii. Researchers need to know more about impact of specific maturational changes in brain and specific kinds of experience
   e. Gave limited attention to social influences on cognitive development
      i. Child often viewed as isolated scientist exploring the world alone
      ii. Parents, teachers, peers, siblings and others likely impact development, but Piaget's model saw little cognitive growth from interaction with adults

VII Vygotsky's Sociocultural Perspective
A. Brief Biography of Vygotsky
1. Russian psychologist Lev Vygotsky was born in 1896, same year as Piaget
2. Active scholar during 1920s and 30s, when Piaget formulating his theory
3. Work banned by for political reasons by both the former Soviet Union
   a. North American scholars did not have access to English translations of his work
   b. Limited consideration of Vygotsky's work until recent decades
   c. Died at age 38
4. Basic argument—cognitive growth occurs in a sociocultural context and evolves out of the child's social interactions
B. Culture and Thought
1. Intelligence is held by group, not individual
   a. Vygotsky's colleague Alexander Luria found environment provides conditions that allow for the emergence of thinking and differed between rural children and those raised in large cities
   b. Knowledge depends on social experience
2. Vygotsky would not be surprise that formal-operational thought is rarely used in some countries as he expected cognitive development to vary by culture,

© 2012 Cengage Learning. All Rights Reserved. May not be copied, scanned, or duplicated, in whole or in part, except for use as permitted in a license distributed with a certain product or service or otherwise on a password-protected website for classroom use.

depending on the mental tools (like language and cultural values) that are available

 C. Social Interaction and Thought
  1. Example of four-year-old receiving a jigsaw puzzle and receiving assistance from her father (e.g., suggestions to put the corner pieces together first) exemplifies the type of social interactions that Vygotsky believed fostered cognitive growth
  2. Zone of proximal development—gap between what one can accomplish alone vs. with assistance of more skilled partner
   a. Knowledge not fixed (cannot be tested by single test)
   b. Upper limit of knowledge moves in response to cultural change
   c. Children's performance on assisted learning tasks is a good predictor of their future achievement
  3. Guided participation—learning by actively participating in culturally relevant events with aid and support of parents and knowledgeable guides
  4. Scaffolding—structuring learning situation so learning is easier
  5. Vygotsky rejected Piaget's view of children as independent explorers

 D. The Tools of Thought
  1. Mental activity is mediated by "tools"
   a. Key to learning is to equip with tools
   b. If child practices and masters tools, then child will adopt tools as his or her own
  2. Language (spoken and written) is an important tool
   a. Faulkner and colleagues (2000)—children with computer as tool think and act different than those with physical materials alone
   b. Vygotsky—language shapes thought, and thought fundamentally changes once we begin to use words
   c. Disagreed with Piaget's emphasis on nature of egocentric speech
    i. Piaget saw this speech as evidence that preoperational thinkers cannot take the perspective of others
   d. Vygotsky called children's recitations "private speech"—guides own thought and behavior
    i. Not sign of cognitive immaturity, but cognitive maturity
    ii. Forerunner of silent thinking-in-words engaged in by adults
    iii. This regulatory speech gradually becomes internalized
    iv. Private speech more common when children are struggling to solve a difficult problem
    v. Incidence of private speech varies with age (four-year-olds more than three-year-olds) and task demands (more on unfamiliar and open-ended activities)
    vi. Intellectually capable children more likely to engage in private speech
    vii. Private speech contributes to effective problem-solving (allows one to think through problems and to incorporate own thinking with problem-solving strategies learned during collaborations with adults)
   e. Social speech (conversation) gives rise to private speech

E. Evaluation of Vygotsky
   1. Placed needed emphasis on role of social environment in cognitive development
   2. Too much emphasis on social interactions at expense of individually constructed knowledge

SUGGESTIONS FOR CLASS DISCUSSIONS OR PROJECTS

1. Have students work in pairs or small groups on Piagetian tasks. Holbrook (1992) describes a demonstration of a standard conservation of liquid task, as well as a "conservation-like" problem for adults. Student responses on this task are analyzed using Piagetian concepts of centration, irreversibility, and perceptual dominance. Students might also work on the pendulum problem (described in the text). Within each pair or group of students, one or two might try working on the problem while another student keeps track of the problem-solving approach (this is easiest if those working on the problem verbally describe what they are thinking as they work through the problem).

Holbrook, J.E. (1992). Bringing Piaget's preoperational thought to the minds of adults: A classroom demonstration. *Teaching of Psychology,* 19, 169-170.

2. An alternative or add-on to suggestion 1 is to provide an opportunity to observe children of various ages working on Piagetian tasks, such as conservation or object permanence. Depending on access, students may be able to actually test some infants or children on Piagetian tasks and report on their findings. This is an excellent option if you assign an observational or interviewing project in the course. If young children are not readily accessible to a large number of students, it may be possible to videotape children of friends or children at a local preschool (or bring the children into the classroom).

If videotaping, be sure to get permission to show the tape to the class. You also should contact your school's Institutional Review Board or Human Subjects committee for rules on using tapes of underage students. To avoid IRB issues, you might just have students view a few examples of Piagetian tasks available on YouTube that can be found by searching with "Piaget and conservation." A few examples are listed below. You will notice that some children appear to be able to solve the tasks at younger ages than Piaget predicted. These findings support one of the criticisms of Piaget's theory.

http://www.youtube.com/watch?v=zd3mh7mT9xs
http://www.youtube.com/watch?v=Te5qpRyVxpE

3. Students may find traditional formal operational tasks such as the pendulum problem difficult. Kuhn and Brannock (1977) used a formal operational task that had more familiarity, or external validity, for adolescents than traditional Piagetian tasks. In this task, participants are given a description of four plants that are treated differently and have different outcomes. Based on this, participants are asked what to do with a fifth plant (see questions below for task description). The problem is constructed so that one variable (plant food) influences plant outcome and the other variables are irrelevant to plant outcome. The Kuhn and Brannock article provides sample answers for four different levels of performance on this task.

Plant Problem

Imagine you have five plants, all of the same type.

Plant A gets a large glass of water each week and a light-colored plant food. It is doing well.

Plant B gets a large glass of water, dark-colored plant food, and leaf lotion. It appears to be dying.

Plant C gets a small glass of water, light-colored plant food, and leaf lotion. It is doing well.

Plant D gets a small glass of water and dark plant food. It seems to be dying.

Plant E is new. How should you treat it?

On what basis do you draw your conclusions?

Kuhn, D., & Brannock, J. (1977). Development of the isolation of variables scheme in experimental and "natural experimental" contexts. *Developmental Psychology, 13*, 9-14.

4. At a time in history when the theory of evolution is under attack and the distinction between humans and other animals is a hot topic of conversation, an interesting class discussion could focus on differences and similarities in problem-solving strategies (specifically, the ability to solve Piagetian tasks) between species. The Suda and Call (2004) study of conservation of liquid skills in apes, and the Watson, Gergely, and Csanyi (2001) study of invisible displacement comparing dogs and children, provide a starting point for such a discussion.

Suda, C., and Call, J. (2004). Piagetian liquid conservation in the Great Apes (*Pan paniscus, Pan troglodytes*, and *Pongo pygmaeus*). *Journal of Comparative Psychology, 118*(3), 265-279.

Watson, J.S., Gergely, G., and Csanyi, V. (2001). Distinguishing logic from association in the solution of an invisible displacement task by children (Homo sapiens) and dogs (*Canis familiaris*): Using negation of disjunction. *Journal of Comparative Psychology, 115*(3), 219-226.

5. One method of enhancing students' understanding of postformal thinking is by providing them with "hands-on" experience with solving logical problems (like those found in section 7.5) that demand relativistic thinking. For examples of the types of items that can be used to enhance such thought, you may wish to check out Sinnott (1998).

Sinnott, J.D. (1998). *The Development of Logic in Adulthood.* NY: Springer Publications.

6. Vygotsky suggested that culture plays a major role in cognitive development. Have students identify 5-10 characteristics that they believe are highly impacted by culture and 5-10 characteristics that they believe are not influenced by culture. These lists will give students some insight into their own beliefs concerning the nature-nurture issue.

This project can also be linked to Piaget's formal stage of thinking by having students respond to the following hypothetical situation. How would you change if, as of tomorrow, you lived in a country with 1) no computer technology, 2) a belief that females were superior to males, 3) a hatred for the wealthy and educated, and 4) no organized religions?

SUGGESTED FILMS AND VIDEOS

The Age of Reason: Cognitive Development during The School Years (2003, Insight Media, VHS, 30 minutes): Covers characteristics of Piaget's concrete operational stage of development along with Kohlberg's moral reasoning theory.

The Little Scientists: The First Two Years of Cognitive Development (2003, Insight Media, VHS, 30 minutes): This video focuses on development during the sensorimotor stage.

Piaget's Developmental Theory: An Overview (1989, Insight Media, DVD, 25 minutes): This DVD offers an excellent overview of the works of Piaget and Elkind.

What If? Cognitive Development in Adolescence (2003, Insight Media, VHS, 30 minutes): Video highlights cognitive development in the teen years, including the transition from concrete to formal operational thought.

Vygotsky's Developmental Theory: An Introduction (1994, Insight Media, DVD 28 minutes): Nice review of the basic concepts of Vygotsky's theory of cognitive development.

SUGGESTED WEBSITES

Jean Piaget's Genetic Epistemology: Appreciation and Critique
http://hubcap.clemson.edu/%7Ecampber/piaget.html

Jean Piaget
http://www.indiana.edu/~intell/piaget.shtml

Piaget's Theory of Cognitive Development
http://www.edpsycinteractive.org/topics/cogsys/piaget.html

Vygotsky Archives
http://www.marxists.org/archive/vygotsky/

Vygotsky Resources
http://www.kolar.org/vygotsky/

SUGGESTED READINGS

Brunstein, A. (2008). Egotistical you. *New Scientist*, 197(2648), 32-35.

Daniels, H., Cole, M., and Wertsch, J.V. (Eds). (2007). *The Cambridge Companion to Vygotsky*. New York, NY: Cambridge University Press.

Kagan, J. (2008). In defense of qualitative changes in development. *Child Development*, 79(6), 1606-1624.

Kuhn, D. (2008). Formal operations from a twenty-first century perspective. *Human Development*, 51(1), 48-55.

Pass, S. (2007). When constructivists Jean Piaget and Lev Vygotsky were pedagogical collaborators; a viewpoint from a study of their communications. *Journal of Constructivist Psychology*, 20(3), 277-282.

MEMORY AND INFORMATION PROCESSING

LEARNING OBJECTIVES

After reading and studying the material in this chapter, you should be able to answer the following questions.

THE INFORMATION-PROCESSING APPROACH

1. What is the general orientation of the information-processing model to cognition? What are the specific components of the model, and how does information "flow" through the system?

2. What are the different forms or types of memory?

3. What are the basic information processing elements of problem-solving?

THE INFANT

4. How do researchers assess infant memory? What information can infants typically remember? What are the limitations of infants' memory?

THE CHILD

5. What are four major hypotheses about why memory improves with age? Is there evidence to support each hypothesis?

6. When do autobiographical memories begin, and what possible explanations can account for childhood amnesia?

7. How do scripts influence memory?

8. How do problem-solving capacities change during childhood? What explanation does Siegler propose for changes in problem-solving?

THE ADOLESCENT

9. What developments occur in the information-processing abilities of adolescents?

THE ADULT

10. How is expertise developed in adulthood?

11. In what ways do memory and cognition change during adulthood? What are the strengths and weaknesses of older adults' abilities?

12. What factors help explain the declines in abilities during older adulthood? And what can be done to minimize losses with age?

13. How are problem solving-skills affected by aging?

I The Information-Processing Approach
  A. Memory From an Information-Processing Approach
    1. Memory—our ability to store and later retrieve information about past events
    2. Cognitive psychologists were influenced by rise of computer technology and began to think of brain as a computer that processes input and converts it to output
    3. Based on inadequacies of behaviorist approach and emerging computer technology
    4. Information-processing approach to human cognition—emphasis on basic mental processes involved in attention, perception, memory, and decision-making
    5. More highly developed computers have greater capacity and do more highly developed humans (i.e., adults better memory abilities than children)
  B. Memory Systems
    1. Computer analogy includes hardware (brain and nervous system) and software (rules and strategies)
    2. Atkinson and Shiffrin (1968) model of memory
      a. Sensory register—holds incoming information for fraction of second
      b. Short-term memory—holds about seven items for several seconds
      c. Working memory—active form of short-term memory "mental scratch pad"
      d. Long-term memory—relatively permanent store of information
    3. Four steps to learning and memory
      a. Encoding—getting information into system
      b. Consolidation—information organized into a form suitable for long-term storage
        i. Event becomes long-lasting memory trace
        ii. Process facilitated by sleep
      c. Storage—holding information (in long-term)
        i. Memories fade if not appropriately stored
        ii. Constructive (not static) process
      d. Retrieval—getting information out of long-term memory
    4. Types of retrieval
      a. Recognition memory—recognize among options (multiple choice test)
      b. Recall memory—active retrieval without cue (essay question)
      c. Cued-recall—active retrieval with cue (hint)
  C. Implicit and Explicit Memory
    1. Implicit (nondeclarative) memory—unintentional, automatic
    2. Explicit (declarative) memory—deliberate, effortful
      a. Two types of explicit memories: semantic (general facts; knowing that Twin Towers collapsed on 9-11-2001) and episodic (specific experiences; remembering where you were when the Twin Towers collapsed)
    3. Implicit memory
      a. Often tested without learner knowing
      b. Amnesia more likely to impact explicit memory
      c. Implicit may develop earlier

        d. Two types of memory involve different parts of the brain
            i. Procedural memory (type of implicit) mediated by the striatum
            ii. Explicit largely localized in medial temporal lobe, area crucial in
                consolidating information into memory trace for long-term store
            iii. Damage to hippocampus area of medial temporal lobe leads to
                impairments in creating new episodic memories
            iv. Storage and retrieval tied to original cortex area that first registered the
                memory
        e. Two types of memory may follow different developmental paths
            i. Implicit develops earlier in infancy than explicit
            ii. Explicit capacity increases from infancy to adulthood then declines
            iii. Implicit memory capacity does not change much across the lifespan
    D. Problem-Solving
        1. Problem-solving—using information-processing system to arrive at decision
        2. Executive control processes—part of system that plans and monitors activity
            a. Executive processes include selection, organization, manipulation, and
                interpretation of information
        3. Humans are parallel processors—can carry out several mental activities at
            same time
        4. Information-processing theorists appreciate that different processing
            approaches are used in different domains of knowledge
        5. Information-processing approach focuses on how problem-solving is done
        6. Many processes improve between infancy and adulthood, then show some
            decline

II **The Infant**
    A. Memory
        1. Assessment of infant memory—often with imitation, habituation, or operant
            conditioning techniques
        2. Imitation—measure memory by having infant repeat activity it has seen
            a. Infants imitate tongue thrust
                i. Some argued that this was a reflex action and not imitation, but has
                    been replicated consistently
            b. Deferred imitation—ability to imitate a novel act after a delay
                i. Appears at six months of age
                ii. May be a form of explicit memory
        3. Habituation—learn not to respond to a repeatedly presented stimulus (get
            bored, ignore dripping faucet)
            a. Measure of recognition memory that newborns are capable of performing
            b. As they age, infants need less "study time" to retain information (leading to
                longer retention times)
        4. Operant conditioning
            a. Rovee-Collier and colleagues demonstrated recall memory in infants
                i. Shown mobile
                ii. Ribbon tied to infant's leg; when leg kicks, mobile moves
                iii. Ribbon removed
                iv. Days later infant kicks at site of mobile

Chapter 8

        v. Three-month-olds recall for one week, six-month-olds remember for two weeks, 18-month-olds remember for three months
    b. Memory strongest when cued (cue dependent); by 15 months, cues can be verbal
        i. Infants shown mobile two to four weeks after original experience kicked up a storm
    c. Memory appears cue-dependent and context-specific (i.e., have difficult recalling when cues are insufficient or too different)
  5. Recall—"pure recall" involves retrieval without cue
    a. Six-month-old infants can imitate novel behavior
    b. Thirteen-month-olds recall sequence of events for as long as three months
    c. Two-year-olds use words to reconstruct earlier events
B. Problem-Solving
  1. By nine months, infants can solve the problem of reaching an object that is out of reach
  2. Older infants increasingly pay attention to cues provided by adults and let adults know they need assistance by doing things like pointing or reaching

III The Child

A. Explaining Memory Development
  1. Four major hypotheses
    a. Changes in basic capacities
        i. More memory space
        ii. Increasing speed of processing
    b. Changes in memory strategies; increasing use of effective encoding and retrieval strategies
    c. Increased knowledge about memory
        i. Know how long to study (i.e., which tasks take longer)
        ii. Better at selection of strategies
    d. Increased knowledge about world
        i. Expertise leads to improvements in memory
        ii. Familiar material easier to recall
  2. Do basic capacities change?
    a. Little change in long-term memory capacity
    b. Sensory memory in place very early so sensory register itself an unlikely source of developmental variation
    c. Basic features of working memory in place by age four
    d. Significant improvements in short-term memory capacity during childhood
    e. Speed of processing increases
    f. Piagetian "centration" may be due to working memory limitations
    g. Short-term memory increases may be domain-specific
        i. The more you know about a subject, the faster you can process information related to the subject
    h. Improvement due to biological maturation of brain (frontal lobes) and experience

3. Do memory strategies change?
    a. Children as young as two can deliberately remember things
        i. Young children more likely to use memory aids
        ii. Are not effective at switch strategies
        iii. Make preservation errors—continue same unsuccessful strategy (e.g., if previously found favorite toy under sofa will search there the next time the item is lost)
    b. Rehearsal—repeating items in memory, dramatic increase between ages five and seven
    c. Organization—memory strategy that involves classifying items into meaningful categories (e.g., animals) emerges as effective tools around age nine
        i. Chunking—organizational strategy in which a long number is broken into manageable subunits (e.g., 6065551843 = 606-555-1843; telephone sequence)
        ii. Organization mastered later in childhood than rehearsal
    d. Elaboration—actively creating meaning
        i. Add meaningful link between items
        ii. Helpful in learning foreign languages
    e. Four phases of memory strategy development
        i. Mediation deficiency—don't spontaneously use or benefit even when taught how to use a strategy
        ii. Production deficiency—can use strategy, but do not produce any on their own
        iii. Utilization deficiency—can spontaneously produce strategy, but do not benefit from strategy use
        iv. Finally exhibit effective strategy use in all areas
        v. Utilization deficiencies due to a number of factors like strategy is too mentally taxing, leaving no room for the use of other cognitive resources
    f. Retrieval strategies—methods of accessing long-term memory
        i. Young children tend to rely on external cues for encoding and retrieval
4. Does knowledge about memory change?
    a. Metamemory—knowledge about process of remembering
    b. Metacognition—knowledge about cognitive processes
        i. Two- to three-year-olds demonstrate some metacognitive skills and understand that in order to remember something, you have to work at it
        ii. Simpler and more familiar tasks lead to highest levels of memory in childhood
        iii. Language skills and general knowledge impact memory
5. Does knowledge of the world change?
    a. Knowledge base—what someone knows
        i. Affects learning and memory
        ii. Difference between reading about something new vs. something familiar
    b. Chi study showed knowledge of chess could impact memory for chess positions but not memory for sequence of digits
        i. Children with chess expertise form more and larger mental chunks (meaningful groups) of chess pieces, which allows them to remember

117

   ii. Expert children perform similarly to adult chess experts
  c. Memory may improve in childhood because know more about all kinds of things than younger children
  d. Expertise can improve memory for related materials, even in children with low general intellectual ability
 6. Revisiting the explanations
  a. Older children are faster information processors and can juggle more items in working memory
  b. Older children use more effective memory encoding and retrieving strategies
  c. Older children know more about how memory works (metamemory skills)
  d. Older children have larger knowledge base
  e. Most effective predictors of memory performance include basic capacities, strategies, and metamemory

B. Autobiographical Memory
 1. Autobiographical memory—episodic memories of personal events
 2. When do autobiographical memories begin?
  a. Childhood (or infantile) amnesia—most older children and adults have few autobiographical memories for events occurring during first few years of life (lower limit may be two years for adults)
   i. Limited early autobiographical memories may be due to lack of working memory space
   ii. Lack of language skills may impact autobiographical memory
   iii. Lack of sense of self in very early child might make it difficult to organize events as "things that happened to me"
   iv. Fuzzy-trace theory—store verbatim (exact word for word) and general accounts separately
   v. Verbatim memories more unstable and memory for gist better
   vi. With age, children make transition from verbatim to gist
   vii. Young children encode information, but issues like lack of sufficient working memory, language skills, sense of self, and encoding on a fuzzy trace of what really happened do not allow children the opportunity to undergo the consolidation needed to store robust memories
  b. Scripts—general event representations (GERs) or typical sequence of actions related to an event (e.g., fast-food restaurant script: wait in line, tell person at counter you want food, pay for food, carry food to table, open package, eat food, gather trash, throw trash away before leaving)
   i. Children as young as three years report general sequences vs. specific experience
   ii. Experiences lead to better (richer and more detailed) scripts
  c. Eyewitness memory
   i. Reconstructed nature of memory interferes with accuracy of eyewitness testimony—reporting of experienced events
   ii. Young children are more suggestible and influenced by information presented after the event
   iii. Young children are fairly accurate but report less information than older children

        iv. General prompts can elicit recall of more information (e.g., "tell me more about…")

        v. Specific questions elicit more information, but accuracy may slip (especially true of more directed or leading questions

        vi. Preschooler tend to be asked a larger number of directed questions and are subjected to repeated questioning (both of which increase reporting errors)

        vii. A study in which five- and six-year-old were "cross-examined" after a delay of eight months, when asked many irrelevant, leading, or ambiguous questions, "cracked" and changed responses in reaction to the questions (one in three changed all of their answers)

C. Problem-Solving
  1. Memories (especially working memories) vital to problem-solving
  2. Piagetian balance beam problem used to assess problem-solving skills
    a. Concrete thinkers focus on either amount of distance of weights from fulcrum or on the amount of weight
    b. Formal-operational thinkers focus on decreasing weight and moving it farther from fulcrum or increasing weight and moving it close to fulcrum
  3. Ziegler's rule-assessment approach—focus on what children take in and the rules they formulate on tasks like the balance beam problem
    a. Siegler's findings
      i. Young children use no rules
      ii. Four- and five-year-olds rule based on weight
      iii. By eight, also consider distance
      iv. By 12, rule dependent on both weight and distance that is successful on simple problems
      v. By 20, rule dependent on both weight and distance that is successful on complex problems
      vi. Improvements in accuracy result in increase in time needed to solve problem
    b. Most children use multiple rules or problem-solving strategies, and their use of a strategy's efficiency tends to increase over multiple task trails
  4. Overlapping waves theory—development not a series of stages but "process of variability, choice, and change"
    a. Development of problem-solving involves knowing and using a variety of strategies
    b. With experience, problem-solving strategies become more effective
    c. With age, children not only choose the most useful strategy but also become more effective at executing the strategies
  5. Piaget vs. Siegler's information-processing explanations
    a. Piaget emphasizes qualitative change, with new strategies replacing old all at once
    b. Siegler argues that strategies emerge gradually and become more effective with time, also multiple strategies available any time

IV The Adolescent

A. Strategies
1. New learning and memory strategies emerge in adolescence (e.g., elaboration)
2. Use of strategies is more deliberate, selective, and spontaneous
   a. Will deliberately organize a list of words rather than relying on a list they are given
3. Better able to push irrelevant information out of working memory so that it does not interfere with task performance

B. Basic Capacities
1. Adolescents perform any number of cognitive operations faster than children do
2. Have greater functional use of working memory (due to brain maturation)
3. Better than young on highly complex cognitive tasks that require them to use recalled information to strategically direct search behavior

C. Metamemory and Knowledge Base
1. Knowledge base continues to expand during adolescence
2. Metamemory and metacognition improve
   a. Better able to tailor strategies and to monitor strategy choice
   b. Typically choose elaboration over rote repetition when they realize former is more effective
   c. Teens typically allocate more study time to information judged to be difficult
   d. When pressed for time, devote more time to easy items
3. Extent to which metacognition is employed varies by gender and socioeconomic background
   a. Adolescent girls consider using metacognitive strategies more than adolescent boys (may explain higher school grades in girls)
   b. Students from higher SES background report using more metacognitive strategies than those from low SES backgrounds

V The Adult

A. Developing Expertise
1. Effect of knowledge base on memory and problem-solving
   a. Experts have larger, more organized knowledge base, and use information efficiently
      i. Seems to take about 10 years of training and experience to develop expertise
   b. Effects of knowledge base
      i. Experts recall information central to task
      ii. Experts recall more detail
      iii. Experts elaborately organize and complete knowledge bases to solve problems effectively
   c. Knowledge and processing is domain-specific
      i. Experts in math are good at numeric memory, but performance does not translate to other domains
      ii. Domain-specific knowledge can hinder performance if solution violates common principle

     d. Experts know more than novices, have more organized knowledge bases, and

        are better able to use this knowledge to solve problems in their areas of expertise

     e. Expertise can allow adults to compensate for losses in information-processing capacities

  B. Autobiographical Memory

    1. Bauer (2007) identified factors that influence autobiographical memories

      a. Personal significance—has little impact on ability to later recall

      b. Distinctiveness or uniqueness—the more unique, the more likely to be recalled with relevant details

      c. Affective or emotional intensity of event—events with highly positive or highly negative emotions recalled better

        i. Effect tends to dissipate with time

        ii. Emotions may activate neural components associated with enhanced encoding

      d. People tend to recall more information from their teens, 20s, and near present, and this may be due to the fact that this time is full of memorable events that are instrumental in shaping one's life, making these memories more easily accessible

  C. Memory and Aging

    1. Common trouble recalling names and items that will later be needed

    2. Become more upset at memory loss, seen as indicator of aging

    3. Areas of strength and weakness

      a. Memory pattern in adulthood

        i. Use of cross-sectional research may mean that declines could be the result of factors other than age

        ii. Declines most noticeable in older adulthood (70s)

        iii. Difficulties in memory most severe in oldest elderly people

        iv. Not all older people experience memory difficulties

        v. Not all memory tasks cause older adult difficulties

        vi. (Exploration Box on forgetting: what is normal and what is not?)

      b. Timed tasks—older slower, hurt by time limits

      c. Unfamiliar or artificial (laboratory task) content

        i. Older slower when unfamiliar tasks or meaningless (ones that cannot be tied to existing knowledge)

        ii. Artificial tasks performance poorer but likely related to meaningfulness of task

        iii. In naturalistic environments, older adults can outperform younger adults

        iv. When task is meaningful, older adults may be able to draw on greater experience and knowledge base to enhance performance

      d. Unexercised skills—less practice leads to disadvantage

        i. Age differences small when well-practiced skills are assessed

      e. Recall vs. recognition—recognition superior to recall

        i. Excellent example from study of identification of high school classmates with and without cues

      f. Explicit memory tasks—more trouble with explicit (those requiring effort) than on implicit tasks

       i. Older adults retain good semantic memory (general factual knowledge) but show steady declines in episodic memory (specific events tied to time and place)

    g. Cognitively demanding tasks more difficult in older age

4. Explaining declines in old age

    a. Knowledge base

       i. Semantic memory increases until about age 65

       ii. Older adults know more than younger individuals about real-world categories of information

       iii. Amazing retention of foreign vocabulary learned in high school or college

       iv. Deficiencies on knowledge base probably not the source of most memory problems in older age

       v. Older have more general knowledge, which helps compensate for loss of memory skills

       vi. Knowledge is power

    b. Metamemory

       i. Older adults seem to know as much as younger adults about which memory strategies are best and which memory tasks are hardest

       ii. Older adults more likely to misjudge accuracy of some aspects of their memory

       iii. Older people express more negative beliefs about own memory abilities

       iv. Negative stereotypes of intellectual aging contribute to metamemory

       v. Culture plays role—Chinese adults and deaf American adults perform better than hearing American adults, who tend to hold more negative stereotypes about aging

       vi. Believing that aging brings memory loss causes older individuals to perform poorer on memory tasks and to express less confidence in their memory skills

    c. Memory strategies

       i. Less spontaneous generation of strategies

       ii. Older adults' biggest problem is effective retrieval, not original encoding (see in increased episodes of the tip-of-the-tongue phenomenon).

       iii. Retrieval strategies may be more susceptible to aging

    d. Basic processing capacities

       i. Working memory capacity peaks around age 45 and then begins to decline

       ii. Greater difficulty ignoring irrelevant information may be the result of age-related changes in areas of the brain associated with inhibition of task-irrelevant information

       iii. Slowing central nervous system may hinder working and long-term memory

       iv. Experience can enhance performance but older simply become able to keep up with demands of complex learning and memory tasks

       v. Underactivity in older brain may result from deficiencies in "hardware" or "software"

     vi. Overactivity may indicate that the older brain is trying to compensate for age-related losses

     vii. Slow neural transmissions may underlie limitations in working memory which may limit range of performance (e.g., problem-solving, intelligence)

   e. Sensory changes

     i. Loss of vision and hearing lead to memory deficits

     ii. Vision and hearing predictive of cognitive performance (sensory loss at any age may tax available processing resources)

   f. Contextual contributors

     i. Learning and memory are the product of an interaction between learner characteristics (e.g., motivation, health), task characteristics, and characteristics of broader environment

     ii. Cohort differences in education and IQ—older are less educated (education can partially compensate for age-related cognitive loss)

     iii. Cohort differences in health and lifestyle—older more likely to have chronic or degenerative diseases (fitness training can enhance cognitive ability in older adults)

     iv. Older adults who remain mentally active outperform other adults

     v. Declines in information-processing not inevitable or universal

     vi. Older adults may experience loss of basic capacities but may compensate for such loss

     vii. (Exploration Box: Can you teach an "old dog" new tricks?)

D. Problem-Solving and Aging

 1. Familiar vs. unfamiliar tasks

   a. In laboratory, older adults tend to do worse on unfamiliar problem-solving tasks

   b. Older adults use fewer constraint-seeking questions—ones that rule out more than one item (e.g., "Is it an animal?" vs. "Is it a pig?")

   c. Performance on unfamiliar tasks decreases, but performance on meaningful, everyday tasks is stable or improves in middle and old age

 2. Selection, optimization, and compensation (SOC)

   a. SOC framework for understanding older individuals' problem-solving

     i. Compensation—finding ways to make up for cognitive skills that have gotten rusty

     ii. Selection and optimization—maintain and strengthen skills most useful in everyday life (choose to complete tasks that are most important)

   b. SOC model supported in research on implicit memory training with Alzheimer's patients in which memory for names was enhanced by having the patients name photos of the staff members

Chapter 8

SUGGESTIONS FOR CLASS DISCUSSIONS OR PROJECTS

1. Ask students to report their earliest memories, including their age at the time of the occurrence and the content of these memories. Do students really recall the experience, or do they recall the feelings associated with the experience? Do they remember because the events have been retold, captured in pictures, or otherwise been made memorable for them?

For an excellent sampling of the first memories recalled by scores of people, try the following website: http://www.exploratorium.edu/memory/earlymemory/index.html. What sort of events does it seem we tend to remember? Which senses predominate? What sorts of emotions are involved? If possible, have students check on the accuracy of memories by having them compare their memory for an event to that of an adult (e.g., parent) who also witnessed the event. A related activity would involve students checking out and discussing the A Memory Artist: An Artist Paints His Childhood website at: http://www.exploratorium.edu/memory/earlymemory/index.html This fascinating site does a masterful job of combining visual art and cognitive psychology. At this site, students will learn about Franco Magnani who was born in Italy but moved to the United States as a child. This self-taught artist paints pictures of Italy from memory. By comparing the artist's painting to actual photographs, the developers of the site are able to demonstrate both strengths and limitation of human memory.

2. For a hands-on memory experience, create an overhead containing pictures of 20 or more items. Be sure that some of the items are related (e.g., types of fruit, types of furniture), while others cannot be categorized with the other items. Show the overhead for 15 seconds, remove the overhead, and ask students to write down all the items they can recall. This is a good way to stimulate discussion of memory strategies such as rehearsal, organization, elaboration, and memory reconstruction.

3. To demonstrate constraint-seeking strategies, have pairs or small groups of students try the 20 Questions Game in which student thinks of a target item, and others ask yes-no questions until they can identify the chosen item. Have them try this several times and note if strategies improve. What are the most efficient constraint-seeking approaches (e.g., Is it in the top two rows? Is it an animal?)? If possible, ask students to try the game with younger subjects and report the outcome in class. If enough students do this with children of different ages, the class can pool their data to see if any developmental trends in constraint-seeking questions emerge.

4. To replicate Siegler's rule-assessment approach, bring in a balance beam and present students with different types of problems (e.g., ones in which distance from fulcrum alone is varied, ones in which the amount of weight alone is varied, and ones in which both distance and weight are varied). Compare the students' responses and explanations to those found by Siegler.

5. Muir-Broaddus (1998) describes a great in-class demonstration of the effect of knowledge on memory. This simple demonstration provides an excellent way to show the powerful influence of knowledge on memory. You may want to use yourself (and the topic of psychology) as another example of the impact of expertise.

This demonstration might also be used to demonstrate the positive impact of experience on the memory abilities of older people. You could, for example, have students in class list as many concepts related to World War II as fast as they can, in one minute. You could then have students find an adult (at least age 50) and have them complete the same task. It would be great to get at least some older individuals (born prior to 1930 who lived through WWII) and see how their pattern of responses compares to younger adults and college students.

Muir-Broddus, J.E. (1998). Name seven words: Demonstrating the effects of knowledge on rate of retrieval. *Teaching of Psychology,* 25(2), 119-120.

6. In chapter 8, students read about some advantages of expertise. The goal of this assignment is to have them delve further into the factors related to the development of expertise and advantages that experts have over novices. To complete the assignment, students should search the Web for articles using the terms *expertise*, *novice*, *wisdom*, and *aging/elderly*. Based on what they find, students should write a paper in which they identify 10 ways in which experts' thinking or behavior differs from novices in real-life areas (e.g., business decision-making).

SUGGESTED FILMS AND VIDEOS

The Becoming Years: Adolescence to Older Adults (2006, Insight Media, DVD, 30 minutes): This program presents information on the development of cognitive and social skills from adolescence through old age.

Preschoolers: Cognitive Development (2008, Insight Media, DVD, 28 minutes): Informative presentation of cognitive growth (e.g., language development) and related neural development in the preschool years.

Thanks for the Memories (2002, Insight Media, DVD, 60 minutes): This DVD offers an interesting review of memory development in young children.

The Mind's Storehouse: Memory (2006, Insight Media, DVD, 30 minutes): This DVD focuses on several interesting aspects of memory including repressed memories and the reliability of memory.

Thinking About Thinking: Metacognition (2003, Insight Media, DVD, 30 minutes): From Annenberg/CPB, this program presents an interesting discussion of the benefits of teaching metacognitive skills to students.

Chapter 8

SUGGESTED WEBSITES

Academic Tips: Ways of Improving Memory
http://www.academictips.org/memory/index.html

Fuzzy-Trace Theory
http://epse501.freeservers.com/fuzzy-trace.htm

Improving Memory: Understanding Age-Related Memory Loss
http://www.patienteducationcenter.org/aspx/HealthELibrary/HealthETopic.aspx?cid=IM0306

Mental Fitness: Exercise for the Brain
http://www.bellydoc.com/articles/article7.htm

Memory Improvement Techniques
http://www.mindtools.com/memory.html

SUGGESTED READINGS

Cohen-Mansfield, J., Regier, N.G., Peyser, H., and Stanton, J. (2009). Wisdom of generations: A pilot study of the values transmitted in ethical wills of nursing home residents and student volunteers. *Gerontologist*, 49(4), 525-535.

Geraci, L., and Barnhardt, T.M. (2010). Aging and implicit memory: Examining the contribution of test awareness. *Consciousness & Cognition*, 19(2), 606-616.

Ofen, N., Yun-Ching, K., Sokol-Hessner, P., Heesoo, K., Whitfield-Gabrieli, S., and Gabrieli, J.D.E. (2007). Development of the declarative memory system in the human brain. *Nature Neuroscience*, 10(9), 1198-1205.

Schlagman, S., Kliegel, M., Schulz, J., and Kvavilashvili, L. (2009). Differential effects of age on involuntary and voluntary autobiographical memory. *Psychology & Aging*, 24(2), 397-411.

Strough, J., McFall, J.P., Flinn, J.A., and Schuller, K.L. (2008). Collaborative everyday problem solving among same-gender friends in early and later adulthood. *Psychology and Aging*, 23(3), 517-530.

INTELLIGENCE AND CREATIVITY

LEARNING OBJECTIVES

After reading and studying the material in this chapter, you should be able to answer the following questions.

DEFINING INTELLIGENCE AND CREATIVITY?

1. What is the psychometric approach to intelligence, and how have different psychometric theorists defined intelligence?

2. What are the traditional measures of intelligence, and what are some of the advantages and disadvantages of these approaches? What are some alternatives to these traditional measures of intelligence?

3. What is creativity, and how does it relate to intelligence?

THE INFANT

4. What methods have been used to assess infant intelligence, and how successful is each method? To what extent is infant intelligence related to later intelligence?

THE CHILD

5. Are IQ scores stable during childhood? What factors contribute to gains and losses in IQ scores?

6. What are the typical characteristics of creative children?

THE ADOLESCENT

7. How well do IQ scores predict school achievement and intellectual abilities in adulthood? To what extent is IQ related to occupational success?

8. How can creativity be fostered?

THE ADULT

9. What is the relationship between IQ and occupational success?

10. How do IQ and mental abilities change with age? What factors predict declines in intellectual abilities in older adults?

11. To what extent does wisdom exist in older adults?

12. How does creativity change throughout adulthood?

FACTORS THAT INFLUENCE IQ SCORES

13. What evidence shows genetic influence on IQ scores? What other factors influence IQ scores?

THE EXTREMES OF INTELLIGENCE

14. How are intellectual disability and giftedness defined? What are the outcomes for individuals who have an intellectual disability or who are gifted?

INTEGRATING COGNITIVE PERSPECTIVES

15. How can the major approaches to cognition be integrated?

CHAPTER OUTLINE

I Defining Intelligence and Creativity
   A. Early Definitions of Intelligence
      1. Piaget defined intelligence as thinking or adaptive behavior
      2. Early definitions of intelligence generally reflected the assumption that intelligence is an innate ability (genetically determined and fixed at conception)
      3. No single accepted universal definition of intelligence
   B. The Psychometric Approach
      1. Psychometric approach—spawned the development of standardized intelligence tests
         a. Focus on measurement of intelligence (defined as set of traits that characterize individual)
         b. Goal is to identify and measure these traits
      2. Spearman theory—two-factor theory (g and s)
         a. Intelligence includes general mental ability (g) that contributes to performance on many different tasks
         b. Intelligence includes special (s) abilities specific to a task
            i. By adolescence, processes underlying (g) may become automated
      3. Horn and Cattell's theory—fluid versus crystallized intelligence
         a. Fluid intelligence—use of mind to actively solve problems
            i. Verbal analogies, relations among geometric figures
            ii. Skills not taught and relatively free of cultural influence
         b. Crystallized intelligence—use of knowledge acquired through life experience (e.g., school, life experience) like general information, word comprehension, numeric abilities
         c. Fluid involves using mind in new and flexible ways, crystallized involves using what one has already learned
      4. Emerging consensus on intelligence
         a. A "top" general ability factor that influences performance on wide variety of cognitive tasks
         b. A few broad dimensions that are distinguishable on factor analyses (e.g., fluid, crystallized intelligence)
         c. On the "bottom," specific skills (e.g., spatial discrimination) that impact performance on specific task

5. Binet and Simon commissioned in 1904 by French government to devise a test to identify "dull" children in need of special education
    a. Battery of tests measuring skills believed to be critical for classroom learning (e.g., attention, memory)
    b. Test generated a mental age—level of age-graded problems that a child is able to solve (i.e., a 6-year-old child who solves problems at 5-year-old level has a mental age of 5)
    c. Stanford-Binet Intelligence Scale—adaptation of Binet's test that was developed by Lewis Terman at Stanford University for use with American children
        i. Terman developed a method of calculating an intelligence quotient (IQ)—calculated by dividing mental age (MA) by chronological age (CA) and multiplying by 100 (IQ=MA/CA x 100)
        ii. IQ score of 100 indicates average level of intelligence
        iii. Eight-year-old child with mental age of 10 has an IQ of 125
        iv. Stanford-Binet now in fifth edition
        v. Test norms—standards of performance expressed as average scores and the range of scores around the average that are based on the performance of a large, representative sampled.
    d. David Wechsler developed the Wechsler Scales
        i. Wechsler Preschool and Primary Scale of Intelligence (WPPSI) for children between ages 3 and 8
        ii. Wechsler Intelligence Scale for Children (WISC-IV) for schoolchildren ages 6 to 16
        iii. Wechsler Adult Intelligence Scale (WIAS-IV) use with adults
        iv. Test yields a verbal IQ (based on factors like vocabulary), a performance IQ (based on nonverbal skills like puzzle assembly), and full-scale IQ (combination of verbal and performance)
    e. Scores on both Sanford-Binet and Wechsler Scales form a normal distribution—bell-shaped spread around average score of 100
        i. Scores around average are most common, very high and low scores are rarer
        ii. Two-thirds of people have IQ scores between 85 and 115 (correspond to a spread of one standard deviation above and below the average)
        iii. Fewer that 3% score above 130 (sometimes used as a criteria for giftedness) or below 70 (sometimes used as a criteria for intellectual disability)
    f. Emphasis on intelligence tests that summarize intellect into a single IQ score
    g. Critics—psychometric tests do not fully describe what it means to be intelligent
    h. Exploration Box on alternatives to traditional intelligence tests
        i. Sternberg's Triarchic Abilities Test (STAT)
        ii. Information-processing theory focuses on *how* children solve problems rather than *why* they solve problems
        iii. STAT uses variety of question formats, including essays

C. Gardner's Theory of Multiple Intelligences
   1. Rejects single IQ model in favor of at least eight distinct kinds of intelligences
   2. Many of the types of intelligence are not found on standard intelligence tests
      a. Linguistic—language skills
      b. Logical-mathematical—abstract thinking
      c. Musical—sensitivity to sound patterns
      d. Spatial—object perception
      e. Bodily-kinesthetic—body movement skills
      f. Interpersonal—social skills
      g. Intrapersonal—understanding one's own feeling
      h. Naturalistic—world of plants and animals
   3. Does not claim that this is *the* definitive list of intelligence
   4. Savant syndrome—extraordinary talent in a mentally retarded person
      a. Leslie Lemke, blind, retarded, cerebral palsy, but can perfectly imitate music on piano even if he only hears it once
      b. Savants cannot be explained by theories emphasizing a "g" (general intelligence) factor
      c. Each type of intelligence may have a unique developmental course
         i. Musical and athletic intelligence revealed in childhood
         ii. Logical-mathematical intelligence revealed in later life
   5. Distinct intelligences linked to distinctive brain structures
D. Sternberg's Triarchic Theory
   1. Triarchic Theory—emphasis on three aspects of intellectual behavior (practical/contextual, creative/experiential, analytic)
   2. Practical component—intelligence defined by sociocultural context in which it is displayed (e.g., people who have adapted well to environment have "street smarts")
      a. Intelligent behavior varies by context (e.g., numerical abilities less important now that calculators and computers more widely available)
      b. Definition of intelligence in childhood different from definition in adulthood
      c. Definition of intelligent behavior depends on sociocultural context in which it is displayed
   3. Creative component—impact of experience (e.g., what is intelligent the first time a task is encountered may not be intelligent after extensive experience with the task)
      a. Response to novelty requires active, conscious information processing
      b. Sternberg suggests that novel tasks best measure of intelligence
      c. Automatization—increased efficiency with practice (familiarity effect)
         i. Little "programs in the mind" for performing common actives efficiently and unthinkingly
         ii. Must know how familiar an individual is with a task before assessing a behavior
      d. Cultural bias in intelligence testing—familiarity of items varies by culture
   4. Analytic component—information-processing skills assessed by traditional intelligence tests
      a. People high on this component can plan what to do, monitor progress, filter irrelevant information, and compare new information to existing knowledge

        b. Sternberg focus is on *how* people produce intelligent answers
          i. Must consider the processes used to arrive at an answer
          ii. Must consider context in which action is performed
          iii. Must consider analytic strategies used
     5. Theory of successful intelligence—intelligence is the extent to which an individual succeeds in life, according to his or her own definition of success within his or her sociocultural context (not just doing well in school)
        a. Individuals with successful intelligence are strong in practical, creative, and analytical areas
        b. Intelligent people optimize strengths and minimize weaknesses
        c. Intelligent people select or modify environments to fit them
        d. Today's widely used tests of intelligence do not reflect Sternberg's sophisticated view of intelligence
  E. Creativity—ability to produce novel, appropriate, and valued responses
     1. Creative thinking distinct from, and not well correlated with, IQ scores and grades
     2. IQ tests measure divergent thinking—variety of solutions when there is no one correct answer
     3. Creativity tests assess convergent thinking—finding a variety of solutions
        a. Responses on divergent tasks analyzed along three dimensions
          i. Originality or uniqueness
          ii. Flexibility or number of different categories expressed
          iii. Ideation fluency—sheer number of different ideas one can generate
     4. Confluence—coming together of several factors to form a new product
        a. Sternberg argues that creativity is a confluence of factors
          i. Knowledge of the field in which creativity may emerge
          ii. A thinking style open to new ways of thinking
          iii. Personality characteristics that include calculated risk-taking and willingness to pursue and overcome obstacles
          iv. Motivation
          v. Environment that is supportive of creative ideas
        b. Sometimes having more of one component can compensate for having less of another
          i. High motivation to create new ideas may overcome environment that does not support this activity
        c. Minimum of intelligence probably required for creativity but in those with higher IQ, there is little relationship between intelligence and creativity

II The Infant
  A. Developmental Quotients
     1. None of the standard intelligence tests can be used with children younger than 3 because of the required verbal and attention skills
     2. Bailey Scales of Infant Development (1 to 42 months)
        a. Most widely used scale of developmental milestones (has three parts/scales)
          i. Motor scale (e.g., grasping)
          ii. Mental scale (e.g., searching for hidden object)
          iii. Behavioral record scale (e.g., emotional regulation)

b. Developmental quotient (DQ)—performance compared to norms based on performance of a large group of infants of the same age

B. Infant Intelligence and Later Intelligence
1. Low correlation between DQ scores and later IQ scores
2. Explanations for this lack of relationship
    a. Tests tap qualitatively different domains
    b. Infant intelligence based on universal maturation
    c. Infants "straying from path" are on temporary deviation
3. Some relationship between measures of infant attention and later IQ; predictors include
    a. Speed of habituation
    b. Preference for novelty
    c. Reaction time
4. "Smart" infant is a speedy processor, gets quickly bored by the same old thing, seeks novel experiences, and soaks up information rapidly

III The Child

A. How Stable Are IQ Scores During Childhood?
1. IQ scores are fairly stable starting at about age 4
    a. High short-term predictability
2. Correlations reflect groups of children, not individuals
    a. Within group, stability but individual variation
    b. One study, one-third of participants showed changes of 30 points
3. IQ scores influenced by nonintellectual factors (e.g., motivation, testing procedures)

B. Causes of Gains and Losses
1. Fluctuation in individual IQ score greatest if child in unstable environment
2. Cumulative-deficit hypothesis—IQ scores of children from impoverished environments decrease as negative effects accumulate
3. Effects worse if living in poverty with low intellectually functioning parents

C. Emergence of Creativity
1. Developmental course of creativity
    a. Preschool children display high levels of divergent thinking
    b. Fourth-grade slump in creativity
    c. Levels of divergent thinking rise after age 12
    d. Actual peaks and valleys not as large as originally reported
2. What a creative child is like
    a. Creative children have more humor, originality, playfulness than high-IQ children
    b. More success oriented
    c. Tend to engage in more fantasy or pretend play
    d. Parents tend to be tolerant of unconventional ideas
3. Creativity influenced by different factors than IQ
    a. Genetic factors do not appear to impact creativity
    b. Creative children appear to value nonconformity and independence
    c. Some research suggested that childhood adversity (e.g., distant parents) is driving force behind creativity but not true for all individuals

4. Factors that impact creativity quite distinct from the cognitive abilities measured on IQ tests

IV The Adolescent
  A. Continuity between Childhood and Adulthood
    1. Rapid intellectual growth in early adolescence, then levels off
      a. Piaget's formal operations stage
      b. Brain development may provide needed speed and working-memory capacity
      c. Brain development may underlie variety of cognitive advances
    2. Increasing stability of individual differences during the teen years
  B. IQ and School Achievement
    1. Original purpose of IQ was to estimate how well children would do in school
    2. General intellectual ability is one of the best predictors of academic achievement
      a. Adolescents with high IQ scores less likely to drop out of college
      b. IQ scores predict high school grades but not college grades
      c. Overall IQ is good predictor of academic achievement
      d. IQ scores do not reflect habits, motivations, and interests
  C. Fostering Creativity
    1. Timing of creativity dependent on culture and pressure to conform
    2. Creativity impacted by type of task
    3. Creative thinking stable from fourth to ninth grade, but creative *feelings* (e.g., curiosity, imagination) increase significantly in adolescence
    4. Multiple factors involved in fostering creativity
      a. On the nature side, talent and motivation both important
      b. Internal motivation and thirst for challenge are crucial
      c. Willingness to take risks important
      d. Key is to be in environment that recognizes, values, and nurtures creativity
      e. Building a knowledge base necessary but not sufficient
      f. Some parents may be too pushy (e.g., movie *Shine*)
    5. Do tests of creativity predict actual creative accomplishments?
      a. While there is some evidence, mistake to expect tests of creativity to predict so with much accuracy
        i. Creativity expressed in different ways at different points in the lifespan
        ii. Tests of creativity require assessment of specific talents and distinct skills

V The Adult
  A. IQ and Occupational Success
    1. Some occupations require more intellectual ability than others (more complexity)
      a. General intelligence is significantly related to both income and occupational prestige
      b. Gap between those with higher and lower intelligences increases with time
      c. Prestige or status of occupation is not as important as the complexity of the work
      d. IQs vary considerably with every occupation

2. Performance on the job also related to IQ
   a. Intellectually capable adults do their jobs better
   b. Those with greater intellectual ability tend to earn more money

B. IQ and Health
   1. People who score higher on intelligence tests tend to live healthier and longer lives
      a. Less likely to have lung cancer and cardiovascular or coronary disease
      b. Common explanation is that the connection between IQ and health involves socioeconomic status
      c. When you control for socioeconomic status, still a connection between intelligence and health
   2. Monitoring health may require same skills as doing well on intelligence tests
      a. Better monitoring may lead to successful management of disorder
      b. Intelligent people with diabetes learn more about the disorder

C. Change in IQ with Age
   1. Individual IQ scores remain relatively stable from pre-adolescence until well into old age
   2. Depends on type of research design
      a. Cross-sectional design—decline in later life, but verbal IQ is essentially unchanged until late in life (Kaufman, 2001)
      b. Longitudinal design—some abilities decline in later life (Kaufman, 2001); verbal IQ stable, performance peak 20-24
      c. Sequential design (Schaie)
         i. Different cohorts tested at different times
         ii. When a person is born has great impact on intellect (cohort effect)
         iii. Different generations may have special edge in different areas
         iv. Young cohorts outscore older cohorts on most tests
         v. Older cohorts outscore younger cohorts on tests of numeric abilities
         vi. Scores of verbal meaning increased until 1952 but have dropped in recent cohorts
         vii. Fluid (skills to solve novel problems) shows decline
         viii. Crystallized (general knowledge) shows increase
      d. Performance on speeded tests declines more
         i. Speed loss may be related to slowing of central nervous system
   3. Declines in intellectual abilities generally minor until late 60s or 70s
   4. Declines are not universal
   5. Range of differences in intellectual functioning of older adults extremely large

D. Predictors of Decline
   1. Poor health
      a. Chronic illness and diseases related to intellectual decline
      b. Terminal drop—rapid loss of IQ within a few years of death
   2. Unstimulating lifestyle
      a. Disengagement has negative impact on intellect
      b. Married couples can provide intellectual stimulation for each other
      c. Over the years, IQ scores of partners become more similar (lower-functioning partner rises to higher)
      d. "Use it or lose it!"—more you use intellect, the less the loss

E. Potential for Wisdom
   1. Erikson, older adults gain wisdom facing death and meaning of life
      a. Term "wise" seldom used to describe children or young adults
   2. Wisdom—expert knowledge in fundamental pragmatic of life
   3. Sternberg's aspects of a wise person is someone who can combine successful intelligence with creativity to solve problems
   4. Staudinger, Smith, and Baltes study of well-educated women found that
      a. Wisdom is rare
      b. Wisdom related more to expertise (large knowledge base) than age
   5. Age does not predict wisdom
      a. Older adults who have had life experiences that sharpen insight into the human condition are more likely to display wisdom
      b. Immediate social context influences degree to which wisdom is expressed
         i. Wiser solutions generated when adults have the opportunity to discuss problems with someone whose judgment they value and when they reflect after the discussions
   6. Wisdom best thought of as combination of intelligence, personality, and cognitive style factors
F. Creative Endeavors
   1. Creative production usually greatest from 20s to early 40s in most fields and then gradually declines
   2. Actual peak times of creativity vary by field
      a. Creative productivity of scholarship in the humanities continues well into old age
      b. Creative productivity in the arts often peaks in 30s and 40s
      c. Creative productivity in the sciences peaks in the 40s and declines thereafter
      d. Many creators are still producing outstanding works in old age (e.g., Michelangelo)
   3. Creative achievement requires both enthusiasm and experience (most likely to occur in people in their 30s and 40s)
   4. Simonton suggests creativity requires both ideation and elaboration
      a. Ideation—generating creative ideas
      b. Elaboration—executing ideas to real problems
      c. Older people may use up stock-pile of potential ideas
      d. Elderly adults do not differ from younger adults in originality of ideas, just generate fewer ideas

VI Factors that Influence IQ Scores
A. Flynn Effect
   1. Flynn effect—during the 20th century, IQ scores in many countries increased
      a. United States, 3 to 4 IQ point increase per decade
         i. Adults born in 1980 will soon score 6 to 8 points higher than those born in 1960
         ii. Full-scale IQ scores increased 18 points in last 50 years
         iii. Subscales as much as a 24-point increase
      b. Improved nutrition and living conditions important

135

       c.   Children have been more the focus of their parents
       d.   Children more educated

B. Genes and Environments
    1. Pioneers of the IQ testing movement believe that differences exist simply because some people inherit better genes (hereditarians position)
       a.   Identical twin IQ scores more similar than fraternal IQ scores
       b.   Adopted children's IQ (once they reach adolescence) more similar to biological parents than adoptive parent
       c.   As much as half of variation in IQ score attributed to genetic differences
       d.   Even if the genetic influence is strong, no trait is set in stone
          i.   Genes may set upper and lower limits of behavioral expression
    2. Environmental influences on intelligence
       a.   Environmental risk factors (e.g., unemployed head of household, family with four or more children, father absent from home) predict lower IQ scores
       b.   Home Observation of Measurement of the Environment (HOME) inventory developed by Caldwell and Bradley assess various aspects of environment
          i.   Parental stimulation and responsiveness is critical
          ii.   Amount of stimulation parents provide not as important as whether that stimulation is responsive to child's behavior
          iii.   More intelligent parents tend to provide more stimulating environment for their children
       c.   Parents with greater intellect more likely to provide stimulating environments and to pass along gene related to higher intelligence
          i.   Maternal IQ is correlated with child's IQ at age 3 years
          ii.   Father's IQ less reliable predictor
       d.   Intellectual development best when motivated, intellectually capable child receives intellectual nourishment from responsive parents

C. Poverty
    1. Child poverty involves low parent income and low levels of meeting a child's basic needs
       a.   Children living in poverty often have inadequate healthcare, live in overcrowded and unsafe neighborhoods, have families in chronic stress, and lack opportunities for cognitive stimulation
          i.   Studies with animals show direct relationship between being raised in an impoverished environment and impaired brain development (e.g., fewer neurons, fewer connections between neurons)
          ii.   Brain clearly influenced by development
       b.   Children living in poverty average IQ are 10 to 20 points below middle-class age-mates
    2. Socioeconomic status affects IQ scores and rate of intellectual growth
    3. *Neuroplasticity*—brain's responsiveness to environment
       a.   Adoption from lower-class into middle-class homes associated with higher IQ

D. Race and Ethnicity
    1. Studies finding ethnic differences in IQ spark controversy
    2. Some studies show differences shrinking, others see similar historic gap (e.g., Asian and European-American students score higher than African-American, Native-American, and Hispanic-American children)

3. Different subcultural groups sometimes show distinctive profiles of mental abilities
   a. Must remember that differences involve *group averages*
4. Cannot predict individual IQ merely on basis of racial or ethnic identity
5. Racial and ethnic difference in IQ scores may involve biased test
   a. Culture bias—possible bias in test questions
      i. Questions may be more appropriate for middle-class children
      ii. Children who speak Ebonics or Spanish at home may not understand some test instructions or items
      iii. Level of cultural exposure may negatively impact IQ scores
      iv. Culture-fair IQ tests included familiar and unfamiliar items from all ethnic or social groups
      v. Racial and ethnic difference still found on culture-fair tests
      vi. IQ scores predict school success for most populations (including minority population)
   b. Motivational factors—minority students not motivated to do their best because of anxiety or fear of being judged by examiner who is often of different racial/ethnic background
      i. Disadvantaged children score 7 to 10 points higher when with a friendly examiner and when given questions that are a mix of easy and hard items
      ii. African-American children less comfortable in testing situations
      iii. Poor performance by African-American children may be the result of a fear that the test would reveal their level of intellect
      iv. Steele and colleagues have suggested that negative stereotypes of one's own group may decrease scores; may be especially a problem for African-American students
      v. Stereotype threat—fear that one will be judged by the qualities associated with negative stereotypes (often racial or ethnic in nature)
      vi. A meta-analysis found that a 40-point difference on the SAT between majority and non-majority students may be the result of stereotype threat
      vii. Positive stereotypes about a group can increase performance for members of that group (including racial minorities and women)
      viii. Effects of stereotype threat may be reduced by providing students with a mentor
6. Genetic factors?
   a. Heated debate in psychology about role of genetics in intelligence
   b. Most psychologists do not think that evidence that heredity contributes to *within-group* differences says much about the reasons for *between-group* differences
   c. Example of seeds planted in two environment and how this is used to determine the impact of genetics versus the environment
   d. No direct evidence that race differences in test scores due to genetics
7. Environmental influences?
   a. Adoption research supports critical impact of environment placement in advantaged homes' positive impact on lower-income African-American children

137

        b. Intellectually stimulating environment a key to explaining "racial differences" in IQ scores

        c. IQ gap between African Americans and Caucasians may be decreasing

        d. Living in poverty and having limited learning opportunities has a lot to do with racial differences in IQ scores

VII The Extremes of Intelligence

A. Intellectual Disabilities

1. Intellectual disabilities referred to as "mental retardation" for decades)

2. Significantly below-average intellectual functioning (i.e., IQ score below 70-75) and limitations in meeting age-appropriate expectations in everyday functioning (e.g., self-care)

3. Mental retardation not merely a deficiency within person but a product of the interaction between the person and their environment

4. Impact can range from mild to profound

        a. Individual with mild intellectual disability can live independently or with occasional help and can learn academic and practical skills in school

        b. Individual with profound intellectual disability shows major delays in all areas of development and require basic care (and possibly institutionalization)

5. Organic intellectual disability—due to biological cause (heredity, disease, injury)

        a. Down syndrome—extra 21st chromosome

        b. Phenylketonuria (PKU)

        c. Maternal alcohol consumption

        d. Rubella

6. Most cases on intellectual disability have no identifiable organic cause

        a. Likely a combination of genetic and environmental factors

            i. Living in poverty

           ii. Neglectful or abusive families

          iii. Frequently have a parent or sibling who is disabled

7. Historically about 3% of school-age children classified with intellectual disability

        a. Often have associated impairments (e.g., cerebral palsy, sensory disorders)

        b. Parents have both positive and negative reactions to having their child diagnosed with an intellectual disability

            i. Mothers report higher levels of stress

8. Children with intellectual disabilities tend to follow same developmental sequence as other children

        a. Individuals with Down syndrome may experience greater deterioration of intellect in later life

9. "Camberwell Cohort" was a group of English individuals with intellectual disabilities studied for 25 years

        a. When in their 40s, about 50% in community group homes, 25% lived with families, 20% in larger residential facilities

        b. Social skills remained largely unchanged, but for those with the worst level of impairment, skills worsened with age because of diminished social supports

        c. Overall quality of life lower for individuals diagnosed with intellectual disabilities early in life; there has, however, been a marked improvement in the quality of life for these individuals compared to previous decades

B. Giftedness
1. Use to be identified solely be IQ score (at least 130)
2. Increased recognition that gifted children have special abilities rather than high general intelligence
3. Giftedness—having a high IQ or special abilities in areas valued by society (e.g., mathematics, visual arts, leadership)
4. Renzulli states giftedness as combination of above-average ability, creativity, and task commitment
5. Gottfried's research
   a. Identified potentially gifted children at age 18 months
   b. Longitudinal study showed that gifted children tend to have similar characteristics that distinguish them from average children
      i. Characteristics include extensive vocabulary, rapid learning, good memory, longer attention span
6. Silverman and colleagues research
   a. Used the Characteristics of Giftedness Scale
   b. Identified common characteristics of gifted children including rapid learning, extensive vocabulary, good memory, perfectionism, sense of humor, preference for older companions, early interest in reading, strong ability with puzzles, maturity, and task perseverance
7. German's research
   a. Study of 1,500 gifted children (*Termites*) begun in 1921
   b. Intellectually gifted children also better adjusted, better-than-average health, earlier puberty
   c. Gifted children quick to take on leadership roles
   d. Destroyed stereotype of intellectuals as weak and frail
8. Gifted students who skip grades and entered U. of Washington early were socially mature and well adjusted and most thrived in school
9. As adults, Termites were different from average individuals
   a. Lower rates of ill health, mental illness, alcoholism
   b. Impressive occupational achievements (professional and high-level business jobs)
   c. Termites aged well, with both men and women in their 60s and 70s highly active and involved
   d. Contrary to stereotype, gifted do not tend to burn out early
10. Some with high IQs (closer to 180 than 130) are unhappy and socially isolated
11. Most well-adjusted adults had highly educated parents who offer love and intellectual stimulation

VIII Integrating Cognitive Perspectives
1. Piaget—modes of thought change qualitatively with age (like a caterpillar into a butterfly)
2. Vygotsky—highlights importance of culturally transmitted modes of thinking and interactions with others
3. Information-processing—explains why young children cannot remember as much information or solve problems as effectively as adults
4. Psychometric approach—tasks can be used to recognize distinct mental abilities that each person displays in greater or lesser amounts

5. Sternberg—pushed us to look beyond traditional psychometric tests of intelligence, which emphasize analytic skills, and to consider creative and practical intelligence

SUGGESTIONS FOR CLASS DISCUSSIONS OR PROJECTS

1. Ask your students to name behaviors and traits that they associate with highly intelligent adults and with unintelligent adults. Sternberg and his colleagues did this and found that the named behaviors fell into three categories: practical problem-solving skills, verbal skills, and social competence. Examples of practical problem-solving include making good decisions, keeping an open mind, and using original sources for information. Examples of verbal ability include conversing well, reading with high comprehension, and having a good vocabulary. Examples of social competence include being on time for appointments, admitting mistakes, and sensitivity to other people's needs. Sternberg (1986) presents a checklist of behaviors in each category that students can use to evaluate themselves on a nine-point scale. Sternberg notes that higher ratings on the checklist are associated with better performance.

The class might also try to generate lists of behaviors and traits associated with creative and non-creative people. Are the concepts of creativity and intelligence in any way related?

Sternberg, R. (1986). *Intelligence Applied*. NY: Harcourt, Brace and Jovanovich.

2. An interesting variation on project 1 would be to have students generate a list of intelligent and nonintelligent behaviors of infants. You could then compile this list and compare to some standard form of intelligence tests for infants (e.g., the Bayley Scales of Infant and Toddler Development III).

3. This chapter describes the relationship between home environment and intellectual performance and provides sample items from the HOME inventory. Ask students to expand on this by "designing" (on paper) environments that would be rated high, moderate, and low on intellectual stimulation. There are often examples of environments shockingly low on appropriate stimulation in the news.

4. Some people have recently argued that providing stimulation has gone overboard when parents begin coaching infants and young children with flashcards and enrolling them in numerous programs designed to promote some aspect of development. The Better Baby Institute, founded by Glenn Doman (author of *How to Teach Your Child to Read*), provides a good illustration of a program that uses early structured stimulation with infants to accelerate mental growth. In this program, parents are trained to educate their infants by using flashcards presented to the infants three times a day. Discuss pros and cons of such efforts. What do students think would be the effects of such a program (on intellectual and also other types of functioning)?

5. Given the many criticisms of IQ tests reflected in the chapter, have students discuss in small groups whether it is a good or a bad idea to have some method of assessing individual intelligence. When are intelligence tests used? Should they be used for those purposes? What alternatives to these tests might exist? Ask students to try to design a "new and improved" test

that taps typical aspects of intelligence as well as aspects not well represented in current tests. The test should relate to everyday intellectual functioning, be practically administered, predict what students design it to predict, and be fair to such groups as minority children and older adults. This exercise often makes students appreciate why none of the current intelligence tests are perfect; tests that are high in one desired feature are often low in another desired feature.

6. Have students generate a list of 10 of the most famous geniuses of all time. After students have generated a list, have them share their ideas with the class. Do the lists that students generate better fit with an IQ or Gardner's model of intelligence? Is there a lot of agreement on who belongs on the list?

7. If you have a number of students from different ethnic or geographic backgrounds, have each student create a 10-item culturally biased intelligence test that individuals from their background would find easy and those from other backgrounds might find difficult. Have students give their "tests" to other members of the class as a way to promote the role of culture in testing and the difficulty in creating a "culture-fair" test.

8. To spur a discussion on the definition of "creativity," have students each write down an example of a behavior that they have engaged in that they believe illustrates that they are creative. Collect each of the examples and then randomly draw and read aloud a few. After each, have the class rate whether the example illustrates true creativity.

SUGGESTED FILMS AND VIDEOS

Different Kinds of Smarts: Multiple Intelligences (2003, Insight Media, VHS, 30 minutes). Features discussion of Gardner's theory of multiple intelligences.

Intelligence and Creativity (2001, Insight Media, VHS, 30 minutes). Focuses on the way culture and environmental factors define intelligence.

Minor Keys (2004, Insight Media, DVD, 53 minutes). Examines the lives of two violin prodigies and sheds light on the lives of gifted children and their parents.

Smarter than the Rest of Us (2004, Insight Media, DVD, 46 minutes). Uses famous individuals (e.g., Einstein) to explore the issues of why certain individuals are smarter than others, and whether intelligence can be increased.

The Search for Intelligence (2006, Insight Media, DVD, 30 minutes). Focuses on whether intelligence tests actually measure intelligence. Includes discussion of triarchic theory and theories of multiple intelligences.

Bayley Scales of Infant and Toddler Development (3rd Edition)
http://harcourtassessment.com/haiweb/cultures/en-us/productdetail.htm?pid=015-8027-23X

Classics in the History of Psychology: Binet on Intelligence
http://psychclassics.yorku.ca/Binet/binet1.htm

Creativity Portal
http://www.creativity-portal.com/

Free IQ Test
http://www.funeducation.com/Tests/IQTest/TakeTest.aspx

Parenting of K-6 Children: Gifted Children
http://childparenting.about.com/od/giftedchildren/

SUGGESTED READINGS

Deary, I. J., Penke, Lars, and Johnson, W. (2010). The neuroscience of human intelligence differences. *Nature Reviews Neuroscience*, 11(3), 201-211.

Flood, M., and Phillips, K. D. (2007). Creativity in older adults: A plethora of possibilities. *Issues in Mental Health Nursing*, 28(4), 389-411.

Henshon, S.-E. (2010). Giftedness across the lifespan: An interview with Rena Subtnik. *Gifted Child Today*, 33(1), 27-31.

Rodgers, K. A. (2008). Racial identity, centrality and giftedness: An expectancy-value application of motivation in gifted African American students. *Roeper Review*, 30(2), 111-120.

Vaillend, C., Poirier, R., and Laroche, S. (2008). Genes, plasticity, and mental retardation. *Behavioural Brain Research*, 192(1), 88-105.

LANGUAGE AND EDUCATION

LEARNING OBJECTIVES

After reading and studying the material in this chapter, you should be able to answer the following questions.

MASTERING LANGUAGE

1. What is the typical developmental course of language development?

2. How do neurobiologist, learning, nativist, and interactionist perspectives explain the acquisition of language? Which explanation is best supported by research?

THE INFANT

3. What factors influence mastery motivation of infants? How is this related to later achievement?

4. What are the pros and cons of early education?

THE CHILD

5. What factors contribute to differences in levels of achievement motivation during childhood, and what can be done to foster achievement motivation?

6. What are the components of learning to read? Is there a most effective way of teaching reading? What distinguishes skilled and unskilled readers?

7. How does school affect children? What factors characterize effective schools?

THE ADOLESCENT

8. What changes in achievement motivation occur during adolescence? What factors contribute to these changes?

9. How does science and math education in the United States compare to science and math education in other countries?

10. What are the pros and cons of integrating work with school during adolescence?

THE ADULT

11. How does achievement motivation change during adulthood?

12. How do literacy, illiteracy, and continued education affect adults' lives?

I Mastering Language
 A. Definition of Language
  1. Language—communication system of limited sounds, letters, gestures, combined in agreed upon rules; produces infinite number of messages
   a. Linguists have not yet fully defined the rules to any language
 B. What Must Be Mastered?
  1. Key aspects of language to be mastered
   a. Phoneme—basic units of sounds from any given language
    i. English /b/ as in bit
    ii. More phonemes than letters as some letters can be pronounced in different ways
    iii. Each language defines which sounds can be combined (e.g., in English "br" combination is okay but "bm" is not
   b. Morphemes—basic units of meaning that exist in a word
    i. Some words have one morpheme (e.g., view)
    ii. Adding a different morpheme (e.g., pre) can result is a word consisting of two morphemes (e.g., preview)
    iii. Morphemes are not syllables
   c. Syntax—systematic rules for formation of sentences
    i. Order of words can lead to different meaning (e.g., Fang bit Fred versus Fred bit Fang)
   d. Semantics—meaning of words or symbols or sentences
   e. Pragmatics—rules for specifying how language is appropriately used in different social context
   f. Prosody—how sounds are produced
    i. "Melody" of speech including pitch, intonation, or accentuation of certain syllables
    ii. Tone makes a statement sarcastic
 C. When Does Language Develop?
  1. Before the first words
   a. Very young infants show preference for speech over nonspeech and for their native language
   b. Very young infants can distinguish phonemes
   c. Before they can speak, infants are sensitive to the pause between words
   d. By 7½ months, infants demonstrate word segmentation—ability to detect a target word in a stream of speech
   e. Sensitive to cues marking the beginning and end of words
   f. Early sounds include cries, burps, grunts
   g. Early vocalization exercises vocal chords
   h. Parents tend to respond to prelinguistic sounds as if infant attempting to genuinely communicate
   i. Around 6-8 weeks begin cooing—repeating vowel-like sound "aaah"
   j. Around 3-4 months begin babbling—consonant-vowel combination "baba"
   k. Deaf children initially sound like hearing children, but without auditory experience/feedback, they eventually show delay in language development

l. Advanced babblers restrict sounds to phonemes of language they are hearing and pick up intonation of language

m. Infants attempt to master semantics—meaning of language

    i. Understand words before they can produce them

    ii. Comprehension (reception) precedes production (expression)

n. Before speaking first word, seem to understand familiar words

o. Joint attention—infant and parent attend to vocalization and visual image at same time

    i. Infants direct gaze toward object connecting words and their referents

p. Syntactic bootstrapping—use the syntax (placement of a word in a sentence) to determine the meaning of a word

2. The first words

   a. Holophrases—single words convey many things (single-word sentences)

     i. Way a holophrase is said and the context in which it is said determines its meaning

     ii. Accompanying intonation and gesture pattern help convey meaning of holophrase

     iii. At holophrase phase, infants have mastered basic functions like naming, questioning, requesting, and demanding

   b. One-year-olds mainly talk about familiar objects and actions

     i. Often involve common nouns about objects interacted with each day (e.g., *mommy*), objects the infant manipulates (e.g., *ball*), and words facilitating social interactions (e.g., *bye-bye*)

   c. Vocabulary spurt—increase in vocabulary size around 18 months (e.g., 18 months = 30-50 words, 24 months = 300 words)

   d. Overextension—use word too broadly (e.g., "dog" for all four-legged animals)

   e. underextension—use word too narrowly (e.g., "dog" for only the family pet and no other dogs)

   f. Over- and underextension are examples of Piagetian assimilation and may be due to small vocabularies or not yet learning the name of an object

   g. Large individual variations in vocabulary size

     i. Referential style—lots of nouns

     ii. Expressive style—lots of personal pronouns and social routines

   h. Culture exerts influence on language

     i. Infants learning English produce more nouns

     ii. Infants learning Korean produce more verbs

     iii. Quality and quantity of speech interactions impact young children's vocabulary size

3. Telegraphic speech

   a. Telegraphic speech—early combinations of two to four words into sentences that are like telegrams

     i. Normally seen around 18 to 24 months; combine two or three words in simple sentences

     ii. Sentences contain critical content and omit frills

     iii. Follow systematic rules

b. Functional grammar—emphasizes semantic relationship between words, the meaning expressed, and the function served by sentences

c. Major advancement in complexity of sentences between ages 2 and 5 years
    i. Sentences are longer, more grammatically correct, but not without errors

d. Begin to infer morphological rules for forming plural and past-tense words
    i. Often engage in overregularization—applying rules to exceptions (e.g., says "foots" or "goed")

e. Transformational grammar—rules of syntax for transforming basic underlying thoughts into a variety of sentence forms
    i. Three stage rules for questioning
    ii. Stage one: two- or three-word sentences with rising intonation
    iii. Stage two: use auxiliary or helping verbs
    iv. Stage three: move auxiliary verb ahead of subject

4. Later Language Development

a. School-age children show improved pronunciation, larger vocabulary, can infer meaning
    i. Average first-grader has vocabulary of 10,000 words and add between 5 and 13 words a day through elementary school years

b. With help of formal operational thought, teens better able to understand and
define abstract terms

c. School-age children begin to be able to interpret passive sentences and show greater command of grammar

d. By middle childhood to adolescence, show increased metalinguistic awareness—increased knowledge of language itself
    i. Able to define abstract words
    ii. Can better distinguish grammatically correct and grammatically incorrect sentences

e. Changes in adulthood
    i. Knowledge of phonology, grammar, syntax usually retained in adulthood
    ii. May have trouble distinguishing sounds if hearing becomes impaired
    iii. Knowledge of semantics (word meaning) expands into adulthood (at least until 70s or 80s)
    iv. Older adults have more "tip-of-the-tongue" experiences
    v. Refinement of linguistic pragmatics (ability to adjust language to fit social situations) into adulthood
    vi. Command of language holds up well in later life unless there are other major declines in cognitive functioning

D. How Language Develops

1. Neurobiology of language

a. Language is often largely a product of left hemispheric activity in Broca's area (associated with speech production) and Wernicke's area (associated with comprehension of language)

b. Based on new brain imaging techniques (functional magnetic resonance imaging [fMRI] and event-related potentials [ERPs]), can craft more precise picture of neural activity of language

c. Those successful at leaning new words show more connectivity between left and right supramarginal gyrus in the parietal lobe

d. fMRIs show more balance of left and right hemisphere activity during language for women, but more left than right for men

e. Wernicke's and Broca's areas connected by fibers

    i. Incoming language first comprehended in Wernicke's area and sent to Broca's area via "arcuate fasciculus" fibers

f. Damage of arcuate fasciculus fibers can lead to aphasia—language disorder in which person might hear or understand linguistic input but be unable to vocally repeat the information

g. Neurons in Broca's area are active during speech production and when a person sees or hears someone speaking

h. It appears that both heredity and environmental factors combine to impact language development

2. Nurture: the contributions of the environment and learning

    a. Environmental influences on language acquisition

        i. Children learn words that they hear

        ii. Explains why children speak language of parents down to regional accent

        iii. Children are more likely to use a word if reinforced for using the word

        iv. Children encouraged to ask questions tend to ask questions

    b. Learning theorists have easy time explaining the development of phonology and semantics, but harder time accounting for acquisition of syntactical rules

        i. Parents often reinforce sentences that are not grammatically correct

        ii. Imitation cannot explain all of language acquisition as children say sentences that they have never heard

        iii. Saying "repeat after me" to a child not a good idea for teaching syntax

        iv. Young children do imitate speech, but imitation and reinforcement alone cannot account for grammar acquisition

3. Nature: the contributions of biology

    a. Chomsky's theory proposed that humans have a unique genetic capacity to learn language

        i. Equipped with universal grammar—system of common rules and properties for learning any of the world's languages (e.g., most languages have basic word order of subject-verb-object or subject-object-verb)

        ii. Most languages are based on grammar that starts with a subject

        iii. Language acquisition device (LAD)—area of the brain assisting in acquisition of universal features of language; tailors brain to process specific language spoken in the child's environment

    b. Evidence supporting nativist perspective

        i. "Learnability factor"—children acquire an incredibly complex communication system rapidly and without formal training

        ii. Similar stages of linguistic progression occurring at similar ages

        iii. Similar pattern of development despite significant cultural differences in pattern of verbal interaction between adults and children

        iv. Children learn native language with ease but struggle later to learn a second language (may be a critical period for language acquisition)

        v. In deaf children, mastery of American Sign Language morphology, syntax, and semantics better in children exposed to ASL in infancy or young childhood

Chapter 10

      vi. Similar critical period found in second-language learning (e.g., native Korean speakers learning English)

     vii. Learning a language earlier better (e.g., puberty worse outcome than in young childhood, middle-age outcome worse than in young adulthood)

   viii. (Exploration Box on language development in deaf versus hearing children)

  c. Critical period in language acquisition?

      i. May not be a critical period in language acquisition, difference may be related to level of exposure and emersion (which is much greater at younger ages)

     ii. Better thought of as an "optimal" or "sensitive" period

  d. Fact that some primates have primitive language skills supports idea of genetic component

  e. FOXP2 gene has been identified as important in the muscle skills necessary for speech

4. Nature and nurture working together

  a. Combination of learning and nativist position

      i. Both nature and nurture are critical

     ii. Acquisition of language skills dependent on other capabilities (e.g., cognitive and social skills)

    iii. Piaget took an interactionist-like position on language acquisition but he did not emphasize the impact of social interactions with adults (something Vygotsky did acknowledge)

    iv. Infants learn turn-taking before they use words

  b. Child-directed speech—style of speech used by adults when talking with children

      i. Simple, short sentences

     ii. Repetition and high-pitched voice (with exaggerated emphasis on words)

    iii. Infants pay attention to high-pitched sounds and varied intonation patterns

    iv. Caregiver–child-directed speech is dynamic (constantly changing in response to the child's utterances)

  c. Ability to pick up grammar requires more than mere exposure, children must be actively involved in using language

      i. Dutch-speaking children watching German television did not acquire German words or grammar

     ii. Child-directed speech simplifies child's task of figuring out the rules of language

  d. Expansion—adult method for improving language by encouraging children to expand on their verbalizations

      i. Effective adult conversation practices provide corrective feedback that is often subtle

  e. Language acquisition requires interaction between biologically prepared child with at least one conversational partner who ideally tailors his or her own speech to the child's level of understanding

  f. Complete mastery best with early exposure to language

  g. Language acquisition lays foundation for acquisition of writing, reading, and other skills

II The Infant

A. Mastery Motivation
   1. Mastery motivation—intrinsic (internal) motivation to succeed
   2. Infants intrinsically motivated to master environment (i.e., are innately curious)
   3. Key influences on mastery motivation
      a. Goal may hold different levels of value for different infants
      b. Mastery motivation higher when parents provide sensory stimulation designed to arouse child
      c. Mastery motivation higher in children with responsive parents (returning smiles, promptly responding to cries)
      d. Parents who stifle a child's initiative may create a child less likely to take on new tasks
   4. Early mastery motivation affects later achievement (i.e., parents can strengthen or weaken inborn motive to act)

B. Early Education
   1. No need to provide special early childhood experiences
      a. Elkind says that too much early stimulation may be detrimental
      b. Children simply need time to play and socialize as they choose
      c. Elkind worries that when their lives are too orchestrated by parents, children may lose self-initiative and intrinsic motivation to learn
      d. One study found that for each hour children spent watching "Baby Einstein" or "Brainy Baby" videos, they understood 6 to 8 less words than babies who did not watch the videos (but no long-term impact was studied)
      e. Highly academic preschool programs raise academic achievement but decrease expectancies of success and pride in accomplishment
      f. Best programs offer mix of play and academic skill building and are especially helpful to disadvantaged children
         i. Abecedarian Project—full-time infancy educational program resulted in impressive cognitive gains during and immediately after the program
      g. Alternative programs that focus on educating parents about importance of early environmental experience benefit children (e.g., "born to learn")
         i. Head Start is a federally funded program aimed at preparing disadvantaged children for school
         ii. Best programs build school-readiness skills but also allow time for play and socialization

III The Child

A. Initial Keys
   1. By age 3, children have internalized standards of performance and experience pride and shame depending on their level of success
   2. Some children are more achievement oriented and are higher achievers than others

B. Achievement Motivation
   1. Mastery orientation—drive to succeed despite challenge (i.e., persist in the face of failure, believe that increased efforts will pay off)
      a. High achievers blame failure on external factors

  b. High achievers credit success to internal factors

  c. Low achievers credit success to external factors (e.g., ease task)

  d. Low achievers blame failure on internal factors (e.g., lack of ability)

  e. Low achievers more likely to exhibit learned helplessness—tendency to avoid challenges (give up when they fail and believe that they can do little to improve)

 2. Child contributions

  a. Before age 7

   i. Unrealistic optimism even after poor performance

   ii. Even with poor performance, they continue to believe that they have the ability (older children tend to become more helpless with failure)

   iii. Young children "protected" from damaging self-perception from failure because they do not yet view ability as a stable capacity

   iv. Mastery (learning) goals—drive to learn new things to improve ability—dominates lower elementary grades' thinking

  b. Older children (late elementary and middle school)

   i. Acquire performance goals—emphasis on proving ability rather than improving ability and seek to be judged as smart and not dumb

   ii. Change is likely the result of cognitive advancement and accumulation of feedback in school

   iii. Focus on mastery/learning goals results in better school performance

   iv. Children high in mastery find the process of learning enjoyable (quenches their curiosity)

   v. Children high on performance goals are more in tune with the outcome (e.g., grade) and not the process of learning

   vi. Children with performance goal focus show more anxiety and boredom

   vii. Different goals may involve different neurological activity in response to performance outcomes

   viii. Children who believe that ability is primarily a fixed entity tend to set up

    performance goals

  c. Child's overall intelligence contributes to academic success (but just a piece of the puzzle)

   i. Motivation and achievement are both higher when children value a subject

 3. Parent contributions for fostering higher levels of achievement motivation

  a. Key to stress independence and self-reliance at early age

  b. Emphasize importance of doing well and meeting high standards

  c. Get involved in child's education and emphasize practices that stimulate curiosity

  d. Provide cognitively stimulating home (e.g., reading material, intellectual discussions, attending cultural events, holding high educational expectations)

  e. Parents can undermine school performance with lack of involvement, nagging, lack of guidance, using bribes for good grades, and criticizing bad grades

 4. Fryer study on whether students could be bribed into earning higher standardized test scores

  a. Test conducted in Chicago, New York, Dallas, and Washington, DC

b. In Chicago, 9th graders could earn up to $2,000 per year ($50 per each A earned on a test, $35 per each B earned on a test, $20 for each C earned on a test; similar scheme in New York)
c. In Washington, DC, students paid for studying and staying out of trouble
d. In Dallas, students paid $2 each time they read a book and passed a quiz on the reading
e. Program a "bust" in Chicago and New York, as students earned lots of money for good grades but showed no improvement on standardized test scores
f. Mixed results in Washington, with improvement in standardized test scores, but only for students rewarded for attendance
g. Biggest bang-for-buck in Dallas (one that paid the least and targeted reading, a behavior controlled by students)
h. Results indicate that best way to encourage students is by rewarding a behavior that they can control and that contributed to greater engagement in the course material

5. School contributions
    a. Focus on external rewards (e.g., grades) may encourage the adoption of performance goals rather than mastery goals
    b. Emphasis on competitive race for best grades a bad practice in that students come to view the grade and not learning as the goal
        i. Need to downplay competitive races for the best grades in class
        ii. Telling kids that the goal of the task is to sharpen the mind might help in school
        iii. Helplessness most likely with child who perceives he or she has low ability and is pursuing a performance goal
    c. Teachers should focus on nurturing intrinsic motivation in students
        i. Slow learners could be taught to view mistakes as a sign that they should change their strategies to improve competence rather than it being seen as a lack of ability
    d. Academic achievement highest when school encourages family involvement and regular parent–teacher interaction

C. Learning to Read
1. Acquiring the ability to read may be the most important achievement in school
2. Reading acquisition is an "unnatural task" that requires formal education
3. Mastering the alphabetic principle—idea that printed letters represent words—is critical step in reading
4. Ehri's four-step process related to alphabetic principle
    a. Prealphabetic phase—memorize specific visual cues (e.g., specific words)
    b. Partial alphabetic phase—learn shapes and letter sounds
    c. Full alphabetic phase—attain phonological awareness; sensitivity to sound system of a language (helps decipher new words)
        i. Phonological awareness of a language helps child to decode work through sight reading
        ii. Sight reading is fast and works well with hard-to-decode words
    d. Consolidation alphabet phase—letters regularly occurring together become grouped as a unit (e.g., ing)

5. Emergent literacy—developmental precursors of reading skills (including knowledge, skills, attitudes)
    a. Children with greater working memory and attention control have higher degree of reading readiness
    b. Repetitious reading enhances a child's vocabulary
        i. Key is to read with, not to, a child
        ii. Asking questions about the story also important
    c. Older children benefit from reading a book multiple times and sharing what they read with parents
    d. Rhyming stories foster phonological awareness
    e. Preschool emergent literacy skills (e.g., phonological awareness, word segmentation) provide fairly accurate idea of later reading skills
    f. Parents can help students get head start on reading by encouraging activities like rhyming, repeating the ABCs, and defining words
6. Skilled and unskilled readers
    a. Skilled readers have a solid understanding of the alphabetic principle (notion that letters must be connected to phonemes)
    b. Phonological awareness level critical (i.e., must connect sound to letter)
    c. Unskilled readers tend to visually skip words or parts of words
    d. Skilled readers do not rely on context to identify word, but may use context to help with comprehension
    e. Dyslexia—reading disability in individuals of normal intelligent and without sensory impairment and emotional difficulty
        i. Difficulty distinguishing similar letters or read word backwards (e.g., "top" becomes "pot")
        ii. More problems in auditory perception versus visual perception
        iii. Some evidence of differential brain responses (i.e., distinctive patterns of neural activity) in children with dyslexia
        iv. Show deficiencies in phonological awareness and tests of word recognition
        v. Life-long disability, not just delay in development
7. How should reading be taught?
    a. Phonetic approach (code-oriented) versus whole-word (look–say)
        i. Phonetic approach emphasizes letter–sound correspondence
        ii. Whole-language method emphasizes recognition of words by sight or using context of surrounding words
    b. Phonetics may be more important
        i. Teaching phonological awareness rules pays off with better reading skills
        ii. Computer games focused on distinguishing hard-to-distinguish sounds may improve phonetic performance
        iii. Whole-word method also important, especially for reading with meaning
D. Effective Schools
    1. No Child Left Behind Act of 2002 created pressure on schools to demonstrate effectiveness through annual increases in student proficiency
        a. Some schools seem to do a better job

2. Less important factors
   a. Level of funding directly aimed at classroom instruction may increase performance (i.e., not just added funds, but funds focused in specific areas)
   b. Average class size little to do with effectiveness of teaching (especially within a range of 18 to 40 students)
   c. Tutoring one-on-one can make big difference, especially for children from disadvantaged groups
   d. Amount of time spent in school (modest increases in time result in modest increases in skills)
   e. Spreading out learning (e.g., year-round schooling) minimal impact
   f. Ability grouping—segregating high- and low-ability students does not have any clear advantages but may have an impact on certain groups
      i. Gifted students can benefit by being grouped with gifted peers for a substantial portion of the school day
      ii. (Exploration Box on school integration and inclusion)
3. Factors that matter
   a. Students
      i. May be affected by genetic factors tied to aptitude
      ii. Schools with preponderance of economically advantaged children do better
      iii. Children from stimulating home environments do better
      iv. Many schools serving disadvantaged populations are highly effective at motivating students and preparing them for future jobs
      v. High achieving parents provide genes and may select stronger schools (example of passive-gene environment interaction)
   b. Teachers
      i. Better-quality teachers (e.g., quality of teacher's undergraduate educational institutions and their licensure exam score) lead to better outcomes
      ii. Good teachers can have significantly positive impacts on students' performance (50 points higher on standardized tests)
      iii. Criteria may be how far teachers can advance students each year
   c. School/classroom environment
      i. Strong emphasis on academics
      ii. Task-oriented but comfortable environment
      iii. Effective management of discipline problems
      iv. Schools supported by parents and communities
   d. Goodness of fit—match between learner and teaching method
      i. Highly distractible students best with computer-assisted instruction
      ii. More positive outcomes when teacher and student share similar backgrounds

IV The Adolescent
   A. Declining Levels of Achievement
      1. Teens (especially in grades 6-9) tend to become less dedicated to academics
      2. Student risk factors include minority group status, low maternal education and mental health, stressful life events, family size, and father absence

3. Students better at analyzing causes of events tend to view strengths and weaknesses more realistically and may lose some academic self-esteem
4. Family characteristics impact achievement
   a. Poorer performance in minority and single-parent families and when mom is less educated or has a mental disorder
   b. Students who believe that parents are involved in their schooling tend to be more academically motivated
5. Increasing peer-group awareness that leads to a motivation to not look dumb and to make parents proud
6. Peer pressures may undermine achievement motivation
   a. Especially negative impact on academics in lower-income minority students
      i. Thought of by peers as "acting white"
      ii. Culture may not value academics
      iii. Parental valuing of academics may cancel negative peer impact
      iv. Minority students with supportive peers show strengthened academic achievement
      v. A strong ethnic identity can help, but cannot overcome the negative effects of discrimination experienced by many minority students
7. Poor person–environment fit may contribute to decline in motivation
   a. Reaching puberty may result in drop in self-esteem
   b. Changes in grade level of transition into middle school do not significantly impact achievement
   c. Most negative impact in middle-school transition if child's developmental needs do not match well with school environment (e.g., look for autonomy while school demands less autonomy)
      i. Giving students a sense of ownership and some degree of control may improve interest and motivation
      ii. Level of support by teachers during middle-school transition is critical (i.e., more supportive teachers, more positive student outlook on learning)
   d. Educators can keep adolescents engaged by providing a better fit between developmental needs and interests of adolescents
   e. Parents can help by remaining supportive and involved in their child's education
B. Science and Math Education
   1. Skills necessary for an industrialized society
   2. Students in the United States score above average (but not at top level) on tests of math and science ability
   3. Poorer cross-cultural showing of U.S. students mainly due to cultural differences in attitudes concerning education and academics (especially when compared to students in Asian nations)
      a. Students in Asian nations spend more time in school and engaging in on-task behavior
      b. Teachers in Asian nations have different approaches to education
         i. Engage in more discourse about correct answers
      c. Students in Asian nations (especially Japan) receive more homework
      d. Parents in Asian nations show strong commitment to education

i. Parents in Asian nations tend to be less satisfied with how their children are doing when compared with American parents
  e. Peers in Asian nations tend to have higher value for achievement and have high standards concerning performance levels
  f. Students, parents, and teachers in Asian nations have strong belief that hard work will pay off
  g. Key cross-cultural finding is that the most effective education occurs when teachers, parents, and students all make education a top priority
C. Integrating Work and School
  1. Many American and Canadian children work outside of school; fewer in other industrialized nations
  2. Working students (at least 20 hours per week) experience positive and negative effects
    a. Working students gain knowledge of work, consumer issues, and financial management
    b. Working students have lower GPAs
    c. Working students are more disengaged from school (e.g., skip class)
    d. Greater risk for psychological distress in working students
    e. Disenchanted students more disenchanted when working more hours
    f. Working associated with academic struggles, poorer academic performance
    g. Some studies have found significantly fewer negative impacts of employment
    h. Nature of job important in determining impact of work
      i. Working routine and repetitive jobs that do not call on academic skills tend to not build character or teach new skills
      ii. Jobs that provide opportunity for advancement and teach useful skills may be of benefit (e.g., increase mastery motivation)
D. Pathways to Adulthood
  1. Educational pathways somewhat constrained by intelligence and aptitude levels
  2. Dropping out of high school can negatively impact career path
  3. Making the most of your abilities is critical
  4. Many factors impact outcome (e.g., quality of school, parental encouragement, extent to which peers value school)
  5. Students with good grades are more likely to complete high school, and number of graduates varies by ethnicity (e.g., 92% of European Americans, 86% of African Americans, 85% of Asian Americans, 70% of Hispanics)
  6. Rates for completing 4-year college degree also vary by culture (e.g., 30% of European American, 17% of African Americans, 49% of Asian Americans, 11% of Hispanics)

V The Adult
A. Achievement Motivation
  1. Achievement motivation stable through adulthood
  2. Women with higher levels of education more likely to be motivated to achieve career success
  3. Achievement motivation more affected by changing work and family contexts than by age

        a. Little evidence that elderly adults inevitably lose their motivation to pursue important goals

B. Literacy—Ability to Use Printed Information to Function
    1. Fourteen percent of adults in United States at lowest level of literacy
        a. One-quarter are immigrants learning English as second language
            i. About two-thirds of illiterate non-immigrants did not finish high school
        b. Twenty-nine percent of adults have rudimentary or basic literacy skills
        c. U.S. also has some of the most highly literate adults and one of the largest pockets of illiterate adults
    2. Literacy important to economic security
        a. Nearly half of adults with lowest literacy live in poverty
        b. Improved literacy does not automatically raise from poverty
    3. Programs to raise literacy in adults are rarely effective
        a. Often unmotivating and have high dropout rates (70-80%)
        b. Adults do not stay; report boredom and that program did not meet needs
        c. Materials often geared toward children

C. Continuing Education
    1. Many adults seek higher education
        a. Forty percent of college students are 25 or older
        b. Number of adults in college (adult learners, nontraditionals, returning students, mature students, lifelong learners) expected to increase
    2. Older students more likely to be motivated by internal factors
        a. Women more likely to return to school for personal enrichment
        b. Men more likely to return to school as work requirement
        c. Internal motivation leads to deeper understanding (better retention)
    3. Lifelong education difficult to fit into schedule
    4. Benefits to lifelong education outweigh drawbacks
        a. Allows adults to remain competitive in rapidly changing fields
        b. Can aid in career advancement
        c. Higher education associated with maintaining or improving physical and mental health

SUGGESTIONS FOR CLASS DISCUSSIONS OR PROJECTS

1. Play samples of children's language (YouTube is a nice source, search using "children's speech"). Ideally, try to capture children of different ages. Have students identify any examples of over- or underextension, overregularization, holophrases, and other early language limitations discussed in the text.

2. Ask students to discuss factors that should or could be used to indicate readiness for school. Traditionally, age 6 years has been used as the indicator, which works fine for the average child. Besides age, what other factors should be considered? You could also ask students about factors that could be used to indicate a readiness for college. Part of this discussion could focus on the types of skills that students would have wished they had when they began college.

3. A lack of achievement motivation is a major detriment to academic performance. It is likely that many students in the class have personal experience and strong opinions on how schools could increase the motivation of students to attend class and succeed in college. Have students make a "top 10" list of things that would/could motivate them to do better in class. Randomly select students to present their lists. Did they differ by grade level (freshman versus senior), sex (male versus female), or age (traditional 18- to 25-year-olds versus middle-aged or older students)? How many items on the list were types of external motivators (likely most to all)? Ask students how they could best change their self to improve performance.

A second, or alterative project would be an exploration/debate over the idea of paying students for high levels of academic performance. The text presents a brief description of recent research on this topic conducted by a team led by Fryer. For this project, have students review the book material and read Ripley's (2010) *Time* magazine article on the subject. The class could then be divided into a "pro-pay" versus "anti-pay" groups for the debate.

   Ripley, A. (2010). Is cash the answer? *Time*, 4/19/2010, 175(15), 40-47.

4. Many classrooms now include students from a wide range of ages. The text authors indicate that traditional-age freshman and older students may be operating under different types of motivation (e.g., internal versus external factors). An interesting exercise would involve having students list the top three reasons for them seeking their degree. This list could then be shared with the class, and comparison across a number of dimensions (e.g., age, race, sex) could be discussed.

5. The "adult education" market is expected to increase significantly in the next few decades, and an increasing number of institutions are marketing directly to this population by focusing on options like online courses, evening course, or credits for prior life experience. Have students learn more about their own campus's effort in this area by reviewing and reporting on ways in which your institution is pursing this market niche. The main source for this information will likely involve a Web search or a visit to the admissions office.

6. In Chapter 10, students are provided with a superb review of the progression of normal language development. In addition, the authors note the existence of two types of deviation; "dyslexia" and "aphasia." In reality, there are numerous speech and language disorders that impact children, adolescents, and adults. The purpose of this assignment is to help students increase their knowledge about a type of speech or language disorder that is not covered in the text. To complete the project, students should conduct a Web search for articles using the terms "speech disorders" and "language disorders." Based on this search, they should select one specific speech or language deviation issue on which to focus (e.g., stuttering, language development in autistics). Once they have selected their topic, they should conduct a more detailed search on it that could include both Web-based and hardcopy research or journal articles. They should then generate a one-page, double-sided pamphlet discussing the disorder. The goal of the pamphlet should be to introduce the reader to the disorder and then provide some advice on the best way to assist individuals with the problem.

Cognitive Coaching: A Process for Teaching and Learning (1997, Films for the Humanities & Sciences, VHS, 39 minutes). Describes and shows demonstrations on methods of improving performance in education settings.

Language Development: Birth to Two-and-a-Half Years (2001, Insight Media, VHS, 29 minutes). Nice video on the impacts of environment and biology on early language development.

Promoting Language and Literacy (2003, Insight Media, DVD, 29 minutes). Follows the impact of caregivers on the development of literacy in children.

Successful Language Development Strategies in the Early Childhood Classroom for English Language Learners and Native Speakers (2003, Insight Media, DVD, 25 minutes). Focuses on strategies for facilitating the acquisition of language in native/non-native speakers.

The Baby Human: To Talk (2003, Insight Media, DVD, 52 minutes). Follows the progression of language over the course of the first years of life.

SUGGESTED WEBSITES

Context for Engagement and Motivation in Reading
http://www.readingonline.org/articles/art_index.asp?HREF=/articles/handbook/guthrie/index.html

How Does Your Child Hear and Talk?
http://www.asha.org/public/speech/development/chart.htm

National Center on Adult Literacy
http://www.literacy.org/

SparkNotes: Language and Cognition
http://www.sparknotes.com/psychology/psych101/languageandcognition/section2.rhtml

Speech and Language Milestones
http://www.ldonline.org/article/6313

SUGGESTED READINGS

Dekeyser, R., Alfi-Shabtay, I, and Ravid, D. (2010). Cross-linguistic evidence for the nature of age effects in second language development. *Applied Psycholinguistics*, 31(3), 413-438.

Ferguson, C., and Johnson, L. (2010). Building supportive and friendly school environments. *Childhood Education 2010 Annual Themes*, 86(5), 302-306.

Fromkin, V., Rodman, R., and Hyams, N. (2011). *An Introduction to Language* (9th ed.). Belmont, CA: Wadsworth Publishing.

Wise, B. (2009). Adolescent literacy: The cornerstone of student success. *Journal of Adolescent & Adult Literacy*, 52(5), 369-375.

Wood, C., Pillinger, C. and Jackson, E. (2010). Understanding the nature and impact of young reader's literacy interactions with talking books and during adult reading support. *Computers and Education*, 54(1), 190-198.

SELF AND PERSONALITY

LEARNING OBJECTIVES

After students have read and studied the material in this chapter, they should be able to answer the following questions:

CONCEPTUALIZING THE SELF AND PERSONALITY

1. How is personality typically defined, and what are the five principles of defining personality?

2. How do psychoanalytic, trait, and social learning theories explain personality development?

THE INFANT

3. How does self-concept emerge during infancy, and how does it change across the lifespan?

4. How has infant temperament been categorized? How do these temperament styles interact with caregiver characteristics? How does temperament relate to later personality?

THE CHILD

5. What changes occur in the development of children's self-esteem? What factors influence self-esteem?

6. How does personality evolve over childhood, and what do children understand of their personality?

THE ADOLESCENT

7. How do adolescents conceptualize their selves, including self-esteem and personality?

8. What factors influence the development of identity during adolescence? How do adolescents make vocational choices, and how does work affect adolescents' identities?

THE ADULT

9. How does personality change during adulthood? Why do people change or remain the same? How does culture influence personality?

10. What is the focus of each of Erikson's psychosocial stages? What factors can influence how each crisis is resolved? Is a "midlife crisis" common?

11. How do career paths change during adulthood? How do adults cope with age-related changes that affect their working selves? How are older adults influenced by retirement?

12. How can we characterize successful aging?

I Conceptualizing the Self and Personality

A. Basic Concepts

   1. Personality—unique, organized combinations of attributes, motives, values, behaviors that make up an individual

   2. Most people describe personality in terms of dispositional traits—relatively enduring traits like extraversion or introversion

   3. People differ in characteristic adaptations—more situation-specific and changeable ways in which people adapt to environment (e.g., motives, self-conceptions)

   4. People differ in narrative identities—unique integrative "life stories" we construct about our past and futures

      a. Cultural and situational influences help shape all aspects of personality

   5. Description of personality often includes

      a. Self-concept—perceptions (positive to negative) of your own characteristics

         i. Self-concept may be unrealistic (e.g., think you are dull while you are actually brilliant)

      b. Self-esteem—evaluation (positive to negative) of self-worth (i.e., "how good am I")

      c. Identity—overall sense on one's self

B. Theories of Personality Development

   1. Psychoanalytic theory

      a. Sigmund Freud

         i. Children progress through universal stages of psychosexual development

         ii. Gist of personality is formed in first five years

         iii. Unfavorable early experience (e.g., harsh parenting) leads to permanent mark on personality

      b. Erik Erikson (neo-Freudian approach)

         i. Personality evolves through challenges associated with different stages of development

         ii. When compared with Freud, Erikson placed more emphasis on social influences (e.g., peers, culture), the adaptive nature of the rational ego, the possibility to overcome effects of harmful early experiences, and the potential for personality growth during the adult years

      c. Trait theory

         i. Psychometric approach—guided by the development of intelligence tests

         ii. Personality is set of measurable traits (e.g., sociable-unsociable)

         iii. Relies on factor analysis—statistical technique to identify items that are correlated with each other but not with other factors

         iv. Big Five factor model—five key dimensions of neuroticism, extraversion, openness to experience, agreeableness, conscientiousness

         v. Big Five traits may be genetically determined and emerge early in life

         vi. Traits seem universal

         vii. Levels of Big Five traits vary by culture (in the way they are expressed)

      d. Social learning theory
         i. Developed by researchers like Albert Bandura and Walter Mischel
         ii. Reject notion of stages of personality and question existence of enduring traits
         iii. People change as environments change—situation is key
         iv. Consistency in personality if situation is consistent, but not necessarily consistent if situation is different
         v. Behavioral tendencies shaped by interactions with others in specific social situations
         vi. Because social context is so powerful, consistency over time is most likely if social environment remains the same (i.e., different personalities in different situations)

II The Infant

  A. The Emerging Self
    1. Pattern of emerging self
      a. Infants born without sense of self, but quickly develop a sense through perceptions of their body and actions
        i. By 2 to 3 months, discover that they can cause things to happen
      b. During first 6 months, infants first discover properties of physical self, distinguish self from rest of the world, and act upon other people and objects
      c. During second 6 months, realize that they are separate beings from others, joint attention—begin sharing perceptual experience with others
    2. Self-recognition—ability to recognize oneself in mirror or photograph
      a. Researched by watching children's reaction to self
      b. Recognition in mirror indicates clear evidence of self-recognition (occurs by 18-24 months)
    3. Categorical self—classification by socially meaningful dimensions (e.g., sex, age) (i.e., figuring out what is "like me" and what is "not like me")
      a. Master skill of awareness of physical self between 18 and 24 months
    4. Self-awareness driven by several factors
      a. Cognitive development (mentally retarded children slower to recognize themselves)
      b. Social experience/interactions (toddlers with secure attachments better able to recognize themselves in a mirror)
    5. Self-awareness at 18-24 months paves way for later social and emotional development
      a. Become able to talk about themselves and assert their will
      b. Experience self-conscious emotions such as pride
      c. Coordinate their own perspectives with those of others
  B. Temperament
    1. Temperament—dimension of "infant personality" early, genetically based tendencies to respond in predictable ways that gives insight into a baby's personality
    2. Easiness and difficultness: theory of temperament by Thomas and Chess
      a. Three categories of temperament (easy, difficult, slow-to-warm-up) found in infants
      b. Easy temperament—typically happy, content, open to new experiences

      c. Difficult temperament—irritable, irregular in habits, and react negatively to change

      d. Slow-to-warm-up temperament—relatively inactive, somewhat moody, and have only moderately regular daily schedules

         i. Slow to adapt to new people and situations

      e. Longitudinal study: 40% easy, 10% difficult, 15% percent slow-to-warm-up, remaining third could not be clearly placed

      f. Temperament in infancy has little to do with adult adjustment

3. Behavioral inhibition—tendency to be extremely shy and reserved in unfamiliar situations (Kagan)

      a. In Big Five terms, inhibited children are low in extraversion but show neuroticism and anxiety

      b. Estimated 15% of toddlers are inhibited and 10% are extremely inhibited

      c. Early tendencies seen by 4 months with fussing and fretting

      d. Impact can be seen into the adolescent years

      e. Kagan and colleagues conclude that behavioral inhibition is biologically rooted

4. Surgency, negative affect, and effortful control (Rothbart): dimensions of temperament that emerge in infancy or toddlerhood/early childhood

      a. Surgency/extraversion—tendency to actively and energetically approach new experiences

      b. Negatively affectivity—tendency to be sad, easily frustrated, and irritable

      c. Effortful control—ability to sustain attention, control one's behavior, and regulate one's emotions

      d. Rothbart's ideas very influential; share similarities with Big Five dimensions

      e. Meaningful connections exist between temperament in infancy/early childhood and personality in later life

5. Goodness of fit—extent to which child's temperament is compatible with demand and expectations of social world

      a. Relationship between child and environment affects continuity of temperament

         i. "Carl" who was studied in Thomas and Chess study was difficult but was with responsive dad who supported his behavior

         ii. Research suggests that behaviorally inhibited children remain inhibited if parents are overprotective or impatient, but can overcome inhibitions if their parents create a good fit by preparing them for potentially upsetting experiences

      b. Parents should get to know baby as an individual and allow for personality quirks

         i. Teaching parents of irritable babies how to better interpret infant cues can produce calmer infants

III The Child

  A. Elaborating on a Sense of Self

    1. Toddlers tell about emerging self-concept through personal pronouns (e.g., "I," "Mine")

2. A sense of categorical self is exhibited when they describe themselves in terms of age and sex and other factors (e.g., "Katie big girl")
3. Preschoolers' sense of self is concrete and physical
   a. Describe selves in terms of physical characteristics ("I have blue eyes"), physical activities and accomplishments ("I can run real fast"), and preferences ("I like pizza")
   b. Few descriptions of psychological traits or inner qualities
4. Self-conceptions become more sophisticated around age 8 due in part to cognitive growth
   a. First begin to describe enduring qualities or traits ("funny")
   b. Form social identities by defining themselves as part of a social unit ("I am a Brownie Scout")
   c. Become capable of social comparison—use information about how they compare to others to characterize and evaluate themselves
      i. Young children tend to believe they are the greatest
      ii. By first grade, are very interested in social comparisons and more aware of their implications

B. Self-Esteem
   1. Harter developed self-perception scale measures
      a. Self-esteem becomes more differentiated or multidimensional with age
         i. Preschoolers' self-esteem defined by competence (physical and cognitive) and personal/social adequacy (social acceptance)
      b. By mid-elementary years, children able to differentiate between five dimensions of self-worth
         i. Scholastic competence—does well in school
         ii. Social acceptance—is popular
         iii. Behavioral conduct—does not get into trouble
         iv. Athletic competence—is good at sports
         v. Physical appearance—feels good-looking
      c. By third to ninth grade, self-esteem is multidimensional and hierarchical
      d. Accuracy of self-evaluations increases steadily over the elementary-school years, but can reflect a desire to be liked or good at activities
         i. Self-evaluations first inflated, then more realistic by school-age (age 8)
      e. Children begin to form a sense of ideal self—idea of who they want to be (versus who they are)
         i. Gap between real and ideal self increases with age
         ii. Older children have greater risk of thinking that they fall short of what they should be
      f. Social comparisons do not always come up well
      g. Tendency for parents and teachers to offer more critical feedback may contribute to decrease in self-esteem from early to middle childhood

C. Influences on Self-Esteem
   1. Differences exist in levels of self-esteem
      a. Levels of self-esteem may lie in genes (i.e., self-esteem may be a heritable trait)

   b. More capable and socially attractive children have more success that can contribute to more positive self-concept and to future academic achievement

   c. More positive social feedback from parents

     i. Parental behavior promoting self-esteem (e.g., parents who are warm and democratic tend to have securely attached children)

     ii. Loving parents communicate approval and acceptance

     iii. Effective parents enforce clearly stated rules

   d. Once established, self-esteem stable over school years and correlated with measures of good adjustment

   e. Despite the importance of self-esteem, some feel that American educators go overboard in making all children feel good about themselves

     i. Damon maintains that self-esteem means nothing unless it grows out of actual achievement

     ii. Children need real opportunities to learn about their limitations and to not give them an inflated and unrealistic sense of their worth

   f. Helping children succeed at tasks can boost self-esteem and lead to future achievements

 D. The Developing Personality

  1. Temperament shaped into predictable personality during childhood

   a. Some links between temperament in early childhood and later personality

     i. Inhibited 3-year-olds shy as teens

     ii. Difficult 3-year-olds may end up as impulsive teens

   b. Link between temperament and Big Five factors (e.g., behavioral inhibition in early childhood predictive of low extraversion in middle childhood)

  2. Cannot accept Freud's view that personality is set by age five

  3. Some stabilization in childhood, but then some traits change while others remain about the same

  4. Some characteristics do not gel until adolescence or adulthood

IV The Adolescent

 A. Self-Conceptions

  1. During adolescence, self-descriptions become

   a. Less physical ("I have brown eyes") and more psychological ("I am lonely")

   b. Less concrete ("I love sports") and more abstract ("I an a pseudoliberal")

   c. More differentiated (splits into more distinct aspects)

   d. More integrated, creating a more coherent self-portrait

   e. More self-aware and reflective (may become painfully self-conscious)

 B. Self-Esteem

  1. Self-esteem tends to decrease from childhood to early adolescence

   a. Drop may be the result of more knowledge and realism about strengths and weaknesses

   b. Drop more common among white females, especially those facing multiple stressors (e.g., puberty, dating, entering middle school)

   c. Self-esteem affected by social context and social comparisons

Chapter 11   166

d. Big-fish-little-pond effect—academic self-esteem tends to be lower when the average academic achievement of one's classmates is high and personal academic achievement is low
    i. Certain academic transitions (e.g., from regular classes to gifted classes) might lead to drop in self-esteem
    ii. Special education students in regular classes with higher-achieving classmates tend to have higher academic self-esteem
2. Adolescence is not as hazardous to self as most people believe
  a. Most adolescents emerging from the developmental period with higher self-esteem than they had at the onset of the period
  b. Opportunities to feel competent in areas they find important and to experience support and approval from important people in their lives can positively impact self-esteem in this age group
  c. As adults, adolescents with low self-esteem tend to have poorer physical and mental health and higher levels of criminal behavior

C. Forging a Sense of Identity
1. Erikson argues that adolescence is a crisis of identity versus role confusion and moratorium period
  a. Adolescence is the time to attempt to form own identity (definition of who you are, where you are going, and where you fit into society)
    i. Must integrate separate perceptions that are part of self-concept into a coherent sense of self
    ii. Search involves grappling with many questions about beliefs
  b. Struggling with issues of self may lead adolescents to experience "identity crisis" resulting from
    i. Changing body image and adjusting to being sexual being
    ii. Cognitive growth allows for more sophisticated understanding of self
    iii. Social demands force children to "grow up"
  c. Society supports "moratorium period"—time of relative freedom from responsibility for adolescents
2. Developmental trends
  a. Marcia expanded on Erikson's theory and proposed four levels of identity statuses
    i. Key to status level is whether person has experienced a *crisis* or achieved *commitment*
    ii. Diffusion status—no crisis, no commitment (common in 12- to 15-year-olds)
    iii. Foreclosure status—a commitment decision without a crisis is made ("I am going to be a doctor like my dad," while never having thought about what suits one best)
    iv. Moratorium status—crisis experienced, no commitment, around age 18; many question religion, drug use, changing majors, and enter a time of active exploration of ideas (but with no decisions)
    v. Identity achievement status—crisis experienced, commitment made (about 20% of 18-year-olds, and 40% of college students)

  b. Females are as concerned as males about establishing a career identity, but are
    more interested than males in identity aspects related with sexuality, interpersonal relationships, and balancing career and family goals
  c. Many people achieve a sense of identity achievement status in late teens or early 20s, but this is not the end of identity formation process
  d. People often reopen the question of who they are and recycle through the identity moratorium and achievement statuses throughout later life
  e. Identify formation occurs at different rates in different domains of identity
    i. Archer found 5% of adolescents in same identity status in all four domains (occupational choice, gender-role attitudes, religious beliefs, political ideology) and 90% were in two or three statuses across the four areas
  f. Life-story approach to studying identity (Exploration Box on life stories)

2. Developing a positive ethnic identity
  a. Ethnic identity—a sense of personal identification with an ethnic group and its values, customs, and traditions
  b. Members of minority groups tend to place more emphasis on ethnic identity, as the members of majority group often do not think of having an ethnic identity
  c. Infants notice difference in different ethnic faces
  d. Preschoolers learn about different racial and ethnic categories and behaviors associated with their culture (e.g., Chicano handshake)
  e. Ethnic identity formed same way as other identities (e.g., vocational)
    i. School-age and young adolescents mostly in foreclosure or diffusion status and mid to late teens may move into moratorium and achievement status
    ii. Some do not reflect ethnic identity until 20s
  f. Positive sense of ethnic identity established when parents teach them about cultural traditions and prepare them to live in a diverse society
  g. Positive ethnic identity can protect from effects of racial discrimination and can reduce symptoms of depression

3. Vocational identity and choice
  a. Central aspect of identity with major implications toward adulthood
  b. Age 10, explore vocational possibilities but not in realistic fashion
  c. Early choices tend to follow gender guidelines (boys-masculine occupations, girls-feminine occupations)
  d. During adolescence, choices more realistic, weighing factors other than just wishes (e.g., interests, capacities, values)
  e. Older adolescents begin to consider realities of job market and the physical and intellectual requirements for a job
  f. Main developmental trend involves increasing realism with age
  g. Adolescents from lower-income families and minority groups have difficulty in forming positive vocational identity
    i. Aim high at first, but then become aware of constraints and lower career aspirations
  h. In adolescence, gender norms still impact vocational choice (especially for girls)

i. More young women are aspiring to high-status jobs (traditionally male careers) but many women continue to aim at feminine stereotypes, lower-status and lower-paying careers

i. Many teens do not follow vocational theorist pattern and explore many options

4. Influences on identity formation

    a. Identity formation product of five factors

        i. Cognitive development enables one to consider possible future identities

        ii. Personality traits impact exploration (e.g., low neuroticism and high openness to experience and conscientiousness)

        iii. Relationships with parents—youth in diffusion most rejected while those in achievement have high support; parents can be "too loving" and allow adolescents few chances to make own decisions; best option is a warm and democratic parenting style

        iv. Opportunities to explore (experiences outside the home)—college often time of moratorium, allows for exposure to diverse ideas

        v. Broader cultural context plays role in formation of identity; Navajo adolescent experience differs from that in Western society

II The Adult

A. Self-Conceptions

    1. Age differences

        a. Self-esteem high in childhood, drops in adolescence, rises gradually in adulthood, and drops in older age

           i. Little truth to stereotype that most older adults suffer from a poor self-image and significant drops in self-esteem

        b. How elderly people maintain positive self-image despite loss

           i. Reduce gap between real selves and ideal selves (i.e., scale down visions of what they can ideally be like and what they will be like)

           ii. Adjust goals and standards of self-evaluation to lessen perception of failure (i.e., apply different measuring sticks in evaluating selves)

           iii. Comparing self to other older adults involves a change in comparison group (e.g., often compare selves to older unhealthy people)

           iv. Not internalizing ageist stereotypes (resist applying negative stereotypes concerning aging that can be damaging to self-perception)

        c. Research on the impact of aging stereotypes

           i. Priming older individuals with negative and positive stereotypes can impact their rate of walking (negative prime led to slower gait)

           ii. Positive attitudes toward aging may increase longevity while negative attitudes are associated with higher risk for cardiovascular events like heart attacks

           iii. Rothmans and Brandtstadter found that holding negative stereotypes at age 54 led to negative self-perceptions in later life, but early self-perceptions did not affect later aging stereotypes

2. Cultural differences
   a. Individualistic culture—individual goal valued above group, typical of North America, Western Europe
   b. Collectivist culture—group goal valued above individual's goals, typical of Asia, Africa, Latin America
   c. Americans tend to focus on unique aspects of general self and attempt to maintain high self-esteem
   d. Japanese tend to focus on behavior in specific context and are more self-critical
   e. Americans describe themselves in terms of generalized personality traits found in most situations; Japanese describe specific behavior in context
      i. Americans adopt trait theory
      ii. Japanese adopt social learning theory
   f. Americans more obsessed with maintaining high self-esteem and tend to see themselves as above average on this trait, while Japanese and other East Asians more modest and self-critical
   g. Cultural differences in self-description seen as early as age 3 to 4
      i. Parents contribute to cultural differences through everyday conversation (e.g., American mothers tell stories in which the child is a star, Chinese mothers discuss experiences of the family group)
   h. Cross-cultural differences challenge many assumptions about healthy personality development
      i. Western assumption is that you cannot function without a well-developed sense of individual identity, but in many other cultures, it's "self-in-relation-to-others" that matters
      ii. Asking individuals about self may be culturally biased form of assessment
B. Continuity and Discontinuity in Personality
   1. Do people retain their rankings?
      a. Big Five personality traits relatively enduring (i.e., good deal of consistency in rankings within a group), but individual change is possible
      b. Tendency to be consistent increases with age; age 50 and beyond quite consistent
   2. Do mean personality scores change?
      a. Focus on stability in the average level of a trait
      b. Younger and older adults tend to have quite different personalities on average
         i. Differences likely due to generational or cohort effects
      c. There is much cross-age consistency in rankings on Big Five, although some small changes possible
         i. Openness to new experience and extraversion decline modestly from adolescence to middle-age
         ii. Emotional stability, agreeableness, and conscientiousness increase from adolescence to middle-age
      d. Big Five traits appear to be biologically based temperaments that undergo a universal process of maturational change
         i. Activity level and openness to new experience both tend to decline after age 50

     ii. Agreeableness tends to increase after age 50
   e. Summary points on Big Five traits
     i. Good deal of cross-age consistency in Big Five traits
     ii. Cohort effects suggest that historical context impacts personality
     iii. Personality growth in adulthood differs by factor
     iv. Little personality change in middle to later adulthood
  3. Why do people change or remain the same?
   a. Stability may be accounted for by
     i. Heredity (genetic inheritance)
     ii. Lasting effects of childhood experiences
     iii. Stability of environments
     iv. Gene-environment correlations promote continuity
   b. Significant changes may be explained by
     i. Biological factors (e.g., diseases)
     ii. Changes in social environments (including major life events)
     iii. Poor fit between person and the environment (e.g., independent women lacking traditional feminine traits show more midlife change personality than those fitting stereotypical feminine roles)
   c. Although several factors contribute to stability, change in personality is common (especially if there is a change in the environment or a poor fit between personality and lifestyle)
   d. Personality development impacts physical health and psychological well-being
     i. Good health linked to higher levels of conscientiousness and extraversion and low levels of neuroticism
 C. Erikson Ian Psychosocial Growth
  1. Psychosocial stage theory of personality development with eight psychosocial stages
   a. Both maturational forces and social demands push humans through the eight stages
   b. Later conflicts more difficult to resolve if early conflicts not resolved successfully
   c. Optimal development involves a health balance of conflicts
  2. The path to adulthood
   a. Trust versus mistrust—infants learn to trust caregiver, or mistrust may develop
   b. Autonomy versus shame and doubt—toddlers learn self as they assert themselves and gain sense of autonomy
   c. Initiative versus guilt—4- or 5-year-olds gain sense of self/pride in accomplishment of goals to form initiative
   d. Industry versus inferiority—elementary school students begin to make social comparisons and master cognitive skills, if this goes well, they can acquire a sense of industry
   e. Identity versus role confusion—adolescent crisis of establishing unique sense of self

3. Early adult intimacy
   a. Intimacy versus isolation—first psychosocial conflict in adulthood
      i. Share self through intimacy in relationship with another
      ii. Failure may lead to being threatened by commitment (fear of being "tied down")
      iii. College graduates have better-developed sense of resolution of intimacy issues than college seniors
   b. Women may gain identity by choosing mate and taking on role of wife
   c. Women with masculine gender-role orientation follow identity-before-intimacy route (route that characterizes most men)
   d. Erikson's theory better fit for men than women
4. Midlife generativity
   a. Psychosocial crisis of generativity versus stagnation
      i. Generativity involves the capacity to produce something that will outlive you and to care about welfare of future generations
      ii. Teaching and parenting to younger generation examples of generativity
   b. Research on generativity in midlife
      i. Valliant's research found that 50-something males expressed more interest in caring for their own children or younger people at work than 40-somethings
      ii. Adults who have achieved a sense of identity and intimacy more likely to achieve generativity as well
      iii. Generativity can be thought of in terms of successful parenting, but it can be achieved by those without children
      iv. Research supports idea of impressive psychological growth during middle age
5. Old age integrity
   a. Psychosocial crisis of integrity versus despair—finding meaning of life that will help them face the inevitability of death
      i. Sense of identity in early adulthood predicts generativity and integrity in later life
      ii. Sense of integrity is related to a high sense of psychological well-being and low levels of depression or despair
   b. Life review—process of reflecting on past and resolving conflicts
      i. Life review can help one find meaning and coherence of life and to prepare for death
      ii. Those who reminisce show stronger sense of integrity and better overall adjustment than those who stew about unresolved regrets
      iii. Some use life review as a therapy for use with older adults
      iv. Conducting a life review may help people develop better sense of ego integrity and adjustment
D. Midlife Crisis?
   1. Daniel Levinson proposed stage theory of personality development
      a. Stages are universal and describe an unfolding "life structure"—overall pattern of activities reflecting priorities and relationships
      b. Saw adults as building a life structure across time

c. Midlife crisis—intensely unsettled time of life between age 40 and 45
d. Levinson popularizes concept of "midlife crisis" (especially in men)
   i. Many question existence of genuine "midlife crisis" for majority of people during middle age
   ii. May reflect response to life event such as divorce or job change
   iii. Midlife crisis may be more appropriately referred to as "midlife questioning"

E. Vocational Development and Adjustment
   1. Establishing a career
      a. Early adulthood is time for exploring career possibilities
      b. Mentors can be of great help in getting careers launched
      c. From age 21 to 36, young adults tend to progress from wide-open exploration of careers to trial commitments to stabilization of choices
         i. In one study, by the time they reached age 36, the average adult had held seven full-time or training positions
         ii. Adults often reach career peak in their 40s (e.g., have major responsibilities and define themselves in terms of work)
      d. Personality and person-environment fit can impact job performance
         i. Job performance correlated with scores on Big Five dimensions of conscientiousness, extraversion, and emotional stability
         ii. Person-environment fit also critical
      e. Gender can negatively impact vocation
         i. Women in U.S. continue to earn about 80 cents for every dollar earned by men
         ii. Gender-role norms affect expectations and choice of subordinate careers
         iii. Women more likely to interrupt careers for families, to drop down to part-time work, and to decline promotions that would involve a transfer to a new location
         iv. Women with children at home may show reduced productivity at work
         v. Women at the top of their careers may have to remain single and childless to achieve this success
         vi. Women less likely to enjoy career boost associated with non-working spouse
      f. Discrimination can limit women's vocational development by
         i. Leading to less pay for female jobs (even when as intellectually demanding as male jobs)
         ii. Limiting how far a woman can rise in an organizations
      g. Work can have positive impact on personality; lack of employment can increase the risk for stress, depression, and other psychological problems
   2. The aging worker
      a. Older workers as competent as younger workers and more satisfied with their jobs
      b. Older workers outperform younger workers in areas like good citizenship and safety and have lower levels of aggression, substance use on the job, tardiness, and absenteeism
      c. Older workers use strategies to compensate for cognitive and physical decline

          i. Compensation sometime referred to as "selective optimization with compensation" (SOC) pattern

              (i) Selection (focus on limited set of goals and skills necessary to achievement them)

              (ii) Optimization (practice those skills to keep sharp)

              (iii) Compensation (develop ways around the needed skills)

          ii. One study of SOC coping strategy found that older adults with highly stressful job who relied on the SOC maintained a high level of performance and achieved their workplace goals

          iii. Competence of older workers has led to raise or elimination of mandatory retirement ages and to an increase in the age of eligibility for receiving Social Security

    3. Retirement

       a. Introduction of Social Security in 1934 made retirement financially possible

          i. 50% of workforce retired by age 62-64, 90% of those 70 or older are retired

       b. Some workers retire "cold turkey" (all at once), but many retire by gradually cutting back on work hours

       c. Atchley proposed model of retirement said to proceed in stages

          i. Preretirement—getting ready for retirement (e.g., gather information about retirement options)

          ii. Actual point of retirement may be by choice or the result of poor health or being pushed out of a job

          iii. Honeymoon phase—initial pleasure following retirement, the result of newfound freedom

          iv. Disenchantment—novelty wears off and unhappiness sets in

          v. Reorientation—set more realistic lifestyle

       d. Research supports this basic pattern (i.e., early honeymoon and later satisfaction)

       e. Most consistent impact is loss of income

       f. Declines in health not directly the result of retirement, but poor health may actually lead to retirement

       g. Retirement does not disrupt social life, frequency of social contacts, or mental health

       h. Huge individual difference in retirement

       i. Most favorable retirement when it is voluntary, person is in good health, financially secure, and married or with strong support

       j. (Exploration Box on his versus her retirement)

F. Personality and Successful Aging

    1. Activity theory—aging adults more satisfied if they can maintain previous lifestyle and/or activity level, may involve substitution of new activity with old

       a. Defying aging is the primary way to go about aging

    2. Disengagement theory—successful aging involves planned withdrawal from society/activity; aging involves reducing activity and leaving old roles behind

    3. Most successful way to age

       a. Remain physically and intellectually active, however, many inactive individuals are satisfied with their life

  b. Quality of activity more important than quantity

  c. Most older people voluntarily withdraw from certain roles and activities

 4. Both models have some merit and neither says enough about the role of personality in influencing well-being in old age

  a. People high in extraversion, conscientiousness, and emotional stability have a greater sense of well-being in later life

 5. Optimal satisfaction experienced when good fit between lifestyle, needs, and personality and engaging in selective optimization with compensation; helps older individuals maintain a high sense of well-being

SUGGESTIONS FOR CLASS DISCUSSIONS OR PROJECTS

1. Thomas, Chess, and Birch (1968) introduced the labels "difficult," "easy," and "slow-to-warm-up" to characterize different temperament styles of infants and young children. The labels convey much value-laden information that might inspire the following questions:

- What are the messages implicit in these labels?
- Would any parent want to have a difficult or slow-to-warm-up infant?
- Would there be advantages to informing parents of their child's temperament style?
- How might the label affect parent-infant interactions?
- Are there other, less value-laden labels that might describe the same temperament styles?
- What would be a good fit for a child with one of these temperaments?

  Thomas, A., Chess, S., and Birch, H.G. (1968). *Temperament and Behavior Disorders in Children*. New York, NY: New York Press.

2. Have students write 10 answers to the question, "Who am I?" and then have them analyze their answers to determine how much they emphasize physical traits, social roles (e.g., student, mother), psychological traits, and membership in social groups (e.g., gender, ethnicity, religion). You might capitalize on diversity within the classroom to see if people in different groups (males versus females, students in early versus late adulthood, ethnic minority versus majority students) use different types of descriptors. Students might also pose the "Who am I?" question to children and adults of different ages to see if they can identify the developmental trends in self-descriptions delineated in the text.

3. For many people, ethnic identity is an important part of their sense of self. Jean Phinney (1992) has developed a measure of ethnic identity that is relevant to diverse ethnic groups. This questionnaire enables students to think about the importance of ethnic identity in their own lives. Discussion questions might include the following:

- Why do members of minority groups more often feel their ethnic identity is an important part of who they are, as compared to members of majority groups?
- How does ethnic identity develop?
- How is ethnic identity the same and different from other aspects of the self-concept?

  Phinney, J.S. (1992). The multigroup ethnic identity measure: a new scale for use with diverse groups. *Journal of Adolescent Research, 7(2)*, 156-176.

4. The headline of an article in a local newspaper proclaimed "Personality change after 30 unlikely." The article described a study showing that personality changes very little after about the age of 30. The article concluded by saying that if you have a personality trait that you are not happy about, work on changing it before you hit your late 20s. Ask students to discuss the extent to which personality can be modified. Is there a point when it becomes more or less fixed? Does the research discussed in the text provide any support for the somewhat dire warnings in the newspaper? Can students think of cases where individuals have changed features of their personality? What factors influence personality change? Are some aspects easier to modify than others?

5. Most people receive their "education" in human development through media depictions (i.e., television shows and movies). Have students identify television shows that they believe are good (realistic) portrayals of humans and personality issues across the lifespan (e.g., teen angst, the midlife crisis, retirement). They could then compare these portrayals to a list of media examples they classify as the worst (most misleading or unrealistic) portrayals.

6. In Chapter 11, students are provided with an introduction to the topic of self-esteem and its potential impact on human development. It should come as no surprise that a great deal of advice exists concerning the most effective way to raise esteem in children and adults. The purpose of this assignment is to help students identify some of the esteem-raising strategies that have been identified by researchers. This will be accomplished by conducting a Web search or journal entry using the term *self-esteem* in combination with restrictive terms like *children*, *adolescents*, *boys*, or *girls* (e.g., *self-esteem and children*). Students should use the information they identify via the search to create a list of 10 specific strategies that have been shown to raise esteem in various populations.

7. Today's economic situation has made job opportunities scarce, and many individuals (both young and old) have become involuntarily unemployed (e.g., been fired or laid off). As we look forward, many people are asking, "Where are the hot job prospects?" Have students gain insight into the future of employment opportunities by reviewing at data from the most recent *Occupational Outlook Handbook* (the 2010-2011 edition is referenced below). After reviewing the information, you could have the class develop a list of the "top 10" and "bottom 10" job prospects for the 2010s.

Occupational Outlook Handbook, 2010-11. Overview of the 2018-18 Projections. Retrieved from the Bureau of Labor Statistics: http://www.bls.gov/oco/oco2003.htm

SUGGESTED FILMS AND VIDEOS

Identity Crisis (2005, Films for the Humanities & Sciences, VHS/DVD, 60 minutes): This film discusses the topic of identity formation by focusing on the development of 25 five-year-olds.

Looking Beyond Race, Looking Beyond Border: Explorations into the Multicultural Personality (2007, Insight Media, DVD, 60 minutes): This film looks at how individuals adapt to the evolving multicultural society.

Personality: All about Me (2003, Insight Media, DVD, 60 minutes): This DVD describes the acquisition of personality traits across the lifespan.

The Enduring Self: Personality (2006, Insight Media, DVD, 30 minutes): This DVD presents a review of personality from Bandura's Social Learning Theory perspective.

Who am I? Psychological Development During Adolescence (2003, Insight Media, VHS, 30 minutes): This video examines the process of identity formation during the adolescent years.

SUGGESTED WEBSITES

Big Five Quickstart: Introduction to the Five-Factor Model of Personality
http://www.centacs.com/research-development/the-big-five-quickstart/

Developing Your Child's Self-Esteem
http://www.kidshealth.org/parent/emotions/feelings/self_esteem.html

Erik Erikson
http://www.ship.edu/~cgboeree/erikson.html

Great Ideas in Personality
http://www.personalityresearch.org/

Temperament: Different Drums, Different Drummers
http://www.keirsey.com/

SUGGESTED READINGS

Duffy, R.D. (2009). Beyond the self: External influences in the career development process. *Career Development Quarterly*, 58(1), 29-43.

Jackson, K.F. (2009). Beyond race: Examining the facets of multiracial identity through a life-span developmental perspective. *Journal of Ethnic & Cultural Diversity in Social Work*, 18(4), 293-310.

McAdams, D.P. (2010). Personality development: Continuity and change over the life course. *Annual Review of Psychology*, 61(1), 517-542.

Reef, J. (2010). Predicting adult emotional and behavioral problems from externalizing problem trajectories in a 24-year longitudinal study, *European Child & Adolescent Psychiatry*, 19(7), 577-585

Zentner, M. (2007). Origins of adolescents' ideal self: An intergenerational perspective. *Journal of Personality and Social Psychology*, 92(3), 557-574.

GENDER ROLES AND SEXUALITY

LEARNING OBJECTIVES

After students have read and studied the material in this chapter, they should be able to answer the following questions:

SEX AND GENDER
1. What are gender norms and stereotypes? How do they play out in the behaviors of men and women?

2. What actual psychological differences and behaviors exist between males and females?

3. How does Eagly's social role hypothesis explain gender stereotypes?

THE INFANT
4. How do gender-role stereotypes influence infants' behavior and treatment?

THE CHILD
5. How do children acquire gender-role stereotypes? In what ways do children exhibit gender-typed behavior?

THE ADOLESCENT
6. What theoretical explanations account for adherence to gender-typed behaviors during adolescence?

7. How do biosocial, social learning, and cognitive/cognitive developmental theories explain gender-role development? How can these approaches be integrated into a more coherent approach to understanding gender roles?

THE ADULT
8. How do gender roles change throughout adulthood?

9. What are the parental imperative and androgyny? To what extent do they shape gender development?

SEXUALITY OVER THE LIFESPAN
10. How are infants affected by their sex? What do we know about infant sexuality?

11. What do children know about sex and reproduction? How does sexual behavior change during childhood?

12. How does abuse impact children?

13. What factors contribute to the development of sexual orientation?

14. What are adolescents' sexual attitudes today? How would you characterize the sexual behaviors of today's teens?

15. What changes occur in sexual activity during adulthood?

CHAPTER OUTLINE

I Sex and Gender
  A. Differentiating Sex and Gender
   1. Biological sex—physical characteristics that define male and female
   2. Gender—all features that a society associates with or considers appropriate for being men or women
       a. Menstruation in females and larger muscle mass in males are sex differences
       b. Women earning less than men is a gender difference
   3. Zygote receives sex chromosome from each parent
       a. Genetically, XX is male and XY is female
         i. Some individuals with XXY and XYY pattern
       b. Sex chromosomes impact prenatal hormone levels
         i. Hormones responsible for genitalia
         ii. Females can bear children and live longer
         iii. Males typically larger, taller, more muscular
   4. Gender roles—patterns of behavior for males and females expected by society
       a. Gender-role norms—society expectation standards (what males and females should be like)
       b. Gender-role stereotypes—overgeneralizations or inaccurate beliefs about what males and females are like
  B. Gender Norms and Stereotypes
   1. Feminine gender role
       a. Communality (communion)—orientation emphasizing connectedness to others (e.g., emotionality, sensitivity)
         i. Preparation for role as wife and mother
   2. Masculine gender role
       a. Agency—orientation toward individual action (e.g., independence, assertiveness, competitiveness)
         i. Roles tied to husband and father including providing for family and protecting family from harm
         ii. Male brain may systemize—analyze and explore how things work
   3. Gender stereotypes still exist
       a. Boys more likely to endorse traditional stereotypes
       b. Males and females continue to define themselves differently
  C. Gender Differences or Similarities?
   1. Gender similarities hypothesis (Hyde and others)—males and females are similar on most psychological variables
       a. Differences are often group differences (i.e., not all members of a sex display the same levels of a trait)

2. Research findings concerning gender differences
    a. Females sometimes display greater verbal abilities than males, but on most tasks the difference is small
        i. Females tend to consistently outperform males on reading tasks (occurs across many cultures, and difference often quite large)
    b. Males outperform females on many tests of spatial ability
        i. Some differences often emerge in adolescence
        ii. Differences in mental rotation seen in childhood
        iii. Training can reduce or eliminate gender differences on most spatial tasks
    c. Historically, males outperformed females on average tests of mathematical ability, but difference has disappeared in U.S. and many other countries
        i. Males and females perform similarly on most standardized math tests
        ii. Females tend to score slightly higher grades in math classes
        iii. Educational opportunity differences may explain gender differences in math in some cultures
        iv. More males are also low math achievers
    d. Girls display greater memory abilities than boys
        i. Female advantage at remembering object location and recalling facial features
        ii. Women have advantage in odor recognition
    e. Males engage in more physical and verbal aggression than females, starting as early as 17 months
        i. Effect found in nearly all countries
        ii. Males commit more serious and violent crimes
        iii. Females tend to use more subtle relational forms of aggression (e.g., gossip) but so do males
    f. Boys are more physically active and more hyperactive
    g. Boys more developmentally vulnerable (prone to illness or death)
    h. Girls more tactful, cooperative, and compliant
    i. Males and females view females as more nurturant and empathic
    j. Females more prone to anxiety disorders, depression, and phobias
    k. Males more likely to engage in antisocial behavior and to abuse drugs
    l. Males use computers more and are more confident in computer abilities
3. Differences tend to be small and in "average" levels of behaviors between females and males
    a. Impossible to accurately predict a behavior if all you know about someone is their sex
    b. Most sex differences small
4. Gender stereotypes bias our perceptions (notice behaviors confirming our perceptions)
5. Eagly's social-role hypothesis—different roles males and females play in society create and maintain gender-role stereotypes
    a. Traditional business and industry role of men requires dominance and forcefulness
    b. Traditional role of homemaker requires nurturance and sensitivity
    c. Differences part of social role not one's "nature"
    d. Reversing roles may result in different gender roles

        i. Men in role of homemaker perceived to be just as caring and affectionate as women in same role

        ii. Gender segregation in workforce (i.e., women more likely to be in nursing profession, men more likely to be construction workers) may contribute to notion of gender roles

6. Although many gender stereotypes are unfounded, they still have a great impact on the way we perceive ourselves and others

7. Society does steer each sex toward different goals
   a. In childhood, boys and girls conform to gender roles, segregating themselves by biological sex and developing different interests and play activities
   b. Women remain under-represented in many traditionally male-dominated fields
   c. Occupations remain highly gender segregated (e.g., 2009 top U.S. female professions are secretary, nurse, teacher, cashier, and nursing/health aide)
   d. Despite significant social change, couples tend to divide labor along traditional lines

II The Infant

A. Initial Differences between Boys and Girls
   1. Other than the obvious anatomical ones, few differences between males and females
   2. Shortly after birth, newborns labeled as girls and boys for gender stereotypes to affect how they are perceived and treated

B. Differential Treatment
   1. Adults respond differently to infants on basis of perceived sex beginning in the delivery room (e.g., calling sons "big guy")
   2. Although few objective differences between male and female children in infancy, adults tend to perceive boys as strong and coordinated while girls as perceived as weaker and more awkward
      a. Study of college students watching a videotape of a 9-month-old reacting to jack-in-the-box; when infant introduced as "David," reactions seen as anger, but when infant introduced as "Dana," same reaction seen as fear
   3. Stereotypic treatment may partly be part of the cause of differences between the sexes

C. Early Learning
   1. Young infants actively trying to know the social world
      a. 3- to 8-month old infants: males look longer at trucks while females look longer at dolls
         i. May represent a rudimentary recognition of gender stereotypic information
   2. By end of first year, infants look longer at a face when it matches the correct sex (i.e.. male face and male voice), indicating possibility of cross-modal association of gender-related information
   3. By 24 months, look longer at gender-inconsistent information (e.g., male putting on makeup)
   4. Begin early categorization of the sexes and begin to figure out which sex they are

             182

5. Development of gender identity, awareness that you are a boy or girl, by age 2½ to 3 years

6. Gender identity awareness accompanied by differences in behavior (e.g., toy selection)

III The Child

A. Early Gender-Role Development

1. Young children rapidly acquire gender stereotypes (ideas about what males and females are supposed to be like) and show tendencies to favor "gender-appropriate" activities and behaviors through the process of gender-typing

   a. Gender-typing—awareness of biological sex and acquisition of motives, values, and patterns of behavior that a culture considers appropriate for members of one's biological sex

      i. Susie learns the gender norm that women should be good mothers and adopts traditional role by devoting herself to the task of mothering

B. Acquiring Gender Stereotypes

1. Child learns gender stereotypes around the time they become aware of their basic gender identities

   a. 3-year-olds understand masculine stereotype (boys play with GI Joe dolls) and feminine stereotypes (girls play with Barbie dolls)

2. 4- to 6-year-olds understand masculine (car mechanic) and feminine (secretary) stereotyped occupations

   a. Children see those in gender-stereotype role (e.g., male pilot) as more competent that those from the other sex (e.g., female pilot)

3. Rigid adherence to gender norms and stereotypes at ages 4 to 6 years may be followed by more flexibility in thinking by age 8 or 9

   a. Some children are particularly offended when a peer steps outside of traditional gender-stereotypic behavior and will act to "enforce" the correct role

      i. Rigidity about gender stereotypes highest in preschool years and then decline

4. Young children may exaggerate gender roles to help cognitively clarify them; once gender identity more firmly established, they can be more flexible in their thinking about what is "for boys" or "for girls"

5. Some believe that rigidity about a gender-role violation may depend on how essential the behavior is to a given gender identity

   a. Bad for boy to wear a dress because that is strongly associated with being feminine, but alright to play in the kitchen because that is not an essential aspect of the feminine gender role

B. Gender-Typed Behavior

1. Behaving in "gender-appropriate" manner often precedes establishment of clear sense of own identity (e.g., a baby has a preference for "boy toys" before having clearly established a clear male identity)

   a. In childhood, gender-congruent toy preference still evident, but rules are violated (e.g., girl prefers a "boy toy")

2. Young children tend to prefer and form friendships with same-sex partners

a. Gender segregation—strong preference for interactions with same-sex peers
   i. Gender-segregation occurs in a variety of cultures
   ii. Gender roles incompatible due to differences in play styles (e.g., boys are too rowdy and domineering to suit the tastes of many girls)
   iii. Socialization pressure may encourage drift into boy-only or girl-only playgroups
b. Strong adherence to gender-role boundaries tend to be seen in children who are socially competent and popular while children who violate gender-segregation rules tend to be less well-adjusted and run risk of peer rejection
   i. Boys face stronger pressure to adhere to gender-role expectations

IV The Adolescent
A. Adhering to Gender Roles
   1. Adolescents tend to continue to be highly intolerant of certain gender-role violations
      a. Tend to make negative judgments about peers who violate rules by engaging in cross-sex behavior or cross-sex interests
         i. Study on boy wearing a barrette or girl with a crew haircut; kindergartners and adolescents judged behavior as most wrong while third- and fifth-graders were more tolerant
         ii. Adolescents begun to conceptualize gender violation as sign of psychological abnormality
   2. Gender intensification—sex differences are magnified by increased pressure to conform around the time of puberty (linked to hormonal changes)
      a. Higher levels of "femininity" found in teen girls vs. teen boys
      b. Teen boys and girls report similar levels of "masculinity"
   3. Peers critical as conforming to traditional roles seen as appealing to opposite sex; traditional roles linked to popularity
      a. "Tomboy" may feel need to become more feminine and attract boys
   4. Social pressure to conform to traditional roles may explain more noticeable differences in cognitive abilities in adolescence
   5. Social pressure to conform to gender stereotypes does not have to be real to have an impact (i.e., perceptions of pressure just are influential)
   6. Later adolescence, more comfort with identity and more flexibility in thinking
B. Explaining Gender-Role Development
   1. Nature/nurture of gender
      a. Taylor study on perceptions on nature of gender
         i. Children told story of Chris, girl raised on an island of all men and boys; children asked about Chris's toy preferences
         ii. 4- to 8-year-olds took nature side expecting the fact that Chris was a girl to result in her preferring feminine toys
         iii. 9- and 10-year-olds took nurture side, expecting her to prefer masculine toys like the other people with whom she was raised
      b. Freud saw gender-role behaviors shaped in phallic stage and resolved through resolution of conflict involving incestuous love for opposite-sex parent and identification with same-sex parent

2. Biosocial theory (Money and Ehrhardt)
   a. Chromosomes (male XY or female XX), hormones, and social labeling
      i. Presence of genes on Y chromosome leads to the development of testes (otherwise you get ovaries)
      ii. Testes of male embryo normally secretes testosterone, which stimulates growth of male internal reproductive system and inhibits the development of female organs (without hormone, female organs will develop)
      iii. 3 to 4 months postconception, release of hormones leads to development of penis and scrotum
      iv. Relative amount of hormone release critical (e.g., if no hormones released, the fetus will develop female external genitalia)
      v. Fertilized eggs have potential to acquire features of either sex
      vi. Society labels and differential treatment of child on basis of male or female genitals creates gender roles
      vii. Puberty leads to release of more hormones that stimulate reproductive system and secondary sex characteristics, providing basis for adult gender identity and role behavior
   b. Evidence of biological influences
      i. Evolutionary psychologists notice that most societies socialize males to have agentic traits and females to have communal traits; also suggest that 20-50% of extent to which individual self-describes as masculine or feminine is the result of hereditary factors
      ii. Studies of children exposed to "wrong hormones" prenatally
      iii. Androgenized females (exposed to excessive levels of "male associated" androgens) have an XX endowment: female internal organs, but external organs that resemble a male
      iv. Money and Ehardt found that androgenized females display more male-like actions (e.g., toy preference)
      v. As adolescents, androgenized females dated later, felt marriage should be delayed, and described themselves as homosexual or bisexual
      vi. Androgenized females may outperform other females on tests of spatial ability
      vii. Testosterone levels and levels of other male hormones may affect aggression (e.g., female rhesus monkeys exposed to testosterone were more threatening and aggressive with other monkeys)
      viii. Men with high testosterone levels have high rates of delinquency and violence, but this effect is most evident in males of low socioeconomic status; results are correlational so they cannot show the direction of the relationship
      ix. Difficult to establish unambiguously that high concentrations of testosterone results in aggressive or competitive actions
      x. Prenatal exposure of brain to male and female hormones does have lasting effect on its development and on sexual behavior, aggression, and cognitive abilities

      xi. While influential, biological factors alone do not dictate gender-role development, but rather gender-role development evolves from a complex interaction between biology, social experience, and the individual's behavior

    c. Evidence of social-labeling influences

      i. How a child is labeled and treated can considerably affect gender development

      ii. Fewer problems with children "relabeled" prior to 18 months (e.g., an androgenized female who was surgically corrected and labeled a "girl"); after age 3, sexual reassignment exceedingly difficult because the child experiences prolonged masculine gender-typing and has labeled himself as a boy

      iii. Proposed critical period of self-gender labeling between 18 and 36 month but may not be "critical period" as much as "sensitive" period (Exploration box on social labeling and biological destiny)

3. Social learning theory

    a. Masculine and feminine identities learned through differential reinforcement for sex-appropriate behaviors (reward for sex-appropriate behavior and punishment for sex-inappropriate behavior) and observational learning—model same-sex behavior seen in same-sex models (e.g., parents, peers, media)

    b. Differential reinforcement

      i. By second year, parents encourage sex-appropriate play and discourage cross-sex play

      ii. By 20 to 24 months, parents reinforce sex-appropriate behavior and reprimand for engaging in sex-inappropriate behavior (e.g., boy reinforced for playing with truck but not encouraged to play with dolls)

      iii. Parents provide differential discipline (more physical for boys and more verbal for girls)

      iv. Parents have different emotions toward male and female children (anger at sons, disappointment at daughters); see risky behavior as being in a boy's "nature" while a girls behavior could be influenced by rule enforcement

      v. Overall pattern of parents' attempt to instill traditional roles called "gender curriculum"

      vi. Fathers tend to play a great role in gender socialization (e.g., more likely to reward gender-appropriate behavior)

      vii. Women in nontraditional careers more likely to have fathers who encouraged them to be assertive and competitive

      viii. Eccles and colleagues found that parental expectations about gender differences in math do have impact; as a result of societal stereotypes, parents expect sons to do better at math, attribute boys' math success to being male and females' to hard work

      ix. Children internalize parents' views, thinking they lack ability, girls become less interested in math

   x. 12- to 25-month-old peers provide differential reinforcement by belittling boys for playing with "feminine" toys and disapproving of girls who play with boys

  c. Observational learning

   i. Children watch others to determine which activities are "for girls" and which are "for boys"

   ii. Begin to pay closer attention to same-sex models around age 6 years

   iii. Watch parents to determine gender roles

   iv. Child with opposite-sex siblings have less gender-typed activity preferences

   v. Children learn gender roles from observing media sources (e.g., television, video games, books)

   vi. Children's picture books often continue to depict males and females in stereotypic ways (e.g., boys active bike riders, girls passive flower pickers)

   vii. Popular children's picture books are more likely to portray fathers (but not mothers) as absent

   viii. In recent decades, blatant gender stereotyping of television characters has decreased, but male characters still dominate many programs

   ix. Television characters still reinforce stereotypic sex roles (men working at a profession and women managing a home)

   x. Children who watch more television more likely to hold stereotypic views of men and women

   xi. Strong traditional gender stereotypes found in video games (which are played at higher rates by males); games tend to portray females as helpless and sexually provocative and males are strong and aggressive

   xii. Men do not find offensive stereotypes in video games as offensive as do women

  d. Criticism is that model does not place enough emphasis on child's own role in gender socialization/acquisition (i.e., child too passive)

 4. Cognitive theories

  a. Cognitive-developmental theory (Kohlberg)

   i. Gender-role development depends on stage-like changes in cognitive development

   ii. Children engage in self-socialization

   iii. Three stages in the acquisition of gender constancy—an understanding of what it means to be a boy or girl

   iv. Stage one: basic gender identity—by age 2 to 3, able to recognize and label self as male or female

   v. Stage two: gender stability—around age 4, understand that boys become men and girls become women

   vi. Stage three: gender consistency—realize that one's own sex does not change and cannot be altered by superficial means (e.g., dressing as a member of the opposite sex)

   vii. Children age 3 to 5 say a boy could become a mommy and that if a girl cut her hair, she could be a boy

viii. As children enter Piaget's concrete-operational stage, they are able to conserve gender (i.e., know it remains constant despite changes in appearance)

ix. One criticism is that children who are just acquiring gender labels are already engaging in gender-typed behavior

x. A second criticism is that children do not have to be concrete-operational thinkers to understand gender stability and consistency

xi. Most controversial idea is that it is only when a child fully grasps that biological sex is unchangeable that he or she actively seeks same-sex models and attempts to acquire their values and behaviors

xii. Children appear to learn many gender-role stereotypes and develop clear preferences for same-sex activities long before they master gender stability and gender consistency

b. Gender schema theory (Martin and Halverson)

i. Like Kohlberg, believe that children are intrinsically motivated to acquire values and behaviors consistent with judgments about the self, but believe that self-socialization begins as soon as children acquire a basic gender identity (around age 2-3 years)

ii. Key is the acquisition of gender schema—organized set of beliefs and expectations about males and females that influence the kinds of information to which a child will attend and remember

iii. Children form a simple in-group-out-group schema based on gender that allows them to classify the appropriateness of an object or action (e.g., cars are for boys)

iv. Begin to seek information about the role of their own sex while constructing a gender self-schema

v. Compare world to own sex schema with the intent of acting consistently according to one's gender schemata

vi. Young children are interested in learning about objects that fit their own-sex schemata (e.g., boys more likely to explore an object that is labeled as a "boy" item) and are more likely recall items associated with their own-sex schemata

vii. Once gender schemata are in place, children may distort reality to fit schema (e.g., study in which children saw pictures including a girl sawing wood, later recalled that they saw a boy sawing wood)

5. An attempt at integration

a. Biosocial model key focus on biology, labeling, and how labeling impacts treatment

b. Socializing agents teach children how to be boys or girls well before they understand that they are boys or girls

c. Social learning experiences can explain why some children are more gender-typed than others

d. Cognitive growth and self-socialization processing contribute to gender development

      i. Children want to learn about appropriate roles

      ii. Parents who avoid socializing children into traditional roles often amazed to see children turn into traditional boys and girls

   e. Summation is that biological endowment guides development, active socialization impacts development, and children actively socialize themselves to behave in ways consistent with their self-schema of being a girl or a boy

V The Adult

  A. Changes in Gender Roles

    1. In early adulthood, male and female gender roles differ little because both sexes play similar roles (i.e., single and in school or working)

    2. Roles tend to become more distinct in adulthood, especially in married couples with children

      a. Wives typically do most of the housework (about 17-18 hours per week for her and about 10 hours for her husband, adding up to 400-hour difference a year)

      b. Birth of a child makes even egalitarian couples adopt more traditional gender-role attitudes

        i. Women have primary responsibility for childcare and household tasks

        ii. Men focus energy on providing for the family

    3. Roles tend to become more similar starting in middle age (when children are grown and the nest empties)

  B. Androgyny?

    1. Early assumption that masculine and feminine traits were at opposite ends of a single continuum and were mutually exclusive

    2. Androgyny—blending of both agentic and communal traits

      a. Agentic and communal traits are two separate dimensions of personality

        i. Masculine gender-type—many agentic traits and few communal traits

        ii. Feminine gender-type— many communal traits and few agentic traits

        iii. Androgynous gender-type—both agentic and communal traits

        iv. Undifferentiated gender-type—lacking both agentic and communal traits

      b. Generational changes in gender roles

        i. In the 1970s, about one-third of adults were androgynous and another third were traditionally gender-typed; 20 years later, men rated themselves higher on 9 of 22 agentic traits than women

        ii. Women and men both rate themselves at near identical levels on the criteria "acts as a leader"

      c. Advantages of androgyny

        i. Most college students believe that the ideal person is androgynous

        ii. Androgynous individuals have more trait flexibility and seem more adaptable and are viewed by others as warmer

      d. Disadvantages of androgyny

        i. In childhood, expressing too many traits appropriate to the opposite sex may result in peer rejection and low self-esteem

        ii. In college students, psychological well-adjustment is associated with gender-congruent personality traits

iii. Need to distinguish between positive agentic and communal traits and one who possesses negative agentic and communal traits; positive score higher on mental health measures

3. Changes with age
   a. Parental imperative—gender-role distinctions adopted by parents to successfully raise their children
      i. Young and middle-aged men must emphasize masculine qualities to feed and protect family; young and middle-aged women must express feminine qualities to nurture the young and meet emotional needs of the family
      ii. After children leave, and in order to free themselves from the parental imperative, men shift to become more passive and sensitive while women become to become more domineering and assertive (i.e., the two sexes flip-flop)
   b. Androgyny shift—don't give up old traits in middle age, simply retain old and add traditional qualities associated with the other sex (more androgynous)
      i. Some support for this hypothesis in grandparents
      ii. Compared to young age groups, men over 70 are more likely to view androgyny positively and to adopt androgynous traits; interesting since the younger generation grew up in an era of more flexible gender norms

VI Sexuality Over the Lifespan
A. Are Infants Sexual Beings?
   1. Freud championed idea of infant sexuality (a seemingly outrageous claim)
   2. Infants in oral stage are biologically equipped and derive pleasure from oral activities and genital stimulation
   3. Infants find stimulation of genitals pleasurable, they enjoy touching all parts of their body, and appear to experience orgasms, but are not aware that their behavior was sexual
   4. Infants will continue to touch themselves unless discouraged by parents or other grown-ups
B. Childhood Sexuality
   1. Knowledge of sex and reproduction
      a. Learn that sexual anatomy is key differentiator of males and females and the vocabulary of sex organs
      b. Young children assume either babies there all along or somehow manufactured
      c. Young children construct their own reality concerning the understanding of reproduction long before being told the "facts of life"
      d. By age 12, most have fundamental understanding of sexual intercourse and egg and sperm role in process
      e. Cognitive advancement leads to better understanding of sexuality
   2. Sexual behavior
      a. Phallic stage (Freud) is time of genital interest (including masturbation)
         i. Sexual interest quite common
         ii. Latency stage (Freud) time when sex drive is repressed
         iii. Freud was correct that preschoolers are curious about their bodies, masturbate, and engage in same- and cross-sex sex play

Chapter 12   190

    iv. Freud was wrong to believe that such activities occur infrequently among school-age children (two-thirds of adolescents have masturbated by age 13 and some are engaging in "light" sexual activity)

  b. Around 10, children often experience first sexual attraction (can be heterosexual or homosexual)

    i. May be influenced by adrenal gland development and release of androgens

    ii. Comes well before maturation of sex organs

    iii. Society does little to encourage sexual thoughts in younger children (especially about the same sex), so hormones may be best explanation of early sexual interest

  c. Societal differences contribute to diversity in sexual attitudes and behaviors

    i. Teens less likely to use condoms if sexually active friends do not use them

    ii. "Teen permissive" and "sexually conservative" societies impact teens in different ways

    iii. Sexual behavior driven by hormones and mediated by social context and personal beliefs

    iv. Learn how to relate to other sex using peers

3. Childhood sexual abuse

  a. Prevalence and reporting

    i. Estimates of prevalence vary, but may be widespread (one study found that 25% of women and 16% of men reported having been sexually molested)

    ii. Many children do not tell anyone (one estimate is that only one in four children report being abused within first 24 hours of abuse, while one in four remain silent forever)

  b. Impact

    i. No one distinct "syndrome" for all abuse victims, but rather many common problems like anxiety, depression, aggression, withdrawal, and school learning problems

    ii. Many aftereffects involve a lack of self-worth and difficulty trusting

    iii. Sexual acting out, behaving seductively, and promiscuously (one-third of victims)

    iv. Some display posttraumatic stress disorder symptoms—clinical disorder involving nightmares, flashbacks, helplessness, anxiety

    v. In a few cases, result of abuse is severe psychological damage

    vi. Impact may be most severe when abuse involves penetration, force, occurs over a long period of time, and perpetrator is close relative

  c. Recovery factors

    i. High-quality relationship with mom and friends may lead to better recovery

    ii. Psychotherapy aids in treatment of abuse victims

  d. Some offenders are juveniles taking advantage of peers or somewhat younger children

    i. Can learn acceptable behaviors

  ii. Effective intervention involving working with the survivors, the offenders, and all children on prevention of sexual abuse may be behind recent decline in reports of abuse

C. Adolescent Sexuality
  1. Sexual orientation—preference for sex partner as same, opposite, or either sex
    a. Continuum of sexual orientation, although our culture tends to recognize only three: heterosexual, homosexual, and bisexual
    b. Most teens establish heterosexual orientation
    c. Establishing homosexual orientation more difficult
      i. Establishing a positive attitude in the face of negative societal attitudes can be long and torturous
      ii. Often do not "come out" until after high school (mid-20s)
    d. Sexual experimentation with same sex may be common, but only about 5-6% establish an enduring homosexual or bisexual orientation
    e. Homosexuality influenced by genetic and environmental factors
      i. Identical twins more alike in sexual orientation than fraternal twins (indicates a genetic link), however, environmental factors contribute at least as much as genes
      ii. Gay men and lesbian women show strong cross-sexed interest when young despite pressure to adopt traditional gender role
      iii. Being masculine or feminine in childhood not a predictor of later sexual orientation
      iv. Lesbian and bisexual orientation tends to be an enduring characteristic
      v. Not the result of domineering mom and weak dad, or seduction by older adult
      vi. Having a gay or lesbian parent has little impact on a child's sexual orientation
      vii. Prenatal hormones like androgens may predispose an individual to an orientation
      viii. It is unclear which pre- or postnatal environmental factors contribute with genes to produce a homosexual orientation
  2. Sexual morality
    a. In adolescence, sex with affection in the context of a committed relationship is acceptable
      i. Males may have a slightly more permissive attitude concerning casual sex
      ii. The first sex partner for most adolescents is someone with whom they are romantically involved
      iii. Casual and frequent sex with multiple partners is not the norm among adolescents
    b. Decline (but not disappearance) of the double standard—sexual behavior appropriate in males and inappropriate in females
      i. May continue because it is entrenched in societal expectations
      ii. Actual data suggests little actual difference in sexual behavior among teens (e.g., one study found 66% of female and 63% of male 12th graders were sexually active)

    c. Increased confusion about sexual norms due to mixed societal messages: sex makes you popular versus the value of virginity and avoiding STDs

3. Sexual behavior

    a. Rate of teen sexual activity climbed between 1960s and 80s, leveled off, and is now declining

    b. Percent of teens having intercourse increased steadily in 20th century

    c. Sexual behavior of females changing faster than males

    d. Cognitive schema for "having sex" may not include oral sex as defined by high school students

       i. May explain increasing rate of oral sex

       ii. Can engage in sex without having "sex"

       iii. Oral sex now seen as less intimate than intercourse (a change from past generations)

       iv. Inaccurate perception that oral sex is "safer" (still may result in transmission of sexually transmitted disease)

       v. Oral sex only may lead to less positive feelings about self

    e. Risk for early sexual activity/antecedents of early sexual behavior

       i. Early sex more likely in children of unmarried mother

       ii. Greater risk in homes in which parents were less emotionally responsive

       iii. Low-risk teens (sexually active, but always using protection) looked more mature; mature appearance may have led others to respond to them in a different manner (e.g., sexual involvement, use of alcohol)

       iv. Cooper's research on sexual risk-taking in teens identified key within-person, situational, and combination factors

       v. Within-person factors that elevated risk of sexual behavior include low levels of impulse control and communality and high levels of adventuresomeness and negative emotionality

       vi. Situation factors including drinking alcohol

       vii. Teens and young adults from minority groups (especially males) at greater risk of engaging in risky practices

    f. Lack of contraception use partially related to cognitive immaturity of adolescent couples and not taking seriously the potential long-term consequences of one's actions

       i. Condom use is increasing but is still lower than what healthcare professionals would like to see

       ii. Adolescent couples in long-term relationships become less likely to use condoms as they no longer fear transmission of HIV or STDs

    g. Negative consequences of teens giving birth include long-term economic disadvantage and interrupted education

    h. STDs are one consequence of poorly planned sexual activity

    i. Teens who feel close to their parents are more likely to delay initiating sexual activity

       i. Mothers pointing out negative consequences of sex at early age especially effective

       ii. Many parents do not communicate information about sex because they fear it will encourage sexual activity and it would be too embarrassing

D. Adult Sexuality
    1. Adult sex lives quite varied
       a. Some many partners, some few
       b. Small decline in quality of sex life for married couples
       c. Men's satisfaction with sex tied to frequency of activity
       d. Middle-aged women report more positive moods and less stress levels on days following sexual behavior with a partner
    2. Tend to stereotype older individuals as sexless or asexual
       a. Most people are sexual beings throughout the lifespan
       b. Older men appear to be more sexually active and interested in sex than their female age peers
       c. Activity level does decline with age
    3. Longer and healthier lifespans have increased sexual activity in middle and older adults with some unexpected consequences
       a. STD rates in those 45 and older have doubled
       b. Many older adults do not get tested for STDs nor get potential life-saving treatment
       c. Jane Fowler: story of 47-year-old divorcee who dated and contracted HIV from a man she knew, prompting her to found the organization HIV Wisdom for Older Women
    4. Explanations for declining activity
       a. Physical changes
          i. Male sexual peak responsiveness is in teens and 20s (i.e., more intense organism and shorter refractory period—period of time before one is again capable of sexual activity)
         ii. Older male is slower to arouse, ejaculate, and recover after ejaculation
         iii. Some decline in male hormone release with age
         iv. Female physiological changes less dramatic (e.g., continuation of little or no refractory period)
         v. Menopause tends to not reduce interest in sex or sex activity
         vi. Infirmity, diseases, and disabilities may limit function (e.g., may lead to impotence in men)
         vii. Health problems like high blood pressure, coronary disease, and diabetes and psychological problems like stress and depression can result in impotence in middle-aged and elderly adults
       b. Concerns about social attitudes (sex in old age is ridiculous) may contribute to a reduction in sexual activity
         i. Elderly stereotyped as sexless or sexually unappealing ("dirty old men")
         ii. Negative attitudes may be internalized by elderly
         iii. Older females further inhibited by the double standard
       c. Lack of partner or willing partner will diminish sexual activity
         i. Especially problematic for older women as number of available older men significantly declines
       d. Lack of sexual experience in young adulthood predicts less sex in later life ("use it or lose it")

1. In a classic study, Broverman and colleagues (1970) asked trained clinicians about their definitions of healthy adults, healthy males, and healthy females. They found that if women lived up to their gender-role prescriptions, they were also, by definition, maladjusted adults. What do students think has and has not changed since this study was conducted? What does this study have to say about the power of psychologists to define abnormality? What special responsibilities might psychologists have? How can psychologists (and others) guard against biases about social groups (e.g., based on gender, age, sexual orientation, social class, disability status) with which we *all* grow up?

Broverman, I.K., Broverman, D.M., Clarkson, E.E., Rosenkrantz, P.S., & Vogel, S.R. (1970). Sex-role stereotypes and clinical judgments of mental health, *Journal of Consulting and Clinical Psychology, 34,* 1-7.

2. Gender roles and stereotypes are easily apparent in the media, especially in advertising. Bring in (and ask students to bring in) advertisements from magazines and/or clips from commercials. Questions to consider: How are males and females portrayed? Does the age of the person affect this portrayal? Does the portrayal of males and females by the media accurately reflect societal views? What role does one's age play concerning stereotypes?

You might consider following the lead of Signorielli and McLeod (1994) or Miller, Leyell, and Mazachek (2004) and have a class discussion of the types of commercials aimed at young people and the types of stereotypes of older individuals found in commercials. You could expand your discussion to gender-related stereotypes and include information like that reported by Sterns ad Mastro (2004).

Miller, D.W., Leyell, T.S., and Mazachek, J. (2004) Stereotypes of the elderly in U.S. television commercials from the 1950s to the 1990s. *International Journal of Aging & Human Development, 58(4),* 315-340.

Signorielli, N., and McLeod, D. (1994). Gender stereotypes in MTV commercials: The beat goes on. *Journal of Broadcasting & Electronic Media, 38(1),* 91, 101.

Stern, S.R., and Mastro, D.E. (2004). Gender portrayals across the life span: a content analytic look at broadcast commercials. *Mass Communication & Society, 7(2),* 215-236.

3. If possible, obtain a copy of the BEM Sex-Role Inventory. The BEM Inventory (available for a fee at http://www.mindgarden.com/products/bemss.htm) has 20 items that are feminine stereotyped (e.g., affectionate, sympathetic, warm), 20 items that are masculine stereotyped (independent, assertive, dominant), and 20 items that are gender neutral. Respondents rate themselves on each item using a seven-point Likert-type scale ranging from "never or almost never true" to "always or almost always true" of me. Someone who is androgynous would have high scores on both the feminine and masculine scales. Have students complete the inventory and calculate their femininity and masculinity scores to determine if they are androgynous. Many students are surprised at their results. Ask them to comment on factors that they think may have contributed to their sex-role profile.

4. In order to examine gender-role stereotypes, have students respond to the following statement: "Suppose that you are going to meet someone for the very first time and all you know about this person is that she is a woman. Write down the first five traits that you would expect this person to possess." "Suppose that you are going to meet someone for the very first time and all you know about this person is that he is a man. Write down the first five traits that you would expect this person to possess." The teacher can then create a list of common "beliefs" and see if they match any of the data on gender-role stereotypes (which they likely will).

5. One argument for the development of gender roles involves differential treatment by parents and others during the first years of life. Have students observe the manner in which individuals interact with infants in their family and document ways in which girls and boys are differentially treated. You might want to share these lists in class to see if the type's differential treatment is common across a variety of family types. You may also want to discuss whether males or females appear to be more likely to treat infants differentially based on the baby's sex.

6. Have students discuss what they would consider "appropriate" sexual behavior for the following people: 15-year-old Greg, 25-year-old Marcia, 45-year-old Peter, 65-year-old Jan, and 100-year-old Bobby. During this likely "lively" discussion, you can tap into the issues of sexual morality and age-based cultural norms concerning sex.

SUGGESTED FILMS AND VIDEOS

Being Gay: Coming Out in the 21st Century (2003, Films for the Humanities and Sciences, VHS, 25 minutes): This award-winning video explores the many obstacles faced by gays, lesbians, bisexuals, and transgendered individuals when they "come out."

Divide of the Sexes: Gender Roles in Childhood (2008, Insight Media, DVD, 60 minutes): This interesting video explores numerous aspects influencing gender development (e.g., celebrity culture, media treatment of sexuality and gender roles).

How Boys and Girls Differ: The First Six Years (2002, Insight Media, DVD, 20 minutes): This video highlights early childhood physical and psychological differences between boys and girls.

Portraits in Human Sexuality (2006, Insight Media, DVD, 35 minutes): This "mature audience" video offers a frank discussion of sexual issues across the lifespan.

Sex and Sexuality (2007, Insight Media, DVD, 30 minutes): This video explores U.S. attitudes concerning sex and sexuality across a wide range of topics.

SUGGESTED WEBSITES

APA Online: Aging and Human Sexuality Resource Guide
http://www.apa.org/pi/aging/resources/guides/sexuality.aspx

Biological and Sociological Views and Consequences of Gender Stereotyping
http://www.unc.edu/~lorelei/sexroles.html

Electronic Journal of Human Sexuality
http://www.ejhs.org/

Oxford Journals of Human Reproduction
http://humrep.oxfordjournals.org/

Sexual Orientation and Homosexuality
http://www.apa.org/helpcenter/sexual-orientation.aspx

SUGGESTED READINGS

Balsam, K.F. (2007). Adaptation to sexual orientation stigma: A comparison of bisexual and lesbian/gay adults. *Journal of Counseling Psychology*, 54(3), 306-319.

Barker, G., Ricardo, C., Nascimento, M., Olukoya, A., and Santos, C. (2010). Questioning gender norms with men to improve health outcomes: Evidence of impact. *Global Public Health*, 5(5), 539-553.

Corby, B.C. (2007). Gender identity and adjustment in Black, Hispanic, and White preadolescents. *Developmental Psychology*, 43(1), 261-266.

Garrity, J.M. (2010). A review of *Older, Wiser, Sexually Smarter: 30 Sex Ed Lessons for Adults Only. American Journal of Sexuality Education*, 5(1), 88-95.

Tenenbaum, H.R., Hill, D.B., Joseph, N., and Roche, E. (2010). 'It's a boy because he's painting a picture': Age differences in children's conventional and unconventional gender schemas. *The British Journal of Psychology*, 101(1), 137-154.

SOCIAL COGNITION AND MORAL DEVELOPMENT

LEARNING OBJECTIVES

After students have read and studied the material in this chapter, they should be able to answer the following questions:

SOCIAL COGNITION

1. What is a theory of mind? How is it assessed? What role does desire and desire-belief psychology play in this process? What developmental changes occur in acquiring a theory of mind, and what factors affect its emergence?

2. How do person perception, role-taking , and other social cognitive skills develop? Why are these skills important? How do they change over the lifespan?

PERSPECTIVES ON MORAL DEVELOPMENT

3. What is morality? What are the three basic components of morality?

4. What is Freud's explanation for the development of morality?

5. How do cognitive developmental psychologists assess moral reasoning? What are the important characteristics of each level and stage of both Piaget and Kohlberg's theories of moral development? What are examples of responses at each stage of reasoning?

6. How do social learning theorists explain moral behavior?

7. According to evolutionary theory, what are the functions of morality?

THE INFANT

8. What do infants understand about morality and prosocial behavior?

THE CHILD

9. What changes in moral reasoning and behavior occur during childhood? What factors influence children's moral thinking?

10. What parenting characteristics contribute to the development of morality? Which parenting
   style is "best"?

THE ADOLESCENT

11. What changes in moral reasoning occur during adolescence? How is moral development related to antisocial behavior of adolescents? What other factors influence antisocial behavior?

12. What changes in moral reasoning and behavior occur during adulthood?

13. How does Kohlberg's theory of moral reasoning fare in light of research findings? In what ways might the theory be biased or incomplete? What are some new approaches to morality?

14. What differentiates spirituality and religiosity? How do each impact development across the lifespan?

CHAPTER OUTLINE

I   Social Cognition
   A. Introduction Material
       1. John Gibbs (author of *Moral Development and Reality*) spent a summer at a camp where a mildly mentally retarded adult named Edward was tormented by other campers and wondered why he never interceded
       2. Social cognition—thinking about the perceptions, thoughts, emotions, and behaviors of self and others (e.g., taking the perspectives of others like Edward)
   B. Developing a Theory of Mind
       1. False belief task—assesses understanding that people can have, and be influenced by, incorrect beliefs
       2. Theory of mind—understanding that people have mental states (e.g., desires, beliefs) that guide behavior
           a. Rely on theory of mind (called mind-reading skills) to predict and explain human behavior
           b. Passing false belief task indicates possession of theory of mind
               i.   One false belief task involves finding a hidden marble
       3. Research on normal development as well as autism
           a. Despite normal levels of intelligence, autistics often fail the false belief task, while children with Down syndrome with lesser mental ages pass the task
           b. Appear to have "mind blindness" as they appear to lack theory of mind
               i.   Lack of theory of mind would make life difficult
           c. Professor with autism indicates that she has to create a memory bank of how people behave and what emotions they express in various situations and then to compute how people might be expected to behave in similar situations
       4. First steps in infancy
           a. Although it is not until around age 4 years that children can pass the false belief task, forerunners of theory occur in the first two years
               i.   Joint attention—at 9 months, infants begin to look at objects being looked at by caregivers
               ii. In first months of life, infants come to understand that other people have intentions—set goals and achieve them
               iii. Pretend play in infancy begins between 1 to 2 years of age

iv. Imitate others during first year of life

v. Comforting a playmate provides evidence of emotional understanding

b. Some evidence for ability to solve false belief task as young as 15 months (i.e., surprised when an actor looks in the wrong box in order to find a toy)

c. Infants know more about the world than we give them credit for

5. Desire and belief-desire psychologies

a. By age 2, begin to ask others, "Why?" (reflects understanding of the concept of desire)

b. By age 2½, begin to attempt to deceive others by planting false beliefs in others (deliberate deception)

c. Desire psychology—by age 2, children begin to talk about/explain their wants and desires

i. 18-month-olds express happiness at Goldfish crackers and disgust (mostly) at broccoli

d. Belief-desire psychology—by age 4, children begin to pass along false ideas and attempt to fulfill their own desires

i. Understand that beliefs do not always reflect reality

ii. Appreciate what others do because they desire things and believe that certain actions will help fulfill those desires

e. 4-year-olds more sophisticated students of psychology than the egocentric beings described by Piaget

f. Theory of mind better thought of as set of understandings that are constantly being refined

6. Nature and nurture

a. Nature evidence

i. Support from evolutionary perspective from primates like chimps, gorillas, and other apes who show the capacity to deceive

ii. Theory of mind due to maturing neurological systems and cognitive advancement along with abnormal brain development in autistic children may be responsible for lack of theory of mind

iii. Research using functional magnetic resonance imaging (fMRI) has been used to identify areas of prefrontal cortex and temporoparietal areas involved in thinking about people's beliefs

iv. Areas of adult brain that respond during a false belief task do not respond during questioning about false photographs

v. Areas of prefrontal cortex active in adults' ability to think about others' beliefs are active in 4- to 6-year-olds who are able to pass the false belief task

vi. Mirror neurons—activated both when we perform an action and when we observe someone else perform the same action appear to be involved in theory of mind understanding and empathy (all areas of difficulty for autistics)

vii. (Exploration Box on mirror neurons and the theory of mind)

b. Nurture evidence

i. Acquisition of theory of mind requires experience with other humans (participating in a "community of minds")

    ii. Deaf children of deaf parents who communicate effectively with children (often through sign) result in child developing a theory of mind on schedule; deaf children of hearing parents who do not converse in sign early show delays in ability to perform false belief tasks (may struggle until age 8 to 10 years)

    iii. Preschoolers who interact more with siblings tend to acquire theory of mind skills quicker (engaging in pretend play may be especially instructive)

    iv. Parents can impact development of theory of mind

    v. Parental "mind-mindedness," talking in elaborate ways about their children's mental states, tends to lead to advanced theory of mind skills

    vi. Cultures in which children do not have experience talking about thoughts and beliefs show delayed acquisition of theory of mind skills (i.e., culture plays role in acquisition of this skill)

  c. Acquiring a theory of mind, the foundation for all future social cognitive development, begins in infancy and toddlerhood through a combination of nature and nurture factors (e.g., joint attention, mirror neurons)

  d. Children who have mastered theory of mind tend to have more advanced social skills and are more socially adjusted

  e. Theory of mind can be used for "bad" ends as bullies and liars often prove adept at "mind reading"

C. Describing and Evaluating Other People

  1. Children younger than 7 to 8

    a. Can describe people primarily in physical terms

    b. Tend to perceive others in terms of physical appearance, possessions, and activities

    c. When using "psychological" terms to describe others, tend to make global versus specific statements (i.e., "bad person" or "good person")

    d. Do not view traits as enduring (i.e., predictive of future behavior)

  2. Children at 7 to 8 begin to infer enduring traits in others

  3. Children age 11 or 12

    a. More use of personality traits to explain why people behave the way they do

    b. Become more psychologically minded

  4. Adolescents more advanced

    a. Offer personality profiles that are more psychological

    b. See others as having unique personalities

    c. Able to analyze how diverse and often inconsistent traits in others fit together

  5. Basic progression in perceptions of others

    i. Physical and global description in preschool

    ii. More differentiated and psychologically orientated at 7 to 8

    iii. More integrated personalities; see how seemingly inconsistent traits fit together

D. Social Perspective-Taking

  1. Social perspective-taking (role-taking) skills—ability to adopt other people's perspectives and understanding their thoughts and feelings in relations to one's own

       a. Social perspective-taking skills example of theory of mind in action

       b. Essential in the ability to think about moral issues, to predict the consequences of one's actions, and to empathize with others

    2. Selman contributed greatly to understanding of role-taking using interpersonal dilemmas (e.g., story of Holly, her father to whom she promises to not climb trees, and a kitten in a tree)

    3. Selman's findings indicate that social perspective-taking abilities develop in a stagelike manner (consistent with Piaget's theory)

       a. 3- to 6-year-old children highly egocentric

       b. 8- to 10-year-olds' ability to appreciate that two people can have different ideas emerge with concrete operations (due to reduction in egocentrism)

       c. Adolescents at formal operations stage of thought can juggle multiple perspectives, including perspectives of "generalized other" or the broader social group

    4. Advances in social cognition more likely if parents good models of social perspective taking, consider thoughts of children, and rely on explanations

    5. Role-taking advancement has important implications on relationship skills

    6. Interacting with peers sharpens role-taking, and role-taking advancements make child more sensitive to peers

E. Social Cognition in Adulthood

    1. Involves both gains and losses

       a. Adults better able to integrate multiple and discrepant perspectives (i.e., see both sides of an issue)

       b. Older adults may be better able to infer traits like honesty in others

          i. Performance is enhanced by accumulated expertise about the world of people

       c. Losses in older adults may be result of declines in basic cognitive functioning (e.g., working memory, processing speed)

    2. For the most part, social cognitive abilities hold up in later life

       a. Area of the brain associated with these skills ages slowly

       b. Older adults come to rely on simple rules of thumb about people

       c. Skills may hold up well because they are exercised every day

    3. Older adults vary greatly in social cognitive abilities

       a. Sharpest social cognitive skills are seen in those who remain socially active

       b. Poorer social cognitive skills in isolated or inactive adults

II Perspectives on Moral Development

A. Defining Morality

    1. Morality—ability to distinguish right from wrong, act on this distinction, and experience pride when doing right and shame when doing wrong

    2. Three basic developmental components of morality

       a. Affective (feelings concerning self and others)

       b. Cognitive (thoughts of right and wrong)

       c. Behavioral (our actions)

B. Moral Affect: Psychoanalytic Theory and Beyond

    1. Moral affect—emotions felt when one does wrong (e.g., shame, guilt) or right (e.g., pride)

a. Empathy—vicariously experiencing others' feelings
  i. Empathy can motivate prosocial behavior
b. Prosocial behavior—positive acts of helping or sharing, reflecting concern for others
2. Freud sees formation of superego (conscience) during phallic stage as critical
  a. Superego forms in order to resolve conflict over love for same-sex parent and one result is taking on the moral standards of one's parents as one's own
    i. Superego like having parent "inside of head"
3. Many Freudian ideas unsupported
  a. Cold and punishing parents who make children anxious about losing their parents' love do not raise more morally mature children
  b. Males do not have stronger superegos
    i. Freud predicted this difference because males have stronger fear of castration and are more motivated to internalize parental values
  c. Moral development occurs long before phallic stage and extends long after age 6 or 7
4. Despite lack of support, Freud's main themes still taken seriously
  a. Moral emotions part of morality and motivate moral behavior
  b. Early relationships with parents contribute to moral development
  c. Children must internalize moral standards in order to behave morally when no authority figure present
C. Moral Reasoning: Cognitive Developmental Theory
1. Cognitive developmental approach
  a. Moral reasoning—thinking process underlying decisions to act right or wrong
  b. Move beyond egocentrism to construct reciprocity—mutual give and take in relationships
  c. Moral reasoning is thought to progress through an invariant sequence (i.e., fixed and universal order of stages)
  d. Cognitive focus is on how we decide to do right/wrong, not what we actually decide to do
2. Piaget's view in terms of premoral period and two moral stages
  a. Premoral period—preschool time when children show little understanding of rules and cannot be considered moral beings
  b. Heteronomous morality—ages 6-10
    i. Begin to take rules seriously
    ii. See rule of authority figures (e.g., parents) as sacred
    iii. Heteronomous—under the rule of another
    iv. Judge rule violation in terms of extent of damage done
  c. Autonomous morality—ages 10-11
    i. Appreciate that rules are agreements between individuals
    ii. Pay attention to intentions of acts
3. Kohlberg's view—universal, invariant sequences (inspired by Piagetian ideas)
  a. Presented 10- to 16-year-old males with dilemmas
  b. Analyzed and created model with three levels and two stages within each level

     c. Stages of moral reasoning
        i. One example of dilemma involves Dr. Jefferson and the issue of mercy killing
     d. Level 1: preconventional morality—focus on personal satisfaction
        i. Punishment and obedience orientation (stage 1)—focus on possible consequence to self
        ii. Instrumental hedonism (stage 2)—focus on gaining rewards
     e. Level 2: conventional morality—focus on internalized values set by others
        i. "Good boy" or "good girl" morality (stage 3)—focus on following approved social roles set by others
        ii. Authority and social-order-maintaining morality (stage 4)—focus on adherence to rules of legitimate authority (e.g., laws)
     f. Level 3: postconventional morality—focus on personal set of broadly defined principles that are not set by some other authority
        i. Morality of contract, individual rights, and democratically accepted law (stage 5)—focus on "social contract"
        ii. Morality of individual principles of conscience (stage 6)—focus on respect for all
     g. Progression though stages based, in part, on development of perspective-taking abilities
  4. Influences on moral development
     a. Kohlberg saw two main influences on moral development: cognitive growth and social interactions with equals
     b. Required cognitive growth
        i. To reach conventional level of moral reasoning, must be able to take other people's perspectives
        ii. To gain the capacity for postconventional thinking, must have solid command of formal-operational thinking
     c. Required social interactions
        i. Working out differences with peers or equals contributes more to moral development than one-sided interactions with authority figures (e.g., parents)
        ii. Advanced schooling (i.e., college) contributes to general cognitive growth and exposes students to more diverse perspectives
D. Moral Behavior: Social Learning Theory
  1. Primary interest of social cognitive theory is the behavior exhibited (what we actually do) when facing temptation or opportunity to act in a prosocial manner
  2. Social learning theorists like Bandura suggest that moral behavior is learning (i.e., acquired through experience) through observational learning and reinforcement/punishment and is strongly influenced by situational factors
  3. Moral thinking is linked to moral action through cognitive self-regulatory mechanism—those monitoring and evaluating own actions
     a. Apply consequences to ourselves and become able to exert self-control (i.e., gain ability to inhibit urges to misbehave)
     b. Moral disengagement—in order to avoid condemning ourselves, may engage in immoral behavior (e.g., underpaid employee pilfers from company)

    i. People who have perfected techniques of moral disengagement tend to engage in the most antisocial and unethical behavior

  E. The Functions of Morality: Evolutionary Theory

   1. Evolutionary theories like Krebs' have contributed to our understanding of moral development

    a. Focus on aspects of morality that helped with adaptation (e.g., living in groups and socializing to increase corporation changes if obtaining food or protecting from harm)

     i. Social animals like dogs and wolves may be a "moral code" that governs fairness; those not "playing by the rules" become outcasts

   2. "Survival of fittest" implies raw selfishness

    a. Evolutionary theorists argue that we have a genetic self-interest to act altruistically toward kin because they will pass on family genes to the next generations

    b. Cooperation with others to obtain resources that we could not get on our own makes genetic sense as does abiding by rules to avoid punishment

   3. Unlike the dark portrayal of humans by Freud, evolutionary theory views humans as predisposed to empathy and prosocial behavior (humans may be uniquely altruistic species)

   4. Theoretical approaches to why a teenager named Bart will cheat on exam

    a. Freud focus on strength of superego and sense of guilt

    b. Kohlberg interested in individual's current stage of moral thinking

    c. Bandura interested in reinforced moral behavior, observed models, if he has well-developed self-regulatory mechanisms that cause him to take responsibility for his actions

    d. Evolutionary perspective focuses on adaptive functions of cheating

II The Infant

  A. Early Moral Training

   1. Infants amoral—lack sense of morality (right and wrong) and are not expected to be "good"

   2. Infants must learn to

    a. Experience negative emotions when they violate rules

    b. Exert self-control

    c. Inhibit impulses when tempted to violate rules

    d. 18- to 24-month-olds begin to show visible signs of distress when they violate standards of behavior

    e. Even younger infants seem capable of judging moral actions (Exploration Box on infants judgment)

   3. Mutually responsive orientation—close, affectively positive, and cooperative relationship between child and parent best situation for moral development

    a. Mutually responsive relationships make children want to comply with adult rules and adopt their values, learn moral emotions like guilt and empathy, and develop the capacity for advanced moral reasoning, to help them resist temptation when no one is around to catch them

      b. Parents should discuss toddlers' behavior in an open way, with focus on emotion-centered discussions

      c. Parents who have close mutual relationship and discuss emotional consequences with their children assist those children in developing a conscience

B. Empathy and Prosocial Behavior

    1. At birth, infants show primitive empathetic response by becoming distressed when they hear other babies cry

    2. Between ages 1 and 2, truer form of empathy emerges

      a. React to distress in friend by providing comfort (e.g., giving them a teddy bear)

      b. 18-month-olds help adults pick up objects that they have dropped

      c. With age, empathy become less egocentric and more sophisticated

III The Child

A. Thinking through Kohlberg's Dilemmas

    1. Piaget believed that children did not understand the importance of assessing intent of wrongdoers until age 10 or 11

    2. Kohlberg did not have much to say about children other than they are mostly preconventional reasoners taking egocentric perspectives on morality

    3. Both underestimated children's moral understanding

B. Weighing Intentions

    1. Piaget suggests that young children (heteronomous thinkers) judge moral behavior on basis of consequences, and older children (autonomous thinkers) judge on basis of intention

    2. Flaw in that issues of intention and amount of damage confounded

    3. Nelson conducted study on intention (good, bad) and consequence of action (positive, negative)

      a. 3-year-olds' positive consequences more favorable

      b. Piaget correct that young children assigned more weight to consequences, but wrong to conclude that young incapable of considering intention

C. Understanding Rules

    1. Piaget stated that 6- to 10-year-old heteronomous children view rules as sacred, laid down by respected authority figures

      a. Turiel found that children distinguish between moral rules and social-conventional rules

          i. Moral rules—focus on welfare and rights of others

          ii. Social-conventional rules—standards determined by social consensus

          iii. Preschool children distinguish between types of rules, viewing moral rules as more compelling and unalterable (e.g., wrong to hit = a moral rule, but ok to leave seat at preschool = a social-conventional rule)

      b. 6- to 10-year-olds can understand that rules are not sacred (something Piaget did not expect in children at this age), and they do not blindly accept any dictate offered by an authority figure as legitimate

D. Applying Theory of Mind

    1. 4-year-olds have theory of mind and understand intention of others

2. Understanding of wrongdoers' beliefs at time of harmful act impacts judgments
    a. Children with well-developed theory of mind better able to distinguish between a lie and someone who simply has a wrong fact
    b. Theory of mind helps children understand people's emotional reactions (e.g., bad to give puppy to someone who fears puppies)
    c. Young children need to link behavioral choice and emotions

E. Moral Socialization
    1. Social learning theory suggestions to parents
        a. Reinforce moral behavior, punish immoral behavior, avoid being overly harsh (side effect of anxiety or teaching aggression), and model moral behavior
    2. Hoffman compared three approaches to discipline
        a. Love withdrawal—withhold affection after misbehavior (create anxiety by threatening loss of reinforcement by parent)
        b. Power assertion—use power (e.g., administer spanking, take privileges)
        c. Induction—explain why behavior is wrong and emphasize how behavior affects others
    3. Best approach to foster moral development?
        a. Induction superior to love withdrawal or power assertion because it breeds empathy
        b. Love withdrawal tends to not be that effective
        c. Power assertion often associated with moral immaturity than moral maturity
            i. Children of abusive parents feel less guilt and engage in more immoral behavior
            ii. Even at mild levels, power tactics are generally ineffective
            iii. Power assertion interferes with internalization of rules and undermines ability to exert self-control
            iv. Power assertion works best in loving and mutually responsive parent-child relationship
    4. Effective parenting use of proactive parenting strategies—tactics designed to prevent misbehavior and reduce the need for correction or discipline—to prevent misbehavior (e.g., distracting from temptation)
        a. (Exploration Box on a case study in raising a moral child)
    5. No one best method of discipline with impact dependent on child, parent, situation, and culture
        a. Parent needs to maintain high-quality relationship with child and to know which approach to use in a given situation
    6. Child's temperament also impacts degree of moral trainability
        a. Children are easiest to socialize if they are by temperament fearful or inhibited (i.e., become distressed when disciplined and want to avoid such distress in the future), when they are capable of effortful control and are able to inhibit their urges to engage in wrongdoing
        b. Fearful, inhibited children can be socialized through a gentle touch, capitalizing on their anxiety but not terrorizing them
        c. Fearless children do not respond well to being treated harshly and are most likely learn to comply with rules and requests when parents engage in a mutually responsive orientation
        d. Goodness of fit between child and social environment critical

IV The Adolescent

A. Changes in Moral Reasoning

1. Kohlberg stages

a. Preconventional (stages 1 and 2) dominate until the teen years

b. Conventional reasoning dominates (Kohlberg stages 3, good boy or girl, and 4, authority and social order-maintaining morality) by late teens

c. Older adolescents show broader societal perspective on justice and greater concern over maintaining the social system

d. Basic change, shift from preconventional to conventional

    i. Express genuine concern over living up to moral standards they have been taught

    ii. Postconventional reasoning does not emerge until adulthood (if at all)

e. Attempt to live up to standards (e.g., laws taken more seriously)

f. Teens view being moral as important part of identity, and those with strong moral identity are capable of more advanced moral reasoning

B. Antisocial Behavior

1. Few adolescents involved in serious antisocial conduct (e.g., rape, assault, robbery), but crime rates peak during adolescence in most societies (especially for "hell-raising" crimes like vandalism)

a. Most severely antisocial adults start antisocial careers in adolescence with early misbehavior cumulating in juvenile delinquency—law breaking by a minor

b. Some individuals qualify for a psychiatric diagnosis of a conduct disorder—a persistent pattern of violating the rights of others or age-appropriate societal norms through such behaviors as fighting, bullying, and cruelty; others may receive a diagnosis of antisocial personality disorder

    i. Most children and adolescents who engage in antisocial behavior do not grow up to be antisocial adults

c. Two subgroups of antisocial youth

    i. Persistent antisocial behavior across the lifespan

    ii. Larger group that shows antisocial behavior only during adolescence (perhaps in response to peer pressure)

d. Some relationship between moral reasoning and antisocial behavior but likely involves factors other than immature moral reasoning

    i. Aggressive teens or those with conduct disorders are less likely than other teens to show empathy and concern for others in distress and often feel little guilt or remorse about their acts

2. Dodge's Social Information-Processing Model

a. Key to understanding aggression behavior is how an individual processes and interprets social information

b. Six steps to the process

    i. Encoding of cues—taking in information

    ii. Interpretation of cues—making sense of information

    iii. Clarification of goals—deciding what to achieve

    iv. Response search—thinking of actions to achieve goals

    v. Response decision—weighing pros and cons of actions

Chapter 13

vi. Behavioral enactment—doing something

 c. Do not have to go through steps in a specific order (can cycle among them or work on two or more simultaneously)

 d. Skills in each area tend to increase with age

 e. Deficient or biased processing at any step can result in an interpretation of a social situation that leads to aggression (often found in highly aggressive youth)

 f. Example of highly aggressive adolescent tripped by classmate is likely to

  i. Process few cues and hold bias suggesting trip was deliberate

  ii. Make attribution of "hostile intent"

  iii. Set goal of getting even

  iv. Think of only a few responses, mostly aggressive

  v. Conclude that aggressive response will have positive outcome

  vi. Carry out aggressive act selected

 g. Many respond impulsively and aggressively "without thinking"

 h. Severely aggressive youth often have experienced abandonment, neglect, abuse, or other trauma that helps them morally justify negative actions against any threat and feel morally justified in taking antisocial action because they believe that they are only retaliating against students who are "out to get them"

 i. Basic problem with Dodge's model is that it does not clarify whether aggression is the result of "how one thinks, "what one thinks," or "whether one thinks"

3. Patterson's coercive family environments

 a. Coercive family environments—family members locked in power struggle trying to control others through negative and coercive tactics

 b. Parents learn that they can stop child's behavior (at least temporarily) by yelling or hitting (form of negative reinforcement)

 c. As coercive tactics become more common, they have less effect on child's behavior

 d. Antisocial children are rejected by peers, become unpopular, and may become more delinquent and aggressive

 e. No doubt that ineffective parenting in childhood contributes to behavioral problems, peer rejection, involvement with antisocial peers, and antisocial behavior in adolescence

4. Nature and nurture

 a. Males are overall more aggressive

  i. Shows up in many cultures and is evident as early as infancy

  ii. Aggressive male tendencies may be evolutionarily related to adolescents being more successful at mating, increasing their ability to pass on genes to future generations

 b. Some males and females more genetically predisposed to have difficult temperaments, impulsive tendencies, that contribute to aggression, delinquency, and criminal behavior

    c. Behavioral geneticists suggest genetics account for 40% of variation among individual antisocial behavior, with remaining 60% accounted for by environmental influences

    d. Gene-environment interaction—child with genetic predisposition toward aggression in dysfunctional family may result in antisocial behavior

        i. MAOA gene on X chromosome may contribute to inability to control temper

        ii. Children with this gene variant who are provoked are less able to control their anger and show higher levels of antisocial behavior

    e. Gene-environment correlation—child with genetic predisposition toward aggression may evoke coercive parenting

    f. Evocative gene-environment correlation—child's antisocial behavior and negative parenting influence each other reciprocally

    g. Prenatal environment (e.g., exposure to alcohol, lead poisoning) may contribute to unhealthy behavioral trajectory in children

    h. Culture can play a role

        i. Collectivist cultures (like Japanese, Hispanic) children taught to value social harmony; result is less antisocial behavior

        ii. Exposure to violent media may increase violence

        iii. United States is generally violent nation

        iv. Aggression and violence two to three times higher in low socioeconomic neighborhoods

        v. School environment can play a role

        vi. Bullying—repeatedly inflicting harm (through words or actions) on weaker peers who are often unable to defend themselves

        vii. Bullying somewhat of an epidemic in schools with lower standards of achievement and in which no one attempts to stop the bullying

    i. Dodge and Pettit have aggression model that integrates all influences in a biopsychosocial model based on a dynamic cascade model in which aggression results from the interplay between numerous biological, individual, and social factors (e.g., genes, living in violent area, antisocial peers, coercive parents, cognitive factors including a databank of social knowledge about topics related to aggression) more risk factors, greater likelihood of aggression against an adult

        i. Antisocial adults stand a good chance of becoming the kind of negative and coercive parents who raises antisocial children

    j. Prevention of antisocial behavior should be a national priority

        i. Fast Track Program designed by Dodge and members of the Conduct Problems Prevention Research Group to foster social-information processing and social skills

        ii. Effective in reducing antisocial behavior and preventing the diagnoses of conduct disorder and other psychiatric problems

V The Adult
  A. Changes in Moral Reasoning

    1. Postconventional moral reasoning (Kohlberg stage 5) may emerge in young adulthood, but seldom does

2. No real major changes in complexity of moral thinking in relatively educated individuals
3. Older adults have greater sense of having learned life lessons
4. Spirituality—ultimate search for meaning of life may or may not be carried out
5. Spirituality and postconventional thinking both related to wisdom

B. Kohlberg's Theory in Perspective
   1. Theory made tremendous contribution to field of psychology for many years
      a. Weak support for developmental progression in moral thought (e.g., only a minority of people shift from conventional to postconventional perspective in adulthood)
   2. Charges of bias
      a. Claims of cultural bias—biased against collectivist cultures that emphasize social harmony and place good of group ahead of good for the individual
         i. People in collectivist cultures are scored in stage 3 yet may have sophisticated concepts of justice
         ii. Hindu children and adults rate getting a haircut the day after a father dies as a very morally offensive act (Americans don't)
         iii. Americans view beating a wife for being disobedient and going to a movie without permission as a serious moral violation, Hindus do not
         iv. Results challenge the notion of moral development as universal but rather point our the fact that moral judgments are shaped by the social context in which we develop
      b. Political bias—some believe that highest stages only achievable if you have liberal attitude toward issues that are biased against political conservatives (e.g., oppose capital punishment)
      c. Gender bias—possible bias against women
         i. Carol Gilligan argued that Kohlberg's stages (initially developed using only male subjects) are biased against women (i.e., women tend to be stage 3 and males stage 4)
         ii. Gilligan suggests socialization leads to morality of justice (focus on laws, rules, individual rights, and fairness) in men and morality of care (focus on obligation to selflessness and welfare of others) in women
         iii. Little support that Kohlberg's model systematically biased against women
         iv. Few actual sex differences in moral reasoning (i.e., both men and women tend to use care-based reasoning when pondering relationship dilemmas and justice-based reasoning when pondering issue of rights)
         v. Gilligan did increase awareness of looking at both morality of care and morality of justice
      d. Underemphasizing emotion and behavior
         i. Kohlberg's theory has a primary focus on moral thinking and devotes little attention to moral emotions and moral behavior
         ii. Higher rate of moral reasoning found in those who behave more prosocially and less likely to engage in delinquent behavior
         iii. When relationships between moral reasoning and behavior are found, they tend to be weak

        iv. Kohlberg underestimated children's moral development, and the later stages are not that supported

C. New Approaches to Morality
1. New emphasis on role of empathy in motivating moral action
   a. Haidt suggests that humans have evolved to have quick moral intuitions based on emotions or disgust; such intuitions more important than deliberate moral reasoning
   b. Dual-process models of morality—both deliberate thought and emotion/intuition inform decisions about moral issues and motivate behavior
      i. (Exploration Box on dual-process morality)

D. Religion and Spirituality
1. Kohlberg viewed moral development and religious development as distinct, but others see the two as clearly interrelated
   a. Fowler proposed stages in the development of religious faith from infancy to adulthood, which paralleled Kohlberg's stages (e.g. concrete images of God in childhood to universal perspective on faith in adulthood)
2. Exploring religious and spiritual issues part of identity formation (children adopt beliefs of parents and then may reject them when they develop their own belief system)
   a. Religiosity (religiousness)—sharing the beliefs and participating in the practices of an organized religion
   b. Spirituality—a quest for ultimate meaning and a connection with something greater than one's self
      i. Spirituality may be carried out within or outside the context of a religion
3. Dillon and Wink investigated developmental changes in religiosity and spirituality
   a. Religiosity strong in adolescence, decreased somewhat in middle age and rose again in the late 60s and early 70s
   b. Spirituality was judged to be at lower levels that religiosity throughout adulthood but increased significantly from middle age to later adulthood (especially in women)
   c. Levels of religiosity and spirituality tend to be highly consistent within individuals
      i. Highly religious individuals tend to be conscientious and agreeable (if women)
      ii. Highly spiritual individuals tend to be highly open to new experiences
   d. Religiosity in later adulthood correlated with a sense of well-being stemming from positive relationships with others, involvement in social and community activities, and qualities associated with generativity
      i. Highly religious individuals are very involved in their religious communities and tend to have good physical health, good mental health, and high levels of prosocial behavior
   e. Highly spiritual individuals have a high sense of well-being that is derived from personal growth
      i. Spiritual adults tend to be highly involved in activities that allow them to express creativity, build their knowledge or skills, and display qualities like wisdom and insightfulness

    f. Religion and spirituality especially important to older adults in certain
        minority groups
        i. African-American and Caribbean blacks report more religious
            participation, more use of prayer, and more spirituality than non-
            Hispanic whites

SUGGESTIONS FOR CLASS DISCUSSIONS OR PROJECTS

1. Students might report on moral dilemmas they have experienced in their own lives. Do they
remember any early moral dilemmas? Do they remember how they chose to act and the
reasons for their actions? Was there any difference between how they thought about the
dilemma (e.g., what they knew they should do) versus how they acted (what they did do)? Is
their thinking about the dilemma different now? Would their course of action be different
now? If so, what accounts for these cognitive and behavioral changes? What about more
recent moral dilemmas? How are they the same and different from earlier dilemmas? Do
students think that if a recent dilemma occurred again later in life, they would behave the
same way? Why or why not?

You might consider focusing this discussion on childhood and adolescent incidences in which
the student was a bully or allowed bullying to take place (paralleling the opening section of
the text in which John Gibbs describes his experience at a camp at which a mentally retarded
adult was the victim of bullying).

2. An excellent film by Pierre Sauvage (VHS, 1997) allows students to think about moral
dilemmas of the most serious kind. *Weapons of the Spirit* tells the story of a Christian
mountain community in France that defied the Nazis and turned itself into a haven of refuge
for 5,000 Jews, including the filmmaker and his parents. One of the intriguing aspects of this
experience is that an entire town of people made the decision to help the Jews, largely without
conferring with each other. This would be a good opportunity to revisit Bronfenbrenner and
think about moral decision-making beyond the individual level. Other questions for
discussion: What in the development of these individuals might have prepared them to make
the choices they made? Why do these rescuers resist the label of "hero"? There are a number
of books available on the subjects, as well. Here are a few:

   Block, G., and Drucker, M. (1992). *Rescuers: Portraits of Moral Courage in the
Holocaust*. Holmes & Meier.

   Fogelman, E. (1995). *Conscience & Courage: Rescuers of Jews during the Holocaust*.
Anchor.

   Hallie, P.P. (1994). *Village of Le Chambon and How Goodness Happened There*.
Harperperennial.

3. Many students have trouble relating to the traditional Kohlberg moral dilemmas such as the
"Heinz dilemma" because they find them out of date or unrealistic. This and other moral
dilemmas can be found in Colby, Kohlberg, Gibbs, & Lieberman, 1983. Pick a more
contemporary topic, such as obeying (or disobeying) social networking rules (i.e., posting

something unflattering about someone else on Facebook) or cheating (or not cheating) on a test using your cellphone to transmit answers, and ask students to generate responses that fit into each stage of Kohlberg's theory.

Gump, Baker, and Roll (2000) claim to have developed a potentially better measure of moral development. Have students look over their findings and discuss the pros and cons of this alternative approach.

Colby, A., Kohlberg, L., Gibbs, J., & Lieberman, M. (1983). A longitudinal study of moral judgment. *Monographs of the Society for Research in Child Development, 48* (Nos. 1-2, Serial No. 200).

Gump, L.S., Baker, R.C., and Roll, S. (2000). The morality justification scale: reliability and validity of a new measure of care and justice orientation. *Adolescence, 35(137),* 67-76.

4. Have students discuss whether moral education or values clarification should be included in both the school curriculum (at the elementary, middle school, high school, and college levels) and workplace (e.g., job place rules). What are the pros and cons of such programs? At what age should children be exposed to values clarification? How can values be presented so that they are not offensive to students with different cultural and religious backgrounds? Do we have the right to tell adults how to behave? For some real fireworks, have the class attempt to make a list of five values that all children and adults must possess!

5. Use the crisis of school violence (e.g., the Columbine or Virginia Tech shootings) to discuss the role of nature and nurture in explaining antisocial behavior. What factors have been used to explain the behavior of these children? A partial list would include peer rejection, poor parenting, access to weapons, media exposure to violence, and genetic predisposition to violence. Have students weigh the impact of these factors and any other factors they generate. You might contrast this list to one generated to explain the behavior of an adult in a similar situation (e.g., select any recent case of an adult killing their coworkers).

6. Given the violence on middle school, high school, and college campuses, the issue of bullying and bullies has come to the forefront of psychology and popular press debate. An interesting class discussion could focus on the issue of bullying in academic settings. Students may wish to discuss their personal experiences (as either bully or victim). You could also solicit suggestions for methods of reducing bullying in school. To get things started, you might discuss the Steps to Respect program described by Frey (2005).

Frey, K.S. (2005). Reducing playground bullying and supporting beliefs: An experiment trail of the Steps to Respect Program. *Developmental Psychology*, 41(3), 479-491.

A related activity involves a project in which students attempt to answer the question, "Can individuals who are aggressive be taught not to display antisocial behavior?" To complete this assignment, students should conduct a Web or library search on the effectiveness of anger management programs. Based on their findings, they should write a three- to four-page paper in which they either defend or condemn the use of violence prevention programs.

7. As noted in the text, spirituality is hard to define. Have students explore their and their classmates' conceptions of this concept by having everyone in class write down three characteristics of someone who they would consider spiritual. These definitions can then be shared in small groups and/or with the class as whole as the foundation for a discussion of the topic.

SUGGESTED FILMS AND VIDEOS

Anger (2002, *Insight Media*, VHS/DVD, 37 minutes): This video explores various factors that contribute to negative emotions and aggression.

Encouraging Moral Development in Children (2006, *Insight Media*, DVD, 14 minutes): This short video focuses on the moral development in preschoolers.

Morality: Judgments and Actions (2002, *Insight Media*, DVD, 30 minutes): This program reviews key theories of moral development (e.g., Piaget, Kohlberg) and considers the moral decision-making of individuals from diverse cultural backgrounds.

Religion and Spirituality (2008, *Insight Media*, DVD, 30 minutes): This program provides contrasting definitions of religiosity and spirituality and discusses the psychological and social functions of these belief systems.

Taking a Stand: The Bullying Prevention Series (2006, Films for the Humanities & Sciences, DVD/VHS, three videos 18–20 minutes each): This compelling series of videos focuses on the topic of bullying among boys, girls, and online cyberbullying.

SUGGESTED WEBSITES

A Discussion about Theory of Mind: From an Autistic Perspective
http://www.autistics.org/library/AE2000-ToM.html

Kohlberg's Stages of Moral Development
http://faculty.plts.edu/gpence/html/kohlberg.htm

Moral Development: Answers.com
http://www.answers.com/topic/moral-development?cat=health

Parenting in America: Fostering Goodness
http://parenthood.library.wisc.edu/Berkowitz/Berkowitz.html

The Measurement of Family Religiosity and Spirituality
http://aspe.hhs.gov/hsp/connections-papers04/paper1.htm

SUGGESTED READINGS

Greenfield, E.A. (2009). Do formal religious participation and spiritual perceptions have independent linkages with diverse dimensions of psychological well-being? *Journal of Health and Social Behavior*, 50(2), 196-212.

Killen, M., and Smetana, J.G. (Eds). (2006). *Handbook of Moral Development*. Mahwah, N.J.: Lawrence Erlbaum Associates.

Konijn, E.A. (2007). I wish I were a warrior: The role of wishful identification in the effects of violent video games on aggression in adolescent boys. *Developmental Psychology*, 43(4), 1038-1044.

Shore, K. (2009). Preventing bullying. *Education Digest*, 75(4), 39-44.

Takagishi, H., Kameshima, S., Schug, J., Koizumi, M., and Yamagishi, T. (2010). Theory of mind enhances preference for fairness. *Journal of Experimental Child Psychology*, 105 (1/2), 130-137.

ATTACHMENT AND SOCIAL RELATIONSHIPS

LEARNING OBJECTIVES

After students have read and studied the material in this chapter, they should be able to answer the following questions:

PERSPECTIVES ON RELATIONSHIPS

1. How do relationships with others contribute to development?

2. How does Bowlby's attachment theory explain attachment? In this model, how do nature and nurture contribute to the development of attachment?

3. In what way are peers part of the two worlds of childhood?

THE INFANT

4. In what ways are infants emotional beings? How are emotions socialized and regulated?

5. How do infants become attached to a caregiver? What are some observable signs of infant attachment?

6. What types of attachment relationships can develop between infants and caregivers? What infant, caregiver, and contextual factors determine the quality of early attachments?

7 How do early relationships relate to later development? What are the consequences of early social deprivation? How are the first peer relationships best characterized?

THE CHILD

8. What features characterize parent-child attachments and peer relations in childhood?

9. What different types of play evolve during the first few years of life? What are the developmental benefits of play?

10. What factors contribute to peer acceptance, popularity, and friendship or to peer rejection during childhood? How are sociometric measures used to place individuals into social status categories? What are the main categories?

THE ADOLESCENT

11. How do relationships with parents and friends change during adolescence?

12. How do social networks change between late childhood and late adolescence? What are the phases of dating?

13. How do social networks and friendships change during adulthood? How does socioemotional
    selectivity theory explain these changes?

14. What is the process of romantic relationship formation in adulthood? How do filter theory and homogamy explain this process? How does the triangular theory describe love?

15. What types of attachment styles are found in adulthood? In what ways do they impact development?

16. How do adult friendships and other relationships change in old age?

CHAPTER OUTLINE

I   Perspectives on Relationships
  A. Opening Vignette on Morality Issues
    1. Mike Pohle, fiancée of Marcy Crevonis, was a victim of the mass murder of students at Virginia Tech University
    2. Seung Hui Cho, a lonely child who spoke little, spent days writing about violence and death before killing 32 people at Virginia Tech University
    3. Poet John Donne wrote, "No man is an island, entire of itself"
    4. No human can become entire without the help of other humans
  B. What Do We Gain from Social Relationships?
    1. Social relationships important, but theoretical disagreement over which relationships most critical to development
      a. Freud—stable relationship between mother and child critical
      b. Erikson—development of trust in parent-child relationship
  C. Attachment Theory
    1. Attachment theory (Bowlby and Ainsworth)—influential ethological theory of parent-child relationship
      a. Draws on components of psychoanalytic (contribution mother-child relationship) and cognitive (expectations of self and others) theory
    2. Attachment—strong affectional tie that binds a person to an intimate companion
      a. First attachment is to caregiver around 6 or 7 months of age
      b. Attachments are expressed in different ways
        i. Maintenance of proximity, preference for mom over other people, target of smile when baby is upset, confident to explore if mother there for security
      c. Throughout the lifespan, attachments are to special, irreplaceable people with whom we seek proximity and from whom we derive security
    3. Nature, nurture, and attachment
      a. Ethologists assume all species (including humans) born with behavioral tendencies to assist in survival
      b. Ethological theory proposes existence of biological predisposition to form attachments

  c. Imprinting—innate form of learning in which a young animal will follow and become attached to a moving object (often seen in chicks, ducks, or goslings)
    i. Groundbreaking imprinting research by Lorenz using goslings
    ii. Imprinting in goslings is automatic and irreversible and involves following a particular object (mother or Lorenz)
    iii. Imprinting has survival value
    iv. Imprinting may have a "sensitive period" and can be reversed
    v. Human infants do not become imprinted to their mothers, but rather come equipped with behaviors (e.g., clinging, smiling, vocalizations) that will promote adults to love and stay with them
    vi. Adults biologically programmed to respond to infant's signals (e.g., baby's grin)
    vii. Hormone oxytocin plays a role in facilitating parent-infant attachments and other relationships (Exploration Box on oxytocin as the love hormone)
    viii. Infants programmed to respond to sight, sound, and touch of caregiver
    ix. Sensitive period (first 3 years)—infant ready to attach but needs responsive caregiver (interaction between the two)
  d. Attachment in human infants may involve sensitive period
    i. Sensitive period (first 3 years)—time during which attachment likely but does not automatically form
    ii. Caregiver-infant interactive responses important to establishing early relationship
  e. Bonding—more of a biologically-based process (than attachment) in which parents and infants form a connection within the first few hours after birth
    i. Klaus and Kennell suggested that skin-to-skin contact immediately after birth was necessary for bonding
    ii. Subsequent research shows that early physical contact not necessary, and early bonding does not have much significance for later development
 4. Attachments and later development
  a. Bowlby proposed the existence of internal working models—cognitive representations of self and others constructed by infants—that guide the processing of social information and behavior in relationships
    i. Securely attached infants form internal working models suggesting that they are loveable
    ii. Insecurely attached infants form internal working models that they are difficult to love and that others are unreliable
    iii. Insecurely attached infants are expected to have difficulty participating in close relationships later in life
  b. Bowlby and Ainsworth summary
    i. Capacity to form relationships part of evolutionary heritage
    ii. Attachments unfold as interaction between biology and environment
    iii. First attachment types shape later attachments
    iv. Internal model of self affects later development
D. Peers and the Two Worlds of Childhood
 1. Peer—a social equal who functions at a similar level of behavioral complexity

2. "Two social worlds of childhood"—one adult-child and one child-peer
3. Some theorists view peer relationships as significant as infant-parent relationship
4. Piaget
   a. Peer relationships help children understand that relationships are reciprocal and are forced to learn role-taking skills
5. Neo-Freudian Harry Stack Sullivan
   i. Interpersonal relationships are important throughout the lifespan, but social needs change with age
   ii. Parent-child relationship central up until about age 6, but peers are becoming important
   iii. Children first need playmates, then peer acceptance, and then around 9 to 12 years of age, they need intimacy in the form of a close childhood friendships—chumships
   iv. Having a chum teaches children to take the perspective of others, can protect them from a poor child-parent relationship and from peer rejection
   v. Chumships pave the way for romantic relationships in adolescence

II The Infant
A. Early Emotional Development
   1. Izard maintains that basic emotions play critical role in motivating and organizing behavior
      a. Studied by videotaping infants' reactions to events (e.g., toy taken away)
      b. Infants express distinct "primary emotions"— contentment (smiling), interest (staring intently at objects), distress (grimaces in response to pain)
      c. Within the first 6 months, different emotions evolve from these primary emotions
         i. Commitment becomes joy or excitement
         ii. Interest becomes surprise
         iii. Distress becomes disgust then sadness
         iv. Anger develops around 4 months
         v. Fear develops around 5 months
      d. Self-conscious emotions—"secondary emotion" (e.g., embarrassment) come with self-awareness and emerge around 18 months
      e. Around age 2, self-conscious emotions based on judgment of performance emerge (e.g., pride, shame, guilt)
   2. Nature, nurture, and emotions
      a. Primary emotions (e.g., interest and fear) seem biologically programmed
      b. Timing of emergence of emotions tied to cognitive maturation
      c. Basic emotions likely evolved as way for ancestors to appraise and respond appropriately to novel stimuli
      d. Infants' emotional signals help ensure that caregivers respond to them
      e. Nurture also helps shape patterns of emotional expression (e.g., attachment relationship between infant and caregiver)
      f. Infants display range of emotions (positive to negative) that change quickly
      g. Mothers tend to display positive emotions (e.g., surprise, joy) and elicit positive emotions from infants

h. By age 1, begin social referencing—monitor companions' emotional reactions or companions in ambiguous situations and use information to decide how to act and feel

i. Infants especially attentive to stimuli that provoke negative emotional reactions in their parents (as if they know that these emotions are a warning signal)

j. Parents also socialize their child's emotions by reacting (sympathetically or critically) to their child's expressions of emotion

3. Emotion regulation
   a. Emotion regulation—process of initiating, maintaining, and altering emotions
   b. Very young infants reduce negative arousal by turning from unpleasant stimuli or sucking on a pacifier
   c. By end of the first year, infants can regulate emotions by rocking themselves or moving away from upsetting events
   d. By 18 to 24 months, toddlers try to control actions and objects that upset them
      i. Push away offending person or object
      ii. Knit brow or compress lips to suppress anger
      iii. As children gain symbolic logic and language, become able to regulate distress symbolically (e.g., repeating soothing word like "mommy coming soon")
   e. Emotional development influenced by infant temperament and caregiver behavior
      i. Attachments help infants regulate emotions and teach them how to do so
      ii. With age, infants gain control of emotions using methods learned in the context of the child-parent relationship (e.g., being rocked by a parent is basis for rocking one's self)
      iii. Attachment figures arouse powerful emotions (e.g., can overstimulate infants during play or distress them if they leave)
      iv. Infants develop their own distinct styles of emotional expression designed to keep attachment figures close

B. An Attachment Forms
   1. The caregiver's attachment to the infant
      a. Caregivers' emotional attachment may form before birth
      b. Parents with opportunity to have skin-to-skin contact with newborns feel a special bond (although such contact is not necessary to form an attachment)
      c. Infant characteristics (e.g., sucking, grasping) help endear them to caregivers
         i. Smiling is an especially important social signal
      d. Synchronized routines—turn-taking, or responding between infants and caregivers (e.g., playing peek-a-boo), promotes social interactions
      e. Caregiver-infant synchrony most likely to develop when caregiver is sensitive and infant alert (not being pushed)
   2. The infant's attachment to the caregiver
      a. Four phases of attachment
         i. Undiscriminating social responsiveness—birth to 2-3 months; infants responsive to voices and faces

   ii. Discriminating social responsiveness—2-3 months to 6-7 months; begin to express preference for familiar companion

   iii. Active proximity seeking/true attachment—6-7 months to about 3 years; form first attachments (often to mothers) and then to others; infant will stay close to attached individuals and will protest when they leave

   iv. Goal-corrected partnership—advanced cognitive skills allow for consideration of other peoples' goals in considering relationship behavior; 3 years and older; goal-corrected partnership phase lasts a lifetime

 3. Attachment-related fears

  a. Separation anxiety—fear when separated from attached individual; appears when attachments are forming and peaks around 14-18 months

  b. Stranger anxiety—wary or fretful when approached by unfamiliar individual; becomes common between 8-10 months

 4. Exploratory behavior

  a. Attachment facilitates exploration

  b. Attachment figure becomes secure base—point of safety from which to explore environment

C. Quality of Attachment

 1. Four types assessed in the strange situation

  a. Strange situation—method of assessing attachment involving child, parent, and stranger interacting in different combinations

  b. Ainsworth found four types of attachments

   i. Secure attachment—60-65% of infants comfortable exploring and using mom as base (stay close and continuously monitor); proximity maintenance, safe haven, separation distress, secure base

   ii. Resistant attachment—10% of infants have ambivalent reaction to caregiver (referred to as anxious/ambivalent attachment), very distressed when separated from mom, ambivalent when mom returns (i.e., remains close but resists attempts at physical contact), wary of strangers

   iii. Avoidant attachment—up to 15% of infants avoid contact with mom, do not explore, not wary of strangers; appear to be either denying need for affection or have learned to not express emotions

   iv. Disorganized/disoriented attachment—up to 15% of infants (more in high-risk families); associated with later emotional problems; dazed or immobile when reunited with mothers following separation or may seek contact and then abruptly move away; possess few strategies for regulating negative emotions like separation anxiety

 2. The caregiver's contributions

  a. Freud suggests importance of oral stage pleasure

   i. Whomever provides infant with oral pleasure will be the individual who will be the target of the bond/attachment

   ii. Best situation is mom with relaxed and generous feeding practices

  b. Harlow and Zimmerman (working with infant monkeys and surrogate mothers, one cloth and one wire) suggest importance of contact comfort

   i. Half monkeys fed by wire mom and half by cuddly cloth mom, yet all show preference to cloth mother over wire mom

        ii. Comfort contact—pleasurable tactile sensation more powerful contribution to attachment than feeding or reduction of hunger

       iii. Contact comfort promotes human attachments

       iv. Infants do become attached to someone other than the adult who feeds them

    c. Parenting styles contribute to attachment formation

       v. Secure attachments found in sensitive and responsive parents

       vi. Parenting style inconsistency contributes to insecure, resistant pattern of attachments

       vii. Depressed moms have difficultly responding to infant's signals and do not provide comfort

       viii. Resistant attachment style linked to the development of negative internal working images of self and parents in children as young as 3 years

       ix. Excess (intrusive) or insignificant amounts of stimulation contribute to avoidant attachment, parents may also find infant's cry extremely aversive

       x. Some parents are "overzealous" and provide high levels of stimulation even when an infant is uncomfortably aroused

       xi. Infants with avoidant style may make few emotional demands of adults

       xii. Disorganized/disoriented attachment evident in up to 80% of infants who have experienced physical abuse or maltreatment by parent

       xiii. Disorganized/disoriented attachment may involve severely depressed or drug-abusing mother

3. The infant's contributions

    a. Infants' cognitive development key to attachments

       i. Must recognize caregiver

       ii. Must have acquired person permanence—form of object permanence concerning people

       iii. Temperament of infant contributes to attachment; less secure if infant is fearful, irritable, or unresponsive

    b. Caregiver (e.g., depression) and infant traits interact to contribute to attachment type (e.g., mother with low sense of self-efficacy paired with infant with colic who cries endlessly may result in insecure attachment)

    c. Caregiver reactions appear most important for determining quality of attachment; little evidence that genes influence quality of attachment

4. Contextual contributions

    a. Poverty can make it difficult for parents to be sensitive and may contribute to insecure attachment formation

    b. Culture (society's expectations concerning appropriate parenting) can play role in attachment

       i. Western, individualistic cultures (e.g., German) emphasize strong sense of independence

       ii. The strange situation may underestimate the number of securely attached German infants as those who make few emotional demands of parents are often classified as "avoidant"

       iii. Eastern, collectivist cultures (e.g. Japan) encourage children to be dependent

    iv. The strange situation may overestimate the number of resistantly attached Japanese infants who are encouraged to be very dependent on parents and who often become highly distressed upon separation

    v. The main prediction of attachment theory, that there is a relationship between parental sensitivity and security of attachment, holds up well in cross-cultural research

 D. Implications of Early Attachment

  1. Social deprivation

   a. It is better to have loved and lost than to never have loved at all (i.e., infants raised in deprived institutional settings may never be able to form attachments)

   b. Research on Romanian infants raised in orphanages and adopted into U.S., Canadian, or U.K. homes

    i. Ratio of children to caregiver was often 1 caregiver for every 10-20 children, result was that children spent most of the day with no human contact and rocked themselves for stimulation

    ii. Some infants in such deprived orphanages for more than 6 months or more of life after birth overcame their problems once they were in adoptive homes, however, others displayed many problems (e.g., lack of normal cognitive development, withdrawn, overwhelmed in social situations)

    iii. Impact may be due to lack of stimulation of brain

    iv. Rapid recovery is possible, but many never recover; the longer the early deprivation, the worse it is

    v. Problems related to formation of disinhibited attachment— indiscriminate friendliness, lack of appropriate wariness of strangers, and difficulty participating in real, reciprocal, social interactions

    vi. Children will approach stronger, but then back off warily

    vii. Impact of early lack of social stimulation on attachment lends support to Bowlby's claim of a "sensitive period" for attachment formation

   c. Reason for damage from institutional deprivation

    i. Lack of proper nutrition, hygiene, and medical care, but even those with proper care who lack a stable team of caregivers often experience developmental delays and have long-lasting social and emotional difficulties

    ii. Normal development in an institution requires placing children into small groups with a consistent set of caregivers who interact with the children in a caring manner

    iii. Resilience possible given later opportunities to socialize and find someone to love

  2. Separation

   a. Long-term separation

    i. Infants who become separated from the caregiver to whom they have attached via illness, war, or other circumstances go through a grieving process but tend to recover once they are reunited with loved one

    ii. Infants permanently separated (e.g., caregiver dies) normally recover if they form attachment to someone else

        iii. The earlier the separation, the better
        iv. Infants who experience a series of separations may be permanently marred (e.g., withdrawn from human relations)
    b. Daycare
        i. Daycare can have positive or negative effects, but does not normally damage child development
        ii. Major longitudinal study by the National Institute of Child Health and Human development found that infants who received alternative forms of care, even over 20 hours per week, were no less secure than infants tended to by parents
        iii. Quality of parenting a stronger influence on attachment security than daycare experience
        iv. Children who spend a good deal of time in quality daycare perform better than home-reared children on measures of cognitive and language skills along with some social skills, but they also tend to display more behavioral problems
        v. Characteristics of a quality daycare include a reasonable child-to-caregiver ratio (e.g., 3:1 for infants, 8:1 for preschoolers), well-trained caregivers who are warm and responsive, stable staff (i.e., little turn-over), planned and age-appropriate activities
        vi. Quality of home environment interacts with quality of daycare
        vii. Infants fare poorly if their mothers are insensitive and unresponsive, and they were subjected to poor-quality daycare

3. Later development of securely and insecurely attached infants
    a. Secure attachment may lead to more social competence in later childhood
        i. Securely attached preschoolers are described as curious, self-directed, and eager to learn
        ii. Securely attached preschoolers more often popular with peers, curious, self-directed
        iii. Related to healthy emotional development
        iv. Secure attachment linked to positive emotional development and greater capacity to cope with stress
        v. Some evidence of relationship between infant attachment and later relationships (e.g.. Simpson and colleagues (2007) found link between secure attachments in infancy, peer relationships in elementary school, quality of friendships in adolescence, and emotional quality of romantic relationships in early adulthood through an indirectly associated chain of influences)
    b. Children unlikely to develop normally if they never have the opportunity to form an attachment or first relationships involve repeated separations
    c. Infant securely attached to mothers are not "forever blessed" nor are insecurely attached to moms "doomed"
        i. Affectionate ties to fathers can compensate for insecure infant-mother relationship
        ii. Negative life event (e.g., divorce) can convert secure into insecure attachment; positive events can convert insecure into secure (internal working models are subject to revision)
    d. All things considered, Bowlby-Ainsworth attachment theory well supported

E. First Peer Relations
   1. Infants have evolutionary-based capacity for forming attachments to caregivers and for establishing social relationships
      a. Infants show an interest in other babies at an early age
      b. By 6 months, infants will smile and babble at tiny companions, they will at times share nicely and other times squabble, and they begin to relate in meaningful way to one or two peers
      c. By 18 months, engage in simple reciprocal (complementary play) with peers and can adopt and reverse roles in their play
      d. Around 2 years, begin taking turns and demonstrate reciprocal exchange
      e. Some infants will show special, distinctive relationships with certain preferred playmates (friends)
         i. Infants raised in kibbutz with other infants may show true attachment to other infants as early as 1 year of age

III The Child
   A. Parent-Child Attachments
      1. Attachments change qualitatively during childhood
      2. Preschooler learn to negotiate separations from parents to make sure rituals take place (e.g., reading a book before going to bed)
      3. Older preschoolers seek attention from parents but become increasingly dependent on peers for social and emotional support
      4. Parents are there to be turned to in time of need, but elementary school children call on them less frequency
   B. Peer Networks
      1. From 2 to 12 years, increasing time spent with peers and less with adults (10% of interactions in toddlerhood and 30% of interactions in middle school involve peers)
      2. Gender segregation (play with same-sexed peer) increases with age
      3. Children experience different social worlds in sex-segregated play
         a. Boys in packs and girls in pairs
   C. Play
      1. Four general types of play in childhood
         a. Locomotor play (e.g., tag), object play (e.g., stacking blocks), social play (e.g., playing broad games), pretend play (e.g., enacting roles)
         b. Ages 2 to 5 are called the play years (time of exuberant and fanciful play)
      2. Play becomes more social
         a. Parten's model of social development in play
            i. Unoccupied play—child stands idly by
            ii. Solitary play—play alone and are highly involved
            iii. Onlooker play—begin to take interest in others but not very active
            iv. Parallel play—child plays next to other children, not really with them
            v. Associative play—play involves interaction of conversation and material, but still not mutual goal
            vi. Cooperative play—play involves common goal, collaboration

  b. Play becomes increasingly social and socially skilled with age
  c. Paten sees older children engaging in solitary play in order to build skills
  d. Older children work their way into groups first as onlookers and then in parallel play before joining the activity
 3. Play becomes more imaginative
  a. Pretend play—one actor and/or object stands for something else
   i. By 2 years, will wipe up an "imaginary spill" of tea
   ii. Toddlers capable of using symbolic capacity to construct mental representation of pretend event and to act on this representation
   iii. Pretend play fully blossoms at 2 to 5 years, enact elaborate dramas depicting heroes and heroines using fewer props
  b. Social pretend play—by age 2 to 3, begin more elaborate and cooperative play with caregivers and classmates
   i. Social pretend play universal and more frequent with age, but the actual quality of play highly influenced by culture (e.g., U.S. children like to play superhero; Korean children like to play family)
   ii. Individualistic culture—play aimed at asserting own identity
   iii. Collectivist culture—play aimed at increasing harmony of ego
 4. Play becomes more rule-governed
   i. Once in school, kids play more games with rules (e.g., tag, board games)
   ii. May need to reach concrete stage of development to follow rules
 5. What is good play?
  a. 19th century American children discouraged from play because it was thought to be frivolous; today play thought to mold little Einstein
  b. Play is evolved behavior helping children prepare for adulthood
   i. Girls playing with dolls grooming themselves for traditional role as mom
  c. Pretend play fosters cognitive, motor, and social skill development
   i. Playing contributes to the development of bone density and neural maturation
   ii. Pretend play linked to better performance on tests of creativity and language
   iii. Engaging in social pretend play allows children to hone social skills and construct theory of mind
   iv. Play contributes to positive emotional development (e.g., resolving emotional conflict, regulating emotions)
D. Peer Acceptance and Popularity
 1. Sociometric techniques—research methods for determining who people like and dislike within a group (e.g., classmates)
 2. Distinct categories of social status
  a. Popular—well liked, rarely disliked
  b. Rejected—rarely liked, often disliked
  c. Neglected—neither liked nor disliked (invisible to classmates)
  d. Controversial—liked by some and disliked by others (e.g., fun-loving leader who bullies peers)
  e. Average—in middle on like and dislike scale

229   Chapter 14

© 2012 Cengage Learning. All Rights Reserved. May not be copied, scanned, or duplicated, in whole or in part, except for use as permitted in a license distributed with a certain product or service or otherwise on a password-protected website for classroom use.

3. Popularity affected by personal characteristics like physical attractiveness, intelligence (relatively intelligent children more popular), and who have social competence—the ability to apply social cognitive skills successfully in initiating social interactions and resolving interpersonal conflict
4. Rejected children are often highly aggressive, although some are socially isolated, submissive children who are overly sensitive to teasing and are seen by others as "easy to push around"
5. Neglected children are nonaggressive, shy, unassertive (unnoticed)
6. Controversial children interesting as they may show good social skills while also showing aggressive bullying behavior
7. Popular children tend to hold back, assess social situation, and then blend in
8. Children rejected by peers tend to be pushy and disruptive
9. Neglected children tend to hang around edge of a group
10. Same type of child may be popular in one culture but not in another (e.g., shy unpopular in Canada and popular in China)
11. Way of gaining popularity changes with age (e.g., interest in opposite sex unpopular in childhood but popular in adolescence)
12. Rejection in early childhood due to aggressive behavior is associated with peer rejection in later grades
    a. Rejected children may become more poorly adjusted as a result of the rejection
    b. Rejected children have lower self-esteem, develop negative attitudes toward others, hang out with antisocial children, and perform more poorly on academic tasks
    c. Children who are rejected by peers may end up positively adjusted if they develop a niche outside of school where they are liked
E. Friendships
    1. Unpopular children may have a reciprocated social relationship, while popular kids may not have any
    2. Having friends increases odds of happiness and reduces the odds of loneliness and depression
    3. Friendships can be source of social support and comfort
    4. Secure attachment to parents better predicts having friends than it predicts being accepted by wider peer group

IV The Adolescent
A. Attachment to Parents
    1. Continue to need security and support from parents to become independent
        a. Adolescents may feel conflicted as they seek greater autonomy from parents while continuing to need their support
        b. Secure attachment to parents translates to stronger sense of identity, higher self-esteem, better social competence, better emotional adjustment, and fewer behavioral problems
    2. Going off to college qualifies as "naturally occurring strange situation"
        a. Some separation anxiety normal and adaptive
        b. Preoccupation with parents typically decreases in first semester
        c. College students who are securely attached to parents more psychologically sound and better socially adjusted

B. Friendships
  1. Early friendships based on enjoying common activities, mutual loyalty and caring in late childhood, and intimacy and self-disclosure in adolescence
  2. Adolescents tend to choose friends with similar psychological qualities (e.g., interest, values, personalities)
  3. Begin to form more cross-sexed friendships
     a. Same-sexed tend to be more intimate
     b. Girls report more emotional intimacy in cross-sexed relationships
     c. May be a downside to intimate friendships as it can promote co-rumination—excessive discussion of personal problems with a friend—which may aggravate rather than relieve symptoms of depression and anxiety (especially in females)
     d. Co-rumination in males tends to have only positive effects
C. Changing Social Networks
  1. Dunphy five stages of evolution of peer groups during adolescence from isolated unisex cliques to crowd disintegration
     a. Stage 1: in late childhood begin with same-sex cliques—small group of friends—that have little to do with opposite sex
     b. Stage 2: boy and girl clique members begin to interact
        i. Same-sex cliques provide a secure base for romantic relationships
     c. Stage 3: most popular males and females form heterosexual cliques
     d. Stage 4: development of crowd—collection of several heterosexual cliques—that is involved in arranging organized social activities (e.g., parties)
        i. Adolescents who become members of mixed-sexed cliques and crowds have many opportunities to get to know members of both sexes both as friends and as romantic partners
     e. Stage 5: crowds begin to disintegrate into couples
     f. Different types of high school "crowds" (e.g., "populars," "druggies")
        i. Type of crowd a child belongs to is important
        ii. "Brains" tend to graduate from college and have high self-esteem
        iii. "Basket cases" more psychological problems
        iv. "Jocks" often financial success but also at risk for criminality
     g. Crowd membership partly reflects personality traits and values that existed before entry into the crowd, but experiences in a crowd also shape future development
     h. Common misconception that peers are negative influence on adolescent development
        i. "Druggies" do encourage drug use, but "brains" discourage it
        ii. Getting into trouble due to peer pressure is less likely among teens who are securely attached to warm and authoritative parents
     i. Adolescents with deviant friends and without friends more prone to deviance and depression (Exploration Box on the dark side of peer relations)
D. Dating
  1. Basics facts concerning teen dating
     a. Many teens (70% of 18-year-olds) involved in "special romantic relationship"
     b. Early adolescent dates superficial and short-lived
     c. Brown's phases of adolescent romantic relationships

© 2012 Cengage Learning. All Rights Reserved. May not be copied, scanned, or duplicated, in whole or in part, except for use as permitted in a license distributed with a certain product or service or otherwise on a password-protected website for classroom use.

  i. Initiation phase—early focus on self and seeing self as capable of relating to members of opposite sex

  ii. Status phase—middle adolescence status derived from having the right kind of partner

  iii. Affection phase—focus on relationship rather than group status, relationships more caring, set in smaller mixed-sex cliques

  iv. Bonding phase—young adulthood emotional intimacy, long-term commitment, lasting bond

  v. Supporting evidence found in longitudinal study

  vi. Romantic relationships in early teens tend to be low-quality and unstable while relationships in late teens are more emotionally intimate and supportive

  vii. Having a committed romantic relationship has positive effects for all teenagers (e.g., more positive self-concept)

  viii. Supportive parents important in predicting positive love relationships

 d. Dating at early age appears to have more negative consequences (either because troubled teens date earlier or because someone gets hurt)

 e. Involvement in steady relationship good for self-esteem and overall adjustment

V The Adult

A. Social Networks

 1. Larger social convoys—social networks and support systems—in young adulthood than in middle or old age

  a. Infant's social convoy may only include parents

  b. As we age, new members are added to social convoy while others leave

  c. Relationships within social convoys change with age

 2. Social interaction patterns

  a. Young adults busy forming romantic relationships

  b. Young women tend to form closer ties than young men

  c. Single young adults tend to have more friends than middle-aged or older adults

  d. Social network size varies by ethnic group (e.g., African Americans' networks tend to be smaller and more dominated by kin than European Americans')

 3. Socioemotional selectivity (Carstenson)—theory that shrinking networks represent choice to better match emotional needs (sacrifice quantity for quality)

  a. Perception by older individuals that there is limited time left prompts them to put less emphasis on the goal of acquiring knowledge for future use and more emphasis on fulfilling current emotional needs

  b. Younger people focus on social stimulation and new information provided by others and may sacrifice some emotional well-being to have many social contacts

  c. Older focus on choosing narrow range of social partners on emotional well-being

  d. Older adults' emotional lives benefit from socioemotional selectivity

   i. Elderly do not have more dismal or depressing emotional lives than young adults

        ii. Negative emotions less common in older adults

       iii. Older individuals have longer-lasting positive emotions and fleeting negative emotions

    e. Older individual may achieve emotional gratification goals through positivity effect—information processing involving paying more attention to, better remembering, and putting more priority on positive information

        i. Downside is that the focus on positive information and ignoring or avoiding of negative information can result in biased decisions

B. Romantic Relationships

  1. Mate selection

    a. Evolutionary theorists suggest that men are more likely than women to emphasize physical attractiveness while women are more likely to place emphasis on a potential mate's resources and social status

    b. Filter theories of mate selection see process as involving a filtering from all possible partners to one partner

        i. Early in the process, decisions are based on similarity of qualities (e.g., physical appearance, religion, race)

       ii. Next partners disclose more about their inner qualities (e.g., values, beliefs); if compatible, the relationship may survive; if not it may end

       iii. Mate selection does not appear to unfold in the stagelike manner suggested by filter theories

    c. Mate selection influenced by homogamy—similarity

        i. Once homogamy is assured, people may also prefer partners who complement them in some way

       ii. "Birds of a feather" more valid than "opposites attract"

    d. Love

        i. Sternberg proposed a triangular theory of love based on three key components: passion, intimacy, and decision/commitment

       ii. Passion—sexual attraction, romantic feelings, excitement

       iii. Intimacy—feelings of caring, closeness, trust, and respect in a relationship

       iv. Decision/commitment—deciding that one is in love and then committing to a long-term relationship

       v. In U.S. culture, couples often first experience passion, then move to intimacy, and finally to commitment

       vi. Consummate love—high levels of passion, intimacy, and decision/commitment

       vii. With time, many couples experience companionate love—high intimacy and commitment but not much passion

C. Attachment Styles

  1. Attachment is important component of love relationships

    a. Attachments between love partners is biologically adaptive and increases the odds of having children and the odds that the children will have two parents to help them survive

    b. Attachment styles can be described in terms of the dimensions of anxiety (extent of concern about the availability and responsiveness of a partner) and avoidance (extent of discomfort in being intimate with and depending on a partner)

    c. Adults with secure working model feel good about self and willing to enter intimate relationships

    d. Adults with preoccupied working model have a positive view of others but feel unloved

    e. Adults with a dismissing style of attachment have a positive view of self but do not trust others (fear of abandonment)

    f. Adults with a fearful internal working model have a dim view of self and others and show an unpredictable mix of neediness and fear of closeness

  2. Adult attachments related to love and romantic relationships

    a. Secure attachment predicts positive relationships

    b. Avoidant lovers fear intimacy while resistant individuals tend to be obsessed with their partner

    c. Avoidant and resistant attachment represent jealousy and extremes of love and pain in relationships

    d. Secure individuals tend to calmly share feelings, avoidant-style adults inhibit their true feelings, and resistant-style adults become highly emotionally aroused

    e. Quality of parent-child attachment relationship in early life predicts adult attachment style and romantic relationship quality

  3. Adult internal working models predict extent to which adults have confidence and curiosity to explore and master their environments

    a. Secure attachments in adulthood associated with strong achievement motivation

    b. Securely attached adults enjoy work more and are better at it, resistantly attached adults want approval and grumble about not being valued enough, avoidant adults bury them selves in work and don't socialize with coworkers

  4. Internal working models affect adult capacity for caregiving

    a. Secure relationships in adulthood linked to being sensitive and responsive parent

    b. Mothers with preoccupied style are more anxious and more intrusive with their infants; dismissing mothers derive little pleasure from their babies

  5. Attachment styles have a bearing on adjustment in old age

    a. Older people in dismissing-avoidant category express some discomfort with closeness and tend to be more compulsively self-reliant (may involve a desire to avoid dependency in old age)

    b. Elderly people with secure or dismissive attachment style tend to be happier than those with preoccupied or fearful styles

 D. Friendships

  1. Important across the lifespan but take on different characters at different ages

    a. Young adults typically have more friends than older adults, but even very old adults tend to have one or more close friends

  2. Friendships can be strained as older adults develop significant health problems

  3. Equity—balance of contributions and gains—impacts the quality of a relationship

    a. Growing importance of equity (balance of contributions) in older adults' overbenefited (overly dependent) friendships more distressing than underbenefited relationships

b. Males more interested in independence and react more negatively to receiving help

c. Older adults tend to call on family, not friends, for help (perhaps over concern that the inequity of assisting will threaten the friendship)

E. Adult Relationships and Adult Development

1. Quality, not quantity, of social relationships affects well-being

2. Apparent need for confidants—individual to whom one is closely attached and with whom feelings and thoughts can be shared

    a. Spouses are important confidants

        i. Males particularly dependent on spouses

        ii. Females rely on friends, siblings, and children for emotional support

        iii. Number of adults who say that they have no one with whom they can discuss important matters increasing dramatically (25% of adults in U.S. indicate that they have no confidant)

3. Key to life satisfaction is whether interacting with close companion is rewarding or stressful

    a. Positive relationships in one friendship tend to predict positive relationships in other friendships

    b. Interactions in relationships can undermine emotional well-being if exchanges mostly negative

4. Social supports can have positive impact on psychological and health status

    a. Positive impact on cardiovascular, endocrine, and immune systems (improving body's ability to deal with illness)

    b. Close relationships can help maintain levels of physical and cognitive functioning

5. People may have evolved to be with other people, and isolation and loneliness wears the body down

    a. Programs to reduce loneliness in isolated elderly may be effective

SUGGESTIONS FOR CLASS DISCUSSIONS OR PROJECTS

1. In 1993, a 2½-year-old known as "Baby Jessica" was permanently separated from her adoptive parents after her biological parents succeeded in regaining custody of her. Many were haunted by the image of a screaming Jessica being driven off in a van from the only family she had known. Ask students to predict this little girl's short- adjustment and long-term adjustment based on Bowlby's attachment theory. Then report that eight months later, Jessica, now named Anna Jacqueline, was apparently thriving and had experienced none of the serious traumatic effects (e.g., eating problems, sleeping problems, weepiness) that had been predicted by all the experts (see *Newsweek*, March 21, 1994).

The course of Baby Jessica's transition into her new family appears to be quite different than the courses experienced by internationally adopted children as described in *New York Times Magazine* (May 24, 1998). What are some of the differences in these situations that might account for the poorer prognosis of the children described in the *Times*?

2. Hazan and Shaver (1990) have done research on adult attachment. Students might enjoy seeing the short descriptors of avoidant, anxious/ambivalent, and secure adults. Do these adult styles seem to map well to the infant styles? How much continuity in styles would students expect to exist across the lifespan? What experiences *after* infancy might alter one's attachment style? Do these attachments really impact self-concept and mental health status?

Hazan, C. and Shaver, P.R. (1990). Love and work: an attachment-theoretical perspective. *Journal of Personality and Social Psychology,* 59, 270-280.

3. Have students complete a "create a best friend" exercise in which they list the five characteristics that they would instill in a person if they were trying to build a "best friend." You could also have them attempt to create a best friend for people of different ages (e.g., 15-year-olds, 35-year-olds, 65-year-olds, 95-year-olds). You could then use these characteristics to discuss differences in expectations concerning friendships across the lifespan. You might also touch on any sex differences found between the lists of males and females.

4. What makes someone popular at different points of the lifespan? One way to explore this question is to have students interview people from across the lifespan and ask these individuals to describe characteristics that make one popular at their age. After generating the information, a class discussion could focus on one or more of the following questions:
  • What are the characteristics of popular peers at different ages?
  • Do these characteristics remain stable across the lifespan?
  • Do students expect the "in-crowd" from their high school to still be "in" when they return for their 10th or 25th class reunion?

You could also consider the issue of rejection by asking which characteristics would most likely lead to rejection by peers. Again, you could have the class discuss whether the dynamics of rejected status is consistent versus inconsistent across the lifespan.

5. To help students think more about friendship development, have them reflect on their first friend. Before beginning the class discussion, you might ask for a show of hands in response to the following questions so that students can assess the diversity in the classroom:
  • How old were the students (preschool, middle childhood, preadolescent, other)?
  • Were their friends younger, older, or the same age?
  • Were these friends the same sex?
  • Were they biologically related?
  • How long did the friendship endure (less than a year…a lifetime)?
  • What made that person a friend?
  • What factors are important at different ages?
  • What led to the end of the friendship (if it ended) and what contributed to its maintenance for as long as it lasted?
  • For friendships that lasted, how did the interpersonal dynamics change over time?

6. In Chapter 14, students are introduced to cliques and their impact on social and emotional development during the middle and high school years. In most cases, cliques are viewed in negative terms and seen as detrimental, but the text points out that belonging to some cliques is associated with positive outcomes. The goal of this assignment is to introduce students to

research on effective methods of dealing with cliques. To complete the assignment, students should search the Web and or research journals using the term *cliques*. They should then read five articles related to cliques in middle school, high school, and college. Based on these readings, students should write a paper in which they identify five negative impacts of cliques and five techniques that can be used to reduce these impacts.

7. Sternberg (1986) suggested the existence of seven types of love: liking (intimacy only), Infatuation (passion only), empty love (commitment only), romantic love (intimacy and passion), companionate love (intimacy and commitment), fatuous love (passion and commitment), and consummate love (intimacy, passion, and commitment). Have students work in class to develop a brief (5- to 10-item) survey that they believe would be able to identify the type of love relationship a person is in. Once developed, you could then have students use this survey to interview individuals in current relationships with the goal of determining their "love relationship type" and (perhaps more interestingly) if both members of the couple view themselves as being in the same type of relationship. If you decide to go the research route with this assignment, please follow all of the Institutional Review Board policies in place at your institution.

Sternberg, R.J. (1986). A triangular theory of love. *Psychological Review*, 93, 119-135.

SUGGESTED FILMS AND VIDEOS

Attachment Relationships: Nurturing Healthy Bonds (2010, Magna Systems, DVD, 29 minutes, available in Spanish): This video offers an excellent overview of the Bowlby and Ainsworth approach to attachment.

Infancy: Early Relationships (2003, Magna Systems, VHS or DVD, 21 minutes, available in Spanish): This video focuses on numerous aspects of attachment and temperament.

Mary Ainsworth: Attachment and the Growth of Love (2005, Insight Media, DVD, 35 minutes): This interesting video focuses on the way Ainsworth's fieldwork influenced Bowlby's theory of attachment.

Preschoolers: Social and Emotional Development (2008, Insight Media, DVD, 25 minutes): This DVD focuses on the development of social skills and emotions during the preschool years.

The Social Convoy: In Their Own Words (2002, Magna Systems, DVD, 29 minutes): This video provides first-hand descriptions of social relationships (e.g., marriages) of elderly individuals.

SUGGESTED WEBSITES

Adult Attachment Lab
http://psychology.ucdavis.edu/labs/Shaver/PWT/index.cfm

Better Kid Care: Play in the Business of Kids
http://www.nncc.org/Curriculum/better.play.html

Cliques
http://www.massgeneral.org/children/adolescenthealth/articles/aa_cliques.aspx

Types of Love
http://dataguru.org/love/fehrtyp.asp

What Is Attachment?
http://psychology.about.com/od/loveandattraction/a/attachment01.htm

SUGGESTED READINGS

Alterovitz, S.S. (2009). Partner preference across the life span: Online dating by older adults. *Psychology and Aging*, 24(2), 513-517.

Buote, V.M. (2009). Exploring similarities and differences between online and offline friendships: The role of attachment styles. *Computers in Human Behavior*, 25(2), 560-567.

Miller, E. (2009). Crisis in kindergarten: Why children need play in school. *The Education Digest*, 75(19), 42-45.

Wong, M.S. (2009). Parental beliefs, infant temperament, and marital quality: Associations with infant-mother and infant-father attachment. *Journal of Family Psychology*, 23(6), 828-838.

Yeung, R. (2010). Adults make a difference: The protective effects of parents and teacher emotional support on emotional and behavioral problems of peer-victimized adolescents. *Journal of Community Psychology*, 38(1), 80-98.

THE FAMILY

LEARNING OBJECTIVES

After students have read and studied the material in this chapter, they should be able to answer the following questions:

UNDERSTANDING THE FAMILY

1. How is the family viewed by the family systems theory?

2. How do individual family systems change? How have families in general changed during the 20th century?

THE INFANT

3. How is the father-infant relationship similar to and different from the mother-infant relationship?

THE CHILD

4. What are two basic dimensions of parenting? What patterns of childrearing emerge from these dimensions? How do these parenting styles affect children's development? How does social class affect parenting style?

5. What effects do parents have on their children, and what effects do children have on their parents? What is the transactional model of family influence?

6. What features characterize sibling relationships across the lifespan? How do siblings contribute to development?

THE ADOLESCENT

7. What are relationships like between adolescents and their parents?

THE ADULT

8. How does marriage and parenthood affect adults? What changes occur in the family as children mature and leave home?

9. What sorts of roles do grandparents establish with their grandchildren?

10. How do various family relationships (e.g., spouses, siblings, parent-child) change during adulthood?

DIVERSITY IN FAMILY LIFE

11. What sorts of diversity exist in today's families? What is the life satisfaction of people in these different types of families?

12. How does divorce affect family relationships?

13. Why might family abuse occur? What can be done to reduce spouse abuse and child abuse?

CHAPTER OUTLINE

I Understanding the Family

A. The Family as a System within Systems

1. Family systems theory—family as "whole" made up of interconnected parts, each affecting the other

   a. Family is a dynamic system—a self-organizing system that adapts to changes in members

   b. In the past, developmentalists did not adopt a family systems approach but focused almost exclusively on the mother-child relationship

2. Nuclear family—two-generation system (i.e., father/mother/at least one child)

   a. Reciprocal influence—each member influences all others (e.g., baby smiles, mom smiles in response, baby grins in response to mom)

   b. Must consider all combinations of influences: mother-child, father-child, mother-father (everyone affects each other)

   c. Coparenting—ways in which parents coordinate their parenting and function well (or poorly) as a team

      i. Communication and mutual support of each other makes a big difference (can head off problems in children)

3. Extended family household—nuclear family system plus other kin (e.g., grandparents, aunts/uncles)

   a. More common in cultures outside the United States

   b. More common in African-American and Hispanic-American families

      i. Single African-American mothers obtain needed support to help with child care

4. The family as a system within other systems

   a. Bioecological approach (Bronfenbrenner)—must take into account many levels of the environment (e.g., family is embedded into other systems like the neighborhood, community, and culture)

   b. Familial experiences in one culture differ from that in other cultures (e.g., in some cultures, a bride becomes an underling in the household of her mother-in-law)

   c. Near infinite variety of family forms and context

B. The Family as a Changing System

1. Family best defined as dynamic, developing system (i.e., thing, including members, change)

   a. Early family developmental theories featured notion of family life cycle—sequence of changes in composition, role and relationships within family over time

   b. Duvall's eight stages of family life cycle

      i. Married without children

        ii. Childbearing family

       iii. Family with preschool children

       iv. Family with school-aged children

       v. Family with teenagers

       vi. Family launching young adults

       vii. Family without children

       viii. Aging family

   c. Increasing numbers of people do not experience the "traditional" life cycle

       i. Some remain single or childless while others marry multiple times

       ii. Many now find fault with models that view a family life cycle in which a nuclear family remains intact and moves through each of the life phases in sequence

       iii. New concept is that we lead linked lives—our development as individuals is intertwined with that of other family members

       iv. Most theorists now embrace concept that families function as systems, developing and changing over the lifespan

C. A Changing Family System in a Changing World

   1. Families are embedded in a changing world

      a. Several dramatic social changes have altered makeup of typical family and the quality of family experience

        i. Now more single adults (but 90% of adults will marry)

        ii. More people are postponing marriage (2009 average age of marriage was 26 for women and 28 for men)

        iii. More unmarried parents (40% of births to single women)

        iv. People are having fewer children

        v. More working mothers (60% of married women with children younger than 6 work outside the home)

        vi. Substantial increase in divorces (4 in 10 new marriages will end in divorce)

        vii. More single-parent families (23% of children under age 18 live with mom alone and 3% live with dad alone)

        viii. More children living in poverty (35% of African American, 29% of Hispanic, and 10% of nonhispanic white children are poor; 43% of children in female-headed household are poor)

        ix. More remarriages and reconstituted (blended) families—those including stepparent and/or stepsiblings

        x. More years without children (modern couples are compressing their childbearing into a smaller number of years, and with improved health, people are living longer)

        xi. More multigenerational families

        xii. Fewer caregivers for aging adults

   2. Some see change as "decline of the family" (i.e., negative effects of divorce, single-parent families, poverty)

      a. Some see instability of family (e.g., parents going from married to single to remarried) as "dizzying" for children

   3. Some see change as good news

      a. Postponing marriage greater chance of success

b. Men and women have more similar roles
c. More interaction between grandparents/great-grandparents and their grandkids
d. With two wage earners, families better off financially
4. Once "traditional" nuclear family (1960 – 45%) now represents small proportion of families (1995 – 12%)

II The Infant

A. The Mother-Infant and Father-Infant Relationship
1. Despite gender stereotypes, fathers are as capable of caring for infants as mothers (fathers and mothers more similar than different); fathers good at feeding, become objects of their infant's love
2. Mothers and fathers do differ in both quantity and quality of interactions with infants
   a. Mothers tend to spend more quantity of time with children (but fathers are more involved with children than they were in the past, with some even sharing equal responsibility for childcare)
   b. Mothers and fathers typical styles are qualitatively different
      i. Mothers tend to spend time caregiving (e.g., food, changing diapers)
      ii. Fathers spend more time in playful interactions (e.g., tickling, bouncing)
      iii. Fathers can adopt "mother-like" role if they have primary responsibility for childcare
      iv. Fathers tend to contribute financially to support children
      v. Fathers who are warm contribute to achievement levels in their children
      vi. Fathers tend to challenge children during play and to egg on into taking risks
      vii. Children with caring and involved fathers tend to have fewer psychological disorders
   c. Forty percent of babies now born to unmarried mothers, creating a large group of unmarried fathers
      i. Unmarried fathers tend to not live with the child's mother and are not very involved parents
      ii. Odds of being an involved parent high if unmarried man still has a strong relationship with the mother
      iii. Involvement as a father greatest when father does not use drugs, is employed, is not engaging in criminal activity, and is participating in a religion
      iv. Unmarried fathers involved before birth tend to be involved after birth
      v. Becoming a father seems to help some men mature and make positive changes in their lives

B. Mothers, Fathers, and Infants: The System at Work
1. Parents also have "indirect effect"—in which effect on child involves parent influence on third party, who in turn influences child
   a. Mothers with supportive relationships with husbands more patient with children
   b. Fathers who have just argued with wives tend to be less supportive with their children
   c. When parents compete rather than cooperate, infants may show signs of insecure attachments

III The Child

    A. Parenting Style

        1. Two dimensions of childrearing include acceptance-responsiveness and demandingness-control

            a. Acceptance-responsiveness—extent of parents' support, show sensitivity to needs, and praise or encourage children

            b. Demandingness-control (permissive-restrictiveness)—amount of control parents have over decisions concerning a child

                i. Less controlling and less demanding parents called "permissive parents"

            c. Four patterns (based on crossing two dimensions above)

                i. Authoritarian parenting—highly demanding, with expectations for strict obedience, low acceptance-responsiveness (i.e., impose rules, expect strict obedience, rarely explain why child should comply, and rely on power tactics like physical punishment)

                ii. Authoritative parenting—parents set and explain rules, listen to their children, and are flexible (reasonable and democratic)

                iii. Permissive parenting—high in acceptance-responsiveness, these parents make few demands, encourage children to express their feelings, and exert little control over children

                iv. Neglectful parenting—low demanding-control and low acceptance-responsiveness, these parents are uninvolved in the upbringing of their children

            d. Baumrind research on child outcomes associated with parenting patterns

                i. Best outcomes from warmth combined with authoritative style (e.g., children more cheerful, socially responsible, achievement oriented, and cooperative with peers and adults)

                ii. Children of authoritarian parents moody, unhappy, easily annoyed

                iii. Children of permissive parents impulsive, aggressive, without self-control, but can be effective with older independent children

                iv. Worst outcomes from neglectful parents, with children displaying aggression and temper tantrums as early as age 3 years and hostility and drug abuse in their teens

            e. "Love and limits" best combination for parents

                i. Overall link between authoritarian parenting and positive developmental outcomes evident in most ethnic groups

                ii. Some cultural and subcultural differences in effectiveness of parenting styles exist (Exploration box on parenting in cultural and subcultural context)

    B. Social Class, Economic Hardship, and Parenting

        1. Class differences (lower and working-class versus middle and upper-class) associated with different socialization goals, values, and parenting styles

            a. Lower- and working-class tend to stress obedience and respect

            b. Lower- and working-class tend to be more restrictive and authoritarian and tend to reason with children less frequently

            c. Lower- and working-class tend to show less warmth/affection

2. Socioeconomic differences in parenting styles and child outcomes
   a. Parents experiencing financial problems tend to become more depressed and engage in more conflict; marital conflict disrupts each partner's ability to be supportive and effective parents (example of indirect family effect)
      i. Negative impacts on children include low self-esteem, poor school performance, and adjustment problems
      ii. Lower- and working-class may be under more stress (especially financial)
      iii. Parents living in poverty tend to be more restrictive, punitive, inconsistent, and neglectful (sometimes to the point of abuse)
      iv. In high-crime poverty areas, parents may engage in more authoritarian and controlling behavior to protect their children from danger
      v. Poverty also associated with poorer physical environment (e.g., pollution, noise, crowds, unsafe conditions)
      vi. Poor environment linked to health, emotional, and behavioral problems in children
   b. Low SES parents have fewer resources to invest in their children's development
   c. High and low SES parents may emphasize different qualities in preparing children for work (because of their work experience); lower SES parents emphasize obedience to authority because it is what their jobs require; higher SES parents emphasize initiative and creativity as these are the attributes of executives, professionals, and other white-collar workers

C. Models of Influence in the Family
   1. Parent effects model
      a. Assumes that parent's action causes child's behavior (a one-way influence from parent to child)
   2. Child effects model
      a. Assumes that child's action influences parenting style
         i. Infant requires more care than older child
         ii. Parents tend to become less restrictive as children age
         iii. Difficult children may cause parents to reject or harshly rule children (authoritarian style)
         iv. "Good" children less in need of harsh parental involvement
         v. Research shows that child's behavior can lead to differential treatment (e.g., college students used more induction with attentive girls and more power-assertion techniques with inattentive parents, parents of juvenile delinquent girls became less warm and less controlling as their daughters aged)
   3. Transactional model—hypothesis that parents and children influence each other reciprocally (e.g., child genetically predisposed to aggression elicits negative and coercive parenting, which results in more aggressive acts by the child)
      a. Includes potential impact of genes on behavior of both parents and children
         i. Child problems develop when the relationship between parent and child goes bad over time; optimal development results when parent-child transactions evolve in positive directions
      b. Parents do not single-handedly control the developmental process (but are influential)

D. Sibling Relationships
   1. A new baby arrives
      a. Mothers pay less attention to other children
         i. "Dethroning" of firstborn can be stressful on the child
      b. Children become more demanding, clingy, and develop problems in their routines (e.g., eating, toileting)
         i. Siblings may become targets of aggression
      c. Decreases security of attachment in children 2 years or older
      d. Child's increased insistence on doing things independently increases
      e. Parents need to guard against ignoring older children following birth of sibling
         i. Parents should encourage older children to become aware of new baby's needs
   2. Ambivalence in sibling relationships
      a. Sibling rivalry—competition, jealousy, and resentment between siblings common and normal reaction
         i. May be rooted in evolution, with siblings competing with one another for parental resources
         ii. Siblings may be at odds because of close proximity
      b. Level of sibling conflict high between young siblings but tends to decrease in early adolescence
      c. Personalities and parenting behaviors affect sibling relationships
         i. Sibling relationships friendlier when parents get along with each other and respond warmly and sensitively to all their children
   3. Sibling influences on development
      a. Siblings can provide emotional support (e.g., siblings often confide in each other)
         i. Even preschoolers jump in to comfort infant siblings
      b. Siblings often provide caretaking (babysitting) services of siblings
      c. Older siblings serve as teachers (but some siblings not skilled at teaching as parents)
      d. Siblings provide social experience (having at least one sibling to interact with tends to have positive effects on a child's social-cognitive development)
      e. Siblings can have indirect impact via their interactions with parents; older sibling sets negative chain of events in motion, which can lead to negative impact on younger siblings (or positive events that have positive impacts)

IV The Adolescent
  A. Ripples in the Parent-Child Relationship
   1. Most parent-adolescent relationships are close and retain the quality they had during earlier childhood
      a. Rare for parent-child relationships to suddenly turn bad
   2. Decrease in time together can make adolescents feel less emotionally close to parents
      a. Modest increase in parent-child conflict common around onset of puberty
      b. Some bickering but tends to be over minor matters (e.g., homework, household chores)

B. Achieving Autonomy
   1. Task of achieving autonomy—capacity to make independent decisions and manage own life
   2. Achieving autonomy part of the establishment of identity described by Erikson
   3. As children reach puberty, they attempt to assert themselves more and parents become less dominant, but best if they continue to maintain close attachments with parents even as they gain autonomy
      a. Gaining autonomy from parents is healthy
      b. Blend of autonomy (independence) and attachment (interdependence) is more desirable
   4. Amount of autonomy granted by parents varies by culture
      a. Filipino- and Mexican-American adolescents more likely to believe that they should not disagree with their parents
      b. Chinese-American adolescents do not expect freedom to go to parties
      c. Japanese-American adolescents strongly socialized to accept limits on autonomy
      d. In collectivist Asian cultures, parents continue to impose many rules and remain dominant power
   5. Achievement, autonomy, well-adjusted behavior found in adolescents whose parents set reasonable goals and monitor their children's behavior
      a. Authoritative parenting style fosters greater autonomy and achievement in adolescents, but in some cultures and subcultures, a more authoritarian or permissive style may achieve good results
      b. Rejecting and extremely strict parents or extremely lax parenting associated with adolescents in psychological distress, socializing with the wrong crowd, and getting into trouble

V The Adult
A. Establishing the Marriage
   1. Most adults in the United States marry (over 90%)
      a. U.S. marriages tend to be based on love; not true in all cultures
      b. In some cultures, marriage arranged by leaders and involve acquiring property or rights or forming allies
   2. Is a significant life transition with new roles
      a. Rejoice at weddings; is a time when couple feels on top of the world
      b. May struggle with autonomy and results in an unwanted need to compromise with partner and adapt to fit each other's personality and preferences
      c. Honeymoon is short-lived, and satisfaction with marriage and sex life tends to decline
      d. Most couples do remain satisfied but must learn to adapt to strains of marriage
      e. Blissful marriages evolve into less idealized ones
   3. Quality of couple's early relationship predicts later relationships
      a. Couples unhappy after 13 years of marriage tend to have relatively poor relationships all along
      b. Some marriages turn sour and some start out sour

4. Establishment phase of life cycle involves loss of enthusiasm for most couples
   a. Some couples on the path to long-term mutual satisfaction while others on the path to divorce

B. New Parenthood
  1. Additional children create added stress on the family involving positive and negative changes
    a. Positive side is that parents claim that having a child brings them joy, fulfillment, and contributes to their individual growth
    b. Negative side of being a couple with children
      i. New roles (mother and father) added to existing roles of spouse, worker; juggling roles is difficult
      ii. Often less sleep, less time to themselves, and some face financial difficulties
      iii. Division of labor often along gender lines (she-feminine caregiver, he-masculine provider)
    c. Marital satisfaction declines when baby enters household
      i. Greater decline in females due to additional childcare burden and feeling overwhelmed by responsibilities
  2. Some adjust to new parenthood as "bowl of cherries" other as "the pits"
  3. Coping to addition of child related to several factors
    a. Difficult babies create more stress and anxiety
    b. Adopted children pose special challenge (e.g., parents do not have 9 months of pregnancy to prepare for the child)
  4. Parents' characteristics matter
    a. Parents with better problem-solving skills better equipped to handle stress
      i. More realistic expectations, less stress
      ii. Mentally healthy parents (e.g., those not depressed) fare better
    b. Attachment style is important
      i. Warm and accepting attachment has best outcome
      ii. Mothers with preoccupied (resistant) style of attachment express more anxiety
    c. Social support can make a big difference
      i. Partner support is critical
      ii. Social support from friends and relatives helps new parents cope

C. The Childrearing Family
  1. Additional children increase workload and stress
    a. Stress of caring for toddler more than for an infant
    b. Arrival of second child increases stress
    c. More hassles of feeding, cleaning, playing
    d. Birth of second child may result in increased father involvement
    e. Mothers with less involved fathers find themselves without a moment's rest
  2. Additional challenges when kids become adolescents
    a. Conflict over how to raise their adolescent can lead to conflict between parents
    b. Living with an adolescent who is becoming physically and sexually mature may cause parent to engage in midlife questioning
    c. Middle-aged parents are troubled when children experience adolescence, and children are at risk for trouble when parents troubled

      d. Parents are impacted by how well-adjusted their teens are

      e. Parents who are unhappy or experiencing marital problems can negatively impact their teens, causing the children to be at risk for problems like delinquency, drug use, anxiety, and emotional disorders

      f. Children complicate their parents' lives by claiming and demanding time that might go to nourish the marital relationship

      g. Although parenting is challenging, most parents emphasis the positives and feel that parenthood has contributed a great deal to their personal development

D. The Empty Nest

    1. Empty nest—departure of last child from family (phase of life that first became common in the 20th century)

    2. Results in changing role and lifestyle of parent

    3. Overall, parents generally respond positively to children leaving home

      a. Often an increase in marital satisfaction

      b. Women may feel that marriages more equitable and spouses more accommodating of their needs

      c. Minority of parents find empty nest transition disturbing

      d. More time to focus on relationship and engage in activities together

      e. Empty nest is evidence that they have done a good job

      f. Most parents maintain contact with children after they leave

    4. Refilling or "boomerang effect"—launched child returns to family (often as young adult) can be stressful for parents

      a. Refilling typically the result of unemployment, financial difficulties, divorce

      b. Can be distressing, but most empty nesters adapt if children are responsible (rather than being seen as freeloaders)

E. Grandparenthood

    1. Styles of grandparenting (Cherlin and Furstenberg)

      a. Remote—only occasionally seen, emotionally and geographically distant

      b. Companionate—frequently seen, shared activities with grandchildren, rarely involved in parenting issues

      c. Involved—assumed parent-like involvement often giving advice; some actually act as parents to grandchildren

    2. Most grandparents see grandchildren often and gain pleasure from these experiences; more frequent visits associated with more positive view

    3. "Family National Guard"—grandparents often needed in times of crisis (e.g., pregnancy of unmarried granddaughter)

    4. "Called to duty" grandparents can make real contribution to development of grandchildren (e.g., mentor teen or coparent)

      a. Child raised by single mom with assistance from at least one grandparent have better outcome than those raised without grandparent

    5. Grandmothering can take a toll as well (e.g., depression as grandchildren move in and need a substitute parent)

      a. Grandparents may benefit from intellectual and emotional rewards that parenting brings, but can also become overwhelmed

F. Changing Family Relationships
  1. Marital relationships
     a. Dips and recoveries in marital satisfaction, more so for women
        i. Dips after honeymoon period, drops as children added, recovers with empty nest
        ii. Frequency of intercourse declines (passion decrease) and intimacy increases; relationship more companionate (elderly couples often more affectionate than middle-aged couples)
     b. Personality better predictor of happiness than marital satisfaction
        i. In happy marriages, personalities of marital partners tend to be similar and stable over the years
        ii. Partners affect each other's development (e.g., depressed wife may lead to depressed symptoms in husband)
     c. Family life cycle ends with widowhood
        i. By age 65, 73% of men are married while only 42% of women are married
        ii. Serious health problems with spouse can negatively affect satisfaction
        iii. Most spouses are able to cope with death of spouse and rebuild their lives
     d. Marital relationship central to adult development
        i. Overall married adults "happier, healthier, and better off financially"
  2. Sibling relationships
     a. Typically the longest-lasting relationship in one's life
     b. Sibling relationships tend to change with time
        i. In adulthood, less contact and conflict and more warmer feelings than during childhood
        ii. Most siblings remain in contact in adult years
        iii. Seldom discuss intimate ideas or help one another but usually feel that they can count on each other in a crisis
     c. Relationships remain ambivalent
        i. May compete as they build their lives
        ii. May be drawn closer after significant life event (e.g., parent's death)
        iii. Adult siblings feel closer when they feel their parents treat them equally (i.e., no favorites)
  3. Parent-child relationships
     a. Parent-child relationships take many forms (some strained and some close)
        i. Quality of relationship stays much the same as in adolescence
        ii. Parents become stressed when their children have problems, children can become irritated if parents meddle in their lives or are demanding
        iii. Most parents report some tension with their adult children
        iv. Adulthood may represent a chance for children to negotiate a new relationship with parents
        v. Mutual and friendly relationship most common if parents were supportive and authoritative earlier in the child's life
        vi. Aging mothers more connected with children than fathers
        vii. Many ethnic minority groups (e.g., African American, Hispanic American) often have better relationships with elderly parents than European Americans

        viii. Common belief of role reversal (parent being dependent on children) in late adulthood, but it is a rare occurrence and tends to occur only when parent reaches an advanced age and develops serious physical or mental problems

    b. Caring for aging parents
      i. Middle generation squeeze (or sandwich generation)—middle-aged adults experiencing heavy demands from young and older generation
      ii. Spouses first in line for care, but ailing parents often cared for by adult daughter or daughter-in-law (female's traditional role as "kinkeeper")
      iii. In many collectivist Asian cultures, daughters-in-law are first choice to be care providers
      iv. China's former one-child policy has led to elders having no one to care for them (especially those living in rural areas)
      v. In our individualistic society, most aging parents resist having to live with or be dependent on children; today's families continue to meet their responsibility to meet needs of oldest individuals
      vi. Caregiver burden—psychological distress from caring for someone with physical or cognitive impairments
      vii. Burden greatest in those experiencing physical, emotional, or financial strain
      viii. Caregiver burden worse if parent engages in disruptive or socially inappropriate behavior
      ix. Are cultural differences (e.g., European-American caregivers devote fewer hours elderly care than African-American caregivers)
      x. Helping out of love is a lot less stressful than helping out of sense of duty

VI Diversity in Family Life
  A. Singles
    1. "Typical" single adult impossible to describe due to delay in marriage; number of young singles is on the rise
      a. Majority of adults between ages 18 to 29 are unmarried
    2. Cohabitation—living with romantic partner without being married
      a. Many cohabiting couples have children (4 out of 10 children will live in a household headed by a cohabiting couple)
      b. Some live together as a matter of convenience while others look at cohabitation as an alternative to marriage (later group includes previously married individuals, those who do not want to jeopardize their financial situation, and those whose children may be upset by remarriage)
      c. Couples who cohabitate (especially with multiple partners) and then marry often more dissatisfied with marriage
    3. Ten percent of adults never marry
      a. Stereotype of single adult as lonely and maladjusted is unsupported but divorced or widowed single adults tend to be most lonely and least happy (versus never-married individuals)
  B. Childless Married Couples
    1. Growing number of childless couples especially among highly educated adults with high status (childless by choice)

2. Childless couples tend to have higher marital satisfaction than couples with children
3. Children do not guarantee happiness nor does having children doom people to be unhappy in old age
4. Elderly widows without children may find themselves without needed supports in adulthood

C. Dual-Career Families
1. Spillover effects—when workplace events impact home life and vice versa
   a. Most research has found that events at home can carry over and undermine work effectiveness (negative spillover effect)
2. Positive effects of working
   a. No indication that a mother's working itself damages child development, and it can produce positive spillover effects (children adopt less stereotyped views of men and women and set higher educational and vocational goals)
   b. Living in dual-career family positive if it increases income, if moms are happy with the choice, and if dads become more involved with their children
3. Negative effects of working
   a. Can be negative if parents cannot share "quality time" with children
4. Impact of working parents on child development could result in less negative impact if U.S. provided paid leave for parents and other family caregivers and supported parents through flexible work hours, daycare, and after-school programs

D. Gay and Lesbian Families
1. Very diverse group
   a. May become parents through previous heterosexual relationship, adoption, or artificial insemination
   b. Some raise as single parents, others in families with two same-sex parents
2. Gay and lesbian couples face special challenges
   a. National controversy over ability to marry
   b. Some are not recognized by family or society
   c. May be victims of discrimination
   d. Lesbian mothers worried about legal status and possible discrimination at risk for depression
3. Gay and lesbian couples similar to heterosexual couples
   a. Tend to be in happy and sustained relationships
   b. Egalitarian division of labor—partners share equally (work without division of labor)
   c. Pattern of marital satisfaction similar to that of heterosexual couples
4. Implications of being raised by a gay or lesbian parent
   a. While very similar to heterosexual moms, lesbians less likely to hit children but more likely to engage in imaginative play
   b. Living with two parents (even when both gay) advantage over single-parent household
   c. Gay and lesbian parents are as likely as heterosexual parents to raise competent and well-adjusted children
   d. Children not more likely to become homosexual

E. Divorcing Families
 1. Before the divorce
  a. Only 70% of marriages make it to 10-year mark; divorce more likely in marriages when teens, short courtship, baby before marriage, low socioeconomic status (contribute to high levels of financial and psychological stress)
  b. Reasons for divorce include lack of communication, lack of emotional fulfillment, lack of compatibility
   i. Wives tend have longer list of complaints and tend to initiate breakup
  c. Divorce use to be taken as a drastic step (e.g., reaction to adultery), but in recent times is more like an action taken when people do not feel personally fulfilled in their marriage
 2. After the divorce
  a. Most families experience a genuine crisis (period of considerable disruption lasting at least 1 to 2 years)
  b. Wife, who usually has custody of child, is angry, depressed, and distressed
  c. Husband upset if he did not want the divorce or is cut off from the children
  d. Both husband and wife may feel isolated from friends
  e. Custodial moms with children often see standard of living decline by a third while financial situation of former husbands improve
  f. Higher risk for depression and health problems in divorced adults
  g. Distressed parents can cause disturbance of parent-child relations
   i. Children often angry, fearful, guilty, especially if they believe that they have some responsibility for divorce
   ii. Custodial mothers may become preoccupied with own problems and impatient toward children; may become less responsive, more authoritarian, but less consistent as parent
   iii. Transactional family influence: child's behavior problems make parenting difficult, deterioration in parenting aggravates child's behavioral problems
  h. Most problems disappear a couple of years post-divorce (by 6 years post divorce), but negative effects can continue
   i. About 20-25% of children of divorce carry emotional and psychological scars into adulthood
   ii. Increased risk of divorce when child in divorced family marries
  i. Positive impact
   i. Not all families experience a crisis, and most parents and children do rebound from the crisis and adapt well in the long run; some even undergo impressive growth as a result of the experience
   ii. Conflict-ridden two-family household usually more detrimental to child development than a cohesive single-parent family
  j. Influences on adjustment (factors that facilitate a positive adjustment to divorce and prevent lasting damage)
   i. Adequate financial support by noncustodial parent (usually the father)
   ii. Good parenting by the custodial parent (remain warm, authoritative, and consistent)

   iii. Good parenting by the noncustodial parent (must provide a quantity of quality interactions to child)

   iv. Minimal conflict between parents (protect children from continuing marital conflict)

   v. Additional social support to divorcing adults (e.g., confidant or close friend) and children of divorce (e.g., close friend or support group)

   vi. Minimal other life changes

   vii. Personal resources (e.g., intelligence, emotional stability, and good coping skills)

   viii. Ultimately, adjustment to divorce will depend on total configuration of stressors an individual faces and the resources he or she has to cope with these stressors

 F. Reconstituted Families

  1. Seventy-five percent of divorced people remarry within 3 to 5 years following a divorce

  2. Sixty percent of remarried couples divorce

   a. Remarriage of divorced parent can be source of stress for children; impact is worse if both parents bring children into the family

   b. Girls may have harder time as they may resent the stepfather or competing for mom's attention with the stepfather

   c. Most children adapt with time to being in the reconstituted family

VII The Problem of Family Violence

 A. Types of Family Violence

  1. Child abuse is the most visible form, with estimates of 11 of every 1,000 children a victim of substantiated maltreatment—broad term including both abuse and neglect of the child's basic needs; 2009 data found 71% neglected, 16% physically abused, 9% sexually abused, 7% emotionally or psychologically abused, and 8% experienced other types of abuse (as some children experience multiple forms, percents add to more than 100%)

  2. Abuse can come in many forms, impacting all possible family relationships

   a. Children and adolescents batter and kill parents

   b. Siblings abuse each other

   c. Spouse or partner abuse is commonplace

    i. Globally, about one-third of women are beaten, coerced into sex, or emotionally abused by partners

    ii. Sixteen percent of U.S. couples experience at least one case of marital violence

    iii. Much mild spousal abuse is mutual; in rarer cases, the violence is serious and one-sided

   d. Millions of children witness domestic violence and some get hurt (sometimes trying to protect their mother)

  3. Elderly abuse

   a. Elderly also at risk for abuse (especially when frail or impaired)

   b. Types of elderly abuse include physical or psychological maltreatment, neglect, financial exploitation, and being stripped of one's rights (often by adult children or spouses serving as caretakers)

B. Why Does Family Violence Occur?
 1. The abuser
  a. Only one in 10 abusers severely psychologically disturbed
  b. Most often, young mother, in poverty, unemployed, with no partner
  c. Child abusers tend to be former victims of child abuse
   i. About 30% abuse their children
   ii. Cycle not inevitable and can be broken if individual receives emotional support from parent substitutes, therapists, or spouses and are spared stress in adulthood
   iii. Intergenerational transmission of parenting—passing down of abusive and nonabusive parenting styles from one generation to another (Exploration box on intergenerational parenting styles)
  d. Abusive mothers often battered by partners (e.g., abused mother abuses her children)
   i. Adults more likely to abuse if they were the victim of abuse as a child or witnessed abuse as a child
  e. Abusers tend to have low levels of self-esteem
   i. Unhappy experiences may reinforce negative experiences in romantic relationships and lead to the formulation of negative internal models concerning self and others
  f. Abusive parents often have unrealistic expectations and twisted perceptions about normal behavior of their children (e.g., mother interpreting 3-month-old's babbling as "talking back")
 2. The abused
  a. Typically one child per family singled out (but that child is not to blame)
  b. Children with medical problems or difficult temperaments are at risk
  c. Combination of high-risk parent and high-risk child spells trouble
   i. Parent who feels powerless in controlling the child or who has a child with a disability or illness is prone to overreact and use harsh discipline
   ii. Powerless parents experience higher levels of stress as measured by high cortisol levels and faster heart rates
   iii. Parental uneasiness makes children less responsive, and this transactional chain of events may produce use of power tactics by the parent
 3. The context
  a. Abuse is most likely when parent under stress (e.g., lost job) and has little support
  b. Abuse highest in deteriorating neighborhood culture (e.g., poor, transient, social isolation, lack community services)
  c. Larger macroenvironment critical (e.g., violent society); abuse less common in cultures that discourage physical punishment and advocate nonviolence
C. What Are the Effects of Family Violence?
 1. Impact of physical abuse and maltreatment can involve physical damage to brain or other parts of the body; cognitive deficits; social, emotional and behavioral problems; and psychological disorders
  a. Intellectual and academic problems common in mistreated children

       i. Children exposed to high levels of domestic violence have lower IQ scores

   b. Social, emotional, and behavioral problems common in physically abused children

       i. Some abused children are explosively aggressive and rejected by peers

       ii. Experience with an abusive parent makes then supersensitive to angry emotions (may perceive anger in peers that is nonexistent)

       iii. Abused children tend to show higher rates of depression and anxiety

   c. Consequence of abuse may involve a lack of empathy in response to distress of others

2. Many maltreated children are resilient and turn out fine

   a. Genes may protect some children from negative psychological effects of abuse

       i. Genes may equip with personal resources like intelligence, social skills, or emotional stability that allow mistreated children to demonstrate resilience in face of adversity

       ii. Close relationship with at least one nonabusive adult helps protect against impact of abuse

SUGGESTIONS FOR CLASS DISCUSSIONS OR PROJECTS

1. The impact of divorce is mediated by many factors. Have students gain some appreciation for these factors by writing a 5-page review paper in which they answer some of all of the following questions.

    • How is the experience of divorce related to the child's age at the time of the divorce?

    • What about the age of the parents?

    • How are the effects of divorce the same and different for male versus female children and parents?

    • How does culture come into play? What about historical factors (e.g., the effects of divorce now versus 10 years ago, versus 30 years ago)?

2. Have students consider how parents using different parenting styles (e.g., authoritarian, permissive) would respond to various family situations. For example, what if a child is watching television or playing with friends and the parent says it is time to go to bed and the child does not want to go? Or, suppose parents have repeatedly told the child not to keep going through the fence into the neighbor's yard and the child continues to do so? Or, a child who knows she is supposed to make her bed in the morning before going to school but always waits until it's too late, meaning she'll miss the school bus and will need a ride to school. How would parents using Baumrind's (1991) different styles of parental control respond in these situations?

   Baumrind, D. (1991). Parenting styles and adolescent development. In J. Brooks-Gunn, R. Lerner, & A.C. Petersen (Eds.), *The Encyclopedia of Adolescence* (pp. 746-758). New York: Garland.

Chapter 15

3. Have students write a paper in which they argue for competency testing for parents. This issue emerges in several contexts, for example, when a child who has been abused on numerous occasions and removed from the abusive home is returned to the home, only to be killed by the abusive parents. As another example, the competency of parents has been questioned in cases of mildly retarded parents of children with normal intelligence. The paper should include a list of the exact requirements and why each is important.

4. Consider the "sandwich" generation—middle-aged adults caring for their children and their aging parents. What impact do aging parents have on their children? What effect is this situation likely to have on grandchildren? Ask students if any of their parents are experiencing middle generation squeeze. What stresses does this place on the entire family? What benefits are realized from this experience? Under which circumstances should a person be able to tell a parent that he or she cannot move in?

5. Discuss how changes in society such as geographic mobility, daycare, and divorce have contributed to changes in the quality of grandparent-grandchildren relationships. If possible, have students interview people of different ages about their experiences with their grandparents (and grandchildren, if any). Is it possible to identify the different styles of grandparenting noted in the text? Are there other styles of grandparenting that are evident from students' descriptions of their relationships with grandparents? How many factors can they identify that contribute to different patterns of grandparent-grandchildren relationships?

6. A common belief is that parenting is mostly a maternal process (i.e., "woman's work"). At the same time, we are seeing a movement in which men are being actively encouraged to become active in the lives of their children. Have students write a paper in which they address the question, "Who is more important to the development of a child, mom or dad?"

7. In Chapter 15, students are introduced to the issue of family violence, including an application section on the use of empowerment as a method of reducing child abuse by mothers. It is clear that being a victim of violence can negatively impact an individual at any time of life. It is also clear that reducing violence has great benefits at both the individual and societal levels. The goal of this assignment is to introduce students to research additional ways (beyond empowerment) for reducing violent behavior within families. To complete the assignment, students should search for journal or Web articles using the terms *child abuse and prevention*, *sexual abuse and prevention*, *elderly abuse and prevention*, and *spouse abuse*. Students should use information in these articles to write a paper in which they will identify different methods that have been shown to reduce family violence in at least two different types of family violence.

SUGGESTED FILMS AND VIDEOS

Changing Families (2007, Insight Media, DVD, 30 minutes): This video offers a look at the changing nature of the American family in the 21st century.

Common Sense Parenting: Building Relationships (2006, Insight Media, DVD, 28 minutes): The goal of this program is to highlight the components that underlie the development of positive relationships between parents and children.

Discovering What Motivates You: How Your Family Upbringing Influenced You (2005, Insight Media, DVD, 30 minutes): This DVD examines the impact of numerous familial factors on development.

Fatherhood: The Influence on the First Two Years (2003, Insight Media, VHS, 30 minutes): This video examines the eroding role of the father and how the parenting style of a father often differs from that of a mother.

The Roots of Violence, Addiction, and Neglect (2006, Magna Systems, DVD, 33 minutes): This interesting film explores the lives of children raised in abusive environments.

SUGGESTED WEBSITES

Divorce 360
http://www.divorce360.com/

Families
http://www.families.com/

Foundation for Grandparenting
http://www.grandparenting.org/

Marriage
http://marriage.about.com/

Prevent Child Abuse
http://www.preventchildabuse.org/index.shtml

SUGGESTED READINGS

Attar-Schwartz, S. (2009). Adolescent's perspectives on relationships with grandparents: The contribution of adolescent, grandparent, and parent-grandparent relationship variables. *Children & Youth Services Review*, 31(9), 1057-1066.

Goddard, C. (2010). Intimate partner violence and child abuse: A child-centered perspective. *Child Abuse Review*, 19(1), 5-20.

Suitor, J. J. (2009). The role of perceived maternal favoritism in sibling relationships in midlife. *Journal of Marriage and Family*, 71(4), 1026-38.

Thornberry, T. P. (2009). Intergenerational linkages in antisocial behavior. Criminal *Behaviour & Mental Health*, 19(2), 80-93.

Wallerstein, J. S. (2008). Divorced fathers and their adult offspring: Report from a twenty-five-year longitudinal study. *Family Law Quarterly*, 42(4), 695-711.

16

DEVELOPMENTAL PSYCHOPATHOLOGY

LEARNING OBJECTIVES

After students have read and studied the material in this chapter, they should be able to answer the following questions:

WHAT MAKES DEVELOPMENT ABNORMAL?

1. What criteria are used to define and diagnose psychological disorders?

2. What is the perspective of the field of developmental psychopathology? What sorts of questions or issues do developmental psychopathologists study?

3. How does the diathesis-stress model explain the causes of psychopathology?

THE INFANT

4. What are the characteristics, suspected causes, treatment, and prognosis for individuals with autism and its related syndromes?

5. In what ways do infants exhibit depression-like conditions? How is depression in infants similar to, or different from, depression in adults?

THE CHILD

6. What differentiates externalizing and externalizing disorders? How are they explained in terms of nature vs. nurture and continuity vs. discontinuity?

7. How is depression during childhood similar to, or different from, depression during adulthood?

THE ADOLESCENT

8. Are psychological problems more prevalent during adolescence than other periods of the lifespan? Explain.

9. What are the characteristics, suspected causes, and treatment of eating disorders such as anorexia nervosa?

10. What are the characteristics of substance abuse and substance abuse in adolescence? How does the cascade model describe the progression of substance abuse? What is this model missing?

11. What is the course of depression and suicidal behavior during adolescence? What factors influence depression during adulthood?

12. What is the prevalence of depression in older adulthood? What makes depression difficult to diagnose during this time of life? How is it treated?

13. What are the characteristics and causes of Alzheimer's disease? How is it treated?

14. What differentiates dementia and delirium? Why is the distinction so important, especially in later life?

CHAPTER OUTLINE

I   What Makes Development Abnormal?

A. Criteria for Diagnosing Psychological Disorders
  1. Three criteria for diagnosis
     a. Statistical deviance—does the person's behavior fall outside the normal range of behavior?
     b. Maladaptiveness—does the person's behavior interfere with personal and social adaptation or pose a danger to self or others?
     c. Personal distress—does the behavior cause personal anguish or discomfort?
  2. DSM-IV Diagnostic Criteria
     a. *Diagnostic and Statistical Manual of Mental Disorders* (DSM-IV-TR)—fourth edition of book (with text revision in 2000) used by professionals to diagnosis psychology disorders
     b. Changes in this edition include single category of "autism spectrum disorder (rather that subcategories of autism), replace term "mental retardation" with intellectual disability," and use of label "addition and related disorders" to distinguish between compulsive drug seeking and withdrawal from prescribed drugs
     c. Depression is a family of affect or mood disorders
        i. DSM-IV characteristics of major depressive disorder—at least one episode of feeling profoundly sad, depressed, and hopeless and/or the loss of ability to derive pleasure for almost all activities for at least two weeks and at least five of the following symptoms: depressed mood (e.g., sad), greatly decreased interest/pleasure in activities (e.g., quit participating), significant change in weight (e.g., weight loss), insomnia or too much sleep, fatigue and loss of energy, feeling of worthlessness or extreme guilt, decreased ability to concentrate, recurrent thoughts of death (e.g., suicidal thoughts or attempts)
     d. Not just "a little down" or symptoms due to substance use
     e. Not the result of dealing with death of another (bereavement)—this criteria may be dropped in DSM-V as death can trigger major depression
  3. Greater need to consider cultural and developmental conditions (DSM-IV addresses but does not say enough) (e.g., depressed Asians more likely to complain about somatic symptoms—bodily symptoms like loss of appetite or disruption of sleep—than psychological symptoms like guilt)
  4. Depression is fundamentally the same in children and adults, but children may express depression by being irritable rather than sad

B. Developmental Psychopathology
   1. Major theories of human development attempted to understand and treat psychological disorders
      a. Freudian psychoanalytic theory once guided clinical practice
      b. Behavioral theory applied learning principles to understanding and treatment
      c. Cognitive theory called attention to individual interpretation of experience
      d. More recently, evolutionary theory asked questions of the adaptive nature of psychological disorders
         i. Depression may help conserve energy after stress
         ii. Attention deficit/hyperactivity disorder—energetic and willing to take risks
         iii. Inheriting too many ADHD genes not as adaptive today
   2. New field forged to study abnormal behavior from a developmental perspective called developmental psychopathology—study course of maladaptive development as compared with normal development
      a. Major focuses on the origin and course of maladaptive development (i.e., how do disorders arise, how does their expression change as the individual develops)
      b. Is a lifespan, interdisciplinary, and systems perspective
   3. Psychopathology as development, not disease
      a. Some developmentalists fault DSM-IV for being rooted in a medical and disease model of psychopathology (i.e., the notion that psychological problems are diseaselike entities a person has or does not have); alternative is that it is the outcome of some developmental process with some branches leading to more or less optimal outcomes
         i. Many different paths for developmental disorders to take
         ii. Some individuals at risk for developing disorder stay on route to adjustment
         iii. Some start off with slight maladaptive course and deviate even further from the norm
      b. Lines between normal and abnormal may be blurred (i.e., different pathways can lead to same disorder and same risk factors can lead to a variety of outcomes)
      c. March has recently suggested that due to relationship between genes, brain, and behavior, psychological disorders need to be view as lifespan neurodevelopmental disorders
         i. Neurodevelopmental perspective looks at normal and abnormal pathways of brain development
         ii. Early intervention with those at risk may put them on healthier developmental trajectories
   4. Social norms and age norms
      a. Social norms—expectations about how to behave in particular situation
      b. Definition and incidence of abnormal behavior are culturally bound
         i. Depressed Thai children show more symptoms of inner distress and less acting out due to cultural standards that emphasize need to internalize negative emotions

Chapter 16

        ii. Hints at the fact that definitions, rates, and developmental course of abnormal behavior vary from culture to culture

    c. Age norms—societal expectations about appropriate behavior for one's age that must be considered in order to understand "normal" before defining "abnormal"

5. Developmental issues

    a. Concerned with nature-nurture issue (origin) of maladaptive behaviors

        i. How do biological, psychological, and social interact?

        ii. What are the risk factors?

    b. Concerned with continuity-discontinuity (progression) of maladaptive behaviors

        i. Are childhood problems passing phases that have no bearing on adjustment in adulthood?

        ii. How does expression of psychopathology change with developmental status?

6. The diathesis-stress model

    a. Proposes that psychopathology results from interaction over time of predisposition or vulnerability to psychological disorder (diathesis) and environmental pressure (stress)

    b. Diathesis-stress description of depression

        i. Genetics factors manifested in outcomes like serotonin imbalance estimated to account for 40 percent of variation in group of people with major depressive disorder; leads to individual highly emotionally reactive to stress (including the high production of the stress hormone cortisol) and self-defeating patterns of thinking in the face of negative events

        ii. Genetically vulnerable individual must then experience multiple (chronic) significant environmental stressors (e.g., death of loved one), and if they do, they are likely to become depressed

        iii. Individuals without depression diathesis (a vulnerability to depression) may be able to handle the high levels of stress without becoming depressed

    c. In one study of individuals with one or two high-risk genes for depression, 10% depressed with no significant negative life event and 33% depressed with four or more stressful events; in same study, only 17% of individuals with two low-risk genes became depressed

    d. Key is combination of these factors (in Figure 16.2) (e.g., genes both predispose some to depression and influence the extent to which they experience stressful life events)

        i. Extreme stress and high vulnerability (severe disorder)

        ii. Extreme stress and high resiliency (mild disorder)

        iii. Low stress and high vulnerability (mild disorder)

        iv. Low stress and high resiliency (no disorder)

        v. Stress and disorder reciprocal relationship (one aggravates the other)

        vi. A depressive episode early in life in response to intense stress may change gene activity and neurobiology of the stress system

    e. Diathesis stronger in some disorders

    f. The environment can shape the course of a disorder and effect functioning and later development

II The Infant

A. Autism

    1. Autism first identified by Leo Kanner in 1943 and characterized by abnormal social development, impaired language and communication, and repetitive behavior

    2. Three defining features of autism in DSM-IV

        a. Abnormal social development

           i. Difficulty forming normal social relationships, responding to social cues, and sharing social experiences with others

           ii. Less eye contact, joint attention with social partner, seeking others for contact, snuggling when held, and making friends

           iii. Difficulty reading the emotions of others, responding with empathy, and demonstrating self-awareness and self-consciousness

           iv. Many display disorganized-disordered attachments

           v. Parents no less sensitive and child's social deficits largely governed by security level of parent-child relationship

        b. Impaired language and communicative skills

           i. Some mute—others acquire speech but have trouble communicating

           ii. Do not babble or gesture as infants

           iii. Autistic children speak in flat tone, reverse pronouns (e.g., "I" for "you"), and engage in echolalia—parroting (repeat) back what someone else says

        c. Repetitive, stereotyped behavior and restricted interests

           i. Seek sameness and repetition (great distress when environment changed)

           ii. Stereotypic behaviors (e.g., rock back and forth, flap hands, and/or spin repeatedly and without purpose

           iii. May carry out elaborate rituals (e.g., particular sequence of dressing their self)

           iv. May become obsessed with particular object of interest

           v. Become highly distressed when physical environment is altered

    3. Autism varies greatly in level of impact (some refer to it as "autisms")

        a. Autism spectrum disorder, ASD—family of conditions within DSM-IV category of "pervasive developmental disorders" that all involve social and communication problems

        b. Asperser syndrome is also an ASD with several unique characteristics

           i. Normal or above-average intellect, good verbal skills, serious deficit in emotion-reading and social skills

           ii. "Little professor" who talks stiffly and at length about topics that obsess them

           iii. Until recently, have been largely ignored, although were seen as odd or socially aloof

    4. Is there are autistic epidemic?

        a. Rates have been rising

           i. Autism in broadest sense (9 out of 1,000 8-year-olds in the U.S.) and broader sense (1 in 110 8-year-olds in the U.S.)

      ii. Four to five boys affected for every girl

    b. Debate over cause of increase

      i. One theory involves mercury-based preservative (thimerosal) in vaccines for measles, mumps, and rubella or the measles virus itself but evidence does not support the idea; the main study linking MMR vaccine and autism has been withdrawn from the medical journal in which it was published due to errors and irregularities; rates climbed after the preservative was removed from the vaccine

      ii. More accepted theory is that the increase is the result of broadening of the definition of autism and greater awareness of the disorder (in past, cases were likely misdiagnosed as language impairments, learning disabilities, or odd personalities)

      iii. Autism not added to U.S. list of disabilities eligible for special education services until 1991; Asperger syndrome not added to DSM-IV until 1994

      iv. It is possible that the number of actual cases is still increasing

5. Characteristics of autistic individuals

    a. Diagnosis does not typically take place until around age 2 to 3 years

      i. Working on an earlier screening and detection measures as early treatment may steer development to a more normal pathway

    b. Autistic infants given away by lack of normal interest in and response to social stimuli and delayed language development

      i. Fail to orient to human voices

      ii. Fail to babble and use first word

      iii. Fail to make eye contact and tend to focus on background objects

      iv. Socially fail to engage in joint attention, reciprocity of turn-taking, and mutual smiling

      v. Longer they go without diagnosis, the more severe the social and communicative problems

    c. Intelligence level varies greatly

      i. Judging intelligence can be challenging (IQs have likely been underestimated in the past); perform better on Raven's Progressive Matrices test (nonverbal test involving comparison of geometric patterns) than on IQ tests

      ii. More higher-functioning children being diagnosed today; less than 50% have intellectual disability (IQ of 70 or lower)

      iii. Some autistics show special ability (e.g., calculating days of the week on calendar or memorizing large amounts of information)

    d. Autism used to be viewed as clear example of path of development that qualitatively deviates from the norm but is now seen as extreme end of genetically influenced continuum of social responsiveness (a quantitative difference)

6. Suspected causes

    a. Early "refrigerator mom" theory (rigid and cold) is now known to be a harmful myth

    b. Parental factors

i. Interaction with parents may cause parent to be frustrated
ii. Parent's genes may contribute (and parents may have mild autistic spectrum traits)
iii. Bad parenting not a factor
iv. One study found concordance rate for broader spectrum of autism traits was 92% in identical twins and 10% in fraternal twins

c. Genetic factors
i. Many genes on different chromosomes have been implicated (most likely that individual with autism inherits several of these genes)
ii. Distinct genes may contribute to the three major impairments (social, communication, repetitive behaviors)
iii. In some cases, genes related to neural communication are copied too many time or too few times during meiosis
iv. Autism more likely when mother and especially father is older and more prone to errors in DNA copying

d. Environmental factors
i. When one identical twin is autistic, the other sometimes is not, indicating that the environment contributes to autism
ii. Environmental trigger (e.g., virus or chemical) might interact with genetic predisposition
iii. Is possible that epigenetic influences that turn gene on and off may play a role
iv. Prenatal exposure to rubella, alcohol, and thalidomide may contribute
v. Maternal bleeding and other birth complications may contribute

e. Neurological-brain factors
i. Neurological abnormalities common, and many autistics have epilepsy
ii. Leading hypothesis is that neurons in frontal lobe and other areas of the brain proliferate wildly during early sensitive period of brain development in infancy and do not properly connect to other areas of the brain; focus on amygdala in forebrain that is implicated in social and emotional behavior; toddlers with autism have especially larger amygdales, and extent of social and communication impairment is correlated with size of amygdala
iii. Mirror neuron hypothesis—autism the result of malfunctioning of mirror neurons located in number of brain areas account for deficits in imitation, theory-of-mind skills, empathy, and language; mirror neurons allow us to make sense of others' feelings and thoughts by reacting as if they were experienced ourselves (e.g., view picture of angry facial expression and automatically mimic the expression)
iv. Too soon to conclude that lack of brain connectedness, overgrowth of amygdala, or improperly functioning mirror neurons at heart of ADS display

f. Executive dysfunction hypothesis
i. Deficiency in executive functions—planning and organizing ability based in prefrontal cortex of brain
ii. May explain repetitive behavior and tendency to focus on details and fail to see "big picture"

g. Extreme male brain hypothesis
  i. Autism is a pervasive disorder (i.e., impacts a number of core areas and has multiple causes)
  ii. (Exploration box on the hypothesis of autism as an extreme version of a male brain)
7. Developmental outcomes and treatment
  a. Can improve, but long-tem prognosis usually poor, especially if accompanied by intellectual disability (autistic for life)
    i. Positive outcomes most likely in autistics with IQ over 70 who can communicate
  b. Antipsychotic and antidepressant drugs treat some symptoms but do not cure autism
  c. Nasal administration of oxytocin (type of hormone) may have short-lived ability to improve attention and social interest in high-functioning individuals with autism
  d. Most effective programs involve intensive behavioral and educational training beginning as early in life as possible
    i. Goal is to make most of plasticity of infant brain
    ii. Lovaas has used reinforcement principles to teach children with autism to reduce aggression and self-stimulation, to imitate others, to play effectively with peers, and to master language; parents taught to use same behavioral techniques at home
    iii. "Astounding results" (e.g., IQ scores 30 points higher in treatment group versus the control group)
    iv. Study criticized because it was not a true experiment with random assignment to control and treatment groups
    v. Early behavioral interventions usually do not convert children with autism into typically functioning children
    vi. Can be taught social scripts and how to make eye contact, but training does not generalize easily to other situations
    vii. Many young children without severe intellectual disabilities make significant gains if they receive intensive cognitive and behavioral training and comprehensive family services in early life

B. Depression
1. Still debating whether "true depression" can occur in infancy (i.e., may not be capable of negative cognitions common among depressed adults like low self-esteem, guilt, hopelessness but can exhibit behavioral symptoms like loss of interest and psychomotor slowing)
2. Symptoms of depression most likely in infants who lack secure attachment to caregiver
3. Infants of depressed mothers or fathers at risk
  a. Babies adopt style of depressed caregivers (e.g., vocalize little and look sad)
  b. May be a combination of genes and stressful experiences
  c. Early life stress can produce overactive stress response in those easily distressed and who cannot regulate their own emotions

4. Failure to thrive—neglected, abused, separated from attachment figures, or otherwise stressed infants that fail to grow normally, lose weight, and become seriously underweight for their age
   a. Often developmentally delayed
   b. Cause may be more emotional than physical
   c. Babies with nonorganic failure to thrive may gain weight and overcome depression-like symptoms quickly if removed from homes but relapse quickly if returned to insensitive care
   d. Intervening to change family system is critical

III The Child
A. Externalizing and Internalizing Problems
   1. Many children experience developmental problems (e.g., temper tantrums) but smaller portion officially diagnosed with a psychological disorder
   2. Two general categories of developmental problems: externalizing and internalizing
      a. Externalizing (undercontrolled) disorders (acting out, more disturbing to others)—aggression, disobedience, disruptive, hyperactive (includes ADHD and conduct disorder)
      b. Internalizing (overcontrolled) disorders (inner distress, more destructive to self)—anxiety, phobias, severe shyness, depression
      c. Internalized bottle up, externalized express
      d. Externalizing tends to decline in frequency between ages 4 and 18 and is more common among boys
      e. Internalizing tends to increase in frequency between ages 4 and 18 and is more prevalent among girls
      f. Children from low SES show more internalizing and externalizing problems
   3. Nature and nurture
      a. Societal and parental tendency to believe in "parental effect" and blame parents (especially mom) if children are sad or "bratty"
         i. Parents feel guilt because they assume they are at fault
      b. Must view developmental disorders from family systems perspective, appreciating how emerging problems affect and are affected by family interactions
      c. Depressed children and children with many psychological disorders tend to come from problem-ridden families and to have insecure attachments with their parents; are more likely to have parents with histories of psychological disorders
      d. Child might have genetic predisposition to disorder
      e. Poor parenting may be the effect of a child's disorder and not the cause (e.g., child's behavioral problem can negatively impact parent's mood, marital relationships, and parenting behavior)
      f. Stress and ineffective parenting can contribute to and aggravate many childhood problems
         i. (Exploration box on stress from Hurricane Katrina and rise in rate of externalizing and internalize problems in children)

g. Children predisposed to internalizing and externalizing problems can be protected by warm and loving parents but hurt by rejecting parents

4. Continuity and discontinuity
   a. Research by Caspi found that externalizing problems at age 3 (e.g., irritable, impulsive, rough) were more likely to be diagnosed with antisocial personality disorders and records of criminal behavior in young adulthood
   b. Same study found that internalizers at age 3 (e.g., shy, anxious) were more likely to be depressed (but not suffering from anxiety disorders) as young adults
   c. These results suggest continuity in susceptibility to problems and that early problems have significance for later development
   d. However, most children with risk-related temperaments did not have diagnosable disorders as young adults, suggesting discontinuity
   e. Children with mild symptoms who receive help may see problems disappear
      i. Targeting young children with internalizing and externalizing problems for treatment is critical
   f. Some children show remarkable resilience and function well despite exposure to risk factors for disorders or can overcome severe early problems
      i. Resilient children benefit from protective factors (e.g., competencies like intellectual ability and social skills) and strong social support (e.g., stable family with one caring parental figure)

B. Depression
   1. Psychoanalytic theorists argued that infants were incapable of experiencing depression but now know that children as young as age 3 can meet criteria for major depressive disorders using adult diagnostic criteria
   2. Depression rarer in childhood than in adolescence
      a. Many youngsters with symptoms of depression also show other disorders like attention deficit disorder and anxiety disorder; comorbidity—co-occurrence of two of more psychiatric conditions in same individual
   3. Depression expresses itself differently in young children than adults; more likely to display behavioral and somatic problems (e.g., losing interest in activities) and less likely to display cognitive symptoms (e.g., hopelessness)
      a. Prone to more anxiety; children as young as age 3 years express shame or guilt
   4. Very young children (2-3 years) capable of attempting suicide
      a. Jump from high places, stab themselves, run into traffic
      b. Those who attempt suicide once are more likely to try again
      c. Parents, teachers, and professionals need to appreciate childhood is not always happy
   5. Most children make it through mild episodes of sadness, and carryover of depression problems from childhood to adolescence not as strong as from adolescence to adulthood
   6. Childhood depression can disrupt intellectual, academic, and social adjustment
   7. Multiple types of therapies
      a. Cognitive-behavioral therapy—focus on identifying and changing distorted thinking and maladaptive emotions and behavior

           i.   Especially effective but requires more cognitive and verbal ability of children than strictly behavioral treatments

      b.   Antidepressant medication (e.g., Prozac), many of which are selective serotonin reuptake inhibitors (correct for low levels of serotonin in the brain)

           i.   Not as effective with children as with adults

          ii.   Some concern that medications can increase risk of suicide in children and adolescents

        iii.   Are now prescribed less often and with more careful monitoring

      c.   Combination of Prozac and cognitive-behavioral therapy appears to be the best treatment for seriously depressed children and adolescents

IV The Adolescent

    A. Storm and Stress?

       1. Founder of developmental psychology G. Stanley Hall viewed adolescence as emotional time of "storm and stress," and this depiction has been with us since 1904

       2. Most adolescents actually well-adjusted; only about 20% of teens have significant mental health problems

           a.   Many teens with significant mental health problems were maladjusted in childhood and will continue to have problems in adulthood

       3. Adolescence is time of heightened vulnerability to substance abuse and delinquency and a heightened sense of vulnerability to certain psychological disorders

           a.   20% rate of diagnosable disorders in adolescence higher than 10% rate in childhood

       4. Teens face greater stress due to factors like physical growth, changing brain and cognitive abilities, dating, family dynamics, challenges at school, and assumption of adult roles and responsibilities

           a.   Most adolescents cope with challenges remarkable well

           b.   For a minority of adolescents, stressors build and can precipitate serious psychopathology

       5. Risk for behavioral problems in teen years comes in several areas including overuse of drugs and engaging in delinquent behavior, but they tend not to reach the level of seriousness that would constitute definition as a psychological disorder

           a.   Problem behaviors may peak in adolescence in part because brain development at this time endows adolescents with strong sensation- and regard-seeking tendencies but immature self-regulatory capabilities

           b.   Impulsive pursuit of enjoyment without must self-control or thought of consequences

    B. Anorexia Nervosa

       1. Highly associated with adolescence (specifically, female adolescents); often first seen in transition from childhood to adolescence or adolescence to adulthood

       2. Eating disorders (e.g., anorexia nervosa) have become more common in several industrialized countries, and these conditions can be potentially fatal

       3. Anorexia nervosa—literally means "nervous loss of appetite"

Chapter 16

a. Refusal to maintain body weight (e.g., significant loss of weight resulting in 85% or less of expected weight), fear of becoming overweight, distorted body image (tendency to see one as fat even when emaciated)

b. Distinguished from bulimia nervosa—"binge/purge syndrome" involving recurrent binge-eating of huge quantities of food followed by purging activities using self-induced vomiting, laxatives, or rigid dieting and fasting

c. Anorexia nervosa often begins as diet during or shortly after puberty and continues (even when weighing 60-70 pounds and looking like a cadaver)
   i. Initially receive praise from parents for weight loss
   ii. Become increasingly obsessed with diet and exercise
   iii. Gain sense of power by resisting urge of parents and friends to eat more

d. Affects both men and women but is especially prevalent in females in late adolescence (3 in 1,000 adolescent girls, 11 females for every 1 male victim)

e. Myth that anorexia nervosa only found in European-American females from upper-middle class backgrounds
   i. Some cultural variation in incidence (e.g., less common in African-American females than in European- or Asian-American females)

4. Suspected causes
   a. Nurture side focuses on cultural factors like social pressures and value to be thin (especially in Westernized cultures)
      i. Media presentations of thinness as ideal women to Fiji; females altered traditional view of plump body as status symbol to feeling of fatness and need to control weight
      ii. Fear of fatness seen in preschool girls
      iii. Desire to be thin and feelings about their bodies influenced by how much emphasis their peers place on thinness and how much television focused on appearance
      iv. Ultra-thin Barbie dolls with unattainable body proportions may contribute to young girls' dissatisfaction with their bodies
      v. One study: one-fourth of second-grade girls dieted
   b. Nature side
      i. Normal puberty changes involve fat gain and may explain why adolescence is a prime time for emergence of eating disorders
   c. Genes
      i. Why do so few adolescent females develop anorexia even though almost all experience social pressure to be thin?
      ii. Genes may serve as diathesis (predisposition)
      iii. Twin and adoption studies suggest that half of variation in risk for eating disorders attributed to genes
      iv. A number of biochemical abnormalities found in individuals with anorexia
      v. Genes may contribute to low levels of serotonin (associated with eating disorders and mood) and levels of dopamine (implicated in brain's reward system)
      vi. Genes may contribute to personality profile that puts them at risk (e.g., anxiety and obsessive perfection)

    d. Interaction of genes and environment
       i. Genetically predisposed girl living in a weight-conscious culture
       ii. Early stress (prenatal and perinatal complications) increases risk of anorexia
    e. Family factors
       i. Often found in families who tend to be preoccupied with weight and where mothers model disordered eating
       ii. May have insecure attachments with parents
    f. Pileup of stressors (e.g., relationship issues, school, changing body in puberty) pushes person over the edge
  5. Treatment
    a. Effective treatment of anorexia starts with behavior modification to alter eating (i.e., gain weight) and dealing with medical problems associated with the disorder; then moving on to psychotherapy designed to help understand and gain control of the problems and family therapy to change parent-child relationships; medications for depression and related psychological problems
    b. Maudsley approach to family therapy (named after the hospital in London where it originated)
       i. Focuses squarely on initial weight gain and views family as part of the treatment team rather than the cause of the problem (puts parents in charge of temporarily getting child to eat until she is ready to take over that responsibility)
       ii. Requires cooperation of all family members, who must see problem as serious and stop blaming themselves
       iii. Once sufficient weight is gained, control of eating is returned to adolescent
    c. Individuals with anorexia more difficult to treat; strong resistance in admitting they have a problem
    d. Treatment most effective if begun prior to age 18 (before it is chronic)
    e. Prevention might be possible
       i. Body Project—dissonance-producing anorexia nervosa intervention
       ii. Get adolescent girls who have body image concerns to stop viewing thin bodies as ideal by having them critique thinness in essays and in role-playing
       iii. Psychological dissonance created by coming out against ideal expected to motivate the individual to stop pursuing thinness as goal
       iv. Study using this technique effective at reducing the internalization of thin as ideal body type, reducing body dissatisfaction, dieting efforts, and eating disorder symptoms
       v. Some evidence that Internet-based prevention programs based on cognitive-behavioral principles succeeded in reducing risk of eating disorders in at-risk and high school and college students
C. Substance Abuse Disorders
  1. Some adolescents explore identity and strive for peer acceptance by experimenting with smoking, drinking, and drug use

2. DSM-IV substance abuse—when use of a substance has adverse consequences such as putting the person in physical danger, interfering with school or work performance, or contributing to interpersonal problems
3. Substance dependence—continuing use despite significant problems as indicated by compulsive use, increased drug tolerance, withdrawal symptoms if use terminated, and the inability to quit (worse than substance abuse)
4. Heavy toll of substance abuse and dependence
   a. Teens under influence of alcohol make risky choices including risky sex, driving under the influence, riding with others who are drinking, fighting, and engaging in illegal behavior
   b. Drugs can have toxic effects on nervous system at key time of brain development, negative impacts on academic achievement, occupational success, and interpersonal relationships
   c. Drug use in childhood or early adolescence predicts later problems with abuse and dependence
5. Use patterns
   a. Current rate of substance abuse in adolescence not as high as in the 1970s but represents an increase since the early 1990s
   b. Typical increase in use with age, exception is inhalants (e.g., glue, nail polish remover) used more often by young teens than older teens (reason likely due to the fact that inhalants are cheap and readily attainable)
   c. If inhalants included in list of "illegal drugs," then one quarter of 8th graders and half of 12th graders have used illegal drugs
   d. Binge-drinking—5 or more alcohol drinks in a row—8% of 8th graders, 16% of 10th graders, 25% of 12th grades; even a bigger problem in college students
   e. Native-American youth have high rate of drug use, Hispanic and non-Hispanic white youth have medium rates, Asian- and African-American youth have the lowest rates
   f. Males have traditionally had higher rates than females, but the gap is narrowing
   g. Cascade model of substance abuse—transactional and multifactor model
      i. Begins with child at risk due to difficult temperament
      ii. Child born into an adverse family environment characterized by problems like poverty, stress, and substance abuse
      iii. Child exposed to harsh parenting and family conflict
      iv. Child develops behavioral problems, especially aggression and conduct problems
      v. Child is rejected by peers and gets into more trouble at school
      vi. Parents, perhaps in frustration, give up monitoring and supervision of now difficult-to-control adolescent child
      vii. Ends with child's involvement in a deviant peer group in which adolescent is exposed to and reinforced for drug use and other deviant behavior
      viii. Study on cascade model in children from 7th to 12th grade found correlation between many factors that predicted both the next step in the model and involvement in substance abuse

        ix. Research indicates that behavioral and psychological disorders do not spring out of nowhere but grow out of accumulating effects of transactions between an individual and parents, peers, and other aspects of the social environment over many years

        x. Model indicates that there are opportunities to intervene at each step in the cascade model

   h. Genetic factors

      i. Behavioral genetics research suggests that a genetic predisposition to drink alcohol may cause teens to associate with other peers who drink

      ii. Drug abuse is the developmental outcome of interactions between many genes and many environmental factors

   i. Substance use disorder often combined with other disorders like depression and anxiety disorders (same genes contributing to both substance abuse and internalizing and externalizing behaviors)

      i. Substance abuse may develop as a way to cope with psychological disorders, but substance abuse then aggravates the mental health problem, creating a vicious cycle

      ii. Good news is that preventative interventions delay drinking and drug abuse and head off problematic substance use in adulthood

D. Depression and Suicidal Behavior

  1. Adolescents more vulnerable to depression than in childhood (especially females)

    a. Rate in girls about 1% at age 12 but 17% at age 19

    b. Up to 35% of adolescents experience some depressive mood and 7% diagnosable depression

    c. Depressed adolescents sometimes act out and look more like delinquents than victims of depression

  2. Factors in depression

    a. Rise in risk possibly due to genetic influences related to timing of puberty may explain greater risk to females who mature earlier

    b. Interpersonal stressful adolescent events (divorce in family, breakups) result in increase in depression rates

    c. Females more likely to experience an accumulation of stressful events in early adolescence (especially interpersonal issues involving divorce and relationship breakups), which predicts increased depressive symptoms

      i. Girls more likely to rely on ruminative coping—dwelling unproductively on problems when attempting to solve them

      ii. Ruminative coping may make problems seem worse and does not typically result in problem being solved

      iii. Ruminative coping predicts future depression and binge-eating in adolescent girls

  3. Suicidality

    a. Increase in depression between childhood and adolescence leads to increase in suicidal thoughts, attempts, and actual suicides

    b. Suicide third leading cause of death in teens (far behind accidents and homicide)

    c. Most suicide attempts unsuccessful

d. Almost 12% of males and 22% of females in grades 9 to 12 have seriously considered suicide

e. Age and rate of suicide
   i. Peak suicide rate in females is middle age and in white males the rate climbs throughout adulthood; white men aged 65 and over most likely to commit suicide

f. Males more likely to commit suicide (3 to 1 ratio), while females more likely to attempt suicide (3 to 1 ratio); males more successful because they use more lethal techniques (especially guns)

g. Hear more about teen suicide because of more attempts, seen as "cry for help"
   i. Adolescents who attempt suicide often want a better life, not death
   ii. Message: "I've got serious problems; wake up and help me!"

4. Adolescent suicide behavior is product of diathesis/stress

a. Four risk factors for suicide are youth psychological disorder, family pathology, stressful events, and access to firearms

b. Additional suicide factors: genetic predisposition, substance abuse, anxiety disorders, other diagnosable psychological disorder

c. Many suicide attempters have history of family problems, and suicide may run in the family

d. Often preceded by buildup of stressful events (e.g., deteriorating relationships with parents and peers, academic or social failure, run-ins with the law)

e. Availability of firearms makes it easier to act on suicidal impulses

f. Professional intervention important after unsuccessful event

V The Adult

A. Life Strains Change with Age
1. Stressful experiences in childhood and adolescence increase a person's chances of psychological disorders in later life
2. Psychological problems emerge when a vulnerable individual faces overwhelming stress

   a. Adults typically experience the greatest amount of stress in early adulthood
   b. Life strains tend to decrease from early to middle adulthood
   c. Elder adults report fewer hassles and strains than middle-aged adults
   d. Age differences in stressful events may explain age differences in rate of psychological disorders
   e. Some decrease in incidence of certain disorders (e.g., affect disorders, alcohol abuse, depression, mood disorders, schizophrenia, and anxiety disorders) as we get older
   f. Cognitive impairments (e.g., dementia) tend to increase in frequency with age

B. Depression
1. Age and sex differences

   a. By age 75, 28% of Americans experience diagnosable mood disorder, but elderly adults become less vulnerable to stress
   b. Mental health in old age is likely good unless an individual develops physical health problems that contribute to depression or experiences increasing levels of stress

c. Reasons to be concerned about depression in old age
   i. Elderly depressed most likely age group to take own life
   ii. Reports of depression increase beginning when people reach age 70
   iii. While only 1-2% of older adults have major depressive disorder, 15-25% have symptoms of depression
d. May be difficult to diagnose depression in older adults
   i. Symptoms of depression include fatigue, sleeping, somatic complaints that are common in normally aging older adults, (i.e., symptoms may be missed as they are seen as normal aging)
   ii. Elderly adults may hide depression by denying problem
   iii. Clinicians need to be sensitive to differences between normal aging, disease, and psychopathology
   iv. While few suffer from sever, diagnosable depression, many elderly adults (especially very old women who are physically ill, poor, and/or socially isolated) feel depressed or demoralized
e. Women more likely to be diagnosed with depression (margin of two to one)
   i. Possible reasons for sex difference in diagnosis of depression include differences in hormones, biological reactions to stress, levels of stress, ways of expressing distress, coping styles (e.g., women more likely to ruminate)

2. Treatment
   a. Big challenge is to get depressed adults to seek treatment
   b. Elderly most likely to go undiagnosed and untreated (especially if they are members of minority groups)
   c. Elderly and family believe that depression and anxiety are a normal part of aging
   d. Elderly benefit from treatment
      i. Those treated with antidepressants tend to both overcome the depression and show improved cognitive functioning
      ii. Combination of drug treatment and psychotherapy (especially cognitive-behavioral therapy) best approach

C. Aging and Dementia
   1. Dementia—term for senility, a progressive deterioration of neural functioning and associated traits (memory, thinking, personality changes)
      a. Senility not a normal part of aging, yet incidence of dementia increases with age (less than 1% in the 60-64 age group to around 30% in the 85 and older group)
      b. Dementia not single disorder; many conditions can produce symptoms associated with senility
   2. Alzheimer's disease or dementia of Alzheimer's type—most common form of dementia (70% of cases)
      a. Can strike in middle age, but becomes more likely with advanced age (5% of population at age 65, 40% at age 90)
      b. Related brain changes
         i. Senile plaques—masses of dying neural material with toxic protein call beta-amyloid at their core

      ii. Neurofibrillary tangles—twisted strands of neural fibers within the body of neural cells

     iii. Both symptoms normal in older adults but number, type, and location of differences separate normal aging from Alzheimer's disease

     iv. Effects of Alzheimer's disease progressive and irreversible

  c. Alzheimer's symptoms

      i. First symptoms involve mild cognitive impairment in learning and recalling recently encountered verbal information like names and phone numbers; detectable 2 to 3 years before dementia in diagnoses; such mild cognitive impairment is common and may not lead to Alzheimer's

      ii. In early stages, free recall tasks become difficult but can be improved with use of recall cues; eventually cuing does not help and individual will become increasingly frustrated

     iii. Progresses to trouble recalling old information and coming up with words during conversation; may not know where or when they are

     iv. Progresses to inability to care for self and loss of verbal abilities

      v. Death is typically about 8-10 years following diagnosis

     vi. Tests the patience of caregivers because of wandering, taking off clothes in public, highly agitated and uncontrollable behavior, depression, and psychotic symptoms like hallucinations

  d. Causes and contributors

      i. Has a genetic basis but there is no single "Alzheimer's gene"

      ii. Early-onset form (prior to age 60) more linked to genetic factors including a dominant gene on the 21st chromosome pair (early onset only account for 2% of cases)

     iii. Late onset type much more common than early onset type, and a number of genes increases risk; genes account for 60% of the variation in Alzheimer's

     iv. Presence of a gene on 19th chromosome responsible for Ape—protein involved in processing cholesterol—increases risk factor; having two variants of the APoE4 gene increases risk level by 15 times; another version of ApoE4 gene linked to good chance of maintaining cognitive function in very late adulthood

      v. Signs of brain atrophy can be detected in people with two ApoE4 gene; may increase the build-up of beta-amyloid and step the progression of Alzheimer's, but not everyone with the ApoE4 gene or pair of genes develops Alzheimer's disease (indicating that additional genes and/or environmental factors are likely at play)

     vi. Environmental risk factors include head injury at younger age and diets that increase odds of high blood pressure, high cholesterol, and cardiovascular disease

  e. Reserve capacity—extra brain power or cognitive capacity that people can fall back on as aging and disease take a toll

  f. People with advanced education, high intelligence, good health, and who are socially active tend to have higher levels of reserve capacity

  g. Preventions and treatments

        i.   Early detection the best

       ii.   Drugs increase levels of acetylcholine (shown at deficit levels in many with Alzheimer's disease), which is essential for normal learning and memory

      iii. No pills can prevent or reverse Alzheimer's; drugs like Aricept and Namenda improve cognitive function

      iv. Anti-oxidants (e.g., vitamin E and C) and statin drugs may be used to improve cognitive function, reduce behavioral problems, and slow the progression of the disease

       v.   Changes in lifestyle (especially those contributing to cardiovascular disease) may reduce risk for Alzheimer's

      vi. Physical and mental exercise may delay onset and progression of dementia

   h. If Alzheimer's disease is not preventable, researchers hope to learn to slow the onset and progression

       i.   Much can be gained by making the disease more bearable

3. Other causes of cognitive impairment

   a. Vascular dementia (multi-infarct dementia)—series of continuing strokes

       i.   Unpredictable pattern of development (deterioration after each stroke) that can damage the functions based in the affected brain area

       ii. Less strongly influenced by genes and more related to environmental factors like smoking, diet high in fat that increase risk for cerebrovascular disease

   b. Huntington's disease, Parkinson's disease, and multiple sclerosis are among many other possible causes of dementia

   c. Perhaps 10% or more of cases are reversible or curable; alcoholism, toxic reactions to medications, infections, malnutrition can cause symptoms of dementia but may be correctable and a once "senile" person can be restored to normal

   d. Some elderly who are diagnosed with dementia actually suffer from delirium—treatable condition developing rapidly over course of the day that may be characterized by disorientation, wandering attention, and hallucinations

       i.   Many hospital patents experience delirium in reaction to stressors like illness, surgery, drug overdoses, interactions of drugs, or malnutrition; essential to identify this condition before patient is sent home as those who do not receive treatment have higher death rates

   e. Depressed elderly individuals sometimes misdiagnosed with dementia

   f. Vital to accurately diagnose and differentiate between irreversible dementia, reversible dementia, delirium, depression, and other conditions mistaken for irreversible dementia (including old age itself)

   g. Diagnosis of Alzheimer's disease should be made only after all other causes have been ruled out

SUGGESTIONS FOR CLASS DISCUSSIONS OR PROJECTS

1. Much debate has centered on Hall's (1904) notion that adolescence is a period of storm and stress. Entertain the possibility that adolescence *is* a period of storm and stress, but for the *parents*, not the adolescent. How many reasons can students think of as to why this period might be stressful for parents? Examples include adolescent rebellion, financial stress of college, the parents' own midlife crisis, and ambivalence about having an "empty nest." Have students discuss how other times of life (e.g., infancy, middle age, old age) might also be characterized as time of "storm and stress."

Hall, G. S. (1904). *Adolescence: Its Psychology and Its Relations to Physiology, Anthropology, Sociology, Sex, Crime, Religion, and Education.* New York, NY: Appleton-Century-Crofts.

2. Students generally have some personal experience with delinquent behavior or illicit drug use. Ask them to be the "experts" and analyze why adolescents become involved in such activities. Encourage them to consider theoretical concepts such as Erikson's conflict of identity versus role confusion and Elkind's (1984) concept of adolescent egocentrism. Students are also likely to know people who have crossed the line between experimental drug use and abuse. Discuss where the line between normal and abnormal lies and what factors explain why some of their fellow students become drug abusers and others do not. What role and responsibility do parents play in this process? Are they part of the problem? Part of the solution? Miller and Plant (2010) suggest that they may be both. What do your students think about this issue?

Elkind, D. (1984). *All Grown Up and No Place to Go: Teenagers in Crisis.* Reading, MA: Addison-Wesley.

Miller, P., and Plant, M. (2010) Parental guidance about drinking: Relationship with teenage psychoactive substance use. *Journal of Adolescence*, 33(1), 55-68.

3. Have students write a paper on how psychological disorders are portrayed by the media. Are the portrayals stereotypical or accurate? What television shows, commercials, or movies have the most and the least accurate portrayals? Those portrayals that are not negative are often inaccurate or uninformative because they highlight a single case study that may not be representative of the group of people with a particular condition. To what extent do students find this to be the case in their analyses of the representation of disorders? Research shows that viewers believe these portrayals *are* representative of the larger group. This may have practical consequences because the belief structures people form from watching television and movies affect their future actions. Do students have any ideas on how to address this problem?

You might consider having students read a short article by Gard (2001) on this issue. Interestingly, the article includes a brief (three-item) assessment of the reader's understanding of mental illness.

Gard, C. (2001). How the media portray the mental illness. *Current Health 2*, 28(1), 24-25.

4. For a practical and interesting activity, follow the following suggestion also adapted from a *Current Health* source. This suggested activity involves having students find out what resources exist at their school and community to turn to if they or someone they know is showing signs of a mental illness. Examples of resources likely include a school nurse, a school-based clinic, a school psychologist(s), and/or a guidance counselor(s).

Media and Mental Illness (2001) *Current Health 2*, *Teacher's Guide*, 28(1), 2-3.

5. The *Diagnostic and Statistical Manual of Mental Disorders-IV-TR* (2000), published by the American Psychiatric Association, delineates that defining characteristics of psychological disorders and is generally viewed as the standard for the field. Standards do, however, change. A brief history of attention-deficit/hyperactivity disorder (ADHD) as described in the DSM demonstrates how changes in the depiction of disorders reflect ongoing research discoveries and philosophical changes in how we view the disorder.

Researchers, diagnosticians, and therapists have wrestled over whether inattention or hyperactivity is the primary problem in ADHD. In DSM-II (1968), the label was hyperkinetic reaction of childhood, and the main characteristic was hyperactivity. In DSM-III (1980), there were two different categories. One was attention deficit disorder with hyperactivity (ADDH), and the characteristics were inattention, impulsivity, and motor hyperactivity. The second category was attention deficit disorder without Hyperactivity (ADD/noH), and the characteristics were inattention, disorganization, and difficulty completing tasks, but no hyperactivity. In the revision of DSM-III (1987), the category was changed to attention-deficit hyperactivity disorder (ADHD) because there seemed to be a lack of clinical cases of ADD/noH and a shift in thinking about the relative importance of hyperactivity and inattention. DSM-III-R did include a category of undifferentiated attention deficit disorder (U-ADD) that focused on developmentally inappropriate and marked inattention for children who didn't quite fit ADHD. In DSM-IV (1994), a child can show inattention *or* hyperactivity-impulsivity to be classified as ADHD. There are three subtypes of ADHD in DSM-IV: 1) ADHD, combined type for children who show roughly equal symptoms of both inattention and hyperactivity-impulsivity; 2) ADHD, predominantly inattentive type for children who show numerous inattention symptoms and few hyperactivity-impulsivity symptoms; and 3) ADHD, predominantly hyperactive-impulsive type for children who show numerous symptoms of hyperactivity-impulsivity symptoms and few inattention symptoms.

After discussing ADHD, students might look up descriptions of disorders mentioned in the text in DSM-IV and perhaps compare them to descriptions in earlier versions of the manual. Some questions to consider:
- What has changed in the descriptions over time?
- What assumptions are embedded in current descriptions?
- Is there any recent research that might affect how we think about disorders?
- What sorts of research studies might be helpful?

6. There are typically students in the class who have aging relatives with dementia (Alzheimer's or another form). You might ask them to describe their relatives' symptoms and

how they progressed over time to help impress on students the nature of the disease. You could also discuss the impact of the disorder on those caring for the relative (caregiver burden originally discussed in Chapter 15).

7. The purpose of this assignment is to have students expand their knowledge of psychopathology by exploring the topic of school phobia, a type of anxiety disorder associated with academic settings. To complete the project, students should search for articles using the terms *school phobia*. The student should then select and read at least five articles on the topic with the goal of producing a 3- to 4-page paper addressing the cause, symptoms, and effective types of interventions for school phobia. This paper should focus on the phobia in younger children and high school and college students.

8. Most student are probably familiar with the Amber Alert system, in which a national alert is issued in response to missing and abducted children, but far fewer may be aware of the Silver Alert system, which is designed to issue an alert when a cognitively impaired adult is missing. As of 2008, 17 states in the U.S. had this system in place. As this topic may be unfamiliar but of interest to students, consider a discussion of the topic based on Carr's (2010) article.

Carr, D. (2010). Silver alerts and the problem of missing adults with dementia. *The Gerontologist,* 50(2), 149-157.

SUGGESTED FILMS AND VIDEOS

Alzheimer's and Dementia: Caring for the Caregiver (2003, Films for the Humanities & Sciences, DVD/VHS, 55 minutes): This video focuses on the impact of Alzheimer's disease and other forms of dementia on the caregiver.

Am I Normal? Teens and Emotional Health (2008, Insight Media, DVD, 22 minutes): This DVD takes a look at the range of issues facing modern teens and teaches ways of coping with anxiety, anger, and depression.

Autism: The Unfolding Mystery (2005, Insight Media, DVD, 26 minutes): This program discusses signs and symptoms of autism in child and presents information on treatment types.

Eating Disorders: Causes, Symptoms, and Treatment (2002, Insight Media, DVD, 22 minutes): This video investigates why teenagers suffer from eating disorders and includes a discussion of possible treatments.

The Biological Mind: Deeply Depressed (2006, Insight Media, DVD, 46 minutes): This program prevents information on various aspects of depression, including cause, symptoms, and treatments (antidepressants and psychotherapy).

SUGGESTED WEBSITES

Autism Information Page
http://www.ninds.nih.gov/disorders/autism/autism.htm

Attention Deficit Disorder Association
http://www.add.org/

Dementia
http://www.nlm.nih.gov/medlineplus/dementia.html

Depression Screening
http://www.depression-screening.org/

Eating Disorders
http://www.mayoclinic.com/health/eating-disorders/DS00294

SUGGESTED READINGS

Garcia, C. (2010). Conceptualization and measurement of coping during adolescence: A review of the literature. *Journal of Nursing Scholarship*, 42(2), 166-185.

Hall, L.J. (2010). Training paraprofessionals to use behavioral strategies when educating learners with autism spectrum disorders across environments. *Behavioral Interventions*, 25(1), 37-51.

Keel, P.K. (2007). A 20-year longitudinal study of body weight, dieting, and eating disorder symptoms. *Journal of Abnormal Psychology*, 116(2), 422-432.

Kessler, R.C. (2010). Age differences in prevalence and co-morbidity of DSM-IV major depressive episodes: Results from the WHO World Health Survey Initiative. *Depression & Anxiety*, 27(4), 351-364.

St. John, P.D. (2010). Cognitive impairment and life satisfaction in older adults. *International Journal of Geriatric Psychiatry*, 25(8), 814-821.

Chapter 16

THE FINAL CHALLENGE: DEATH AND DYING

LEARNING OBJECTIVES

After students have read and studied the material in this chapter, they should be able to answer the following questions:

MATTERS OF LIFE AND DEATH

1. How is death defined? Why is the definition of death controversial? How does the social meaning of death vary across groups?

2. What are the major causes of death at different periods of the lifespan?

3. What is the main difference between programmed theories of aging and damage theories of aging? What is an example of each type of theory?

4. What factors influence life expectancy? Is it possible to extend life expectancy?

THE EXPERIENCE OF DEATH

5. What are Kübler-Ross's stages of dying? How valid and useful is this theory?

6. What is the Parkes/Bowlby attachment model of bereavement? Is there evidence to support this model?

THE INFANT

7. What is the infant's understanding of separation and death?

THE CHILD

8. How do children's conceptions of death compare to a "mature" understanding of death? What factors might influence a child's understanding of death?

9. What is a dying child's understanding of death? How do dying children cope with the prospect of their own death? How do children grieve?

THE ADOLESCENT

10. What is the adolescent's understanding of death? Is an adolescent's reaction to death different from the reactions of a child or adult?

THE ADULT

11. How do family members react and cope with the loss of a spouse, a child, and a parent?

12. What factors contribute to effective and ineffective coping with grief?

13. What can be done for those who are dying and for those who are bereaved to better understand and face the reality of death?

14. What are the major themes of lifespan development that have been covered throughout the text?

CHAPTER OUTLINE

I   Matters of Life and Death

   A. What Is Death?

   1. Biological definitions of death

   a. Biological death is a process, not a single event

   i.   Basic bodily process can be maintained by life-supporting machines in people who are in a coma and whose brains have ceased to function

   b. 1968 Harvard Medical School committee defined criteria for total brain death—irreversible loss of functioning in entire brain (both higher centers of the cerebral cortex that involve thought and lower centers controlling basic life processes like breathing)

   c. Following four criteria must be met for a person to be judged dead

   i.   Body is totally unresponsive to stimuli

   ii. Failure to move for 1 hour and failure to breathe for 3 minutes after removed from ventilator

   iii. No reflexes

   iv. Register a flat electroencephalogram (EEG) indicating there is no activity within the brain

   v.   With added precaution, process is repeated after 24 hours and reversible coma as the result of drug overdose or abnormally low body temperature

   d. Debate over what parts of the brain must cease to function for a person to be pronounced dead

   i.   Karen Ann Quinlan famous case in 1975

   (i) Lapsed in coma at a party (possibly due to alcohol or drug consumption) and became symbol of controversy over meaning of death

   (ii) Unconscious but bodily functions maintained with aid of ventilator or other life-support methods; court granted parents permission to turn off respirator

   (iii) Lived in persistent vegetative state being fed by tube for 10 years until she died

   ii. Terri Schiavo's case led to the question of whether feeding and hydration should be stopped

   (i) Suffered cardiac arrest in 1990 (possibly as a result of an eating disorder) that resulted in irreversible and massive brain damage

   (ii) Like Quinlan, Schiavo was not dead according to the Harvard criteria because her brain stem allowed her to breathe, swallow, and undergo sleep-wake cycles

(iii) Husband wanted tube removed but parents fought the decision; courts supported husband, and after long court battle, tube removed and Schiavo died in 2005

  e. Different positions on issues of when a person is dead

    i. Harvard position is quite conservative (as is laws of most states)

    ii. More "liberal" criteria for death would be when cerebral cortex is irreversibly dead, even if primitive body functions still maintained by primitive area of brain

  f. Defining life and death more complicated when it was demonstrated that at least some people in a coma or "vegetative states" may have more awareness than suspected

    i. Young woman in coma was shown (using brain imaging) to have brain function like a health adult on some tasks, suggesting some degree of consciousness

    ii. Additional support in research on 54 patients in either "vegetative" or "minimally conscious" states found some level of brain response, indicating possible levels of awareness

2. Life and death choices

  a. Euthanasia—meaning "happy, or good, death" in which process of death is hastened in person who is suffering

    i. Active euthanasia or "mercy killing"—deliberately and directly causing death (e.g., administering lethal dose of drug to pain-racked patient in late stages of cancer)

    ii. Passive euthanasia—allowing a terminally ill individual to die of natural causes (e.g., removal of Terri Schiavo's feeding tube ultimately led to her death)

    iii. Assisted suicide—making available to someone who wishes to die the means by which to do so; includes physician-assisted suicide (e.g., physician writing a prescription for sleeping pills at the request of a terminally ill patient, knowing that the patient will intentionally overdose)

  b. Society view of euthanasia and assisted suicide

    i. Overwhelming support among medical professionals and general public for passive euthanasia

    ii. 70% of U.S. adults support doctor's right to end life of a patient with a terminal illness

    iii. Minority groups less accepting, possibly as the result of less trust in medical establishment or for religious/philosophical reasons

    iv. Active euthanasia still viewed as murder in U.S. and most countries

    v. In most states, legal to withhold extraordinary life-extending treatments from the terminally ill and to "pull the plug" on life-support equipment when that is the wish of the individual or when family member can show that it was the desire of the terminally ill individual

    vi. Living will—a type of advanced directive allowing people to state that they do not want extraordinary medical procedures applied to them

    vii. Advanced directives can also be written to specify who can make decisions if ill patient is not able, to decide whether organs will be donated and other post-death instructions

     viii. Oregon became first state to legalize physician-assisted suicide; individuals who are terminally ill with 6 or fewer months to live can request lethal injection (same request is available in some European countries); few people in Oregon have taken this option; Washington state has followed suit with a similar law

     ix. 40 states have enacted laws against assisted suicide; terminally ill individuals are sometime in no shape to make life-or-death decisions and others speaking for them may not have their best interest at heart

     x. Right-to-die advocates maintain that people should have a say in how they die while right-to-life advocates say everything possible should be done to maintain life

3. Social meanings of death

  a. Social and psychological differences in meaning of death

    i. Societies have evolved some manner of reacting to the universal experience of death (e.g., interpreting its meaning, disposing of the corpse, expressing grief)

    ii. Social meaning of death changed with history

    iii. Middle Ages, people bid farewell to life surrounded by friends and dying with dignity

    iv. Late 19th century in Western society, death taken out of home and put into hospitals ("denial of death"); now have less experience with death

    v. Right-to-die and death with dignity advocate going back to the old ways (i.e., death out in the open and naturally experienced by families)

    vi. Trending away from funerals with caskets toward cremation

  b. Experience of dying varies by culture

    i. Cross-cultural study of 41 cultures found that in 21 there was some kind of practice (e.g., not sharing food, stabbing, driving from their homes) to hasten death in frail, elderly individuals

    ii. Funeral and grieving activities vary by culture (e.g., laughing to weeping; holding parties to avoiding people)

    iii. No single biologically mandated grieving process; grieving may involve holding parties, avoiding people, having sexual orgies, or weeping

    iv. Most cultures have some concept of spiritual immortality

    v. Differences in social meaning of death seen within North American cultural groups

    vi. Puerto Ricans (especially women) tend to display intense, hysterical emotions, while Japanese Americans have more restraint to grief expression (smile as to not burden others with their pain)

    vii. Different ethnic and racial mourning practices; Irish Americans believe that dead deserved a good send off as in a wake with food, drinks, and jokes; African Americans express grief in rowdy celebration; Jews have a restrained week of mourning for the dead (a shivah) then honor the person at 1-month and 1-year marks

B. What Kills Us and When?

1. Life expectancy at birth—average number of years a newborn is expected to live

  a. 2010 U.S. estimate life expectancy at birth is 78 years

      b. Increased this century in U.S. to 76 for white men and 81 for white women
         i. Female hormones may protect individuals from high blood pressure and heart problems; women less vulnerable to violent deaths and accidents, and the effects of smoking
         ii. Life expectancy for African Americans lower than for European Americans (but the gap is narrowing); may be due to health hazards related to poverty
      c. Historic increase in expectancy from 30 in ancient Rome to 80 in modern affluent societies
      d. Less-developed nations in Africa hit by AIDS, malaria, famine (e.g., Mozambique, Zambia) lag well behind, with life expectancy about 30 years less than those in the longest lived nations (e.g., Asia-Japan, Europe-Sweden)

2. Infancy is most vulnerable period for dying
      a. Current infant mortality rate about 7 per 1,000 live births (lower for European Americans; higher for African Americans)
      b. After infancy, relatively small chance of dying in childhood or adolescence; death rates then climb steadily throughout adulthood

3. Leading causes of death change across life
      a. Infant deaths typically the result of complication of birth or congenital abnormalities
      b. Leading cause of death in preschool and school-aged children is accidents (e.g., car accidents, poisoning, falls)
      c. Adolescence time of good health (car accidents, homicide, suicide leading causes of death)
      d. Young adults killed by accidents, cancer, and some by heart disease
      e. Age 45 to 65, cancer, heart disease, and chronic diseases
         i. Genetic endowment and lifestyle may place individual at risk
         ii. Incidences of chronic diseases climb steadily with age
      f. Age 65 and older, heart disease, cancers, cerebrovascular disease (strokes)

C. Theories of Aging: Why Do We Age and Die?
1. Two key categories of aging theories: programmed theories of aging (emphasize systematic, genetic control over aging) and damage theories of aging (more haphazard and due to errors in cells and organ deterioration)
2. Programmed theories
      a. Maximum lifespan—ceiling number of years anyone within a species can live
      b. About 120 years in humans (French woman 122 years, quit smoking at 119 when she could not see well enough to light her cigarette)
      c. Maximum lifespan not increased much in past century, despite the fact that average life expectancy increasing by almost 30 years
      d. Humans comparatively long-lived (maximum life—mouse 3½, Galapagos tortoise 150)
         i. Fact that different species have different lifespans suggests a specieswide genetic influence
      e. Genetic makeup and environment combine to determine length of life
         i. Genetic variation accounts for more than 50% of variance in the ability to stay free of major chronic diseases at age 70 or older

ii. Average longevity of parents and grandparents good estimate of one's longevity

f. Many genes likely involved in aging process through regulation of cell division

    i. Genes that become less active with age in normal adults are inactive in children with progeria—premature aging disorder caused by a spontaneous (rather than inherited) mutation in a single gene

    ii. Babies with progeria appear normal at first but age prematurely and die on the average in their teens (often due to heart disease or stroke)

g. "Evolutionary puzzle" concerning genes and lifespan

    i. Genes that act late in life to extend life will not be selected for

    ii. Genes that proved adaptive to ancestors in early life but have negative outcomes could become common in a species over time because they would be selected for due to their positive impact on reproduction

    iii. A gene that limits creation of new cells through cell division could protect against the proliferation of caner cells in early life but also contributes to cell aging later in life

h. Possibility of "aging clock" in every cell

    i. Hayflick limit—human cells can divide a limited number of times (50 times plus or minus 10)

    ii. Capacity for cell reproduction related to differences in maximum lifespan by species (mouse 14 to 28; tortoise 90 to 125 divisions)

    iii. May be due to shortening of telomeres—stretches of DNA on end of chromosomes

    iv. Telomeres—stretches of DNA that form the tips of chromosomes and shorten until cells cease to replicate causing them to malfunction and die (telomere is a yardstick of biological aging)

    v. Chronic tress may lead to shortening of telomeres (is concrete emphasis that stress speeds cellular aging)

    vi. Lack of exercise, smoking, obesity, and low SES (all risk factors for aging) are also associated with short telomeres

i. Other programmed theories

    i. Genetically driven systematic changes in neuroendocrine system and immune system

    ii. Possible that hypothalamus serves as an aging clock, systematically altering levels of hormones and brain chemicals in later life so that we die

    iii. Possible that aging is related to genetically governed changes in the immune system associated with the shortening of telomeres; may decease immune system's ability to defend against life-threatening infections, may cause it to mistake normal cells for invaders (as in autoimmune diseases) and contribute to inflammation and disease

3. Damage theories

a. Damage theories view aging in terms of an accumulation of haphazard or random damage to cells and organs over time (wear and tear)

    i. Early cells replicate faithfully, late cells show random damage

    ii. Biological aging is about random change rather than genetically programmed change

b. Free radicals—toxic and chemically unstable byproducts of everyday metabolism, or the everyday chemical reactions in cells such as those involved in breaking down food
  i. Free radicals produced when oxygen reacts with certain molecules within cells; they have extra or "free" electrons that react with other molecules to produce substances that damage cell and its DNA
  ii. Over time, genetic damage becomes more chaotic and the body cannot repair the damage; results in cells functioning improperly and eventual death of the organism
  iii. "Age spots" on skin are visible examples of free radical damage
  iv. Free radicals implicated in major disease common with aging (e.g., cardiovascular diseases, cancer)
  v. Some question the impact of free radicals on aging as there is no clear relationship between metabolic rate and longevity
4. Nature and nurture conspiring
  a. Programmed theories view aging and dying as part of natures' plan
    i. Maximum lifespan, Hayflick's limit, changes in gene activity with aging suggest that aging and dying are genetically controlled
  b. Damage theories hold that we succumb to haphazard destructive processes
  c. Neither programmed nor damage theories are the explanation of aging and dying
  d. Aging is result of interaction between biological and environmental factors
5. Extending life?
  a. Lifespans of 200 to 600 years unlikely, but average age of death could move toward 112, and individuals at that age may function like modern 78-year-olds
  b. Stem cells may allow us to replace aging cell or modify aging processes
  c. The enzyme telomerase can be used to prevent telomerase from shortening and this will keep the cell replicating and working longer (downside is that it make cancer cells divide more rapidly)
  d. Antioxidants
    i. New focus on preventing damage from free radicals using antioxidants like vitamins E and C that prevent oxygen from combining with other molecules to produce more free radicals
    ii. Antioxidants may increase longevity (although not for a long time) by inhibiting free radical activity; caution is advised as exceptionally high levels of vitamin E may shorten rather than lengthen life
  e. Caloric restriction
    i. Most successful life-extending technique is caloric restriction—a highly nutritious but severely restrictive diet representing a 30-40% cut in normal caloric intake
    ii. Lab tests using caloric restriction on primates and rats suggest that it extends both the average longevity and maximum lifespan of a species and it can delay the progression of many age-related diseases
    iii. 40% reduction in daily calories leads to a 40% decrease in body weight, a 40% increase in average longevity, and a 49% increase in species maximum lifespan

289

Chapter 17

      iv. Caloric restriction works by reducing the number of free radicals and other toxic products of metabolism; it also may alter gene activity and trigger the release of hormones that slow metabolism and protect cells against oxidative damage

      v. Long-lived humans are rarely obese

      vi. Individuals who lived in Biosphere II and who consumed about 1,800 calories a day lost 15-20% of their body weight; they experienced significant improvement in several physiological indicators, but the impact disappeared once they went back to normal diets

      vii. Experimenting with self-starvation is unwise

      viii. Some worry about the social consequences if average longevity were pushed to 100 to 120 years due to high healthcare costs, overpopulation, bankruptcy of Social Security system

      ix. (Exploration box on centenarian (people who live to be 100) secrets)

II The Experience of Death

  A. Perspectives on Dying

    1. Kübler-Ross's stages of dying

    2. Book *On Death and Dying* in 1969 revolutionized the care of dying people

    3. Based on interviews with terminally ill patients, Kübler-Ross detected a common set of emotions in terminally ill individuals and thought that similar reactions might occur in response to any major loss

    4. Her five "stages of dying" of the terminally ill

      a. Denial and isolation—"No, it can't be"

        i. Common first response

        ii. Denial—mechanism for keeping anxiety-provoking thoughts from conscious awareness

        iii. Individual may insist that the diagnosis is wrong or may be convinced that he or she will beat the odds and recover

        iv. Care provider and family member often engage in their own denial

      b. Anger—"Why me?"

        i. Rage or resentment often directed at doctors or family members

        ii. Family and friends need to be sensitive to this reaction

      c. Bargaining—"Okay, me, but please…"

        i. Beg with God, medical staff, others for cure, more time, less pain, or provisions for children

      d. Depression

        i. Grief focuses on losses that have already occurred, loss of ability to function, and losses to come

      e. Acceptance

        i. Accept the inevitability of death in a calm and peaceful manner

        ii. Almost devoid of feelings

      f. Hope, a sixth response that runs throughout the other five responses

    4. Problems with Kübler-Ross's theory

      a. Kübler-Ross deserves credit for sensitizing society to emotional needs of the dying

        b. Main criticism—dying process simply not stage-like
           i. Many do not display all the stages
          ii. Death responses seldom unfold in a standard order
         iii. Overzealous physicians often try to push patients to die in the correct "stage" order
         iv. Shneidman argues that dying patients experience complex interplay of emotions alternating between denial and acceptance
          v. Additional reactions include disbelief, terror, bewilderment, and rage
         vi. Dying people experience unpredictable emotional changes rather than distinct stages of dying

    2. Second criticism—little attention on how responses or trajectory of responses are shaped by specific illnesses and events
        a. Pattern different for those with slow, steady progression toward death versus more erratic pattern

    3. Third criticism—overlooks influences of personality on how a person experiences dying
        a. People who previously have faced life's problems directly and effectively and maintain good interpersonal relationships tend to be less angry and less depressed when dying
        b. Personality traits, coping abilities prior to death, and social competence may cause some to be bitter to the end, others to be crushed by despair, and others to display incredible strength

B. Perspective on Bereavement
    1. Key terms
        a. Bereavement—state of loss
        b. Grief—emotional response to loss
        c. Mourning—culturally defined ways of expressing grief
        d. Anticipatory grief—grieve for a terminally ill person prior to death (does not eliminate grief felt after actual death)
    2. Parkes/Bowlby attachment model
        a. Conceptualizing grieving in context of attachment theory (influenced by Bowlby's ethological theory of attachment)
          i. Parkes, "loss and love are two sides of the same coin"
        b. Model of bereavement includes four predominant reactions that overlap considerably and as such should not be viewed as clear-cut stages
          i. Numbness—sense of unreality and shock experienced during first few hours or days following death; bereaved struggling to defend against weight of loss
          ii. Yearning—pangs or waves of grief coming from 5 to 14 days after death as form of separation anxiety; includes uncontrollable weeping, physical aches and pains, and pining and yearning for the loved one (a longing to be reunited); signs of separation anxiety—distress at being parted from object of attachment; common reactions include anger, guilt, feelings of irritability, and intense rage at loved one for dying
         iii. Disorganization and despair—passage of time, yearning and grieving less frequent and less intense, predominant emotions include depression, despair, and apathy

        iv. Reorganization—begin to invest less energy in grief for deceased and transition into life without person; if married, begin to make the transition to being without spouse and engage in new activities and possibly new relationships

    c. Research shows reaction peaks occur at times predicted by theory, however, acceptance was the strongest response at all stages, yearning was the second strongest response, and remaining responses relatively weak; worst of grieving process is over in first 6 months after loss

  3. The dual-process model of bereavement
    a. Pattern of grief "messier" and more individualized than Parkes/Bowlby phases suggest
    b. Dual-process model of bereavement—bereaved oscillate between coping and emotional blow of the loss
    c. Loss-oriented coping—dealing with one's emotions and reconciling to loss
    d. Restoration-oriented coping—focus on managing daily living and mastering new roles
    e. Both loss- and restoration-oriented issues need to be confronted but they also need to be avoided at times
    f. Over time, tend to shift from loss-oriented to restoration-oriented coping

  4. Bereavement is complex and multidimensional process involving many ever-shifting emotions that vary greatly from one person to another and that often takes a long time
    a. Modest disruptions in cognitive, emotional, physical, and interpersonal functions common (last for a year or so)
    b. Sympathetic toward bereaved immediately after death but grow quickly weary of someone who is depressed, irritable, or preoccupied (think the person needs to cheer up and get on with life)
    c. Must understand that reactions to bereavement might linger

III The Infant

A. Notion of Objects Being and "Missing" to Begin to Understand Death
  1. First form global category of things may be "all gone" (i.e., dead) and later divide it into subcategories that includes "dead"
  2. Disappearance of the loved one is the most direct evidence of death for infants, and at this level Bowlby's attachment theory helpful
    a. Distress similar to symptoms of separation anxiety (e.g., protest loss by crying, yearning, and searching)
    b. Separation from attachment figure same reaction as bereaved adults
       i. Initial vigorous protest phase, yearning, and searching for loved one
      ii. After hours or days of protest and unsuccessful searching, infants begin to show despair—depression-like symptoms (e.g., lose hope, end search, become apathetic and sad)
     iii. Eventually enter detachment phase—renewed interest in toys and companions
     iv. Complete recovery if infant can rely on existing attachment figure

IV The Child

A. Grasping the Concept of Death

1. Young children highly curious about death, yet beliefs considerably different than adults

2. Children must acquire a "mature" understanding of death that is characterized by
   a. Finality—end of movement, thought, sensations, and life
   b. Irreversibility—cannot be undone
   c. Universality—inevitable
   d. Biological causality—result of internal processes (that may be caused by external forces)

3. Preschool children
   a. Understand the universality of death
   b. Believe the dead retain some life functions, are living under altered circumstances, but still have hunger, wishes, and love their moms
   c. View death as reversible (i.e., liken to sleep or a trip, with right medical care or magic can come back)
   d. Death viewed as being caused by external agent (e.g., eating a dirty bug) not biological causes

4. School-age children (5-7 years) have more advanced conceptualization of death
   a. Understand finality, irreversibility, and universality
   b. Understanding functions of the body helps preschoolers grasp concept of death
   c. Infer that death is opposite of life
   d. Do not completely understand biological causality of death (e.g., heart stops) until around age 10

5. Understanding of death depends on level of cognitive development, culture, and life experiences
   a. Breakthrough in death understanding tied to transition from preoperational to concrete operational stage and IQ
   b. Understanding of death influenced by cultural factors
      i. Christian and Jewish children in Israel who are taught Western concept of death have more "mature" understanding
      ii. In cultures promoting idea of reincarnation, death often not viewed as irreversible
   c. Own life experience (especially a life-threatening illness in childhood) can impact thoughts and behaviors concerning death and dying
   d. Adult use of euphemisms (e.g., "grandma has gone to live with God") can confuse and frighten children
   e. Simple and honest answers to children's questions about death are best

B. The Dying Child

1. Typically more aware that they are dying than adults realize
   a. Over time, preschoolers with leukemia understand that death irreversible
   b. Despite secretiveness, terminally ill children notice change in their treatment and pay close attention to what is happening to other children with the same disease
   c. Children stop talking about long-term future including celebration of holidays

293

Chapter 17

2. Terminally ill children often not "models of bravery" that some suppose them to be, but rather experience many emotions of dying adults
   a. May demonstrate fear in play behavior through tantrums
   b. Seek normalcy in school and athletic activities so that they do not feel inadequate with peers
   c. Terminally ill children need love and support of others
      i. Benefit from strong sense that parents care for them and from opportunity to talk about their feelings
C. The Bereaved Child
   1. Children do grieve, however, their grief is expressed differently than an adult's grief
      a. Lack some of the coping skills that adults have
      b. Particularly vulnerable to long-term negative effects of bereavement
   2. Common reactions of bereaved child
      a. Often misbehave or strike out at others
      b. Ask endless questions about death and deceased
      c. Experience anxiety concerning separation, including worry that other family members might die
      d. Some children go about activities as if nothing happened (denying loss)
      e. Lack of cognitive abilities impact coping skills, and they may not understand what is going on
         i. Young children mainly have behavioral or action coping strategies (e.g., put picture of deceased mom by pillow at night and return to frame during the day); older children able to use cognitive coping strategies like conjuring up mental representations of their lost parents
   3. Common grief symptoms vary from person to person and by age
      a. For preschoolers, common reactions include daily routine problems (e.g., sleeping, eating), negative moods, dependency, and temper tantrums
      b. For older children, there is more direct expression of sadness, anger, fear, and physical ailments
   4. Some carry negative adjustment pattern into adolescence and adulthood (e.g., depression, insecurity in attachments)
   5. Most bereaved children with effective coping skills and solid social supports adjust well
      a. Best adjustment when the receive good parenting, if caregivers communicate that they will be loved and cared for, and if they have the opportunity to talk about and share their grief

V The Adolescent
A. More Mature Thinking about Death
   1. Typically understand death as irreversible cessation of biological processes and can think abstractly about death
   2. Cognitive advancement (i.e., achievement of formal-operational stage thought) leads to ability to ponder hypothetical afterlife
   3. Like younger children, may believe that knowing, believing, and feeling continue after bodily functions have ceased

4. Adolescent reaction to dying reflects advanced developmental capacities
   a. Worry how illness might affect appearance (e.g., hair loss, amputation)
   b. Want to be accepted by peers and may feel like "freak"
   c. Eager to be more autonomous (distressed if they have to be dependent on parent or medical personnel)
   d. May be angry or bitter at having dreams snatched from them
5. Reaction to loss of friend or family member reflect themes of adolescent period
   a. May carry on internal dialogue with dead parent
   b. Often devastated if loss involves a close friend
      i. 32% of teens with friend who committed suicide experienced clinical depression during the month after the suicide
      ii. Grief over loss of family member may be taken more seriously, and parents, teachers, and others may not appreciate how much the teen is hurting
6. Adolescents are sometimes reluctant to express grief for fear of seeming abnormal or losing control
   a. Adolescents who yearn for dead parent may feel like they will be sucked back into dependency of childhood

VI The Adult
A. Death in the Family Context
   1. The loss of a spouse or partner
      a. Marital relationship is central one for most adults, and loss of marital partner or other romantic attachment figure can mean a great deal
      b. Precipitates other changes (e.g., changes in residence, job status)
         i. Bereaved must redefine roles and identities
         ii. Women will likely see substantial decline in income
      c. Widow and widower reactions
         i. Widows and widowers show overlapping phases of numbness, yearning, despair, and reorganization
         ii. Increased risk for illness and physical symptoms (e.g., loss of appetite)
         iii. Tend to overindulge in alcohol, tranquilizers, and cigarettes
         iv. Cognitive functions and decision-making may be impaired
         v. Emotional problems like loneliness and anxiety are common
         vi. Most bereaved partners do not become clinically depressed but display increased symptoms of depression
         vii. Modest level of disruption that tends to last for a year, followed by less sever but recurring grief reactions for several years
         viii. Great variation in individual pattern of response to loss
      d. Five most prevalent patterns of widows and widowers adjustment
         i. A resilience pattern—distress at low levels all along
         ii. Common grief—heightened then diminished distress after loss
         iii. Chronic grief—loss brings distress and distress lingers
         iv. Chronic depression—individuals depressed before loss remain so after
         v. Depressed-improved pattern—depressed before loss, less depressed after (relieved of stress of coping with unhappy marriage or spouse illness)

e. Biggest surprise is that the resilience pattern is the most common response
   i. Resilient grievers experienced some emotional pangs, but more comforted by positive thoughts of the deceased
   ii. No signs of defensive denial or avoiding pain in this group
f. Those with symptoms of depression tend to have been depressed before the loss and tend to remain depressed for years later
   i. Those who became depressed in response to the death often recover within a year or two
g. Depressed-improved individuals may have been experiencing caregiver burden before the death and relief afterwards
h. Do partners of gay men who die of AIDS experience similar patterns of bereavement?
   i. Half of the bereaved showed resilience (whether they were HIV positive themselves did not seem to matter)
i. Disenfranchised grief—grief that is not recognized or appreciated by other people and therefore may not result in much support—sometimes experienced by gays and lesbians who lose partners
   i. Losses of ex-spouse, extramarital lovers, foster children, fetuses, and pets can lead to disenfranchised grief
   ii. Disenfranchised grief common when loss is not recognized or acknowledged, bereaved is excluded from mourning activities, and when loss is stigmatized (e.g., suicide)
j. Overall, most bereaved individuals experiencing significant loss begin to show signs of recovery after a year or so
k. A minority of bereaved may experience complicated grief—less common form involving prolonged or intense grief that impairs functioning
   i. Often diagnosed with depression, or if death was traumatic, with posttraumatic stress disorder; may see this as a distinct condition that some believe should be considered a distinct disorder from depression of PTSD
2. The loss of a child
   a. No loss seems more difficult for an adult; even with forewarning, experienced as unexpected, untimely, and unjust
      i. Sense of failed role as parent
      ii. Failure to find meaning in the death even long after the death; one study of children who died of an accident, suicide, or homicide found that only 57% of parents had found meaning in the death after 5 years
      iii. Age of child has little impact (severe grief may occur for a miscarriage, especially for mothers)
   b. Death alters family system
      i. Effects on marriage—strains relationships; strain worse in marriages shaky before death
      ii. Increased risk for marital problems and divorce, although most couples stay together and become closer
      iii. Parents who focus on restorative-oriented coping and less on loss-oriented coping may fare better

      c. Effects on siblings—may feel neglected by parents, anxious about own health, guilty about feeling of sibling rivalry, pressure to replace lost child in their parent's eye

      d. Effects on grandparents—a "double whammy" involving guilt over out surviving their grandchild and helplessness to protect adult child from pain

  3. The loss of a parent

      a. Not as difficult an adjustment as death of spouse or child, as it commonly occurs in middle age when individuals better prepared to deal with loss

      b. Can be turning point effecting identity and relationships with many family members

      c. Adult children may feel vulnerable and alone

      d. Guilt about not doing enough for parent is common

B. Challenges to the Grief Work Perspective

  1. Grief work perspective—in order to cope with death, the bereaved must confront loss (model grew out of Freudian psychoanalytic theory)

      a. Chronic grief (long-lasting and intense) and absence, inhibition, or delay of grief (lack of common reactions) both associated by Freudians with pathological or complicated grief

      b. Grief-work perspective under attack as many question the assumption that there is a "right way" to grieve, that bereaved people must experience and work through intense grief to recover, and that they must sever their bonds with the deceased in order to move on with their lives

         i. Cross-cultural research showing wide variety of successful grief patterns (e.g., Egyptian mother conforms to norms by sitting alone and mute for years after child's death, Balinese mother is following her cultural norms if she is seemingly cheerful after her child's death)

         ii. Little support for assumption the bereaved individual must confront loss and experience painful emotions to cope successfully; those who are most resilient display little distress at any point in bereavement; too much grief work might result in effect like ruminative coping and prolong psychological distress rather than relieve it

         iii. Do not need to completely break from the deceased but rather revise internal working model of self/others to compensate for loss; continuing bonds—indefinite attachment driven by reminisce and sharing of memories of deceased tend to result in feelings of comfort

      c. Some forms of continuing attachment healthier than others

         i. Sharing fond memories of deceased and feeling that loved one is watching over and guiding experience means less distress

         ii. Use of deceased's possessions for comfort led to higher levels of distress

         iii. Continuing bonds helpful when they are in the form of internal memories of the deceased that provide a secure base for becoming more independent but not when they involve hallucination and illusions that reflect a continuing effort to reunite with the deceased; cultural influences may impact adjustment

2. Flaws in traditional grief-work perspective
   a. Norms for expressing grief vary by culture—no one normal and effective way to grieve
   b. Little evidence that bereaved must do intense "grief work"
   c. People do not need to sever attachments to the deceased to adjust to loss and may benefit from some continuing bonds
   d. Most do not experience pathological grief symptoms; more common to experience positive emotions along with negative emotions
C. Who Copes and Who Succumbs?
   1. Personal resources influence an individual's ability to cope with bereavement
      a. Attachment style is an important resource (or liability)
         i. Secure attachment associated with coping relatively well
         ii. Resistant or preoccupied styles of attachment associated with over dependence and extreme displays of chronic grief and anxiety following a loss, ruminating about the loss, and clinging to the loved one rather than revising the attachment bond
         iii. Avoidant or dismissing attachments linked to greater difficulty in expressing emotions and seeking comfort; may disengage from or devalue the person lost
         iv. Disorganized attachment style associated with being especially unequipped to cope; may turn inward and harm self or abuse alcohol
      b. Personality and coping style
         i. Those with a low sense of self-esteem tend to have difficulty coping with loss
         ii. Depression and other chronic psychological disorders may increase difficulty in dealing with loss
         iii. Optimistic individuals find positive ways to interpret loss and tend to use active and effective coping strategies
   2. Loss of someone with whom you have a close relationships (e.g., spouse) hits people hardest
   3. Cause of death influences bereavement; senseless or violent deaths are worse (e.g., death of child)
      a. Sudden death is not necessarily harder to cope with because the advantages of being forewarned are offset by the stress of caring for the dying loved one
   4. Presence of strong social support systems and life stressors can positively impact grief reaction
      a. Social support (e.g., parents, siblings, friends) helps at all ages
         i. Simple ways to be supportive include indicating sorrow about the loss, asking how things are going, and allowing bereaved to express feelings of pain is helpful
      b. Additional stressors hurt recovery
         i. Widow and widowers more troubled if they must single-handedly care for a child, find job, or move
D. Bereavement and Human Development
   1. Although painful, grief has potential to foster growth in self, religiosity, family relationships, and appreciation of life

a. Many widows may master new skills, become more independent, and emerge with new identities and higher self-esteem

b. From tragedy sometimes comes meaning

VII Taking the Sting Out of Death

A. For the Dying

1. Hospice option—program to support dying individuals

a. Philosophy of "care" rather than "cure" founded at St. Christopher's Hospital in London and quickly spread to North America

b. Hospice care may take place at care facility or at home

c. Hospice care is part of a larger palliative care movement—emphasis of care aimed not at curing disease or prolonging life but at meeting physical, psychological, and spiritual needs of patients with incurable illness

d. Key features of hospice care (whether at home or in a facility)

i. Dying person and family the decision-makers (not medical care "experts")

ii. Deemphasis on attempting to cure disease or prolonging life (but death not hastened)

iii. Emphasis on pain control

iv. Emphasis on comfort of setting being as normal as possible (preferable in home or homelike facility)

v. Bereavement counseling available to entire family

2. Impact of hospice care different from medical care

a. Less interest in physician-assisted suicide

b. More emotional support (something often lacking in home healthcare agencies, nursing homes, and hospitals)

c. Fewer medical interventions

d. Fewer symptoms of family grief from spouses, partners, parents, and relatives of dying individual

3. Hospice not for everyone, but is death with dignity that's free of pain and while surrounded by others; good option for some

4. Next challenge of hospice philosophy involves children dying of cancer with uncontrolled pain

B. For the Bereaved

1. Most bereaved individuals do not need psychological intervention, but options are available

2. At-risk individuals (with depression, other psychological disorders, or lacking support) may benefit from counseling designed to reduce depression

3. Family therapies most effective

a. Family Bereavement Program—for children and adolescents (and surviving parent) who had lost a parent

4. Many specific support programs like Companionate Friend, Partners without Parents, and They Help Each Other Spiritually (THEOS) offer bereaved with advice on a variety of issues from finances to emotional support

5. Participation in support groups tends to be beneficial (e.g., less depression, less use of medication, greater sense of well-being); other bereaved individuals may be helpful because they understand what the individual is going through (i.e., are in the "same boat")

C. Taking Our Leave
   1. Reminders of these themes echoed throughout book
      a. Nature and nurture truly interact in development (environment an biology interact reciprocally)
      b. We are whole people throughout the lifespan (advances in one area have implications for other areas)
      c. Development proceeds in multiple directions
      d. There is both continuity and discontinuity in development
      e. There is much plasticity in development
      f. We are individuals, becoming even more diverse with age
      g. We develop in a culture and historical context
      h. We are active in our own development
      i. Development is a lifelong process
      j. Development is best viewed from a multiple perspective

SUGGESTIONS FOR CLASS DISCUSSIONS OR PROJECTS

1. Have students discuss medical and moral concerns raised by euthanasia. They will need to distinguish among passive euthanasia, active euthanasia, and assisted suicide. Assisted suicide has gotten a great deal of media attention because of Dr. Jack Kevorkian's role (who was imprisoned for his activity) in helping several terminally ill patients to commit suicide, and more recently around the legalization of assisted suicide in Oregon. If the right to die becomes more firmly established, what safeguards would students like to see to ensure that this option is used responsibly? To aid in this discussion, you might have students read these articles and the review the EuthanasiaProCon.org website.

Roscoe, L.A.; Malphurs, J.E.; Dragovic, L.J., and Cohen, D.A (2001). Comparison of characteristics of Kevorkian euthanasia cases and physician-assisted suicides in Oregon. *Gerontologist, 41(4),* 439-447.

Teisseyre, N., Mullet, E., and Sorum, P.C. (2005). Under what conditions is euthanasia acceptable to lay people and health professionals? *Social Science & Medicine, 60(2),* 357-368.

http://euthanasia.procon.org/ Should euthanasia or physician-assisted suicide be legal?

2. Have students discuss the understanding of death at different points in the lifespan. Compare a young child's understanding of death to an adolescent's understanding to an adult's understanding, etc. One way to do this would be to use Piaget's stages of cognitive development as a framework. Another way to approach this issue would be to have students role-play explaining death to people of different ages.

3. The last two decades saw numerous high-profile incidents of students killing students and faculty members. In May 1998, a 15-year-old boy killed both his parents and then opened fire on his fellow students in the school cafeteria in Springfield, Oregon, leaving one classmate dead. Perhaps the most infamous of these events in the 1990s was the massacre at Columbine

High School on April 20, 1999 in which two teenage students murdered 12 students and 1 teacher. In 2007, a 23-year-old gunman killed 27 students and 5 faculty members at Virginia Tech, in what was the deadliest peacetime shooting by an individual gunman in U.S. history.

These tragedies have received a great deal of attention as we try to understand factors that contribute to such behavior. An interesting assignment option would be to have students write a paper in which they explore whether our knowledge of preadolescent and adolescent views of death and dying contribute anything to our understanding of why these children kill.

4. Jonathan Swift once commented that we all want to live long lives but none of us wants to become old. Ask students to respond to this. How old do they want to become? What factors or conditions are important to students when considering their longevity? What is the optimal trade-off concerning the quantity of life (longevity) and the quality of life (mental and physical heath)?

To spur discussion, you might want to have students read Moody's (2001/02) commentary on the pros and cons of extending life.

Moody, H.R. (2001/02) Who's Afraid of Life Extension? *Generations, 25(4),* 33-37.

5. To encourage a deeper understanding of the impact of dying, have students write a paper in which they describe what they would consider a "perfect" death. Do students wish to have time to say good-bye, or would they rather die suddenly? Where would they like to be, both in their lives (in terms of accomplishments, etc.), and also in terms of physical location (e.g., in own bedroom or in a field, perhaps a favorite song playing)? Would they want someone with them?

6. Chapter 17 introduces students to a wide variety of topics associated with the processes of death and dying. The inclusion of such material reflects a growing societal willingness to discuss death, something that was often taboo in the recent past. As a result of this past attitude, most people were not only ignorant of biological and psychological aspects of death and dying, but were also ignorant of practical issues associated with death, like information related to the disposal of the corpse (e.g., cost of internment, the cremation option). The goal of this assignment is to help students to expand their knowledge of some of the more practical concerns related to the process of dying. To complete the project, students should search for journal or Web articles using the terms *burial and costs, burial and options, cremation, casket costs*, and *funeral home costs*. The students should then select and read at least five articles on these topics with the goal of producing a three- to four-page paper addressing some of the practical funeral-related decisions that families need to make (e.g., costs of caskets). The paper should focus on identifying some of the key practical decisions family members must make and should offer pros and cons concerning decision options (e.g., cremation versus internment).

SUGGESTED FILMS AND VIDEOS

<u>Bereavement, Loss, and Change</u> (2008, Insight Media, 2 DVDs, 484 minutes): This impressive set of materials explores topics associated with normal and pathological responses to bereavement with an emphasis on information critical to nurses, healthcare students, and grief counselors.

<u>Creating a Good Death: Coping with Terminal Illness</u> (2004, Films for the Humanities & Sciences, DVD/VHS, 26 minutes): This ABC news program follows the life and death of a 51-year-old women with a degree in hematology as she copes with her own death.

<u>Death Just Isn't What it Use to Be</u> (2010, insight Media, DVD, 30 minutes): This interesting video covers the diagnosis of death.

<u>Holding Back the Years? The Race to Slow the Aging Process</u> (2006, Insight Media, DVD, 54 minutes): This video focuses on different viewing concerning efforts to slow the aging process.

<u>Teens Dealing with Death</u> (2004, Films for the Humanities & Sciences, DVD/VHS, 29 minutes): This award-winning production focuses on ways of guiding children through their first experience with death.

SUGGESTED WEBSITES

Bereaved Parents of the USA
http://www.bereavedparentsusa.org/

Care of Terminally Ill Children
http://www.mccg.org/childrenshealth/content.asp?PageID=P03050

Children's Understanding of Death
http://www.hospicenet.org/html/understand.html

Hospice Foundation of America
http://www.hospicefoundation.org/

Theories of Aging
http://www.antiaging-systems.com/agetheory.htm

SUGGESTED READINGS

Callahan, D. (2009). Death, mourning, and medical progress. *Perspectives in Biology and Medicine*, 52(1), 103-115.

Feigelman, W. (2009). Stigmatization and suicide bereavement. *Death Studies*, 33(7), 591-608.

Hofer, S.M. (2010). Toward an integrative science of life-span development and aging. *Journals of Gerontology, Series B: Psychological Sciences and Social Sciences*, 65B(3), 269-278.

Lavive d'Epinay, C.J. (2009). Bereavement in very old age: Impact on heath and relationships in the loss of a spouse, a child, a sibling, or a close friend. *Omega*, 69(4), 301-325.

Little, M. (2009). Comparing cognitive, relational and stress mechanisms underlying gender differences in recovery from bereavement-related internalized problems. *Journal of Clinical Child Adolescent Psychology*, 38(4), 486-500

Chapter 17

CHAPTER 1
UNDERSTANDING LIFESPAN HUMAN DEVELOPMENT

MULTIPLE CHOICE

1. John Tatum
   a. generated the first comprehensive theory of lifespan development.
   b. was the first African-American psychologist.
   c. won three gold medals at the 2009 National Senior Games.
   d. was the first black soldier to serve in an all-white unit in World War II.

   ANS: C   DIF: Moderate   REF: 1   OBJ: 1.1

2. Development is best defined as
   a. individual differences in human behavior.
   b. systematic changes and continuities from conception to death.
   c. the way people change in positive ways across time.
   d. the systematic unfolding of genetic potential.

   ANS: B   DIF: Easy   REF: 2   OBJ: 1.1

3. The fact that development often involves continuities speaks to the fact that over time humans tend to
   a. remain the same.   c. become less active.
   b. become more intelligent.   d. undergo orderly patterns of change.

   ANS: A   DIF: Moderate   REF: 3   OBJ: 1.1

4. The three broad domains explored by developmental psychologists are
   a. motor, interpersonal, cognitive.   c. personality, motor, learning.
   b. physical, cognitive, psychosocial.   d. interpersonal, maturational, learning.

   ANS: B   DIF: Easy   REF: 2-3   OBJ: 1.1

5. Albert, a developmental psychologist, conducts research on children's emotional reactions to studying math in school. Albert is concerned with children's _____ development.
   a. cognitive   c. physical
   b. maturational   d. psychosocial

   ANS: D   DIF: Moderate   REF: 3   OBJ: 1.1

6. Which is best categorized as being in the cognitive domain of development?
   a. Physical maturation of the body   c. Poor interpersonal skills
   b. A changing personality   d. Language acquisition

   ANS: D   DIF: Moderate   REF: 2   OBJ: 1.1

7. Which does NOT belong on a list of key aspects of physical development?
   a. Change in motor ability   c. Change in short-term memory
   b. Change in body organ efficiency   d. Change in skin tone (e.g., wrinkling)

   ANS: C   DIF: Moderate   REF: 2   OBJ: 1.1

8. Traditionally, growth has been defined as
   a. physical changes that occur from conception to maturity.
   b. the biological unfolding of genetic potential.
   c. positive changes across the lifespan.
   d. gains, changes, and losses at each stage of the lifecycle.

   ANS: A   DIF: Moderate   REF: 3   OBJ: 1.1

9. _____ aging involves the deterioration of an organism that eventually results in death.
   a. Cognitive   c. Behavioral
   b. Psychosocial   d. Biological

   ANS: D   DIF: Easy   REF: 3   OBJ: 1.1

10. _____ aspects of development follow the "gain-stability-loss" model.
    a. All   c. No
    b. Some   d. Only physical

    ANS: B   DIF: Moderate   REF: 3   OBJ: 1.1

11. Aging is most accurately defined as involving _____ in the maturing organism.
    a. only negative changes   c. both negative and positive changes
    b. only positive changes   d. neither positive nor negative changes

    ANS: C   DIF: Moderate   REF: 3   OBJ: 1.1

12. The term *age grade* refers to
    a. a group of individuals who are all the same mental age.
    b. a socially defined age group, with culture-specific assigned roles, privileges, and responsibilities.
    c. a universally defined age group, with universal roles, privileges, and responsibilities.
    d. a group of children assigned at a specific age to a specific grade in school.

    ANS: B   DIF: Moderate   REF: 4   OBJ: 1.1

13. "Senior" discounts on meals available only to individuals over age 55 provide an excellent example of a(n)
    a. age norm.   c. age grade.
    b. social clock.   d. social convoy.

    ANS: C   DIF: Moderate   REF: 4   OBJ: 1.1

14. The category of "teenager" best exemplifies an age
    a. effect.   c. analysis.
    b. coefficient.   d. grade.

    ANS: D   DIF: Difficult   REF: 4   OBJ: 1.1

15. Male social age grades for the Arusha people of East Africa include
    a. only boy or man.
    b. junior warriors and retired elders.
    c. helpful and helpless.
    d. boyish and girlish.

    ANS: B   DIF: Difficult   REF: 4   OBJ: 1.1

16. A rite of passage marks a transition from one _____ to another.
    a. culture
    b. gender
    c. sex
    d. status

    ANS: D   DIF: Easy   REF: 4   OBJ: 1.1

17. A *quinceañeara*
    a. impacts only males.
    b. is a Jewish rite of passage.
    c. occurs at age 15.
    d. defines parenthood.

    ANS: C   DIF: Moderate   REF: 5   OBJ: 1.1

18. A company requires employees to retire at the age of 65. This policy is an example of
    a. age norms.
    b. age stratification.
    c. the young-old principle.
    d. growth norms.

    ANS: A   DIF: Difficult   REF: 5   OBJ: 1.1

19. When 60-year-old Madonna wore a miniskirt to a wedding, one of her friends commented, "I sure wish Madonna would act her age." This comment best illustrates the concept of
    a. age norms.
    b. age grade.
    c. cohort effects.
    d. maturation.

    ANS: A   DIF: Difficult   REF: 5   OBJ: 1.1
    KEY: WWW

20. The term _____ concerns an individual's sense of the age at which he or she should experience certain events.
    a. age norms
    b. age stratification
    c. social clock
    d. age grade

    ANS: C   DIF: Moderate   REF: 5   OBJ: 1.1

21. Manuel hoped to graduate from college by age 22 but finds himself enrolling for the first time at age 52. The anxiety Manuel feels because of this situation may be best explained by the concept of
    a. biological maturation.
    b. a social clock.
    c. plasticity.
    d. historical change.

    ANS: B   DIF: Difficult   REF: 5   OBJ: 1.1

22. Diversity can be based on
    a. race or ethnicity, but not socioeconomic status.
    b. race or socioeconomic status, but not ethnicity.
    c. ethnicity or socioeconomic status, but not race.
    d. race, ethnicity, or socioeconomic status.

    ANS: D   DIF: Moderate   REF: 5   OBJ: 1.1

23. When compared to those from middle- or upper-income families, individuals from lower-income families tend to
    a. reach milestones of adulthood earlier.
    b. reach milestones of adulthood later.
    c. never reach milestones of adulthood.
    d. reach milestones of adulthood at the same time.

    ANS: A   DIF: Moderate   REF: 5   OBJ: 1.1

24. Which statement concerning the pre-seventeenth century conception of childhood is most accurate?
    a. Pre-seventeenth century adults believed that children were simply miniature adults.
    b. Pre-seventeenth century adults did not discipline their children because infants were thought to be morally pure.
    c. Pre-seventeenth century adults forced children to grow up at a very slow pace.
    d. Pre-seventeenth century adults held views toward childhood that are different from most modern parents.

    ANS: D   DIF: Moderate   REF: 5-6   OBJ: 1.2

25. Which distinct period of development was the first to be recognized?
    a. Childhood   c. Middle age
    b. Adolescence   d. Old age

    ANS: A   DIF: Moderate   REF: 5-6   OBJ: 1.2

26. The term *emerging adulthood* refers to individuals from about age
    a. 11 to 17.   c. 29 to 37.
    b. 18 to 29.   d. 38 to 46.

    ANS: B   DIF: Moderate   REF: 6   OBJ: 1.2

27. Hermes is currently in the "emerging adulthood" stage of development. As such, he would most likely
    a. be leading a very stable life.   c. be focused on others versus himself.
    b. feel adultlike in all ways.   d. believe in a life of limitless possibilities.

    ANS: D   DIF: Difficult   REF: 6   OBJ: 1.2

28. Which statement best characterizes individuals in the "emerging adulthood" period of development?
    a. Young people who are adolescents but not adults.
    b. Young people who are neither adolescents nor adults.
    c. Old people who are adults but not elderly.
    d. Old people who are neither adults nor elderly.

    ANS: B   DIF: Difficult   REF: 6   OBJ: 1.2
    KEY: WWW

29. Which of the following has had the most significant impact on lengthening the average lifespan in the United States?
    a. Improved health care for the elderly
    b. Improved nutritional habits
    c. Major decreases in infant mortality
    d. Disease prevention among school-age children

    ANS: C   DIF: Difficult   REF: 7   OBJ: 1.2

30. The average life expectancy for a newborn in the United States is _____ years.
    a. 73   c. 83
    b. 78   d. 88

    ANS: B   DIF: Moderate   REF: 7   OBJ: 1.2

31. Which United States-born newborn would currently have the longest life expectancy?
    a. Donny, who is a white male
    b. Marie, who is a white female
    c. Michael, who is an African-American male
    d. Janet, who is an African-American female

    ANS: B   DIF: Moderate   REF: 7   OBJ: 1.2

32. The gap between the average life expectancies for _____ have widened in the past decades.
    a. women versus men   c. newborn females and newborn males
    b. Caucasians versus African-Americans   d. high and low socioeconomic groups

    ANS: D   DIF: Moderate   REF: 7   OBJ: 1.2

33. The question of how biological and environmental forces impact development is referred to as the _____ issue.
    a. continuity-discontinuity   c. nature-nurture
    b. passive-active   d. proximal-distal

    ANS: C   DIF: Moderate   REF: 7   OBJ: 1.3

34. Maturation is best defined as
    a. any physical changes that occur from conception to maturity.
    b. the biological unfolding of genetic potential.
    c. physical gains, changes, and losses across the lifespan.
    d. the effects of experience on thoughts, feelings, and behavior.

    ANS: B   DIF: Moderate   REF: 7   OBJ: 1.3

35. Which best describes the relationship between maturation and genes?
    a. Maturation is driven by a plan contained in the genes.
    b. Maturation is the nature side of development, and genes are the nurture side of development.
    c. Maturation is the process by which genes learn.
    d. Genes and maturation are unrelated concepts.

    ANS: A   DIF: Moderate   REF: 7   OBJ: 1.3

36. Which of the following represents a maturational process?
    a. Being taught how to pay attention
    b. Changing one's violent ways as the result of spending time in prison
    c. Learning to tie your shoes
    d. The development of pubic hair during puberty

    ANS: D   DIF: Difficult   REF: 7   OBJ: 1.3

37. Environmental impacts include all _____ that influence our development.
    a. external physical and social conditions   c. internal physical and social conditions
    b. external genetic and social conditions   d. internal genetic and social conditions

    ANS: A   DIF: Moderate   REF: 7   OBJ: 1.3

38. Learning is defined as the process through which _____ brings about relatively permanent changes in actions, thoughts, or feelings.
    a. maturation   c. instincts
    b. genetics   d. experience

    ANS: D   DIF: Moderate   REF: 7   OBJ: 1.3

39. Nature is to nurture as
    a. maturation is to learning.   c. psychology is to biology.
    b. experience is to genetics.   d. positive is to negative.

    ANS: A   DIF: Difficult   REF: 7-8   OBJ: 1.3

40. Maturation is to learning as
    a. genes are to social experience.   c. the environment is to heredity.
    b. knowing is to doing.   d. practice is to instinct.

    ANS: A   DIF: Difficult   REF: 7-8   OBJ: 1.3

41. If all you know is that men commit more violent crimes than women you can most accurately conclude that
    a. genes alone cause aggression.
    b. women elicit violent behavior in men.
    c. gender roles alone cause aggression.
    d. a difference in the level of a behavior exists, but the cause may involve hereditary and/or environmental factors.

    ANS: D   DIF: Moderate   REF: 8   OBJ: 1.3

42. A cross-cultural study on aggression in children from Belize, Kenya, Nepal, and American Somoa by Munro and colleagues (2000) indicated that
    a. boys were only more aggressive in the poorest countries.
    b. boys were more aggressive an all four countries.
    c. girls were more aggressive in female-dominant countries.
    d. girls and boys exhibited equal levels of aggression in the majority of the countries.

    ANS: B   DIF: Moderate   REF: 8   OBJ: 1.3
    KEY: WWW

43. The fact that sex differences in aggression are greatest in patrilineal cultures suggests that
    a. genes for aggression most likely come from fathers.
    b. cultural standards play a significant role in determining aggression.
    c. boys are naturally more aggressive than girls.
    d. primitive societies were likely less aggressive than modern societies.

    ANS: B   DIF: Moderate   REF: 8   OBJ: 1.3

44. Urie Bronfenbrenner is best associated with the _____ model of development.
    a. bioecological
    b. humanistic
    c. psychodynamic
    d. cognitive

    ANS: A   DIF: Easy   REF: 9   OBJ: 1.4

45. The _____ involves the immediate physical environment in which an individual functions.
    a. microsystem
    b. chronosystem
    c. exosystem
    d. macrosystem

    ANS: A   DIF: Easy   REF: 9   OBJ: 1.4
    KEY: WWW

46. The abusive behavior that Crosby perpetrated on his son has definitely negatively impacted his son's development. According to the ecological model, this impact is best explained by events occurring in the child's
    a. exosystem.
    b. mesosystem.
    c. microsystem.
    d. macrosystem.

    ANS: C   DIF: Difficult   REF: 9   OBJ: 1.4

47. Which is best described as a linkage between two microsystems?
    a. Exosystem
    b. Macrosystem
    c. Mesosystem
    d. Chronosystem

    ANS: C   DIF: Easy   REF: 9   OBJ: 1.4

48. A factory decides to cut the pay of all its employees. This loss of pay results in Julia being unable to provide health care for her infant son. According to bioecological theory, this exemplifies the impact that events in the _____ can play on the development of a child.
    a. microsystem
    b. macrosystem
    c. exosystem
    d. chronosystem

    ANS: C   DIF: Difficult   REF: 9-10   OBJ: 1.4

49. Which is the best example of the macrosystem of a child?
    a. The room in which it is raised
    b. The culture in which it is raised
    c. The school in which it is raised
    d. The family in which it is raised

    ANS: B   DIF: Moderate   REF: 10   OBJ: 1.4

50. Differences in Maternal Leave Acts (laws) between the United States and other nations definitely influence children living in those counties. Bronfenbrenner would describe this phenomena in terms of the impact of the
    a. macrosystem.
    b. microsystem.
    c. mesosystem.
    d. exosystem.

    ANS: A   DIF: Moderate   REF: 10   OBJ: 1.4

51. The fact that specific historical events (e.g., living during the AIDS epidemic) can influence development is best explained by the influence of the
    a. mesosystem.
    b. exosystem.
    c. microsystem.
    d. chronosystem.

    ANS: D   DIF: Moderate   REF: 10   OBJ: 1.4

52. According to the bioecological model, researchers need to
    a. focus mainly on unconscious factors.
    b. conduct research in the laboratory and not in "real-life" settings.
    c. the first step is to separate out the contributions of nature and nurture.
    d. consider the relationship between the person, context, time, and the process through which a person interacts with his or her environment.

    ANS: D   DIF: Moderate   REF: 10   OBJ: 1.4

53. Dr. Benjamin Spock wrote a popular book for parents, providing information on what behaviors can be expected of typical infants at specific ages. This sort of publication primarily reflects which goal of developmental psychology?
    a. Prediction
    b. Optimization
    c. Explanation
    d. Description

    ANS: D   DIF: Difficult   REF: 10   OBJ: 1.5

54. The title of Dr. Doublemint's latest bestseller is *Why Identical Twins Differ from Each Other!* Given this title, it is safe to assume that Dr. Doublemint's primary interest is in the _____ goal of psychology.
    a. prediction
    b. optimization
    c. explanation
    d. description

    ANS: C   DIF: Difficult   REF: 10   OBJ: 1.5

55. Vue is a developmental psychologist who is concerned with helping adolescents learn to deal constructively with divorce. Her work focuses primarily on which goal of developmental psychology?
    a. Prediction
    b. Optimization
    c. Explanation
    d. Description

    ANS: B   DIF: Moderate   REF: 10   OBJ: 1.5

56. When making a decision on whether or not to follow the latest diet trend, Jillian focuses on what the best scientific research has to say about the topic of nutrition. This indicates that Jillian believes in engaging in _____ practice.
    a. speculative
    b. ethnocentric
    c. evidence-based
    d. emerging

    ANS: C   DIF: Moderate   REF: 11   OBJ: 1.5

57. In the nineteenth century, scholars began to systematically record the growth and development of their own children. The published form of the observations were known as
    a. quasi-experiments.
    b. time of measurement papers.
    c. meta-analyses.
    d. baby biographies.

    ANS: D   DIF: Moderate   REF: 11   OBJ: 1.5

58. _____ is often cited as the most influential of the baby biographers.
    a. G. Stanley Hall
    b. Charles Darwin
    c. Sigmund Freud
    d. Jean Piaget

    ANS: B   DIF: Moderate   REF: 11   OBJ: 1.5

59. Who is most often cited as the founder of developmental psychology?
    a. G. Stanley Hall
    b. Charles Darwin
    c. Sigmund Freud
    d. Jean Piaget

    ANS: A   DIF: Easy   REF: 11-12   OBJ: 1.5

60. In his book *Adolescence* (1904), G. Stanley Hall described the period between childhood and adulthood as a time of
    a. senescence.
    b. plasticity.
    c. storm and stress.
    d. fun and exploration.

    ANS: C   DIF: Moderate   REF: 12   OBJ: 1.5

61. Francine has just purchased a copy of G. Stanley Hall's 1922 book *Senescence* for herself. This indicates that she is likely very interested in the topic of
    a. mental illness.
    b. language.
    c. bioecology.
    d. old age.

    ANS: D   DIF: Moderate   REF: 12   OBJ: 1.5

62. Dr. Johnson exclusively researches how people adapt to economic, psychological, and physical changes in old age. Given this emphasis, Dr. Johnson appears to be
    a. a lifespan developmentalist.
    b. an anthropologist.
    c. a pubescence specialist.
    d. a gerontologist.

    ANS: D   DIF: Difficult   REF: 12   OBJ: 1.5

63. Which is NOT an assumption of the lifespan perspective?
    a. Development is shaped by historical context.
    b. Development can take multiple directions.
    c. Development focuses on gains not losses.
    d. Understanding development requires multiple disciplines.

    ANS: C   DIF: Moderate   REF: 12   OBJ: 1.5

64. Sixty-year-old Kwan has led a life filled with ups (a prosperous career) and downs (a battle with breast cancer) and continues to maintain the capacity to change in response to such experiences. A lifespan developmental psychologist would likely say that Kwan has
    a. a flawed social clock.   c. minimal longevity.
    b. great plasticity.   d. maturational grief.

    ANS: B   DIF: Difficult   REF: 12   OBJ: 1.5

65. Which best exemplifies the concept of neuroplasticity?
    a. The ability to use your arm to draw after the arm was severely broken
    b. The development of thicker heart muscles in old age after beginning an aerobic exercise class
    c. The production of large amounts of testosterone during puberty
    d. The formation of new brain cell connections as the result of reading a book

    ANS: D   DIF: Moderate   REF: 12-13   OBJ: 1.5

66. The fact that many adult males who lived through the Great Depression later had erratic careers and unstable marriages exemplifies
    a. the impact of historical context on development.
    b. the multidirectional nature of development.
    c. maturation.
    d. the Baby Boom generation.

    ANS: A   DIF: Easy   REF: 13   OBJ: 1.5
    KEY: WWW

67. According to the lifespan perspective, development is
    a. singularly influenced and involves a single discipline.
    b. multiply influenced and involves a single discipline.
    c. singularly influenced and involves multiple disciplines.
    d. multiply influenced and involves multiple disciplines.

    ANS: D   DIF: Easy   REF: 13-14   OBJ: 1.5

68. The scientific method is best characterized as
    a. neither a method nor an attitude.   c. an attitude but not a method.
    b. a method but not an attitude .   d. both a method and an attitude.

    ANS: D   DIF: Moderate   REF: 14   OBJ: 1.6

314

69. The key element of the scientific method is the belief that _____ should determine the merits of an idea.
   a. systematic observation
   b. logic
   c. debate
   d. intuition

   ANS: A   DIF: Moderate   REF: 14   OBJ: 1.6

70. A theory is best defined as a
   a. set of concepts and propositions used to control developmental outcomes.
   b. set of concepts and propositions intended to describe and explain some aspect of experience.
   c. factual description of developmental phenomena.
   d. series of systematic tests of hypotheses.

   ANS: B   DIF: Moderate   REF: 14   OBJ: 1.6

71. Dr. Wells has proposed that the center of the Earth consists of large open areas that contain air and water and may be inhabited by some life form. This proposition is best described as a
   a. fact.
   b. hypothesis.
   c. theory.
   d. correlation.

   ANS: C   DIF: Difficult   REF: 14   OBJ: 1.6

72. A specific prediction about what will hold true if we observe a phenomenon is called a
   a. fact.
   b. hypothesis.
   c. theory.
   d. correlation.

   ANS: B   DIF: Moderate   REF: 14   OBJ: 1.6

73. After observing the interaction between rival street gangs, Jet predicts that fighting between the gangs would decrease significantly if the existing "colors" (clothing) of the two gangs (one black and one red) were changed to pink and yellow. This prediction is most accurately thought of as a
   a. fact.
   b. hypothesis.
   c. theory.
   d. correlation.

   ANS: B   DIF: Moderate   REF: 14   OBJ: 1.6

74. Based on an observation at a local fast-food restaurant Dr. Colby predicts that more people will buy a hamburger if it is covered with cheese. This prediction is most accurately thought of as a
   a. fact.
   b. hypothesis.
   c. theory.
   d. correlation.

   ANS: B   DIF: Moderate   REF: 14   OBJ: 1.6
   KEY: WWW

75. If asked to list the characteristics of a good theory, you should AVOID saying
   a. speculative.
   b. supported by data.
   c. internally consistent.
   d. falsifiable.

   ANS: A   DIF: Easy   REF: 14   OBJ: 1.6

315

76. Dr. Vandepolder is conducting a study on American Midwest college students' radio-listening habits. He doesn't have the resources to survey all college students in the Midwest, so he uses census data to randomly select a group of several thousand students from Michigan, Wisconsin, Illinois, and Minnesota to participate in the study. In this study, the group of all American Midwest college students is called the _____, while the group randomly selected from Michigan, Wisconsin, Illinois, and Minnesota is called the _____.
   a. sample; control group
   b. sample; population
   c. control group; population
   d. population; sample

   ANS: D   DIF: Moderate   REF: 14-15   OBJ: 1.6

77. Reba wants to examine the TV-viewing habits of 18- to 25-year-old males in the United States. As it is quite impossible to include all males of this age group in her study, she selects a smaller group of 18- to 25-year old males to survey. The males included in her study are called a(n)
   a. population.
   b. sample.
   c. control group.
   d. age grade.

   ANS: B   DIF: Moderate   REF: 14   OBJ: 1.6

78. Trojan interviews a group of 50 teen mothers to determine what sort of knowledge they hold regarding use of contraceptives prior to the time they became pregnant. He then writes an article where he speaks in broad terms about what teen mothers know about the use of contraceptives prior to becoming pregnant. In this study, the group of 50 teen mothers is called the _____, while all teen mothers are collectively called the _____.
   a. control group; population
   b. population; sample
   c. sample; control group
   d. sample; population

   ANS: D   DIF: Moderate   REF: 14-15   OBJ: 1.6

79. The major goal behind random sampling is to ensure that the
   a. data is falsifiable.
   b. sample is representative of the population.
   c. project will not be costly.
   d. population is large.

   ANS: B   DIF: Difficult   REF: 15   OBJ: 1.6

80. Which is NOT a major shortcoming of self-reports?
   a. Standardizing the self-report measure results in difficulty in comparing the responses of two different individuals who have completed the self-report.
   b. Respondents may give socially desirable answers so the researchers think more positively of them.
   c. They are difficult to use with very young children.
   d. Language abilities between people of different ages can make interpretation of results difficult.

   ANS: A   DIF: Difficult   REF: 15   OBJ: 1.6

81. Dr. Hu is interested in children's affective responses to studying science. She spends many hours sitting quietly and observing in elementary school classrooms during science instruction, and makes careful notes on all she observes. While observing, Dr. Hu is careful not to interact with the children or to interfere with their behavior in any way. This form of data collection is known as
   a. self-report investigation.
   b. naturalistic observation.
   c. structured observation.
   d. case study analysis.

   ANS: B   DIF: Moderate   REF: 15   OBJ: 1.6

82. Developmental psychologist Dr. Wiggles is interested in preschool children's helping behavior. He spends hours watching children at the campus preschool, taking great care not to interfere with the children or to influence their behavior in any way. What data collection technique is Dr. Wiggles using?
   a. Case study
   b. Naturalistic observation
   c. Meta-analysis
   d. Structured observation

   ANS: B   DIF: Moderate   REF: 15   OBJ: 1.6
   KEY: WWW

83. The greatest advantage of the naturalistic observation method is that it
   a. can tell us what people do in everyday life.
   b. is easily conducted in a laboratory setting.
   c. readily leads to the discovery of cause-effect relationships.
   d. untangles age effects from cohort effects.

   ANS: A   DIF: Moderate   REF: 15   OBJ: 1.6

84. Which is true of ALL structured observations?
   a. The data is analyzed using inferential statistics.
   b. They take place outside of the laboratory setting.
   c. They measure some verbal response.
   d. The researcher creates a special condition to elicit a behavior.

   ANS: D   DIF: Moderate   REF: 15-16   OBJ: 1.6

85. Dr. Dré is very interested in infants' reactions to different music styles. In order to study the phenomena, he built a special lab crib containing audio speakers. He then individually brings six-month-olds into the lab, places them in the crib, plays rap music, and watches each baby's reactions. Given this description, Dr. Dré appears to be using the _____ technique.
   a. self-report investigation
   b. naturalistic observation
   c. structured observation
   d. case study analysis

   ANS: C   DIF: Difficult   REF: 15-16   OBJ: 1.6

86. A brain scan is most accurately categorized as a
   a. naturalistic observation.
   b. physiological measure.
   c. structured observation.
   d. quasi-experiment.

   ANS: B   DIF: Easy   REF: 16   OBJ: 1.6

87. An fMRI uses magnetic forces to measure _____ in an active area of the brain.
    a. blood flow   c. dendritic expansion
    b. neurotransmitter levels   d. hormone output

    ANS: A   DIF: Moderate   REF: 16   OBJ: 1.6

88. The main limitation of physiological measures is that
    a. responses to such measures are easy to fake.
    b. they cannot be used to assess emotional reactions.
    c. it is not always clear what is being assessed.
    d. they cannot be used to study infants.

    ANS: C   DIF: Moderate   REF: 16   OBJ: 1.6

89. Which type of study always involves an in-depth examination of one specific individual or a very small number of individuals?
    a. Cross-sectional study   c. Longitudinal study
    b. Quasi-experimental study   d. Case study

    ANS: D   DIF: Easy   REF: 17   OBJ: 1.6

90. The main limitation of the case study methods is that
    a. results may not generalize to others.
    b. inferential statistics must be used in its analysis.
    c. it is "too artificial" as it is typically conducted in the laboratory.
    d. it does not provide any detail about an individual's behavior.

    ANS: A   DIF: Moderate   REF: 17   OBJ: 1.6

91. In a psychological experiment, a researcher always
    a. manipulates some aspect of the environment and then measures the effect on behavior.
    b. uses a control group.
    c. randomly assigns participants to a minimum of three different DIF:s of the independent variable.
    d. tests the entire population.

    ANS: A   DIF: Easy   REF: 17-18   OBJ: 1.7

92. Professor Plumb is interested in the impact of fruit consumption on memory. He identifies a group of college students to serve as research participants. Then he randomly assigns them to one of three conditions. In condition 1, the students eat no fruit for a week. In condition 2, students eat one pound of fruit each day for one week. Those students assigned to condition 5 eat five pounds of fruit each day for one week. At the end of the week, Professor Plumb measures the students' memory recall for a list of 20 words. Given this description, Professor Plumb appears to be using a(n) _____ research technique.
    a. correlational   c. experimental
    b. meta-analysis   d. biographical

    ANS: C   DIF: Moderate   REF: 17-18   OBJ: 1.7

93. A true experiment involves the _____ of the independent variable.
    a. manipulation
    b. measurement
    c. elimination
    d. correlation

ANS: A   DIF: Easy   REF: 17-18   OBJ: 1.7
KEY: WWW

94. A psychologist measures the IQs of 20 students who ingested a "smart pill" and 20 students who ingested a "sugar pill" in order to determine if the pill had an effect on intelligence. To ensure peak performance, she tests all of the students on Wednesdays. In this experiment, the independent variable is the
    a. day of the week.
    b. pill type.
    c. IQ score.
    d. sex of the researcher.

ANS: B   DIF: Difficult   REF: 18   OBJ: 1.7

95. In the Friedrich and Stein study on the influence of television on aggression, the type of television show watched (aggressive, prosocial, or neutral) represented the _____ variable in the experiment.
    a. extraneous
    b. dependent
    c. independent
    d. confounding

ANS: C   DIF: Moderate   REF: 18   OBJ: 1.7

96. In an experimental design, the behavior being measured is called the _____ variable.
    a. extraneous
    b. dependent
    c. independent
    d. confounding

ANS: B   DIF: Easy   REF: 18   OBJ: 1.7

97. A psychologist measures the IQs of 20 students who ingested a "smart pill" and 20 students who ingested a "sugar pill" in order to determine if the pill had an effect on intelligence. To ensure peak performance, she tests all of the students on Wednesdays. In this experiment, the dependent variable is the
    a. day of the week.
    b. pill type.
    c. IQ score.
    d. sex of the researcher.

ANS: C   DIF: Difficult   REF: 18   OBJ: 1.7

98. A study is done examining whether rewarding children for good behavior increases the amount of time students spend studying. In this study, amount of time spent studying would be the _____ variable.
    a. control
    b. dependent
    c. confounding
    d. independent

ANS: B   DIF: Moderate   REF: 18   OBJ: 1.7
KEY: WWW

99. In the Friedrich and Stein study on the influence of television on aggression, the observed level of aggression the children displayed in the nursery school represented the _____ variable in the experiment.
    a. extraneous
    b. dependent
    c. independent
    d. confounding

    ANS: B   DIF: Moderate   REF: 18   OBJ: 1.7

100. Random assignment helps ensure
    a. cohort effects.
    b. differences exist between treatment groups prior to the treatment.
    c. age effects.
    d. similarity of treatment groups prior to the treatment.

    ANS: D   DIF: Moderate   REF: 18   OBJ: 1.7

101. Which is NOT a hallmark of a true experiment?
    a. Control over responses on the dependent measure
    b. Manipulation of an independent variable
    c. Control over extraneous variables
    d. Random assignment of participants to experimental conditions

    ANS: A   DIF: Moderate   REF: 17-18   OBJ: 1.7

102. Faith wants to know whether there is a cause-effect relationship between the amount of time parents spend reading to their children and their children's attitudes toward reading. What type of research design should Faith use?
    a. Cross-sectional
    b. Experimental
    c. Longitudinal
    d. Naturalistic observation

    ANS: B   DIF: Moderate   REF: 17-18   OBJ: 1.7

103. A key limitation of the experimental method is that it
    a. cannot be used to identify cause-and-effect.
    b. is very expensive.
    c. cannot be used to assess many interesting questions due to ethical reasons.
    d. does an excellent job of explaining real-world experience, but does not do a good job of explaining what happens in the laboratory.

    ANS: C   DIF: Moderate   REF: 18-19   OBJ: 1.7

104. What point was Urie Bronfenbrenner attempting to make when he said that developmental psychology had become, "the science of the strange behavior of children in strange situations with strange adults"?
    a. Modern developmental psychology is too focused on laboratory research.
    b. Modern developmental psychology pays too much attention to exceptional children and not enough to normal children.
    c. Modern developmental psychology is too worried about the impact of early childhood abuse by parents.
    d. Modern developmental psychology conducts far too few experiments.

    ANS: A   DIF: Moderate   REF: 18   OBJ: 1.7

105. The key distinction between a true experiment and a quasi-experiment is that in quasi-experiments,
   a. research is conducted in the "real world" not in the laboratory.
   b. individuals are not randomly assigned to different treatments.
   c. no statistical analysis is conducted.
   d. there is always a control group.

   ANS: B   DIF: Moderate   REF: 19   OBJ: 1.7

106. Dr. Rambo wants to determine whether there are sex differences in reaction to televised violence. He asks male and female participants to watch a 15-minute video clip of a violent program and then complete a rating scale. Rambo's research project is best classified as a(n)
   a. true experiment.   c. naturalist observation.
   b. quasi-experiment.   d. interview.

   ANS: B   DIF: Difficult   REF: 19   OBJ: 1.7

107. The fundamental question addressed by the correlational method is
   a. "Does variable A cause variable B?"
   b. "How is a control group influenced by the absence of an independent variable?"
   c. "What impact does random assignment have on psychological behavior?"
   d. "Are two or more variables related in some systematic way?"

   ANS: D   DIF: Moderate   REF: 19   OBJ: 1.8

108. In the field of developmental psychology, the main reason that the correlational method is used more often than experimental methods is because
   a. correlations are more effective at addressing the issue of cause.
   b. of ethical concerns.
   c. correlational research is significantly more scientifically rigorous.
   d. of the availability of computers.

   ANS: B   DIF: Moderate   REF: 19   OBJ: 1.8

109. Dr. Fill wants to study the relationship between drug addiction and being the victim of child abuse. As Dr. Fill is an ethical researcher, he would have to conduct a(n) _____ study.
   a. experimental   c. laboratory
   b. correlational   d. cross-sectional

   ANS: B   DIF: Difficult   REF: 19   OBJ: 1.8
   KEY: WWW

110. Tom finds a correlation of +.81 between number of years in school and salary of first job. This would mean that
   a. the more education one has, the lower his or her starting salary is likely to be.
   b. the more education one has, the higher his or her starting salary is likely to be.
   c. education level determines whether or not someone will get a job after graduation.
   d. increases in education level cause employers to offer higher salaries.

   ANS: B   DIF: Difficult   REF: 19   OBJ: 1.8

111. If the correlation between listening to country music and passing general psychology is found to be -.8, then one could rightly conclude that _____ country music listeners pass the class.
    a. all
    b. most
    c. few
    d. no

    ANS: C   DIF: Moderate   REF: 19   OBJ: 1.8

112. Mara finds that the correlation between variables A and B is +.43, while the correlation between variables A and C is -.78. These results indicate that
    a. the correlation between A and C is stronger than the correlation between A and B.
    b. the correlation between A and B is stronger than the correlation between A and C.
    c. variable A causes variable B but not variable C.
    d. variable A causes both variables B and C.

    ANS: A   DIF: Difficult   REF: 19   OBJ: 1.8

113. Smoking cigarettes and having lung cancer are highly correlated events, and people often logically conclude that smoking must cause the cancer. It is hypothetically possible, however, that having lung cancer causes one to crave nicotine and thus it leads to smoking. This example illustrates the issue of
    a. the third variable.
    b. a reversed cause-effect relationship.
    c. time of measurement effects.
    d. plasticity.

    ANS: B   DIF: Difficult   REF: 20   OBJ: 1.8

114. Research has shown a positive correlation between the amount of time children spend watching television and their level of aggression. It is possible that the actual cause of this relationship is harsh parents who act aggressively toward children (teaching them to be aggressive) and whose violence leads children to avoid them at all costs (including by watching television). This example illustrates the issue of
    a. the third variable.
    b. a reversed cause-effect relationship.
    c. time of measurement effects.
    d. plasticity.

    ANS: A   DIF: Moderate   REF: 20   OBJ: 1.8

115. A meta-analysis is best described as
    a. a study using numerous previous studies.
    b. a controlled laboratory experiment.
    c. an unstructured interview.
    d. a longitudinal design study.

    ANS: A   DIF: Easy   REF: 20-21   OBJ: 1.8

116. In order to study the effects of television on children's behavior, Dr. Squarepants synthesizes the results from 150 studies looking at the influence of cartoons on children's moral development. Given this description, Dr. Squarepants appears to be using the _____ research technique.
    a. naturalistic observation
    b. meta-analysis
    c. structured observation
    d. sequential design

    ANS: B   DIF: Moderate   REF: 20-21   OBJ: 1.8

322

117. Which best describes the basic premise of the cross-sectional research design?
    a. Assess different age groups (e.g., 5-, 10-, 15-year-olds) at same time (e.g., during same week)
    b. Assess same age group (e.g., only 5-year-olds) at same time (e.g., during same week)
    c. Assess different age groups (e.g., 5-, 10-, 15-year-olds) at different times (e.g., 5-year-olds in 2003, 10-year-olds in 2004, and 15-year-olds in 2005)
    d. Assess same group (e.g., 5-year-olds) at different times (e.g., first test when kids are 5, then when they are 10, and finally when they turn 15)

    ANS: A   DIF: Moderate   REF: 21   OBJ: 1.9

118. Who is using a cross-sectional research design?
    a. Fred, who is assessing study habits in fifth graders in three different countries
    b. Barney, who is assessing the study habits in a group of fifth graders and who will follow and assess this same group when they get to eighth and then eleventh grade
    c. Wilma, who is simultaneously testing the study habits of fifth, eighth, and eleventh graders
    d. Betty, who is assessing the study habits of fifth graders in the year 2003, and plans to assess eighth-graders' study habits in 2004 and eleventh graders' habits in 2005

    ANS: C   DIF: Difficult   REF: 21   OBJ: 1.9

119. For her senior project, Shantae wants to study children's moral reasoning. During the Fall semester, she interviews 20 individuals in each of the following grades: first, fourth, seventh, tenth, and college sophomores. She asks each participant to solve a practical moral dilemma. What sort of research design is Shantae using?
    a. Cross-sectional   c. Longitudinal
    b. Experimental   d. Sequential

    ANS: A   DIF: Difficult   REF: 21   OBJ: 1.9
    KEY: WWW

120. A _____ is a group of people born in a specified, limited span of years (e.g., the 1960s).
    a. cohort   c. population
    b. cross-section   d. sample

    ANS: A   DIF: Moderate   REF: 21   OBJ: 1.9
    KEY: WWW

121. The fact that individuals who were born in 1980 will develop differently than individuals born in 1880 is best explained using the concept of _____ effects.
    a. age   c. cohort
    b. microsystem   d. social clock

    ANS: C   DIF: Moderate   REF: 21   OBJ: 1.9

122. In which research design are age differences and cohort differences hopelessly tangled?
    a. Cross-cultural   c. Longitudinal
    b. Cross-sectional   d. Sequential

    ANS: B   DIF: Moderate   REF: 21   OBJ: 1.9

323

123. While I am the fastest to conduct research design, one big disadvantage I have is that I do not generate information about the development of individuals. Which research method am I?
    a. Cross-cultural
    b. Cross-sectional
    c. Longitudinal
    d. Sequential

    ANS: B   DIF: Moderate   REF: 21   OBJ: 1.9
    KEY: WWW

124. In a(n) _____ research design, the performance of one group of individuals is assessed repeatedly across a portion of the lifespan.
    a. cross-sectional
    b. experimental
    c. longitudinal
    d. sequential

    ANS: C   DIF: Easy   REF: 22   OBJ: 1.9

125. Who is using a longitudinal research design?
    a. George, who is assessing eating habits of 40-year-olds in three different countries
    b. Jane, who is assessing the eating habits in a group of 40-year-olds, and who will follow and assess this same group when they get to ages 60 and 80
    c. Elroy, who is simultaneously testing the eating habits of 40-, 60-, and 80-year-olds
    d. Judy, who is assessing the eating habits of 40-year-olds in the year 2003, and plans to assess 60-year-olds' eating habits in 2008 and 80-year-olds' habits in 2013

    ANS: B   DIF: Moderate   REF: 22   OBJ: 1.9
    KEY: WWW

126. Olga is interested in how people develop strategies for conflict resolution. She selects a group of preschoolers, and uses both interviews and naturalistic observation to explore their approaches to dealing with conflict. Every two years thereafter, Olga again interviews and observes this same group of youngsters, concluding her study when the children reach adolescence. Olga has been using a _____ research design.
    a. behavioral observation
    b. cross-sectional
    c. longitudinal
    d. sequential

    ANS: C   DIF: Moderate   REF: 22   OBJ: 1.9

127. The impact on research findings produced by historical events occurring at the moment the data were collected are referred to as _____ effects.
    a. meta-analysis
    b. placebo
    c. age
    d. time of measurement

    ANS: D   DIF: Moderate   REF: 23   OBJ: 1.9

128. In which type of study are the effects of age and the effects of time of measurement confounded with one another?
    a. Correlational
    b. Cross-sectional
    c. Longitudinal
    d. Sequential

    ANS: C   DIF: Moderate   REF: 23   OBJ: 1.9

129. Measuring different age groups of subjects repeatedly at different periods in time is called a
     _____ design.
     a. longitudinal   c. sequential
     b. cross-sectional   d. cross-cultural

     ANS: C   DIF: Moderate   REF: 23   OBJ: 1.9

130. Sol is investigating the effects of divorce on children's self-esteem. His initial sample consists
     of a group of 10 five-year-olds, which he plans to follow over a period of at least 15 years.
     When this group of children reaches age 15, Sol adds a second group of five-year-olds to his
     study, and plans to follow them for another 15 years. Sol's overall plan is best classified as a
     _____ research design.
     a. correlational   c. longitudinal
     b. cross-sectional   d. sequential

     ANS: D   DIF: Moderate   REF: 23-24   OBJ: 1.9

131. Only the _____ design allows a researcher to potentially separate out effects of age, cohort,
     and time of measurement.
     a. cross-sectional   c. longitudinal
     b. experimental   d. sequential

     ANS: D   DIF: Moderate   REF: 23-25   OBJ: 1.9

132. Socioeconomic status affects the development of
     a. both lower- and higher-SES individuals.
     b. lower-SES but not higher-SES individuals.
     c. higher-SES but not lower-SES individuals.
     d. neither lower- nor higher-SES individuals.

     ANS: A   DIF: Moderate   REF: 25-26   OBJ: 1.10

133. Ethnocentrism is the belief that
     a. it is better to think of others as having a "deficit" than being "different."
     b. one's own culture is superior.
     c. it is easier to understand the position of people different from one's self.
     d. race does not impact behavior.

     ANS: B   DIF: Moderate   REF: 26   OBJ: 1.10

134. While considering a new study, Creed is concerned that the stimulus he is using might
     frighten the infants he is testing. This indicates that Creed is focusing on
     a. meta-analysis.   c. a sequential design.
     b. a correlational design.   d. research ethics.

     ANS: D   DIF: Easy   REF: 26   OBJ: 1.10

325

135. The American Psychological Association and the Society for Research on Child Development guidelines for ethics in research stipulate all of the following EXCEPT
    a. informed consent.
    b. the avoidance of physical and psychological harm.
    c. debriefing participants.
    d. testing participants using multiple measures.

    ANS: D   DIF: Moderate   REF: 27   OBJ: 1.10

136. The fact that a study participant needs to be aware of what they may experience while in a research study illustrates the concept of
    a. informed consent.   c. protection from harm.
    b. debriefing.   d. confidentiality.

    ANS: A   DIF: Moderate   REF: 27   OBJ: 1.10

137. After Mr. Flay has finished filling out a survey that he thought was on cooking skills, he is told that the actual purpose of the survey was to assess his intelligence. This would represent the concept of
    a. informed consent.   c. protection from harm.
    b. debriefing.   d. confidentiality.

    ANS: B   DIF: Moderate   REF: 27   OBJ: 1.10

138. In a study in which participants are tricked into believing that they caused harm to someone else, a researcher is obligated to make sure that the participants are told about the true nature of the study before they leave and also must make sure that the participants do not feel bad about their behavior. These two researcher obligations are referred to as
    a. informed consent and debriefing.   c. protection from harm and confidentiality.
    b. debriefing and protection from harm. d. confidentiality and informed consent.

    ANS: B   DIF: Moderate   REF: 27   OBJ: 1.10
    KEY: WWW

139. Due to the ethical standard concerning _____, a researcher could not tell a parent that the parent's child scored in the "genius" range on an IQ test that the researcher had given.
    a. informed consent   c. protection from harm
    b. debriefing   d. confidentiality

    ANS: D   DIF: Moderate   REF: 27   OBJ: 1.10

TRUE/FALSE

1. Biological aging is defined as the deterioration of organisms that leads inevitably to their death.

    ANS: T   DIF: Moderate   REF: 3   OBJ: 1.1

2. Lisa thinks that age 22 is the perfect time to get married because all of her friends plan to marry at this age. This is an example of an age norm.

   ANS: T   DIF: Moderate   REF: 5   OBJ: 1.1
   KEY: WWW

3. In Western Societies, it took until the beginning of the eighteenth century for "adolescence" to be viewed as a distinct period of the lifespan.

   ANS: F   DIF: Moderate   REF: 6   OBJ: 1.2

4. Maturation refers to the gains that occur across the lifespan as the result of experiences.

   ANS: F   DIF: Moderate   REF: 7   OBJ: 1.3

5. The larger cultural context in which development takes place is called the microsystem.

   ANS: F   DIF: Moderate   REF: 9-10   OBJ: 1.4

6. The notion that development is impacted by the time in which we live is a key element of what Bronfenbrenner referred to as the chronosystem.

   ANS: T   DIF: Moderate   REF: 9-10   OBJ: 1.4
   KEY: WWW

7. Plasticity involves the capacity to change in response to both positive and negative events.

   ANS: T   DIF: Easy   REF: 12   OBJ: 1.5

8. The scientific method is both an attitude and a method.

   ANS: T   DIF: Easy   REF: 14   OBJ: 1.6

9. A theory is a specific prediction generated by a hypothesis.

   ANS: F   DIF: Moderate   REF: 14   OBJ: 1.6
   KEY: WWW

10. A random sample is always smaller than the population from which it is drawn.

    ANS: T   DIF: Moderate   REF: 15   OBJ: 1.6

11. In a structured observation a researcher creates a special condition designed to elicit some behavior of interest.

    ANS: T   DIF: Moderate   REF: 15-16   OBJ: 1.6

12. The greatest advantage of the experimental method is the ability to establish the fact that one thing causes another.

    ANS: T   DIF: Moderate   REF: 18   OBJ: 1.7

13. In an experimental research design, the variable that is manipulated by the experimenter is called the independent variable.

ANS: T   DIF: Easy   REF: 18   OBJ: 1.7
KEY: WWW

14. Random assignment of participants occurs in all quasi-experimental designs.

ANS: F   DIF: Moderate   REF: 18   OBJ: 1.7

15. A correlation of +.2 indicates a stronger relationship between two variables than would a correlation of -.9.

ANS: F   DIF: Difficult   REF: 19   OBJ: 1.8

16. The main advantage of the correlational method is that it can be used to establish cause-effect relationships.

ANS: F   DIF: Moderate   REF: 20   OBJ: 1.8

17. Cohort effects concern the impact of being born in one particular historical context rather than another.

ANS: T   DIF: Moderate   REF: 21   OBJ: 1.9

18. Cross-sectional studies are better suited than longitudinal studies to the examination of individual differences.

ANS: F   DIF: Moderate   REF: 21-23   OBJ: 1.9

19. In a sequential design, time of measurement is confounded with cohort effects.

ANS: F   DIF: Moderate   REF: 23-24   OBJ: 1.9
KEY: WWW

20. Informed consent is typically obtained following a study.

ANS: F   DIF: Moderate   REF: 27   OBJ: 1.10

COMPLETION

1. Development is defined as the systematic changes that take place between _____ and death.

ANS: conception

DIF: Difficult   REF: 2   OBJ: 1.1

2. The status and privileges assigned to individuals of a specific age defines the concept of an age _____.

   ANS: grade

   DIF: Moderate   REF: 4   OBJ: 1.1

3. A rite of _____ is a ritual marking the transition from one age status to another.

   ANS: passage

   DIF: Easy   REF: 4   OBJ: 1.1

4. The "new" period between adolescence and full-fledged adulthood is called _____ adulthood.

   ANS: emerging

   DIF: Easy   REF: 6   OBJ: 1.2   KEY: WWW

5. _____ developed the bioecological model that stresses how biology and environment interact to produce development.

   ANS: Bronfenbrenner

   DIF: Moderate   REF: 9   OBJ: 1.4

6. According to Bronfenbrenner, a local law passed that requires all children to attend school all year round would be an example of the _____ environmental system

   ANS: exosystem

   DIF: Difficult   REF: 9-10   OBJ: 1.5

7. Bronfenbrenner used the concept of the _____ to capture the notion that changes in environmental systems and life events are patterned over a person's lifetime.

   ANS: chronosystem

   DIF: Moderate   REF: 9-10   OBJ: 1.4   KEY: WWW

8. _____ is considered the most famous baby biographer.

   ANS: Darwin

   DIF: Easy   REF: 11   OBJ: 1.5

9. A set of concepts and propositions intended to describe and explain some aspect of experience is a _____.

   ANS: theory

   DIF: Moderate   REF: 14   OBJ: 1.6

329

10. The overall group from which a sample is drawn is called the _____.

ANS: population

DIF: Moderate   REF: 14-15   OBJ: 1.6   KEY: WWW

11. In a _____ observation study, the researcher creates a special condition designed to elicit the behavior of interest.

ANS: structured

DIF: Moderate   REF: 15-16   OBJ: 1.6

12. In an experiment, the researcher manipulates the _____ variable.

ANS: independent

DIF: Moderate   REF: 18   OBJ: 1.7

13. A _____ experiment is an experiment-like study that assesses the impact of different treatments, but does not involve random assignment to treatment groups.

ANS: quasi

DIF: Difficult   REF: 18   OBJ: 1.7

14. The numeric expression $r = +.84$ represents a _____ coefficient.

ANS: correlation

DIF: Moderate   REF: 19   OBJ: 1.8   KEY: WWW

15. In a _____, the results from multiple studies are synthesized to produce some overall conclusion.

ANS: meta-analysis

DIF: Moderate   REF: 20   OBJ: 1.8

16. _____ effects concern the impact of being born as a member of a particular generation in history.

ANS: Cohort

DIF: Moderate   REF: 21   OBJ: 1.9

17. In a _____ design, a single cohort group is assessed repeatedly over time.

ANS: longitudinal

DIF: Moderate   REF: 22   OBJ: 1.9

330

18. A _____ design combines elements of both longitudinal and cross-sectional designs.

   ANS: sequential

   DIF: Moderate   REF: 23-24   OBJ: 1.9

19. Family indicators like education, income, and occupational prestige levels underlie _____ status.

   ANS: socioeconomic

   DIF: Moderate   REF: 25   OBJ: 1.10   KEY: WWW

20. The belief that one's own group and its culture are superior is referred to as _____.

   ANS: ethnocentrism

   DIF: Difficult   REF: 26   OBJ: 1.10

ESSAY

1. Define "development." Then discuss and give examples of the three broad domains of interest to students of human development.

   ANS: Answer not provided   REF: 2-3   OBJ: 1.1

2. Discuss the bioecological model using personal examples for each of the following levels of impact: microsystem, mesosystem, exosystem, macrosystem, and chronosystem.

   ANS: Answer not provided   REF: 8-10   OBJ: 1.4

3. Currently, development is characterized as multidirectional, multiple influenced, and characterized by lifelong plasticity. What does this mean?

   ANS: Answer not provided   REF: 12-14   OBJ: 1.5

4. What is the relationship between theories, hypotheses, and scientific method?

   ANS: Answer not provided   REF: 14   OBJ: 1.6

5. You have been asked to conduct an experiment on whether a pill affects memory development. Please describe your experiment by identifying the independent and dependent variable(s) you would select. Discuss how the variable(s) would be manipulated.

   ANS: Answer not provided   REF: 17-18   OBJ: 1.7

6. What are age effects, cohort effects, and time of measurement effects, and how do researchers design studies to control each effect?

   ANS: Answer not provided   REF: 21-24   OBJ: 1.9

7. Discuss the ethical concerns a researcher must consider before they conduct a study using humans.

   ANS: Answer not provided   REF: 26-27   OBJ: 1.10

8. What are the concepts of age grade, age norms, and a social clock, and how could they be applied to you and your life?

   ANS: Answer not provided   REF: 3-5   OBJ: 1.1   KEY: WWW

9. A researcher is interested in what children of different ages understand about their parents' jobs. Describe the advantages and disadvantages of verbal-report, naturalistic observations, and structured observations in conducting a study on this issue.

   ANS: Answer not provided   REF: 15-16   OBJ: 1.6   KEY: WWW

10. Dr. Newmonic is interested in memory skill development between ages 5 and 25. Please tell Dr. Newmonic about the advantages and disadvantages of using cross-sectional, longitudinal research, and sequential designs in conducting his study.

   ANS: Answer not provided   REF: 21-23   OBJ: 1.9   KEY: WWW

MULTIPLE CHOICE

1. What in the past was often called school phobia is now referred to as
   a. academic passivity.
   c. academic discontinuity.
   b. school refusal behavior.
   d. school paranoia.

   ANS: B   DIF: Easy   REF: 32   OBJ: 2.1

2. School refusal behavior
   a. affects as many as 20 percent of school-age children at any one given time.
   b. peaks in middle school.
   c. can lead to academic difficulty and dropping out of school.
   d. seldom involve emotional distress.

   ANS: C   DIF: Moderate   REF: 32   OBJ: 2.1

3. A theory guides all of the following EXCEPT
   a. what is most important to study.
   b. what can be hypothesized about.
   c. how many times an issue should be studied.
   d. how an issue should be studied.

   ANS: C   DIF: Moderate   REF: 32   OBJ: 2.1

4. A list of the most influential systems theorists would include the name
   a. Gottlieb.
   c. Freud.
   b. Skinner.
   d. Bandura.

   ANS: A   DIF: Moderate   REF: 33   OBJ: 2.1

5. A list of the most influential psychoanalytic theorists would include the name
   a. Erikson.
   c. Bandura.
   b. Bronfenbrenner.
   d. Gottlieb.

   ANS: A   DIF: Easy   REF: 33   OBJ: 2.1
   KEY: WWW

6. A theory that is falsifiable is
   a. coherent.
   c. discontinuous.
   b. testable.
   d. valid.

   ANS: B   DIF: Moderate   REF: 33   OBJ: 2.1

7. If asked to list the key issues on which developmental theorists tend to disagree, you should AVOID saying
   a. activity—passivity.
   b. Longitudinal—cross-sectional.
   c. universality—context specificity.
   d. goodness—badness of human nature.

   ANS: B   DIF: Moderate   REF: 33   OBJ: 2.1

8. Tara and Chris have just brought their infant daughter home from the hospital. They imagine they will have tough times ahead, for they firmly believe that all children are born with selfish tendencies, and they take their job seriously as the ones who must keep their child in line. Tara and Chris hold a view that is most like that of
   a. Thomas Hobbes.
   b. Albert Bandura.
   c. Jean Jacques Rousseau.
   d. John Locke.

   ANS: A   DIF: Difficult   REF: 34   OBJ: 2.1

9. Jean Jacques Rousseau believed that children are
   a. inherently evil.
   b. unaffected by parenting.
   c. innately good.
   d. like miniature adults and should be treated as such.

   ANS: C   DIF: Difficult   REF: 34   OBJ: 2.1

10. As a strong believer of the influence of experience, John Locke emphasized the role of _____ in human development.
    a. fixations
    b. nature
    c. stages
    d. nurture

    ANS: D   DIF: Moderate   REF: 34   OBJ: 2.1

11. When John Locke referred to the mind of a human infant as like a *tabula rasa*, he meant that an infant's mind was
    a. cursed with original sin that made it naturally evil.
    b. more like that of chimps than human adults.
    c. a set of connected living nerves.
    d. empty and to be written on through experience.

    ANS: D   DIF: Moderate   REF: 34   OBJ: 2.1

12. John Locke believed that human nature was
    a. inherently selfish and aggressive.
    b. innately good.
    c. determined by a person's experiences.
    d. determined equally by both genetic and environmental factors.

    ANS: C   DIF: Moderate   REF: 34   OBJ: 2.1
    KEY: WWW

13. With regard to the nature-nurture debate, a strong believer in nature would suggest that
    a. environmental influences are more important than genetic makeup in determining human behavior.
    b. maturation forces are more influential than environmental experiences in determining human behavior.
    c. teaching and enrichment of the environment are often more influential than genetics in determining human behavior.
    d. humans are basically good.

    ANS: B   DIF: Difficult   REF: 34   OBJ: 2.1
    KEY: WWW

14. Miley is a strong believer in the power of nature in determining the way her son Cyrus acts. As a result, she is most likely to agree that Cyrus's aggression is the result of
    a. watching violent television.   c. bad parenting.
    b. too much sugar in his diet.   d. inheriting genes for violence.

    ANS: D   DIF: Moderate   REF: 34   OBJ: 2.1

15. Because Dr. Smith falls on the "nurture" side of the nature-nurture controversy, she is most likely to believe that
    a. if infants are given normal opportunities to move about, their motor skills will naturally unfold in a universal sequence.
    b. teachers' expectations for their students' success will have little effect on how they actually achieve.
    c. while a child's experiences in school will have an impact on his or her intellectual development, what the child is "born with" matters more.
    d. a mother's care can greatly impact the development of a child.

    ANS: D   DIF: Difficult   REF: 34   OBJ: 2.1

16. Which perspective argues that human development takes many paths and is minimally influenced by physiological factors?
    a. Nature perspective only
    b. Nurture perspective only
    c. Both the nature and nurture perspectives
    d. Neither the nature nor nurture perspectives

    ANS: B   DIF: Moderate   REF: 34   OBJ: 2.1

17. A parent who falls on the "activity" side of the "activity-passivity" issue is most likely to believe that
    a. if a child is aggressive, the parents were not active enough in parenting.
    b. if new skills are not regularly used, they will disappear.
    c. we are naturally more active when young and become more passive with age.
    d. children play an important role in shaping their own development.

    ANS: D   DIF: Difficult   REF: 34   OBJ: 2.1

18. Lindsey argues that she is not responsible for any of her bad behavior as she is driven by biological and environmental factors over which she has no control. This belief best exemplifies the _____ position on development.
    a. discontinuity
    b. continuity
    c. passivity
    d. activity

    ANS: C   DIF: Difficult   REF: 34   OBJ: 2.1

19. Which best describes the continuity approach to development?
    a. Small steps without sudden change
    b. The belief that children play no role in their development
    c. Common development across humanity
    d. Biologically driven maturation

    ANS: A   DIF: Moderate   REF: 34   OBJ: 2.1

20. The fact that Goober believes in different stages of development indicates that he views human development as reflecting
    a. activity.
    b. context-specificity.
    c. discontinuity.
    d. human agency.

    ANS: C   DIF: Moderate   REF: 34-35   OBJ: 2.1

21. Jerome believes that development proceeds through a series of developmental stages, each of which represents distinct changes. He might best be called a(n) _____ theorist.
    a. discontinuity
    b. learning
    c. activity
    d. context-specificity

    ANS: A   DIF: Moderate   REF: 34   OBJ: 2.1
    KEY: WWW

22. Qualitative changes are best thought of as changes in _____, while quantitative changes are best thought of as changes in _____.
    a. amount; type
    b. size; shape
    c. kind; degree
    d. continuity; discontinuity

    ANS: C   DIF: Difficult   REF: 35   OBJ: 2.1

23. The universality-context-specificity issue is concerned with whether
    a. we all follow the same or different developmental paths.
    b. environmental or biological factors are more influential in development.
    c. we pass through abrupt developmental stages or develop in small, gradual steps.
    d. we all participate in our developmental outcomes or not.

    ANS: A   DIF: Easy   REF: 35   OBJ: 2.1

24. The belief that the same type of change occurs in all humans best fits with the _____ approach to development.
    a. activity
    b. universality
    c. continuity
    d. passivity

    ANS: B   DIF: Moderate   REF: 35   OBJ: 2.1
    KEY: WWW

336

25. The statement, "Change is different from person to person because cultures differ from person to person" best fits with the _____ approach to development.
    a. discontinuity
    b. passivity
    c. context-specificity
    d. universality

    ANS: C   DIF: Moderate   REF: 35   OBJ: 2.1

26. Anthony believes that his daughter Cleopatra acts the way she does because of the unconscious workings of her mind. This belief best matches with the _____ theory of development.
    a. cognitive-developmental
    b. contextual
    c. behavioral
    d. psychoanalytic

    ANS: D   DIF: Moderate   REF: 36   OBJ: 2.2

27. Dr. Love believes that it is normal for a six-month-old to throw tantrums when she doesn't immediately get what she wants. Dr. Love's views are most in line with those of
    a. Piaget.
    b. Freud.
    c. Skinner.
    d. Bandura.

    ANS: B   DIF: Difficult   REF: 37   OBJ: 2.2

28. Instincts are best described as
    a. inborn biological forces that motivate behavior.
    b. experiences that motivate behavior.
    c. inborn biological forces that inhibit behavior.
    d. experiences that inhibit behavior.

    ANS: A   DIF: Easy   REF: 36   OBJ: 2.2

29. Freud emphasized the importance of _____ in determining behavior.
    a. preoperational thought
    b. observational learning
    c. negative reinforcement
    d. unconscious motivation

    ANS: D   DIF: Easy   REF: 36   OBJ: 2.2

30. Because he holds a psychoanalytic orientation, Dr. Powers would suggest that the true reason for his son's interest in becoming an international spy involves
    a. a conscious wish to become famous.
    b. a genetic predisposition for behaving in dangerous ways.
    c. unconscious sexual and aggressive drives.
    d. the conditioned response of fear.

    ANS: C   DIF: Moderate   REF: 36-37   OBJ: 2.2

31. Freud believed that human infants were born with
    a. only an id.
    b. an id and an ego.
    c. an ego and a superego.
    d. an id, ego, and superego.

    ANS: A   DIF: Easy   REF: 37   OBJ: 2.2

32. According to Freud, I am the component of personality that is impulsive, irrational, and driven to satisfy instincts. I am the
a. id.
b. ego.
c. superego.
d. formal operation.

ANS: A   DIF: Moderate   REF: 37   OBJ: 2.2
KEY: WWW

33. According to Freud, the personality component underlying the crying of a hungry newborn is called the
a. ego.
b. formal operation.
c. id.
d. superego.

ANS: C   DIF: Moderate   REF: 37   OBJ: 2.2

34. According to Freud, the primary mission of the ego is to
a. help the child learn right from wrong.
b. raise the child's self-esteem.
c. help the child find realistic ways to get needs met.
d. provide for immediate gratification.

ANS: C   DIF: Moderate   REF: 37   OBJ: 2.2

35. Lisa and Lyle both want to stay up past their bedtimes to watch a show on TV. When their parents say "No," Lisa throws a fit, while Lyle says, "Please? I'll brush my teeth and get into PJs and be all ready, so I can just pop into bed the minute the show is over!" From a Freudian perspective, Lisa is responding from her _____, while Lyle is communicating through his

_____.
a. id; ego
b. ego; superego
c. id; superego
d. ego; id

ANS: A   DIF: Difficult   REF: 37   OBJ: 2.2

36. I am the "moral" aspect of the personality that helps a person determine the difference between acceptable and unacceptable behavior. Sigmund Freud called me the
a. ego.
b. id.
c. libido .
d. superego.

ANS: D   DIF: Moderate   REF: 37   OBJ: 2.2

37. Five-year-old Theodore is currently internalizing the moral standards of his father Ward and mother June. According to a psychoanalytic theorist, Theodore appears to be developing his
a. superego.
b. id.
c. libido.
d. ego.

ANS: A   DIF: Moderate   REF: 37   OBJ: 2.2
KEY: WWW

38. After her mother says, "No, you may not eat any cookies" Sandra takes some cookies from the cookie jar and eats them when her mother isn't looking. Later, she feels bad because she knows this was not a good thing to do. The fact that she feels bad indicates that her
   a. id is in control.
   b. ability to delay gratification is strong.
   c. superego is reasonably well developed.
   d. logic includes the concept of stagnation.

   ANS: C   DIF: Difficult   REF: 37   OBJ: 2.2

39. According to Freud, in a mentally healthy individual, the
   a. id finds realistic ways to restrain the ego.
   b. superego gives into the id.
   c. ego is ignored by the superego.
   d. ego restrains the id.

   ANS: D   DIF: Difficult   REF: 37   OBJ: 2.2

40. Freud suggested that psychological problems arise when the
   a. superego develops after the id.
   b. supply of psychic energy is unevenly distributed between the id, ego, and superego.
   c. ego emerges in infancy.
   d. a child realistically postpones gratification.

   ANS: B   DIF: Moderate   REF: 37   OBJ: 2.2

41. Libido is best defined as
   a. the collective unconscious.
   b. your morals.
   c. the psychic energy of the sex instinct.
   d. a conditioned stimulus.

   ANS: C   DIF: Easy   REF: 37   OBJ: 2.2

42. Which is the correct order of the psychosexual stages of development?
   a. Genital, anal, latency, phallic, oral
   b. Oral, anal, phallic, latency, genital
   c. Latency, genital, anal, phallic, oral
   d. Anal, latency, oral, genital, phallic

   ANS: B   DIF: Easy   REF: 37   OBJ: 2.2

43. Which of the following best characterizes Freud's position on the nature-nurture issue?
   a. He emphasized nurture more than nature, but recongized the important contributions of nature.
   b. He emphasized nature more than nurture, but recognized the important contributions of nurture.
   c. He emphasized both nature and nurture equally.
   d. He did not really take a stand on this issue.

   ANS: B   DIF: Moderate   REF: 37   OBJ: 2.2

44. When part of the libido remains tied to an earlier stage of development, _____ has occurred.
   a. extinction
   b. conditioning
   c. fixation
   d. constructivism

   ANS: C   DIF: Moderate   REF: 37   OBJ: 2.2

45. Salem, a university professor, smokes like a chimney and bites her nails. Freud would most likely say that Salem
    a. has become fixated at the oral stage of development.
    b. values despair over integrity.
    c. is suffering from an unresolved Electra complex.
    d. lacks a superego.

    ANS: A   DIF: Moderate   REF: 37   OBJ: 2.2
    KEY: WWW

46. When Felix and Oscar go out to dinner with friends, Felix brings a calculator so he can figure out his exact share of the bill. Oscar thinks Felix is a tight-wad and finds his behavior embarrassing. Freud would be most likely to attribute Felix's stingy behavior to
    a. an unresolved Electra complex.   c. the collective unconscious.
    b. stressful toilet-training.   d. a big ego.

    ANS: B   DIF: Difficult   REF: 37-38   OBJ: 2.2

47. According to Freud, the _____ stage is the first psychosexual stage of development.
    a. anal   c. oral
    b. genital   d. phallic

    ANS: C   DIF: Moderate   REF: 37-38   OBJ: 2.2

48. Paris is a 16-year-old who is having difficulty accepting her newfound sexuality. Given this description, Freud would argue that Paris is in the _____ stage of development.
    a. phallic   c. oral
    b. latency   d. genital

    ANS: D   DIF: Moderate   REF: 38   OBJ: 2.2

49. Four-year-old Ed says, "Mommy, when I grow up I want to marry you and be your husband." Given this statement, Ed appears to be experiencing a(n) _____ complex.
    a. Oedipus   c. Electra
    b. senex   d. inferiority

    ANS: A   DIF: Easy   REF: 38   OBJ: 2.2

50. Freudians believe that when experiencing an Oedipus complex, a boy will fear that his father will retaliate by _____ him.
    a. killing   c. castrating
    b. beating   d. abandoning

    ANS: C   DIF: Moderate   REF: 38   OBJ: 2.2

51. The Oedipus complex is successfully resolved through the process of
    a. regression.   c. reaction formation.
    b. identification.   d. projection.

    ANS: B   DIF: Moderate   REF: 38   OBJ: 2.2

52. Who is undergoing psychodynamic identification?
    a. Randy, who is experiencing a midlife crisis
    b. Ellen, who is starting her first job
    c. Simon, who is taking on the behaviors of his father
    d. Kara, who is attacking her mother (whom she has hated all of her life)

    ANS: C   DIF: Moderate   REF: 38   OBJ: 2.2

53. Five-year-old Greta envies the fact that her father has something she doesn't, a penis. Freud referred to what Greta is experiencing as a(n) _____ complex.
    a. Oedipus   c. Electra
    b. senex   d. superiority

    ANS: C   DIF: Easy   REF: 38   OBJ: 2.2
    KEY: WWW

54. Oedipus is to Electra as
    a. power is to sex.   c. boy is to girl.
    b. repression is to regression.   d. conscious is to unconscious.

    ANS: C   DIF: Difficult   REF: 38   OBJ: 2.2

55. Ten-year-old Jordan has few sexual urges and expends most of his energy playing basketball. Jordan appears to be in Freud's _____ stage of development.
    a. phallic   c. oral
    b. latency   d. genital

    ANS: B   DIF: Moderate   REF: 39   OBJ: 2.2

56. To control anxiety, the ego is most likely to
    a. fulfill all of the id's desires.
    b. turn over control to the superego.
    c. progress through different psychosexual stages.
    d. adopt defense mechanisms.

    ANS: D   DIF: Moderate   REF: 39   OBJ: 2.2

57. Brynn is three years old. She has been out of diapers for over a year. When her mother comes home from the hospital with a new baby brother, Brynn begins to suck her thumb and wet the bed at night. According to Freud, Brynn is experiencing
    a. reaction formation.   c. repression.
    b. regression.   d. sublimation.

    ANS: B   DIF: Moderate   REF: 39   OBJ: 2.2

58. Which defense mechanism involves removing unacceptable thoughts from consciousness?
    a. Reaction formation   c. Regression
    b. Projection   d. Repression

    ANS: D   DIF: Moderate   REF: 39   OBJ: 2.2

59. Jasper sees his friend Johns as "paranoid" and "afraid of the world of humans." However, the reality is that Johns is actually normal, while Jasper is the one who is afraid. According to Freud, Jasper is exhibiting the defense mechanism of
a. repression.
b. regression.
c. reaction formation.
d. projection.

ANS: D   DIF: Moderate   REF: 39   OBJ: 2.2

60. In public, Mr. Mistoffelees is a strong advocate of animal rights. In reality, he has an unconscious desire to gratify himself by being cruel to cats. Freud would argue that Mr. Mistoffelees' is exhibiting
a. a reaction formation.
b. repression.
c. a projection.
d. regression.

ANS: A   DIF: Moderate   REF: 39   OBJ: 2.2

61. A reasonable criticism of Freudian psychoanalytic theory is that it puts too little emphasis on the
a. biological instincts or urges that underlie behavior.
b. collection of hard data to support his findings.
c. emotional side of development.
d. effects of early life experiences on development.

ANS: B   DIF: Moderate   REF: 39-40   OBJ: 2.2

62. One strength of Freud's approach to development is his description of how
a. early experience can influence later development.
b. children learn through observation.
c. reinforcement and punishment determine behavior.
d. conscious motivations underlie most decision-making.

ANS: A   DIF: Moderate   REF: 39   OBJ: 2.2

63. Adler, Jung, Horney, and Erikson are all well-known
a. neo-behaviorists.
b. neo-feminists.
c. neo-Freudians.
d. neo-contextualists.

ANS: C   DIF: Easy   REF: 40   OBJ: 2.3

64. In comparison to Freud, Erikson placed greater emphasis on
a. infantile sexuality.
b. social influences..
c. operant conditioning principles.
d. biological determinants of behavior.

ANS: B   DIF: Easy   REF: 40   OBJ: 2.3
KEY: WWW

65. Erikson's theory is different from Freud's because it
a. places greater emphasis on biological influences.
b. describes development in terms of stages.
c. focuses on possibilities for growth beyond adolescence.
d. involves the resolution of crises.

ANS: C   DIF: Easy   REF: 40   OBJ: 2.3

342

66. Maya has recently given birth to a healthy baby boy, Jason. Whenever Jason cries, Maya goes to him, tries to figure out the reason for his crying, and then promptly does all she can to meet his needs. According to Erikson's theory, Jason is well on his way toward mastering the conflict of
    a. autonomy versus shame and doubt.
    b. initiative versus guilt.
    c. industry versus inferiority.
    d. trust versus mistrust.

    ANS: D   DIF: Moderate   REF: 40-41   OBJ: 2.3

67. Erikson emphasized the importance of a caregiver's _____ in predicting the impact of early life experience on later development.
    a. general responsiveness
    b. age
    c. sex
    d. intelligence

    ANS: A   DIF: Easy   REF: 40-41   OBJ: 2.3

68. The preschool-aged child is typically in which of Erikson's psychosocial stages?
    a. Intimacy versus isolation
    b. Identity versus role confusion
    c. Initiative versus guilt
    d. Integrity versus despair

    ANS: C   DIF: Difficult   REF: 41   OBJ: 2.3

69. Rather than a sense of inferiority, eight-year-old Zeke has developed a sense of mastery in all his academic endeavors. Erikson would say that Zeke has a strong sense of
    a. generativity.
    b. integrity.
    c. autonomy.
    d. industry.

    ANS: D   DIF: Difficult   REF: 41   OBJ: 2.3

70. Erikson used the phrase "_____" to characterize the key element of adolescence.
    a. sexual exploration
    b. identity crisis
    c. guilt heaped upon guilt
    d. reciprocal determinism

    ANS: B   DIF: Moderate   REF: 41   OBJ: 2.3

71. Rachel is 15 years old. She spends countless hours alone and in conversation with her peers trying to figure out what it is she wants to do with her life. Rachel is in which of the following of Erikson's psychosocial stages?
    a. Identity versus role confusion
    b. Industry versus inferiority
    c. Initiative versus guilt
    d. Intimacy versus isolation

    ANS: A   DIF: Moderate   REF: 41   OBJ: 2.3

72. Twenty-eight-year-old Serge is a typical young adult. As such, Erikson would suggest that Sergi is most concerned about
    a. dying young.
    b. the shame he experienced as a toddler.
    c. finding a job.
    d. establishing an intimate long-term love relationship.

    ANS: D   DIF: Moderate   REF: 41   OBJ: 2.3

73. Which question provides the best example of the concept of generativity versus stagnation?
    a. Will my work benefit the next generation?
    b. Do I know who I am?
    c. Should I get married?
    d. Will my choice of college major lead to a career in which I will make a lot of money?

    ANS: A   DIF: Difficult   REF: 41   OBJ: 2.3

74. Ruth is 80 years old and terminally ill with cancer. As she reflects back on her life, she comes to the conclusion that she has lived a full and productive life, and that it could not have been better lived in any other way. Ruth has successfully mastered the developmental crisis of
    a. intimacy versus isolation.   c. industry versus inferiority.
    b. generativity versus stagnation.   d. integrity versus despair.

    ANS: D   DIF: Moderate   REF: 41   OBJ: 2.3

75. Bob is currently questioning himself. Which question would indicate that Bob is currently in Erikson's integrity versus despair stage of life?
    a. Can I raise happy children?
    b. Should I marry Hope?
    c. Has my life been worthwhile?
    d. Will my job as a comedian help the younger generation?

    ANS: C   DIF: Moderate   REF: 41   OBJ: 2.3
    KEY: WWW

76. Which of the following is a key criticism of Erikson's theory of personality development?
    a. He is pessimistic regarding one's ability to overcome problems that have their roots in early childhood experiences.
    b. He portrays adulthood as a period of little growth and change.
    c. His theory is rather vague and difficult to test.
    d. His theory focuses too strongly on formal operations in thinking.

    ANS: C   DIF: Moderate   REF: 41   OBJ: 2.3

77. Which theoretical camp suggests that we should study only what we can directly observe and measure (i.e., overt behaviors)?
    a. Behaviorism   c. Constructivism
    b. Psychoanalysis   d. Epigenesis

    ANS: A   DIF: Moderate   REF: 42   OBJ: 2.4
    KEY: WWW

78. Watson believed that
    a. most children progress through a predictable series of stages that are programmed by biological maturation.
    b. children have many inborn tendencies.
    c. how a person turns out depends entirely on the environment in which he or she grows up
    d. elements of the unconscious mind are responsible for moral thought.

    ANS: C   DIF: Moderate   REF: 42   OBJ: 2.4

344

79. Watson and Pavlov's version of learning theory is referred to as _____ conditioning.
    a. operant
    b. instrumental
    c. social
    d. classical

    ANS: D   DIF: Easy   REF: 42   OBJ: 2.4

80. When describing her theory of development, Candice says, "The basic idea is that I take a stimulus that at first has no effect on an individual. Then I pair that stimulus with a second stimulus that does elicit some response. After the two have been paired together a few times, I test to see if the initial stimulus now elicits a response similar to the one elicited by the second stimulus." Given this description, Candice would be best classified as a(n) _____ conditioning theorist.
    a. operant
    b. instrumental
    c. social
    d. classical

    ANS: D   DIF: Difficult   REF: 42   OBJ: 2.4

81. An unconditioned stimulus is best described as a(n)
    a. learned behavior acquired through conditioning.
    b. unlearned event that automatically leads to a response.
    c. unconscious motivation involving the id and ego.
    d. experience that leads to a relatively permanent change in behavior.

    ANS: B   DIF: Moderate   REF: 42   OBJ: 2.4

82. In Pavlov's study on digestion in dogs, the bell became the
    a. unconditioned stimulus.
    b. conditioned stimulus.
    c. unconditioned response.
    d. conditioned response.

    ANS: B   DIF: Moderate   REF: 42   OBJ: 2.4

83. In Watson and Raynor's classical conditioning study with Albert, a steel bar banged with a hammer served as the
    a. unconditioned response.
    b. conditioned response.
    c. unconditioned stimulus.
    d. conditioned stimulus.

    ANS: C   DIF: Moderate   REF: 42   OBJ: 2.4
    KEY: WWW

84. Polly is attending her first birthday party, where she sees her first balloon. While playing with the balloon, she accidentally pops it with a pin. When the balloon pops, she screams, drops her drink, and starts to cry when she sees it stain the carpet. In this situation, the noise produced by the popping balloon would represent a(n)
    a. unconditioned stimulus.
    b. conditioned stimulus.
    c. unconditioned response.
    d. conditioned response.

    ANS: A   DIF: Difficult   REF: 42   OBJ: 2.4

85. When Mr. Earlgray sits on a needle, he instinctively screams and then accidentally knocks over his cup of tea. He then claims that he will never drink tea again, because he finds the act too painful. In this situation, which provides the best example of an unconditioned response?
    a. His scream
    b. Knocking over the cup
    c. The needle
    d. His decision to not drink tea

    ANS: A   DIF: Difficult   REF: 42   OBJ: 2.4
    KEY: WWW

86. In Watson and Raynor's study on Little Albert, a white rat served as the
    a. unconditioned stimulus.
    b. conditioned stimulus.
    c. unconditioned response.
    d. conditioned response.

    ANS: B   DIF: Easy   REF: 42   OBJ: 2.4

87. While attending his first horror movie, Craven begins eating out of his box of popcorn. Craven likes popcorn and continues to eat during the film. After a few minutes, a crazed killer surprises a character in the film. The character's screaming reaction scares Craven, who spills popcorn all over himself. After the movie ends, Craven starts to leave the movie. He glances down, sees an overturned box of popcorn, and screams out in terror. A classical conditioning theorist would argue that popcorn has now become a(n) _____ that elicits a fear reaction.
    a. unconditioned stimulus
    b. conditioned stimulus
    c. unconditioned response
    d. conditioned response

    ANS: B.   DIF: Moderate   REF: 42   OBJ: 2.4

88. Emeril has never tasted spicy shrimp. When he eats his first spicy shrimp, he smiles and decides that he really likes spicy shrimp. A few weeks after tasting the spicy shrimp for the first time, he is in a different restaurant, sees a bowl of spicy shrimp on a table next to him, and smiles. He then tells the waiter that he is going to try a new dish called spicy chicken. In this situation, _____ is best characterized as a conditioned response.
    a. spicy chicken
    b. spicy shrimp
    c. Emeril's smile
    d. the new restaurant

    ANS: C   DIF: Difficult   REF: 42   OBJ: 2.4

89. _____ is best associated with operant conditioning theory.
    a. Piaget
    b. Vygotsky
    c. Bronfenbrenner
    d. Skinner

    ANS: D   DIF: Easy   REF: 43   OBJ: 2.4

90. Hank is upset with his son for keeping his room so messy. His neighbor, Boomhauer, suggests that Hank give his son a dollar for cleaning his room on Saturday mornings, because he believes that doing so will increase the probability of his son cleaning his room in the future. Hank's approach is most similar to research conducted by which of the following theorists?
    a. Bronfenbrenner
    b. Erikson
    c. Piaget
    d. Skinner

    ANS: D   DIF: Moderate   REF: 43   OBJ: 2.4

91. The basic premise of operant conditioning is that
    a. most learning occurs when a person mimics an observed model.
    b. learning takes place over a series of qualitatively different stages.
    c. the consequences that follow a behavior impact the likelihood of the behavior being repeated.
    d. pairing a neutral stimulus with an unconditioned stimulus will lead to a conditioned stimulus.

    ANS: C   DIF: Moderate   REF: 43   OBJ: 2.4

92. Reinforcement
    a. strengthens the likelihood that a behavioral response will occur in the future.
    b. weakens the likelihood that a behavioral response will occur in the future.
    c. strengthens a desired response while weakening an undesired response.
    d. weakens a desired response while strengthening an undesired response.

    ANS: A   DIF: Easy   REF: 43   OBJ: 2.4

93. In operant conditioning terms, a positive consequence is to a negative consequence as
    a. good is to bad.   c. reinforcement is to punishment.
    b. adding is to removing.   d. operant is to classical.

    ANS: B   DIF: Difficult   REF: 43-44   OBJ: 2.4

94. Joy comes home from work exhausted and is surprised to find that her daughter, Michelle, has set the table and started dinner. Joy is thrilled. She praises Michelle and spends an extra half-hour reading with her before bed (something that Michelle likes). The same thing happens the next day, and soon this has become a daily event. This is an example of
    a. classical conditioning.   c. operant conditioning.
    b. observational learning.   d. modeling.

    ANS: C   DIF: Moderate   REF: 43   OBJ: 2.4
    KEY: WWW

95. After Brainiac brings home a report card with all As, his parents (who want to make sure this behavior continues in the future) give him a new car (something that he really wanted). It appears that Brainiac's parents are attempting to use _____ to keep Brainiac's grades up.
    a. positive reinforcement   c. positive punishment
    b. negative reinforcement   d. negative punishment

    ANS: A   DIF: Moderate   REF: 43   OBJ: 2.4

96. Marge wants her daughter Lisa to improve her study skills. How could Marge use positive reinforcement to achieve this goal?
    a. She could give Lisa candy (something Lisa likes) every time she studies.
    b. She could take candy from Lisa (something Lisa likes) every time Lisa does not study.
    c. She could give Lisa spinach for dinner (something Lisa hates) every time she studies.
    d. She could take spinach (something Lisa hates) from Lisa's dinner every time she studies.

    ANS: A   DIF: Difficult   REF: 43   OBJ: 2.4

347

97. Which statement concerning effective positive reinforcement is true?
   a. Continuous schedules are most effective for establishing and maintaining a behavior.
   b. Partial schedules are most effective for establishing and maintaining a behavior.
   c. When first learning a behavior, a partial schedule of reinforcement is best, but when attempting to maintain a behavior, a continuous schedule is most effective.
   d. When first learning a behavior, a continuous schedule of reinforcement is best, but when attempting to maintain a behavior, a partial schedule is most effective.

   ANS: D   DIF: Moderate   REF: 43   OBJ: 2.4

98. In operant conditioning terms, _____ occurs when something unpleasant is removed and the result is an increased response rate.
   a. positive reinforcement   c. positive punishment
   b. negative reinforcement   d. negative punishment

   ANS: B   DIF: Moderate   REF: 43-44   OBJ: 2.4
   KEY: WWW

99. Elizabeth tells her daughter Taylor, "I will stop this nagging, which you find unpleasant, as soon as you clean your room today and continue to clean it in the future." This description indicates that Elizabeth is trying to use
   a. positive reinforcement.   c. positive punishment.
   b. negative reinforcement.   d. negative punishment.

   ANS: B   DIF: Difficult   REF: 43-44   OBJ: 2.4

100. In operant conditioning terms, a negative consequence
   a. reinforces an action.   c. occurs when something is removed.
   b. punishes an action.   d. occurs when something is added.

   ANS: C   DIF: Moderate   REF: 43-44   OBJ: 2.4

101. Punishment
   a. strengthens the likelihood that a behavioral response will occur in the future.
   b. weakens the likelihood that a behavioral response will occur in the future.
   c. strengthens a desired response while weakening an undesired response.
   d. weakens a desired response while strengthening an undesired response.

   ANS: B   DIF: Difficult   REF: 44   OBJ: 2.4

102. In operant conditioning terms, _____ occurs when something unpleasant is added and the result is a decreased response rate.
   a. positive reinforcement   c. positive punishment
   b. negative reinforcement   d. negative punishment

   ANS: C   DIF: Moderate   REF: 44   OBJ: 2.4

103. Which is the best example of positive punishment?
    a. Giving a child money to get her to mow the lawn
    b. Hollering at a child to get him to stop fighting
    c. Grounding a child in order to stop her from staying out late
    d. Spanking a child in order to get him to stop swearing

    ANS: D   DIF: Difficult   REF: 44   OBJ: 2.4

104. Tiffany really likes jewelry. Her parents want Tiffany to stop talking on the phone every night after school. In order to accomplish this task, they take away Tiffany's new watch and tell her that she will lose more jewelry if she does not decrease her phone use. In this situation, Tiffany's parents are attempting to use _____ to alter Tiffany's behavior.
    a. positive reinforcement   c. positive punishment
    b. negative reinforcement   d. negative punishment

    ANS: D   DIF: Difficult   REF: 44   OBJ: 2.4

105. How could an elementary teacher effectively use negative punishment in the classroom?
    a. Give "stars" that can be converted into treats to students who do well on exams
    b. Give a slap on the wrist to kids who lie about cheating
    c. Take away recess time (something kids want) to decrease misbehavior
    d. Take away homework (something the kids find unpleasant) to increase hand-raising behavior

    ANS: C   DIF: Difficult   REF: 44   OBJ: 2.4

106. Extinction impacts a behavior by
    a. making it less likely to occur.
    b. making it more likely to occur.
    c. making desired behavior more likely and undesired behaviors less likely.
    d. making undesired behavior more likely and desired behaviors less likely.

    ANS: A   DIF: Moderate   REF: 44   OBJ: 2.4

107. Which statement best exemplifies the process of extinction?
    a. Just do it.   c. Just ignore it.
    b. Just keep the rewards coming.   d. Just keep the punishments coming.

    ANS: C   DIF: Moderate   REF: 44   OBJ: 2.4

108. Physical punishment tends to be most effective when it is
    a. very harsh.
    b. administered immediately after the offensive act.
    c. not accompanied by verbal explanations.
    d. not combined with other efforts to reinforce behavior.

    ANS: B   DIF: Moderate   REF: 44   OBJ: 2.4

109. One of the elements that distinguished social cognitive theory from operant conditioning theory was the social cognitive theory emphasis on
   a. reinforcement.
   b. qualitative stages.
   c. observational learning.
   d. epigenetic processes.

   ANS: C   DIF: Moderate   REF: 45   OBJ: 2.4

110. How did Bandura demonstrate the existence of "observational learning" in the famous "Bobo" doll study?
   a. He showed that children would model an adult they saw in a film.
   b. He showed that children scared by a loud noise would cry when they heard a bell.
   c. He showed that boys liked dolls as much as girls.
   d. He showed that children regress when they know a new sibling is about to be born.

   ANS: A   DIF: Moderate   REF: 45   OBJ: 2.4

111. Olga goes along with her brother Joe to his gymnastics class and watches closely while he works on the balance beam. One day, Olga's Mom finds her out in the back yard, with a board spread across two big boxes, doing some of the same maneuvers that she has seen Joe do in class. This is an example of
   a. observational learning.
   b. operant conditioning.
   c. passivity.
   d. formal operations.

   ANS: A   DIF: Difficult   REF: 45   OBJ: 2.4
   KEY: WWW

112. Cosmo, age three, has always been cooperative about going to bed at night. Then the family takes a trip and stays with relatives, where Cosmo's cousin, Wanda (also age three), has a royal fit at bedtime. Cosmo watches while Wanda's parents read her extra stories and bring her a glass of juice to calm her down. After Cosmo and his family return home, Cosmo begins to throw tantrums at bedtime. Cosmo's change in behavior is best explained by
   a. observational learning.
   b. classical conditioning.
   c. sensorimotor stage thinking.
   d. latent learning.

   ANS: A   DIF: Difficult   REF: 45   OBJ: 2.4

113. Beckham is watching his first soccer match on television. Despite the fact that he has learned to kick the ball like the players while watching the event, he does not demonstrate this skill in his backyard later that afternoon. Bandura would refer to this situation as demonstrating
   a. repression.
   b. classical conditioning.
   c. identification.
   d. latent learning.

   ANS: D   DIF: Difficult   REF: 45   OBJ: 2.4

114. What is vicarious reinforcement?
    a. When a person's behavior changes based on consequences received directly
    b. When a person's behavior changes based on consequences that happen to an observed model
    c. When a person's behavior changes based on the influence of a collective unconscious
    d. When a person's behavior changes based on the effect of inborn, unfolding genetic factors

    ANS: B   DIF: Moderate   REF: 45   OBJ: 2.4

115. Cindy watches her big sister, Marsha, get ready for a big date by applying a lot of eye makeup. Cindy decides that the eye makeup would look good on her but decides to wait a while to get ready. When Marsha and Cindy come downstairs, their mother Carol screams at Marsha and tells her to go back upstairs and remove the eye makeup. Later, when Cindy is getting ready to go out, she looks at the makeup on her dresser and decides against putting it on. What concept best explains Cindy's decision?
    a. Classical conditioning   c. Vicarious reinforcement
    b. Defense mechanisms   d. Regression

    ANS: C   DIF: Moderate   REF: 45   OBJ: 2.4

116. The key "cognitive" aspect of social cognitive theory involving deliberate exercise of control over both one's environment and one's life is called
    a. human agency.   c. concrete operations.
    b. instrumental conditioning.   d. extinction.

    ANS: A   DIF: Moderate   REF: 46   OBJ: 2.4

117. Which is the best example of Oscar's human agency?
    a. The fact that he learned to act by watching others act
    b. The fact that his ability to be selected to act in movies is heavily influenced by genetic factors like his good looks
    c. The fact that his acting is highly influenced by some unresolved and unconscious sexual desire
    d. The fact that his high sense of self-efficacy concerning acting allows him to believe that he is a good actor

    ANS: D   DIF: Moderate   REF: 46   OBJ: 2.4

118. Self-efficacy is best defined as
    a. feeling great about who you are.
    b. the belief that you can effectively accomplish a specific outcome.
    c. the ability to make fun of one's self.
    d. your self-concept concerning gender, intellect, and sexual orientation.

    ANS: B   DIF: Moderate   REF: 46   OBJ: 2.4

119. Reciprocal determinism refers to a continuous back and forth interaction between
   a. a want and a desire.
   b. genes and environmental experience.
   c. a person, his or her behavior, and the environment.
   d. a reinforcement and a consequence.

   ANS: C   DIF: Moderate   REF: 46   OBJ: 2.4

120. Learning theory explanations for school refusal include all of the following EXCEPT
   a. the influence of unconscious desires of the id.
   b. consequences of staying at home versus going to school.
   c. the positive reinforcement for staying at home provided by a mother.
   d. a child seeing another child who became very anxious at school.

   ANS: A   DIF: Moderate   REF: 47   OBJ: 2.4

121. Which is a common criticism of learning approaches to human development?
   a. Too little emphasis on genetic and maturational factors
   b. Fail to account for the fact that experiences appear to affect behavior
   c. Too much emphasis on unconscious factors
   d. Fail to describe any types of consequences that influence development

   ANS: A   DIF: Moderate   REF: 47   OBJ: 2.4

122. Piaget's interest in cognitive development was impacted during his work on standardizing IQ tests, in which he took notice of
   a. sex differences in intelligence.
   b. the fact that the language spoken by a child (e.g., English, French) predicted their IQ test scores.
   c. racial differences in intelligence.
   d. the fact that children of the same age often gave the same wrong answer.

   ANS: D   DIF: Difficult   REF: 48   OBJ: 2.5

123. _____ championed the position called constructivism.
   a. Skinner   c. Piaget
   b. Freud   d. Bronfenbrenner

   ANS: C   DIF: Easy   REF: 48   OBJ: 2.5

124. Constructivism proposes that children learn best
   a. by doing.   c. when genetics determine a behavior.
   b. when an adult completes a task for   d. through vicarious reinforcement.
      them.

   ANS: A   DIF: Difficult   REF: 48   OBJ: 2.5

125. According to Piaget, cognitive development is characteristic of an invariant sequence of stages that
    a. vary in order from person to person.
    b. move in one direction in youth and then regress back in old age.
    c. follow in a specific order (i.e., cannot be skipped).
    d. differ depending on whether one is male or female.

    ANS: C   DIF: Moderate   REF: 49   OBJ: 2.5

126. During the _____ stage of development, individuals lack the ability to use symbols.
    a. concrete operations   c. preoperational
    b. formal operations   d. sensorimotor

    ANS: D   DIF: Moderate   REF: 49   OBJ: 2.5

127. As a child moves from the sensorimotor stage to the preoperational stage, he or she first becomes able to
    a. conserve.   c. perceive the environment.
    b. think symbolically.   d. use abstract reasoning.

    ANS: B   DIF: Moderate   REF: 49   OBJ: 2.5

128. For Piaget, conservation is the ability to recognize that
    a. certain properties of an object do not change, even when its appearance is altered in a superficial way.
    b. specific sounds are associated with specific symbols (letters).
    c. needs are greater than wants.
    d. liberal ideas tend to be more complicated and more controversial.

    ANS: A   DIF: Moderate   REF: 49-50   OBJ: 2.5

129. Ruby watches as her mom puts a couple of drops of red food coloring into her glass of water. Although Ruby tasted the water just before her mom put in the drops, Ruby now believes that her water will taste like fruit punch. Piaget would most likely argue that Ruby is in the _____ stage of development.
    a. concrete operations   c. preoperational
    b. formal operations   d. sensorimotor

    ANS: C   DIF: Difficult   REF: 49-50   OBJ: 2.5

130. Which best describes the problem-solving approach of the concrete operational thinker?
    a. Systematic hypothesis testing   c. Trial and error
    b. Scientific   d. Cannot devise solutions to problems

    ANS: C   DIF: Moderate   REF: 50   OBJ: 2.5

353

131. Molly has just entered the stage of formal operational thought. Something she can do now that she could not do before is
    a. engage in trial-and-error problem-solving.
    b. mentally classify objects in her head.
    c. think symbolically.
    d. deal effectively with purely hypothetical situations.

    ANS: D   DIF: Moderate   REF: 50   OBJ: 2.5

132. A major criticism of Piaget's theory is that it
    a. has few practical applications.
    b. focuses too heavily on the importance of social relationships in determining the course of development.
    c. portrays children as passive learners.
    d. underestimates the cognitive abilities of young children.

    ANS: D   DIF: Moderate   REF: 50   OBJ: 2.5

133. Because Rooney has a strong belief in a sociocultural view of cognitive development, he would be most likely to say, "_____."
    a. It's all about genes
    b. You have to consider the important impact of historical context on development
    c. Development clearly follows a specific set of stages
    d. Unconscious motives underlie most decisions

    ANS: B   DIF: Moderate   REF: 51   OBJ: 2.5

134. Which type of theorist would be most likely to describe the human mind in terms of "mental hardware and software"?
    a. Psychoanalytic   c. Information-processing
    b. Constructivist   d. Operant conditioning

    ANS: C   DIF: Easy   REF: 51   OBJ: 2.5

135. A theorist with a(n) _____ perspective would be most likely to focus on the interaction between a changing environmental context and a person who is producing changes in the environment.
    a. psychoanalytic   c. discontinuity
    b. systems   d. operant conditioning

    ANS: B   DIF: Moderate   REF: 51   OBJ: 2.6

136. If asked to name an influential evolutionary/systems theorist, you would be correct if you said the name
    a. Pavlov.   c. Erikson.
    b. Rayners.   d. Gottlieb.

    ANS: D   DIF: Easy   REF: 51   OBJ: 2.7

354

137. The field of ethology was founded on research inspired by
    a. Darwin.   c. Rousseau.
    b. Locke.   d. Freud.

    ANS: A   DIF: Easy   REF: 52   OBJ: 2.7

138. _____ are most likely to emphasize the impact of species-specific behaviors that are products of evolutionary history.
    a. Ethologists   c. Behaviorists
    b. Constructivists   d. Operant theorists

    ANS: A   DIF: Easy   REF: 52   OBJ: 2.7
    KEY: WWW

139. Ethologists argue that
    a. no behaviors are adaptive.
    b. a behavior is adaptive only in relationship to a particular environment.
    c. a behavior that is adaptive to one species cannot be adaptive to another species.
    d. all behaviors are adaptive.

    ANS: B   DIF: Moderate   REF: 52   OBJ: 2.7

140. When asked to describe development, Tyson says, "I believe that a person's genes impact his basic traits; these traits are also impacted by environmental experiences, and as these factors are interactive, it is tough to predict the outcome of development." Given this statement, Tyson is best classified as a(n) _____ theorist.
    a. epigenetic psychobiological systems   c. classical conditioning
    b. social cognitive   d. psychoanalytic

    ANS: A   DIF: Moderate   REF: 52   OBJ: 2.7

141. As a fan of the concept of epigenesis, Tegan would argue that
    a. only genes matter.
    b. you are what happens to you.
    c. your genes and environment combine in ways that make predicting behavioral outcomes easy.
    d. your genes and environment combine in ways that make predicting behavioral outcomes difficult.

    ANS: D   DIF: Difficult   REF: 53   OBJ: 2.7

142. Which was NOT emphasized in Gottlieb's epigenetic psychobiological systems approach?
    a. The activity of genes   c. The organism's behavior
    b. The activity of neurons   d. The organism's unconscious mind

    ANS: D   DIF: Moderate   REF: 53   OBJ: 2.7

143. Research showing that ducklings who had been denied access to their mother's call but who did hear the call of a chicken actually preferred to chicken-call after they were hatched, providing empirical evidence in support of the _____ approach to development.
    a. operant conditioning
    b. epigenetic psychobiological systems
    c. sociocultural
    d. cognitive-developmental

    ANS: B   DIF: Moderate   REF: 53   OBJ: 2.7

144. Which statement best represents the basic premise of the evolutionary/ethologist systems approach?
    a. The unconscious mind rules all.
    b. Normal development requires normal genes and normal early experience.
    c. Life is about moving up a set of qualitatively distinct stairs (stages).
    d. Reinforce what you desire and punish what you despise.

    ANS: B   DIF: Moderate   REF: 53-54   OBJ: 2.7
    KEY: WWW

145. The greatest weakness of the systems theory of development is that it
    a. places too great an emphasis on genes.
    b. shows no appreciation for development during adulthood.
    c. offers only generalization and will never be able to accurately predict future development.
    d. views conscious factors as being as influential as unconscious factors.

    ANS: C   DIF: Moderate   REF: 54   OBJ: 2.7

146. As a strong believer in learning theory, Bea would be most likely to describe parents as _____ of their children.
    a. trainers
    b. supporters
    c. partners
    d. genetic-precursors

    ANS: A   DIF: Moderate   REF: 55   OBJ: 2.7

147. Which statement best exemplifies the perspective held by most 21st century developmentalists?
    a. Extreme black-and-white positions are in vogue.
    b. Freudian ideas (especially those concerning the issues of child sexual fantasy) are more accepted than ever.
    c. Learning approaches are effective at describing the development of thoughts but not effective at explaining the acquisition of behaviors.
    d. Humans and their environments mutually interact to influence development.

    ANS: D   DIF: Easy   REF: 55   OBJ: 2.8

148. Dr. Zaius believes that no one theory can explain human development and has developed an approach that incorporates elements from many of the major theories. Given this description, Dr. Zaius is best classified as a(n) _____ theorist.
    a. psychodynamic
    b. ethological
    c. eclectic
    d. sociocultural

    ANS: C   DIF: Moderate   REF: 57   OBJ: 2.8

356

TRUE/FALSE

1. The term *tabula rasa* is best translated as "blank slate."

   ANS: T   DIF: Easy   REF: 34   OBJ: 2.1

2. Discontinuity theorists believe that development involves primarily quantitative changes in human behavior.

   ANS: F   DIF: Moderate   REF: 34-35   OBJ: 2.1

3. The universality-context specificity issue concerns whether we all follow similar or unique paths of development.

   ANS: T   DIF: Moderate   REF: 35   OBJ: 2.1

4. Freud believed that unconscious motivation played no role in human behavior.

   ANS: F   DIF: Moderate   REF: 36   OBJ: 2.2

5. The ego is the irrational, impulsive component of personality that serves only to satisfy one's instincts.

   ANS: F   DIF: Moderate   REF: 37   OBJ: 2.2

6. When exhibiting a projection, an individual expresses motives that are just the opposite of their real motives.

   ANS: F   DIF: Difficult   REF: 39   OBJ: 2.5

7. Regression is one example of a defense mechanism.

   ANS: T   DIF: Easy   REF: 39   OBJ: 2.2
   KEY: WWW

8. Erikson suggested that humans develop over a series of psychosexual stages.

   ANS: F   DIF: Easy   REF: 40   OBJ: 2.3

9. A major weakness of Erikson's theory is that they do not adequately explain how development comes about.

   ANS: T   DIF: Moderate   REF: 41   OBJ: 2.3

10. According to Erikson, teenagers struggle with the crisis of generativity versus stagnation.

    ANS: F   DIF: Difficult   REF: 41   OBJ: 2.3

11. In Watson and Raynor's study with Little Albert, a white rat served as a conditioned response.

    ANS: F   DIF: Easy   REF: 42   OBJ: 2.4

12. If effective, negative reinforcement leads to an increase in the frequency of a behavior.

    ANS: T   DIF: Difficult   REF: 43-44   OBJ: 2.4

13. Negative punishment involves the removal of something pleasant that results in behavior decreasing in frequency.

    ANS: T   DIF: Moderate   REF: 44   OBJ: 2.4
    KEY: WWW

14. According to Bandura, the phrase "human agency" refers to any group that offers assistance to children or adults.

    ANS: F   DIF: Moderate   REF: 46   OBJ: 2.4

15. Bandura was highly critical of the notion of reciprocal determinism.

    ANS: F   DIF: Moderate   REF: 46   OBJ: 2.4
    KEY: WWW

16. According to Piaget, children construct their own understanding of the world based on their experiences.

    ANS: T   DIF: Moderate   REF: 48   OBJ: 2.5

17. According to Piaget, a child who is unable to use symbols to help solve problems mentally is in the preoperational stage of development.

    ANS: F   DIF: Moderate   REF: 49   OBJ: 2.5
    KEY: WWW

18. The main focus of ethology is in understanding the evolved behavior of a species in its natural environment.

    ANS: T   DIF: Moderate   REF: 52   OBJ: 2.7

19. Epigenetic systems theorists argue that genes completely dictate human behavior.

    ANS: F   DIF: Moderate   REF: 52-53   OBJ: 2.7

20. Stage theorists tend to view parents as supporters of development, while learning theorists tend to view parents as supporters of behavior.

    ANS: T   DIF: Difficult   REF: 55   OBJ: 2.8
    KEY: WWW

COMPLETION

1. The debate between stage theorists and those who view development as being without sudden change is called the _____ issue.

   ANS: continuity-discontinuity

   DIF: Moderate   REF: 34   OBJ: 2.1

2. Freud is credited with developing _____ theory.

   ANS: psychoanalytic

   DIF: Easy   REF: 36   OBJ: 2.2   KEY: WWW

3. According to Freud, the component of personality containing internalized moral standards is called the _____.

   ANS: superego

   DIF: Moderate   REF: 37   OBJ: 2.2

4. Freudians believe that boys love their mothers and fear castration by their fathers in a process called the _____ complex.

   ANS: Oedipus

   DIF: Moderate   REF: 38   OBJ: 2.2

5. The defense mechanism of _____ involves mentally going back in time to a less stressful period in one's life.

   ANS: regression

   DIF: Moderate   REF: 39   OBJ: 2.2

6. According to Erikson, the last psychosocial stage of development involves the conflict of _____ versus despair.

   ANS: integrity

   DIF: Difficult   REF: 41   OBJ: 2.3

7. In Pavlov's study on dogs' digestion, food served as the _____ stimulus.

   ANS: unconditioned

   DIF: Moderate   REF: 42   OBJ: 2.4

8. In operant conditioning, _____ occurs when something unpleasant is removed from a situation and, as a result, the likelihood of a behavior reoccurring is strengthened.

   ANS: negative reinforcement

   DIF: Difficult   REF: 43   OBJ: 2.4

9. In operant conditioning, _____ occurs when something pleasant is added to a situation and, as a result, the likelihood of a behavior reoccurring is strengthened.

   ANS: positive reinforcement

   DIF: Difficult   REF: 41   OBJ: 2.4   KEY: WWW

10. When a behavior is ignored (not reinforced), it tends to go away. This statement describes the operant consequence of _____.

    ANS: extinction

    DIF: Moderate   REF: 44   OBJ: 2.4

11. Bandura is best known for developing _____ cognitive theory.

    ANS: social

    DIF: Easy   REF: 45   OBJ: 2.4   KEY: WWW

12. Acquiring a behavior by watching a model perform the act is called _____ learning.

    ANS: observational

    DIF: Moderate   REF: 45   OBJ: 2.4

13. The ability to learn about a consequence by observing it being experienced by a model is referred to as _____ reinforcement.

    ANS: vicarious

    DIF: Moderate   REF: 45   OBJ: 2.4

14. Bandura used the phrase _____ when describing the ways in which humans exercise deliberate cognitive control over their lives and environments.

    ANS: human agency

    DIF: Difficult   REF: 46   OBJ: 2.4

15. The belief that one can effectively produce a desired outcome in a particular area of life is called self-_____.

    ANS: efficacy

    DIF: Moderate   REF: 46   OBJ: 2.4

16. The _____ stage is the first of Piaget's stages of cognitive development.

    ANS: sensorimotor

    DIF: Easy   REF: 49   OBJ: 2.5   KEY: WWW

17. Piaget suggested that individuals in the _____ operations stage of development are able to effectively think about abstract concepts and can formulate sophisticated hypothesizes.

    ANS: formal

    DIF: Moderate   REF: 49-50   OBJ: 2.5

18. The field of _____ focuses on understanding the development of evolved behaviors displayed in the natural environment.

    ANS: ethology

    DIF: Moderate   REF: 52   OBJ: 2.7

19. Gottlieb suggested that development depends on the joint interaction between genetic and environmental factors in what he called the _____ process.

    ANS: epigenetic

    DIF: Moderate   REF: 52-53   OBJ: 2.7

20. A theorist who relies on a combination of theories rather than relying on a single theory is said to be taking an _____ approach.

    ANS: eclectic

    DIF: Moderate   REF: 57   OBJ: 2.8   KEY: WWW

ESSAY

1. Compare and contrast the developmental assumptions of nature versus nurture, activity versus passivity, continuity versus discontinuity, and universality versus context-specificity.

    ANS: Answer not provided   REF: 34-35   OBJ: 2.1

2. On which elements of learning would Watson, Skinner, and Bandura agree? Where would their differences lie?

   ANS: Answer not provided   REF: 42-47   OBJ: 2.4

3. Many people suggest that violence in teenagers is due to the violent images they view in movies and video games. How would Skinner, Bandura, and Vygotsky react to this suggestion?

   ANS: Answer not provided   REF: 43-47 & 51   OBJ: 2.4 & 2.5

4. Describe Piaget's preoperational, concrete operations, and formal operations stages of development using examples from children or adults you have met (including yourself).

   ANS: Answer not provided   REF: 49-50   OBJ: 2.5

5. Describe the differences between Bronfenbrenner's and Gottlieb's approaches to development. Then discuss why they can both be categorized as systems theories.

   ANS: Answer not provided   REF: 51-54   OBJ: 2.6 & 2.7

6. How would you create a new theory using the ideas of the theorists presented in this chapter? Which concepts would you keep and which would you eliminate?

   ANS: Answer not provided   REF: 55-57   OBJ: 2.7

7. Susie, age four, climbed into her parents' bed one night because she was frightened by a scary dream. Because it was so late and Susie was obviously distressed, her parents comforted her and let her sleep with them. Now Susie does not want to sleep in her own bed, and every night has been a battle of wills, usually ending with Susie sleeping in her parents' bed. How would psychoanalytic, learning, cognitive-developmental, and systems theorist explain what is going on with Susie?

   ANS: Answer not provided   REF: 55-57   OBJ: 2.7

8. Use Freud's stages of psychosexual development to discuss the development of a child from birth through age 25. Be sure to include at least one example of fixation.

   ANS: Answer not provided   REF: 37-39   OBJ: 2.2   KEY: WWW

9. Erikson and Freud both have psychoanalytic theories of development. What are the key similarities and differences of their approaches?

   ANS: Answer not provided   REF: 36-41   OBJ: 2.2 & 2.3
   KEY: WWW

10. Explain and provide examples of the concepts of negative reinforcement, positive punishment, and extinction.

   ANS: Answer not provided   REF: 43-45   OBJ: 2.4   KEY: WWW

MULTIPLE CHOICE

1. The genetic endowment that most members of a particular species have in common is called
   a. a phenotype.
   b. the collective unconscious.
   c. eugenics.
   d. species heredity.

   ANS: D   DIF: Easy   REF: 64   OBJ: 3.1

2. Most dogs bark but don't speak, and most humans speak but don't bark. This is best explained by
   a. species heredity.
   b. meiosis.
   c. individual heredity.
   d. mitosis.

   ANS: A   DIF: Moderate   REF: 64   OBJ: 3.1

3. All human babies, regardless of which culture they live in or which language is spoken around them, begin to babble at about the same age. This is an example of
   a. species heredity.
   b. natural selection.
   c. mutation.
   d. recessive genetics.

   ANS: A   DIF: Moderate   REF: 64   OBJ: 3.1
   KEY: WWW

4. Which of the following is NOT a major claim of Darwin's theory of evolution?
   a. There is genetic variation in a species.
   b. Some genes aid in adaptation to the environment more than other genes do.
   c. New species emerge on their own and are not related to earlier species.
   d. Genes that aid in adaptation to the environment are more likely to be passed on to future generations.

   ANS: C   DIF: Moderate   REF: 65   OBJ: 3.1

5. The idea that some genes aid in adaptation more than others is known as
   a. genetic counseling.
   b. natural selection.
   c. shared environmental influences.
   d. crossing over.

   ANS: B   DIF: Moderate   REF: 65   OBJ: 3.1

6. Kettlewell's research on the color of moths and their geographic location demonstrates the principle of
   a. cultural evolution.
   b. social learning theory.
   c. natural selection.
   d. concordance.

   ANS: C   DIF: Moderate   REF: 65   OBJ: 3.1

7. In Kettlewell's research, the proportion of dark-colored moths increased as _____ increased.
   a. pollution
   b. the use of outdoor lights
   c. dark-colored beetles
   d. the number of trees

   ANS: A   DIF: Easy   REF: 65   OBJ: 3.1

8. The main point of evolution is that development
   a. is driven solely by genetics.
   b. of nonhumans can be easily explained, while human development is unexplainable.
   c. involves an interaction between genetic and environmental forces.
   d. seldom aids in adaptation.

   ANS: C   DIF: Moderate   REF: 65   OBJ: 3.1

9. The belief that we inherit tried and true ways of adjusting to the environment from past generations is referred to as
   a. crossing over.
   b. incomplete dominance.
   c. concordance.
   d. cultural evolution.

   ANS: D   DIF: Moderate   REF: 66   OBJ: 3.1

10. Which best exemplifies the process of cultural evolution?
    a. The fact that different eye shapes are found within individuals in the same ethnic group
    b. Inheriting a stronger left arm than a right arm because in the past this allowed for the faster cutting of grains and more food for families
    c. The dramatic shift from Communism to Democracy seen in the Soviet Union in the 1980s
    d. Greater height in current generations than in past generations because in past generations, food that needed to be gathered was closer to the ground

    ANS: B   DIF: Difficult   REF: 66   OBJ: 3.1

11. Conception is defined as the moment when the
    a. egg is fertilized by a sperm.
    b. ovum undergoes its first cell division.
    c. sperm enters the fallopian tube.
    d. ovary encounters a sperm.

    ANS: A   DIF: Moderate   REF: 66   OBJ: 3.2

12. At conception, the genetic material of the mother's ovum and the genetic material of the father's sperm unite, creating a new cell called a(n)
    a. embryo.
    b. gamete.
    c. juvenile cell.
    d. zygote.

    ANS: D   DIF: Easy   REF: 66   OBJ: 3.2

13. Which is the most genetically complex structure?
    a. A gene
    b. A chromosome
    c. A zygote
    d. A sperm

    ANS: C   DIF: Difficult   REF: 66-67   OBJ: 3.2

14. Which statement concerning the genetic code is FALSE?
    a. Zygotes consist of many genes.   c. DNA strands consist of many zygotes.
    b. Genes consist of many DNA strands.   d. Chromosomes consist of many genes.

    ANS: C   DIF: Moderate   REF: 66-67   OBJ: 3.2

15. Which statement is true?
    a. Genes consist of thousands of chromosomes.
    b. Chromosomes consist of thousands of genes.
    c. Ovum consists of thousands of eggs.
    d. Eggs consist of thousands of ovum.

    ANS: B   DIF: Moderate   REF: 66-67   OBJ: 3.2
    KEY: WWW

16. Dr. Spock is using a microscope to observe a reproductive germ cell. He suddenly remarks,
    "That cell just underwent meiosis!" What has Dr. Spock just seen?
    a. One cell ingesting another cell
    b. A cell dividing into new cells with twice as many chromosomes as the original
       reproductive cell
    c. The process of fertilization
    d. A cell dividing into new cells with half of the chromosomes of the original
       reproductive cell

    ANS: D   DIF: Moderate   REF: 66   OBJ: 3.2

17. A sperm cell and an ovum each contribute 23, rather than 46, chromosomes to a zygote
    because they
    a. were produced through the process of meiosis.
    b. were produced through the process of mitosis.
    c. have undergone the process of crossing over.
    d. have undergone the process of canalization.

    ANS: A   DIF: Difficult   REF: 66   OBJ: 3.2

18. The typical outcome of a female reproductive cell that has undergone meiosis is
    a. one egg and three nonfunctional cells.   c. three eggs and one nonfunctional cell.
    b. two eggs and two nonfunctional cells.   d. four eggs.

    ANS: A   DIF: Moderate   REF: 66   OBJ: 3.2

19. Following mitosis, each daughter cell has _____ number of chromosomes as the mother cell
    had.
    a. half of the   c. four times the
    b. twice the   d. the same

    ANS: D   DIF: Moderate   REF: 66-67   OBJ: 3.2

20. Mitosis is to meiosis as
    a. egg is to sperm.
    b. doubling is to halving.
    c. chromosomes are to genes.
    d. sex cell is to normal cell.

    ANS: B   DIF: Difficult   REF: 66-67   OBJ: 3.2
    KEY: WWW

21. Which is NOT one of the genetic code bases of human DNA?
    a. Adenine
    b. Cytosine
    c. Guanine
    d. Phenylalanine

    ANS: D   DIF: Moderate   REF: 67   OBJ: 3.2

22. Scientists estimate that the average human cell contains about _____ genes.
    a. 200-250
    b. 20,000-25,000
    c. 200,000-250,000
    d. 2,000,000-250,000,000

    ANS: B   DIF: Moderate   REF: 67   OBJ: 3.2

23. Alleles are
    a. types of karyotypes.
    b. versions of enzymes.
    c. variants of a gene.
    d. examples of autosomes.

    ANS: C   DIF: Moderate   REF: 67-68   OBJ: 3.2

24. A gene
    a. is made of hormones and neurotransmitters.
    b. can also be referred to as an ovum.
    c. when combined with a second gene will produce a chromosome.
    d. provides instructions for the production of amino acids.

    ANS: D   DIF: Moderate   REF: 67-68   OBJ: 3.2

25. The purpose of the Human Genome Project was to
    a. map the sequence of strands of DNA in human chromosomes.
    b. determine how many different bases were contained in human DNA.
    c. identify the "double helix" shape of DNA.
    d. verify the existence of dominant genes.

    ANS: A   DIF: Easy   REF: 68   OBJ: 3.2

26. It is estimated that about _____ percent of the human genome consists of what are traditionally defined as genes.
    a. 2
    b. 32
    c. 62
    d. 92

    ANS: A   DIF: Moderate   REF: 68   OBJ: 3.2

27. The majority of the human genome consists of "_____" DNA.
    a. protein-building
    b. stem
    c. junk
    d. fragile

    ANS: C   DIF: Moderate   REF: 68   OBJ: 3.2

28. According to data generated by the Human Genome Project, all humans share about _____ out of 1,000 DNA bases.
   a. 999
   b. 499
   c. 99
   d. 6

   ANS: A   DIF: Easy   REF: 68   OBJ: 3.2

29. Due to the nature of chromosomes, the odds of a couple producing two children with identical genes is a minimum of 1 in
   a. 640.
   b. 64,000.
   c. 64,000,000.
   d. 64,000,000,000.

   ANS: D   DIF: Moderate   REF: 68   OBJ: 3.2

30. As the genetic material in two cells pair up just prior to meiosis, parts of the chromosome are exchanged with a second chromosome. This is called
   a. karyotyping.
   b. concordance.
   c. crossing over.
   d. cloning.

   ANS: C   DIF: Moderate   REF: 68   OBJ: 3.2

31. Identical twins occur when a(n) _____ divides to form two separate, individual cells.
   a. gene
   b. fertilized ovum
   c. gamete
   d. autosome

   ANS: B   DIF: Easy   REF: 68   OBJ: 3.2

32. Statistically, for every 500 births, you would expect _____ pair(s) of identical twins.
   a. 1
   b. 2
   c. 10
   d. 20

   ANS: A   DIF: Moderate   REF: 68   OBJ: 3.2

33. We know that two people have precisely 50 percent of their genes in common if they are
   a. fraternal twins.
   b. identical twins.
   c. parent and child.
   d. grandchild and grandparent.

   ANS: C   DIF: Moderate   REF: 68   OBJ: 3.2

34. Fraternal twin siblings share
   a. precisely 50 percent of their genes.
   b. on average about 50 percent of their genes.
   c. on average about 25 percent of their genes.
   d. nearly 100 percent of their genes.

   ANS: B   DIF: Moderate   REF: 68   OBJ: 3.2
   KEY: WWW

35. In order to produce fraternal twins you must have two
   a. X chromosomes.
   b. sperm.
   c. Y chromosomes.
   d. recessive genes.

   ANS: B   DIF: Moderate   REF: 68   OBJ: 3.2

36. While Click and Clack are brothers and look somewhat alike, they have only about 50 percent of their genes in common. This would mean that Click and Clack are most likely
    a. identical twins.
    b. conjoined twins.
    c. fraternal twins.
    d. adopted.

    ANS: C   DIF: Moderate   REF: 68   OBJ: 3.2

37. Concerning twins, monozygotic is to dizygotic as
    a. common is to uncommon.
    b. one egg is to two eggs.
    c. nonshared environment is to shared environment.
    d. fraternal is to identical.

    ANS: B   DIF: Difficult   REF: 68   OBJ: 3.2

38. A typical human being has _____ pairs of chromosomes that constitute autosomes.
    a. 46
    b. 44
    c. 23
    d. 22

    ANS: D   DIF: Moderate   REF: 69   OBJ: 3.2

39. Most cells of a typical male contain
    a. two X chromosomes.
    b. two Y chromosomes.
    c. one X and one Y chromosome.
    d. neither an X nor Y chromosome.

    ANS: C   DIF: Easy   REF: 69   OBJ: 3.2

40. Which statement concerning human sex chromosomes is true?
    a. The X chromosome has more genes.
    b. The Y chromosome has more genes.
    c. The X and Y chromosome have the same number of genes.
    d. The difference between the number of genes on the X and Y chromosome has not been established.

    ANS: A   DIF: Easy   REF: 69   OBJ: 3.2

41. Who has the set of chromosomes found in a typical female?
    a. (XX) Rose
    b. (XY) Daisy
    c. (YY) Lily
    d. (XXY) Ivy

    ANS: A   DIF: Easy   REF: 69   OBJ: 3.2

42. If you are told that you are about to see a karyotype, you should expect to look at a
    a. set of identical twins.
    b. phenotype.
    c. photograph of a complete set of chromosomes.
    d. full-term fetus.

    ANS: C   DIF: Moderate   REF: 69   OBJ: 3.2

43. What determines the chromosomal sex of a child?
    a. Random chance
    b. An X chromosome carried by the mother
    c. An X or Y chromosome carried by the mother
    d. An X or Y chromosome carried by the father

    ANS: D   DIF: Easy   REF: 69   OBJ: 3.2
    KEY: WWW

44. Jack desperately wants to have a son. He and his wife already have three children, all girls.
    Jack divorces his wife and remarries. He expects that his new wife will be more successful in
    providing him with a son. Which of the following is true?
    a. Jack's chances of having a son are better with his new wife.
    b. Jack's chances of having a son are worse with his new wife.
    c. Jack's chances of having a son are not changed by a change in wife.
    d. Jack will be unable to have a son no matter how many children he fathers.

    ANS: C   DIF: Difficult   REF: 69   OBJ: 3.2

45. Genotype is most accurately described as
    a. your inherited genes.
    b. a visual representation of chromosomes.
    c. the manner in which genes are expressed.
    d. incomplete dominance.

    ANS: A   DIF: Easy   REF: 69   OBJ: 3.3

46. Which is the best example of a genotype?
    a. Blonde hair
    b. High IQ
    c. Your general personality traits (e.g., being shy or aggressive)
    d. The genes on your X chromosome

    ANS: D   DIF: Moderate   REF: 69   OBJ: 3.3
    KEY: WWW

47. How many of the following (your age, your race, your personality, genes related to height)
    represent a genotype?
    a. 1   c. 3
    b. 2   d. 4

    ANS: A   DIF: Difficult   REF: 69   OBJ: 3.3

48. The term _____ refers to the actual characteristics a person exhibits.
    a. autotype   c. genotype
    b. dominant inheritance   d. phenotype

    ANS: D   DIF: Easy   REF: 69   OBJ: 3.3

49. When Topaz comments on Azure's "blue eyes," Topaz is describing an example of a(n)
   a. karyotype.
   b. genotype.
   c. sex-linked trait.
   d. phenotype.

   ANS: D   DIF: Moderate   REF: 69   OBJ: 3.3

50. How many of the following (your height, your hair color, your way of thinking, your sex chromosomes) represent a phenotype?
   a. 1
   b. 2
   c. 3
   d. 4

   ANS: C   DIF: Difficult   REF: 69   OBJ: 3.3

51. It was noted in the text that the genetic "code" is best thought of as written in
   a. mud.
   b. stone.
   c. erasable pencil.
   d. indelible ink.

   ANS: C   DIF: Easy   REF: 70   OBJ: 3.3

52. The activation of a particular gene in a particular cell at a particular time of life is referred to as gene
   a. expression.
   b. migration.
   c. plasticity.
   d. pruning.

   ANS: A   DIF: Easy   REF: 70   OBJ: 3.3

53. Gene expression is affected by
   a. only genetic factors.
   b. only environmental factors.
   c. both genetic and environmental factors.
   d. neither genetic nor environmental factors.

   ANS: C   DIF: Easy   REF: 70   OBJ: 3.3

54. Fraga and colleagues (2005) study on aging and RNA in identical twins found that
   a. the pattern of genetic expression was nearly identical in both very young and older twins.
   b. the pattern of genetic expression was quite different in both very young and older twins.
   c. the pattern of genetic expression was nearly identical in very young twins but differed in older twins.
   d. the pattern of genetic expression differed in very young twins but was nearly identical in older twins.

   ANS: C   DIF: Moderate   REF: 70   OBJ: 3.3

55. The fact that Orson is extremely obese appears to be completely due to one pair of genes that he received (one from mom and one from dad). In this case, Orson's obesity is best explained by
   a. single gene-pair inheritance.
   b. polygenetic effects.
   c. dominant genes.
   d. sex-linked traits.

   ANS: A   DIF: Moderate   REF: 70   OBJ: 3.3

56. During his groundbreaking genetic work with peas, 19th-century monk Gregor Mendel found that dominant characteristics
    a. were uncommon in pea plants.
    b. appeared more often in later generations than opposite traits.
    c. resulted in very wrinkled peas.
    d. disappeared within a few generations.

    ANS: B   DIF: Moderate   REF: 70   OBJ: 3.3

57. If a person needs one matching pair of genes in order to express a characteristic carried by a pair of genes, the characteristic is considered
    a. recessive.   c. a mutation.
    b. dominant.   d. polygenic.

    ANS: A   DIF: Moderate   REF: 70   OBJ: 3.3
    KEY: WWW

58. Tongue-curling is a _____ trait.
    a. recessive   c. dominant
    b. polygenetic   d. incomplete dominance

    ANS: C   DIF: Easy   REF: 70-71   OBJ: 3.3

59. When a dominant gene is paired with a recessive gene, the characteristic associated with the dominant gene will be
    a. repressed.   c. expressed.
    b. absent.   d. dominated.

    ANS: C   DIF: Moderate   REF: 70-71   OBJ: 3.3

60. If blonde hair is dominant and designated as "B" and brunette hair is recessive and designated as "b," probability would predict that if a couple each with a "Bb" hair color genotype had four children, _____ would have blonde hair.
    a. 1   c. 3
    b. 2   d. 4

    ANS: C   DIF: Difficult   REF: 70-71   OBJ: 3.3

61. A human trait is influenced by a single pair of genes, with "T" representing the dominant gene and "t" representing the recessive gene. Joe (genotype Tt) and Meg (genotype Tt) decide to have children. According to the principles of Mendelian heredity, what percentage of their children would exhibit the trait?
    a. 25   c. 75
    b. 50   d. 100

    ANS: C   DIF: Difficult   REF: 70-71   OBJ: 3.3
    KEY: WWW

62. If green eyes are dominant and designated as "G" and gray eyes are recessive and designated as "g," probability would predict that if a couple each with a "Gg" eye color genotype had four children, _____ would have gray eyes.
a. 0
b. 1
c. 2
d. 4

ANS: B   DIF: Moderate   REF: 70-71   OBJ: 3.3

63. Incomplete dominance occurs when
a. a recessive gene overpowers a dominant gene.
b. there is a compromise between the effect of two genes.
c. a dominant gene overpowers a recessive gene.
d. genetic effects are overpowered by environmental factors.

ANS: B   DIF: Moderate   REF: 73   OBJ: 3.3

64. Olive has very red eyes, while her husband Skye has very blue eyes. Interestingly, their son's eyes are best described as purple. The eye color of their child best exemplifies the concept of
a. incomplete dominance.
b. mutation.
c. polygenic inheritance.
d. codominance.

ANS: A   DIF: Difficult   REF: 73   OBJ: 3.3

65. Children of black/white interracial marriages can have a skin tone that is somewhere between their mother's skin color and their father's skin color. This is an example of
a. incomplete dominance.
b. mutation.
c. polygenic inheritance.
d. codominance.

ANS: A   DIF: Moderate   REF: 73   OBJ: 3.3
KEY: WWW

66. The fact that type AB blood appears to be the result of a compromise between genes for type A and type B blood provides a good example of
a. incomplete dominance.
b. mutation.
c. polygenic inheritance.
d. codominance.

ANS: D   DIF: Moderate   REF: 73   OBJ: 3.3

67. Which is the best example of codominance?
a. When a yellow flower and a blue flower are crossed and produce a yellow and blue flower.
b. When a yellow flower and a blue flower are crossed and produce a green flower
c. When a yellow flower and a blue flower are crossed and produce a purely blue flower.
d. When a yellow flower and a blue flower are crossed and produce no flower.

ANS: A   DIF: Difficult   REF: 73   OBJ: 3.3

68. A sex-linked characteristic most likely involves a problem with the _____ chromosome.
a. X
b. 3rd
c. 17th
d. 21st

ANS: A   DIF: Easy   REF: 73   OBJ: 3.3

372

69. Michael is color blind. Whose genes caused this to happen?
    a. Only his father's genes
    b. Only his mother's genes
    c. Either of his parents' genes could have caused this
    d. Neither parent's genes, as color blindness is not inherited

    ANS: B   DIF: Easy   REF: 73   OBJ: 3.3

70. Color blindness and hemophilia are examples of
    a. chromosomal abnormalities.   c. polygenic inheritance.
    b. dominant inheritance.   d. sex-linked inheritance.

    ANS: D   DIF: Easy   REF: 73   OBJ: 3.3

71. As a hemophiliac, Charles has a deficiency in his blood's ability to
    a. form the desired round shape.   c. generate white cells.
    b. clot.   d. fight infections.

    ANS: B   DIF: Moderate   REF: 73   OBJ: 3.3

72. The key characteristic of polygenetic traits is that they ALWAYS involve
    a. a mutation.   c. multiple pairs of genes.
    b. sex cells.   d. recessive genes.

    ANS: C   DIF: Moderate   REF: 73   OBJ: 3.3
    KEY: WWW

73. Most complex human characteristics, such as personality and intelligence, are inherited via
    a. a single gene pair.   c. polygenic inheritance.
    b. sex-linked inheritance.   d. mutation of one or more genes.

    ANS: C   DIF: Moderate   REF: 73   OBJ: 3.3

74. As it suddenly appeared in the bloodline of the royal family of Europe, hemophilia is best explained in terms of
    a. polygenic inheritance.   c. sex-linked inheritance.
    b. chromosomal abnormalities.   d. a genetic mutation.

    ANS: D   DIF: Moderate   REF: 73   OBJ: 3.3

75. Marcia has just given birth to a baby girl. She is concerned because she is a carrier for hemophilia. Which of the following is true?
    a. Marcia has good cause for concern because hemophilia is most often transmitted to female offspring.
    b. Marcia has little cause for concern because hemophilia is most often transmitted to male offspring.
    c. Marcia has little cause for concern because hemophilia cannot be transmitted to offspring unless both parents are carriers.
    d. Marcia should not worry because hemophilia almost always skips a generation.

    ANS: B   DIF: Moderate   REF: 73   OBJ: 3.3

373

76. When looking at the unusual protrusion sticking out of a newborn's head, Dr. Natas says, "I am sure that the growth is due to some sudden change in the structure of the genes that was not passed on by the parents." This means that Dr. Natas suspects that the growth is due to
    a. mutation.
    b. some nutritional problem.
    c. a recessive gene.
    d. codominance.

    ANS: A   DIF: Difficult   REF: 73   OBJ: 3.3

77. What might make a physician suspect that the person from whom she has just drawn blood has sickle-cell disease?
    a. The blood is very dark in color
    b. There is an elevated DIF: of phenylalanine in the blood
    c. The blood cells are not round
    d. The blood cell each contain only 45 chromosomes

    ANS: C   DIF: Moderate   REF: 73   OBJ: 3.3

78. Sickle-cell disease likely arose as a mutation that was passed along because it protected individuals from
    a. hemophilia.
    b. malaria.
    c. diabetes.
    d. influenza.

    ANS: B   DIF: Moderate   REF: 73   OBJ: 3.3

79. Who is LEAST likely to have a chromosomal abnormality?
    a. Tom, who has a total of 22 pairs of chromosomes
    b. Dick, who has a total of 23 pairs of chromosomes
    c. Harry, who has a total of 24 pairs of chromosomes
    d. Sally, who has a total of 25 pairs of chromosomes

    ANS: B   DIF: Moderate   REF: 74   OBJ: 3.3
    KEY: WWW

80. Which disorder is the result of a chromosomal abnormality?
    a. Hemophilia
    b. Malaria
    c. Sickle-cell disease
    d. Down syndrome

    ANS: D   DIF: Moderate   REF: 74   OBJ: 3.3

81. Trisomy 21 is another name for a common form of
    a. Down syndrome.
    b. Duchenne's muscular dystrophy.
    c. Hemophilia.
    d. Tay-Sachs disease.

    ANS: A   DIF: Easy   REF: 74   OBJ: 3.3
    KEY: WWW

82. Maria gives birth to a child with trisomy 21. Which of the following is true?
    a. Maria must have given her child an extra 21st chromosome.
    b. The child's father must have given the child an extra 21st chromosome.
    c. The child received an extra 21st chromosome from either her mother or her father.
    d. Both parents contributed an extra 21st chromosome.

    ANS: C   DIF: Moderate   REF: 74   OBJ: 3.3

83. The odds of having a child with Down syndrome increase with maternal
    a. consumption of alcohol.
    b. exposure to mercury.
    c. age.
    d. weight.

    ANS: C   DIF: Easy   REF: 74   OBJ: 3.3

84. Meg was born with only one X chromosome. She is short, of average verbal intelligence, and lacking in spatial reasoning skills. Meg has
    a. Down syndrome.
    b. Tay-Sachs.
    c. Klinefelter syndrome.
    d. Turner syndrome.

    ANS: D   DIF: Moderate   REF: 75   OBJ: 3.3

85. Margo and John are told that their infant daughter has been diagnosed with Turner syndrome. Which of the following should they expect?
    a. Their daughter will die prior to reaching puberty.
    b. Their daughter will be very tall and large-breasted.
    c. Their daughter will most likely develop decidedly masculine tendencies.
    d. Their daughter will score below average on tests of mathematical reasoning.

    ANS: D   DIF: Moderate   REF: 75   OBJ: 3.3

86. Yao has an extra X chromosome. He is tall, sterile, and has enlarged breasts. Yao would be most accurately diagnosed as having
    a. Tay-Sachs.
    b. PKU.
    c. Klinefelter syndrome.
    d. Turner syndrome.

    ANS: C   DIF: Moderate   REF: 75   OBJ: 3.3

87. Tony and Tina can tell at birth that something is wrong with their son. Genetic tests indicate that the child has an extra chromosome in his cells and that chromosome is a sex chromosome. Which of the following does the child have?
    a. Klinefelter syndrome
    b. Down syndrome
    c. Hemophilia
    d. Turner syndrome

    ANS: A   DIF: Moderate   REF: 75   OBJ: 3.3
    KEY: WWW

88. Which of the following is an accurate comparison of people with Down syndrome and people with Klinefelter syndrome?
    a. They both have cells with 47 chromosomes, but the extra chromosome in Klinefelter syndrome is a sex chromosome and in Down syndrome it is one of the other chromosomes.
    b. They both have cells with 47 chromosomes, and in both cases it is an extra sex chromosome.
    c. There is an extra chromosome in Down syndrome, while there are fewer than the normal number of chromosomes in Klinefelter syndrome.
    d. There is an extra X chromosome in Klinefelter syndrome and a missing X chromosome in Down syndrome.

    ANS: A   DIF: Difficult   REF: 74-75   OBJ: 3.3

89. _____ is the most common hereditary cause of mental retardation.
    a. Turner syndrome   c. Klinefelter syndrome
    b. Fragile X syndrome   d. Down syndrome

    ANS: B   DIF: Moderate   REF: 75   OBJ: 3.3

90. Which statement concerning fragile X syndrome is true?
    a. It is a non-sex-linked trait.
    b. It occurs as the result of an extra X chromosome.
    c. It involves a depletion in the number of duplications in the DNA code.
    d. It is more common in males.

    ANS: D   DIF: Moderate   REF: 75   OBJ: 3.3

91. A service that provides potential parents with information on the risk of a child of theirs being born with an inherited disorder is called _____ counseling.
    a. genetic   c. gene therapy
    b. selective breeding   d. relational

    ANS: A   DIF: Easy   REF: 75   OBJ: 3.4

92. A individual inheriting _____ would have the SHORTEST life expectancy.
    a. Turner syndrome   c. Huntington's disease
    b. Tay-Sachs disease   d. Klinefelter's syndrome

    ANS: B   DIF: Difficult   REF: 76   OBJ: 3.4

93. Which statement concerning cystic fibrosis is true?
    a. It is caused by the presence of two dominant genes.
    b. The mutated gene causing cystic fibrosis may have protected individuals from deadly diarrhea.
    c. It is a sex-linked trait.
    d. It is best classified as a chromosome abnormality.

    ANS: B   DIF: Difficult   REF: 76   OBJ: 3.4

94. Diana and Phillip are in their late 20s. They are also Jewish and of Eastern European ancestry. They seek genetic counseling before they attempt to become pregnant. They are most likely concerned about the possibility of their child having
    a. PKU.   c. sickle-cell disease.
    b. hemophilia.   d. Tay-Sachs disease.

    ANS: D   DIF: Difficult   REF: 76   OBJ: 3.4

95. An individual who is a carrier of a trait has
    a. two dominant genes, both calling for the presence of the trait.
    b. two recessive genes, both calling for the presence of the trait.
    c. one dominant gene calling for the absence of the trait and one recessive gene calling for the presence of the trait.
    d. one dominant gene calling for the presence of the trait and one recessive gene calling for the absence of the trait.

    ANS: C   DIF: Moderate   REF: 76-77   OBJ: 3.4

96. Tony and Tina are both carriers of the same defective gene for a genetic disorder. As knowledgeable individuals, they know that each time they have a child there is a _____ risk that child will be a carrier for the disorder.
   a. 25 percent
   b. 50 percent
   c. 75 percent
   d. 100 percent

   ANS: B   DIF: Moderate   REF: 76   OBJ: 3.4
   KEY: WWW

97. Despite the fact that it is the result of recessive genes, some carriers of sickle-cell disease possess both normal and sickle-shaped blood cells. This phenomenon is best explained by
   a. polygenetic effects.
   b. meiosis.
   c. incomplete dominance.
   d. concordance rate.

   ANS: C   DIF: Moderate   REF: 76-77   OBJ: 3.4

98. If a physician wanted to get a visual image of a developing fetus' limbs, her best option would be to use a(n)
   a. preimplantation genetic diagnosis.
   b. ultrasound.
   c. chorionic villus sampling.
   d. amniocentesis.

   ANS: B   DIF: Moderate   REF: 78   OBJ: 3.4

99. When describing a recent medical procedure, Katrina says, "The worst part was the thought of that needle being stuck through my abdomen." Given this description, Katrina appears to have undergone a(n)
   a. maternal bOBJ:od sampling.
   b. preimplantation genetic diagnosis.
   c. amniocentesis.
   d. chorionic villus sampling.

   ANS: C   DIF: Moderate   REF: 78   OBJ: 3.4

100. When describing her last prenatal visit, Yang says, "They basically inserted a tube into my uterus via my vagina and took a tissue sample from the sack surrounding my fetus." Given this description, Yang appears to have undergone
   a. maternal blood sampling.
   b. preimplantation genetic diagnosis.
   c. amniocentesis.
   d. chorionic villus sampling.

   ANS: D   DIF: Difficult   REF: 78   OBJ: 3.4

101. Which type of prenatal testing is the LEAST invasive?
   a. Maternal blood sampling
   b. Gene therapy
   c. Chorionic villus sampling
   d. Amniocentesis

   ANS: A   DIF: Difficult   REF: 78   OBJ: 3.4

102. During a preimplantation genetic diagnosis, a(n)
   a. mother's blood is checked for pathogens.
   b. amniotic sac is punctured.
   c. fertilized egg is inspected.
   d. catheter is inserted.

   ANS: C   DIF: Moderate   REF: 78   OBJ: 3.4

103. If Huxley is ethically opposed to the creation of "designer babies" through DNA manipulation, he would likely be strongly opposed to
    a. maternal blood sampling.
    b. chorionic villus sampling.
    c. amniocentesis.
    d. preimplantation genetic diagnosis.

    ANS: D   DIF: Moderate   REF: 78   OBJ: 3.4

104. _____ involves conducting DNA tests on the first cells after the mitosis of a fertilized egg.
    a. Maternal blood sampling
    b. Chorionic villus sampling
    c. Amniocentesis
    d. Preimplantation genetic diagnosis

    ANS: D   DIF: Moderate   REF: 78   OBJ: 3.4
    KEY: WWW

105. Which procedure involves the assessment of cells that have passed through the placenta?
    a. Maternal blood sampling
    b. Preimplantation genetic diagnosis
    c. Amniocentesis
    d. Chorionic villus sampling

    ANS: A   DIF: Moderate   REF: 78   OBJ: 3.4

106. What makes Huntington's disease an unusual genetic disorder?
    a. It can be effectively treated through a blood transfusion.
    b. It is a sex-linked trait.
    c. It is found in females of Jewish decent.
    d. The genetic impact does not occur until a person reaches middle age.

    ANS: D   DIF: Moderate   REF: 77   OBJ: 3.4

107. Forty-year-old Chester has just begun to show symptoms indicating a deterioration of his nervous system. Chester most likely has
    a. Klinefelter syndrome.
    b. Cystic fibrosis.
    c. Turner syndrome.
    d. Huntington's disease.

    ANS: D   DIF: Moderate   REF: 77   OBJ: 3.4
    KEY: WWW

108. If one parent has the dominant gene for Huntington's disease, the odds of one of their children having the disease are one out of
    a. one.
    b. two.
    c. three.
    d. four.

    ANS: B   DIF: Easy   REF: 77   OBJ: 3.4

109. If you were being tested for Huntington's disease, the geneticist would focus on chromosome
    a. 4.
    b. 11.
    c. 18.
    d. 21.

    ANS: A   DIF: Difficult   REF: 77   OBJ: 3.4

110. Behavioral genetics is best described as the scientific study of how _____ impact development.
    a. genetics alone
    b. environmental factors alone
    c. genetic and environmental factors together
    d. non-genetic and non-environmental factors together

    ANS: C   DIF: Moderate   REF: 79   OBJ: 3.5

111. Heritability refers to
    a. how much of a trait is influenced by genetic factors for a specific individual.
    b. the proportion of the differences in a trait among a group of people that is due to genetic differences among these people.
    c. the percentage of pairs of people where, if one person in the pair has the trait in question, the other person in the pair also has the trait in question.
    d. the degree to which one trait increases with increases in another trait.

    ANS: B   DIF: Moderate   REF: 79   OBJ: 3.5

112. When looking at Fluffy the cat's family tree, Kitka notices that over several generations, owners have deliberately cultivated the characteristic of extremely black fur. This appears to have been accomplished by careful mating combinations in a process called
    a. mutation.   c. chorionic villus biopsy.
    b. selective breeding.   d. gene therapy.

    ANS: B   DIF: Moderate   REF: 79   OBJ: 3.5

113. When studying heritability in humans, an ethical behavior geneticist would be LEAST likely to
    a. study identical twins reared apart.
    b. compare the behavior of adopted children to their biological parents.
    c. conduct a selective breeding experiment.
    d. investigate the relationship between behaviors of unrelated siblings (step family members).

    ANS: C   DIF: Easy   REF: 79   OBJ: 3.5

114. Tryon's classic 1940 study on *maze bright* and *maze dull* rats demonstrated that maze learning
    a. varied by the age of the rat.   c. varied by the sex of the rat.
    b. was a totally learned behavior.   d. was influenced by genetics.

    ANS: D   DIF: Easy   REF: 79   OBJ: 3.5

379

115. Which one of the following sets of data would show a strong genetic influence on the development of a trait?
   a. Identical twins raised together score more similarly to one another than identical twins raised apart.
   b. Fraternal twins raised apart score as similarly to one another as do biological siblings who are raised together.
   c. Identical twins raised apart score more similarly to one another than fraternal twins raised together.
   d. Fraternal twins raised together score more similarly to one another than fraternal twins raised apart.

   ANS: C   DIF: Moderate   REF: 79   OBJ: 3.5
   KEY: WWW

116. Which is a common criticism of twin studies?
   a. Twin studies are better suited to identify environmental influences than genetic influences.
   b. Fraternal twins tend to be treated more similarly than identical twins.
   c. Twin studies overestimate the role of prenatal experiences on deveOBJ:pment.
   d. Similarity in environmental experiences, not genetic similarity, may be the more important contributor to the similarity seen in twins.

   ANS: D   DIF: Moderate   REF: 79   OBJ: 3.5

117. The logic behind adoption studies is that
   a. only personality factors can be inherited.
   b. if adopted children are similar to their adoptive parents on a given characteristic, then the expression of that characteristic is likely to be influenced by genetic factors.
   c. only physical factors can be inherited.
   d. if adopted children are similar to their adoptive parents on a given characteristic, then the expression of that characteristic is likely to be influenced by environmental factors.

   ANS: D   DIF: Moderate   REF: 79   OBJ: 3.5

118. A limitation of adoption studies is that they
   a. tend to be based on selective breeding research.
   b. need to recognize that adoptive homes tend to provide below-average environmental experiences.
   c. may underestimate the full range of environments experienced by a child.
   d. tend to take a long time to complete.

   ANS: C   DIF: Moderate   REF: 79-80   OBJ: 3.5

119. Which type of study would be most likely to compare unrelated siblings living in the same household?
   a. Selective breeding studies   c. Adoption studies
   b. Family studies   d. Twin studies

   ANS: B   DIF: Moderate   REF: 80   OBJ: 3.5

120. Your text reveals that if one identical twin is gay, there is almost a 50 percent chance that the other identical twin will also be gay. On the other hand, if a fraternal twin is schizophrenic, there is only about a 20 percent chance the other fraternal twin will be schizophrenic. The measure of likelihood that twins will share this mental illness in common is called a(n)
a. concordance rate.
b. correlation coefficient.
c. dominant trait.
d. heritability factor.

ANS: A   DIF: Moderate   REF: 80   OBJ: 3.6

121. A high concordance rate between identical twins for schizophrenia would suggest that the disorder
a. has a genetic basis.
b. is a life choice.
c. results from childhood experiences.
d. cannot be accurately studied.

ANS: A   DIF: Moderate   REF: 80   OBJ: 3.6

122. Research by Lomin and colleagues indicated that the highest heritability correlation concerning the emotion of anger was found between
a. identical twins raised together.
b. identical twins reared apart.
c. fraternal twins raised together.
d. fraternal twins reared apart.

ANS: A   DIF: Moderate   REF: 80   OBJ: 3.6

123. If genes alone contribute to a trait, which of the following patterns of correlations would be observed?
a. 1.00 for identical twins raised together but a lower correlation for those raised apart
b. 1.00 for both identical and fraternal twin pairs raised together but a lower correlation for those pairs raised apart
c. 1.00 for identical twins and .50 for fraternal twins raised together and raised apart
d. No significant correlation between identical twins or fraternal twins, regardless of whether they are raised together or apart

ANS: C   DIF: Moderate   REF: 80   OBJ: 3.6

124. If shared environmental influences alone contribute to the expression of a trait, which of the following patterns of correlations would be observed?
a. 1.00 for identical twins raised together but a somewhat lower correlation for those raised apart
b. 1.00 for both identical and fraternal twin pairs raised together but no correlation for those pairs raised apart
c. 1.00 for identical twins and .50 for fraternal twins raised together and raised apart
d. no significant correlation between identical twins or fraternal twins, regardless of whether they were raised together or apart

ANS: B   DIF: Moderate   REF: 80-81   OBJ: 3.6

125. The consistent parenting style exhibited by parents toward all their children would represent a _____ for the children.
    a. shared environmental experience
    b. genetic effect
    c. nonshared environmental experience
    d. crossing over effect

    ANS: A   DIF: Easy   REF: 80-81   OBJ: 3.6

126. Experiences unique to an individual and not experienced by other family members are referred to as
    a. shared environmental experience.
    b. genetic effect.
    c. nonshared environmental experience.
    d. crossing over effect.

    ANS: C   DIF: Easy   REF: 80-81   OBJ: 3.6
    KEY: WWW

127. Suppose identical twins raised apart have a correlation of .40 on a measure of some aspect of personality, and identical twins raised together have a correlation of .60 on this same measure. From these data, what can we logically conclude about this trait?
    a. Nonshared environment has an impact because, even raised together, the identical twins do not show a perfect 1.00 correlation.
    b. Nonshared environment has no impact because the identical twins raised apart have a lower correlation than the identical twins raised together.
    c. Shared environment has no impact because identical twins raised apart have a correlation lower than 1.00.
    d. Shared environment has an impact because identical twins raised apart have a correlation of .40.

    ANS: A   DIF: Moderate   REF: 81   OBJ: 3.6

128. Molecular genetics is best described as the study of the
    a. number of genes in a chromosome.
    b. molecular shape of a gene.
    c. first cellular division following conception.
    d. impact of particular genes on particular traits.

    ANS: D   DIF: Easy   REF: 81   OBJ: 3.6

129. The apolipoprotein E or apoE gene is associated with an increased risk for developing
    a. Down syndrome.
    b. Alzheimer's disease.
    c. Turner's syndrome.
    d. Huntington's disease.

    ANS: B   DIF: Moderate   REF: 82   OBJ: 3.6

130. Research from behavioral geneticists has found that as we get older, genetic influences on intelligence are _____ in importance, shared influences are _____ in importance, and nonshared environmental influences are _____ in importance.
    a. decreasing; decreasing; increasing
    b. decreasing; increasing; decreasing
    c. increasing; increasing; decreasing
    d. increasing; decreasing; increasing

    ANS: D   DIF: Moderate   REF: 81-82   OBJ: 3.7

131. Which environmental factor appears to have the greatest positive impact on the IQs of children?
    a. Having biological parents with very high IQs
    b. Having adoptive parents with very high IQs
    c. Being raised in a highly stimulating environment
    d. Being raised in a highly passive environment

    ANS: C   DIF: Easy   REF: 82-83   OBJ: 3.7

132. Which term is best defined as an infant's tendency to respond in predictable ways?
    a. Genotype   c. Codominance
    b. Temperament   d. Crossing over

    ANS: B   DIF: Easy   REF: 83   OBJ: 3.7

133. Which of the following statements is true regarding the effects of genes and environment on temperament and personality?
    a. Genes contribute little to no individual differences in temperament.
    b. Genes account for nearly all of the individual differences in temperament.
    c. Nonshared environmental influences contribute nothing to individual differences in temperament.
    d. The shared environment of the home does not appear to make siblings more similar in temperament or personality.

    ANS: D   DIF: Moderate   REF: 83   OBJ: 3.7

134. Which statement concerning schizophrenia is FALSE?
    a. It involves disturbed thinking and emotional expression.
    b. It has a concordance rate of about 98 percent for identical twins.
    c. It typically emerges in late adolescence or early adulthood.
    d. It is not caused by cold and inconsistent parenting.

    ANS: B   DIF: Moderate   REF: 84   OBJ: 3.7

135. If one or both biological parents have schizophrenia, we can conclude that their child will
    a. not develop the disorder as long as he or she is raised in a separate environment.
    b. definitely develop the disorder regardless of the environment.
    c. have a greater than average risk of developing the disorder in response to an environmental trigger.
    d. develop the disorder at a much younger age than another child who develops the disorder but has no family history of schizophrenia.

    ANS: C   DIF: Moderate   REF: 84-85   OBJ: 3.7

136. Some traits are more influenced by genetic factors than other traits, as reflected in the correlations between the traits of identical twins raised apart. Which one of the following series of traits is arranged from most to least heritable?
    a. Height, brain activity, IQ scores, creativity
    b. Brain activity, height, creativity, IQ scores
    c. Brain activity, IQ scores, height, creativity
    d. Height, creativity, IQ scores, brain activity

    ANS: A   DIF: Difficult   REF: 85   OBJ: 3.8

137. Which statement concerning heritability is true?
    a. Heritability explains more of the variation in IQ among children from poor families.
    b. Heritability is a fixed quality.
    c. Heritability differs by socioeconomic status but not by age.
    d. Heritability estimates differ by environment.

    ANS: D   DIF: Easy   REF: 85   OBJ: 3.8

138. Concerning depression,
    a. some genes predispose a person to depression but no genes protect from depression.
    b. some genes protect a person from depression but no genes predispose a person to depression.
    c. some genes protect a person from depression and others predispose a person to depression.
    d. no genes protect a person from depression and no genes predispose a person to depression.

    ANS: C   DIF: Moderate   REF: 87   OBJ: 3.9

139. The belief that genotype expression depends on environmental experience and how we respond to the environment depends on the genes we possess defines the concept of
    a. single gene-pair inheritance.   c. gene-environment interaction.
    b. shared environmental influence.   d. polygenetic inheritance.

    ANS: C   DIF: Easy   REF: 87   OBJ: 3.9

140. Which does NOT belong on a list of the basic types of gene-environment correlations?
    a. Active genotype-environment   c. Passive genotype-environment
    b. Evocative genotype-environment   d. Negative genotype-environment

    ANS: D   DIF: Easy   REF: 87-88   OBJ: 3.10

141. Laurie is a shy child who avoids social gatherings and seeks out solitary activities such as stamp collecting and reading a good book. Laurie's development will be influenced by this pattern of behavior. In terms of genetic-environmental, this example best illustrates a(n)
    a. active genotype-environment.   c. passive genotype-environment.
    b. evocative genotype-environment.   d. negative genotype-environment.

    ANS: A   DIF: Moderate   REF: 88   OBJ: 3.10

142. Baby Gerber smiles and coos so often and is so delightful that his parents feel compelled to smile and chatter right back at him. Which sort of genetic environmental does this best illustrate?
   a. Active genotype-environment
   b. Evocative genotype-environment .
   c. Passive genotype-environment
   d. Negative genotype-environment

   ANS: B   DIF: Moderate   REF: 88   OBJ: 3.10

143. The fact that parents provide their children with both their genes and an environment that is impacted by their own genetic make-up defines the gene-environment correlation of
   a. active genotype-environment.
   b. evocative genotype-environment.
   c. passive genotype-environment.
   d. negative genotype-environment.

   ANS: C   DIF: Moderate   REF: 88   OBJ: 3.10
   KEY: WWW

144. _____ gene-interactions become increasingly important as we age.
   a. Passive
   b. Evocative
   c. Active
   d. No

   ANS: C   DIF: Moderate   REF: 88   OBJ: 3.10

145. What was the main point made by Reiss et al., (2000) in the text *The Relationship Code*?
   a. Genes make females more relationship oriented.
   b. Genes have no impact on complex human behavior like relationships.
   c. Genes explain virtually all of what we are.
   d. Genes and family environment both significantly influence development.

   ANS: D   DIF: Moderate   REF: 89   OBJ: 3.10

146. Special diets can be used to diminish the likelihood of brain damage in individuals with
   a. phenylketonuria (PKU).
   b. cystic fibrosis.
   c. Tay-Sachs disease.
   d. Huntington's disease.

   ANS: A   DIF: Difficult   REF: 90   OBJ: 3.11

147. Oswald hears his doctor say that he plans to treat Oswald's cystic fibrosis using an aerosol spray to deliver normal genes to the lungs. This treatment is best categorized as
   a. chorionic villus sampling.
   b. preimplantation genetic diagnosis .
   c. amniocentesis.
   d. gene therapy.

   ANS: D   DIF: Difficult   REF: 90   OBJ: 3.11

148. What makes stem cells so special?
   a. They are the largest cell produced by the body
   b. They can divide an unlimited number of times
   c. They have the potential to develop into many different types of specialized cells
   d. They are the only cells found in the immune system

   ANS: C   DIF: Difficult   REF: 90   OBJ: 3.11

149. A common criticism of genetic research is that
    a.   chromosomal aberrations cannot be accurately identified.
    b.   no single gene has been shown to impact behavior.
    c.   it tells us too little about epigenesist.
    d.   it is too reliant on conditioned learning processes.

ANS: C   DIF: Moderate   REF: 89-91   OBJ: 3.11

TRUE/FALSE

1.   Species heredity is very important to our understanding of individual differences in human growth and development.

    ANS: F   DIF: Moderate   REF: 64   OBJ: 3.1

2.   Some genes aid in adaptation more than others.

    ANS: T   DIF: Easy   REF: 65   OBJ: 3.1

3.   Genes are made up of chromosomes.

    ANS: F   DIF: Moderate   REF: 66-67   OBJ: 3.2
    KEY: WWW

4.   The process of mitosis results in daughter cells that have half the number of cells as the original one.

    ANS: F   DIF: Moderate   REF: 67-68   OBJ: 3.2

5.   The process of meiosis results in the development of cells that have half the number of cells as the original one.

    ANS: T   DIF: Moderate   REF: 66   OBJ: 3.2
    KEY: WWW

6.   Fraternal twins are no more alike genetically than brothers and sisters born at different times.

    ANS: T   DIF: Moderate   REF: 68   OBJ: 3.2

7.   Phenotype represents the characteristics expressed by an individual.

    ANS: T   DIF: Easy   REF: 69   OBJ: 3.3

8.   In cases of incomplete dominance, a dominant trait is expressed but its recessive counterpart is not expressed.

    ANS: F   DIF: Moderate   REF: 73   OBJ: 3.3
    KEY: WWW

9.   A polygenetic effect is due to the actions of a single pair of genes.

    ANS: F   DIF: Easy   REF: 73   OBJ: 3.3

10. A typical child with Down syndrome will have cells with 47 chromosomes.

    ANS: T   DIF: Easy   REF: 74   OBJ: 3.3

11. An individual with Turner's syndrome has one X chromosome and no Y chromosome.

    ANS: T   DIF: Moderate   REF: 75   OBJ: 3.3

12. If Marty has an XXY chromosome pattern, he would be accurately diagnosed with Klinefelter syndrome.

    ANS: T   DIF: Moderate   REF: 75   OBJ: 3.3
    KEY: WWW

13. During an amniocentesis, a catheter is inserted into the mother's vagina and cervix.

    ANS: F   DIF: Moderate   REF: 78   OBJ: 3.4

14. Concordance rates show the likelihood that if one member of a pair has a particular trait, the other member of the pair also has it.

    ANS: T   DIF: Easy   REF: 80   OBJ: 3.6

15. Shared environmental influences are those common to members of a family.

    ANS: T   DIF: Easy   REF: 80-81   OBJ: 3.6

16. Schizophrenia appears to be the result of possessing an apoE gene.

    ANS: F   DIF: Moderate   REF: 82   OBJ: 3.6

17. The heritability of IQ scores appears to increase between infancy and adulthood.

    ANS: T   DIF: Moderate   REF: 82-83   OBJ: 3.7

18. Concerning mental illness, people appear to inherit a predisposition for a disorder, not the actual disorder.

    ANS: T   DIF: Moderate   REF: 84-85   OBJ: 3.7
    KEY: WWW

19. In an active gene-environment interaction, children's genetically based traits provoke a certain kind of reaction from their environment.

    ANS: F   DIF: Moderate   REF: 88   OBJ: 3.10

20. Some researchers believe that techniques for calculating heritability attribute too much importance to genes.

    ANS: T   DIF: Moderate   REF: 91   OBJ: 3.11

387

COMPLETION

1. I am the initial organism created by the fertilization of an egg by a sperm. I am called the
   _____.

   ANS: zygote

   DIF: Moderate   REF: 66   OBJ: 3.2

2. The cells of a normal zygote consist of a total of _____ chromosomes.

   ANS: 46

   DIF: Easy   REF: 66   OBJ: 3.2

3. The process by which a zygote initially becomes a multiple-celled organism is called _____.

   ANS: mitosis

   DIF: Moderate   REF: 66-67   OBJ: 3.2

4. Human chromosomes appear to contain about 25,000 _____.

   ANS: genes

   DIF: Difficult   REF: 67   OBJ: 3.2   KEY: WWW

5. Of the two sex chromosomes, the _____ chromosome, carries the fewest genes.

   ANS: Y

   DIF: Moderate   REF: 69   OBJ: 3.2

6. A genotype is a person's genetic make-up, while a _____ are the actual traits he or she
   expresses.

   ANS: phenotype

   DIF: Moderate   REF: 69   OBJ: 3.3   KEY: WWW

7. Howdy has inherited a recessive gene that causes freckles and a dominant gene that prevents
   freckle formation. Despite this fact, Howdy's genetic makeup results in him having a few
   freckles. Howdy's freckles are best explained by the process of _____ dominance.

   ANS: incomplete

   DIF: Moderate   REF: 73   OBJ: 3.3

388

8. Characteristics that result from the influence of multiple pairs of genes are called _____ traits.

    ANS: polygenetic

    DIF: Easy   REF: 73   OBJ: 3.3

9. A change in the structure or arrangement of one or more genes that produces a new phenotype is called a _____.

    ANS: mutation

    DIF: Moderate   REF: 73   OBJ: 3.4

10. _____disease appears to have developed as a mutation that helped protect people from malaria.

    ANS: Sickle-cell

    DIF: Moderate   REF: 73 & 76   OBJ: 3.3

11. _____ syndrome is also known as trisomy 21.

    ANS: Down

    DIF: Moderate   REF: 74   OBJ: 3.3

12. _____ syndrome is the most common hereditary cause of mental retardation.

    ANS: Fragile X

    DIF: Difficult   REF: 75   OBJ: 3.3   KEY: WWW

13. An individual who has the ability to transmit a recessive trait to his children but who does not actually express the trait, is called a _____.

    ANS: carrier

    DIF: Moderate   REF: 76   OBJ: 3.3

14. During an _____, a needle is inserted through a pregnant woman's abdomen and a sample of fluid containing cells shed by the fetus are extracted.

    ANS: amniocentesis

    DIF: Moderate   REF: 78   OBJ: 3.4

15. During a _____ genetic diagnosis, the first cells from a fertilized egg are examined for genetic defects.

    ANS: preimplantation

    DIF: Moderate   REF: 78   OBJ: 3.4   KEY: WWW

389

16. Tyron (1940) was able to create *maze bright* rats using the process of selective _____.

    ANS: breeding

    DIF: Moderate   REF: 79   OBJ: 3.5

17. Experiences unique to an individual are referred to as _____ environmental influences.

    ANS: nonshared

    DIF: Moderate   REF: 81   OBJ: 3.6

18. An _____ gene-environment relationship exists when a child's genotype causes him or her to seek out some specific environment.

    ANS: active

    DIF: Moderate   REF: 88   OBJ: 3.10

19. An _____ gene-environment relationship exists when a child's genotype elicits specific reactions from others.

    ANS: evocative

    DIF: Moderate   REF: 88   OBJ: 3.10   KEY: WWW

20. _____ cells have the unique ability to become many different types of specialized cells.

    ANS: Stem

    DIF: Moderate   REF: 90   OBJ: 3.11

ESSAY

1. Provide insight into human reproduction by comparing and contrasting meiosis with mitosis, zygote with ovum, and the X chromosome with the Y chromosome.

   ANS: Answer not provided   REF: 66-69   OBJ: 3.2

2. Differentiate genotype from phenotype using yourself as an example.

   ANS: Answer not provided   REF: 69-70   OBJ: 3.2

3. Compare and contrast Down syndrome, Turner syndrome, and Klinefelter's syndrome.

   ANS: Answer not provided   REF: 74-75   OBJ: 3.4

4. Three friends have just told you they were recently diagnosed with genetic disorders. One has PKU, one has Tay-Sachs disease, and the other has Huntington's disease. None of them knows anything about these disorders. Please explain to each how they got the disease and their general prognosis (i.e., how will the disorder affect them in the future?).

   ANS: Answer not provided   REF: 75-77   OBJ: 3.4

5. Why do children growing up in the same home often turn out to be quite different from one another?

   ANS: Answer not provided   REF: 80-81   OBJ: 3.6

6. What would be the strongest piece of evidence you could gather to show that genetic factors influence personality?

   ANS: Answer not provided   REF: 83-85   OBJ: 3.7

7. Compare and contrast passive gene-environment correlations, evocative gene-environmental correlations, and active gene-environmental correlations.

   ANS: Answer not provided   REF: 87-88   OBJ: 3.10

8. Describe and give an example of a recessive and a dominant gene. Then differentiate between incomplete dominance and codominance.

   ANS: Answer not provided   REF: 70-71   OBJ: 3.3   KEY: WWW

9. Discuss three different techniques for detecting prenatal abnormalities. Be sure to identify the strengths and weaknesses of each technique.

   ANS: Answer not provided   REF: 78   OBJ: 3.4

10. How would you design a study to determine the contributions of genes, shared environment, and nonshared environment on alcoholism?

    ANS: Answer not provided   REF: 80-81   OBJ: 3.6   KEY: WWW

MULTIPLE CHOICE

1. Ovulation tends to occur _____ of the menstrual cycle.
   a. on the first day
   b. within the first week
   c. near the midpoint
   d. at the end

   ANS: C   DIF: Moderate   REF: 96   OBJ: 4.1

2. Conception results in the immediate creation of a(n)
   a. embryo.
   b. neonate.
   c. fetus.
   d. zygote.

   ANS: D   DIF: Easy   REF: 96   OBJ: 4.1
   KEY: WWW

3. A fertile male will deposit about 300 _____ sperm during intercourse.
   a. thousand
   b. million
   c. billion
   d. trillion

   ANS: B   DIF: Moderate   REF: 96   OBJ: 4.1

4. Infertility is defined as inability to become pregnant after
   a. being off birth control for two months.
   b. previously giving birth.
   c. one year of trying.
   d. artificial insemination.

   ANS: C   DIF: Easy   REF: 96   OBJ: 4.1

5. Everett has been informed that his has infertility issues. As he is seeing a competent doctor, what bit of advice should he most likely hear?
   a. You need to cut down on your red meat consumption.
   b. You need to lose your underwear and go without for a few months.
   c. You need to increase your intake of folic acid.
   d. You need to start taking your thalidomide prescription.

   ANS: B   DIF: Moderate   REF: 96-97   OBJ: 4.1

6. The most common first medical step in assisted reproductive technology is to have a women take a drug that
   a. increases the size of her cervix.
   b. straightens the lining of her fallopian tubes.
   c. decreases her testosterone levels.
   d. stimulates the ovaries to ripen and release eggs.

   ANS: D   DIF: Moderate   REF: 97   OBJ: 4.1

7. During artificial insemination, the sperm
   a. can only come from a woman's partner.
   b. can only come from a donor.
   c. can come from either the woman's partner or a donor.
   d. must come from neither the woman's partner nor a donor.

   ANS: C   DIF: Moderate   REF: 97   OBJ: 4.1
   KEY: WWW

8. José is quite knowledgeable about ARTs, thus when he is informed that his friend's new baby was conceived in a laboratory dish, he knows that this process had to involve
   a. in vitro fertilization.   c. a donor egg.
   b. artificial insemination.   d. multiple births.

   ANS: A   DIF: Moderate   REF: 97   OBJ: 4.1

9. Which statement concerning ARTs is true?
   a. The cost of most IVF pregnancies is comparable to that of a typical pregnancy.
   b. Most couples who are unable to become pregnant using ART experience major depression.
   c. For women over age 42, the odds of a live birth following ART are about 1 in 10.
   d. Fathers of ART infants tend to be less attached to their children.

   ANS: C   DIF: Moderate   REF: 97   OBJ: 4.1

10. The three periods of prenatal development are (from earliest to latest)
    a. germinal, embryonic, fetal.   c. fetus, latency, germinal.
    b. latency, germinal, embryo.   d. embryo, germinal, fetus.

    ANS: A   DIF: Moderate   REF: 97-99   OBJ: 4.1

11. On average, the germinal period ends about _____ days after conception.
    a. 4   c. 24
    b. 14   d. 48

    ANS: B   DIF: Moderate   REF: 97   OBJ: 4.1

12. The germinal period ends when the
    a. blastocyst burrows into the lining of the chorion.
    b. blastocyst is implanted in the wall of the uterus.
    c. zygote divides into two cells through mitosis.
    d. zygote travels through the fallopian tube into the uterus.

    ANS: B   DIF: Moderate   REF: 97   OBJ: 4.1
    KEY: WWW

13. I am the hollow ball of cells formed in the days just after conception. Technically, I am referred to as the
    a. blastocyst.   c. uvula.
    b. embryo.   d. chorion.

    ANS: A   DIF: Moderate   REF: 97   OBJ: 4.1

394

14. About _____ percent of recognized pregnancies end in miscarriage, while about _____ percent of unrecognized pregnancies suffer the same fate.
   a. 20; 80
   b. 50; 50
   c. 80; 20
   d. 20; 50

   ANS: D   DIF: Difficult   REF: 97   OBJ: 4.1

15. About _____ of all fertilized ova are successfully implanted in the uterus.
   a. one fifth
   b. one fourth
   c. one third
   d. one half

   ANS: D   DIF: Moderate   REF: 97   OBJ: 4.1

16. The _____ period of prenatal existence technically begins with implantation into the uterus.
   a. germinal
   b. embryonic
   c. fetal
   d. zygotic

   ANS: B   DIF: Moderate   REF: 97   OBJ: 4.1

17. Natalie is six weeks pregnant. At this point, the organism growing inside of her is most properly referred to as a(n)
   a. blastula.
   b. embryo.
   c. fetus.
   d. zygote.

   ANS: B   DIF: Moderate   REF: 97   OBJ: 4.1

18. All major organs initially develop in some fashion during the _____ period.
   a. germinal
   b. zygotic
   c. fetal
   d. embryonic

   ANS: D   DIF: Moderate   REF: 97   OBJ: 4.1

19. While observing developing cells, Dr. House shouts, "I am seeing actual organogenesis taking place!" In simple terms, Dr. House is viewing
   a. meiosis.
   b. the formation of a blastula.
   c. the initial formation of major body organs.
   d. a breech presentation.

   ANS: C   DIF: Moderate   REF: 97   OBJ: 4.1

20. The outer layer of the embryo forms the
   a. amnion and chorion.
   b. placenta and umbilical cord.
   c. brain and spinal cord of the fetus.
   d. heart and internal organs.

   ANS: A   DIF: Difficult   REF: 97   OBJ: 4.1

21. The function of the amnion is to
    a. connect the placenta to the developing fetus.
    b. provide a cushion of protection for the developing embryo.
    c. provide nutrients and oxygen to the developing embryo.
    d. remove waste products from the developing fetus.

    ANS: B   DIF: Moderate   REF: 97   OBJ: 4.1
    KEY: WWW

22. An embryo is directly nourished by root-like extensions from the
    a. amnion.   c. blastula.
    b. chorionic villi.   d. zygote.

    ANS: B   DIF: Difficult   REF: 97   OBJ: 4.1

23. The lining of the _____ originates as tissue called the chorion.
    a. amnion   c. blastula
    b. placenta   d. zygote

    ANS: B   DIF: Difficult   REF: 97   OBJ: 4.1

24. The umbilical cord connects the
    a. amnion and chorion.   c. heart and lungs.
    b. blastula and zygote.   d. embryo and placenta.

    ANS: D   DIF: Difficult   REF: 97   OBJ: 4.1

25. In her human development class, Dr. Ayers shows students several photographs of prenatal
    development. She points out the placenta and explains that its main purpose is to
    a. provide the fetus with carbon dioxide and oxygen.
    b. enable the maternal and fetal blood to mix so they will become compatible.
    c. provide the fetus with oxygen and nutrients and remove carbon dioxide and wastes
       from the fetus.
    d. protect and cushion the fetus from shock.

    ANS: C   DIF: Difficult   REF: 97   OBJ: 4.1

26. What is the most important factor in determining what crosses the "placental barrier"?
    a. The size of a molecule   c. The shape of the molecule
    b. The age of the fetus   d. The age of the mother

    ANS: A   DIF: Difficult   REF: 97   OBJ: 4.1

27. The formation of a primitive heart would take place during the _____ period of development.
    a. zygotic   c. fetal
    b. germinal   d. embryonic

    ANS: D   DIF: Moderate   REF: 97-98   OBJ: 4.1
    KEY: WWW

28. The brain first becomes apparent around four weeks after conception when the neural _____ folds up to form the neural _____.
    a. plate; tube
    b. tube; cup
    c. cup; spike
    d. spike; tube

    ANS: A   DIF: Difficult   REF: 98   OBJ: 4.1

29. _____ occurs when the neural tube fails to close and the spinal cord is not encased in the spinal column.
    a. Spinal meningitis
    b. Anencephaly
    c. Spina bifida
    d. Encephalocele

    ANS: C   DIF: Moderate   REF: 98   OBJ: 4.1

30. Due to her accurate knowledge of prenatal physiology, Amber knows that since her unborn child suffers from anencephaly, the child will be born with
    a. an exposed spinal cord.
    b. a brain protruding from its skull.
    c. fluid on the brain.
    d. no developed brain above the brain stem.

    ANS: D   DIF: Moderate   REF: 98   OBJ: 4.1

31. Spina bifida is best described as a defect of the _____ of the neural tube, while anencephaly is best described as a defect of the _____ of the neural tube.
    a. top; bottom
    b. bottom; top
    c. inside; outside
    d. outside; inside

    ANS: B   DIF: Moderate   REF: 98   OBJ: 4.1

32. A deficiency in maternal levels of _____ during early pregnancy has been linked to a risk for neural tube disorders.
    a. vitamin A
    b. calcium
    c. folic acid
    d. iron

    ANS: C   DIF: Moderate   REF: 98   OBJ: 4.1

33. By secreting the hormone _____, the male embryo stimulates the development of a male reproductive system.
    a. estrogen
    b. teratogen
    c. surfactant
    d. testosterone

    ANS: D   DIF: Easy   REF: 98   OBJ: 4.1

34. In order for an embryo to construct testes, that embryo must have at least _____ at conception.
    a. one X chromosome
    b. two X chromosomes
    c. one Y chromosome
    d. two Y chromosomes

    ANS: C   DIF: Moderate   REF: 98   OBJ: 4.1

35. In a normally developing XY-chromosome embryo, the absence of testosterone would
    a. result in the complete absence of either a "male" or "female" reproductive system.
    b. result in a "male" baby with a "female" internal reproductive system.
    c. result in a "female" baby with a "male" internal reproductive system.
    d. not have any impact on reproductive development.

    ANS: B   DIF: Difficult   REF: 98   OBJ: 4.1

36. Sexual differentiation (due to hormonal activity) first begins during the _____ period of development.
    a. conception   c. fetal
    b. germinal   d. embryonic

    ANS: D   DIF: Moderate   REF: 98   OBJ: 4.1
    KEY: WWW

37. Which statement about development in the embryonic stage of development is true?
    a. The placental barrier first forms during this stage of development.
    b. The eyes and nose take shape at this time of development, but the ears form much later.
    c. The heart forms but is not yet beating.
    d. At this end of this period, the organism is about 10 inches long.

    ANS: B   DIF: Moderate   REF: 98-99   OBJ: 4.1

38. The fetal period is best defined as
    a. the middle three months of pregnancy.
    b. all of the pregnancy that follows the implantation of the blastula in the uterine wall.
    c. the part of the pregnancy that extends from the age of viability to birth.
    d. the period from the ninth week of pregnancy to birth.

    ANS: D   DIF: Moderate   REF: 99   OBJ: 4.1

39. Morgana is now 25 weeks pregnant. At this point, the organism growing inside of her would best be classified as a(n)
    a. blastula.   c. fetus.
    b. embryo.   d. zygote.

    ANS: C   DIF: Moderate   REF: 99   OBJ: 4.1
    KEY: WWW

40. One of the main roles of glial cells is to
    a. provide support for neurons.   c. create a functioning respiratory system.
    b. produce the spinal cord.   d. determine the sex of a fetus.

    ANS: A   DIF: Difficult   REF: 99   OBJ: 4.1

41. When a brain cell differentiates, it
    a. doubles in size.
    b. pairs up with a glial cell.
    c. takes on a specialized purpose.
    d. reaches it age of viability .

    ANS: C   DIF: Difficult   REF: 99   OBJ: 4.1

42. The key to determining the functioning of a new neuron appears to be
    a. the shape of the cell.
    b. where the cell migrates.
    c. the amount of testosterone in the cell.
    d. the genetic make-up of the cell.

    ANS: B   DIF: Difficult   REF: 99   OBJ: 4.1
    KEY: WWW

43. If a cell can be transplanted into any area of the body where it will take on the function of other cells in that area, that cell is most likely a _____ cell.
    a. glial
    b. myelin
    c. stem
    d. renal

    ANS: C   DIF: Easy   REF: 99   OBJ: 4.1

44. The reason that stem cells hold potential promise for treatment of disorders like Parkinson's and diabetes is that these cells
    a. divide uncontrollably.
    b. are not yet specialized.
    c. have already undergone migration.
    d. cannot mutate.

    ANS: B   DIF: Moderate   REF: 99   OBJ: 4.1

45. Dominique is told that her unborn child has bones, distinguishable sex organs, and may be turning somersaults. This description indicates that Dominique's unborn child is best classified as a(n)
    a. zygote.
    b. embryo.
    c. fetus.
    d. neonate.

    ANS: C   DIF: Easy   REF: 99-101   OBJ: 4.1

46. Maria, who just found out she is pregnant, wonders at what point her baby will be able to hear. A competent doctor would tell her that her baby's sensory organs
    a. begin to function during the embryonic phase.
    b. will be functioning by the end of the second trimester.
    c. do not function prior to the eighth or ninth month of pregnancy.
    d. will not function prior to birth.

    ANS: B   DIF: Difficult   REF: 101   OBJ: 4.1

47. The term "age of viability" refers to the point at which
    a. a child will definitely survive if born.
    b. survival outside the uterus might be possible.
    c. the embryo no longer requires oxygen from its mother.
    d. the heart starts beating.

    ANS: B   DIF: Moderate   REF: 101   OBJ: 4.1

48. Who has just reached the current "age of viability" for a human?
    a. Ben, who has survived 6 weeks past conception
    b. Hoss, who has survived 12 weeks past conception
    c. Joe, who has survived 23 weeks past conception
    d. Adam, who has survived 30 weeks past conception

    ANS: C   DIF: Moderate   REF: 101   OBJ: 4.1
    KEY: WWW

49. As of 2007, the most premature infant to survive weighed _____ when she was born.
    a. 2 ounces   c. 20 ounces
    b. 10 ounces   d. 100 ounces

    ANS: B   DIF: Difficult   REF: 101   OBJ: 4.1

50. The seventh month of a human pregnancy would fall in the _____ trimester of that pregnancy.
    a. first   c. third
    b. second   d. fourth

    ANS: C   DIF: Easy   REF: 101   OBJ: 4.1

51. Myelin improves a neuron's ability to transmit by
    a. providing an insulating cover to the neuron.
    b. increasing the number of neurons.
    c. assisting in the migration of neurons to their proper location.
    d. organizing neurons into specific areas of the cortex (e.g.. the auditory cortex).

    ANS: A   DIF: Moderate   REF: 101   OBJ: 4.1

52. Coherent patterns of waking and sleeping are known as infant
    a. states.   c. protective factors.
    b. trimesters.   d. methods.

    ANS: A   DIF: Easy   REF: 101   OBJ: 4.2
    KEY: WWW

53. Sunny is a 20-week-old fetus. Sol is a 32-week-old fetus. If they were both normally developing fetuses, one would expect that Sol would _____ than Sunny.
    a. have a significantly less surfactant
    b. spend less time in distinct states of activity
    c. have significantly less myelin
    d. spend significantly more time in the distinct state of being awake

    ANS: D   DIF: Moderate   REF: 101-102   OBJ: 4.2

54. By the end the fetal period, fetuses spend the majority of their time
    a. in no distinct state.   c. conserving energy in anticipation of birth.
    b. snoozing.   d. intentionally moving.

    ANS: B   DIF: Moderate   REF: 101   OBJ: 4.2

55. Research on infant states shows that
  a. these develop soon after birth.
  b. there is a marked shift at birth from sleep states to waking states.
  c. fetuses who spend a lot of time in active states tend to be active as infants.
  d. infants who were born prematurely do not develop predictable states.

  ANS: C   DIF: Moderate   REF: 102   OBJ: 4.2

56. Which best describes the "fetal position?"
  a. Head up, limbs stretched out   c. Head down, limbs stretched out
  b. Head up, limbs curled in   d. Head down, limbs curled in

  ANS: D   DIF: Moderate   REF: 102   OBJ: 4.2

57. Your psychology professor asks you to write a paper on the prenatal environment. Which search topic should you use for your Web search?
  a. The mother's womb   c. The process of birth
  b. The hospital birthing room   d. The newborn's crib

  ANS: A   DIF: Moderate   REF: 102   OBJ: 4.3

58. In the United States, until the 1940s, it was widely believed that _____ was/were able to protect the developing fetus from the effects of viruses and nicotine.
  a. teratogens   c. maternal exercise
  b. thalidomide   d. the placenta

  ANS: D   DIF: Moderate   REF: 102-103   OBJ: 4.3

59. A teratogen is best defined as
  a. any medication taken during labor and delivery.
  b. anything that can cross the placental barrier.
  c. any drug, disease, or environmental agent that causes a birth defect.
  d. a birth defect caused by genetic abnormalities.

  ANS: C   DIF: Easy   REF: 103   OBJ: 4.3

60. Which of the following is true?
  a. The quality of a postnatal environment has little impact on the effect of a teratogen.
  b. The genetic makeup of a fetus can influence the impact of a teratogen.
  c. The effects of a teratogen do not appear to be related to the "dose" received.
  d. An organ system is least vulnerable to the effects of a teratogen when it is developing rapidly.

  ANS: B   DIF: Moderate   REF: 103   OBJ: 4.3

61. The time of rapid growth of an organ system is called its _____ period.
  a. critical   c. resilience
  b. germinal   d. prenatal

  ANS: A   DIF: Moderate   REF: 103   OBJ: 4.3

62. Which organism is most vulnerable to organ systems damage?
 a. The blastula   c. The fetus
 b. The embryo   d. The zygote

 ANS: B   DIF: Moderate   REF: 103   OBJ: 4.3

63. While under a doctor's care prescription drugs are _____ safe.
 a. never   c. usually
 b. sometimes   d. always

 ANS: C   DIF: Moderate   REF: 103   OBJ: 4.3

64. Why would a pregnant woman be most likely to have taken thalidomide?
 a. She had morning sickness.   c. She was having trouble sleeping.
 b. She wanted to lose weight.   d. To get pregnant (it is a fertility drug).

 ANS: A   DIF: Moderate   REF: 103   OBJ: 4.3

65. Myrna started taking the drug thalidomide in her sixth month of pregnancy. Chances are her baby will
 a. be mentally retarded.   c. have deformed or missing limbs.
 b. have heart problems.   d. suffer no harmful effects.

 ANS: D   DIF: Difficult   REF: 103   OBJ: 4.3

66. Which teratogen would most likely result in a baby being born with a missing limb?
 a. Thalidomide   c. Rubella
 b. Alcohol   d. Syphilis

 ANS: A   DIF: Moderate   REF: 103-104   OBJ: 4.3
 KEY: WWW

67. Although it is associated with the development of birth defects, Thalidomide is currently used to treat all of the following EXCEPT
 a. leprosy.   c. tuberculosis.
 b. morning sickness.   d. forms of cancer.

 ANS: B   DIF: Moderate   REF: 104   OBJ: 4.3

68. Virginia smoked heavily throughout her pregnancy. Her husband was very worried about this because of the possible effects on his unborn child. Which of the following is the most likely outcome that he should be concerned about?
 a. The child's low birth weight   c. Visual impairment
 b. Missing limbs   d. Attention deficit disorder

 ANS: A   DIF: Moderate   REF: 104-105   OBJ: 4.3

69. On an average day, Jenna smokes about 24 cigarettes and has done so throughout her pregnancy. Consequently, she has put her baby at increased risk for all of the following EXCEPT
 a. hearing levels.   c. central nervous system impairment.
 b. growth retardation.   d. susceptibility to respiratory infection.

 ANS: A   DIF: Moderate   REF: 104-105   OBJ: 4.3

402

70. When baby Hughie was put down for his afternoon nap, he seemed in good health. While sleeping, Hughie's breathing stopped and he died. What is the best explanation for Hughie's death?
    a. AIDS
    b. PKU
    c. FAS
    d. SIDS

    ANS: D   DIF: Moderate   REF: 105   OBJ: 4.3

71. Which maternal behavior places an infant at risk for sudden infant death syndrome?
    a. Smoking cigarettes
    b. Alcohol consumption
    c. Exposure to rubella
    d. Using Thalidomide

    ANS: A   DIF: Easy   REF: 105   OBJ: 4.3

72. Rice, Thapar, and colleagues (2007, 2009) attempted to uncouple the effects of genetics and the effects of smoking while pregnant on birth weight and elevated antisocial behavior. They found that
    a. birth weight was unrelated to smoking.
    b. antisocial behaviors elevated the risk for smoking.
    c. antisocial behavior could be linked to genes but not to smoking.
    d. genetic factor appear to cause smoking.

    ANS: C   DIF: Difficult   REF: 106   OBJ: 4.3

73. Ruth has just given birth to a baby girl. Right away, it appears that something is wrong—the child looks odd. She has a small head, widely spaced eyes, and a flattened nose. What are the doctors most likely to suspect?
    a. Ruth consumed considerable quantities of alcohol during the pregnancy.
    b. Ruth had rubella during the second month of her pregnancy.
    c. Ruth had syphilis and did not seek treatment for it.
    d. Ruth did not eat properly throughout the pregnancy.

    ANS: A   DIF: Moderate   REF: 105-107   OBJ: 4.3

74. A child with fetal alcohol syndrome will most likely
    a. be blind or deaf.
    b. have a small head, widely spaced eyes, and a flattened nose.
    c. be at risk for SIDS.
    d. be born missing limbs.

    ANS: B   DIF: Moderate   REF: 105-107   OBJ: 4.3
    KEY: WWW

75. Mineko did not know she was pregnant until she was about three months along. During those first three months, she drank alcoholic beverages quite frequently. While prenatal alcohol consumption can influence the developing embryo and fetus in a number of ways, Mineko should be LEAST concerned about having a newborn who
    a. is hyperactivity.
    b. has lowered intelligence.
    c. has seizures.
    d. has a deformed heart.

    ANS: D   DIF: Difficult   REF: 105-107   OBJ: 4.3

403

76. When compared to a child with fetal alcohol syndrome, a child diagnosed with alcohol-related neurodevelopmental disorder would
   a. show more symptoms.
   b. be more severely impacted.
   c. show fewer symptoms.
   d. be much smaller.

   ANS: C   DIF: Moderate   REF: 105-107   OBJ: 4.3

77. Whose behavior would have the greatest NEGATIVE impact on a baby's brain development?
   a. A mother who consumes one bottle of beer a day during the first five days of the infant's embryonic period
   b. A mother who consumes five bottles of beer during the first day of the infant's embryonic period
   c. A mother who consumes one bottle of beer a day for five days during her seventh month of pregnancy
   d. A mother who consumes five bottles of beer a day during the first day of her seventh month of pregnancy

   ANS: D   DIF: Difficult   REF: 107   OBJ: 4.3

78. One critical factor in determining whether a mother's alcohol consumption will have a negative impact on her fetus concerns the mother's
   a. previous exposure to syphilis.
   b. rate for metabolizing alcohol.
   c. surfactant DIF:.
   d. placenta size.

   ANS: B   DIF: Moderate   REF: 107-108   OBJ: 4.3

79. The main impact of paternal consumption of alcohol (i.e., father's drinking) on a child involves the fact that fathers who drink tend to have
   a. no viable sperm.
   b. a greater potential to pass along the recessive gene related to Duchenne Muscular Dystrophy.
   c. poor parenting skills.
   d. genetic defects they pass on to their children.

   ANS: C   DIF: Moderate   REF: 108   OBJ: 4.3

80. Maria frequently used cocaine while she was pregnant. The most likely effect on her baby would be
   a. fetal strokes.
   b. extreme mental retardation.
   c. blindness.
   d. a hearing impairment.

   ANS: A   DIF: Moderate   REF: 108   OBJ: 4.3

81. Holly's newborn appears malnourished, has a low birth weight, and is showing withdrawal-like symptoms. Given this description, Holly most likely _____ while she was pregnant.
   a. contracted syphilis
   b. abused alcohol
   c. contracted HIV
   d. abused cocaine

   ANS: D   DIF: Difficult   REF: 108   OBJ: 4.3
   KEY: WWW

82. The best statement concerning the impact of drugs on prenatal development is that
   a. the drug alone is the best predictor of whether or not damage with occur.
   b. the combination of the drug and perinatal environment is the best predictor of whether or not damage with occur.
   c. the combination of the drug, perinatal and prenatal environments is the best predictor of whether or not damage with occur.
   d. the combination of the drug, perinatal and prenatal environments, and the genetic make-up of the fetus is the best predictor of whether or not damage with occur.

   ANS: D   DIF: Easy   REF: 108   OBJ: 4.3

83. Rubella is also know as
   a. German measles.
   b. mumps.
   c. typhoid.
   d. otitis media.

   ANS: A   DIF: Moderate   REF: 108   OBJ: 4.3

84. Thelma and Louise are best friends. Thelma contracts rubella, and Louise catches it from her. At the time they have the disease, Thelma is seven weeks pregnant and Louise is seven months pregnant. What is the most likely outcome?
   a. Thelma's child will be born unharmed, but Louise's child will have some sort of birth defect resulting from rubella.
   b. Louise's child will be born unharmed, but Thelma's child will have some sort of birth defect resulting from rubella.
   c. Thelma and Louise will both give birth to children with birth defects resulting from rubella.
   d. There is no need for Thelma or Louise to worry about birth defects as a result of having rubella.

   ANS: B   DIF: Difficult   REF: 108   OBJ: 4.3

85. Maternal diabetes
   a. is a fairly common complication during pregnancy.
   b. is very difficult to control during pregnancy.
   c. tends to result in very small fetuses.
   d. results from a lack of glucose in the mother's blood stream.

   ANS: A   DIF: Moderate   REF: 108   OBJ: 4.3

86. Rubella and syphilis both
   a. can be successfully treated with penicillin.
   b. have the greatest impact late in the pregnancy.
   c. cause heart problems and blindness.
   d. are commonly classified as sexually transmitted diseases.

   ANS: C   DIF: Moderate   REF: 108-110   OBJ: 4.3

87. Maggie, who just found out she is four weeks pregnant, has syphilis. A competent doctor would most likely advise her to
   a. have an abortion, as the child will be severely deformed from the disease.
   b. take penicillin treatments that will significantly reduce the chances that the syphilis will impact her baby.
   c. be prepared for a baby that will be born blind, as she has already passed the point where treatments are effective.
   d. not treat the disease until the child is delivered, as the medications used would cross the placental barrier and cause more damage to the unborn child than would the disease itself.

   ANS: B   DIF: Moderate   REF: 109-110   OBJ: 4.3

88. An infant born with AIDS will always have a compromised _____ system.
   a. immune   c. cardiovascular
   b. respiratory   d. central nervous

   ANS: A   DIF: Moderate   REF: 110-111   OBJ: 4.3

89. Fanny, who lives in the United States, has AIDS. When her son Alexander is born, he also tests positive for HIV. Fanny wonders what this means for Alexander's life expectancy. Fanny's competent doctor is most likely to tell her that as the result of the development of more effective drug treatments, Alexander will
   a. die within a few weeks.
   b. live one to two years.
   c. have over a 75 percent chance of living to age five years.
   d. be unlikely to ever die of the complications of AIDS.

   ANS: C   DIF: Moderate   REF: 111   OBJ: 4.3

90. Sally, who is pregnant, tests HIV-positive. When her daughter Jesse is born, she does not have the HIV virus. Sally's doctor is most likely to tell her
   a. she should breast feed her daughter so she can benefit from natural immunities to infection that breast milk often provides.
   b. she should not breast feed her daughter, as she might transmit the HIV virus through her breast milk.
   c. she and her daughter are very fortunate, and she need no longer worry about transmitting the virus to her.
   d. since she did not transmit the HIV virus to this child, it is unlikely that she would transmit the virus to another child, should she become pregnant again.

   ANS: B   DIF: Moderate   REF: 110-111   OBJ: 4.3

91. The AIDS virus CANNOT be contracted
   a. at conception through a chromosomal abnormality.
   b. during the prenatal period, when the HIV virus crosses the placental barrier.
   c. during the birth process, when maternal and fetal blood may mix.
   d. following birth, through breast feeding.

   ANS: A   DIF: Moderate   REF: 110-111   OBJ: 4.3
   KEY: WWW

92. When HIV is transmitted to a baby through blood it encounters during the birth process, the transmission is best classified as
   a. neonatal.
   b. prenatal.
   c. perinatal.
   d. postnatal.

   ANS: C   DIF: Easy   REF: 110-111   OBJ: 4.3

93. Hoshi is an X-ray technician. She takes special care to avoid exposure to radiation in her work environment, because she is trying to get pregnant and she knows that there can be negative effects from exposure to radiation on her baby. Which impact should she be LEAST concerned about?
   a. Spontaneous abortion
   b. Mutations
   c. Mental retardation
   d. Anoxia

   ANS: D   DIF: Moderate   REF: 111   OBJ: 4.3

94. Research on the impact on fetuses as the result of their mothers being exposed to potentially toxic pollutants during the collapse of the World Trade Center during the 9/11 attack found that the combination of the exposure to the toxins and prenatal exposure to _____ resulted in the most harmful effects.
   a. alcohol
   b. cocaine
   c. cigarette smoke
   d. rubella

   ANS: C   DIF: Difficult   REF: 111   OBJ: 4.3

95. The main danger of postnatal lead exposure is
   a. mutation.
   b. lower mental functioning.
   c. respiratory failure.
   d. sensory levels (e.g., deafness or blindness).

   ANS: B   DIF: Moderate   REF: 111-112   OBJ: 4.3

96. The presence of _____ in vaccines containing thimerosal (a discontinued practice), led some parents to question whether there may be a link between being vaccinated and being autistic.
   a. lead
   b. dioxins
   c. thalidomide
   d. mercury

   ANS: D   DIF: Moderate   REF: 112   OBJ: 4.3

97. The most dangerous time for a baby to be exposed to most chemical teratogens is
   a. at conception.
   b. during birth.
   c. at the age of viability.
   d. when the child's organs are growing most rapidly.

   ANS: D   DIF: Moderate   REF: 112   OBJ: 4.3

98. Claire and her husband are taking classes to prepare them for the birth of their first child. They are learning to do exercises, to focus breathing, and to relax through the contractions of labor. Their instructor tells them that what they are learning will help them to have an easier delivery, with less pain and less need for obstetrical medications. This best demonstrates the _____ method of childbirth.
    a. Leboyer
    b. Lamaze
    c. Neugarten
    d. Brazelton

    ANS: B   DIF: Difficult   REF: 113   OBJ: 4.4

99. What appears to be the optimal range of maternal age for childbearing (i.e., the "safest" time to bear a child)?
    a. 15 to 35
    b. 20 to 40
    c. 25 to 45
    d. 30 to 50

    ANS: B   DIF: Easy   REF: 112   OBJ: 4.4

100. Which is the best definition of stillbirth?
    a. Any miscarriage
    b. Any fetal death occurring on or after 20 weeks of gestational age
    c. Only fetal death occurring during the birth process
    d. Only fetal deaths that occur within the first two days following birth

    ANS: B   DIF: Easy   REF: 112   OBJ: 4.4

101. Trisha, age 25, is wondering what the best age would be for her to begin a family. If the only consideration is physical (in other words, factors such as emotional readiness are not an issue), her doctor is most likely to respond by saying,
    a. "Now would be a perfect time."
    b. "You better get working on it, because you only have a few good years left."
    c. "It would have been best to start your family sooner."
    d. "You would do well to wait until you are in your 30s."

    ANS: A   DIF: Moderate   REF: 112-113   OBJ: 4.4

102. Young teenage mothers (those age 15 or less) are at an increased risk for having a
    a. thalidomide baby.
    b. baby with rubella.
    c. low-birth-weight baby.
    d. baby with PKU.

    ANS: C   DIF: Easy   REF: 112   OBJ: 4.4

103. Barbara was six months pregnant when her mother called to say her father was in a car accident and had been taken to the hospital. Barbara believed that her father was probably not badly hurt, but flew home to visit her parents anyway. When she arrived, she found that her father was going to be just fine, though he did have some bad breaks and lacerations. This stress-related experience would most likely
   a. have no lasting effect on Barbara's unborn child.
   b. contribute to sleep and feeding problems that Barbara's baby exhibited following birth.
   c. cause Barbara to deliver her baby three weeks early.
   d. result in Barbara's baby being somewhat hyperactive during the preschool years.

   ANS: A   DIF: Moderate   REF: 114   OBJ: 4.4

104. The impact of maternal stress during pregnancy is most devastating on the fetus when the stress is
   a. brief and mild.   c. brief and severe.
   b. prolonged and mild.   d. prolonged and severe.

   ANS: D   DIF: Easy   REF: 114   OBJ: 4.4
   KEY: WWW

105. Moesha has been extremely stressed throughout her pregnancy. Her husband left her, she was laid off from work, and her mother died. Her doctor informs her that the extreme stress she has been under may have caused hormonal secretions of adrenaline that could affect her child. What would be the most likely impact on Moesha's baby?
   a. Deafness   c. Mild mental retardation
   b. Impaired vision   d. Increased irritability and crying

   ANS: D   DIF: Moderate   REF: 114   OBJ: 4.4

106. What would be an optimal weight gain for a normal-weight woman during pregnancy?
   a. 15 to 20 pounds   c. 25 to 30 pounds
   b. 20 to 25 pounds   d. 30 to 35 pounds

   ANS: C   DIF: Easy   REF: 114-115   OBJ: 4.4

107. Sofia, who used to suffer from anorexia,, is pregnant. She is still hung up about her body and is determined not to "get fat" while pregnant. Consequently, she puts herself on a strict diet and only gains 12 pounds during her pregnancy. Her physician is most concerned that when the baby is born, it will be
   a. cognitively impaired.   c. hyperactive.
   b. physically deformed.   d. blind or deaf.

   ANS: A   DIF: Difficult   REF: 115   OBJ: 4.4

108. Severe maternal malnourishment during later pregnancy puts a newborn most at risk for
   a. cerebral palsy.   c. stunted growth.
   b. sensory deficits (e.g., blindness). d. respiratory failure.

   ANS: C   DIF: Moderate   REF: 115   OBJ: 4.4

109. In order to decrease the incidence of neural tube disorders, United States and Canadian official mandated with fortification of _____ with folic acid.
    a. cereal
    b. milk
    c. "sports drinks" (e.g., Gatorade)
    d. baby formula

    ANS: A   DIF: Moderate   REF: 115   OBJ: 4.4

110. Having an older father increases the risk for a child being born with _____ syndrome.
    a. Klinefelter's
    b. Turner
    c. Tay Sachs
    d. Down

    ANS: D   DIF: Moderate   REF: 116   OBJ: 4.4

111. If a birth defect is said to be due to a perinatal effect, that means that the defect
    a. led to a miscarriage.
    b. was physical not cognitive.
    c. occurred during the birth process.
    d. affected the mother not the fetus.

    ANS: C   DIF: Easy   REF: 116   OBJ: 4.5

112. In the United States, most women give birth with the sole assistance of a
    a. midwife.
    b. physician.
    c. family member.
    d. spouse.

    ANS: B   DIF: Easy   REF: 117   OBJ: 4.5

113. Thora introduces herself as a perinatologist. This means that she likely spends most of her time
    a. analyzing results from chorionic villus sampling tests.
    b. researching the impact of exposure to lead from tap water on the cognitive development of children.
    c. performing in vitro fertilization procedures.
    d. attending to high-risk pregnancies.

    ANS: D   DIF: Moderate   REF: 117   OBJ: 4.5

114. Lexie is accurately described as a "doula." This means that Lexie
    a. was exposed to German measles when she was a fetus.
    b. assists women throughout the childbirth process..
    c. has used artificial insemination to become pregnant.
    d. can read but is mute (cannot talk).

    ANS: B   DIF: Moderate   REF: 117   OBJ: 4.5

115. Nastia is in the process of having her first baby. As she has read a lot about birthing, when the doctor tells her that the baby's head is now passing through the cervix, she would correctly recognize that she is in the _____ stage of the labor process.
    a. initial contraction
    b. delivery
    c. delivery of placenta
    d. afterbirth

    ANS: B   DIF: Moderate   REF: 117   OBJ: 4.5

410

116. Which event tends to occur the earliest in the labor process?
    a. Dilation of the cervix
    b. Mother told to "push"
    c. Delivery of placenta
    d. Fetus head at vaginal opening

    ANS: A   DIF: Moderate   REF: 117-118   OBJ: 4.5

117. The lack of oxygen during birth is called
    a. ataxia.
    b. apraxia.
    c. atonia.
    d. anoxia.

    ANS: D   DIF: Easy   REF: 117   OBJ: 4.5
    KEY: WWW

118. Who has experienced anoxia?
    a. B.J., whose umbilical wrapped around his neck during birth and cut off the oxygen supply to his body
    b. Margaret, who was exposed to high levels of radiation while she was an embryo
    c. Frank, whose mother drank five glasses of Scotch a day while Frank was a zygote
    d. Hawkeye, who ate lead paint chips as an infant

    ANS: A   DIF: Moderate   REF: 117   OBJ: 4.5

119. A child who is positioned for birth feet or buttocks first is said to be
    a. in normal vaginal delivery position.
    b. a Cesarean baby.
    c. in breech position.
    d. in vitro.

    ANS: C   DIF: Easy   REF: 117   OBJ: 4.5

120. Severe perinatal anoxia places a newborn at great risk for
    a. Tay Sachs.
    b. organogenesis.
    c. cerebral palsy.
    d. muscular dystrophy.

    ANS: C   DIF: Moderate   REF: 117   OBJ: 4.5

121. If Lillana has been accurately diagnosed with cerebral palsy, her most prominent symptom would involve
    a. great difficulty in controlling muscle movement.
    b. lungs incapable of metabolizing oxygen molecules.
    c. a severely compromised immune system.
    d. blindness and deafness.

    ANS: A   DIF: Moderate   REF: 117   OBJ: 4.5

122. A cesarean section is best described as a
    a. birthing position.
    b. surgical procedure.
    c. artificial insemination.
    d. teratogen.

    ANS: B   DIF: Easy   REF: 117   OBJ: 4.5

411

123. When describing the birth of her son Tyler, Liv says, "The coolest part was when the physician put the suction cup on Tyler's head and pulled him out during my contraction." Given this description, Liv appears to have undergone a
   a. vacuum extraction.   c. forceps delivery.
   b. breech birth.   d. Cesarean section.

   ANS: A   DIF: Moderate   REF: 119   OBJ: 4.5

124. Regarding C-section deliveries,
   a. most mothers prefer this method because it leads to a quicker recovery than a vaginal delivery.
   b. doctors conduct C-sections only in clear cases of emergencies.
   c. the number of C-sections has steadily and significantly decreased over the past 30 years.
   d. they continue to be popular as doctors and mothers prefer having a scheduled rather than an unexpected birth.

   ANS: D   DIF: Moderate   REF: 119   OBJ: 4.5

125. Who is at the optimal age for having an elective C-section?
   a. Teri, who is 35 weeks pregnant   c. Eva, who is 39 weeks pregnant
   b. Marcia, who is 37 weeks pregnant   d. Felicity, who is 41 weeks pregnant

   ANS: C   DIF: Moderate   REF: 119   OBJ: 4.5

126. Concerning childbirth, the biggest advantage of regional analgesics versus general sedatives is that the analgesics
   a. deaden pain but allow a mother to maintain complete muscle control.
   b. can be used in conjunction with C-sections, while sedatives cannot.
   c. have less impact on the baby.
   d. last significantly longer.

   ANS: C   DIF: Moderate   REF: 120   OBJ: 4.5

127. Which drug is most commonly used to assist in labor?
   a. Lithium   c. Folic acid
   b. Oxytocin   d. Phenylalanine

   ANS: B   DIF: Moderate   REF: 120   OBJ: 4.5

128. Research has shown that most birthing women experience pain and anxiety and _____ view the experience as positive.
   a. few   c. most
   b. some   d. all

   ANS: C   DIF: Moderate   REF: 120   OBJ: 4.6

129. Since China instituted its "one-child policy,"
   a. its population has dramatically increased.
   b. the ratio of male to female births has tipped dramatically in favor of males.
   c. more midwives have gotten involved in birthing.
   d. the incidence of maternal depression has increased significantly.

   ANS: B   DIF: Moderate   REF: 120   OBJ: 4.6

130. In parts of India, poorly paid and despised "dais" are used in childbirth because
   a. only the wealthy can afford doctors.
   b. it is believed that the poorer the delivery, the richer the life.
   c. giving birth is thought to increase strength, and doing it with little assistance is valued.
   d. the process involved in birth is seen as polluting.

   ANS: D   DIF: Moderate   REF: 120   OBJ: 4.6

131. Which statement about infant mortality rates is FALSE?
   a. The current rate is less than 1% in Western, industrialized nations.
   b. Medicalization of birth has significantly increased the infant mortality rate.
   c. The rate is twice as high for black infants than for white infants.
   d. In some areas of sub-Saharan Africa, the infant mortality rate is about 15%.

   ANS: B   DIF: Moderate   REF: 120-121   OBJ: 4.6

132. Sheila gave birth to a healthy baby boy two months ago. Today (like most days), she is sobbing uncontrollably and feeling irritable, resentful, and depressed. Her husband has no idea what is going on. He consults with the family doctor who would most likely tell him that Sheila is suffering from _____ depression.
   a. prenatal   c. neonatal
   b. perinatal   d. postpartum

   ANS: D   DIF: Easy   REF: 121   OBJ: 4.6

133. Maternal postnatal depression
   a. is common (i.e., found in about 50 percent of first-time moms).
   b. has few long-term effects on a child.
   c. tends to be found in individuals with a history of depression.
   d. strengthens the infant-maternal attachment.

   ANS: C   DIF: Moderate   REF: 121   OBJ: 4.6

134. Helio is currently experiencing symptoms of couvades. As such, you would expect him to complain about
   a. feeling bloated.   c. feeling very energetic.
   b. hair loss.   d. weight loss.

   ANS: A   DIF: Moderate   REF: 122   OBJ: 4.6

135. Concerning pregnancy and new parenthood for fathers,
    a. stress levels tend to be low during pregnancy and then increase significantly after birth.
    b. most fathers report feeling confident and well prepared during the mother's labor period.
    c. many new fathers experience symptoms of depression as do mothers.
    d. the one aspect of behavior that appears unaffected by fatherhood is their sex life.

    ANS: C   DIF: Moderate   REF: 122-123   OBJ: 4.6

136. Which microsystem variable appears most important in insulating older children from the effects of becoming a new sibling?
    a. A strong father-child relationship
    b. Living in a culture in which siblings are valued
    c. The amount of time their mother receives off from work to care for the newborn
    d. The sex and age of the sibling

    ANS: A   DIF: Moderate   REF: 123   OBJ: 4.7

137. The social support available to new parents would represent a _____ .
    a. microsystem   c. exosystem
    b. mesosystem   d. chronosystem

    ANS: C   DIF: Moderate   REF: 123   OBJ: 4.7

138. The neonatal period is best described as the
    a. first days after conception.   c. first months after birth.
    b. last weeks prior to birth.   d. last days of infancy.

    ANS: C   DIF: Easy   REF: 124   OBJ: 4.8

139. In which culture is a newborn most likely to be given daily enemas using a chili pepper solution?
    a. !Kung   c. Beng
    b. Chinese   d. No culture uses this practice

    ANS: C   DIF: Difficult   REF: 124   OBJ: 4.8

140. One of the most striking differences between the treatment of babies by !Kung and treatment of infants in most cultures is the
    a. significant amount of time babies are touched in this culture.
    b. fact that this culture does not believe in breast feeding.
    c. notion that until babies are able to speak, they are considered animals.
    d. this culture heavily stresses the importance of "training schedules."

    ANS: A   DIF: Difficult   REF: 124   OBJ: 4.8

141. The Brazelton Neonatal Behavioral Assessment Scale is designed to assess a baby's
    a. odds of dying from SIDS.   c. basic competencies.
    b. physical features (e.g., height, weight). d. IQ.

    ANS: C   DIF: Moderate   REF: 124   OBJ: 4.8

142. Which is NOT an advantage of breast feeding over bottle feeding?
a. Breast fed children tend to have fewer ear infections.
b. Breast feeding mothers are at a lower risk for ovarian cancer.
c. Breast feeding mothers tend to retain the healthy fat weight gained during pregnancy.
d. Breast milk positively impacts the infant's immune system.

ANS: C   DIF: Moderate   REF: 125   OBJ: 4.8

143. Concerning breast feeding,
a. most women fail to breast feed because of a concern over their baby receiving too many nutrients from their breast milk
b. black mothers are significantly more likely to breast feed than white mothers.
c. mothers with lower levels of education are more likely to breast feed than highly educated mothers.
d. Hospitals may be sending a mixed message by encouraging breast feeding while including formula in the gift packs they send home with new parents

ANS: D   DIF: Moderate   REF: 125   OBJ: 4.8

144. _____ is NOT assessed on the Apgar.
a. Size
b. Color
c. Muscle tone
d. Heart rate

ANS: A   DIF: Moderate   REF: 125   OBJ: 4.9

145. Frieda receives an Apgar rating of 8. This means she
a. is having difficulty breathing.
b. is doing just fine.
c. will likely die without extraordinary intervention.
d. has visual and auditory deficits.

ANS: B   DIF: Moderate   REF: 125-126   OBJ: 4.9

146. Baker was born 34 weeks after conception and weighed eight pounds at birth. If born in the United States, Baker would best be classified as
a. both low birth weight and premature.
b. low birth weight but not premature.
c. premature but not low birth weight.
d. neither low birth weight nor premature.

ANS: C   DIF: Moderate   REF: 126   OBJ: 4.9

147. _____ is the leading cause of infant mortality.
a. Prematurity
b. Down syndrome
c. Rubella
d. Fetal alcohol syndrome

ANS: A   DIF: Difficult   REF: 126   OBJ: 4.9

148. Which assisted reproduction technique is associated with having low-birth-weight infants?
a. Ovulation-stimulating drugs
b. In vitro fertilization
c. Artificial insemination
d. Sperm donorship

ANS: A   DIF: Difficult   REF: 126   OBJ: 4.9

149. Who is most likely to give birth to low-birth-weight infants?
   a. Samantha, who is carrying a set of identical twins
   b. Carlotta, who is carrying a set of fraternal twins
   c. Daniela, who is carry a single fetus
   d. Fredrica, who is carrying triplets

   ANS: D   DIF: Moderate   REF: 126-127   OBJ: 4.9

150. Extremely low-birth-weight infants are
   a. defined as having a birth weight of less than three pounds.
   b. unlikely to have medical issues that last beyond childhood.
   c. at risk for blindness, deafness, and autism.
   d. becoming significantly rarer.

   ANS: C   DIF: Difficult   REF: 127   OBJ: 4.9

151. Respiratory problems in premature infants may be the result of their inability to produce enough
   a. amnion.   c. chorion.
   b. stem cells.   d. surfactant.

   ANS: D   DIF: Moderate   REF: 127   OBJ: 4.9
   KEY: WWW

152. At birth, Kammi's body has an extremely low level of surfactant. What immediate impact will this have on Kammi?
   a. She will have great difficulty breathing.
   b. She will be classified as being of very low birth weight.
   c. She will be severely mentally retarded.
   d. She will show no attachment behavior toward her mother.

   ANS: A   DIF: Difficult   REF: 127   OBJ: 4.9

153. Kangaroo care involves
   a. putting a premature infant into a warm protective pouch.
   b. keeping an infant up at night and asleep during the day.
   c. skin-to-skin contact between infant and mother.
   d. parents jumping from one game to another in order to grab the interest of an infant.

   ANS: C   DIF: Moderate   REF: 128   OBJ: 4.9

154. The fate of premature and low-birth-weight infants
   a. depends solely on their biological condition.
   b. depends solely on the quality of their postnatal environment.
   c. depends on their biological condition and their postnatal environment.
   d. is unrelated to their biological condition or their postnatal environment.

   ANS: C   DIF: Easy   REF: 128-129   OBJ: 4.9 & 4.10

155. Werner and Smith's longitudinal study of Hawaiian children indicated that the two most important protective factors that help at-risk children overcome their disadvantage are
    a. a supportive postnatal environment and continued stress.
    b. continued stress and a two-parent household.
    c. a two-parent household and high-DIF: personal resources.
    d. high-DIF: personal resources and a supportive postnatal environment.

    ANS: D   DIF: Moderate   REF: 129   OBJ: 4.10
    KEY: WWW

156. Despite being abused by her mother when she was an infant, Sybil has become a mentally healthy adolescent. This successful outcome was to a large extent due to the positive social support provided by Sybil's foster family. This story provides an excellent example of the impact of _____ factors.
    a. prenatal   c. teratogen
    b. protective   d. genetic

    ANS: B   DIF: Moderate   REF: 129   OBJ: 4.10

TRUE/FALSE

1. In-vitro fertilization takes place in a laboratory dish.

    ANS: T   DIF: Moderate   REF: 97   OBJ: 4.1

2. The germinal stage of development occurs from the third to the eighth week after conception.

    ANS: F   DIF: Moderate   REF: 97   OBJ: 4.1

3. Every major organ begins to take shape during the embryonic period.

    ANS: T   DIF: Moderate   REF: 97   OBJ: 4.1
    KEY: WWW

4. The embryo is fed by villi that are located on the chorion.

    ANS: T   DIF: Difficult   REF: 97   OBJ: 4.1

5. The fetus is surrounded by a protective structure called the placenta.

    ANS: F   DIF: Moderate   REF: 97   OBJ: 4.1

6. In anencephaly, the brain below the brain stem fails to develop.

    ANS: F   DIF: Moderate   REF: 98   OBJ: 4.1
    KEY: WWW

7. The fetus first reaches the age of viability at around 34 weeks after conception.

    ANS: F   DIF: Easy   REF: 101   OBJ: 4.1

8. The same teratogen may have different effects on different fetuses.

   ANS: T   DIF: Moderate   REF: 103   OBJ: 4.3

9. Thalidomide typically causes babies to be born deaf and mentally retarded.

   ANS: F   DIF: Moderate   REF: 103-104   OBJ: 4.3

10. Maternal smoking appears to increase the risk of an infant experiencing sudden infant death syndrome.

    ANS: T   DIF: Moderate   REF: 105   OBJ: 4.3
    KEY: WWW

11. Fetal alcohol syndrome symptoms include facial deformities and central nervous system damage.

    ANS: T   DIF: Moderate   REF: 105-107   OBJ: 4.3

12. Babies born to mothers with syphilis often suffer from blindness.

    ANS: T   DIF: Moderate   REF: 109-110   OBJ: 4.3
    KEY: WWW

13. AIDS can be transmitted from mom to a birthing baby during the exchange of blood common during the birth process.

    ANS: T   DIF: Moderate   REF: 110-111   OBJ: 4.3

14. Physically, the safest age for a woman to have a baby is somewhere between 30 and 40 years.

    ANS: F   DIF: Moderate   REF: 112-113   OBJ: 4.4

15. Perinatal damage occurs during the time of birth.

    ANS: T   DIF: Moderate   REF: 116   OBJ: 4.5

16. Cerebral palsy may result from perinatal anoxia.

    ANS: T   DIF: Moderate   REF: 117   OBJ: 4.5

17. In some cultures, childbirth is seen as a shameful event.

    ANS: T   DIF: Easy   REF: 120   OBJ: 4.6
    KEY: WWW

18. Most first-time mothers experience postnatal depression.

    ANS: F   DIF: Moderate   REF: 121   OBJ: 4.6

19. Because of its superior nutritional value, bottle feeding tends to be recommended more often by physicians than breast feeding.

ANS: F   DIF: Easy   REF: 125   OBJ: 4.8

20. Maternal responsiveness is positively correlated with the resilience of at-risk infants.

ANS: T   DIF: Moderate   REF: 129   OBJ: 4.10

COMPLETION

1. The assisted reproductive technology involving the injection of sperm into a woman is called
_____.

ANS: artificial insemination

DIF: Easy   REF: 97   OBJ: 4.1

2. The process involving the formation of all major organs is called _____.

ANS: organogenesis

DIF: Moderate   REF: 97   OBJ: 4.1

3. The _____ is a fluid filled membrane that protects the embryo.

ANS: amnion

DIF: Difficult   REF: 97   OBJ: 4.1

4. Five weeks after conception the developing organism is best classified as an _____.

ANS: embryo

DIF: Moderate   REF: 97   OBJ: 4.1   KEY: WWW

5. The embryo receives oxygen and nutrients through the placenta and the _____.

ANS: umbilical cord

DIF: Moderate   REF: 97   OBJ: 4.1

6. The male hormone _____ is primarily responsible for allowing the production of a male reproductive system.

ANS: testosterone

DIF: Moderate   REF: 98   OBJ: 4.1

7. The _____ period is the longest stage of prenatal development.

ANS: fetal

DIF: Moderate   REF: 99   OBJ: 4.1

8. The point at which a fetus has the possibility of surviving outside the uterus is referred to as the age of _____.

ANS: viability

DIF: Moderate   REF: 101   OBJ: 4.1

9. Any drug, disease, or environmental agent that can harm a developing fetus is called a _____.

ANS: teratogen

DIF: Moderate   REF: 103   OBJ: 4.3

10. The morning sickness drug _____ was found to cause children to be born with missing limbs and deformed eyes and ears.

ANS: Thalidomide

DIF: Moderate   REF: 103-104   OBJ: 4.3

11. A physician would likely suspect _____ syndrome if a seemingly healthy infant dies in its sleep.

ANS: sudden infant death

DIF: Easy   REF: 105   OBJ: 4.3

12. German measles, also known as _____, can cause significant damage to a developing embryo.

ANS: rubella

DIF: Moderate   REF: 108   OBJ: 4.3

13. The sexually transmitted disease _____ can cause fetal blindness, deafness, and brain damage but can often be treated with penicillin.

ANS: syphilis

DIF: Moderate   REF: 109-110   OBJ: 4.3   KEY: WWW

14. The lack of oxygen during birth is called _____ or asphyxia.

ANS: anoxia

DIF: Easy   REF: 117   OBJ: 4.5

15. A baby who emerges from mom butt first is classified as being in a _____ position.

    ANS: breech

    DIF: Moderate   REF: 117   OBJ: 4.5

16. _____ is a neurological disorder affecting muscle control that can be caused by severe anoxia.

    ANS: Cerebral palsy

    DIF: Difficult   REF: 117   OBJ: 4.5   KEY: WWW

17. Pregnancy symptoms experienced by fathers are referred to by the French term _____.

    ANS: couvade

    DIF: Difficult   REF: 122   OBJ: 4.6

18. The _____ test is a 10-point assessment often given to newborns.

    ANS: Apgar

    DIF: Moderate   REF: 125-126   OBJ: 4.9   KEY: WWW

19. _____ is a substance that prevents air sacs of the lungs from sticking together.

    ANS: Surfactant

    DIF: Difficult   REF: 127   OBJ: 4.9

20. The therapeutic body position in which a newborn is resting chest-on-chest on a mother is referred to as _____ care.

    ANS: Kangaroo

    DIF: Difficult   REF: 128   OBJ: 4.9

ESSAY

1. Today's prospective parent has options unlike any time in the past. Describe the benefits and concerns related to assisted artificial insemination and in vitro fertilization.

    ANS: Answer not provided   REF: 96-97   OBJ: 4.1

2. Discuss the major physiological changes that take place during the fetal stage of development.

    ANS: Answer not provided   REF: 99-102   OBJ: 4.1

3. Describe any five prenatal teratogens and their impact of the developing embryo and fetus.

    ANS: Answer not provided   REF: 103-112   OBJ: 4.3

4. What advice regarding prenatal care would you give to a woman who has just found out that she is pregnant?

   ANS: Answer not provided   REF: 112-115   OBJ: 4.4

5. Discuss how various cultures react to childbirth.

   ANS: Answer not provided   REF: 120-121   OBJ: 4.6

6. Describe normal and abnormal maternal and paternal reactions to childbirth.

   ANS: Answer not provided   REF: 121-123   OBJ: 4.6

7. To what extent are infants resilient? What factors increase or decrease resilience?

   ANS: Answer not provided   REF: 129   OBJ: 4.10

8. Identify and describe the basic development that takes place during the zygotic (germinal) and embryonic stages of prenatal development.

   ANS: Answer not provided   REF: 97-99   OBJ: 4.1   KEY: WWW

9. The acronyms SIDS, AIDS, and FAS are associated with negative events during prenatal development. Demonstrate your knowledge of this time of existence by describing the potential impact of SIDS, AIDS, and FAS on a newborn.

   ANS: Answer not provided   REF: 105-108 & 110-111   OBJ: 4.3
   KEY: WWW

10. Describe the three-stage process of childbirth. Be sure to discuss the C-section option (i.e., what is it and when is it used?).

   ANS: Answer not provided   REF: 116-120   OBJ: 4.6

MULTIPLE CHOICE

1. The average female in the United States is about _____ tall.
   a. 5 feet 2 inches
   b. 5 feet 4 inches
   c. 5 feet 6 inches
   d. 5 feet 8 inches

   ANS: B   DIF: Moderate   REF: 134   OBJ: 5.1

2. Emilee has been diagnosed with celiac disease. This means that Emilee will likely display stunted growth due to her
   a. inability to absorb certain nutrients.
   b. genetically based small bone structure.
   c. inability to differentiate between nutritious and non-nutritious food.
   d. genetically based small muscle structure.

   ANS: A   DIF: Difficult   REF: 135   OBJ: 5.1

3. A child with _____ would be most likely on a gluten-free diet.
   a. celiac disease
   b. PKU
   c. autism
   d. sickle-cell disease

   ANS: A   DIF: Moderate   REF: 135   OBJ: 5.1
   KEY: WWW

4. During his second year of life, Titus suffered a long and severe illness that left him well below his expected weight and height. After recovering from the illness, Titus suddenly experienced rapid gains in both height and weight. This event is best explained by
   a. plasticity.
   b. the proximodistal principle.
   c. catch-up growth.
   d. the secular trend.

   ANS: C   DIF: Easy   REF: 135   OBJ: 5.1

5. Catch-up growth is most likely to occur
   a. in males.
   b. following hormone replacement therapy.
   c. during late puberty.
   d. following a period of malnutrition or illness.

   ANS: D   DIF: Moderate   REF: 135   OBJ: 5.1

6. The endocrine glands
   a. secrete hormones directly into the bloodstream.
   b. secrete neurotransmitters into the brain.
   c. are instrumental in producing myelin, which protects the neurons.
   d. transmits information from the sensory organs to the brain.

   ANS: A   DIF: Moderate   REF: 135   OBJ: 5.1

7. The endocrine system is most accurately thought of as a _____ system.
   a. neurotransmitter
   b. hormonal
   c. respiratory
   d. cardiovascular

   ANS: B   DIF: Moderate   REF: 135   OBJ: 5.1
   KEY: WWW

8. I am the "master gland" that triggers the release of hormones from all other endocrine glands. I am the _____ gland.
   a. pituitary
   b. thyroid
   c. adrenal
   d. testes

   ANS: A   DIF: Moderate   REF: 135   OBJ: 5.1

9. The pituitary gland is located
   a. next to the testes/ovaries.
   b. in a chamber near the heart.
   c. at the base of the brain.
   d. in the upper chest.

   ANS: C   DIF: Easy   REF: 135   OBJ: 5.1
   KEY: WWW

10. The endocrine gland that regulates growth and triggers the growth spurt during adolescence is(are) the
    a. pituitary gland.
    b. thyroid gland.
    c. adrenal gland.
    d. testes and ovaries.

    ANS: A   DIF: Moderate   REF: 135   OBJ: 5.1

11. If left untreated, children who lack adequate growth hormones tend note to exceed _____ in height in adulthood.
    a. 4 feet
    b. 4 feet 6 inches
    c. 5 feet
    d. 5 feet 6 inches

    ANS: A   DIF: Moderate   REF: 135   OBJ: 5.1

12. Maya was born with a thyroid deficiency that was not diagnosed as such until she was three years old. What is the likely outcome for Maya?
    a. Maya will be mentally handicapped to some extent.
    b. There will be no long-lasting effects as long as Maya receives treatment once the problem is diagnosed.
    c. Maya will grow to be over 6 feet tall.
    d. Maya will become blind and deaf.

    ANS: A   DIF: Difficult   REF: 135   OBJ: 5.1

13. Androgens do all of the following EXCEPT
    a. trigger the adolescent growth spurt.
    b. contribute to sexual motivation in adulthood.
    c. cause ovulation in women.
    d. trigger the development of male sex organs.

    ANS: C   DIF: Easy   REF: 135   OBJ: 5.1

14. Which statement is true?
    a. Estrogen is an androgen.
    b. Progesterone is an estrogen.
    c. Testosterone is an androgen.
    d. Androgen is a progesterone.

    ANS: C   DIF: Moderate   REF: 135   OBJ: 5.1
    KEY: WWW

15. _____ is the primary female hormone.
    a. Testosterone
    b. Androgen
    c. Progesterone
    d. Estrogen

    ANS: D   DIF: Easy   REF: 135   OBJ: 5.1

16. Melissa is 15 years old. All of her friends have become notably "adolescent" in appearance. They have pubic hair and underarm hair and have experienced the "adolescent growth spurt." Melissa has no pubic or underarm hair, and still looks much more like a young girl than an adolescent. The most likely culprit for Melissa's plight is a malfunction of the
    a. central nervous system.
    b. ovaries.
    c. testes
    d. thyroid.

    ANS: B   DIF: Moderate   REF: 136   OBJ: 5.1

17. Male is to female as
    a. adrenal gland is to androgen.
    b. estrogen is to testosterone.
    c. testosterone is to androgens.
    d. testosterone is to estrogen.

    ANS: D   DIF: Moderate   REF: 135   OBJ: 5.1

18. Which is most responsible for the maturation of bones and muscles?
    a. Adrenal gland androgens
    b. Ovary-released estrogen
    c. Brain released acetylcholine
    d. Thyroid-released thyroxine

    ANS: A   DIF: Moderate   REF: 136   OBJ: 5.1

19. During middle adulthood, the most likely impact of thyroid hormones would be to
    a. generate growth spurts.
    b. help metabolize food.
    c. create myelin.
    d. drain reserve capacity.

    ANS: B   DIF: Difficult   REF: 136   OBJ: 5.1

20. The basic cellular unit of the nervous system is the
    a. dendrite.
    b. axon.
    c. synapse.
    d. neuron.

    ANS: D   DIF: Easy   REF: 136   OBJ: 5.1

21. The statement, "I am just a gap between neurons," best describes a
    a. dendrite.
    b. axon.
    c. synapse.
    d. gland.

    ANS: C   DIF: Moderate   REF: 136   OBJ: 6.1

22. Neurons communicate with one another
    a. by releasing neurotransmitters into the synapse.
    b. by releasing hormones from the hypothalamus.
    c. through the pituitary gland.
    d. using androgens.

    ANS: A   DIF: Moderate   REF: 136   OBJ: 5.1

23. Myelin is important to the nervous system because it
    a. transmits neural impulses from the brain to the body.
    b. directs the release of hormones from the endocrine glands.
    c. increases the transmission speed of neural impulses.
    d. is where memories are stored.

    ANS: C   DIF: Moderate   REF: 136   OBJ: 5.1
    KEY: WWW

24. If a cell is experiencing myelination, it is
    a. migrating into its proper place in the brain.
    b. dividing uncontrollably.
    c. developing a fatty covering encasing its axon.
    d. releasing neurotransmitters.

    ANS: C   DIF: Moderate   REF: 136   OBJ: 5.1

25. What part of an overhead projector would be most like the myelin found in the brain?
    a. The rubber insulation covering the extension cord, as this insulation helps transmit
       the electrical energy more efficiently
    b. The light bulb, as myelin becomes highly active when it receives energy
    c. The reflecting mirror, as the purpose of myelin is to reflect away neurotransmitters
    d. The long arm holding up the reflecting mirror, as the main function of the myelin
       is as a conduit through which electrical chemical energy flows within the neuron

    ANS: A   DIF: Difficult   REF: 136   OBJ: 5.1

26. Myelination has been implicated in the increase in _____ in teenagers.
    a. suicide   c. the vocabulary spurt
    b. the generation of hypothetical   d. a major increase in sex drive
       questions

    ANS: B   DIF: Difficult   REF: 136   OBJ: 5.1

27. Changes in the _____ of the brain in adolescents may help explain the increase in risk-taking
    behavior in that group.
    a. somatosensory cortex   c. prefrontal cortex
    b. occipital lobe   d. temporal lobe

    ANS: C   DIF: Moderate   REF: 138   OBJ: 5.1

28. At birth, the average brain weighs about _____ percent of its adult weight.
    a. 10
    b. 25
    c. 35
    d. 50

    ANS: B   DIF: Moderate   REF: 138   OBJ: 5.1

29. Which best exemplifies the concept of brain plasticity?
    a. The fact that the brain changes in response to experience
    b. The fact that a rat brain has the same basic components as a human brain
    c. The fact that, as the result of hormonal differences, the male brain is smaller than the female brain
    d. The fact that the brain is built on a plan that is genetically determined

    ANS: A   DIF: Moderate   REF: 139   OBJ: 5.1

30. Plasticity results in the immature brain being
    a. vulnerable to damage and highly non-adaptable.
    b. invulnerable to damage and highly non-adaptable.
    c. vulnerable to damage and highly adaptable.
    d. invulnerable to damage and highly adaptable.

    ANS: C   DIF: Moderate   REF: 139   OBJ: 5.1
    KEY: WWW

31. Propensity for plasticity is greatest in
    a. infancy.
    b. middle childhood.
    c. late adolescence.
    d. middle age.

    ANS: A   DIF: Moderate   REF: 139   OBJ: 5.1

32. Lateralization refers to the
    a. specialization of the two hemispheres of the cerebral cortex.
    b. organizational structure of the nervous system.
    c. plasticity of the spinal cord.
    d. number of neurons produced during prenatal development.

    ANS: A   DIF: Moderate   REF: 139   OBJ: 5.2

33. The right brain hemisphere generally controls
    a. the right side of the body and is skilled at sequential processing.
    b. the left side of the body and is skilled at sequential processing.
    c. the right side of the body and is skilled at simultaneous processing.
    d. the left side of the body and is skilled at simultaneous processing.

    ANS: D   DIF: Moderate   REF: 139   OBJ: 5.2
    KEY: WWW

34. An overly simplistic way to describe the brain is that the left side is the "_____" side, and the right side is the "_____" side.
    a. behaving; desiring
    b. thinking; emotional
    c. desiring; behaving
    d. emotional; thinking

    ANS: B   DIF: Moderate   REF: 139   OBJ: 5.2

427

35. Which structure is accurately described as the "superhighway" connecting the two hemispheres of the brain?
    a. Pons
    b. Endocrine gland
    c. Brain stem
    d. Corpus callosum

    ANS: D   DIF: Moderate   REF: 139   OBJ: 5.2

36. With regard to brain lateralization, a majority of people
    a. rely primarily on the left hemisphere of the brain to carry out language activities.
    b. rely primarily on the left hemisphere of the brain for spatial perception and listening to music.
    c. rely on the left hemisphere for both language and spatial perception.
    d. rely on the right hemisphere for both language and spatial perception.

    ANS: A   DIF: Moderate   REF: 139   OBJ: 5.2

37. Jill came tumbling down the hill and sustained a serious head injury. As a result, her language skills have been seriously impaired. Which part of Jill 's brain was most likely damaged?
    a. Left hemisphere
    b. Right hemisphere
    c. Hypothalamus
    d. Brain stem

    ANS: A   DIF: Moderate   REF: 139   OBJ: 5.2

38. Brain lateralization is first evident
    a. in embryos.
    b. at birth.
    c. at age two.
    d. at age five.

    ANS: B   DIF: Moderate   REF: 139   OBJ: 5.2

39. Newborn Newton's parents, Isaac (his dad) and Fig (his mom), both have been left-handed throughout their lives. The probability that Newton will be left-handed is closest to
    a. 1 in 4.
    b. 1 in 2
    c. 3 in 4.
    d. 4 in 4.

    ANS: B   DIF: Difficult   REF: 139   OBJ: 5.2

40. Brain development
    a. is completed around age five.
    b. is completed during later childhood.
    c. is completed during late adolescence.
    d. is never completed.

    ANS: D   DIF: Easy   REF: 139   OBJ: 5.2

41. A researcher says, "The video you are about to watch contains scenes of neurogenesis." As such, you should expect to see
    a. the creation of new neurons.
    b. the migration of neurons.
    c. the destruction of neurons.
    d. the differentiation of neurons.

    ANS: A   DIF: Moderate   REF: 139   OBJ: 5.2

428

42. Neurogenesis
    a. only occurs in science fiction movies.
    b. results in the loss of key brain cells.
    c. is incompatible with increased blood flow in the brain.
    d. may be possible in humans.

    ANS: D   DIF: Moderate   REF: 140   OBJ: 5.2
    KEY: WWW

43. The neurogenesis of the brain continues
    a. until age 5.   c. through adolescence.
    b. until age 10.   d. well into adulthood.

    ANS: D   DIF: Easy   REF: 140   OBJ: 5.2

44. Which is the most UNEXPECTED occurrence in the normal aging brain?
    a. Alzheimer's disease and other forms of dementia
    b. Some decrease in the number of neurons
    c. Reduced blood flow to the brain
    d. Some decreased levels of neurotransmitters

    ANS: A   DIF: Easy   REF: 140   OBJ: 5.3

45. Which change is NOT normally seen in the aging brain?
    a. Loss of neurons   c. Formation of senile plaques
    b. Increased brain weight   d. Reduced blood flow

    ANS: B   DIF: Easy   REF: 140   OBJ: 5.3
    KEY: WWW

46. Which of the following characterizes the typical aging brain?
    a. Degeneration only   c. Both degeneration and plasticity
    b. Plasticity only   d. Neither degeneration nor plasticity

    ANS: C   DIF: Moderate   REF: 140   OBJ: 5.3

47. Cephalocaudal involves development proceeding from
    a. head toward tail.   c. brain to behavior.
    b. body to limbs.   d. legs to arms.

    ANS: A   DIF: Moderate   REF: 141   OBJ: 5.4

48. Which is the best example of cephalocaudal development?
    a. Infant gains control over the arms before the hands.
    b. Infant can sit up before it can walk.
    c. Infant can roll over before it can grasp a small object.
    d. Infant can hear before it can see.

    ANS: B   DIF: Difficult   REF: 141   OBJ: 5.4
    KEY: WWW

429

49. When lying flat, babies can hold their heads up before they can lift their hips or legs. This illustrates the _____ direction of growth.
   a. cephalocaudal
   b. cephalodistal
   c. proximodistal
   d. proximocaudal

   ANS: A   DIF: Difficult   REF: 141   OBJ: 5.4

50. Proximodistal involves development proceeding from the
   a. head toward tail.
   b. body to limbs.
   c. brain to behavior.
   d. legs to arms.

   ANS: B   DIF: Moderate   REF: 141   OBJ: 5.4

51. Infants can flail their arms around before they can move their hands and fingers with any precision. This illustrates the _____ direction of growth.
   a. cephalocaudal
   b. cephalodistal
   c. proximodistal
   d. proximocaudal

   ANS: C   DIF: Difficult   REF: 141   OBJ: 5.4

52. According to the orthogenetic principle, growth
   a. occurs from the inside to the outside.
   b. occurs in a head-to-toe direction.
   c. is increasingly distinct and organized.
   d. consists of gains and losses.

   ANS: C   DIF: Moderate   REF: 141   OBJ: 5.4

53. Humans begin their existence as a single undifferentiated cell and proceed to become a highly complex and organized billion-cell organism. This change best exemplifies the _____ principle.
   a. orthogenetic
   b. proximodistal
   c. cephalocaudal
   d. reality

   ANS: A   DIF: Moderate   REF: 141   OBJ: 5.4

54. Which does NOT belong on a list of the summarization of a lifespan model of health?
   a. Health is a life-long process.
   b. Health is determined by both genetic and environmental influences.
   c. Changes in health due to aging involve only losses.
   d. Health can be enhanced by social and historical factors.

   ANS: C   DIF: Easy   REF: 142   OBJ: 5.5

55. Colleen is playing a guessing game at a friend's baby shower. If Colleen correctly guesses the birth weight and length of her friend's newborn, she will win a great prize. Based on typical full-term newborn size in the United States, Colleen's best guess would be
   a. 5 pounds and 15 inches.
   b. 5 pounds and 17 inches.
   c. 7 pounds and 17 inches.
   d. 7 pounds and 20 inches.

   ANS: D   DIF: Moderate   REF: 142   OBJ: 5.6

56. During its first few months after birth, an average newborn gains about an ounce per
   a. minute.   c. day.
   b. hour.   d. week.

   ANS: C   DIF: Moderate   REF: 142   OBJ: 5.6

57. If Webster is an average child, he will have achieved half his adult height around his _____
   birthday.
   a. second   c. fourth
   b. third   d. fifth

   ANS: A   DIF: Moderate   REF: 142   OBJ: 5.6

58. Concerning the development of bones and muscles,
   a. at birth infants have cartilage but not bone.
   b. cartilage needs to soften to become bone.
   c. infants have all of the muscle cells that they will ever possess.
   d. the strength of a newborn is proportionally identical to that of an adult.

   ANS: C   DIF: Moderate   REF: 142   OBJ: 5.6

59. Which of the following is the best definition of a reflex?
   a. A behavior that has been repeated over and over
   b. An automatic response to stimulus
   c. A voluntary muscle movement
   d. The first type of sense developed after birth

   ANS: B   DIF: Moderate   REF: 143   OBJ: 5.6

60. A reflex is best described as
   a. unlearned and voluntary.   c. unlearned and involuntary.
   b. learned and voluntary.   d. learned and involuntary.

   ANS: C   DIF: Moderate   REF: 143   OBJ: 5.6
   KEY: WWW

61. Which is NOT a survival reflex?
   a. The breathing reflex   c. The toe-fanning reflex
   b. The sucking reflex   d. The eye-blink reflex

   ANS: C   DIF: Moderate   REF: 143   OBJ: 5.6

62. The defining feature of a survival reflex is that it
   a. has clear adaptive value.
   b. is linked to eating.
   c. is learned in the first three months after birth.
   d. does not fade with age.

   ANS: A   DIF: Moderate   REF: 143   OBJ: 5.6

63. Primitive reflexes
    a. are found in non-human primates but not in humans.
    b. allow for the use of language and spatial reasoning.
    c. are acquired through experience.
    d. serve no clear purpose.

    ANS: D   DIF: Moderate   REF: 143   OBJ: 5.6

64. Molly strokes the bottom of her baby Martin's foot and watches his toes fan out and then curl. Martin is exhibiting the _____ reflex.
    a. Babinski   c. Palmer
    b. Moro   d. stepping

    ANS: A   DIF: Difficult   REF: 144   OBJ: 5.6

65. Which reflex disappears first as the infant matures?
    a. Grasping reflex   c. Pupillary reflex
    b. Swallowing reflex   d. Breathing reflex

    ANS: A   DIF: Moderate   REF: 143-144   OBJ: 5.6

66. Which reflex is permanent?
    a. eye-blink   c. Swimming
    b. Babinski   d. Stepping

    ANS: A   DIF: Difficult   REF: 143   OBJ: 5.6

67. An organized and individualized pattern of daily activity found in an infant is called a
    a. reflex.   c. rhythmic stereotype.
    b. secular trend.   d. behavioral state.

    ANS: D   DIF: Moderate   REF: 143   OBJ: 5.6

68. Concerning sleep, REM stands for
    a. rapid eye movement.   c. remembering every minute.
    b. rotational emotional manipulation. d. reflexive evoked moment.

    ANS: A   DIF: Easy   REF: 143   OBJ: 5.6

69. As an average newborn, Kit would spend about _____ percent of his sleeping hours in REM sleep.
    a. 25   c. 75
    b. 50   d. 100

    ANS: B   DIF: Difficult   REF: 143   OBJ: 5.6

70. Mauer and Mauer (1988) suggest that the purpose of REM sleep in infants is to
    a. allow for the formation of a strong id.
    b. allow their nervous systems to mature in a less overloaded state.
    c. keep their bodies moving about.
    d. ensure that the infant keeps breathing.

    ANS: B   DIF: Moderate   REF: 143   OBJ: 5.6

71. What is the currently recommended amount of sleep by age?
    a. Two- to five-year-olds (12 hours), school-age (10 hours), teens (9 hours), adults (8 hours)
    b. Two- to five-year-olds (8 hours), school-age (9 hours), teens (10 hours), adults (12 hours)
    c. Two- to five-year-olds (9 hours), school-age (10 hours), teens (12 hours), adults (8 hours)
    d. Two- to five-year-olds (12 hours), school-age (8 hours), teens (9 hours), adults (10 hours)

    ANS: A   DIF: Difficult   REF: 146   OBJ: 5.6

72. The average age when most infants have mastered a skill or milestone is referred to as the
    a. developmental norm.   c. modal norm.
    b. normative curve.   d. growth period.

    ANS: A   DIF: Moderate   REF: 145   OBJ: 5.7

73. If developmentally delayed children begin to talk at 24 months, the average child begins to talk at 18 months, an above-average child talks at 12 months, and a gifted child talks at 6 months, the developmental norm for talking would be _____ months.
    a. 24   c. 12
    b. 18   d. 6

    ANS: B   DIF: Difficult   REF: 145   OBJ: 5.7

74. The fact that activities of a toddler's arms are mastered before activities of their fingers illustrates the _____ principle.
    a. cephalocaudal   c. proximodistal
    b. cephalodistal   d. proximocaudal

    ANS: C   DIF: Moderate   REF: 145   OBJ: 5.7

75. Whole body or large muscle movements are typically classified as _____ motor skills.
    a. fine   c. proximodistal
    b. gross   d. cephalocaudal

    ANS: B   DIF: Easy   REF: 145   OBJ: 5.7

76. Which is the best example of a gross motor skill?
    a. Kicking a ball   c. Writing in cursive
    b. Picking up a tiny rock   d. Performing brain surgery

    ANS: A   DIF: Moderate   REF: 145   OBJ: 5.7

77. Precise movements of fingers or toes are best classified as _____ skills.
    a. gross   c. survival
    b. primitive   d. fine

    ANS: D   DIF: Easy   REF: 145   OBJ: 5.7

78. Which is the best example of a fine motor skill?
   a. Looking at a painting
   b. Painting the wall of a barn with a large brush
   c. Painting a large red blob on a piece of paper using your whole hand
   d. Painting a highly detailed picture of a large group of people

   ANS: D   DIF: Moderate   REF: 145   OBJ: 5.7
   KEY: WWW

79. When a typical infant attempts to kick a ball, it tends to do so with its "whole body." When a typical first-grader attempts to kick a ball, he or she tends to do so only using a foot. The change best exemplifies the _____ principle.
   a. orthogenetic   c. cephalocaudal
   b. epigenetic   d. Babinski

   ANS: A   DIF: Difficult   REF: 145   OBJ: 5.7

80. Two-year-old Tiki has acquired the ability to spin one arm in a large circle while holding the other arm perfectly still. This exemplifies the orthogenetic principle element of
   a. a differentiated response.   c. integration.
   b. global responding.   d. reserve capacity.

   ANS: A   DIF: Difficult   REF: 145   OBJ: 5.7

81. The ability to coordinate separate body movements into a functional whole best describes the concept of
   a. a differentiated response.   c. an integrated response.
   b. global responding.   d. reserve capacity.

   ANS: C   DIF: Difficult   REF: 145   OBJ: 5.7

82. _____ is best defined as movement from one place to another.
   a. Locomotion   c. Lateralization
   b. Differentiation   d. Involution

   ANS: A   DIF: Easy   REF: 145   OBJ: 5.7

83. Concerning infant movement,
   a. initial modes of movement vary greatly, but by about 10 months most infants are crawling on their hands and knees
   b. initial modes of movement vary greatly, but by about 10 months most infants are walking
   c. the initial mode of movement almost always involves rolling, but by about 10 months most infants are crawling on their hands and knees
   d. the initial mode of movement almost always involves rolling, but by about 10 months most infants are walking

   ANS: A   DIF: Moderate   REF: 145   OBJ: 5.7

84. The "Back to Sleep" campaign aimed at reducing sudden infant death syndrome has resulted in a reduction in infant's
    a. REM sleep.
    b. eating.
    c. hearing loss.
    d. crawling.

    ANS: D   DIF: Moderate   REF: 145   OBJ: 5.7

85. In order to walk, newborns
    a. only require a more mature nervous system.
    b. require only a more mature nervous system and more muscle.
    c. require only a more mature nervous system, more muscle, and becoming less top-heavy.
    d. require a more mature nervous system, more muscle, becoming less top-heavy, and near adult-like vision.

    ANS: C   DIF: Moderate   REF: 145   OBJ: 5.7

86. After reviewing an enormous number of observations of infants' movement, Adolph and colleagues (2008) concluded that
    a. consistent performance of a motor skill develops in a single instance .
    b. it takes about 13 starts and stops over a period of time to develop consistent performance of a motor skill.
    c. it takes about 130 starts and stops over a period of time to develop consistent performance of a motor skill.
    d. it takes about 1,300 starts and stops over a period of time to develop consistent performance of a motor skill.

    ANS: B   DIF: Moderate   REF: 148   OBJ: 5.7

87. Research has found that the average 14-month-old takes about 2,000 steps an hour, traveling the equivalent of seven
    a. times around an average size merry-go-round.
    b. miles.
    c. football fields.
    d. yards.

    ANS: C   DIF: Moderate   REF: 148   OBJ: 5.7

88. The ulnar grasp involves only the use of one's
    a. thumb and little finger.
    b. palm and other palm.
    c. little finger and pointer finger.
    d. palm and outer fingers.

    ANS: D   DIF: Moderate   REF: 148   OBJ: 5.7

89. When reaching for a piece of candy that has fallen, Tony attempts to pick up the item by grabbing it between his palm and all fingers (except the thumb). Tony's terrific attempt best exemplifies
    a. a gross motor skill.
    b. the pincer grasp.
    c. lateralization.
    d. the ulnar grasp.

    ANS: D   DIF: Moderate   REF: 148   OBJ: 5.7

435

90. The pincer grasp involves only the use of one's
   a. thumb and forefinger.
   b. forefinger and little finger.
   c. little finger and palm.
   d. palm and thumb.

   ANS: A   DIF: Moderate   REF: 148   OBJ: 5.7

91. Ten-month-old Dora delights in her newly found ability to turn the TV on and off by grabbing the TV's on/off button with her thumb and forefinger and pushing. This developmental change involves Dora's use of a
   a. gross motor skill.
   b. pincer grasp.
   c. lateralization.
   d. ulnar grasp.

   ANS: B   DIF: Moderate   REF: 148   OBJ: 5.7

92. The defining element of a rhythmic stereotype is
   a. integration.
   b. lateralization.
   c. repetition.
   d. involuntary nature.

   ANS: C   DIF: Moderate   REF: 149   OBJ: 5.7

93. While lying in her crib, 18-month-old Rosie loves to rock back and forth. She also spends a lot of time swinging her arms in large circles. Rosie's behavior best exemplify the concept of
   a. reserve capacity.
   b. plasticity.
   c. fine motor movement.
   d. rhythmic stereotypies.

   ANS: D   DIF: Moderate   REF: 149   OBJ: 5.7

94. According to the dynamic systems approach of motor development, infants
   a. learn motor skills by watching others.
   b. develop motor skills in a universal, invariant sequence.
   c. modify their movements in response to sensory feedback regarding their attempted movements.
   d. must be taught how and when to perform various motor skills.

   ANS: C   DIF: Moderate   REF: 149   OBJ: 5.7

95. Ten-month-old Mattel wants to get across the room to reach a favorite toy. He figures out that rolling over doesn't really get him where he wants to go, but pulling himself along on his belly does. Mattel's behavior can best be explained in terms of
   a. dynamic systems perspective.
   b. lateralization.
   c. the proximodistal principle.
   d. developmental norms.

   ANS: A   DIF: Difficult   REF: 149   OBJ: 5.7
   KEY: WWW

96. When toddlers had to walk up a slope wearing a vest with "saddlebags," they were able to compensate for the change and successfully negotiate the slope. This adaptation best exemplifies the
   a. dynamic systems approach.
   b. proximodistal principle.
   c. neural plasticity.
   d. cephalocaudal principle.

   ANS: A   DIF: Moderate   REF: 149   OBJ: 5.7

97. How do falls affect walking proficiency in toddlerhood?
    a. They significantly delay the normal pattern of walking acquisition.
    b. They have little impact because they are actually quite rare.
    c. They provide key feedback concerning which surfaces are safe to traverse.
    d. They tend to make toddlers walk straighter when they get up.

    ANS: C   DIF: Moderate   REF: 150   OBJ: 5.7

98. The best description of the dynamic systems approach to motor development is that thought and action are
    a. independent.   c. integrated.
    b. innate.   d. innocuous.

    ANS: C   DIF: Moderate   REF: 150   OBJ: 5.7

99. Congenital malformations are always
    a. genetic.   c. fatal.
    b. present at birth.   d. adaptive.

    ANS: B   DIF: Moderate   REF: 150   OBJ: 5.8

100. What do Down syndrome, spina bifida, and cleft palates have in common?
    a. They are all caused by tetragons.
    b. They are all congenital malformations.
    c. They are all the result of recessive genes.
    d. They are all preventable through proper diet.

    ANS: B   DIF: Difficult   REF: 150   OBJ: 5.8
    KEY: WWW

101. In recent years, the incidence of polio, measles, and diphtheria in the United States have declined dramatically as the result of
    a. a reduction in chemical teratogens.   c. the administration of vaccinations.
    b. better maternal prenatal nutrition.   d. genetic engineering.

    ANS: C   DIF: Easy   REF: 150   OBJ: 5.8

102. The pattern of grow in childhood is best characterized as
    a. slow and steady.   c. fast and steady.
    b. slow and disjointed.   d. fast and disjointed.

    ANS: A   DIF: Easy   REF: 151   OBJ: 5.9

103. How is a toddler likely to compare to a 10-year-old child in terms of physical behavior?
   a. The toddler can control movements as long as the world around her is stationary, while the 10-year-old can control movements even when the environment around her is changing.
   b. The toddler will have superior eye/hand coordination to the 10-year-old.
   c. The toddler has developed fine motor skills that are as coordinated as the older child, but is just beginning to use gross motor skills.
   d. The toddler is able to move more quickly than the older child, but is less coordinated in her movements.

   ANS: A   DIF: Moderate   REF: 151   OBJ: 5.9

104. Which behavior is most difficult for a child to perform?
   a. Walking in a straight line   c. Skipping
   b. Hopping on one foot   d. Tapping a pen

   ANS: C   DIF: Difficult   REF: 151   OBJ: 5.9

105. Differences between throwing and kicking abilities of male and female children are best explained as being the result of
   a. size differences.   c. differential levels of practice.
   b. hormonal factors.   d. genetics.

   ANS: C   DIF: Moderate   REF: 151   OBJ: 5.9

106. Which statement concerning reaction time differences between toddlers and older children is true?
   a. Toddlers tend to have faster reaction times.
   b. Toddlers tend to have slower reaction times.
   c. Toddlers and older children tend to have identical reaction times.
   d. There is no systematic relationship between age and reaction times.

   ANS: B   DIF: Easy   REF: 153   OBJ: 5.9
   KEY: WWW

107. _____ is the leading cause of death in childhood.
   a. Cancer   c. Influenza
   b. Physical abuse   d. Unintentional injury

   ANS: D   DIF: Moderate   REF: 153   OBJ: 5.10
   KEY: WWW

108. If you wanted to prevent the most common cause of death of a child, you should always
   a. avoid fast-food restaurants.
   b. fasten the child's car seat/seat belt.
   c. make sure to sleep your child on his or her back.
   d. have your child inoculated.

   ANS: B   DIF: Moderate   REF: 153   OBJ: 5.10

109. If you want your child to eat healthy, you should purchase food items high in
    a. sugar.
    b. fat.
    c. nutritional value.
    d. carbohydrates.

    ANS: C   DIF: Easy   REF: 153   OBJ: 5.10

110. Concerning eating habits in childhood,
    a. children tend to eat less "comfort food" when they are under stress.
    b. consumption of sugary soda between meals makes children twice as likely to become overweight.
    c. parents have little impact on what children eat.
    d. children who eat breakfast at school are at risk for becoming overweight.

    ANS: B   DIF: Moderate   REF: 153-154   OBJ: 5.10

111. The BMI is a very good indicator of
    a. intelligence.
    b. depression.
    c. processing speed.
    d. body fat.

    ANS: D   DIF: Easy   REF: 154   OBJ: 5.10

112. In order to fight obesity, school are being asked to increase
    a. the number of vending machines.
    b. physical activity opportunities.
    c. levels of sodium in food.
    d. soda consumption.

    ANS: B   DIF: Easy   REF: 154   OBJ: 5.10

113. Who has just reached the point at which they would be classified as "obese"?
    a. Donald, who is now 10 percent above the ideal weight for his height, weight, and sex
    b. Hughie, who is now 20 percent above the ideal weight for his height, weight, and sex
    c. Dewey, who is now 30 percent above the ideal weight for his height, weight, and sex
    d. Louie, who is now 40 percent above the ideal weight for his height, weight, and sex

    ANS: B   DIF: Moderate   REF: 154   OBJ: 5.10

114. Puberty is best defined as a
    a. social process resulting in adult-like thinking.
    b. biological process resulting in adult-like thinking.
    c. social process resulting in the ability to produce a child.
    d. biological process resulting in the ability to produce a child.

    ANS: D   DIF: Easy   REF: 155   OBJ: 5.11

115. As a typical adolescent growing up in the United States, Maxwell (a male) would most likely achieve his peak growth spurt in height around _____ years of age.
    a. 10.5
    b. 12
    c. 13.5
    d. 15

    ANS: C   DIF: Difficult   REF: 155   OBJ: 5.11

116. Which of the following typical adolescent females growing up in the United States would have most recently achieved her adult height?
    a. 14-year-old Meg
    b. 16-year-old Jo
    c. 18-year-old Beth
    d. 20-year-old Amy

    ANS: B   DIF: Difficult   REF: 155   OBJ: 5.11

117. Adrenarche
    a. involves the release of hormones from the pituitary gland.
    b. determines a child's external genitalia.
    c. contributes to the development of secondary sex characteristics.
    d. is found exclusively in males.

    ANS: C   DIF: Moderate   REF: 155   OBJ: 5.11

118. If Sissy has just experienced menarche, she has
    a. ovulated for the first time.
    b. had her first menstruation.
    c. shown her first secondary sex characteristic (most likely pubic hair).
    d. produced her first seminal fluid.

    ANS: B   DIF: Moderate   REF: 155   OBJ: 5.11

119. Statistically, _____ girls tend to experience breast development at the earliest age.
    a. African-American
    b. Asian-American
    c. European-American
    d. Mexican-American

    ANS: A   DIF: Difficult   REF: 155-156   OBJ: 5.11

120. The defining behavior that marks the onset of semenarche is
    a. initial production of sperm.
    b. first ejaculation.
    c. initial production of testosterone.
    d. first sign of pubic hair.

    ANS: B   DIF: Easy   REF: 156   OBJ: 5.11

121. Nick has just experienced semenarche. Jessica has just experienced menarche. Which statement is most likely true?
    a. Nick and Jessica are now fully capable of producing a child.
    b. Nick is currently capable of producing a child, but Jessica is not.
    c. Jessica is currently capable of producing a child, but Nick is not.
    d. Neither Nick nor Jessica is fully capable of producing a child.

    ANS: D   DIF: Difficult   REF: 156   OBJ: 5.11

122. The mark of sexual maturation for a boy that is most comparable to menarche for a girl is
    a. deepening of the voice.
    b. first ejaculation of seminal fluid.
    c. the appearance of pubic hair.
    d. the release of androgens from the testes.

    ANS: B   DIF: Moderate   REF: 155-156   OBJ: 5.11
    KEY: WWW

123. Over the past 100 years or so, people in industrialized societies have been maturing earlier, as well as growing heavier and taller than in the past. This phenomenon is referred to as the
    a. dynamic systems approach.
    b. rhythmic stereotype.
    c. cephalocaudal principle.
    d. secular trend.

    ANS: D   DIF: Moderate   REF: 157   OBJ: 5.11

124. Which of the following best explains the secular trend?
    a. Better nutrition and medical advances
    b. Genetic variation
    c. Neural plasticity
    d. Reserve capacity

    ANS: A   DIF: Moderate   REF: 157   OBJ: 5.11

125. Anorexia nervosa has been linked to _____ in females.
    a. the production of defective eggs
    b. excessive levels of estrogen
    c. excessive ovulation
    d. a lack of menstruation

    ANS: D   DIF: Difficult   REF: 157   OBJ: 5.11

126. How is family stress, like conflict with a stepfather, most likely to impact the timing of puberty-related issues for a girl?
    a. It will result in excessive menstruation.
    b. It will lead to earlier sexual maturity.
    c. It will delay puberty.
    d. It will have no effect on any puberty-related behaviors.

    ANS: B   DIF: Moderate   REF: 157   OBJ: 5.11

127. Overall, what can we conclude about boys' and girls' body images during adolescence?
    a. Girls' body images are influenced by other people's reactions to them but not to actual physical changes, while boys show the opposite pattern.
    b. Both boys and girls experience puberty as an equally positive event.
    c. Girls show benefits from going through puberty but not from the changes associated with their growth spurt, while boys show the opposite pattern.
    d. Boys hold more positive personal body images than girls.

    ANS: D   DIF: Moderate   REF: 158   OBJ: 5.11

128. Being at or below the fifth percentile on a growth chart in the teen years characterizes the concept of
    a. constitutional growth delay.
    b. the secular trend.
    c. reserve capacity.
    d. rhythmic stereotypes.

    ANS: A   DIF: Moderate   REF: 158   OBJ: 5.11

129. A knowledgeable psychologist would be able to identify a teen exhibiting a constitutional growth delay by noting that they are one of the _____ kids in their class.
   a. smartest
   b. heaviest
   c. tallest
   d. smallest

   ANS: D   DIF: Moderate   REF: 158   OBJ: 5.11

130. Parent-child relationships tend to _____ once puberty is completed.
   a. become confrontational
   b. warm
   c. fade away
   d. ebb-and-flow

   ANS: B   DIF: Moderate   REF: 158   OBJ: 5.11

131. Which groups of adolescents would likely have the greatest difficulties adjusting to the changes of puberty?
   a. Late-maturing boys and early-maturing girls
   b. Late-maturing boys and late-maturing girls
   c. Early-maturing boys and late-maturing girls
   d. Early-maturing boys and early-maturing girls

   ANS: A   DIF: Moderate   REF: 158-159   OBJ: 5.11
   KEY: WWW

132. The greatest long-term negative impact of being an early-maturing female involves an increased risk of
   a. poorer academic performance.
   b. engaging in "risky behaviors" (e.g., sex and alcohol consumption).
   c. athletic injury.
   d. being unpopular with peers.

   ANS: B   DIF: Difficult   REF: 158-159   OBJ: 5.11

133. During adolescence, the physical activity levels of males continue to increase, while those of females tend to level off, or even decline. This is most likely due to
   a. degeneration of muscle tissue in females.
   b. traditional gender-role socialization of females in our culture that discourages physical activity (especially in athletics).
   c. hormone changes across the period of adolescence.
   d. the secular trend.

   ANS: B   DIF: Moderate   REF: 159-160   OBJ: 5.11

134. Concerning physical health,
   a. the rate of obesity among teens has steadily declined in the past two decades.
   b. modern teens lead a more sedentary lifestyle and consume more empty calories than in decades past.
   c. high blood pressure and diabetes remain virtually unheard of in teenage populations.
   d. genetic factors appear to play little role in the levels of obesity found in teens.

   ANS: B   DIF: Moderate   REF: 160   OBJ: 5.12

135. If asked to list the top three causes of death in teens, you should AVOID saying
   a. car accidents.
   b. murder.
   c. suicide.
   d. infections.

   ANS: D   DIF: Easy   REF: 160   OBJ: 5.12

136. Research has shown that when teens are under the influence of alcohol, they are LESS likely to
   a. get into a physical fight.
   b. smoke cigarettes.
   c. avoid engaging in risky sexual behavior.
   d. get into a car accident.

   ANS: C   DIF: Moderate   REF: 160   OBJ: 5.12

137. As a typical 70-year-old, Heston should expect to begin to
   a. lose muscle mass and gain fat.
   b. gain muscle mass and gain fat.
   c. lose muscle mass and lose fat.
   d. gain muscle mass and lose fat.

   ANS: C   DIF: Moderate   REF: 161   OBJ: 5.13

138. Most physical systems peak sometime between
   a. infancy and childhood.
   b. childhood and early adulthood.
   c. early adulthood and middle adulthood.
   d. middle adulthood and older adulthood.

   ANS: B   DIF: Easy   REF: 161   OBJ: 5.13

139. Reserve capacity tends to be most important in _____ situations.
   a. resting
   b. cognitively demanding
   c. social
   d. emergency

   ANS: D   DIF: Moderate   REF: 162-163   OBJ: 5.13

140. Despite being in top condition, 65-year-old Lane notices that his maximum heart rate during an aerobic exercise has declined significantly from when he was in his 20s. This change is best explained in terms of diminished
   a. reserve capacity.
   b. dopamine level.
   c. neural plasticity.
   d. estrogen level.

   ANS: A   DIF: Moderate   REF: 162-163   OBJ: 5.13

141. Although she is 85 years old and in great physical and mental health, Gerta strongly believes that "old people" are stupid and frail. This belief provides a good example of
   a. plasticity.
   b. ageism.
   c. the secular trend.
   d. a delusional state of mind.

   ANS: B   DIF: Easy   REF: 163   OBJ: 5.13

142. Many elderly people do not consider themselves as "old." This is particularly the case for individuals who
   a. still own their home.
   b. have grandchildren.
   c. are socially and physically active.
   d. are over age 90.

   ANS: C   DIF: Easy   REF: 163   OBJ: 5.13

443

143. Three of the most common premenstrual symptoms reported by women are
   a. acne, bloating, and hallucinations.
   b. hallucinations, breast tenderness, and bloating.
   c. bloating, moodiness, headaches, and breast tenderness.
   d. headaches, breast tenderness, and acne.

   ANS: C   DIF: Moderate   REF: 164   OBJ: 5.13

144. Which best describes the Englander-Golden et al. (1986) finding on PMS?
   a. Most PMS is caused by a defect on the 21st chromosome.
   b. Males experience PMS about half as often as females.
   c. Severe PMS appears to be totally psychosomatic (mental not physiologically-based).
   d. Expectations, not hormones, play a bigger role in many cases of PMS.

   ANS: D   DIF: Moderate   REF: 164   OBJ: 5.13

145. For most women, menopause
   a. is no big deal.
   b. results in long-term psychological problems.
   c. results in long-term physical problems.
   d. has more grave consequences if a woman has others with which she is sharing her experiences.

   ANS: A   DIF: Easy   REF: 164   OBJ: 5.13

146. After going through menopause, a woman
   a. does not ovulate and no longer menstruates.
   b. does ovulate but no longer menstruates.
   c. does not ovulate but still menstruates.
   d. both ovulates and menstruates.

   ANS: A   DIF: Easy   REF: 164   OBJ: 5.13
   KEY: WWW

147. Xavier (who is going through menopause) sometimes experiences a sensation of warmth that is unexpected and often centers on her face. This experience is technically referred to as
   a. hot flashes.   c. facism.
   b. hot points.   d. facial lateralization.

   ANS: A   DIF: Easy   REF: 164   OBJ: 5.13

148. The two hormones typically used in hormone replacement therapy related to menopause are
   a. progestine and testosterone.   c. androgen and estrogen.
   b. testosterone and androgen.   d. estrogen and progestine.

   ANS: D   DIF: Moderate   REF: 165   OBJ: 5.13

149. HRT appears to help relieve the physical symptoms of menopause, including
   a. mood swings and breast tenderness.   c. hot flashes and vaginal dryness.
   b. irritability and hot flashes.   d. mood swings and irritability.

   ANS: C   DIF: Moderate   REF: 165   OBJ: 5.13

150. The underlying physiological reason why older adults are slower on many tasks than younger adults is
    a. the loss of androgens.
    b. slowing of the nervous system.
    c. a change from an impulsive style to a reflective style.
    d. an increase in visual acuity.

    ANS: B   DIF: Moderate   REF: 165-166   OBJ: 5.13

151. Which statement concerning aging and health is true?
    a. Alcohol abuse has significant short-term impact, but does little long-term damage.
    b. Most older individuals are in excellent health (i.e., have no chronic illness).
    c. Even healthy older adults show significant losses in functioning.
    d. Aging in the absence of disease has little impact on physical or psychological functioning.

    ANS: D   DIF: Moderate   REF: 166-167   OBJ: 5.13

152. Masters and Johnson proposed the maxim "_____" when describing sexual function in adulthood.
    a. What is gone, is gone   c. Use it or lose it
    b. You can't teach an old dog, new tricks d. Never had it, never will

    ANS: C   DIF: Moderate   REF: 167   OBJ: 5.13

153. Osteoporosis occurs when
    a. the cushioning between joints wears out and the joints become stiff.
    b. maximal heart rates decrease so that any sort of workout requires more effort.
    c. lost minerals result in less bone mass.
    d. vitamin deficiencies lower the efficiency of the major organs.

    ANS: C   DIF: Moderate   REF: 168   OBJ: 5.14

154. Which is NOT known to help prevent or slow osteoporosis?
    a. Calcium supplements   c. Hormone replacement therapy
    b. Weight-bearing exercise   d. MAO inhibitors

    ANS: D   DIF: Moderate   REF: 168   OBJ: 5.14

155. Eighty-year-old Sylvester has begun to complain about his knees. To him, his knees now often feel, "Stiff as a board!" Given this description, Sylvester would appear to have
    a. Turner syndrome.   c. Klinefelter syndrome.
    b. osteoarthritis.   d. osteoporosis.

    ANS: B   DIF: Moderate   REF: 168   OBJ: 5.14

156. One of the more interesting findings from the "Nun Study" was that _____ levels affected both longevity and health.
    a. sex   c. education
    b. religiosity   d. wine consumption

    ANS: C   DIF: Moderate   REF: 168-169   OBJ: 5.14

445

TRUE/FALSE

1. Celiac disease involves an allergy to peanuts.

   ANS: F   DIF: Easy   REF: 135   OBJ: 5.1

2. Endocrine glands secrete chemicals called neurotransmitters.

   ANS: F   DIF: Moderate   REF: 135   OBJ: 5.1
   KEY: WWW

3. The fatty substance that covers the axon of a neuron is called synapse.

   ANS: F   DIF: Moderate   REF: 136   OBJ: 5.1

4. The "plasticity" of the brain means that it is impervious to harm.

   ANS: F   DIF: Moderate   REF: 139   OBJ: 5.1
   KEY: WWW

5. In most people, the processes of language tend to take place in the left hemisphere.

   ANS: T   DIF: Moderate   REF: 139   OBJ: 5.2

6. Neurogenesis involves the generation of new neurons.

   ANS: T   DIF: Moderate   REF: 139   OBJ: 5.1
   KEY: WWW

7. Cephalocaudal means head-to-tail.

   ANS: T   DIF: Moderate   REF: 141   OBJ: 5.4

8. Primitive reflexes have clear adaptive value.

   ANS: F   DIF: Moderate   REF: 143   OBJ: 5.6

9. Newborns spend half of their sleep in REM sleep.

   ANS: T   DIF: Moderate   REF: 143   OBJ: 5.6

10. Fine motor skills tend to be more difficult to perform than gross motor skills.

    ANS: T   DIF: Easy   REF: 145   OBJ: 5.7

11. The ulnar grasp occurs when the palm is pressed to the outer fingers.

    ANS: T   DIF: Moderate   REF: 148   OBJ: 5.7

12. Rocking and swaying are examples of rhythmic stereotypies.

    ANS: T   DIF: Moderate   REF: 149   OBJ: 5.7

446

13. Accidents are the leading cause of death in childhood

    ANS: T   DIF: Moderate   REF: 153   OBJ: 5.10

14. Puberty is a biological process that results in the ability to produce a child.

    ANS: T   DIF: Moderate   REF: 155   OBJ: 5.11
    KEY: WWW

15. The first male ejaculation is called andropause.

    ANS: F   DIF: Moderate   REF: 156   OBJ: 5.11
    KEY: WWW

16. Constitutional growth delays result in an individual being in the top fifth percentile for size for their peer group.

    ANS: F   DIF: Easy   REF: 158   OBJ: 5.11

17. Boys who mature early are at a distinct social advantage as compared to those who mature late.

    ANS: T   DIF: Moderate   REF: 158-159   OBJ: 5.11

18. American teens are more fit today than at any time in history.

    ANS: F   DIF: Moderate   REF: 160   OBJ: 5.12

19. Menopause is a cause of major psychological crisis for most women.

    ANS: F   DIF: Moderate   REF: 164-165   OBJ: 5.13

20. Osteoarthritis is a disease that results in a loss of minerals that leaves bones fragile.

    ANS: F   DIF: Moderate   REF: 168   OBJ: 5.14

COMPLETION

1. The _____ gland is referred to as the "master gland" of the body.

    ANS: pituitary

    DIF: Moderate   REF: 135   OBJ: 5.1

2. Male hormones like testosterone are called _____.

    ANS: androgens

    DIF: Moderate   REF: 135   OBJ: 5.1

3. The asymmetrical development of the two hemispheres of the brain is referred to as _____.

ANS: lateralization

DIF: Moderate   REF: 139   OBJ: 5.2   KEY: WWW

4. The fact that the ability to control one's head develops before the ability to control one's legs illustrates the _____ principle.

ANS: cephalocaudal

DIF: Moderate   REF: 141   OBJ: 5.4

5. The _____ principle refers to the fact that, with development, humans tend to become more differentiated and show greater hierarchical integration.

ANS: orthogenetic

DIF: Moderate   REF: 141   OBJ: 5.4   KEY: WWW

6. Eye-blinking and sucking are examples of _____ reflexes.

ANS: survival

DIF: Difficult   REF: 143-144   OBJ: 5.6

7. The average age at which children show mastery of some ability is called the _____ norm.

ANS: developmental

DIF: Moderate   REF: 145   OBJ: 5.7

8. The ability to pick up a piece of rice with a set of chopsticks would indicate superb _____ muscle control of the fingers.

ANS: fine

DIF: Moderate   REF: 145   OBJ: 5.7

9. Infants often spend a great deal of time repetitively rocking or swaying. Such behaviors are called _____ stereotypes.

ANS: rhythmic

DIF: Moderate   REF: 149   OBJ: 5.7   KEY: WWW

10. The _____ systems approach to motor development argues that development involves "self-organization" in conjunction with sensory feedback.

ANS: dynamic

DIF: Difficult   REF: 149   OBJ: 5.7

11. _____ malformations are defects that are present at birth.

ANS: Congenital

DIF: Moderate   REF: 150   OBJ: 5.8

12. _____ is the technical term for the first menstruation.

ANS: Menarche

DIF: Moderate   REF: 155   OBJ: 5.11

13. A boy's first ejaculation is technically referred to as _____.

ANS: semenarche

DIF: Moderate   REF: 156   OBJ: 5.11   KEY: WWW

14. The fact that today's teenagers are significantly taller than teens living 100 years ago illustrates the _____ trend.

ANS: secular

DIF: Difficult   REF: 157   OBJ: 5.11

15. _____-maturing teenage males tend to show the most positive adjustment to puberty.

ANS: Early

DIF: Moderate   REF: 158-159   OBJ: 5.11   KEY: WWW

16. Stereotypes or prejudice against the elderly are referred to as _____.

ANS: ageism

DIF: Moderate   REF: 163   OBJ: 5.13

17. The ending of a woman's menstrual cycle is called _____.

ANS: menopause

DIF: Easy   REF: 164   OBJ: 5.13

18. During _____ replacement therapy, estrogen and progestine are given to reduce the symptoms of menopause.

ANS: hormone

DIF: Easy   REF: 165   OBJ: 5.13

19. Some men experience symptoms similar to menopause in a process referred to as _____.

    ANS: andropause

    DIF: Difficult   REF: 165   OBJ: 5.13

20. _____ is an age-related disorder that leaves bones fragile and easily fractured.

    ANS: Osteoporosis

    DIF: Moderate   REF: 168   OBJ: 5.14

ESSAY

1. Describe the developing human brain from conception through older age. Be sure to discuss issues like neurogenesis, neuron migration, organization plasticity, and lateralization.

    ANS: Answer not provided   REF: 136-140   OBJ: 5.1 & 5.2

2. Lucy and Ricky are both looking forward to the birth of their first child. Tell them about the physical growth-related changes they can anticipate their child will go through as she or he progresses through infancy, childhood, and adolescence.

    ANS: Answer not provided   REF: 142 & 151-152 & 155   OBJ: 5.6 & 5.9 & 5.11

3. Discuss the development of basic motor and locomotion skills during infancy and childhood.

    ANS: Answer not provided   REF: 145-148 & 151-153   OBJ: 5.7 & 5.9

4. Describe why motor development in childhood is accurately characterized by dynamic systems theory.

    ANS: Answer not provided   REF: 149-150   OBJ: 5.7

5. Demi (a female) and Moore (a male) are about to enter puberty. Tell them what physiological changes each is expected to experience. Also tell them about the advantages and disadvantages of early and late puberty.

    ANS: Answer not provided   REF: 155-159   OBJ: 5.11

6. What is PMS, and what does modern research have to say about its impact on the typical female?

    ANS: Answer not provided   REF: 164   OBJ: 5.12

7. Describe why obesity should be considered a lifespan problem. Then discuss different intervention methods that might be used to reduce the incidence of obesity at various times of life.

ANS: Answer not provided   REF: 153-155 & 160 & 161-163
OBJ: 5.10 & 5.12 & 5.13

8. The main patterns of early development are cephalocaudal, proximodistal, and orthogenetic. Define and provide examples of each of these patterns.

ANS: Answer not provided   REF: 141   OBJ: 5.4   KEY: WWW

9. Newborn humans have many reflexes. Describe three survival reflexes and three primitive reflexes.

ANS: Answer not provided   REF: 143-144   OBJ: 5.6   KEY: WWW

10. What major reproductive system changes can young adult males and females look forward to as they enter middle and old age?

ANS: Answer not provided   REF: 164-165   OBJ: 5.12   KEY: WWW

MULTIPLE CHOICE

1. Sensation refers to
   a. interpretation of incoming sensory messages.
   b. stimulation of sensory neurons in the sense organs.
   c. perceiving the surrounding environment.
   d. innate processes of understanding the world.

   ANS: B   DIF: Moderate   REF: 174   OBJ: 6.1

2. A wave of light proceeds through to the back of the eye where it encounters and stimulates a receptor neuron. What process has taken place?
   a. Perception   c. Cognition
   b. Thinking   d. Sensation

   ANS: D   DIF: Moderate   REF: 174   OBJ: 6.1

3. Nerves are stimulated during the process of _____, and the brain interprets this information in the process of _____.
   a. sensation; perception   c. perception; sensation
   b. stimulation; selection   d. selection; stimulation

   ANS: A   DIF: Moderate   REF: 174   OBJ: 6.1
   KEY: WWW

4. Perception is best defined as the interpretation of
   a. memory.   c. unconscious thoughts.
   b. sensory input.   d. an abstract idea.

   ANS: B   DIF: Moderate   REF: 174   OBJ: 6.1

5. Which of the following is the best example of a perceptual process?
   a. Hearing a sound in the room
   b. Detecting that a light has been turned on in a dark room
   c. Sensing that someone has touched your arm
   d. Realizing that the odor you smell is vanilla

   ANS: D   DIF: Moderate   REF: 174   OBJ: 6.1

6. A wave of sound proceeds through the auditory canal to the inner ear where receptor neurons on the basilar membrane are stimulated. The neurons send a message to the brain. When the brain receives the message, the result is a person thinking, "That sounds like my mom calling me for dinner." What has taken place?
   a. Sensation and perception   c. Perception but not sensation
   b. Sensation but not perception   d. Neither sensation nor perception

   ANS: A   DIF: Moderate   REF: 174   OBJ: 6.1

7. Constructivists are likely to say that perceptions are
   a. innate.
   b. false.
   c. built with sensory experience.
   d. developed prior to sensations.

   ANS: C   DIF: Difficult   REF: 174   OBJ: 6.1

8. If an adult were cloned, a constructivist would predict that once born, the clone would
   a. have to learn to perceive the world as meaningful.
   b. awaken with a meaningful understanding of the world.
   c. not be able to function.
   d. think and perceive like an adult.

   ANS: A   DIF: Moderate   REF: 174   OBJ: 6.1

9. Who would be most likely to develop a theory hypothesizing that in order to interpret music, a person would have to hear many versions of the sound?
   a. A nativist
   b. A constructivist
   c. A humanist
   d. A Fruedian

   ANS: B   DIF: Difficult   REF: 174   OBJ: 6.1

10. Nativists believe that
    a. humans have innate perceptual abilities.
    b. all knowledge comes from experience.
    c. infants come into the world unknowing and uncaring.
    d. genes play no role in development.

    ANS: A   DIF: Moderate   REF: 174   OBJ: 6.1

11. If an adult were cloned, a nativist would predict that once born, the clone would
    a. have to perceive the world as meaningful
    b. awaken with a meaningful understanding of the world.
    c. be unable to learn because it has the brain of an adult rather than an infant.
    d. have a mind like a blank slate.

    ANS: B   DIF: Moderate   REF: 174   OBJ: 6.1
    KEY: WWW

12. Peter believes that his newborn already detects a difference between when he walks away from her and when he walks toward her, and that she understands that these two actions will lead to different outcomes for her. Peter's beliefs are most similar to those of a(n)
    a. empiricist.
    b. psychoanalyst.
    c. humanist.
    d. nativist.

    ANS: D   DIF: Moderate   REF: 174   OBJ: 6.1

13. Today, most developmental psychologists believe that sensations begin
    a. before birth and that early perceptions are coherent not chaotic.
    b. after birth and that early perceptions are coherent not chaotic.
    c. before birth and that early perceptions are chaotic not coherent.
    d. after birth and that early perceptions are chaotic not coherent.

    ANS: A   DIF: Moderate   REF: 175   OBJ: 6.2

14. Habituation is best defined as the process of "learning to be _____" with a stimulus.
    a. smart
    b. you
    c. bored
    d. free

    ANS: C   DIF: Moderate   REF: 175   OBJ: 6.2

15. Glinda jingles her keys in front of baby Elphaba's face, and she watches and smiles. Glinda continues to bring her keys up and jingle them in front of Elphaba because she appears to enjoy this game. After a while, though, Elphaba seems to lose interest in the game and no longer focuses on the keys when Glinda jingles them. This illustrates the process of
    a. cross-modal perception.
    b. constancy.
    c. preferential looking.
    d. habituation.

    ANS: D   DIF: Moderate   REF: 175   OBJ: 6.2

16. If you turn on a floor fan, an infant will orient toward the sound. After a while, it will appear to lose interest in the spinning blades. The phenomenon underlying the loss of interest is known as
    a. habituation.
    b. discrimination.
    c. generalization.
    d. maturation.

    ANS: A   DIF: Moderate   REF: 175   OBJ: 6.2
    KEY: WWW

17. Dr. Violet is interested in how young children perceive color. In her study, Dr. Violet simultaneously shows young children two blobs of different color and measures the amount of time they focus on each blob. Dr. Violet's technique is knows a(n) _____ task.
    a. habituation
    b. preferential looking
    c. evoked potentials
    d. operant conditioning

    ANS: B   DIF: Moderate   REF: 175-176   OBJ: 6.2

18. On a preferential looking task, a researcher measures
    a. how fast an infant gets used to an object.
    b. the brains response to the presentation of an object.
    c. the length of time it takes for an infant to learn to choose the reinforced stimulus.
    d. how long an infant views each of the objects presented.

    ANS: D   DIF: Moderate   REF: 175-176   OBJ: 6.2

19. A(n) _____ task always involves attaching an electrode to a subject.
    a. habituation
    b. preferential looking
    c. evoked potentials
    d. operant conditioning

    ANS: C   DIF: Easy   REF: 176   OBJ: 6.2

20. In an effort to study the acquisition of speech, Dr. Verball reinforces an infant every time it makes a sound. Given this description, Dr. Verball's research method would best be described as a(n) _____ task.
    a. habituation
    b. preferential hearing
    c. evoked potentials
    d. operant conditioning

    ANS: D   DIF: Easy   REF: 176   OBJ: 6.2

21. Within a minute after birth, a typical infant
    a. sees colors and can track slow-moving objects.
    b. sees colors but cannot track any moving objects.
    c. can visually track slow-moving objects but sees only in black/white (no color vision).
    d. cannot track any moving objects and sees only in black/white (no color vision).

    ANS: A   DIF: Moderate   REF: 176   OBJ: 6.3

22. Visual acuity is defined as the ability to perceive
    a. color.
    b. movement.
    c. detail.
    d. depth.

    ANS: C   DIF: Easy   REF: 176   OBJ: 6.3

23. If you want your two-week-old child to see you as clearly as possible, you should
    a. have very bright light on your face.
    b. move back and forth quickly so the child focuses on movement.
    c. put your face within about eight inches of her eyes.
    d. wear colorful makeup.

    ANS: C   DIF: Moderate   REF: 176   OBJ: 6.3

24. Visual accommodation involves the ability of the _____ of the eye to change shape and bring objects into focus.
    a. retina
    b. lens
    c. iris
    d. fovea

    ANS: B   DIF: Moderate   REF: 176   OBJ: 6.3

25. Which of the following is true regarding newborn infants' vision?
    a. Infants do not have color vision until around six months of age.
    b. Much of what young infants see is blurry.
    c. Pattern complexity has no impact on infants' visual preferences.
    d. Initial visual accommodation skills allow infants to focus clearly on far objects but not near objects.

    ANS: B   DIF: Moderate   REF: 176   OBJ: 6.3
    KEY: WWW

26. In a normally developing human, mature color vision is achieved
    a. near the end of the fetal stage.
    b. within a day after birth.
    c. about two to three months after birth.
    d. around a child's first birthday.

    ANS: C   DIF: Moderate   REF: 176   OBJ: 6.3

27. Visual contour is specifically defined as the amount of _____ of a visual object.
   a. curvature
   b. light/dark transition
   c. size
   d. movement

   ANS: B   DIF: Moderate   REF: 177   OBJ: 6.3

28. Which object would have the greatest amount of visual contour?
   a. A series of black circles on a white background
   b. A gray ship on the ocean
   c. A pillow with pastel blobs of blue and yellow
   d. A clear baby-bottle filled with breast milk

   ANS: A   DIF: Difficult   REF: 177   OBJ: 6.3

29. Which of the following is LEAST likely to draw the visual attention of a young infant?
   a. A moving object
   b. A high contour object
   c. A highly complex object
   d. A face

   ANS: C   DIF: Difficult   REF: 177   OBJ: 6.3

30. Human infants prefer "top-heavy" patterns, including human faces. What makes a human face top-heavy?
   a. The large color contrast between the skin, teeth, and eyes
   b. The contrast between the size of the mouth and nose
   c. The eyes, hair, and upper part of the ear
   d. The fact that mommy's head is significantly larger than another infant's head

   ANS: C   DIF: Moderate   REF: 177-178   OBJ: 6.3

31. Martin Banks and colleagues suggest that _____ is the most important overall factor in determining what an infant will stare at the longest.
   a. the degree of contours that the object has
   b. whether the object is moving or not
   c. how complex the object is in terms of colors and patterns
   d. whether or not the infant can see it well

   ANS: D   DIF: Moderate   REF: 178   OBJ: 6.3

32. The ability of an infant to perceive a meaningful facial form tends to occur
   a. within a few minutes of birth.
   b. about one week after birth.
   c. around two to three months after birth.
   d. between one and two years of age.

   ANS: C   DIF: Moderate   REF: 179   OBJ: 6.3

33. The tendency to perceive an object as not growing when it approaches our eyes, or shrinking as it moves away, is _____ constancy.
   a. location
   b. size
   c. brightness
   d. form

   ANS: B   DIF: Moderate   REF: 179   OBJ: 6.3

34. Which child has acquired perceptual size constancy?
   a. Raven, who looks out a window on a plane and says, "Those people on the ground look like ants but they are really big people"
   b. Robin, who knows that she will get bigger when she is older
   c. Jay, who can perceive the difference in size between a 1-story building and a 10-story building
   d. Loon, who uses Lego building blocks to create a tower that is taller than he is

   ANS: A   DIF: Moderate   REF: 179   OBJ: 6.3

35. Three-month-old Jordan reacts as if he believes that the basketball he is playing with actually shrinks as it rolls away from him. This reaction would indicate that Jordan lacks
   a. object permanence.   c. attention.
   b. cross-modal perception.   d. size constancy.

   ANS: D   DIF: Easy   REF: 179   OBJ: 6.3
   KEY: WWW

36. Gibson and Walk's visual cliff experiment demonstrated that infants develop _____ before their first birthday.
   a. depth perception   c. location constancy
   b. size constancy   d. shape constancy

   ANS: A   DIF: Moderate   REF: 179   OBJ: 6.3

37. When describing her research, Dr. Rebhuhn says, "Basically, I take young infants and place them on a supported piece of clear glass several feet off the ground. Then I measure whether the kid seems scared or not." Dr. Rebhuhn's research sounds like it involves the use of a
   a. habituation task.   c. longitudinal design.
   b. strange situation paradigm. d. visual cliff.

   ANS: D   DIF: Moderate   REF: 179   OBJ: 6.3

38. Ester is in a swimming pool. Her nine-month-old son Williams is sitting on a blanket three feet from the edge of the pool. Ester coaxes her child to crawl to her. If the depth of the water is lower than the top lip of the pool, Williams is most likely to
   a. crawl off the edge of the pool and fall into his mother's arms.
   b. crawl to the edge of the pool and stop.
   c. crawl away from his mother because her whole body isn't visible.
   d. not do anything because of lack of location constancy.

   ANS: B   DIF: Difficult   REF: 179-181   OBJ: 6.3

39. Testing infants of different ages with the visual cliff apparatus has found that
   a. six- to seven-month-old infants perceive drop-offs but do not fear them.
   b. two-month-old infants perceive drop-offs but do not fear them.
   c. six-month-old infants show no response to the deep side of the cliff.
   d. both two- and six-month-old infants will crawl across the shallow side of the cliff but will cry when enticed to crawl over the deep side of the cliff.

   ANS: B   DIF: Moderate   REF: 179-181   OBJ: 6.3

40. Research by Campos and colleagues indicates that in infancy the fear of drop-offs is likely related to the experience of
    a. walking.
    b. being carried by moms.
    c. falling.
    d. playing pee-a-boo.

    ANS: C   DIF: Moderate   REF: 180-181   OBJ: 6.3

41. Four month-old infants can best organize the world into distinct objects when the objects they are trying to make sense of are
    a. stationary.
    b. moving.
    c. identical.
    d. multicolored.

    ANS: B   DIF: Difficult   REF: 181   OBJ: 6.3

42. Four month-old infants appear to use object _____ to determine whether two side-by-side objects are separate.
    a. size
    b. hue
    c. shape
    d. shade

    ANS: C   DIF: Difficult   REF: 181   OBJ: 6.3

43. While sitting in her playpen, four-month-old Kiko watches her cat knock a lamp off a dresser. As the lamp begins to fall, Kiko seems to know that the lamp will drop straight to the floor. This knowledge appears to indicate that Kiko instinctively understands
    a. Piagetian laws of object permanence.
    b. Skinnerian laws of reinforcement.
    c. Newtonian laws of object motion.
    d. Freudian laws of ego formation.

    ANS: C   DIF: Moderate   REF: 181   OBJ: 6.3

44. Six-month-old Barbie watches as two dolls are placed behind a screen. When the screen is removed, Barbie sees either two dolls (possible) or one doll (impossible). Which of the following reactions is the infant likely to show?
    a. Barbie will not notice any difference between the possible and impossible outcomes, as evidenced by no difference in looking times at the two outcomes.
    b. Barbie will look longer at the impossible outcome than the possible outcome.
    c. Barbie will look longer at the possible outcome because it is familiar to her.
    d. Barbie will not look at either outcome because they will have habituated to the original stimulus.

    ANS: B   DIF: Moderate   REF: 181   OBJ: 6.3

45. According to the intuitive theorist perspective, infants
    a. have innate knowledge of the world and can reason about the world like adults do.
    b. must construct their knowledge of the world from a blank slate.
    c. learn what they need to know about the world by observing people around them.
    d. may have some innate knowledge of the world, but do not yet have the capabilities to reason about the world.

    ANS: A   DIF: Moderate   REF: 181   OBJ: 6.3
    KEY: WWW

46. Which of the following is the best example of the infant as an intuitive theorist?
    a. Infants look away when an object disappears from view.
    b. Infants get bored and look away when an object is repeatedly presented.
    c. Infants show surprise when a ball that is dropped behind a screen is later shown to be suspended in the air.
    d. Infants show surprise when a ball rolling down a hill is shown reaching the bottom of the hill.

    ANS: C   DIF: Difficult   REF: 181   OBJ: 6.3

47. Which statement would indicate that Tory is an intuitive theorist?
    a. Infants seem to perceive the world in a very adult-like manner.
    b. Infants are like blank pieces of paper that need to be written on in order to change.
    c. Infants have unconscious, survival-based reflexes.
    d. Infants appear to think but do not know.

    ANS: A   DIF: Moderate   REF: 181   OBJ: 6.3
    KEY: WWW

48. Typically, newborns can
    a. see and hear equally well.   c. hear better than they see.
    b. see better than they hear.   d. neither see nor hear well.

    ANS: C   DIF: Moderate   REF: 181   OBJ: 6.4

49. The fact that newborns turn away from loud sounds indicates that they can
    a. localize sound.   c. perceive speech.
    b. distinguish between phonemes.   d. understand size constancy.

    ANS: A   DIF: Moderate   REF: 181   OBJ: 6.4

50. Concerning the ability of newborns to hear, research has shown that they can discriminate
    a. loudness and frequency, but not direction and duration.
    b. only frequency and loudness.
    c. frequency, loudness, duration, and direction.
    d. only between loud and soft sounds.

    ANS: C   DIF: Moderate   REF: 182   OBJ: 6.4

51. How should you react to a policy that supports the initial testing of hearing at age three years?
    a. Great idea.
    b. Great idea, but since few hearing problems occur before this age, you are unlikely to identify any children with hearing problems.
    c. Bad idea, because by that time those with significant hearing loss reach this age, they are at significant risk for life-long speech and language difficulties.
    d. Bad idea, as accurate assessment of hearing is not possible until age five.

    ANS: C   DIF: Difficult   REF: 182   OBJ: 6.4

52. When describing her son's recent surgery, Sheri says, "They connected a microphone on the outside of his head. Then they surgically ran a wire into his inner ear." This description indicates that Sheri's son had
   a. photo-refractive surgery.
   c. cataract surgery.
   b. a cochlear implant.
   d. a magnetic resonance imaging.

   ANS: B   DIF: Moderate   REF: 183   OBJ: 6.4

53. Cochlear implants work by providing direct stimulation to the
   a. tympanic membrane.
   c. oval window.
   b. auditory nerve.
   d. ossicles.

   ANS: B   DIF: Difficult   REF: 183   OBJ: 6.4
   KEY: WWW

54. Which is a criticism of cochlear implants?
   a. Denies deaf children a chance to be part of the deaf community.
   b. The transplanted cochlea is often rejected by the body.
   c. Direct stimulation of the eardrum may cause permanent damage.
   d. There is no evidence that they improve a child's hearing.

   ANS: A   DIF: Moderate   REF: 182-183   OBJ: 6.4

55. A _____ is a basic sound used in human speech.
   a. cataract
   c. phoneme
   b. dopamine
   d. surfactant

   ANS: C   DIF: Easy   REF: 182   OBJ: 6.4

56. The fact that two-month-olds can detect the difference between the sound "pa" and the sound "ba" indicates that they
   a. can differentiate phonemes.
   c. have semantic awareness.
   b. have cross-modal perception.
   d. possess visual accommodation.

   ANS: A   DIF: Moderate   REF: 182   OBJ: 6.4

57. Three-month-old infants can discriminate between phonemes. This means that they can discriminate between
   a. basic speech sounds.
   c. various familiar odors.
   b. a doorbell and the bell on a telephone.
   d. familiar and novel tastes.

   ANS: A   DIF: Moderate   REF: 182   OBJ: 6.4

58. The advantage of being born with the ability to categorize sounds phonetically is that it
   a. prevents children from making phonetic errors in speaking.
   b. biologically prepares a child to speak all human languages.
   c. ensures that people speak the same language.
   d. allows for ease of second language acquisition in later adulthood.

   ANS: B   DIF: Moderate   REF: 182-183   OBJ: 6.4

59. Thirty-year-old Jiang has lived in China all his life and has only spoken in a common Chinese dialect. Jiang has an infant son named Woo. What linguistic advantage would Woo have over Jiang?
    a. Woo would have a larger vocabulary.
    b. Woo would be better able to distinguish between the "r" and "l" sounds.
    c. Woo would be producing more grammatically correct sentences than Jiang.
    d. Woo would have no linguistic advantages over his father.

    ANS: B   DIF: Difficult   REF: 182-183   OBJ: 6.4

60. What can we conclude regarding developmental changes in speech perception?
    a. With age, we become more sensitive to sound discriminations that are relevant in our own language and less sensitive to sound discriminations that are irrelevant.
    b. With age, we become more sensitive to all sound discriminations.
    c. There are no detectable differences in sound discriminations with age.
    d. With age, we become more sensitive to differences in consonant sounds and less sensitive to differences in vowel sounds.

    ANS: A   DIF: Moderate   REF: 182-183   OBJ: 6.4

61. Within days of their baby's birth, Ben and Jen are having an argument about their son. Jen claims that he recognizes her voice, but Ben says that this is impossible. Knowing the research in this area, you are able to tell them that
    a. Ben is correct (voice recognition does not occur until around six months of age).
    b. both could be correct, as babies can recognize only the first voice that they heard immediately following delivery (if this was Jen's voice, then she is correct; if it was not Jen's voice, then Ben is correct).
    c. Jen is correct (maternal voice recognition is evident a few days after birth).
    d. we do not know who is correct because infants this young cannot be accurately tested.

    ANS: C   DIF: Moderate   REF: 183-184   OBJ: 6.4

62. Mom Billie and dad Bob are discussing the abilities of their two-month-old son Thorton. Billie claims that Thorton can recognize both of his parent's voices. Bob says that Thorton cannot recognize either voice. If Thorton is a typical two-month-old, then who is correct?
    a. Billie
    b. Bob
    c. Neither, as Thorton can likely recognize Billie's voice but not Bob's voice
    d. Neither, as Thorton can likely recognize Bob's voice but not Billie's voice

    ANS: C   DIF: Moderate   REF: 184   OBJ: 6.4
    KEY: WWW

63. What was the key finding of the *Cat in the Hat* study on hearing?
    a. Voice recognition is influenced by prenatal experience.
    b. Infants prefer deeper male voices over higher-pitched female voices.
    c. Newborns prefer rhyming phrases over non-rhyming phrases.
    d. Reading to infants significantly increases their vocabulary size.

    ANS: A   DIF: Moderate   REF: 184   OBJ: 6.4

64. What is the best explanation for young infants' ability to recognize their mother's voices shortly after birth?
   a. An instinctive mother-baby bond
   b. Postnatal linguistic experiences
   c. Innate phonetic receptors
   d. Prenatal exposure to mom's voice

   ANS: D   DIF: Moderate   REF: 184   OBJ: 6.4

65. The senses of _____ both rely on detection of chemical molecules.
   a. taste and smell
   b. smell and vision
   c. vision and hearing
   d. hearing and taste

   ANS: A   DIF: Moderate   REF: 184   OBJ: 6.5

66. Which is NOT one of the four basic taste perceptions?
   a. Salty
   b. Sour
   c. Sweet
   d. Fruity

   ANS: D   DIF: Easy   REF: 184   OBJ: 6.5

67. Newborns will produce certain facial expressions depending on the taste of the liquid that they are offered. They smile when offered sugar water and frown when offered quinine. This demonstrates that newborns
   a. prefer salty tastes to sour ones.
   b. inherit their mother's taste preferences.
   c. can discriminate between various tastes.
   d. learn to avoid substances that might contain poison.

   ANS: C   DIF: Easy   REF: 184   OBJ: 6.5

68. Mennella and colleagues found that infants who were fed sour-tasting formula
   a. were at risk for being obese by age two.
   b. preferred the taste of sour items when they were preschoolers.
   c. were at risk for being anorexic in their teens.
   d. became very picky eaters as adults.

   ANS: B   DIF: Moderate   REF: 184   OBJ: 6.5

69. If a mother wanted to DECREASE the likelihood that her infant would grow into a picky eater later in life, she should
   a. bottle feed.
   b. give the infant a wide variety of foods.
   c. give the infant a diet exclusively consisting of fruits and vegetables.
   d. avoid eating spicy foods.

   ANS: B   DIF: Moderate   REF: 184-185   OBJ: 6.5

70. The sense of smell is also referred to as the sense of
   a. surfaction.
   b. olfaction.
   c. adaptation.
   d. involution.

   ANS: B   DIF: Easy   REF: 185   OBJ: 6.5

71. Which statement is FALSE?
    a. The sense of smell appears to develop by 28 weeks after conception.
    b. Infants prefer the smell of human milk over formula even if they have only consumed formula.
    c. Newborns tend to act favorably to the odor of ammonia.
    d. Mothers can identify their baby solely by the baby's smell.

    ANS: C   DIF: Moderate   REF: 185   OBJ: 6.5

72. Skin receptors allow a person to sense all of the following EXCEPT
    a. pain.   c. pressure.
    b. heat.   d. balance.

    ANS: D   DIF: Easy   REF: 185   OBJ: 6.5

73. Premature infants who are _____ tend to gain weight faster than those not receiving this stimulation.
    a. fed formula with quinine   c. stroked over their entire body
    b. kept in a warm environment   d. hearing soothing music

    ANS: C   DIF: Moderate   REF: 185   OBJ: 6.5

74. If he were a typical baby, Apollo would show the most tactile sensitivity when he is stroked on his
    a. face.   c. stomach.
    b. shoulder.   d. feet.

    ANS: A   DIF: Difficult   REF: 185   OBJ: 6.5

75. Recent research has indicated that infants are more likely to survive heart surgery if they receive _____ during the operation.
    a. deep anesthesia that keeps them unconscious
    b. moderate levels of anesthesia that keeps them semiconscious
    c. light levels of anesthesia that keeps them almost conscious
    d. no anesthesia so that they are completely conscious

    ANS: A   DIF: Moderate   REF: 185   OBJ: 6.5

76. Breast feeding an infant who is receiving a vaccination
    a. leads the infant to produce more antibodies.
    b. is ill advised as it promotes connecting pleasure with pain.
    c. reduces the behavior signs that they are in pain.
    d. has been banned by the American Academy of Pediatrics.

    ANS: C   DIF: Moderate   REF: 185-186   OBJ: 6.5

464

77. Newborns look in the direction of a sound that they hear. They also try to grasp objects that they can see. This suggests that newborns
   a. use the senses of sight, hearing, and touch, more than taste and smell.
   b. use vision to coordinate all the senses.
   c. cannot distinguish between their senses.
   d. can integrate two or more senses.

   ANS: D   DIF: Moderate   REF: 186   OBJ: 6.6

78. Cross-modal perception is the ability to
   a. perceive three-dimensionality from a two-dimensional display.
   b. perceive an object through two senses at the same time.
   c. stop responding to a stimulus that is repeatedly presented.
   d. recognize with one sense an object that was learned through another sense.

   ANS: D   DIF: Moderate   REF: 186   OBJ: 6.6

79. One-month-old infants were given either a smooth pacifier or one with hard nubs on which to suck. Although they had not seen the pacifier while sucking on it, when given the opportunity to look, the infants stared longer at the type of pacifier that they had sucked on. This shows that they have
   a. cross-modal perception.   c. inter-sensory sensation.
   b. dark adaptation.   d. repression.

   ANS: A   DIF: Moderate   REF: 186   OBJ: 6.6

80. Which of the following is NOT an example of cross-modal perception?
   a. Recognizing a person's face in a photograph that you have only seen in person one time
   b. Picking out by sight a toy that you had previously only touched
   c. Identifying which of your two pet cats has jumped onto the bed in the dark by running your hands over it
   d. Correctly identifying a Tootsie Roll pop because of the way it feels in your mouth, after a friend tells you to closer your eyes and open your mouth for a treat

   ANS: A   DIF: Moderate   REF: 186   OBJ: 6.6
   KEY: WWW

81. All of the major sensory systems begin to function
   a. before birth.   c. about one month after birth.
   b. shortly after birth.   d. by a child's first birthday.

   ANS: A   DIF: Moderate   REF: 186   OBJ: 6.7

82. Research by Hubel and Wiesel on visual deprivation in cats demonstrated that
   a. visual deprivation led to permanent vision loss in both kittens and adult cats.
   b. visual deprivation led to permanent vision loss in kittens and but not adult cats.
   c. visual deprivation led to permanent vision loss in adult cats but not kittens.
   d. visual deprivation had no long-term impact on either kittens nor adult cats.

   ANS: B   DIF: Moderate   REF: 187   OBJ: 6.7

83. Rather than using the term *critical period*, it is more accurate to characterize the effects of early experience on vision as a "_____."
   a. sensitive period
   b. critical stage
   c. genetically determined event
   d. once-in-a-lifetime moment

   ANS: A   DIF: Moderate   REF: 187   OBJ: 6.7

84. Lewis and Maurer (2005, 2009) provided evidence for multiple sensitive periods for vision that included all of the following EXCEPT a sensitive period for
   a. visually driven normal development.
   b. damage.
   c. enhancement.
   d. recovery.

   ANS: C   DIF: Difficult   REF: 187   OBJ: 6.7

85. Pearle was born with congenital cataracts. Her mother, Bailey, is a knowledgeable psychologist. As such, Bailey would know that in order to develop normal vision, Pearle should
   a. have cataract surgery as soon as possible.
   b. have cataract surgery around age two, after the eyes have developed.
   c. have cataract surgery around the time he goes through puberty.
   d. be left alone as his cataracts will disappear on their own.

   ANS: A   DIF: Moderate   REF: 187   OBJ: 6.7

86. Research has shown that children who undergo surgery for congenital cataracts, but who missed out on early visual experience,
   a. are unable to see any details of faces.
   b. are able to see details of faces, but have difficulty identifying different orientation of the same face.
   c. are able to see details of faces, but have difficulty telling two different people apart.
   d. have face discrimination abilities identical to children born without cataracts.

   ANS: B   DIF: Moderate   REF: 187   OBJ: 6.7
   KEY: WWW

87. When asked whether it is important for some sensory damage (e.g., congenital cataract) in an infant be treated early, a competent physician would say,
   a. "If you hope to achieve the best results, absolutely!"
   b. "You can delay the procedure, but only until age two."
   c. "The earlier you intervene, the more likely the procedure will actually increase the long-term damage."
   d. "There is no relationship between the timing of intervention and the long-term implications."

   ANS: A   DIF: Moderate   REF: 187   OBJ: 6.7

88. Which describes the "sleeper effect of early visual deficits?"
    a. If an infant does not experience normal visual experience, even after corrective surgery, it may never develop a normal perception of vision
    b. Naps are critical to the development of the depth receptors found on the retina
    c. The brain is so plastic, that even with complete absence of visual stimulation for up to a year, human infants will not show any detrimental effects
    d. Children tend to inherit visual problems that show up suddenly around age six

    ANS: A   DIF: Moderate   REF: 187   OBJ: 6.7

89. Research has shown that _____ need to be detected and corrected as early in life as possible.
    a. only hearing problems   c. both hearing and visual problems
    b. only visual problems   d. neither hearing nor visual problems

    ANS: C   DIF: Easy   REF: 187   OBJ: 6.7

90. Whose exploratory behavior would most likely involve mouthing an object to learn more about it?
    a. 2-month-old Rachael   c. 12-month-old Phoebe
    b. 6-month-old Chandler   d. 18-month-old Ross

    ANS: A   DIF: Moderate   REF: 188   OBJ: 6.7

91. Whose exploratory behavior would most likely just begin to involve exploring an item with both their eyes and hands?
    a. 2-month-old Tom   c. 12-month-old Harry
    b. 6-month-old Dick   d. 18-month-old Sally

    ANS: B   DIF: Difficult   REF: 188   OBJ: 6.7
    KEY: WWW

92. Perceptual development
    a. is impervious to cultural differences.
    b. varies across cultures because of socialization differences.
    c. varies across cultures because of differences in sensory capabilities.
    d. varies across cultures because of differences in levels of intellectual ability.

    ANS: B   DIF: Moderate   REF: 188   OBJ: 6.7

93. When 10- to 15-year-olds in Papua New Guinea are asked to draw pictures of the human body, they are most likely to
    a. refuse, as drawing the human body is against their religion.
    b. draw pictures of their "gods."
    c. scribble or draw tadpole-like forms.
    d. draw museum-quality pictures of humans.

    ANS: C   DIF: Moderate   REF: 188   OBJ: 6.7

94. The best definition of attention is that it involves
    a. unconscious awareness of a stimuli.
    b. intuition.
    c. random acts of perception.
    d. cognitive focus on something in particular .

    ANS: D   DIF: Easy   REF: 189   OBJ: 6.8

95. As a typical four-month-old, Dakota's attention process is best described as
    a. being focused on the most relevant items.
    b. adult-like.
    c. being caught by objects in the environment.
    d. non-existent.

    ANS: C   DIF: Moderate   REF: 189   OBJ: 6.8
    KEY: WWW

96. The fact that infants' attention seems to involve reacting to environmental stimulation (i.e., an
    item catches their attention) rather than being deliberately focused, illustrates the concept of
    a(n) _____ system.
    a. dynamic   c. fail-safe
    b. orienting   d. intentional

    ANS: B   DIF: Moderate   REF: 189   OBJ: 6.8

97. Which of the following is NOT a typical change in attention during childhood?
    a. Attention becomes more selective
    b. Attention span becomes longer
    c. Attention becomes more focused on irrelevant objects
    d. Attention becomes systematic

    ANS: C   DIF: Moderate   REF: 189   OBJ: 6.8

98. _____ attention is best defined as deliberate concentration on one thing while ignoring
    something else.
    a. Divided   c. Reflexive
    b. Selective   d. Cross-modal

    ANS: B   DIF: Moderate   REF: 189   OBJ: 6.8
    KEY: WWW

99. Which indicates that Maria has well-developed selective attention skills?
    a. She can pay attention to two people talking at the same time.
    b. She can pay attention to her teacher's voice while ignoring the voices of other
       students who are talking at the same time.
    c. It takes a great deal of noise to get Maria to notice that someone is talking to her.
    d. It takes her a long time to complete a task that requires vigilance.

    ANS: B   DIF: Moderate   REF: 189-190   OBJ: 6.8

100. The most effective way to increase the performance of a young child on a task requiring attention skills would be to
    a. increase the complexity of the task.
    b. increase the number of senses (e.g., hearing and seeing) involved with the task.
    c. decrease distractions.
    d. decrease time spent on the task.

    ANS: C   DIF: Moderate   REF: 189-190   OBJ: 6.8

101. Vurpillot's (1968) study on the development of visual search found that
    a. female children conduct more efficient visual searches than male children.
    b. young children conduct extremely unsystematic searches.
    c. Russian children were more focused searchers than American children.
    d. young children search details and older children search the "whole."

    ANS: B   DIF: Moderate   REF: 190   OBJ: 6.8

102. If asked to list the three key symptoms of ADHD, you should avoid saying
    a. inattention.   c. hyperactivity.
    b. impulsivity.   d. dysphasia.

    ANS: D   DIF: Easy   REF: 190   OBJ: 6.9

103. Wadsworth is extremely easily distracted, seems to forget whatever he starts to do, and just cannot seem to follow directions. This would suggest that Wadsworth has significant problems with
    a. attentiveness.   c. hyperactivity.
    b. impulsivity.   d. dysphoria.

    ANS: A   DIF: Moderate   REF: 190   OBJ: 6.9

104. Mika's mom describes her as "the girl with the motor that never quits" because she seems to be perpetually running in circles or gabbing. This suggests that Mika is
    a. inattentive.   c. hyperactive.
    b. impulsive.   d. dysphonic.

    ANS: C   DIF: Moderate   REF: 190   OBJ: 6.9
    KEY: WWW

105. Tyler's biggest problem is that he never seems to stop and think before he says anything, and he appears unable to stop from interrupting every conversation he encounters. If this is true, Tyler has significant problems with
    a. attention.   c. hyperactivity.
    b. impulsivity.   d. dysphoria.

    ANS: B   DIF: Easy   REF: 190   OBJ: 6.9

106. Concerning sex difference in rates of ADHD,
    a. boys are significantly more likely to be diagnosed than girls, but girls may be underdiagnosed because they do not act out as much.
    b. girls are significantly more likely to be diagnosed than boys, but boys may be underdiagnosed because they do not act out as much.
    c. boys are significantly more likely to be diagnosed than girls and they may be underdiagnosed because they do not act out as much.
    d. girls are significantly more likely to be diagnosed than boys and they may be underdiagnosed because they do not act out as much.

    ANS: A   DIF: Moderate   REF: 191   OBJ: 6.9

107. Which symptom of ADHD is most likely to reveal itself in infancy?
    a. Impulsivity-inattention
    b. Inattention- hyperactivity
    c. Hyperactivity-impulsivity
    d. All symptoms are equally likely to be seen in infants

    ANS: C   DIF: Moderate   REF: 191   OBJ: 6.9

108. Concerning the outcome of having ADHD as a child,
    a. children who have both ADHD and conduct disorders are at risk for drug abuse and emotional problems in adulthood.
    b. children who are the most aggressive are least likely to continue to show symptoms in later life.
    c. children do not "outgrow" the symptoms in later life.
    d. children with ADHD tend to have problems in school, but these problems do not translate into problems in the workforce.

    ANS: A   DIF: Moderate   REF: 191   OBJ: 6.9

109. Statistically, an estimated _____ percent of ADHD children outgrow their problems, _____ percent continue to have severe problems as adults, and _____ percent have at least some mild problems throughout their lives.
    a. 33; 33; 33   c. 50; 40; 10
    b. 50; 25; 25   d. 20; 20; 60

    ANS: D   DIF: Easy   REF: 191   OBJ: 6.9

110. Barkley (1997, 2000) has suggested that an improperly functioning _____ lobe may be involved in ADHD.
    a. occipital   c. parietal
    b. frontal   d. temporal

    ANS: B   DIF: Moderate   REF: 191-192   OBJ: 6.9

111. Low levels of the neurotransmitters _____ have been linked to ADHD.
    a. GABA and acetylcholine   c. dopamine and norepinephrine
    b. acetylcholine and dopamine   d. norepinepherine and GABA

    ANS: C   DIF: Moderate   REF: 192   OBJ: 6.9

112. Concerning the genetic nature of ADHD,
    a. all types are caused by a defect on the fourth chromosome.
    b. the majority of ADHD is caused by a mutate apoE gene.
    c. genes do not account for any of the variation in ADHD individuals.
    d. no gene directly causes ADHD.

    ANS: D   DIF: Moderate   REF: 192   OBJ: 6.9

113. Whose experience has been identified by scientists as directly contributing to some cases of ADHD?
    a. Pam, who is consuming a beverage that is full of sugar.
    b. Jim, who is eating a muffin that is laced with red food coloring.
    c. Angela, who has always liked watching and playing videogames.
    d. Dwight, who suffered from a lack of oxygen during his birth

    ANS: D   DIF: Moderate   REF: 193   OBJ: 6.9

114. Which statement concerning Ritalin, which is commonly used to treat attention deficit hyperactivity disorder, is FALSE?
    a. It is a stimulant.
    b. It increases level of dopamine.
    c. Its use appears to help individuals concentrate.
    d. It affects function in the occipital lobe.

    ANS: D   DIF: Easy   REF: 193   OBJ: 6.9

115. One of the biggest controversies concerning the use of drugs like Ritalin to treat individuals with ADHD is that
    a. the vast majority of individuals with the disorder are not prescribed the drug.
    b. while Ritalin is a cure for the disorder, most people see it only as a temporary treatment.
    c. so far, there is not much evidence that individuals who took the drug as children function better as adults.
    d. the effects fail to wear off when the drug dose is increased.

    ANS: C   DIF: Moderate   REF: 193   OBJ: 6.9

116. Research from the Multimodal Treatment of Attention Deficit Disorder Study indicates that the most effective treatment for ADHD
    a. involves drug intervention only.
    b. involves behavioral intervention only.
    c. involves both drug and behavioral intervention.
    d. involves letting the disorder simply "run its course."

    ANS: C   DIF: Easy   REF: 193   OBJ: 6.9

117. Attention skills of adolescents are advanced relative to those of children. This advantage appears to be due, in part, to _____ commonly found in adolescents.
   a. improvements in visual acuity
   b. increased distractibility
   c. myelination of brain cells
   d. androgens released by the ovaries/testes

   ANS: C   DIF: Moderate   REF: 194   OBJ: 6.10

118. Which of the following is a typical change in attention seen during childhood?
   a. Attention becomes less selective
   b. Attention span becomes shorter
   c. Attention becomes less focused on irrelevant objects
   d. Attention becomes more unsystematic

   ANS: C   DIF: Moderate   REF: 194   OBJ: 6.10

119. If you were experiencing tinnitus, you would
   a. hear ringing in your ears.
   b. be unable to attend to two auditory images at the same time.
   c. be deaf in one ear.
   d. be unable to hear high-frequency sounds.

   ANS: A   DIF: Easy   REF: 194   OBJ: 6.10

120. Ozzie is planning on attending a very loud rock concert. As such, he should be prepared to experience _____ unless he takes precautions to protect his hearing.
   a. presbyopia
   b. macular degeneration
   c. presbycusis
   d. tinnitus

   ANS: D   DIF: Moderate   REF: 194-195   OBJ: 6.10

121. Programs designed to effectively improve hearing protection in teens should
   a. avoid noting the potential long-term consequences of noise exposure.
   b. not address the misperception that hearing is not a health issue.
   c. reduce the stigma associated with wearing hearing protection.
   d. note that one-time exposure to loud noise cannot cause damage.

   ANS: C   DIF: Easy   REF: 195   OBJ: 6.10

122. What is the new taste that is being considered the fifth basic taste beyond that of sweet, salty, sour, and bitter?
   a. Umami
   b. Spicy
   c. Minty
   d. Fruity

   ANS: A   DIF: Moderate   REF: 195   OBJ: 6.10

123. Which word best describes the taste "umami?"
   a. Creamy
   b. Fishy
   c. Eggy
   d. Brothy

   ANS: D   DIF: Easy   REF: 195   OBJ: 6.10

124. What type of food would be most likely to produce "chemosensory irritation?"
    a. A cold scoop of ice cream
    b. A hamburger hot off of the grill
    c. A pickled pig's foot
    d. A spicy hot jalapeño pepper

    ANS: D   DIF: Moderate   REF: 195   OBJ: 6.10

125. Research has shown that _____ will make people perceive the taste as more flavorful.
    a. pouring a glass of orange juice slowly
    b. putting a few drops of orange food coloring into a glass of orange juice
    c. leaving a glass of orange juice out on the counter for a few hours
    d. telling people that the juice in a glass is sugar-free

    ANS: B   DIF: Moderate   REF: 195   OBJ: 6.10

126. Compared to younger children, adolescents are more likely to
    a. enjoy a food item with a strong taste.
    b. dislike the taste of sour foods.
    c. refuse to try some unfamiliar food item.
    d. show a greater preference for sweets.

    ANS: A   DIF: Moderate   REF: 195   OBJ: 6.10

127. Research on smell in adolescence has shown that
    a. only females use body odor of others as a criteria for mate selection.
    b. only males use body odor of others as a criteria for mate selection.
    c. both females and males use body odor of others as a criteria for mate selection.
    d. neither females nor males use body odor of others as a criteria for mate selection.

    ANS: C   DIF: Moderate   REF: 195-196   OBJ: 6.10

128. Sensory threshold is defined as the
    a. minimum amount of stimulation that can be detected.
    b. maximum amount of sensory stimulation that can be tolerated before pain is experienced.
    c. maximum number of senses that can be stimulated before the person is confused.
    d. minimum amount of energy produced by a neuron.

    ANS: A   DIF: Moderate   REF: 197   OBJ: 6.11

129. As a researcher focused on the issue of sensations, how would you most likely explain why older people tend to raise the volume on their television sets and use more seasoning (e.g., salt and pepper) on their food?
    a. Their sensory thresholds have increased with age.
    b. They cannot concentrate on simple things.
    c. Visual accommodation abilities have declined.
    d. They forget that they already salted their food or raised the volume on the television.

    ANS: A   DIF: Moderate   REF: 197   OBJ: 6.11
    KEY: WWW

130. A study finds that 100 percent of 20-year-olds, 70 percent of 40-year-olds, and only 40 percent of 60-year-olds are able to detect the scent of a single rotten egg in a 10- by 10-foot room. A developmental psychologist would most likely explain this change in terms of a(n)
   a. Decrease in olfactory sensory threshold
   b. Increase in olfactory sensory threshold
   c. Decrease in cross-modality perception
   d. Increase in cross-modality perception

   ANS: B   DIF: Difficult   REF: 197   OBJ: 6.11

131. About _____ percent of adults over age 70 are blind in both eyes.
   a. 2
   b. 12
   c. 22
   d. 32

   ANS: A   DIF: Easy   REF: 197   OBJ: 6.11

132. Which is the most common visual condition for a person over age 70?
   a. Glaucoma
   b. Legally blind in one eye
   c. The need for corrective lens
   d. Cataracts

   ANS: C   DIF: Moderate   REF: 197   OBJ: 6.11

133. Seventy-year-old Vinita has been having difficulty seeing while driving at night. When she is seen by an optometrist, she is told that the problem is the fact that both of her lenses have clouded. The correct specific diagnosis would by that Vinetta has
   a. presbycusis.
   b. myopia.
   c. presbyopia.
   d. cataracts.

   ANS: D   DIF: Moderate   REF: 197   OBJ: 6.11

134. Swen's doctor just informed him that in order to correct his visual problem, Swen must have his clouded lens replaced. This means that Swen's visual problem involves
   a. retinitis pigmentosa.
   b. cataracts.
   c. glaucoma.
   d. macular degeneration.

   ANS: B   DIF: Moderate   REF: 197   OBJ: 6.11
   KEY: WWW

135. A slow-reacting pupil is most likely to be responsible for
   a. glaucoma.
   b. difficulty with dark adaptation.
   c. cataracts.
   d. difficulty with far vision.

   ANS: B   DIF: Moderate   REF: 198   OBJ: 6.11

136. When driving at night, an elderly person may have trouble seeing well when exiting a lighted freeway onto an unlighted road. The most likely cause of this trouble involves
   a. reduced sensory thresholds.
   b. presbycusis.
   c. slower dark adaptation abilities.
   d. trouble with near vision.

   ANS: C   DIF: Moderate   REF: 198   OBJ: 6.11

137. Presbyopia
    a. is caused by inter-ocular pressure.
    b. leads to difficulty in seeing object that are nearby.
    c. is due to an aging iris.
    d. impacts visual acuity but not visual accommodation.

    ANS: B   DIF: Moderate   REF: 199   OBJ: 6.11

138. When grandpa has difficulty reading a newspaper 20 inches from his face, but can clearly see the television that is 20 feet away, he most likely has
    a. presbyopia.   c. glaucoma.
    b. age-related macular degeneration.   d. retinitis pigmentosa.

    ANS: A   DIF: Moderate   REF: 199   OBJ: 6.11

139. Which disorder results in the reduction in the ability to see close objects but does NOT impact the ability to see things at a distance?
    a. Presbyopia   c. Glaucoma
    b. Age-related macular degeneration   d. Retinitis pigmentosa

    ANS: A   DIF: Moderate   REF: 199   OBJ: 6.11
    KEY: WWW

140. Because of recent advancements in surgical techniques to effectively treat cataracts, _____ has now become the leading cause of blindness in older adults in the United States.
    a. age-related macular degeneration   c. retinitis pigmentosa
    b. glaucoma   d. presbyopia

    ANS: A   DIF: Moderate   REF: 199   OBJ: 6.11

141. Webster has just been informed that he is suffering from a visual problem that is destroying retinal cells responsible for central vision and that he will soon find reading nearly impossible. This diagnosis indicates that Webster has
    a. age-related macular degeneration.   c. retinitis pigmentosa.
    b. glaucoma.   d. cataracts.

    ANS: A   DIF: Moderate   REF: 199   OBJ: 6.11

142. Which cannot currently be treated either surgically or through the use of corrective lenses?
    a. Cataracts   c. Age-related macular degeneration
    b. Glaucoma   d. Presbyopia

    ANS: C   DIF: Moderate   REF: 199   OBJ: 6.11

143. Statistically, who is least likely (per mile driven) to be in an accident?
    a. Teenage drivers   c. Elderly drivers
    b. Middle-aged drivers   d. Very old drivers

    ANS: B   DIF: Moderate   REF: 200   OBJ: 6.11

144. _____ is characterized by the deterioration of light-sensitive cells of the retina.
   a. Presbyopia
   b. Age-related macular degeneration
   c. A cataract
   d. Retinitis pigmentosa

   ANS: D   DIF: Moderate   REF: 199 & 201   OBJ: 6.11

145. While they both significantly affect vision, retinitis pigmentosa and age-related macular degeneration differ in that retinitis pigmentosa _____ and age-related macular degeneration _____.
   a. is due to genetics; is due to illness
   b. impacts peripheral vision; impacts central vision
   c. is more likely to be found in males; is more likely to be found in females
   d. impacts close vision; impacts far vision

   ANS: B   DIF: Difficult   REF: 199 & 201   OBJ: 6.11

146. Increased eye pressure that can eventually lead to blindness is called
   a. glaucoma.
   b. retinitis pigmentosa.
   c. cataracts.
   d. presbyopia.

   ANS: A   DIF: Moderate   REF: 201   OBJ: 6.11
   KEY: WWW

147. Older adults seem to have the greatest visual perceptual problems
   a. when tasks consist of color objects rather than black and white objects.
   b. on tasks that are complex and novel.
   c. when they must focus on tasks one at a time, in a sequential manner, rather than in a simultaneous manner.
   d. when they are given oral instructions rather than written instructions.

   ANS: B   DIF: Moderate   REF: 202   OBJ: 6.11

148. Woody has just been diagnosed with presbycusis. What is he most likely experiencing?
   a. He is hearing voices of people who are not there.
   b. He is hearing a continuous ringing sound in his ear.
   c. He is having difficulty hearing low-frequency sounds.
   d. He is having difficulty hearing high-frequency sounds.

   ANS: D   DIF: Moderate   REF: 202   OBJ: 6.12

149. Which best describes the hearing of most older adults?
   a. Minor hearing loss especially for high-frequency sounds
   b. Significant hearing loss especially for high-frequency sounds
   c. Minor hearing loss especially for low-frequency sounds
   d. Significant hearing loss especially for low-frequency sounds

   ANS: A   DIF: Moderate   REF: 202   OBJ: 6.12

150. Which statement concerning speech perception in adulthood is true?
   a. Loud background noise is more distracting to young adults than to older adults.
   b. Older adults are more likely to recall fewer details from a conversation that took place in a noisy restaurant.
   c. Older adults tend to be better at attending to multiple conversations than young adults.
   d. In familiar setting, older adults tend to not use contextual cues to help them interpret what they are hearing.

   ANS: B   DIF: Easy   REF: 202-203   OBJ: 6.12

151. The ability to taste _____ does NOT appear to decline with age.
   a. sour fruit   c. lightly salted crackers
   b. bitter herbs   d. sweet candy

   ANS: D   DIF: Moderate   REF: 204   OBJ: 6.13

152. Research findings from Murphy (1985) suggests that the ability of older individuals to identify food is most negatively impacted by
   a. losses in the ability to taste and smell.
   b. losses in the ability to taste and cognitive declines impacting memory.
   c. losses in the ability to smell and cognitive declines impacting memory.
   d. losses in the ability to see and cognitive declines impacting memory.

   ANS: C   DIF: Moderate   REF: 204   OBJ: 6.13
   KEY: WWW

153. Old people are most likely to keep their homes too hot or too cold because
   a. they tend to be less sensitive to changes in temperature.
   b. changes in temperature tend to induce a loss of balance.
   c. their constant pain will make them seek environments of different temperatures.
   d. the myelin in their brains begins to be destroyed and this leaves them with bodies that crave heat.

   ANS: A   DIF: Moderate   REF: 205   OBJ: 6.13

154. In terms of their ability to sense pain, old people typically experience
   a. less sensitivity to mild pain.
   b. more sensitivity to mild pain.
   c. decreased sensitivity for all types and levels of pain.
   d. increased sensitivity for all types and levels of pain.

   ANS: A   DIF: Moderate   REF: 205   OBJ: 6.13

TRUE/FALSE

1. The brain's interpretation of sensory information is known as sensation.

   ANS: F   DIF: Moderate   REF: 174   OBJ: 6.1

2. Constructivists believe that we need experience in order to learn how to interpret our sensory experiences.

   ANS: T   DIF: Moderate   REF: 174   OBJ: 6.1

3. Nativists believe that we enter the world with knowledge that helps us understand the world.

   ANS: T   DIF: Moderate   REF: 174   OBJ: 6.1
   KEY: WWW

4. Habituation refers to learning to be bored by repeatedly presented stimuli.

   ANS: T   DIF: Moderate   REF: 175   OBJ: 6.2

5. Visual acuity is defined as the ability to see depth.

   ANS: F   DIF: Easy   REF: 176   OBJ: 6.3
   KEY: WWW

6. Young infants appear to prefer visual displays that are dynamic and moderately complex.

   ANS: T   DIF: Easy   REF: 177   OBJ: 6.3

7. When tested on the visual cliff, seven-month-old infants will usually cross the cliff to reunite with their mothers.

   ANS: F   DIF: Moderate   REF: 179-181   OBJ: 6.3

8. Intuitive theorists believe that infants are born with organized systems of knowledge.

   ANS: T   DIF: Easy   REF: 181   OBJ: 6.3

9. Phonemes are the words used to produce a spoken sentence.

   ANS: F   DIF: Moderate   REF: 182   OBJ: 6.3
   KEY: WWW

10. Newborns appear to be able to recognize the voices of both their mother and father.

    ANS: F   DIF: Moderate   REF: 184   OBJ: 6.4

11. Infants fed with sour formula later preferred the taste of sour foods.

    ANS: T   DIF: Easy   REF: 184   OBJ: 6.5

12. Putting infants under deep anesthesia during surgery has been banned by the American Academy of Pediatrics.

    ANS: F   DIF: Easy   REF: 185   OBJ: 6.7

478

13. In order to ensure the most favorable long-term outcome concerning visual acuity, cataract surgery should be delayed until a child reaches at least age four years.

ANS: F   DIF: Easy   REF: 187   OBJ: 6.7

14. A child's attention span is typically more systematic than that of an infant.

ANS: T   DIF: Moderate   REF: 189   OBJ: 6.8

15. When a child is selectively attending, he is focusing on at least two stimuli at the same time.

ANS: F   DIF: Moderate   REF: 189   OBJ: 6.8

16. An impulsive child has a very hard time inhibiting her urges.

ANS: T   DIF: Easy   REF: 190   OBJ: 6.8
KEY: WWW

17. The most effective treatment for ADHD involves both medication and behavioral treatment.

ANS: T   DIF: Easy   REF: 193   OBJ: 6.8

18. For adolescents, the most common outcome of exposure to loud noise is tinnitus.

ANS: T   DIF: Moderate   REF: 194   OBJ: 6.10

19. Age-related macular degeneration results in the destruction of the cells responsible for peripheral vision.

ANS: F   DIF: Moderate   REF: 178   OBJ: 6.11

20. Older adults have the greatest difficulty in processing visual information when the situation is familiar and the task is simple.

ANS: F   DIF: Moderate   REF: 202   OBJ: 6.11
KEY: WWW

COMPLETION

1. The interpretation of sensory information is called _____.

ANS: perception

DIF: Moderate   REF: 174   OBJ: 6.1   KEY: WWW

2. _____ theorists believe that infants enter the world equipped with knowledge that allows them to perceive a meaningful world.

ANS: Nativist

DIF: Difficult   REF: 174   OBJ: 6.1

479

3. The ability of the lens to change shape in order to bring an image into focus is referred to as visual _____.

ANS: accommodation

DIF: Difficult   REF: 176   OBJ: 6.3

4. A black-and-white checkerboard would have a great deal of _____, which is the amount of light-dark transition of an object.

ANS: contour

DIF: Difficult   REF: 177   OBJ: 6.3

5. A child who understands that an object is the same size, despite the fact that it appears to become smaller as it moves into the distance, comprehends the concept of size _____.

ANS: constancy

DIF: Difficult   REF: 179   OBJ: 6.3   KEY: WWW

6. Gibson and Walk used a devise called a _____ to assess depth perception in infants and toddlers.

ANS: visual cliff

DIF: Moderate   REF: 179   OBJ: 6.3

7. Some developmentalists believe that infants are equipped with _____ theories, which are organized systems of knowledge that allow the child to make sense of the world.

ANS: intuitive

DIF: Difficult   REF: 181   OBJ: 6.3

8. The controversial surgery involving the implantation of electrodes designed to stimulate the auditory nerve is called a _____ implant.

ANS: cochlear

DIF: Moderate   REF: 183   OBJ: 6.4   KEY: WWW

9. The sense of smell, or _____, takes place in sensory receptors located in the nasal passage.

ANS: olfaction

DIF: Moderate   REF: 185   OBJ: 6.5

10. The ability to recognize through one sense an object that is familiar through another is referred to as _____ perception.

    ANS: cross-modal

    DIF: Moderate   REF: 186   OBJ: 6.6   KEY: WWW

11. A child with _____ attention can keep deliberate focus on one stimulus while ignoring others.

    ANS: selective

    DIF: Moderate   REF: 189   OBJ: 6.8

12. The ringing that follows exposure to loud noise is called _____.

    ANS: tinnitus

    DIF: Moderate   REF: 194   OBJ: 6.10

13. Researchers have proposed a fifth type of basic "taste" called _____ that is said to be the flavor of "savory."

    ANS: umami

    DIF: Difficult   REF: 195   OBJ: 6.10

14. A sensory _____ is the point at which the lowest amount of stimulation results in detection.

    ANS: threshold

    DIF: Moderate   REF: 197   OBJ: 6.11

15. The process by which the eye becomes more sensitive to low levels of light is referred to as dark _____.

    ANS: adaptation

    DIF: Moderate   REF: 198   OBJ: 6.11

16. _____ is a visual disorder in which the lens thickens and individuals have difficulty viewing nearby items.

    ANS: Presbyopia

    DIF: Moderate   REF: 199   OBJ: 6.11

17. Age-related _____ degeneration involves damage to the retinal cells and results in the loss of central vision.

    ANS: macular

    DIF: Moderate   REF: 199   OBJ: 6.11

18. Retinitis _____ is a hereditary disorder that leads to the loss of peripheral vision.

    ANS: pigmentosa

    DIF: Moderate   REF: 199 & 201   OBJ: 6.11   KEY: WWW

19. _____ is an eye disorder caused by increased fluid pressure.

    ANS: Glaucoma

    DIF: Moderate   REF: 201   OBJ: 6.11

20. _____ is the most common age-related form of hearing loss and involves the inability to detect high-pitched or high-frequency sounds.

    ANS: Presbycusis

    DIF: Moderate   REF: 202   OBJ: 6.12

ESSAY

1. Discuss the basic beliefs of nativists, constructivists, and intuitive theorists concerning sensation and perception.

    ANS: Answer not provided   REF: 174-175   OBJ: 6.1

2. How do researchers use habituation, evoked potentials, and preferential looking to study infant perception?

    ANS: Answer not provided   REF: 175-176   OBJ: 6.2

3. Discuss the changes in visual acuity, pattern perception, and depth during infancy.

    ANS: Answer not provided   REF: 176-181   OBJ: 6.3

4. Discuss the process of the development of speech perception and voice recognition in infants.

    ANS: Answer not provided   REF: 182-184   OBJ: 6.4

5. Describe the quality of the senses of taste, smell, touch, temperature, and pain of the typical one-year-old.

    ANS: Answer not provided   REF: 184-186   OBJ: 6.5

6. What are the basic symptoms of attention deficit hyperactivity disorder? What is the most likely developmental progression of the disorder? How can it be treated?

    ANS: Answer not provided   REF: 190-193   OBJ: 6.9

7. Discuss any four age-related visual problems/disorders found in adults.

   ANS: Answer not provided   REF: 197-201   OBJ: 6.11   KEY: WWW

8. Discuss evidence indicating that early life experience (including culture) can impact perceptual development. Be sure to provide a specific example.

   ANS: Answer not provided   REF: 186-188   OBJ: 6.7   KEY: WWW

9. Describe three types of changes in attention skills that take place between infancy and adolescence.

   ANS: Answer not provided   REF: 189-190   OBJ: 6.8   KEY: WWW

10. How does the sense of hearing change in older adulthood? What is the impact of these changes?

    ANS: Answer not provided   REF: 202-203   OBJ: 6.12   KEY: WWW

MULTIPLE CHOICE

1. Cognition is best defined as the activity of
   a. sensing energy in the environment.
   b. knowing and processing through which knowledge is acquired.
   c. brain maturation.
   d. unconscious influences.

   ANS: B   DIF: Moderate   REF: 210   OBJ: 7.1

2. Dr. Gretzky defines himself as a cognitive psychologist. Given this information, you would most likely believe Dr. Gretzky studies
   a. operant conditioning in rats.   c. children's thinking skills.
   b. the endocrine system.   d. the olfactory system.

   ANS: C   DIF: Easy   REF: 210   OBJ: 7.1

3. Piaget's intrigue concerning _____ initially spurred his interest in cognitive development.
   a. age-related mistakes in children's responses
   b. the relationship between humans and primates
   c. sex differences in the ability to problem-solve
   d. brain lateralization research

   ANS: A   DIF: Moderate   REF: 210   OBJ: 7.1

4. Piaget was most interested in determining
   a. which genes drive development.
   b. social interactions with adults could be shown to determine cognitive development in children.
   c. the most effective way to test for a child's IQ.
   d. how children think.

   ANS: D   DIF: Easy   REF: 210   OBJ: 7.1
   KEY: WWW

5. What 1960s event brought Piaget's theory into the mainstream of American science?
   a. The end of the Cold War
   b. Woodstock, which opened up the society to the acceptance of alternative ways of thinking
   c. Flavell's summary of Piaget's work that was published in English
   d. Piaget's death, which focused attention on his life's work

   ANS: C   DIF: Moderate   REF: 210   OBJ: 7.1

6. Piaget's clinical method involves
   a. uncovering unconscious motives for behavior.
   b. presenting standardized questions to all children tested.
   c. observing children in their natural environment.
   d. a flexible question-and-answer technique.

   ANS: D   DIF: Moderate   REF: 210-211   OBJ: 7.1

7. Ten-year-old Chester has just been asked, "What is 10 plus 10?" He says, "The answer is 22."
   How would a researcher best use Piaget's clinical method to follow-up this response?
   a. She would ask Chester to count the number of fingers on each hand.
   b. She would ask Chester to explain how he came up with the answer of "22."
   c. She would ask Chester to describe any abuse he had endured as a child.
   d. She would ask Chester to give a blood sample.

   ANS: B   DIF: Difficult   REF: 210-211   OBJ: 7.1

8. According to Piaget, intelligence is the ability to
   a. adapt to one's environment.   c. process information.
   b. respond to reinforcement.   d. score well on IQ tests.

   ANS: A   DIF: Moderate   REF: 211   OBJ: 7.1

9. Piaget argued that newborns enter the world with
   a. no means of adaptation.
   b. senses and reflexes that can assist in adaptation.
   c. little interest in investigating the world around them.
   d. an intuitive knowledge of basic biology and physics.

   ANS: B   DIF: Moderate   REF: 211   OBJ: 7.1

10. Which of the following is the best description of a schema?
    a. An organized way of thinking or acting that allows us to interpret our experiences
    b. A standard way of solving a problem in the fewest possible steps
    c. Changing our experiences in order to adapt to our environment
    d. Interpreting new experiences by using previously stored information

    ANS: A   DIF: Moderate   REF: 211   OBJ: 7.1

11. Which of the following is an example of a behavioral schema?
    a. Using a block to represent a car
    b. Asking about grandma even when she's not present
    c. Grasping a block or a bottle of milk
    d. Calling the dog by the cat's name

    ANS: C   DIF: Difficult   REF: 211   OBJ: 7.1

12. Which of the following is an example of a symbolic schema?
    a. Counting the number of holes on a belt
    b. Creating a mental model of a dog or cat
    c. Sucking on the nipple of a bottle of milk
    d. Grasping an adult's finger

    ANS: B   DIF: Difficult   REF: 211   OBJ: 7.1
    KEY: WWW

13. Piaget refers to the process of combining existing schemas into new and more complex ones as
    a. centration.
    b. transitivity.
    c. guided participation.
    d. organization.

    ANS: D   DIF: Moderate   REF: 211   OBJ: 7.1

14. Adam has a schema for saying, "Hi." He has a second schema for holding out his hand. He has another schema for making eye contact. With time, Adam is able to combine the simple schemas into a complex structure of a greeting (i.e., simultaneously making eye contact, saying "Hi," and holding out his hand to be shaken). According to Piaget, Adam is demonstrating
    a. organization.
    b. hypothetical-deductive reasoning.
    c. reversibility.
    d. class inclusion.

    ANS: A   DIF: Difficult   REF: 211   OBJ: 7.1

15. According to Piaget, adaptation is best defined as
    a. adjusting to the demands of the environment.
    b. reducing schemas.
    c. the ability to think about abstract concepts.
    d. the maturation of the mind.

    ANS: A   DIF: Moderate   REF: 211   OBJ: 7.1

16. Piaget stated that adaptation involves the two major processes of
    a. accommodation and symbolic thinking.
    b. assimilation and accommodation.
    c. assimilation and organization.
    d. organization and equilibration.

    ANS: B   DIF: Moderate   REF: 211-212   OBJ: 7.1

17. Assimilation is best defined as the process in which
    a. a conditioned stimulus becomes an unconditioned stimulus.
    b. multiple schemas are combined into a single scheme.
    c. we interpret new experiences in terms of existing schemas or cognitive structures.
    d. the unconscious mind impacts the conscious mind.

    ANS: C   DIF: Difficult   REF: 211   OBJ: 7.1

18. Eighteen-month-old Mickey is visiting a theme park for the first time. At the park, he sees some zebras, an animal with which he is unfamiliar. Despite this, he looks at the animals and shouts, "Look! Horse!" He had previously formed a mental schema for horses. Piaget would say that Mickey's reaction best demonstrates the concept of
    a. accommodation.
    c. assimilation.
    b. reversibility.
    d. formal thought.

    ANS: C   DIF: Difficult   REF: 211   OBJ: 7.1

19. Which of the following is the best example of assimilation?
    a. Naming your dog Barney after the famous purple Barney on TV
    b. Changing the name of your dog after finding out that a classmate has a dog with the same name
    c. Pretending that your dog is a horse
    d. Naming the first dog you meet, "Spot," and then calling all other dogs that you meet "Spot"

    ANS: D   DIF: Difficult   REF: 211   OBJ: 7.1
    KEY: WWW

20. Jerry likes to play with his stuffed animals, dragging them around the house by their arms, ears, or tails. He tries to do this with Tom the cat one day, but Tom hisses at Jerry and runs off, leaving Jerry perplexed and crying. Jerry's original attempt to play with the cat best illustrates the concept of
    a. accommodation.
    c. disequilibrium.
    b. assimilation.
    d. fixation

    ANS: B   DIF: Difficult   REF: 211   OBJ: 7.1

21. Accommodation is best defined as
    a. the process of modifying existing schema to better fit new experiences..
    b. knowing an object continues to exist even after it has left your sensory range.
    c. thinking that everyone else possesses the same experiences as you.
    d. using scientific logic to solve all problems.

    ANS: A   DIF: Moderate   REF: 212   OBJ: 7.1

22. Mabel always thought of herself as being incapable when it came to fixing things. She easily developed the habit of asking her husband, Abel, to do even the simplest "fix-it" tasks, like changing a light bulb. Then one day Mabel got a flat tire on a country road. She managed to struggle through the process of changing the tire all on her own. From then on, she felt much more capable, and started to fix more things around the house. This best illustrates
    a. accommodation.
    c. disequilibrium.
    b. assimilation.
    d. fixation.

    ANS: A   DIF: Difficult   REF: 212   OBJ: 7.1

23. Peggy finds that yelling at her dog is an effective way to get the dog to learn to behave. Peggy has recently taken a job as a substitute Spanish teacher at a local middle school. During her first week of class, Peggy becomes aware that yelling at her students is not an effective way to get them to learn to behave. Piaget would say that Peggy's situation would likely lead her to experience cognitive
   a. inclusion.
   b. conditioning.
   c. realism.
   d. disequilibrium.

   ANS: D   DIF: Difficult   REF: 212   OBJ: 7.1

24. According to Piaget, when our internal thoughts are consistent with the evidence we are receiving from the world, we are experiencing
   a. plasticity.
   b. equilibration.
   c. cognitive dissonance.
   d. fixation.

   ANS: B   DIF: Moderate   REF: 212   OBJ: 7.1

25. Which statement best describes Piaget's theory on intelligence?
   a. Intelligence develops as the result of classical conditioning.
   b. Intelligence develops as the result of interactions between biologically based individuals and their interaction with an environment.
   c. Intelligence is solely the product of biological maturation.
   d. Intelligence is solely the product of experience.

   ANS: B   DIF: Moderate   REF: 212   OBJ: 7.1

26. From first to last, what is the correct order of Piaget's stages of cognitive development?
   a. Sensorimotor, preoperational, concrete operations, formal operations
   b. Preoperational, sensorimotor, formal operations, concrete operations
   c. Sensorimotor, concrete operations, preoperational, formal operations
   d. Preoperational, concrete operations, formal operations, sensorimotor

   ANS: A   DIF: Easy   REF: 212   OBJ: 7.1

27. Almost all of Timmy's cognitive structures appear to involve basic behavioral schemas for coordinating sensory input and motor responses (e.g., put hand near object, if object is hot, then pull hand away from object). Given this description, Timmy is best classified as being in Piaget's _____ stage of development.
   a. formal operations
   b. preoperational
   c. concrete operations
   d. sensorimotor

   ANS: D   DIF: Moderate   REF: 213   OBJ: 7.2

28. Piaget hypothesized that an infant's first schemas for interacting with the environment always begin with
   a. cross-modal reactions.
   b. conservation.
   c. reflexes.
   d. trial-and-error accommodations.

   ANS: C   DIF: Difficult   REF: 213   OBJ: 7.2

29. The key characteristic of a primary circular reaction is that they are
   a. repeated actions related to one's own body that originally happened by chance.
   b. a one-time event related to one's own body that originally happened by chance.
   c. repeated actions related to one's own body that originally happened by choice.
   d. a one-time event related to one's own body that originally happened by choice.

   ANS: A   DIF: Moderate   REF: 213   OBJ: 7.2

30. Baby Jay accidently sucked his thumb, now seems to love to suck his thumb, and has learned to do it over and over again. This best exemplifies the concept of a
   a. beginning of thought.   c. secondary circular reaction.
   b. primary circular reaction.   d. tertiary circular reaction.

   ANS: B   DIF: Moderate   REF: 213   OBJ: 7.2

31. A _____ circular reaction is a repetitive action that involves something in an infant's external environment.
   a. coordination   c. secondary
   b. primary   d. tertiary

   ANS: C   DIF: Moderate   REF: 213-214   OBJ: 7.2
   KEY: WWW

32. Once while she was about to take a nap, baby Carolyn accidentally sucked on her blanket. Now she repeatedly sucks on the blanket when she's going to sleep. This new behavior is an example of
   a. coordination of secondary schemes.   c. a secondary circular reaction.
   b. a primary circular reaction.   d. a tertiary circular reaction.

   ANS: C   DIF: Difficult   REF: 213-214   OBJ: 7.2
   KEY: WWW

33. According to Piaget, _____ occur when an infant combines secondary actions to achieve a simple goal.
   a. secondary circular reactions   c. tertiary circular reactions
   b. coordination of secondary schemes d. beginning of thought

   ANS: B   DIF: Easy   REF: 213-214   OBJ: 7.2

34. A true sense of curiosity and novelty first emerge during the _____ stage of development.
   a. secondary circular reactions   c. tertiary circular reactions
   b. coordination of secondary schemes d. beginning of thought

   ANS: C   DIF: Moderate   REF: 213-214   OBJ: 7.2
   KEY: WWW

490

35. Franco is enjoying a fine lunch in his high chair. He picks up a handful of spaghetti and stuffs it in his mouth. Next, he picks up two handfuls and shoves them in his ears. The next handful goes in his hair, and the one after that is casually thrown on the floor. As his motivation appears to be simply the novelty of each of these acts, Franco's behavior would best be categorized as a
    a. secondary circular reaction.
    b. primary circular reaction.
    c. tertiary circular reaction.
    d. beginning of thought.

    ANS: C   DIF: Difficult   REF: 213-214   OBJ: 7.2

36. Which is the most advanced substage of the sensorimotor stage?
    a. Beginning of thought
    b. Secondary circular reaction
    c. Coordination of secondary schemes
    d. Tertiary circular reaction

    ANS: A   DIF: Easy   REF: 213-214   OBJ: 7.2

37. Saturn has discovered that even though her dad won't let her play with his set of car keys, she can use a ring of metal tabs and pretend that these are his car keys. Saturn's behavior would indicate that she is in the _____ substage of sensorimotor development.
    a. secondary circular reactions
    b. primary circular reactions
    c. tertiary circular reactions
    d. beginning of thought

    ANS: D   DIF: Moderate   REF: 213-214   OBJ: 7.2

38. To a young infant, out of sight is literally out of mind. Piaget stated that this was due to a lack of
    a. reversibility.
    b. insight.
    c. object permanence.
    d. horizontal décalage.

    ANS: C   DIF: Easy   REF: 214   OBJ: 7.2

39. Which infant behavior best demonstrates object permanence?
    a. Crying and reaching for a favorite toy you were playing with after it has been put inside a toy box
    b. Repeatedly swiping at a mobile hanging over the crib
    c. Crying when someone grabs a toy out of your hand
    d. Trying to grab a toy that you can see, but is just out of reach

    ANS: A   DIF: Moderate   REF: 214   OBJ: 7.2

40. The A not B error involves
    a. inability to realize that a bowl of ice cream has the same amount when the ice cream has melted.
    b. tendency to search for an object in a place where it was last found rather than in a new hiding place.
    c. failure to convert a concrete problem into an abstract problem.
    d. valuing adaptation over organization.

    ANS: B   DIF: Moderate   REF: 214   OBJ: 7.2

41. Five-year-old Linus is playing with his baby sister, Lucy. He takes Lucy's teddy bear and hides it behind a pillow while Lucy watches. Lucy quickly finds the bear. Then Linus puts teddy in a bag, puts the bag behind a chair (where he dumps teddy), and then brings out the empty bag. Lucy looks inside the bag, but doesn't look for teddy behind the chair and is surprised when it is not there. According to Piaget, Lucy
    a. is demonstrating object permanence.
    b. is playing to an imaginary audience.
    c. is committing the A not B error.
    d. is a formal operational thinker.

    ANS: C   DIF: Difficult   REF: 214   OBJ: 7.2

42. Piaget argued that object permanence is fully developed at 18 months. Recent research has indicated that
    a. Piaget's time estimate was right on.
    b. object permanence is actually developed at birth.
    c. awareness of object permanence is not apparent at birth but develops well before Piaget thought.
    d. object permanence actually develops around age two years.

    ANS: C   DIF: Moderate   REF: 214-215   OBJ: 7.2

43. Object permanence research using toddlers with spinal muscular dystrophy (SMA) found that
    a. children with SMA tend not to advance beyond the sensorimotor stage.
    b. having SMA did not impact responding on an object permanence task.
    c. motor impulses are faster than cognitive impulses.
    d. object permanence responding may be influenced by the time interval between seeing and being able to reach for it.

    ANS: D   DIF: Moderate   REF: 216   OBJ: 7.2

44. Piaget contended that in infancy,
    a. reaching was a developmental precursor of looking.
    b. reaching and looking represented the same activity.
    c. looking was a developmental precursor of reaching.
    d. reaching and looking were unrelated behaviors.

    ANS: C   DIF: Difficult   REF: 216   OBJ: 7.2

45. The "crowning achievement" of the sensorimotor stage is the ability to
    a. display secondary circular reactions.
    b. deal with a purely abstract task.
    c. conserve.
    d. construct mental symbols to guide behavior.

    ANS: D   DIF: Easy   REF: 216   OBJ: 7.2

46. The ability to use images or words to stand for objects or experiences is called
    a. object permanence.
    b. symbolic capacity.
    c. reversibility.
    d. horizontal décalage.

    ANS: B   DIF: Easy   REF: 216   OBJ: 7.2

47. Which symbolic behavior did Piaget's daughter Lucienne appear to use that assisted her in thinking about who to reach a chain in a box?
    a. She opened and closed her mouth
    b. She drew a picture of a refrigerator with food inside
    c. She said, "chain out box"
    d. She put a piece of cereal in her hand, enclosed it into a fist, and used her other hand to take out the "hidden" pieced of cereal

    ANS: A   DIF: Moderate   REF: 216   OBJ: 7.2

48. Piaget stated that the preoperational stage of development normally begins around
    a. 2 months of age.   c. 2 years of age.
    b. 12 months of age.   d. 12 years of age.

    ANS: C   DIF: Easy   REF: 217   OBJ: 7.3
    KEY: WWW

49. Piaget suggested that the key cognitive acquisition in the preoperational stage of cognitive development is the ability to
    a. comprehend object permanence.
    b. refer to people and objects that are not physically present.
    c. seriate concepts.
    d. construct a personal fable.

    ANS: B   DIF: Moderate   REF: 217   OBJ: 7.3

50. Which childhood activity best illustrates symbolic capacity?
    a. Pretending to be a superhero   c. Kicking a soccer ball
    b. Riding a two-wheeled bicycle   d. Playing with an electric train

    ANS: A   DIF: Easy   REF: 217   OBJ: 7.3

51. Imaginary companions are most likely to first develop during the _____ stage of development.
    a. formal operations   c. sensorimotor
    b. concrete operations   d. preoperational

    ANS: D   DIF: Moderate   REF: 217   OBJ: 7.3

52. Four-year-old Lenny has invented an imaginary companion, an invisible octopus named Squiggy. How would a Piagetian most likely react to Lenny's behavior?
    a. He might suspect that Lenny is cognitively and socially advanced.
    b. He would see it as a sign of possible mental illness.
    c. He would suggest that Lenny cannot decenter from an object.
    d. He would state that it is impossible for a child that young to create any imaginary companions.

    ANS: A   DIF: Moderate   REF: 217   OBJ: 7.3

53. Focus on the most obvious features of an object or situation is referred to as
    a. perceptual salience.   c. decentration.
    b. horizontal décalage.   d. transitivity.

    ANS: A   DIF: Easy   REF: 217   OBJ: 7.3

493

54. Virginia tells her mom that "there is no Santa Claus" and as evidence presents the fact that most of the gifts that are supposed to come from Santa have labels from Target, Wal-Mart, and other retail stores. Virginia's questioning of Santa appears to be based on the concept of
   a. guided participation.
   b. adolescent egocentrism.
   c. seriation.
   d. perceptual salience.

   ANS: D   DIF: Difficult   REF: 217-218   OBJ: 7.3
   KEY: WWW

55. Why might perceptual salience lead a child not to believe in the Easter Bunny?
   a. The fact that Easter is a holiday
   b. The fact that it would be impossible for one rabbit to deliver millions of eggs in one night
   c. The fact that eggs come from chickens
   d. The fact that Easter eggs come in many colors

   ANS: B   DIF: Moderate   REF: 217-218   OBJ: 7.3

56. Conservation is best defined as the ability to
   a. think abstractly.
   b. think the way other people think.
   c. understand that some properties of an object remain the same even if other properties change.
   d. realize that an object continues to exist even if that object has left the sensory range.

   ANS: C   DIF: Moderate   REF: 217   OBJ: 7.3

57. Jimmy watches as his mom pours all of his juice out of a tall skinny glass into a short wide cup. He puts up a fuss, because he now thinks he doesn't have as much juice as he started with. Jimmy is unable to
   a. center.
   b. conserve.
   c. seriate.
   d. animate.

   ANS: B   DIF: Moderate   REF: 217   OBJ: 7.3
   KEY: WWW

58. Asked to choose between two cookies of equal size, one whole, and one broken, Jenny takes the broken cookie, saying that three cookies are better than one. Piaget would say that Jenny lacks
   a. centration.
   b. object permanence.
   c. seriation.
   d. conservation.

   ANS: D   DIF: Difficult   REF: 217   OBJ: 7.3

59. The Piagetian concept of "decentration" refers to the inability to
   a. focus on more than one dimension of a problem at one time.
   b. mentally reverse simple operations.
   c. understand that the amount of something remains the same regardless of a change in shape or position.
   d. take another person's point of view.

   ANS: A   DIF: Easy   REF: 217   OBJ: 7.3

494

60. The tendency to focus on only a single aspect of a problem is called
   a. assimilation.
   b. centration.
   c. conservation.
   d. identification.

   ANS: B   DIF: Easy   REF: 217   OBJ: 7.3

61. Sarah Lee is helping her dad, Jefferson, bake cookies. First, Sarah divides the dough into two equal round piles. Then, as she goes to roll her dough, she trips, flattens her pile, and begins to cry. Her dad asks her if she's hurt, whereupon Sarah tells her dad that she isn't hurt but she's sad because now he has a tall pile with more dough than her. Sarah Lee's response demonstrates
   a. centration.
   b. conservation.
   c. relativistic thinking.
   d. seriation.

   ANS: A   DIF: Difficult   REF: 217   OBJ: 7.3

62. The process of mentally "undoing" an action is referred to as
   a. assimilation.
   b. a personal fable.
   c. egocentrism.
   d. reversibility.

   ANS: D   DIF: Easy   REF: 217   OBJ: 7.3

63. While watching a pizza being cut into 10 pieces, eight-year-old Domino suddenly realizes that the 10 pieces of pizza are actually the same amount as the original one pizza. This realization best reflects the process of
   a. reversibility.
   b. A not B error.
   c. seriation.
   d. static thought.

   ANS: A   DIF: Moderate   REF: 217   OBJ: 7.3

64. Billy always walks to kindergarten. His mom always picks him up at school after kindergarten on her way home from work. One day, mom asks Billy to walk home from kindergarten by himself. Billy insists he does not know how to walk home from kindergarten—he only knows how to walk to kindergarten. Which cognitive operation does Billy apparently lack?
   a. Centration
   b. Equilibration
   c. Reversibility
   d. Transformation

   ANS: C   DIF: Difficult   REF: 217   OBJ: 7.3
   KEY: WWW

65. Transformational thought is best defined as the ability to
   a. think to one's self.
   b. conceptualize processes of change from one state to another.
   c. put two or more objects in some order.
   d. focus on one aspect of a task.

   ANS: B   DIF: Moderate   REF: 217   OBJ: 7.3

495

66. Houdini is watching a magician pour a clear liquid from one glass into another. When the liquid enters the second glass, it magically changes to the color blue. While Houdini finds the trick interesting, he is not surprised that an object can be changed from one state to another. This indicates that Houdini possesses _____ thought.
   a. transformational
   b. egocentric
   c. sensorimotor
   d. animistic

   ANS: A   DIF: Moderate   REF: 217   OBJ: 7.3

67. Oscar, a college student, is checking seven-year-old Meyer to see what cognitive skills he has. He asks him to do some basic conservation tasks. Meyer has correctly responded that there is still the same amount of clay, whether it is in a round ball or rolled out into a hotdog-type shape. When Oscar asks why, Meyer demonstrates how the hotdog-type shaped piece of clay can be rolled back into a ball. This shows that Meyer has a good grasp of
   a. assimilation.
   b. transformational thought.
   c. equilibrium.
   d. primary circular reactions.

   ANS: B   DIF: Moderate   REF: 217   OBJ: 7.3
   KEY: WWW

68. Static thought involves a fixation on the
   a. process of transformation.
   b. end state.
   c. process of egocentrism.
   d. beginning state.

   ANS: B   DIF: Moderate   REF: 217-218   OBJ: 7.3

69. While observing her mother bake cookies, Lorna ignores the process by which eggs, flour, and sugar are combined and baked, but focuses on the end product of a cookie. Lorna's thought best exemplifies
   a. conservation.
   b. class inclusion.
   c. reversibility.
   d. static thought.

   ANS: D   DIF: Moderate   REF: 217-218   OBJ: 7.3

70. The inability to take a point of view other than one's own is referred to as
   a. animism.
   b. egocentrism.
   c. object permanence.
   d. static thought.

   ANS: B   DIF: Easy   REF: 218   OBJ: 7.3

71. When her mommy is sick in bed, Jenna brings her a pacifier and a rattle, thinking these will help mommy feel better since they always make Jenna feel better. Jenna's behavior best demonstrates
   a. centration.
   b. egocentrism.
   c. animism.
   d. formal thought.

   ANS: B   DIF: Moderate   REF: 218   OBJ: 7.3
   KEY: WWW

72. Belle is excited when she receives a telephone call from her grandmother on her birthday. When Belle's grandmother asks Belle how old she is, Belle holds up three fingers in front of the phone. Belle's belief that because she can see her fingers, so can her grandmother, reflects the Piagetian concept of
   a. centration.
   b. egocentrism.
   c. animism.
   d. formal thought.

   ANS: B   DIF: Difficult   REF: 218   OBJ: 7.3

73. A preoperational thinker is most likely to exhibit _____ thought.
   a. decentration
   b. reversible
   c. static
   d. transformational

   ANS: C   DIF: Moderate   REF: 217-220   OBJ: 7.3

74. The logic of class inclusion focuses on understanding that
   a. inanimate objects cannot move.
   b. a simple transformation does not change all aspects of an object.
   c. objects out of perceptual range still exist.
   d. parts are included in the whole.

   ANS: D   DIF: Moderate   REF: 220   OBJ: 7.3

75. Jack is taking a class on Piaget, and as part of an assignment, he is "testing" some youngsters on various Piagetian tasks. He gives four-year-old Meg a bag of white and striped marbles. They discuss the fact that marbles are made of glass. Meg counts the marbles—7 whites and 18 stripes. Jack asks, "Are there more striped marbles or more glass marbles?" Meg answers, "There are more striped marbles." This demonstrates Meg's difficulty with
   a. class inclusion.
   b. conservation.
   c. identity.
   d. transformations.

   ANS: A   DIF: Difficult   REF: 220   OBJ: 7.3

76. Research has demonstrated that when shown a card with a cat on one side and a dog on another side, three-year-olds seemed to correctly understand that when a researcher held the card so that the child saw the dog, the researcher must be seeing a cat. This indicates that children may not be as _____ as Piaget suggested.
   a. animated
   b. schema-driven
   c. logical
   d. egocentric

   ANS: D   DIF: Moderate   REF: 220   OBJ: 7.3

77. Four-year-old Kula is given a puppet and told to teach it all of the names that she can think of for certain animals and food items. At one point, she is asked the following questions about a lion: "Is it an animal?" and "Is it a type of cat?" Her correct response of "yes" to both questions indicates that Kukla understands
   a. object permanence.
   b. seriation .
   c. hypothetical-deductive reasoning.
   d. classification hierarchies.

   ANS: D   DIF: Moderate   REF: 221   OBJ: 7.3

78. A hallmark achievement of concrete operational thought is being able to
    a. solve object permanence tasks.
    b. solve conservation tasks.
    c. solve hypothetical problems.
    d. use relativistic thinking.

    ANS: B   DIF: Moderate   REF: 221-222   OBJ: 7.4

79. Which conservation skills does a concrete operations thinker possess?
    a. The ability to decenter, but neither reversibility nor transformational thought
    b. Reversibility, but neither the ability to decenter nor use transformational thought
    c. Transformational thought, but neither the ability to decenter nor to reverse
    d. The ability to decenter, reversibility, and transformational thought

    ANS: D   DIF: Easy   REF: 221-222   OBJ: 7.4

80. For the first time in his young life, Nemo is able to look at photos of aquatic animals and classify them as mammals or fish. He is also able to order them from smallest to largest. These skills indicate that Nemo has likely just entered the _____ stage of cognitive development.
    a. formal operations
    b. sensorimotor
    c. preoperational
    d. concrete operations

    ANS: D   DIF: Moderate   REF: 221-222   OBJ: 7.4

81. Okezie has just acquired the ability to accurately solve conservation tasks. Given this description, Okezie is best classified as being in Piaget's _____ stage of development.
    a. formal operations
    b. preoperational
    c. concrete operations
    d. sensorimotor

    ANS: C   DIF: Moderate   REF: 221-222   OBJ: 7.4
    KEY: WWW

82. What term did Piaget use to describe the fact that different cognitive skills related to the same stage of development may emerge at different times?
    a. Hypothetical-deductive reasoning
    b. Horizontal décalage
    c. Transformational thought
    d. Seriation

    ANS: B   DIF: Moderate   REF: 222   OBJ: 7.4
    KEY: WWW

83. What is horizontal décalage?
    a. The idea that children believe that inanimate objects can move
    b. The idea that cognitive skills may emerge at different times within the same stage of development
    c. The idea that children cannot think in terms of pure abstraction
    d. The idea that biology guides behavior

    ANS: B   DIF: Moderate   REF: 222   OBJ: 7.4

84. Thao is able to correctly solve conservation tasks involving mass but cannot solve conservation tasks involving volume. How would Piaget explain Thao's behavior?
   a. Typical of someone in the sensorimotor stage of development
   b. As involving animism
   c. Using the concept of horizontal décalage
   d. As a personal fable

   ANS: C   DIF: Moderate   REF: 222   OBJ: 7.4

85. Seriation involves
   a. the realization that properties of objects do not change even though appearance might be altered.
   b. understanding that subclasses are included in the whole class.
   c. understanding the difference between big and small.
   d. mentally arranging elements along a quantifiable scale.

   ANS: D   DIF: Moderate   REF: 222   OBJ: 7.4

86. Bell is shown a set of jars and is asked to arrange a group of them from shortest to tallest. This is a test for
   a. classification.   c. seriation.
   b. conservation.   d. centration.

   ANS: C   DIF: Moderate   REF: 222   OBJ: 7.4
   KEY: WWW

87. Amber can quickly and accurately arrange crayons from lightest to darkest. This demonstrates a capacity for
   a. animism.   c. seriation.
   b. centration.   d. transitional thinking.

   ANS: C   DIF: Moderate   REF: 222   OBJ: 7.4

88. Transitivity is best defined as
   a. the necessary relations among elements in a series.
   b. understanding one's own mental limitations.
   c. private, mental speech.
   d. the ability to convert an object into a mental image.

   ANS: A   DIF: Moderate   REF: 222   OBJ: 7.4

89. "Pete is older than Jill, and Jill is older than Pat. Who is older, Pete or Pat?" The ability to solve problems such as this demonstrates competence in
   a. decentration.   c. centration.
   b. identity.   d. transitivity.

   ANS: D   DIF: Moderate   REF: 222   OBJ: 7.4

90. During which stage of development would a person first be able to understand that her dad is a parent, an uncle, and someone's son (i.e., understand class inclusion)?
   a. Formal operations
   b. Sensorimotor
   c. Concrete operations
   d. Preoperational

   ANS: C   DIF: Moderate   REF: 222   OBJ: 7.4

91. The term "concrete" is used to describe concrete operations because
   a. understating reversibility at this stage is so hard (like concrete).
   b. once a child focuses on one aspect of a task, his thinking appears to be unmovable (set in stone or concrete).
   c. the path of understanding is paved with challenges (like a concrete road).
   d. individuals in this stage can mentally manipulate objects as long as they are present (concrete example).

   ANS: D   DIF: Moderate   REF: 222   OBJ: 7.4

92. One key difference between formal operational thought and concrete operational thought is that formal operational thinkers
   a. show more centration.
   b. can apply thoughts to real objects.
   c. can solve conservation tasks.
   d. can think about hard to imagine hypotheticals.

   ANS: D   DIF: Moderate   REF: 222   OBJ: 7.5

93. Concerning mental actions, concrete operations are to formal operations as
   a. objects are to ideas.
   b. knowing is to doing.
   c. imagined is to real.
   d. centration is to decentration.

   ANS: A   DIF: Difficult   REF: 222   OBJ: 7.5

94. A researcher asked students of different ages, "What would the world be like if there was no gravity?" According to Piaget's theory, which one of the following answers would most likely be heard from an adolescent in the formal operational stage?
   a. There is gravity, so this is a useless exercise.
   b. Things would fall.
   c. We would have to redesign classrooms with desks on the ceiling.
   d. I wouldn't like it if there was no gravity.

   ANS: C   DIF: Difficult   REF: 222-223   OBJ: 7.5
   KEY: WWW

95. On Piaget's famous pendulum task, most concrete operations thinkers use a _____ approach.
   a. random guessing
   b. trial-and-error
   c. guided participation
   d. hypothetical-deductive reasoning

   ANS: B   DIF: Moderate   REF: 223   OBJ: 7.5

500

96. What is the first step in hypothetical-deductive reasoning?
    a. Generate all possible hypotheses
    b. Get a concrete example
    c. Consider what others in your position would do
    d. Guided participation

    ANS: A   DIF: Easy   REF: 224   OBJ: 7.5

97. In what sort of reasoning does one move from general ideas to their specific implications?
    a. Empirical-inductive   c. Hypothetical-inductive
    b. Empirical-deductive   d. Hypothetical-deductive

    ANS: D   DIF: Easy   REF: 224   OBJ: 7.5

98. Which of Gibson's statements indicates that he is engaging in hypothetical-deductive reasoning?
    a. "I can still hear the sound of that guitar after the string has been strummed."
    b. "A guitar is just a larger version of a mandolin."
    c. "I bet that my guitar looks exactly like the one you have."
    d. "If the length of a guitar string matters, then a short string should produce a different sound than a long string."

    ANS: D   DIF: Difficult   REF: 224   OBJ: 7.5

99. Which cognitive skill would a formal operations thinker possess that a concrete operational thinker would lack?
    a. Hypothetical-deductive reasoning   c. Transformational thought
    b. Seriation   d. Class inclusion

    ANS: A   DIF: Easy   REF: 224   OBJ: 7.5
    KEY: WWW

100. Formal operational thinking differs from Piaget's other stages in that a formal thinker gains the ability to
    a. think systematically about abstract concepts.
    b. mentally manipulate objects that they can see.
    c. understand the symbols used in language.
    d. form mental schemas.

    ANS: A   DIF: Easy   REF: 222-224   OBJ: 7.5

101. Findings from the Munich Longitudinal Study of the Ontogenesis of Individual Competencies (LOGIC) demonstrated that most 12-year-olds
    a. could not recognize good or bad examples of scientific research nor could they create a good experiment themselves.
    b. could recognize good or bad examples of scientific research but could not create a good experiment themselves.
    c. could not recognize good or bad examples of scientific research but could create a good experiment themselves.
    d. could recognize good or bad examples of scientific research and could create a good experiment themselves.

    ANS: B   DIF: Moderate   REF: 224 & 226   OBJ: 7.5

501

102. By late adolescence, most individuals
   a. replace intuitive reasoning with scientific reasoning.
   b. replace scientific reasoning with intuitive reasoning.
   c. abandon both scientific reasoning and intuitive reasoning strategies.
   d. utilize both scientific reasoning and intuitive reasoning strategies.

   ANS: D   DIF: Moderate   REF: 226   OBJ: 7.5

103. The ability to separate prior knowledge from the demands of a task at hand is referred to as
   a. egocentrism.   c. decontextualization.
   b. conservation.   d. class inclusion.

   ANS: C   DIF: Easy   REF: 226   OBJ: 7.5

104. Gomer was born and raised in the Midwestern part of the United States. All of his life, he was told that seafood tasted terrible so he avoided it. One day while visiting the East Coast, he goes into a restaurant that features steamed clams. Gomer tells himself, "Those clams do smell good and many people eat seafood, so it can't be terrible to eat. I think I'll order a big bucket of steamers." Gomer's decision to eat the seafood would best be explained by the Piagetian concept of
   a. Reversibility   c. Animism
   b. Decontextualization   d. Horizontal décalage

   ANS: B   DIF: Difficult   REF: 226   OBJ: 7.5

105. One implication of formal operational thought is that adolescents are more likely than children to
   a. have idealized notions about their parent.
   b. rebel against the inconsistencies they are able to detect in the world.
   c. accept the realities of the world.
   d. solve problems by using a trial-and-error approach.

   ANS: B   DIF: Moderate   REF: 226-227   OBJ: 7.5

106. A teenager's difficulty in differentiating his own thoughts and feelings from those of other people is called adolescent
   a. class inclusion.   c. egocentrism.
   b. reversibility.   d. décalage.

   ANS: C   DIF: Moderate   REF: 227   OBJ: 7.5

107. Phillip is moping around because his steady girlfriend, Janet, is going on a date with another boy she's interested in. His dad comes up to him and says, "I know just how you feel, son..." Phillip cuts him off, shouting, "You don't know how I feel. No one knows how I feel! Just leave me alone!" Philip's response demonstrates a phenomenon known as
   a. adolescent egocentrism.   c. preoperational thinking.
   b. object permanence.   d. A not B error

   ANS: A   DIF: Easy   REF: 227   OBJ: 7.5

502

108. Paris spends the last week of summer vacation at the mall, looking for just the right outfit for the first day of 10th grade. Finally, she finds something she likes, and feels sure that everyone will notice her smashing outfit! This is an example of adolescent
   a. class inclusion.
   b. reversibility.
   c. egocentrism.
   d. décalage.

   ANS: C   DIF: Moderate   REF: 227   OBJ: 7.5
   KEY: WWW

109. The phenomenon of the _____ occurs when an individual confuses her own thoughts with those of a hypothesized group of people.
   a. A not B error
   b. personal fable
   c. imaginary audience
   d. class inclusion

   ANS: C   DIF: Moderate   REF: 227-228   OBJ: 7.5

110. Sally has just gotten her hair trimmed, and even though it doesn't look very different than before, she is sure everyone in homeroom will notice a big change and be focusing on her hair all day. This is an example of
   a. imaginary audience.
   b. personal fable.
   c. hypothetical-deductive reasoning.
   d. relativistic thinking.

   ANS: A   DIF: Moderate   REF: 227-228   OBJ: 7.5

111. Which statement best exemplifies the premise of an imaginary audience?
   a. Live hard and die young.
   b. Why ask why.
   c. Why is everyone looking at me?
   d. You don't know me, no one knows me.

   ANS: C   DIF: Moderate   REF: 227-228   OBJ: 7.5

112. The key to a personal fable is the belief that you
   a. are being watched by an imaginary audience.
   b. have an "invisible" friend.
   c. cannot deal with abstract concepts like philosophy or theology.
   d. are unique.

   ANS: D   DIF: Moderate   REF: 228   OBJ: 7.5

113. Which is the best example of a personal fable?
   a. Believing that life is a tragedy, thus every precaution needs to be taken to ensure everyone's safety
   b. Failing to be self-conscious in front of an audience
   c. Knowing that everyone wants you dead
   d. Believing that no one has ever felt grief more strongly than you

   ANS: D   DIF: Difficult   REF: 228   OBJ: 7.5

114. Jamie doesn't worry very much about contracting HIV from unprotected sex, saying "I'm a good guy. It can't happen to me." This is an example of
    a. imaginary audience.
    b. personal fable.
    c. A not B error.
    d. hypothetical-deductive reasoning.

    ANS: B   DIF: Difficult   REF: 228   OBJ: 7.5

115. Elkind suggested that adolescent egocentrism is due to increased
    a. self-consciousness.
    b. self-esteem.
    c. self-efficacy.
    d. self-confidence.

    ANS: A   DIF: Moderate   REF: 228   OBJ: 7.5

116. Recent research on adolescent egocentrism (e.g., Bell and Bromnick, 2003) suggests that teens are most worried about how they present themselves in public because of concerns regarding a(n) _____ audience.
    a. adult
    b. imaginary
    c. overly supportive
    d. real

    ANS: D   DIF: Moderate   REF: 228   OBJ: 7.5

117. Adults are most likely to regularly use formal operational thinking
    a. in making relationship decisions.
    b. in areas where they have some expertise.
    c. in high school and college courses but not on nonacademic tasks.
    d. on novel and complex tasks.

    ANS: B   DIF: Moderate   REF: 229   OBJ: 7.6

118. Some theorists have proposed the existence of a stage of cognitive development beyond the highest level proposed by Piaget. This hypothesized level of thinking is referred to as _____ thought.
    a. private
    b. hypothetical
    c. postformal
    d. decontextualized

    ANS: C   DIF: Easy   REF: 230   OBJ: 7.6

119. Relativistic thinking is best associated with the _____ stage of development.
    a. concrete operations
    b. formal operations
    c. postformal
    d. preoperational

    ANS: C   DIF: Easy   REF: 230   OBJ: 7.6

120. Seefeldt doesn't understand why his psychology instructor doesn't just tell the class the correct answer. When asked, his instructor says that there is no single correct answer, it depends on each individual's interpretation. Seefeldt's difficulty in accepting his professor's answer would indicate that Seefeldt lacks _____ thinking.
    a. class inclusion
    b. systematic
    c. relativistic
    d. concrete

    ANS: C   DIF: Moderate   REF: 230   OBJ: 7.6
    KEY: WWW

121. Which famous statement best illustrates the concept of relativistic thinking?
    a. Beauty is in the eye of the beholder.
    b. Truth is absolute.
    c. What goes up must come down.
    d. All men are created equal.

    ANS: A   DIF: Moderate   REF: 230   OBJ: 7.6

122. An absolutist believes that truth
    a. lies in the nature of reality, and that there is only one truth.
    b. is relative to the experiences of the thinker .
    c. does not exist.
    d. is stranger than fiction.

    ANS: A   DIF: Moderate   REF: 230   OBJ: 7.6

123. Perry's (1970) research with cognitive development in college students found that many
    students tended to be _____ in their thought when they first started college and grow to be
    _____ thinkers by the end of their college careers.
    a. formal; concrete
    b. absolutist; relativistic
    c. nonegocentric; egocentric
    d. decontextualized; contextualized

    ANS: B   DIF: Moderate   REF: 230   OBJ: 7.6

124. _____ thinking is best defined as detecting paradoxes and inconsistencies among ideas and
    attempting to reconcile them.
    a. Absolutist
    b. Static
    c. Preoperational
    d. Dialectical

    ANS: D   DIF: Moderate   REF: 231   OBJ: 7.6

125. Whose statement indicates that they are engaging in dialectic thinking?
    a. Earl, who says, "I love the fact that ice is cold."
    b. Eileen, who says, "I just do not understand how light can be both a wave and an
       individual element, but I will."
    c. Lowell, who says, "Drop a bowling ball and it will fall, can the world get any more
       consistent?"
    d. Rellen, who says, "The moon looks massive tonight."

    ANS: B   DIF: Moderate   REF: 231   OBJ: 7.6

126. Which would NOT typically be on a list of the characteristics of postformal thought?
    a. Understanding that knowledge is relative
    b. Accepting that the world is full of contradictions
    c. Rejecting input from others as it will taint the truth
    d. Integrating contradictions in some larger understanding

    ANS: C   DIF: Moderate   REF: 231   OBJ: 7.6

127. Which of the following statements is true regarding cognitive capacities during later adulthood?
   a. Older adults do not perform as well as younger adults on formal operational tasks.
   b. Older adults perform better than younger adults on novel tasks.
   c. Older adults perform better on laboratory tasks than on applied, everyday tasks.
   d. Older adults perform just as well as younger adults on concrete-operational and formal operational tasks.

   ANS: A   DIF: Moderate   REF: 231   OBJ: 7.6

128. Which is a legitimate question concerning the lack of success of older adults on Piagetian tasks?
   a. Could it be due to a lack of motivation to solve tasks that are so rarely encountered in real life?
   b. Could it be due to the over emphasis on IQ testing common to Piagetian tasks?
   c. Could it be due to slower reaction times commonly found in older study participants?
   d. Could it be due to the fact that normal hearing is required to solve all of Piaget's tasks?

   ANS: A   DIF: Moderate   REF: 231   OBJ: 7.6

129. Piaget's work,
   a. stifled most research on children's cognitive development.
   b. demonstrated that infants are active participants in their development.
   c. pointed out the critical effect that genes play in abnormal trajectories of development.
   d. lent significant support to theories that emphasize the key role of unconscious elements of the mind (e.g. id) .

   ANS: B   DIF: Easy   REF: 232   OBJ: 7.7

130. Piaget's theory
   a. does a nice job describing development, but a poor job explaining it.
   b. ignores the possibility that development may be the result of an interaction between nature and nurture.
   c. emphasizes the role of brain maturation in stage transition.
   d. clearly distinguishes between competence and performance.

   ANS: A   DIF: Moderate   REF: 232-233   OBJ: 7.7

131. Piaget's theory incorrectly overemphasized
   a. broad stages of development.
   b. sex differences.
   c. that knowledge is best thought of as anything but all or nothing.
   d. racial differences.

   ANS: A   DIF: Moderate   REF: 233   OBJ: 7.7
   KEY: WWW

132. Which is a common challenge to Piaget's theory?
    a. It failed to distinguish between competence and performance.
    b. It over estimated young minds.
    c. It place too much emphasis on explaining development rather than describing development.
    d. It over emphasized the role of social influence on cognitive development.

    ANS: A   DIF: Moderate   REF: 233   OBJ: 7.7

133. The main theme of Vygotsky's theory is that cognitive growth is
    a. a product of the child's social interactions within a cultural and historical context.
    b. uninfluenced by language acquisition.
    c. universal, with all children developing at the same rate and in the same sequence.
    d. exclusively shaped by genetic factors.

    ANS: A   DIF: Moderate   REF: 234   OBJ: 7.8

134. Gustav was born and raised in a small fishing village in Sweden. Vygotsky would argue that this experience will
    a. impact both how he thinks and what he thinks about.
    b. impact how he thinks but not what he thinks about.
    c. impact what he thinks about but not how he thinks.
    d. have no impact on this cognitive development.

    ANS: A   DIF: Moderate   REF: 234   OBJ: 7.8

135. Vygotsky referred to the gap between what a learner can accomplish independently and what he can do with guidance and assistance as the
    a. imaginary audience.   c. guided participation.
    b. personal fable.   d. zone of proximal development.

    ANS: D   DIF: Easy   REF: 234   OBJ: 7.9
    KEY: WWW

136. Which of the following is an example of Vygotsky's zone of proximal development?
    a. Figuring out the answer to your math homework after your sister gives you a hint
    b. Getting a better grade on the math test than you usually get
    c. Using trial and error to eliminate incorrect answers to a problem
    d. Thinking about a purely abstract problem like how many digits there are in infinity

    ANS: A   DIF: Difficult   REF: 234   OBJ: 7.9

137. How could Vygotsky's concept of the zone of proximal development be applied to intelligence testing?
a. A blood test could be given before the exam to test for genetic advantages in intellect.
b. All intelligence tests could be given in a standard language, as the effects of culture and language on intelligence are minimal.
c. The test-taker could be denied access to scratch paper and be told to perform all calculation in his or her head.
d. The person giving the test could be allowed to give hints if the test-taker answered incorrectly.

ANS: D   DIF: Difficult   REF: 234   OBJ: 7.9

138. Learning through active involvement in culturally relevant activities with the aid of knowledgeable individuals is referred to as
a. the personal fable.
b. guided participation.
c. transformational thought.
d. class inclusion.

ANS: B   DIF: Moderate   REF: 235   OBJ: 7.9

139. Rana never had any formal training in breeding animals, but had always actively helped his father in the family's business of breeding sheep. Consequently, Rana is now quite skilled at this practice. Vygotsky would refer to this skill acquisition as being the result of
a. a personal fable.
b. imaginary companions.
c. guided participation.
d. transformational thought.

ANS: C   DIF: Moderate   REF: 235   OBJ: 7.9

140. When Vygotsky referred to the concept of scaffolding, he was speaking about
a. guided assistance a skilled individual provides to a less skilled individual.
b. the "intellectual ladder of success" that children are innately drive to climb.
c. the importance of allowing children to "learn on their own" without adult interference.
d. the structures of the mind that hold together lower levels of thought and higher levels of thought.

ANS: A   DIF: Moderate   REF: 235   OBJ: 7.9

141. With respect to children's use of private speech, research suggests that this speech is (may)
a. unrelated to children's cognitive capabilities.
b. a sign of cognitive maturity.
c. a sign of immature egocentrism.
d. indicate that the child is autistic.

ANS: B   DIF: Moderate   REF: 236   OBJ: 7.10

142. Four-year-old Jackie often mutters to herself as she builds things with her blocks. Her utterances (e.g., "the blue one goes first") seem to be a running dialogue of her actions that are guiding her behavior. Vygotsky referred to this activity as _____ speech.
    a. private
    b. social
    c. egocentric
    d. telegraphic

    ANS: A   DIF: Moderate   REF: 136   OBJ: 7.10

143. Which is a legitimate criticism of Vygotsky's theory?
    a. There is no evidence that private speech helps children solve problems.
    b. He placed too much emphasis on the influence of social interactions.
    c. His stages of psychosocial development have received little empirical support.
    d. A model that focuses only on postformal thinking in adulthood is too limited to be considered a major developmental theory.

    ANS: B   DIF: Moderate   REF: 237   OBJ: 7.10

TRUE/FALSE

1. Cognition is the activity of knowing and the processes through which knowledge is acquired and problems are solved.

    ANS: T   DIF: Easy   REF: 210   OBJ: 7.1

2. Assimilation is the process of modifying existing schemas to better fit new experience.

    ANS: F   DIF: Moderate   REF: 211   OBJ: 7.1

3. A tertiary circular reaction involves repetition of interesting acts on objects in an infant's external environment.

    ANS: F   DIF: Moderate   REF: 213-214   OBJ: 7.2

4. The final substage of the sensorimotor period is called the secondary circular reaction period.

    ANS: F   DIF: Easy   REF: 213-214   OBJ: 7.2
    KEY: WWW

5. Toddlers with spinal muscular atrophy are better at some object permanence tasks than non-disabled children.

    ANS: T   DIF: Moderate   REF: 216   OBJ: 7.2

6. Having imaginary companions in childhood is associated with advanced social development.

    ANS: T   DIF: Moderate   REF: 217   OBJ: 7.3

7. Irreversibility and the inability to conserve are common characteristics of a person in the preoperational stage of development.

    ANS: T   DIF: Moderate   REF: 217   OBJ: 7.3

509

8. According to Piaget, centration is the ability to focus on multiple aspects of a task at the same time.

ANS: F   DIF: Moderate   REF: 217   OBJ: 7.3
KEY: WWW

9. An individual engaging in static thought is focused on the beginning state of the problem.

ANS: F   DIF: Moderate   REF: 217-218   OBJ: 7.4

10. Recent research has supported Piaget's conclusions that young children (age three or so) have no ability to take another person's point of view.

ANS: F   DIF: Moderate   REF: 220-221   OBJ: 7.3

11. Concrete operational thinkers can conserve, but they are still unable to use transformational thought.

ANS: F   DIF: Moderate   REF: 221-222   OBJ: 7.4
KEY: WWW

12. Seriation is the ability to arrange items along some quantifiable dimension.

ANS: T   DIF: Moderate   REF: 222   OBJ: 7.4

13. When using hypothetical-deductive reasoning, you begin by generating all possible hypotheses.

ANS: T   DIF: Moderate   REF: 224   OBJ: 7.5

14. A person who can decontextualize is able to separate prior knowledge from the demands of a current task.

ANS: T   DIF: Moderate   REF: 226   OBJ: 7.5
KEY: WWW

15. The tendency to think that your thoughts and feelings are unique underlies the personal fable.

ANS: T   DIF: Easy   REF: 228   OBJ: 7.5

16. Researchers have proposed the existence of a stage of thinking more advanced than any proposed by Piaget. This stage of thinking is referred to as preformal thought.

ANS: F   DIF: Easy   REF: 230   OBJ: 7.6

17. With regard to Piaget's stages of cognitive development, cultural factors have been shown to influence both the rate and sequence of stage acquisition.

ANS: F   DIF: Difficult   REF: 232   OBJ: 7.7

18. Vygotsky stressed the critical role that sociocultural context plays in cognitive development.

ANS: T   DIF: Moderate   REF: 234   OBJ: 7.8

19. Vygotsky referred to the gap between what a learner can accomplish independently and what he or she can accomplish with guidance as the synapse.

ANS: F   DIF: Moderate   REF: 234   OBJ: 7.9

20. Vygotsky saw private speech in toddlers as a sign of cognitive maturity.

ANS: T   DIF: Moderate   REF: 236   OBJ: 7.5
KEY: WWW

COMPLETION

1. The flexible question-and-answer technique used by Piaget was known as the _____ method.

ANS: clinical

DIF: Moderate   REF: 210-211   OBJ: 7.1

2. Piaget used the term _____ to describe the process by which we interpret new experiences in terms of existing schemas.

ANS: assimilation

DIF: Moderate   REF: 211   OBJ: 7.1   KEY: WWW

3. Piaget used the term _____ to describe the process by which we modify existing schemas to better fit our experiences.

ANS: accommodation

DIF: Moderate   REF: 212   OBJ: 7.1

4. The final substage of the sensorimotor stage of development is referred to as the beginning of _____.

ANS: thought

DIF: Moderate   REF: 213-214   OBJ: 7.2

5. Searching in a place where an object was last found rather than its new hiding place is called the _____ error.

ANS: A-not-B

DIF: Difficult   REF: 214   OBJ: 7.2

511

6. Perceptual _____ involves focusing on the most obvious features of a situation or object.

   ANS: salience

   DIF: Moderate   REF: 217   OBJ: 7.3   KEY: WWW

7. Piaget defined _____ as the ability to focus on two dimensions of a problem at the same time.

   ANS: decentration

   DIF: Moderate   REF: 217   OBJ: 7.3   KEY: WWW

8. _____ is the Piagetian term for the ability to mentally undo an action.

   ANS: Reversibility

   DIF: Moderate   REF: 217   OBJ: 7.3

9. Preoperational fixation on the end state of a task rather than the changes that transform one state into another is called _____ thought.

   ANS: static

   DIF: Difficult   REF: 217-218   OBJ: 7.3

10. The tendency to view the world solely from your own perspective is called _____.

    ANS: egocentrism

    DIF: Easy   REF: 218   OBJ: 7.3   KEY: WWW

11. Most 10-year-olds would be in Piaget's _____ operations stage of development.

    ANS: concrete

    DIF: Moderate   REF: 221   OBJ: 7.4

12. Piaget used the term _____ to explain his belief that different cognitive skills related to the same stage of cognitive development could emerge at different times.

    ANS: horizontal décalage

    DIF: Difficult   REF: 222   OBJ: 7.4

13. A person who had just begun to exhibit hypothetical-deductive reasoning would have just entered Piaget's _____ operations stage of development.

    ANS: formal

    DIF: Moderate   REF: 222-224   OBJ: 7.5

14. Extremely self-conscious behavior (e.g., not going to school because you believe that everyone in your class will notice the stain on your shirt) in the teen years is referred to as _____ audience.

ANS: imaginary

DIF: Moderate   REF: 227-228   OBJ: 7.5

15. The adolescent tendency to view your thoughts and feelings as unique is called the personal _____.

ANS: fable

DIF: Moderate   REF: 228   OBJ: 7.5

16. Postformal thought in which an individual understands that knowledge depends on the subjective perspective of the knower is referred to as _____ thinking.

ANS: relativistic

DIF: Moderate   REF: 230   OBJ: 7.6

17. Postformal thought in which an individual focuses on detecting paradoxes among ideas and attempts to reconcile them is referred to as _____ thinking.

ANS: dialectical

DIF: Moderate   REF: 231   OBJ: 7.6

18. Vygotsky called the gap between what a learner can do alone and what he or she can do with guidance and encouragement of a skilled partner the _____ development.

ANS: zone of proximal

DIF: Moderate   REF: 234   OBJ: 7.9

19. Vygotsky emphasized the importance of _____ participation in culturally relevant activities with support from others can lead to improvements in performance.

ANS: guided

DIF: Moderate   REF: 235   OBJ: 7.9   KEY: WWW

20. Vygotsky referred to speech that directs one's thought as _____ speech.

ANS: private

DIF: Moderate   REF: 236   OBJ: 7.10

ESSAY

1. Describe how the organization, adaptation, assimilation, accommodation, and equilibration contribute to the development of intellect.

   ANS: Answer not provided   REF: 211-212   OBJ: 7.1

2. Use Piagetian terminology and concepts to describe cognitive development from birth to age two years.

   ANS: Answer not provided   REF: 213-216   OBJ: 7.1-7.2

3. Describe the negative impact of egocentrism, irreversible thinking, and static thought on a child's ability to solve conservation problems.

   ANS: Answer not provided   REF: 217-218   OBJ: 7.3

4. How do adolescent egocentrism, the imaginary audience, and the personal fable impact the behavior of teenagers?

   ANS: Answer not provided   REF: 227-228   OBJ: 7.5

5. What are the elements of postformal thought?

   ANS: Answer not provided   REF: 229-231   OBJ: 7.6

6. In light of current research, what are some of the main concerns about Piaget's theory?

   ANS: Answer not provided   REF: 233   OBJ: 7.7

7. Suppose you need to design a program to teach six-year-old children a new academic skill. How would you approach this from Vygotsky's perspective?

   ANS: Answer not provided   REF: 234-236   OBJ: 7.9 & 7.10

8. What are the main cognitive advances made during the concrete operational stage of development?

   ANS: Answer not provided   REF: 221-222   OBJ: 7.4   KEY: WWW

9. What are the zone of proximal development, guided participation, and scaffolding, and how are they related?

   ANS: Answer not provided   REF: 211-213   OBJ: 7.9   KEY: WWW

10. Does Piaget or Vygotsky do a better job of describing the importance of private/egocentric speech? Support your answer with some of the research provided in your textbook.

   ANS: Answer not provided   REF: 235-236   OBJ: 7.10   KEY: WWW

514

MULTIPLE CHOICE

1. Research participant "AJ" (real name Jill Price) has the unusual ability to
    a. recall the name of every person she has ever met, regardless of how long they interacted.
    b. "see" a running image of past events as if they were currently happening.
    c. calculate "pi" to 1,000,000 digits.
    d. learn any language within one week's time.

    ANS: B   DIF: Easy   REF: 243   OBJ: 8.1

2. Who would be most likely to describe the process of reading and understanding this test question by focusing exclusively on the concepts of an "external stimulus" and an "overt response," with no discussion of the mind?
    a. Larry, who is a behaviorist
    b. Curly, who is a psychoanalyst
    c. Moe, who is a cognitive-oriented theorist
    d. Shemp, who is a Piagetian

    ANS: A   DIF: Moderate   REF: 244   OBJ: 8.1

3. The information-processing approach to learning
    a. focuses exclusively on the impact of genetics on intelligence.
    b. relies heavily on modeling and imitation.
    c. likens the human mind to a computer.
    d. is concerned primarily with affective responses to the environment.

    ANS: C   DIF: Moderate   REF: 244   OBJ: 8.1

4. In the information-processing approach, hardware is to software as
    a. the nervous system is to the skills used to retrieve information.
    b. memory is to the brain.
    c. feelings are to thoughts.
    d. perception is to sensation.

    ANS: A   DIF: Difficult   REF: 244   OBJ: 8.2

5. An information-processing theorist would most likely refer to _____ as being part of the mind's "software."
    a. the brain   c. neural connections
    b. sensory receptors   d. mental problem-solving strategies

    ANS: D   DIF: Moderate   REF: 244   OBJ: 8.2
    KEY: WWW

6. The information-processing approach stresses all of the following basic mental processes EXCEPT
   a. decision-making.
   b. reinforcers.
   c. perception.
   d. attention.

   ANS: B   DIF: Moderate   REF: 244   OBJ: 8.2

7. Which pair is best known for developing an information-processing-based model of memory?
   a. Young and Helmholtz
   b. Watson and Skinner
   c. Fechner and Weber
   d. Atkinson and Shriffin

   ANS: D   DIF: Easy   REF: 244-245   OBJ: 8.2

8. In the information-processing model, the purpose of the sensory register is to
   a. briefly hold a piece of information for possible processing.
   b. control the activities of long-term memory.
   c. retrieve data from short-term memory.
   d. develop strategies for storing encoded data.

   ANS: A   DIF: Moderate   REF: 245   OBJ: 8.2

9. Shirley is introduced to her friend's mother. While Shirley heard the woman's name, she had no idea what the woman's name was immediately after it was spoken. It is most accurate to say that the woman's name
   a. never made it past Shirley's sensory register.
   b. is trapped in Shirley's short-term memory.
   c. is lost in Shirley's long-term memory.
   d. could be cued for recall later on if Shirley would relax a bit.

   ANS: A   DIF: Difficult   REF: 245   OBJ: 8.2

10. Information typically stays in _____ for the briefest amount of time.
    a. working memory
    b. short-term memory
    c. long-term memory
    d. sensory register

    ANS: D   DIF: Easy   REF: 245   OBJ: 8.2

11. Which is the best description of a typical short-term memory?
    a. Fairly brief duration (seconds) and small capacity (seven or so items)
    b. Fairly long duration (minutes) and small capacity (seven or so items)
    c. Fairly brief duration (seconds) and large capacity (seventy or so items)
    d. Fairly long duration (minutes) and large capacity (seventy or so items)

    ANS: A   DIF: Moderate   REF: 245   OBJ: 8.2

12. Ethel looks up the phone number of a gas station and remembers it just long enough to walk over to the telephone and dial. When she is dialing, the information is contained in her
    a. sensory register.
    b. short-term memory.
    c. long-term memory.
    d. metamemory.

    ANS: B   DIF: Moderate   REF: 245   OBJ: 8.2

516

13. The main distinction between short-term memory and working memory is that working memory is
   a. larger.
   b. unconscious.
   c. actively processed.
   d. sensory based.

   ANS: C   DIF: Moderate   REF: 245   OBJ: 8.2

14. When someone asks you, "What's on your mind?" the response you give would best exemplify the information currently in your
   a. sensory register.
   b. long-term memory.
   c. collective unconsciousness.
   d. working memory.

   ANS: D   DIF: Difficult   REF: 245   OBJ: 8.2
   KEY: WWW

15. Timmy is visiting the dog pound and looking for a new pet. He looks from cage to cage until he suddenly sees a collie sitting in the far corner. He thinks to himself, "That dog looks great. I think I'll bring her home and name her Lassie." At this moment, the best example of what's in Tommy's working memory would be the
   a. the excitement Timmy will feel when he takes Lassie for a walk.
   b. words that Timmy is saying to himself.
   c. image of collies that Timmy has stored in his brain but is not currently accessing.
   d. fact that Timmy will buy the dog before the end of the day.

   ANS: B   DIF: Moderate   REF: 245   OBJ: 8.2

16. Information is stored in _____ memory for a relatively permanent period of time.
   a. short-term
   b. sensory
   c. long-term
   d. working

   ANS: C   DIF: Easy   REF: 245   OBJ: 8.2

17. As you are reading this exam question, what would best represent information in your long-term memory?
   a. The light waves as they excite the cells in your visual system
   b. The words from the question as you read them
   c. The words from the possible answers as you repeat them in your head
   d. The information you access about the concept of long-term memory that you encoded during the previous night's study session

   ANS: D   DIF: Difficult   REF: 245   OBJ: 8.2

18. Which statement concerning memory is true?
   a. The sensory register is located in long-term memory.
   b. Short-term memory has a much larger storage capacity than long-term memory.
   c. Working-term memory provides a temporary space for processing information.
   d. Long-term memory appears not to exist until around age two years.

   ANS: C   DIF: Difficult   REF: 245   OBJ: 8.2

19. Cognitive theorists suggest that the most likely order of the process of memory when information is being processed for the first time would be
    a. encoding, consolidation, storage, retrieval.
    b. retrieval, encoding, consolidation, storage.
    c. consolidation, storage, encoding, retrieval.
    d. storage, retrieval, encoding, consolidation.

    ANS: A   DIF: Easy   REF: 245   OBJ: 8.2
    KEY: WWW

20. Encoding is best described as the process of
    a. cued recall.   c. uncued recall.
    b. putting information into the system.   d. taking information out of the system.

    ANS: B   DIF: Easy   REF: 245   OBJ: 8.2

21. If information fails to be encoded it is _____ to remember.
    a. easy   c. very difficult
    b. a little difficult   d. impossible

    ANS: D   DIF: Moderate   REF: 245   OBJ: 8.2

22. The process during which information is organized into a form suitable for long-term storage is called
    a. retrieval.   c. recognition.
    b. utilization.   d. consolidation.

    ANS: D   DIF: Moderate   REF: 245   OBJ: 8.2

23. Pujols is watching his favorite baseball player in a home run derby and is trying to remember all of the movements that this player makes before he hits a long ball so that he can also become a big league player himself. Which of the following would best represent the consolidation stage of this process?
    a. The attention that he is paying to each movement
    b. His organizing the player's swing into a series of memories for sequential motions that can be stored in long-term memory
    c. Holding of the information in long-term store
    d. His retrieval of past episodes of home runs hit by this player

    ANS: B   DIF: Difficult   REF: 245   OBJ: 8.2

24. Which process would best be described as "holding information"?
    a. Perception   c. Storage
    b. Retrieval   d. Encoding

    ANS: C   DIF: Easy   REF: 245   OBJ: 8.2

25. At one time in his life, Edward could name every province in Canada. Somehow this information has disappeared from where it was being held. Information-processing theorists would most likely argue that this is a failure of the _____ system.
    a. elaboration
    b. storage
    c. metamemory
    d. encoding

    ANS: B   DIF: Moderate   REF: 245   OBJ: 8.2

26. When information is taken out of long-term memory, it is being
    a. scripted.
    b. encoded.
    c. retrieved.
    d. stored.

    ANS: C   DIF: Easy   REF: 245   OBJ: 8.2

27. Which statement would best represent a failure of retrieval?
    a. I never actually learned that information.
    b. I don't know the answer because I never read the book containing the answer.
    c. I know the answer, but I just cannot find it in my mind.
    d. I would know the answer, but the teacher talked so fast about the information that I could not keep up.

    ANS: C   DIF: Moderate   REF: 245   OBJ: 8.2

28. On a recognition task, a person
    a. is presented with a list of alternatives that includes the correct answer.
    b. is not presented with the correct answer but is given a hint.
    c. is neither presented with the correct answer nor given a hint.
    d. must generate the answer completely on his or her own.

    ANS: A   DIF: Moderate   REF: 245-246   OBJ: 8.2

29. Professor Sotomayor gives the students in her law class a multiple-choice test on Supreme Court Justices. This method of assessment requires students to use _____ memory.
    a. recall
    b. cued-recall
    c. repressed
    d. recognition

    ANS: D   DIF: Moderate   REF: 246   OBJ: 8.2
    KEY: WWW

30. In a police lineup, a witness is shown a group of potential perpetrators that includes the actual perpetrator. He or she is then asked to point to the individual who committed the crime. The basic premise of this method involves assessing _____ memory.
    a. recall
    b. cued-recall
    c. implicit
    d. recognition

    ANS: D   DIF: Difficult   REF: 246   OBJ: 8.2

519

31. On a true recall memory task,
    a. no memory cues/aids are presented.
    b. a few hints are presented.
    c. a correct answer is presented along with a few distracters.
    d. a correct answer is presented by itself.

    ANS: A   DIF: Moderate   REF: 246   OBJ: 8.2

32. Regis asks a game show contestant, "In inches, how far is the Earth from the sun?" If no other information is given to the contestant, this task is best classified as an assessment of _____ memory.
    a. recognition   c. recall
    b. metamemory   d. cued-recall

    ANS: C   DIF: Moderate   REF: 246   OBJ: 8.2

33. Which is the best example of a test of recall memory?
    a. An essay test with no hints   c. A multiple-choice test with no hints
    b. An essay test with some hints   d. A multiple-choice test with hints

    ANS: A   DIF: Easy   REF: 246   OBJ: 8.2
    KEY: WWW

34. On a(n) _____ memory task, a person trying to remember some information is given a hint but not the entire answer.
    a. episodic   c. recall
    b. implicit   d. cued-recall

    ANS: D   DIF: Easy   REF: 246   OBJ: 8.2

35. On a political science test, Barack is asked to write down the name of the main democratic presidential candidate in the United States in 2008. He has no idea of the answer, so he asked his teacher for a hint. The teacher says, "I can tell you this, when he won my friend said, "oh mama." With the hint, Barack is now being presented with a _____ memory task.
    a. cued-recall   c. recall
    b. recognition   d. implicit

    ANS: A   DIF: Moderate   REF: 246   OBJ: 8.2

36. Most people find that test questions requiring _____ memory are easier to answer than those requiring _____ memory.
    a. recall; recognition   c. recognition; recall
    b. cued-recall; recognition   d. recall; cued-recall

    ANS: C   DIF: Moderate   REF: 246   OBJ: 8.2

37. At which age do people do better on recall tasks than on recognition tasks?
    a. Adolescence   c. Old age
    b. Middle age   d. No age group does better on recall tasks

    ANS: D   DIF: Moderate   REF: 246   OBJ: 8.2

38. A memory that occurs without any conscious effort is best referred to as
    a. explicit.
    b. implicit.
    c. scripted.
    d. autobiographical.

    ANS: B   DIF: Easy   REF: 246   OBJ: 8.2

39. While sitting in his psychology class and daydreaming as his instructor drones on about memory, Mac suddenly recalls a great hamburger he ate at a fast-food restaurant a month ago. Mac's unintentional recall for this event provides a great example of _____ memory.
    a. explicit
    b. fuzzy-trace
    c. scripted
    d. implicit

    ANS: D   DIF: Moderate   REF: 246   OBJ: 8.2

40. An explicit memory
    a. always has a sexual overtone.
    b. is deliberately recalled.
    c. occurs only after a hint has been given.
    d. involves recalling behaviors but not ideas.

    ANS: B   DIF: Easy   REF: 246   OBJ: 8.2

41. Implicit memory is to explicit memory as
    a. unintentional is to deliberate.
    b. retrieval is to storage.
    c. cued it to uncued.
    d. effort is to automatic.

    ANS: A   DIF: Difficult   REF: 246   OBJ: 8.2
    KEY: WWW

42. Colette is participating in a research study. In the first phase of the study, she is shown a list of 20 French words. She is then asked to count backwards from 50 to 1 by threes. Colette is then asked to write down all of the French words she can remember. She has taken part in a study of _____ memory.
    a. explicit
    b. implicit
    c. cued-recall
    d. recognition

    ANS: A   DIF: Moderate   REF: 246   OBJ: 8.2

43. Semantic memories are for
    a. specific events.
    b. general facts.
    c. early childhood experiences.
    d. how to perform an action.

    ANS: B   DIF: Moderate   REF: 246   OBJ: 8.2

44. Which is the best example of a semantic memory?
    a. Knowing that the first record you ever liked was by the Beatles.
    b. Remembering the time you saw the Beatles perform on the Ed Sullivan show
    c. Recalling how to play the song "A Hard Day's Night" on the guitar
    d. Knowing that the Beatles were a band

    ANS: D   DIF: Difficult   REF: 246   OBJ: 8.2

45. _____ memories always involve personal experiences.
    a. Procedural   c. Implicit
    b. Episodic   d. Cued-recall

    ANS: B   DIF: Moderate   REF: 246   OBJ: 8.2

46. Which is the best example of an episodic memory?
    a. Remembering how to light a candle
    b. Recalling the words to the song "Happy Birthday"
    c. Recalling your 21st birthday party
    d. Naming four kinds of ice cream

    ANS: C   DIF: Moderate   REF: 246   OBJ: 8.2

47. A researcher develops a test in which participants are first given a list of types of fruit that
    includes the words "grapes, bananas, apples, oranges, and cherries" and asked to identify
    which is the longest. A while later, they are given the word stem "ban_____" and are asked to
    complete the word as quickly as possible. When a participant fills out the word by writing
    "banana," he or she is exhibiting what is called a(n) _____ memory.
    a. implicit   c. semantic
    b. procedural   d. recognition

    ANS: A   DIF: Difficult   REF: 246   OBJ: 8.2

48. The fact that some forms of amnesia destroy explicit memory but not implicit memory
    indicates that
    a. these forms of memory operate independently.
    b. implicit memory is learned and explicit is innate.
    c. explicit memory develops earlier than implicit memory.
    d. long-term memory lacks organization.

    ANS: A   DIF: Moderate   REF: 246   OBJ: 8.2

49. Research has indicated that procedural memory is mediated by the striatum. This means that
    a. only information that is attended to is recalled.
    b. language plays a significant role in the development of memory.
    c. memory requires cognitive effort.
    d. the brain is involved in processing memory.

    ANS: D   DIF: Difficult   REF: 246   OBJ: 8.2

50. Carlos has experienced significant damage to his hippocampus (an area located in the medial
    temporal lobe). How would this most likely impact his memory?
    a. He would not be able to recall events from his childhood.
    b. He would have trouble creating new episodic memories.
    c. He would not be able to recall who he is.
    d. He could recall past events but not past factual information.

    ANS: B   DIF: Difficult   REF: 246   OBJ: 8.2

51. Which statement concerning memory is true?
    a. Explicit memory increases in capacity from infancy through adulthood then declines, while implicit memory capacity peaks in childhood then declines.
    b. Explicit memory increases in capacity from infancy through adulthood then declines, while implicit memory capacity is constant across the lifespan.
    c. Implicit memory increases in capacity from infancy through adulthood then declines, while explicit memory capacity peaks in childhood then declines.
    d. Implicit memory increases in capacity from infancy through adulthood then declines, while explicit memory capacity is constant across the lifespan.

    ANS: B   DIF: Difficult   REF: 247   OBJ: 8.2

52. Problem solving is best defined as the use of _____ to achieve a goal.
    a. unconscious motivators   c. information-processing systems
    b. a non-cognitive response   d. operant conditioning

    ANS: C   DIF: Easy   REF: 247   OBJ: 8.3

53. Information-processing theorists use the term _____ to describe the part of the unique element of the cognitive system that plans and monitors problem-solving.
    a. fuzzy-traces   c. executive control processes
    b. sensory registers   d. implicit memory

    ANS: C   DIF: Difficult   REF: 247   OBJ: 8.3

54. The main purpose of the executive control processor is to
    a. store information in long-term memory.
    b. collect sensory input from the environment.
    c. suppress memories that are too painful.
    d. plan and monitor problem-solving.

    ANS: D   DIF: Moderate   REF: 247   OBJ: 8.3
    KEY: WWW

55. Allison is attempting to recall the code number that she uses to unlock her high school locker. As she tries different combinations, a part of her consciously keeps track of the combinations of numbers she has already tried. Information-processing theorists would refer to this aspect of Allison's cognitive system as her
    a. fuzzy-trace.   c. executive control process.
    b. sensory register.   d. implicit memory.

    ANS: C   DIF: Difficult   REF: 247   OBJ: 8.3

56. Cognitive psychologists believe that humans are capable of engaging in "parallel processing." This means that humans can
    a. carry out several mental activities at the same time.
    b. think about complex issues, like religion.
    c. pay selective attention to an event.
    d. encode information into long-term memory.

    ANS: A   DIF: Moderate   REF: 247   OBJ: 8.3

523

57. Carlos's teacher tells the class that they should be sure to listen to an important announcement that is coming in on the school's intercom. Carlos, however, misses the message as he is focused on a fly that is crawling across his desk. Carlos's failure is best blamed on faulty
   a. deferred imitation.
   c. attention skills.
   b. implicit memory.
   d. sensory memory.

   ANS: C　　　DIF: Moderate　　REF: 247　　　OBJ: 8.3

58. In assessing his newborn son's cognitive ability, Cosmo waves his hand at the baby and watches to see if his son reacts by also waving his hand. Cosmo is using a(n) _____ technique to assess his son's abilities.
   a. implicit memory
   c. cued-recall
   b. imitation
   d. operant conditioning

   ANS: B　　　DIF: Moderate　　REF: 248　　　OBJ: 8.4

59. Piaget argued that six-month-olds were incapable of imitating a mother who is intentionally opening her mouth very wide because infants
   a. do not have vision that allows them to accurately see their mother's face.
   b. cannot mentally represent the act of a wide, open mouth at that age.
   c. are not physically capable of opening their mouth very wide until they reach 12 months of age.
   d. refuse to imitate any actions they see.

   ANS: B　　　DIF: Difficult　　REF: 248　　　OBJ: 8.4

60. Research on early infant ability to imitate (e.g., Meltzoff, 2004) has tended to assess the action of
   a. eye blinking.
   c. sticking out the tongue.
   b. rolling over.
   d. smiling.

   ANS: C　　　DIF: Moderate　　REF: 248　　　OBJ: 8.4

61. Deferred imitation always
   a. involves a reflex action.
   b. occurs after a delay between seeing an action and the response.
   c. reflects the method of loci.
   d. indicates that an implicit memory has been activated.

   ANS: B　　　DIF: Moderate　　REF: 248　　　OBJ: 8.4

62. Six-month-old Trent saw his dad blink three times when he held a baby bottle. An hour after this occurred, Trent sees a baby bottle and blinks three times. This action would best be described as _____ imitation.
   a. deferred
   c. serial
   b. implicit
   d. decentered

   ANS: A　　　DIF: Moderate　　REF: 248　　　OBJ: 8.4

63. Habituation is best described as learning
   a. a reflex.
   b. a new response.
   c. not to respond.
   d. in reaction to reinforcement.

   ANS: C   DIF: Moderate   REF: 248   OBJ: 8.4

64. If you turn on a floor fan, an infant will immediately orient its head toward the sound. After awhile, the infant appears to lose interest and turns its head back to its original position. This phenomenon is known as
   a. habituation.
   b. discrimination.
   c. generalization.
   d. sound acuity.

   ANS: A   DIF: Moderate   REF: 248   OBJ: 8.4

65. Six-month-old Frances has been listening to her mother, Connie, singing for the past 20 minutes. How would Frances demonstrate habituation?
   a. While she would be excited when her mom first started singing, she would eventually become disinterested.
   b. She would attempt to imitate the noise her mother is making.
   c. She would become progressively more excited by her mom's singing.
   d. She would begin to exhibit the rooting reflex.

   ANS: A   DIF: Difficult   REF: 248   OBJ: 8.4

66. Carolyn Rovee-Collier's (1997) research on infant memory involved recording kicking behavior when a ribbon was tied to the infant's foot, demonstrating that young children have _____ memory.
   a. repressed
   b. implicit
   c. recall
   d. elaborative

   ANS: C   DIF: Moderate   REF: 249   OBJ: 8.4

67. The research study of infant memory involving a ribbon tied to an infant's foot relied heavily on _____ conditioning techniques.
   a. social-learning-theory
   b. classical
   c. humanistic
   d. operant

   ANS: D   DIF: Easy   REF: 249   OBJ: 8.4
   KEY: WWW

68. Which best describes the memory abilities of an infant human?
   a. Cue-dependent and context-independent
   b. Cue-dependent and context-specific
   c. Cue-independent and context-independent
   d. Cue-independent and context-specific

   ANS: B   DIF: Easy   REF: 249   OBJ: 8.4

69. While attempting to find his lost toy bear, 10-month-old Teddy pulls away a couch's cushion and finds the bear he watched his mother hide there 10 minutes earlier. This best demonstrates the use of _____ memory.
   a. recognition
   b. recall
   c. implicit
   d. sensory register

   ANS: B   DIF: Moderate   REF: 249   OBJ: 8.4

70. By age _____, most infants first begin to verbalize events that happened months earlier.
   a. 6 months
   b. 12 months
   c. 18 months
   d. 2 years

   ANS: D   DIF: Moderate   REF: 250   OBJ: 8.4

71. Flavell and Wellman (1977) suggested four major reasons to explain the improved memory and learning abilities in the aging child. Which was NOT on their list of reasons?
   a. Increased knowledge about how memory works
   b. An increase in general knowledge about the world
   c. A working-term memory that increases from 1 slot at birth to about 10 slots by age five years
   d. Better "software" for effective information retrieval

   ANS: C   DIF: Moderate   REF: 250   OBJ: 8.5
   KEY: WWW

72. Flavell and Wellman (1977) suggested four major reasons to explain the improved memory and learning abilities in the aging child. Which was on their list of reasons?
   a. Larger long-term memory capacity
   b. Increased cognitive impairment
   c. Larger sensory memory capacity
   d. Increased knowledge about the world

   ANS: D   DIF: Moderate   REF: 250   OBJ: 8.5

73. Older children can learn faster and remember more than younger children because older children typically show a significant increase in
   a. the size of their sensory register.
   b. childhood amnesia.
   c. the capacity of long-term memory.
   d. working-memory space available for constructive use.

   ANS: D   DIF: Moderate   REF: 250-251   OBJ: 8.5

74. Short-term memory capacity _____ between ages 6 and 13.
   a. increases significantly
   b. remains steady
   c. decreases slightly
   d. decreases significantly

   ANS: A   DIF: Easy   REF: 251   OBJ: 8.5

75. What seems to underlie the significant increase in processing speed seen during childhood?
   a. Enhanced use of preservation
   b. Vastly improved sensory systems
   c. A greater reliance on implicit memory
   d. Brain maturation

   ANS: D   DIF: Easy   REF: 251   OBJ: 8.5

526

76. Case suggests that a preschooler's tendency to center (as described by Piaget) is likely related to limited _____ memory size.
    a. sensory
    b. working
    c. long-term
    d. implicit

    ANS: B   DIF: Difficult   REF: 251   OBJ: 8.5

77. If short-term memory capacity is "domain-specific," then
    a. all children should have the same short-term memory capacity size.
    b. the more you know about something, the larger short-term memory capacity size will be for related items.
    c. it is solely determined by biological factors, not experience.
    d. it cannot be impacted by the size of working memory.

    ANS: B   DIF: Difficult   REF: 251   OBJ: 8.5

78. Nelson is going to the grocery story with his four-year-old son, Muntz. Nelson wants Muntz to help him recall the items that they need to buy. Research on memory development indicates that Nelson should expect his son to be able to store about _____ item(s) in short-term memory.
    a. one
    b. three
    c. five
    d. seven

    ANS: B   DIF: Moderate   REF: 251   OBJ: 8.5

79. The tendency to keep making the same mistake over and over is referred to as making a(n) _____ error.
    a. preservation
    b. mediation
    c. utilization
    d. organization

    ANS: A   DIF: Moderate   REF: 252   OBJ: 8.5

80. Which statement best exemplifies a "preservation error"?
    a. I have never tried this before, so what the heck.
    b. Trial and error is the way to go.
    c. It worked in the past and even if it does not work in the present, I will still keep doing it.
    d. The best way to remember something is to connect the new idea with some past memory.

    ANS: C   DIF: Moderate   REF: 252   OBJ: 8.5

81. Which best describes the memory strategy of rehearsal?
    a. Take original information, expand on it, and make connections to existing memories.
    b. Repeat to self over and over.
    c. Organize into meaningful categories, then memorize.
    d. See it and be it.

    ANS: B   DIF: Easy   REF: 252   OBJ: 8.5

82. Sam and Sue are shopping for groceries. Sam looks at the list and tells Sue, "I'll get the cat food, soap, toilet paper, and flour, and I'll meet you by the lettuce." Sam takes off, muttering to himself over and over: "Cat food, soap, toilet paper, flour." This best illustrates the use of which memory strategy?
    a. Chunking
    b. Elaboration
    c. Organization
    d. Rehearsal

    ANS: D   DIF: Moderate   REF: 252   OBJ: 8.5

83. Which memory strategy is being used when a long number is memorized by breaking it into manageable subunits each containing three digits?
    a. Chunking
    b. Method of loci
    c. Implicit memory
    d. Rehearsal

    ANS: A   DIF: Easy   REF: 252   OBJ: 8.5

84. Saffron is presented with the following list of items to memorize: bagel, carrot, ham, corn, hot dog, donut, bread, chicken, peas. Her immediate reaction is to think of the items in the following way: (bagel, donut, bread), (carrot, corn, peas), (ham, hotdog, chicken). This reaction would indicate that Saffron is using the strategy of
    a. rehearsal.
    b. elaboration.
    c. organization.
    d. method of loci.

    ANS: C   DIF: Moderate   REF: 252   OBJ: 8.5

85. Which best describes the memory strategy of organization?
    a. Take original information, expand on it, and make connections to existing memories.
    b. Repeat to self over and over.
    c. Classify into meaningful categories, then memorize.
    d. See it and be it.

    ANS: C   DIF: Easy   REF: 252   OBJ: 8.5
    KEY: WWW

86. The best example of elaboration is
    a. repeating "red, chair, dog" several times.
    b. consolidating "red" and "green" into a color group and "chair" and "table" into a furniture group.
    c. noting that the red chair and the green piano remind you of last year's Christmas party.
    d. seeing the color red but perceiving the color green.

    ANS: C   DIF: Difficult   REF: 252   OBJ: 8.5

87. Wayne has trouble remembering the last four digits of his new phone number (4422) until he makes the connection that the last two digits are exactly half of the first two digits. Once he makes this connection, he has no trouble remembering the number! This best demonstrates the memory concept of
    a. chunking.
    b. elaboration.
    c. organization.
    d. rehearsal.

    ANS: B   DIF: Difficult   REF: 252   OBJ: 8.5

88. A child with _____ deficiencies cannot use strategies, even when taught to use them.
    a. mediation
    b. utilization
    c. mediation and utilization
    d. utilization and production

    ANS: A   DIF: Moderate   REF: 252   OBJ: 8.5

89. Nadal teaches his son a great way to serve a tennis ball so the opponent cannot return the serve. However, his son Rafael appears to not benefit whatsoever from the advice and does not even appear to understand what is going on. Rafael is best classified as exhibiting a(n)
    a. mediation deficiency.
    b. utilization deficiency.
    c. production deficiency.
    d. A-B error.

    ANS: A   DIF: Moderate   REF: 252   OBJ: 8.5

90. As Josephine has a production deficiency, she
    a. cannot solve any problems.
    b. doesn't produce useful strategies on her own.
    c. spontaneously produces useless strategies.
    d. spontaneously produces effective strategies.

    ANS: B   DIF: Moderate   REF: 252   OBJ: 8.5

91. A production deficiency is best described as
    a. not producing a strategy but benefiting from guessing.
    b. not producing a strategy but benefiting from strategies you are taught.
    c. producing a strategy but not benefiting from its use.
    d. producing a strategy and benefiting from its use.

    ANS: B   DIF: Difficult   REF: 252   OBJ: 8.5
    KEY: WWW

92. A utilization deficiency is best described as
    a. not producing a strategy but benefiting from guessing.
    b. not producing a strategy but benefiting from strategies you are taught.
    c. producing a strategy but not benefiting from its use.
    d. producing a strategy and benefiting from its use.

    ANS: C   DIF: Difficult   REF: 252   OBJ: 8.5

93. While trying to solve a math problem, Vector is able to come up with a strategy that might work. Unfortunately, Vector's math performance does not improve by using the strategy. This situation best exemplifies
    a. autobiographical memory.
    b. cued recall.
    c. the method of loci.
    d. utilization deficiency.

    ANS: D   DIF: Moderate   REF: 252   OBJ: 8.5

94. Len has a mediation deficiency. Ben has a production deficiency. Ken has a utilization deficiency. How many of these children would be able to both produce and benefit from their own memory strategies?
    a. Zero
    b. One
    c. Two
    d. Three

    ANS: A   DIF: Difficult   REF: 252   OBJ: 8.5

95. Dundee has just returned to the United States from a trip to Australia. His friend asks him, "What was the best food you ate on your trip?" Dundee responds, "I kind of remember eating some great meals but cannot seem to recall any restaurants. Perhaps if I think back about where I stayed each night I'll be able to remember a great meal." Dundee appears to be attempting to use _____ to improve recall.
    a. a retrieval strategy
    b. sensory register
    c. metamemory
    d. implicit memory

    ANS: A   DIF: Difficult   REF: 253   OBJ: 8.5

96. Younger children tend to rely more on _____ than older children.
    a. internal cues for encoding and retrieval
    b. external cues for encoding and retrieval
    c. external cues for encoding and internal cues for retrieval
    d. internal cues for encoding and external cues for retrieval

    ANS: B   DIF: Moderate   REF: 253   OBJ: 8.5

97. Which is NOT an example of metamemory?
    a. Knowing the difference between metaphysics and meta-analysis
    b. Knowing which memory strategies are most effective for you
    c. Knowing which memorization tasks are most difficult for you
    d. Being able to plan and control your memory processes as you learn

    ANS: A   DIF: Moderate   REF: 253   OBJ: 8.5
    KEY: WWW

98. Jack knows that he can more easily memorize and recall a list of 10 familiar words than he can 10 unfamiliar words. This knowledge provides an excellent example of
    a. short-term memory.
    b. chunking.
    c. recall memory.
    d. metamemory.

    ANS: D   DIF: Difficult   REF: 253   OBJ: 8.5

99. Metamemory awareness is most likely to be displayed in young children
    a. who have often been in situations in which they had to remember something and they are facing a task that they find relevant.
    b. who have never been in situations in which they had to remember something and they are facing a task that they find relevant.
    c. who have often been in situations in which they had to remember something and they are facing a task that they find irrelevant.
    d. who have never been in situations in which they had to remember something and they are facing a task that they find irrelevant.

    ANS: A   DIF: Moderate   REF: 254   OBJ: 8.5

100. A person's knowledge base is defined as
    a. unconscious awareness of an event.
    b. the difference between what he or she knows and what he or she can acquire with guided participation.
    c. how much the person knows about a topic.
    d. the rate at which he or she can solve a task.

    ANS: C   DIF: Easy   REF: 254   OBJ: 8.5

101. In comparing memory capabilities in children who were experts at chess with the memories of adults who weren't, Chi (1978) tested both groups on memory of location of chess pieces and on ability to remember sequences of digits. She found that the
    a. children did better on both tests.
    b. adults did better on both tests.
    c. children did better on memory of chess, but not sequences of digits.
    d. children did better on memory of digits, but not on memory of chess.

    ANS: C   DIF: Moderate   REF: 254   OBJ: 8.5

102. The Chi (1978) study on memory for chess pieces indicated that when recalling information in their area of expertise, expert children perform
    a. better than novice adults.   c. worse than novice adults.
    b. the same as novice adults.   d. the same as children who are novices.

    ANS: A   DIF: Moderate   REF: 254   OBJ: 8.5
    KEY: WWW

103. Which is true regarding the development of learning and memory in children?
    a. Older children have a greater information-processing capacity and know more about their memorization strategies than younger children do.
    b. Older children have a greater information-processing capacity, but younger children know more about their memorization strategies than older children do.
    c. Older children know more about their memorization strategies, but younger children have a greater information-processing capacity.
    d. Older children have a lesser information-processing capacity and know less about their memorization strategies than younger children do.

    ANS: A   DIF: Moderate   REF: 254-255   OBJ: 8.5

104. Which statement is true regarding the development of learning and memory in children?
    a. Younger children tend to have a greater information-processing capacity and a larger knowledge base than older children do.
    b. Younger children tend to have a greater information-processing capacity, but older children have a larger knowledge base.
    c. Younger children tend to have a larger knowledge base, but older children have a greater information-processing capacity.
    d. Older children tend to have a greater information-processing capacity and a greater knowledge base.

    ANS: D   DIF: Moderate   REF: 254-255   OBJ: 8.5
    KEY: WWW

105. The best model for explaining recall memory in children includes the factors of
    a. basic capacities and strategies only.
    b. basic capacities and metamemory only.
    c. metamemory and strategies only.
    d. basic capacities, metamemory, and strategies.

    ANS: D   DIF: Easy   REF: 255   OBJ: 8.5

106. An autobiographical memory is a memory for
    a. historical events that occurred before your conception.
    b. other people's lives.
    c. past personal experiences.
    d. future possible events in one's life.

    ANS: C   DIF: Easy   REF: 255   OBJ: 8.6

107. Which is the best example of an autobiographical memory?
    a. Recalling that the War of 1812 was fought in 1812
    b. Recalling the heated argument between you and you mom that broke out at your wedding
    c. Thinking about the hot ham sandwich that you are going to have for lunch
    d. Understanding that numbers are easier to recall when they are chunked into groups

    ANS: B   DIF: Moderate   REF: 255   OBJ: 8.6
    KEY: WWW

108. While daydreaming in her physics class, Dorothy recalls the day the tornado hit her farmhouse last summer. Dorothy's recollection is best classified as a(n) _____ memory.
    a. sensory   c. autobiographical
    b. explicit   d. meta-

    ANS: C   DIF: Easy   REF: 255   OBJ: 8.6

109. Childhood or infantile amnesia is defined as the inability to access _____ memories.
    a. all traumatic   c. autobiographical
    b. insignificant   d. meta-

    ANS: C   DIF: Moderate   REF: 255   OBJ: 8.6

110. Ten-year-old Conrad has difficulty remembering anything that happened between his birth and his second birthday. Conrad is most likely
    a. normal.
    b. having likely suffered some traumatic event early on that has caused him to block off memory of his early years.
    c. mentally impaired.
    d. having an unusually small amount of space in his working memory.

    ANS: A   DIF: Moderate   REF: 255   OBJ: 8.6

111. If Travis is a typical college student, he would have the HARDEST time accurately recalling the
    a. death of his father when he was a year old.
    b. time his family moved when he was two years old.
    c. birth of his brother when he was three years old.
    d. time he was in the hospital when he was four years old.

    ANS: A   DIF: Easy   REF: 255   OBJ: 8.6

112. The text noted that one information-processing-based explanation for infantile amnesia focuses on the lack of space in infant and toddler's _____ memory.
    a. implicit   c. working
    b. sensory   d. long-term

    ANS: C   DIF: Easy   REF: 255-256   OBJ: 8.6

113. Why can't a lack of language be used to fully account for infantile amnesia?
    a. Because the "amnesia" includes the inability to recall non-verbal information like faces
    b. Because language skills do not impact memory abilities, even in adults
    c. Because mute children (those who never speak) do not display infantile amnesia
    d. Because mothers who talk to infants are recalled longer than those who don't

    ANS: A   DIF: Easy   REF: 256   OBJ: 8.6

114. How can a mother's interactions with a toddler result in that child growing into an adolescent with stronger autobiographical memories?
    a. She can avoid contaminating the child's memory by having conversations about events in the toddler's life
    b. She can enhance the child's memory by having conversations about events in the toddler's life
    c. She can focus exclusively on praising the child for major events during toddlerhood
    d. She can't

    ANS: B   DIF: Moderate   REF: 256   OBJ: 8.6

115. The key to the "fuzzy trace" theory of infantile amnesia is the belief that _____ is/are stored separately in memory.
    a. visual and auditory information   c. verbatim and general accounts of events
    b. emotional and behavioral memories d. tactile and spatial events

    ANS: C   DIF: Easy   REF: 256   OBJ: 8.6

533

116. Bon is trying to explain why his four-year-old son, Jovi, cannot recall what happened at an exciting rock concert they attended two years ago. In doing so, Bon says, "Jovi kind of recalls being at some event with a lot of people and singing, but he has no recollection for any details of the concert." Bon's description best matches the _____ theory of childhood amnesia.
    a. fuzzy-trace
    b. working memory capacity
    c. surfactant
    d. constraint-seeking

    ANS: A   DIF: Moderate   REF: 256   OBJ: 8.6

117. Four-year-old Barnum goes to the circus and sees animals that he has never seen before. When asked about the event a year later, Barnum is most likely to recall
    a. a verbatim account of the event.
    b. the gist of the event.
    c. only the linguistically coded parts of the event.
    d. nothing about having gone to a circus.

    ANS: B   DIF: Moderate   REF: 256   OBJ: 8.6

118. The key to a memory script is that it
    a. is almost always stored as a "fuzzy trace."
    b. cannot be mentally rehearsed.
    c. represents a typical sequence of events.
    d. is found in sensory register but not long-term storage.

    ANS: C   DIF: Moderate   REF: 256   OBJ: 8.7

119. Ten-year-old Elisa has several accurate, well-developed scripts, including one for grocery shopping. Which is the most likely example of her shopping script?
    a. Enter store, see piece of candy, beg for candy, parent buys candy
    b. Realizing that people work to earn money so that they can buy things in a store
    c. Envisioning the size of the candy bar that she ate yesterday
    d. Remembering that she needs to buy a carton of chocolate milk by mentally picturing a brown cow drinking out of a glass

    ANS: A   DIF: Moderate   REF: 256   OBJ: 8.7

120. Eight-year-old Hawthorne has several accurate, well-developed scripts, including one for a visit to the doctor's office. Which is the most likely example of her doctor's office script?
    a. Enter clinic, tell mom she feels better, sit in waiting room, see doctor, get shot (inoculation) in arm, cry
    b. Realizing that doctors earn money so that they can buy things
    c. Envisioning herself performing brain surgery on a patient
    d. Remembering that her favorite television show, ER, is also about doctors

    ANS: A   DIF: Moderate   REF: 256   OBJ: 8.7
    KEY: WWW

121. Which statement on children's eyewitness testimony is true?
    a. Older children tend to be more suggestible than young children.
    b. Preschoolers tend to initially offer more information on open-ended questions than older children.
    c. Frequently repeating the same close-ended question tends to increase the accuracy of memory in both young and old children.
    d. Preschool children tend to recall less information about an event than do older children.

    ANS: D   DIF: Difficult   REF: 257   OBJ: 8.7

122. What is the best advice concerning the accuracy of preschoolers' eyewitness testimony?
    a. Leading questions improve accuracy of responding.
    b. If it is a memory for a traumatic event, it is definitely a real memory.
    c. It is very difficult to create a situation where preschool children do not accurately recall basic events like field trips.
    d. Under conditions of questioning with lots of open-ended questions, memory accuracy will likely decline.

    ANS: D   DIF: Moderate   REF: 257   OBJ: 8.7

123. According to Piaget, when a concrete-operational thinker is presented with the "balance beam" problem he or she
    a. can appreciate the significant impact of both weight and distance from center, but cannot understand their inverse relationship.
    b. can appreciate the significant impact of weight but not distance from center.
    c. can appreciate the significant impact of distance from center but not weight.
    d. can appreciate the significant impact of both weight and distance from center, and can understand their inverse relationship.

    ANS: A   DIF: Moderate   REF: 257-258   OBJ: 8.8

124. Robert Siegler investigated the type of information that a child takes in during a problem-solving task and also what strategies he or she formulates when attempting to solve the problem. Siegler called his model the _____ approach.
    a. rule assessment   c. autobiographical
    b. fuzzy-trace   d. method of loci

    ANS: A   DIF: Easy   REF: 257-258   OBJ: 8.8

125. On the "balance beam problem," which child would be most likely to always guess that the side with the more weights will drop?
    a. Warren, who is 5 years old   c. Waldo, who is 50 years old
    b. Walter, who is 15 years old   d. Wayne, who is 85 years old

    ANS: A   DIF: Easy   REF: 258   OBJ: 8.8

126. Sigler concluded that when solving problems, most children
   a. guess.
   b. progress through a series of more sophisticated stages of thought.
   c. use multiple rules and problem-solving strategies.
   d. defer to peers.

   ANS: C   DIF: Moderate   REF: 258   OBJ: 8.8

127. According to Siegler's "overlapping waves theory," cognitive development is best conceptualized as
   a. random in nature.
   b. a set of stages.
   c. controlled by unconscious factors.
   d. a process of variability, choice, and changes.

   ANS: D   DIF: Easy   REF: 258   OBJ: 8.8
   KEY: WWW

128. Because she believes in overlapping waves theory, Serena would most likely argue that her six-year-old daughter, Venus,
   a. is in the formal stage of thinking.
   b. has multiple problem strategies available to her.
   c. cannot recall any event prior to her third birthday.
   d. has no recognition memory.

   ANS: B   DIF: Moderate   REF: 258   OBJ: 8.8

129. How is Piaget's explanation of cognitive development different from that of Siegler's explanation?
   a. Siegler sees cognitive development more in terms of operant consequences (i.e., reinforcement and punishment).
   b. Siegler sees cognitive development more in terms of genetic and biological factors.
   c. Piaget sees cognitive development more in terms of qualitative steps in which new ideas replace old.
   d. Piaget sees cognitive development more in terms of language and less in terms of spatial skills.

   ANS: C   DIF: Moderate   REF: 258-259   OBJ: 8.8

130. If a teacher were to apply Siegler's findings on the use of problem-solving strategies in the classroom, the teacher would
   a. want to find out about the number of books in the child's home.
   b. try to notice just what aspect of a problem is causing the child some difficulty.
   c. discourage the use of metacognitive strategies.
   d. stop using recognition tests in favor of recall exams.

   ANS: B   DIF: Moderate   REF: 259   OBJ: 8.8

131. Indy is a typical 6-year-old and his brother Jones is a typical 16-year-old. How do their information processing skills most likely differ on a memory task?
    a. Indy will be able to learn more than Jones if both are given extra time to study for the task.
    b. Indy will be more likely to utilize deliberate strategies while Jones will rely on unconscious strategies.
    c. Jones will recall both more relevant information and task-irrelevant information.
    d. Jones will recall more relevant information and is less likely to recall task-irrelevant information.

    ANS: D   DIF: Moderate   REF: 259   OBJ: 8.9

132. As a typical teen, between seventh grade and his senior year of high school, Stefano will most likely show increases in
    a. basic information-processing capacities but not knowledge base or metamemory.
    b. metamemory basic but not knowledge base or information-processing capacities.
    c. information-processing capacities and metamemory but not knowledge base.
    d. basic information-processing capacities, knowledge base, and metamemory.

    ANS: D   DIF: Easy   REF: 259-260   OBJ: 8.9

133. As a typical college student, research indicates that Hanna would be most likely to shift her focus to _____ if she suddenly found herself pressed for time when studying for an exam.
    a. the most difficult material   c. another subject
    b. the easiest material   d. friends

    ANS: B   DIF: Moderate   REF: 260   OBJ: 8.9

134. _____ teens are most likely to utilize metacognitive strategies.
    a. Low SES male   c. High SES male
    b. Low SES female   d. High SES female

    ANS: D   DIF: Easy   REF: 260   OBJ: 8.9

135. It was estimated that it takes about _____ of training and expertise to become a true expert in a field.
    a. 10 years   c. 30 years
    b. 20 years   d. a lifetime

    ANS: A   DIF: Moderate   REF: 261-262   OBJ: 8.10

136. Acquiring domain-specific expertise tends to lead to
    a. great improvement in cognitive skills in unrelated areas.
    b. improved cognitive skills in areas related to the domain.
    c. increased fuzzy traces.
    d. utilization deficiency.

    ANS: B   DIF: Moderate   REF: 262   OBJ: 8.10

137. Rajan has practiced until he is able to remember the population of every country in the world. This ability will most likely
    a. greatly increase Rajan's ability to learn and remember foreign words.
    b. have little impact on cognitive abilities unrelated with knowledge for populations.
    c. disrupt his autobiographical memories.
    d. enhance the size of his sensory register.

    ANS: B   DIF: Moderate   REF: 262   OBJ: 8.10
    KEY: WWW

138. Research on autobiographical memory in adulthood has shown that the more _____ an event, the better it will later be recalled.
    a. distant   c. negative
    b. emotional   d. unique

    ANS: D   DIF: Moderate   REF: 263   OBJ: 8.11

139. _____ events tend to have the greatest likelihood of being recalled after the event.
    a. Only positive emotional   c. Both positive and negative emotional
    b. Only negative emotional   d. Non-emotional

    ANS: C   DIF: Moderate   REF: 263   OBJ: 8.11

140. As a typical 80-year-old Irvine would have the greatest number of autobiographical memories from his
    a. early childhood.   c. 30s and 40s.
    b. teens and 20s.   d. 50s and 60s.

    ANS: B   DIF: Moderate   REF: 263   OBJ: 8.11

141. Research on aging and memory has shown that
    a. declines in memory first become noticeable around age 50.
    b. older people experience difficulty on all memory tasks.
    c. reliance on data from cross-sectional studies may mean that what appear to be age differences in memory are due to other factors.
    d. the severity of memory loss is unrelated to age.

    ANS: C   DIF: Moderate   REF: 263   OBJ: 8.11

142. Which statement concerning individuals with mild cognitive impairment is FALSE?
    a. They will be forgetful
    b. They will have difficulty learning
    c. They will show all the symptoms of dementia
    d. They will display deficits in other cognitive areas

    ANS: C   DIF: Moderate   REF: 264   OBJ: 8.11

143. With which of the following tasks would older adults have the LEAST problem?
    a. A memory task where the material is unfamiliar
    b. A task where they are asked to recall rather than recognize names
    c. A memory task where they can use well-practiced memory strategies
    d. A timed memory task

    ANS: C   DIF: Moderate   REF: 265   OBJ: 8.11

144. Which statement is true regarding "recall" memory and "recognition" memory in elderly adults?
    a. They are likely to be more deficient in recall than in recognition memory.
    b. They are likely to be more deficient in recognition than in recall memory.
    c. They are likely to be equally deficient in both types of memory.
    d. Neither type of memory diminishes with age (except in extreme cases).

    ANS: A   DIF: Moderate   REF: 265   OBJ: 8.11

145. Which combinations of memory tasks would prove most difficult to the average older individual?
    a. Exercised and implicit   c. Exercised and explicit
    b. Unexercised and implicit   d. Unexercised and explicit

    ANS: D   DIF: Moderate   REF: 265   OBJ: 8.11
    KEY: WWW

146. A study on the long-term retention of foreign language (Spanish) learned in high school in individuals who are elderly found that
    a. most elderly did not even recall having taking a foreign language in high school.
    b. a few individuals recalled having had a class in a foreign language in high school but could recall no content from the course.
    c. many individuals recalled having had a class in a foreign language in high school and a small percent had retained some vocabulary.
    d. not only did the individuals recall the foreign language courses, but as much as half of the vocabulary was retained nearly 50 years later.

    ANS: D   DIF: Moderate   REF: 266   OBJ: 8.12

147. Research comparing elderly hearing Americans, deaf Americans, and hearing Chinese demonstrated the effect that _____ can have on memory performance.
    a. genetics   c. negative stereotypes
    b. diet   d. disabilities

    ANS: C   DIF: Difficult   REF: 266   OBJ: 8.12

148. Which statement concerning memory strategies and basic processing capacities with age is true?
    a. Verbal knowledge begins to show a steep decline beginning around age 50.
    b. Holding negative stereotypes concerning memory ability actually leads to improved memory abilities in older adulthood.
    c. Memory problems in adulthood are more likely the result of original encoding and not retrieval.
    d. Limitations in working memory in older adulthood may be due to the slowing of the nervous system.

    ANS: D   DIF: Difficult   REF: 267   OBJ: 8.12

149. Limitations in working memory in older adulthood appear to be most directly related to reduced functioning of the _____ system.
    a. visual   c. auditory
    b. nervous   d. pulmonary

    ANS: B   DIF: Easy   REF: 267   OBJ: 8.12

150. Which best fits with a cohort difference explanation concerning the apparent loss of memory abilities in old age?
    a. The visual systems tend to slow with age.
    b. Implicit tasks tend to be easier than explicit tasks.
    c. Elderly people tend to have had less formal education than young people.
    d. Older individuals are more likely to use external memory aids.

    ANS: C   DIF: Moderate   REF: 268   OBJ: 8.12

151. The most accurate summation of declines in information-processing skills in older adults is that they are
    a. both inevitable and universal.   c. inevitable but not universal.
    b. neither inevitable nor universal.   d. universal but not inevitable.

    ANS: B   DIF: Moderate   REF: 268   OBJ: 8.12

152. On which type of problem-solving task would the performance of a middle-aged adult be superior to that of a young adult?
    a. On unfamiliar, meaningless laboratory tasks
    b. On unfamiliar, but meaningful tasks
    c. On familiar and meaningful tasks
    d. Middle-aged problem-solvers never out-perform younger adults

    ANS: C   DIF: Easy   REF: 268-269   OBJ: 8.13
    KEY: WWW

153. Milton is playing a game of "20 Questions" in which he has to try and guess what his friend Bradley is thinking about. Which of Milton's inquiries would best exemplify a constraint-seeking question?
    a. "Is it an animal?"   c. "Is it a frog?"
    b. "Is it green?"   d. "Is it a green frog?"

    ANS: A   DIF: Moderate   REF: 268-270   OBJ: 8.13

540

154. On an everyday problem such as what to do if you cannot pay your electric bill, _____ tend to out-perform other groups.
    a. teenagers
    b. young adults
    c. middle-aged adults
    d. elderly adults

    ANS: C   DIF: Moderate   REF: 270   OBJ: 8.13

155. Seventy-year-old Ace decides that he cannot remain effective at all types of gambling so he decides to focus only on blackjack, with the hopes that this narrow focus will allow him to perform better in this one area. According to the SOC approach, the decision to abandon other forms of gambling represents
    a. selection.
    b. optimization.
    c. compensation.
    d. plasticity.

    ANS: A   DIF: Moderate   REF: 270   OBJ: 8.13

TRUE/FALSE

1. Information-processing theorists use an analogy of a computer when discussing the human mind.

    ANS: T   DIF: Easy   REF: 244   OBJ: 8.2

2. Short-term memory can hold an unlimited amount of information.

    ANS: F   DIF: Moderate   REF: 245   OBJ: 8.2

3. Working memory is an active form of short-term memory.

    ANS: T   DIF: Moderate   REF: 245   OBJ: 8.2
    KEY: WWW

4. The final stage in the three basic steps of the memory process involves storage.

    ANS: F   DIF: Moderate   REF: 245   OBJ: 8.2

5. On a cued-recall task, a person is given a hint to help facilitate retrieval.

    ANS: T   DIF: Easy   REF: 246   OBJ: 8.2

6. Explicit memories occur unintentionally.

    ANS: F   DIF: Moderate   REF: 246   OBJ: 8.2

7. Executive control processes are responsible for monitoring our information-processing behavior.

    ANS: T   DIF: Moderate   REF: 247   OBJ: 8.3

8. Deferred imitation involves the imitation of a novel act after some delay.

    ANS: T   DIF: Moderate   REF: 248   OBJ: 8.4

541

9. Infants demonstrate memory when they habituate to a stimulus that is repeatedly presented.

    ANS: T   DIF: Moderate   REF: 248-249   OBJ: 8.4

10. Early memories tend to be very cue-dependent and context-specific.

    ANS: T   DIF: Moderate   REF: 249-250   OBJ: 8.4

11. A child's increased knowledge about the world can lead to improvements in memory.

    ANS: T   DIF: Moderate   REF: 250   OBJ: 8.5
    KEY: WWW

12. A child making perseveration errors will continue to use the same strategy even though it is not successful.

    ANS: T   DIF: Moderate   REF: 252   OBJ: 8.5

13. Elaboration involves the creation of meaningful links between items that you are attempting to remember.

    ANS: T   DIF: Moderate   REF: 252   OBJ: 8.5

14. If a child has a mediation deficiency, he or she cannot spontaneously use a strategy but can benefit from it.

    ANS: F   DIF: Moderate   REF: 252   OBJ: 8.5

15. Knowing that "1 + 1 = 2" is a good example of an autobiographical memory.

    ANS: F   DIF: Moderate   REF: 255   OBJ: 8.6
    KEY: WWW

16. Eyewitness testimony accuracy in young children is increased when the same question is asked repeatedly.

    ANS: F   DIF: Moderate   REF: 257   OBJ: 8.7

17. The overlapping waves theory argues for conceptualizing of cognitive development in terms of an invariant sequence of stages.

    ANS: F   DIF: Moderate   REF: 258   OBJ: 8.8

18. By adolescence, individuals begin to recall more irrelevant information and less relevant task information.

    ANS: F   DIF: Moderate   REF: 259-260   OBJ: 8.9
    KEY: WWW

19. Older adults tend to perform best on explicit memory tasks that focus on unpracticed skills.

    ANS: F   DIF: Moderate   REF: 265   OBJ: 8.11

20. On average, older adults are faster on timed tasks than young adults.

ANS: F   DIF: Easy   REF: 267   OBJ: 8.12
KEY: WWW

COMPLETION

1. According to Atkinson and Shiffrin, the part of your memory system that holds information for a fraction of a second is called the _____ register.

ANS: sensory

DIF: Difficult   REF: 245   OBJ: 8.2

2. The process of getting information into the memory system is called _____.

ANS: encoding

DIF: Moderate   REF: 245   OBJ: 8.2   KEY: WWW

3. The transformation of a sensory-perceptual experience into a long-lasting memory takes place during the _____ step.

ANS: consolidation

DIF: Difficult   REF: 245   OBJ: 8.2

4. An essay question that contains a hint would best be classified as a _____ recall memory task.

ANS: cued

DIF: Moderate   REF: 246   OBJ: 8.2   KEY: WWW

5. An _____ memory occurs unintentionally and without awareness.

ANS: implicit

DIF: Moderate   REF: 246   OBJ: 8.2

6. An _____ memory occurs as the result of a deliberate, intentional effort.

ANS: explicit

DIF: Moderate   REF: 246   OBJ: 8.2   KEY: WWW

7. Memories for general facts are referred to as _____ memory.

ANS: semantic

DIF: Moderate   REF: 246   OBJ: 8.2

8. The portion of your information-processing system that plans and monitors what you do is referred to as the _____ control processor.

    ANS: executive

    DIF: Moderate   REF: 247   OBJ: 8.3

9. When an infant repeats a novel act that it has seen earlier in the day, it is displaying _____ imitation.

    ANS: deferred

    DIF: Moderate   REF: 248   OBJ: 8.4

10. The memory strategy of _____ involves repeating items that you are trying to learn and remember.

    ANS: rehearsal

    DIF: Moderate   REF: 252   OBJ: 8.5

11. The strategy of making a meaningful link between items in order to help remember them is called _____.

    ANS: elaboration

    DIF: Moderate   REF: 252   OBJ: 8.5

12. A child who can benefit from a strategy, but who is unable to produce one on his or her own, is best classified as having a _____ deficiency.

    ANS: production

    DIF: Moderate   REF: 252   OBJ: 8.5   KEY: WWW

13. Children who cannot benefit from a strategy, even when taught it, are best classified as having a _____ deficiency.

    ANS: mediation

    DIF: Moderate   REF: 252   OBJ: 8.5

14. Memories for our own specific life experiences are called _____ memories.

    ANS: autobiographical

    DIF: Easy   REF: 255   OBJ: 8.6

15. The fact that people are unable to recall events that took place during the first two years after birth is called infantile _____.

   ANS: amnesia

   DIF: Easy   REF: 255   OBJ: 8.6

16. According to _____ theory, children store verbatim and general accounts of events separately.

   ANS: fuzzy-trace

   DIF: Difficult   REF: 256   OBJ: 8.6

17. A _____ or general event representation is a mental representation of the typical sequence of actions related to an event.

   ANS: script

   DIF: Easy   REF: 256   OBJ: 8.7   KEY: WWW

18. Siegler proposed a _____ assessment approach to explain children's behavior on Piaget's balance beam problem.

   ANS: rule

   DIF: Moderate   REF: 257   OBJ: 8.8

19. According to Siegler, rather than picturing development as a series of "stair step" stages, we should picture it as _____ waves.

   ANS: overlapping

   DIF: Difficult   REF: 258   OBJ: 8.8

20. When playing "20 Questions," asking, "Is it bigger than a bread box?" represents a _____-seeking question.

   ANS: constraint

   DIF: Moderate   REF: 270   OBJ: 8.13

ESSAY

1. Discuss the process of human memory by differentiating between sensory register, working memory, short-term memory, and long-term memory.

   ANS: Answer not provided   REF: 244-245   OBJ: 8.2

2. Describe ways of assessing memory development from birth through age one year.

   ANS: Answer not provided   REF: 248-250   OBJ: 8.4

545

3. Describe the potential accuracy of young children's eyewitness testimony. What role does childhood amnesia play in this process?

   ANS: Answer not provided   REF: 257   OBJ: 8.7

4. What problem-solving advancements did Robert Siegler suggest occur between infancy and adolescence?

   ANS: Answer not provided   REF: 257-259   OBJ: 8.8

5. Justine is a typically developing human. What information-processing advances would you expect her to experience between the start of her middle school years and the end of her senior year of high school?

   ANS: Answer not provided   REF: 259-260   OBJ: 8.9

6. What factors contribute to expertise in adulthood?

   ANS: Answer not provided   REF: 261-262   OBJ: 8.10

7. What factors contribute to declines in cognitive abilities in old age?

   ANS: Answer not provided   REF: 265-268   OBJ: 8.12

8. Why are the memory abilities of a 10- to 12-year-old better than the abilities of a 4- to 5-year-old?

   ANS: Answer not provided   REF: 250-256   OBJ: 8.5-8.6 KEY: WWW

9. In what ways are the autobiographical memory young children and older adults similar? How do they differ?

   ANS: Answer not provided   REF: 255-256 & 262-263   OBJ: 8.6 & 8.11
   KEY: WWW

10. What types of memory tasks cause older adults the most problems? On which types of tasks do older individuals have the least difficulty?

    ANS: Answer not provided   REF: 263-265   OBJ: 8.11   KEY: WWW

MULTIPLE CHOICE

1. According to the psychometric approach to intelligence, intelligence
   a. aids in adaptation to the environment.
   b. is made up of traits that vary and can be measured.
   c. is fixed at conception by genetic factors.
   d. is organized by stages or levels.

   ANS: B   DIF: Moderate   REF: 277   OBJ: 9.1
   KEY: WWW

2. Who is most likely to say, "The major focus of my discipline is on the creation and understanding of intelligence tests"?
   a. Sisko, who is a Freudian
   b. Kirk, who is a Piagetian
   c. Janeway, who is an information-processing theorist
   d. Archer, who is a psychometric theorist

   ANS: D   DIF: Difficult   REF: 277   OBJ: 9.1

3. When discussing intelligence, David says, "I subscribe to a psychometric approach on that topic." This means that David would most likely
   a. be against the idea of measuring intelligence.
   b. believe that he is smarter than most other people.
   c. describe a person in terms of measurable traits he or she possesses.
   d. believe that intelligence is inherited.

   ANS: C   DIF: Moderate   REF: 277   OBJ: 9.1

4. The two-factor model argues that intelligence is highly influenced by a factor simply designated as "g." What does "g" stand for?
   a. Global self-worth
   b. Genetic inheritance
   c. Goodness-of-fit
   d. General mental ability

   ANS: D   DIF: Difficult   REF: 277   OBJ: 9.1

5. The intelligence concept of "g" was based on the observation that
   a. IQ scores predict career success.
   b. skill levels are consistent across tasks.
   c. children who take math do better at math.
   d. there are few racial differences in IQ scores.

   ANS: B   DIF: Moderate   REF: 277   OBJ: 9.1

6. Whose "formula" for intelligence is, "intelligence" = "g" + "s"?
   a. Raymond Cattell
   b. Charles Spearman
   c. J.P. Guilford
   d. Louis Thurstone

   ANS: B   DIF: Moderate   REF: 277   OBJ: 9.1

7. Which pair is best associated with concepts of fluid intelligence?
   a. Cattell and Horn
   b. Atkinson and Shiffrin
   c. Fechner and Weber
   d. Spearman and Thurstone

   ANS: A   DIF: Moderate   REF: 277   OBJ: 9.1

8. _____ intelligence is defined as the ability to use your active mind to solve novel problems.
   a. Fluid
   b. Crystallized
   c. Primary
   d. Tertiary

   ANS: A   DIF: Moderate   REF: 277   OBJ: 9.1

9. Fluid intelligence is usually
   a. taught and emphasizes using the mind in new ways.
   b. not taught and emphasizes using the mind in new ways.
   c. taught and emphasizes using the mind to solve familiar tasks.
   d. not taught and emphasizes using the mind to solve familiar tasks.

   ANS: B   DIF: Moderate   REF: 277   OBJ: 9.1
   KEY: WWW

10. Dominique is shown a series of triangles of different sizes and colors and is asked to guess
    what the next triangle in the series might look like. The use of this novel task indicates that the
    person testing Dominique is most likely assessing _____ intelligence.
    a. fluid
    b. crystallized
    c. naturalistic
    d. linguistic

    ANS: A   DIF: Difficult   REF: 277   OBJ: 9.1

11. Crystallized intelligence is the dimension of intellect that includes all of the following abilities
    EXCEPT
    a. word comprehension.
    b. numerical abilities.
    c. recognizing relationships between two objects you have never seen before.
    d. ability to recall general information.

    ANS: C   DIF: Moderate   REF: s   OBJ: 9.1

12. Kao is involved with a project studying intelligence. During the study, she is first asked to
    name the state capitals of Wisconsin and Hawaii. Then she is asked to explain the difference
    between the words "destiny" and "density." Given these tasks, Kao appears to be taking a test
    of _____ intelligence.
    a. interpersonal
    b. crystallized
    c. spatial
    d. fluid

    ANS: B   DIF: Difficult   REF: s   OBJ: 9.1

548

13. The basic distinction between crystallized and fluid intelligence is that
    a. fluid intelligence involves using your mind in new ways, and crystallized intelligence involves using what you have already learned.
    b. fluid intelligence is verbal, and crystallized intelligence is nonverbal.
    c. fluid intelligence is implicit, and crystallized intelligence is explicit.
    d. fluid intelligence tests wisdom, and crystallized intelligence tests genius.

    ANS: A   DIF: Difficult   REF: s   OBJ: 9.1

14. The modern general consensus concerning intelligence is that
    a. a general ability influences how well people do on only one or two tasks.
    b. there are a few broad dimensions of intelligence that can be found in factor analyses.
    c. specific abilities are not part of intelligence.
    d. IQ tests do a better job of explaining intelligence than describing intelligence.

    ANS: B   DIF: Moderate   REF: 278   OBJ: 9.1
    KEY: WWW

15. The intelligence test developed by Binet and Simon (1904) was specifically designed to
    a. measure the intelligence quotient (IQ) of adults.
    b. identify gifted children.
    c. predict which high school students would be successful in college.
    d. determine which school children were likely to be slow learners.

    ANS: D   DIF: Moderate   REF: 278   OBJ: 9.1

16. The intent of the original Binet and Simon intelligence test was to be able to identify
    a. effective soldiers.
    b. women who would make the best teachers.
    c. geniuses.
    d. "dull" children in need of special education.

    ANS: D   DIF: Easy   REF: 278   OBJ: 9.1

17. Concerning the Binet and Simon intelligence test, "age graded" refers to
    a. a test that is scored by same-age peers.
    b. the age at which an average child of a certain age can successfully complete an item.
    c. test items that are similar across cultures.
    d. a child who typically relies on divergent rather than convergent thinking.

    ANS: B   DIF: Moderate   REF: 278   OBJ: 9.1

18. The average level of age-graded problems a person can solve is used to determine the person's
    a. chronological age.   c. mental age.
    b. karyotype.   d. genotype.

    ANS: C   DIF: Moderate   REF: 278   OBJ: 9.1

549

19. An average 10-year-old would have
    a. only a chronological age of 10.
    b. only a mental age of 10.
    c. both a chronological and mental age of 10.
    d. neither a chronological nor mental age of 10

    ANS: C   DIF: Moderate   REF: 278   OBJ: 9.1

20. Who developed the Stanford-Binet Intelligence Scale?
    a. Lewis Terman   c. John Stanford
    b. Alfred Binet   d. Theodore Simon

    ANS: A   DIF: Moderate   REF: 278   OBJ: 9.1

21. The formula for calculating an intelligence quotient is
    a. $IQ = (CA+MA)/100$.   c. $IQ = (MA/CA)*100$.
    b. $IQ = (CA+MA)*100$.   d. $IQ = (MA+CA)/100$.

    ANS: C   DIF: Moderate   REF: 278   OBJ: 9.1

22. Ten-year-old Kookla is found to have a mental age of 12. According to the traditional
    Stanford-Binet Scale, Kookla has an IQ of
    a. 80.   c. 110.
    b. 100.   d. 120.

    ANS: D   DIF: Moderate   REF: 278   OBJ: 9.1
    KEY: WWW

23. Who would have the highest IQ?
    a. Tom, who is 10 years old and has a mental age of 15
    b. Brady, who is 15 years old and has a mental age of 10
    c. Payton, who is 15 years old and has a mental age of 20
    d. Manning, who is 20 years old and has a mental age of 15

    ANS: A   DIF: Difficult   REF: 278   OBJ: 9.1

24. Test norms are
    a. a set of procedures for properly administering a test.
    b. information specifying the number and types of items found on a test.
    c. a statement indicating the purpose of the test along with information on
       appropriate and inappropriate use of test results.
    d. a table of test scores that indicates the average score and how to interpret the range
       of scores around that average score.

    ANS: D   DIF: Moderate   REF: 278   OBJ: 9.1

25. On the fifth edition of the Stanford-Binet test,
    a. mental age is no longer used to calculate IQ.
    b. chronological age is no longer used to calculate IQ.
    c. no IQ score is calculated.
    d. there is a "cultural-balance" scale that equates children who have been raised in different cultures.

    ANS: A   DIF: Difficult   REF: 278   OBJ: 9.1

26. Who is best known for developing a set of intelligence tests that can be used on individuals from toddlerhood to old age?
    a. Alfred Binet   c. Charles Spearman
    b. David Wechsler   d. Howard Gardner

    ANS: B   DIF: Easy   REF: 278   OBJ: 9.1

27. Harold is about to assess the intelligence of his 4-year-old son, Kumar. Which test would be most appropriate him to select?
    a. WPPSI   c. WAIS-IV
    b. WISC-IV   d. MMPI

    ANS: A   DIF: Moderate   REF: 278   OBJ: 9.1
    KEY: WWW

28. Sixty-five-year-old Kint is going to a psychologist to have his verbal IQ assessed. Which test would a competent psychologist select to accomplish this goal?
    a. WPPSI   c. WAIS-IV
    b. WISC-IV   d. MMPI

    ANS: C   DIF: Moderate   REF: 278   OBJ: 9.1

29. Jacque is told that he will be taking the Wechsler Intelligence Scale for Children. What type of task should Jacque expect to complete as part of the assessment of his performance IQ?
    a. Arithmetic reasoning   c. Puzzle assembly
    b. A test of general knowledge   d. Vocabulary

    ANS: C   DIF: Difficult   REF: 278   OBJ: 9.1

30. The Wechsler Intelligence Scale for Children (WISC-IV) test differs from the Stanford-Binet test because only the WISC-IV
    a. is administered in groups rather than individually.
    b. emphasizes verbal abilities.
    c. has separate scores for verbal and performance abilities.
    d. is administered to children.

    ANS: C   DIF: Moderate   REF: 278   OBJ: 9.1
    KEY: WWW

551

31. To say that test scores are normally distributed around the average score means that
    a. most people score in the average range and few people score very high or very low.
    b. there are equal numbers of low, average, and high scores.
    c. scores obtained on repeated testing sessions are fairly consistent.
    d. the test is a good measure of the trait that it is supposed to be measuring.

    ANS: A   DIF: Moderate   REF: 278   OBJ: 9.1

32. On a normal distribution of IQ test scores, the average score would be
    a. 1.   c. 50.
    b. 10.   d. 100.

    ANS: D   DIF: Moderate   REF: s   OBJ: 9.1

33. If the scores from an intelligence test are normally distributed, then you would predict that the FEWEST number of people would receive an IQ score of _____ on that test.
    a. 70   c. 100
    b. 85   d. 115

    ANS: A   DIF: Difficult   REF: s   OBJ: 9.1

34. If the scores from an intelligence test are normally distributed, then you would predict that the largest number of people would receive an IQ score of _____ on that test.
    a. 70   c. 100
    b. 85   d. 115

    ANS: C   DIF: Moderate   REF: s   OBJ: 9.1
    KEY: WWW

35. An information-processing theorist focusing on intelligence testing would be most likely interested in
    a. the statistics used to calculate an IQ score.
    b. how children solve the problems on the test.
    c. a child's full IQ score.
    d. why children solve problems on the test.

    ANS: B   DIF: Difficult   REF: 280   OBJ: 9.2

36. The STAT test
    a. is designed for use with hearing impaired populations.
    b. generates "creativity" IQ score.
    c. avoids assessing acquired knowledge.
    d. includes an essay.

    ANS: D   DIF: Difficult   REF: 280   OBJ: 9.2

37. One of the unique features of Gardner's theory of intelligence is that it
    a. rejects the notion that a single IQ score can meaningfully assess intelligence.
    b. promotes the notion of genetic testing as a form of intelligence testing.
    c. focuses on what someone does not know as opposed to what he or she does know.
    d. completely ignores the impact of experience on intellectual functioning.

    ANS: A   DIF: Moderate   REF: 279   OBJ: 9.2

552

38. According to Howard Gardner, intelligence consists of at least eight distinct abilities. Which of the following is among Gardner's distinct types of intelligence?
   a. Musical
   b. Memory capacity
   c. Creative
   d. Interracial

   ANS: A   DIF: Easy   REF: 279   OBJ: 9.2

39. One of Siggy's most endearing traits is an exceptional sensitivity to other people's motivations and moods. According to Gardner, Siggy would best be classified as having high _____ intelligence.
   a. bodily-kinesthetic
   b. intrapersonal
   c. linguistic
   d. interpersonal

   ANS: D   DIF: Difficult   REF: 279   OBJ: 9.2

40. Given that Charles Darwin's theory of evolution was based on Darwin's extremely insightful observation of animals, it is likely that Gardner would have viewed Darwin as having exceptionally high _____ intelligence.
   a. naturalistic
   b. intrapersonal
   c. spatial
   d. logical-mathematical

   ANS: A   DIF: Easy   REF: 279   OBJ: 9.2

41. His steady hands make Dr. Greene a top-notch surgeon. Given this information, Dr. Greene would appear to have a high level of _____ intelligence.
   a. bodily-kinesthetic
   b. naturalistic
   c. linguistic
   d. interpersonal

   ANS: A   DIF: Easy   REF: 279   OBJ: 9.2

42. Cleopatra has an outstanding sense of her own feelings. This ability is best associated with Gardner's _____ type of intelligence.
   a. bodily-kinesthetic
   b. intrapersonal
   c. linguistic
   d. interpersonal

   ANS: B   DIF: Moderate   REF: 279   OBJ: 9.2
   KEY: WWW

43. Browning's latest book of poems is being hailed as a "triumph in the use of the written word." This indicates that Browning most likely possesses high levels of _____ intelligence.
   a. naturalistic
   b. intrapersonal
   c. linguistic
   d. interpersonal

   ANS: C   DIF: Easy   REF: 279   OBJ: 9.2

44. As a great architect, Mr. Brady has an amazing ability to visual and mentally transform a building in his mind. This suggests that he has superb _____ intelligence.
   a. bodily-kinesthetic
   b. spatial
   c. linguistic
   d. interpersonal

   ANS: B   DIF: Easy   REF: 279   OBJ: 9.2

45. People with savant syndrome illustrate that intelligence
    a. is a single unified ability.
    b. has no genetic basis.
    c. cannot be measured.
    d. consists of multiple and distinct abilities.

    ANS: D   DIF: Moderate   REF: 279   OBJ: 9.2

46. While Dilbert is severely mentally retarded, he has the ability to tell you the day of the week for any future date (e.g., November 27, 2949 = Tuesday). This description indicates that Dilbert
    a. has great wisdom.
    b. possesses superb divergent thinking skills.
    c. has savant syndrome.
    d. is about to experience a terminal drop.

    ANS: C   DIF: Easy   REF: 279   OBJ: 9.2

47. Gardner's theory of intelligence
    a. links distinct types of intelligence to specific areas of the brain.
    b. suggests that all types of intelligence have the same developmental course.
    c. argues that the concept of "g" can be used to explain savant behavior.
    d. is heavily reliant on the use of traditional IQ tests to assess intelligence.

    ANS: A   DIF: Moderate   REF: 279   OBJ: 9.2

48. Sternberg is best associated with _____ theory.
    a. psychodynamic
    b. autistic
    c. triarchic
    d. IQ

    ANS: C   DIF: Easy   REF: 279   OBJ: 9.2

49. Moesha grew up in a society in which women were supposed to always begin a conversation with a man. While traveling in a foreign nation, Moesha learns that in this culture, a woman who begins a conversation with a man is considered stupid. This cultural distinction in the definition of intelligence illustrates what Sternberg called the _____ component of intelligence.
    a. practical
    b. fluid
    c. developmental quotient
    d. information-processing

    ANS: A   DIF: Easy   REF: 281   OBJ: 9.2

50. According to triarchic theory, person with "street smarts" possesses high levels of _____ intelligence.
    a. creative
    b. analytical
    c. socioemotional
    d. practical

    ANS: D   DIF: Easy   REF: 281   OBJ: 9.2

554

51. When describing the practical component, Sternberg argues that an intelligent person will
    a. be successful in all situations.
    b. score high on an IQ test.
    c. show outstanding abilities in the areas of music and interpersonal skills.
    d. shape an environment to better suit his or her skills.

    ANS: D   DIF: Moderate   REF: 281   OBJ: 9.2

52. With regard to experience, Sternberg believes that
    a. the level of intelligence of a response can be accurately assessed only after extensive experience with the tasks.
    b. experience with a task has no impact on ability to intelligently respond to the task.
    c. there is no way to assess familiarity with a task.
    d. the creative component of intelligence is best measured by a person's responses on novel tasks.

    ANS: D   DIF: Moderate   REF: 281   OBJ: 9.2

53. _____ refers to an efficiency of information processing that appears with practice.
    a. Terminal drop   c. Factor analysis
    b. Automatization   d. The Flynn effect

    ANS: B   DIF: Moderate   REF: 281   OBJ: 9.2

54. What would indicate that LeBron's free-throw-shooting has undergone automatization?
    a. He has practiced so many times that he does not even have to pay that much attention to make the shot.
    b. He has never seen the behavior before, but he is busy committing it to memory.
    c. He can show someone else how to shoot free-throws.
    d. He now becomes distracted if fans wave banners while he is shooting.

    ANS: A   DIF: Moderate   REF: 281   OBJ: 9.2

55. Mr. Edam grew up in Wisconsin and knows a lot about Colby cheese. Mr. Cheddar grew up in Cheddar, England, and knows a lot about cheddar cheese. Both are given an intelligence test that contains a question about Colby cheese. The fact that Mr. Edam would be at an advantage due to his familiarity with the subject matter illustrates a problem referred to as
    a. the Flynn effect.   c. culture bias.
    b. savant syndrome.   d. factor analysis.

    ANS: C   DIF: Difficult   REF: 281   OBJ: 9.2

56. The analytic component focuses exclusively on
    a. genetic.   c. operant conditioning.
    b. cultural.   d. information-processing skills.

    ANS: D   DIF: Moderate   REF: 281   OBJ: 9.2
    KEY: WWW

57. Sternberg would argue that an individual who is outstanding at filtering out irrelevant from relevant information excels on the _____ component of intelligence.
   a. practical
   b. experiential
   c. creative
   d. analytic

   ANS: D   DIF: Moderate   REF: 281   OBJ: 9.2

58. A key role of Sternberg's triarchic theory was to _____, something that is not commonly found on traditional IQ tests.
   a. explain how people produce intelligent answers
   b. create questions that tap into different areas of intellectual functioning
   c. describe the key role of genetics in determining intelligence
   d. discuss how a single score could assess intelligence

   ANS: A   DIF: Moderate   REF: 281   OBJ: 9.2

59. The newest aspect of Sternberg's approach to intellect is _____ intelligence.
   a. naturalistic
   b. successful
   c. intrapersonal
   d. bodily-kinesthetic

   ANS: B   DIF: Easy   REF: 281   OBJ: 9.2
   KEY: WWW

60. "Successful intelligence" is BEST summarized as the ability to succeed in
   a. life
   b. school
   c. standardized test situations
   d. familiar settings

   ANS: A   DIF: Moderate   REF: 281   OBJ: 9.2

61. Most widely used traditional tests of intelligence focus on _____ intelligence(s).
   a. creative
   b. analytic
   c. practical
   d. creative, analytic, and practical

   ANS: B   DIF: Moderate   REF: 281   OBJ: 9.2

62. Creativity is usually defined as
   a. high intelligence (as defined by a high IQ)
   b. the ability to come up with the most bizarre answer to a problem
   c. the ability to produce novel responses that are valued by others
   d. factual information gained over years of experience

   ANS: C   DIF: Moderate   REF: s   OBJ: 9.3

63. The production of ideas that are original and meaningful are both defining characteristics of
   a. terminal drop.
   b. creativity.
   c. fluid intelligence.
   d. automatization.

   ANS: B   DIF: Easy   REF: s   OBJ: 9.3
   KEY: WWW

64. IQ and creativity scores are
    a. inversely related.
    b. identical.
    c. highly related.
    d. not well correlated.

    ANS: D   DIF: Easy   REF: 282   OBJ: 9.3

65. Miss Whitney asks her class to name the person who invented the cotton gin. This question best represents a measure of
    a. convergent thinking.
    b. divergent thinking.
    c. creativity.
    d. ideational fluency.

    ANS: A   DIF: Moderate   REF: 282   OBJ: 9.3

66. Which is NOT one of the three dimensions on which divergent thinking is analyzed?
    a. Originality
    b. Flexibility
    c. Ideation fluency
    d. Crystallization

    ANS: D   DIF: Difficult   REF: 282   OBJ: 9.3

67. Which question would be the best method of assessing divergent thinking?
    a. Who is the president of Mexico?
    b. What are some effective ways of studying for a psychology exam?
    c. Where does the equator pass through the continent of Africa?
    d. How much is (212*34)/.948?

    ANS: B   DIF: Difficult   REF: 282   OBJ: 9.3

68. Divergent thinking is to convergent thinking as
    a. a variety of answers are to one answer.
    b. IQ tests are to tests of creativity.
    c. interpersonal intelligence is to intrapersonal intelligence.
    d. DQ is to IQ.

    ANS: A   DIF: Difficult   REF: 282   OBJ: 9.3

69. Ideational fluency refers to one's ability to
    a. pick the most appropriate idea to solve a problem.
    b. quickly recall synonyms when given a word.
    c. solve a problem quickly and accurately.
    d. generate many interesting, novel ideas.

    ANS: D   DIF: Difficult   REF: 282   OBJ: 9.3

70. Who is demonstrating a high level of ideation fluency?
    a. Hugh, who knows four different languages
    b. Stew, who has an IQ of 150
    c. Drew, who quickly generated a list of 20 novel uses for marshmallows
    d. Lou, who can name the day of the week for any date in the 1900s

    ANS: C   DIF: Difficult   REF: 282   OBJ: 9.3

71. How did Sternberg include the notion of confluence into his theory?
    a. He believed that several factors combined to create intelligence.
    b. He saw intelligence as based on cultural differences.
    c. He suggested that the presence of a member of the same race would improve the intelligence score of children from minority groups.
    d. He saw intelligence as a "use it or lose it" proposition.

    ANS: A   DIF: Moderate   REF: s   OBJ: 9.3

72. Luther is developing a test of intelligence. He believes that in order to accurately generate an intelligence test score, he must assess a multitude of factors that will be added together to form the "product" called intellect. This belief indicates that Luther is a strong proponent of
    a. confluence.   c. convergent thinking.
    b. creativity.   d. neuroplasticity.

    ANS: A   DIF: Difficult   REF: s   OBJ: 9.3

73. Research on intelligence and creativity has shown that
    a. highly creative individuals rarely have below-average IQs.
    b. a high IQ is required for creativity.
    c. the more reliance on convergent thinking, the greater the creativity.
    d. motivation cannot compensate for the lack of environmental support for intellectual advancement.

    ANS: A   DIF: Moderate   REF: 283   OBJ: 9.3

74. The major focus of the Bayley Scales of Infant Development is to assess intelligence by measuring
    a. the rate at which infants achieve developmental milestones.
    b. vocabulary size.
    c. creativity.
    d. physiological status at birth (e.g., heart rate, respiration, muscle tone).

    ANS: A   DIF: Moderate   REF: 283   OBJ: 9.4

75. Otis has just been told that his son Goober is going to be assessed using the Bayley Scales of Infant Development. As a knowledgeable psychologist, Otis would know that this test will assess Goober's
    a. savant skills (e.g., ability to calculate future days of the week).
    b. motor skills (e.g., ability to grasp and throw a ball).
    c. physiological skills (e.g., average heart rate, respiration).
    d. sociometric skills (e.g., the number of friends the child has).

    ANS: B   DIF: Moderate   REF: s   OBJ: 9.4

76. Searching for a hidden toy is part of the assessment of _____ scale on the Bayley Scales of Infant Development.
    a. behavioral-rating   c. physiological
    b. motor   d. mental

    ANS: D   DIF: Moderate   REF: 284   OBJ: 9.4

77. Which is NOT one of the scales on the Bayley Scales of Infant Development?
   a. Motor
   b. Mental
   c. Behavioral
   d. Social

   ANS: D   DIF: Easy   REF: s   OBJ: 9.4
   KEY: WWW

78. The use of a test yielding a DQ over a test yielding an IQ is most appropriate when you are assessing
   a. infants.
   b. preschoolers.
   c. adolescents.
   d. the elderly.

   ANS: A   DIF: Easy   REF: 284   OBJ: 9.4

79. If you tested 1,000 infants on a valid test that generated a DQ, what expectation would you have concerning the correlation between the DQ and an IQ taken when these individuals reach age 20?
   a. Expected correlation around 0
   b. Expected correlation around +.5
   c. Expected correlation around −1.0
   d. Expected correlation around +1.0

   ANS: A   DIF: Difficult   REF: 284   OBJ: 9.4

80. Why do scores on infant developmental scales appear to be such poor predictors of later IQs?
   a. Because negative environmental impacts cannot be over come by later experience.
   b. They are actually very good predictors.
   c. They are over-reliant on verbal skills that continue to develop in childhood.
   d. They may tap qualitatively different abilities.

   ANS: D   DIF: Moderate   REF: 284   OBJ: 9.4

81. If you want to predict later intelligence using some infant measure, which of the following measures would be best to use with the infants?
   a. Bayley DQ scores
   b. Stanford-Binet IQ scores
   c. Wechsler performance scores
   d. Speed of habituation scores

   ANS: D   DIF: Difficult   REF: 284   OBJ: 9.4

82. An intelligent infant is best characterized as one whom
   a. prefers familiar information over novel information.
   b. achieves developmental milestones more quickly than other infants.
   c. gets bored quickly with familiar information and seeks out novel information.
   d. slowly habituates to stimuli.

   ANS: C   DIF: Moderate   REF: 284   OBJ: 9.4

83. The stability of IQ scores
   a. is highest in infancy.
   b. becomes fairly high starting at around age four.
   c. is highest with longer times between testing sessions.
   d. is high for individual children but low for large groups of children.

   ANS: B   DIF: Moderate   REF: 285   OBJ: 9.5

84. Whose current IQ score would most likely be highly correlated with their IQ score at age 10?
    a. Dana, who is two years old
    c. Scully, who is six years old
    b. Mulder, who is four years old
    d. Fox, who is eight years old

    ANS: D   DIF: Moderate   REF: 285   OBJ: 9.5

85. Which statement best summarizes the pattern of IQ-score change in childhood?
    a. Overall age group stability but large individual variation
    b. Significant rise in average group IQ score from early to late childhood
    c. Significant drop in average group IQ score from early to late childhood
    d. Overall individual stability but large age-group variation

    ANS: A   DIF: Moderate   REF: 285   OBJ: 9.5

86. Some children show gains in IQ during their school years. Which factor appears to be the primary cause of such gains?
    a. Strict child rearing practices
    c. Parents who foster achievement
    b. Relaxed child rearing practices
    d. Effective schools

    ANS: C   DIF: Moderate   REF: 285   OBJ: 9.5

87. Some children show a lowering of their IQ during their school years. Which factor seems to be the most common cause of this decline?
    a. Accidental injury to the brain
    c. Chronic illness
    b. Living in impoverished environments
    d. Ineffective schools

    ANS: B   DIF: Moderate   REF: 285   OBJ: 9.5

88. The cumulative-deficit hypothesis is often used to explain
    a. how deficits in school funding create ineffective schools.
    b. how people with lower IQs have more children, thus lowering the average IQ in a society.
    c. how the cumulative effects of a superior education create a feeling of never being satisfied.
    d. how the negative effects of an impoverished environment "snowball" over time to create lowered IQ scores.

    ANS: D   DIF: Moderate   REF: 285   OBJ: 9.5

89. Children from impoverished environments may show progressively lower IQ scores over time, a phenomenon called
    a. terminal drop.
    c. cumulative-deficit hypothesis.
    b. savant syndrome.
    d. the factor analysis.

    ANS: C   DIF: Moderate   REF: 285   OBJ: 9.5
    KEY: WWW

560

90. Long-term research on children who were in Project Head Start indicates that
   a. while early changes in IQ are rare, significant increases in IQ are seen during the college years.
   b. compensatory programs like Head Start lead to poorer attitudes about achievement.
   c. children in these programs are more likely to end up in special education classes than their peers.
   d. participation in such programs may reduce the likelihood of teenage pregnancy.

   ANS: D   DIF: Difficult   REF: s   OBJ: 9.5

91. Research has shown that children who participate in early intervention programs
   a. show immediate gains in IQ that last long after the programs end.
   b. show immediate gains in IQ, but the gains fade after the programs end.
   c. show no immediate gains in IQ, but do eventually show long-term gains, even after the programs end.
   d. show no immediate gains in IQ, but do eventually show long-term gains, however the gains fade after the programs end.

   ANS: B   DIF: Difficult   REF: s   OBJ: 9.5

92. The typical pattern of creativity in childhood is
   a. high in preschool, higher in first grade, even higher in fourth grade, and highest by age 12.
   b. highest in preschool, lower in first grade, even lower in fourth grade, and lowest by age 12.
   c. high in preschool, lower in first grade, even lower in fourth grade, and higher by age 12.
   d. low in preschool, higher in first grade, even higher in fourth grade, and lower by age 12.

   ANS: C   DIF: Difficult   REF: s   OBJ: 9.6

93. Which of the following is true of creative children?
   a. They engage in more fantasy or pretend play than other children.
   b. They tend to be less open to new experiences.
   c. They do not have unhappy or lonely childhood experiences.
   d. Their creativity can be predicted by high IQ scores.

   ANS: A   DIF: Moderate   REF: s   OBJ: 9.6

94. Many early studies suggested that childhood _____ was the driving force behind the development of creativity.
   a. vaccinations
   b. nutrition
   c. adversity
   d. peer-friendship

   ANS: C   DIF: Difficult   REF: 287   OBJ: 9.6

95. What physiological event has been associated with the acquisition of Piaget's formal operation stage of thinking?
    a. A spurt in brain development
    b. Menopause
    c. Increased levels of androgens
    d. Spermarche

    ANS: A   DIF: Easy   REF: 288   OBJ: 9.7

96. IQ scores obtained during adolescence are best at predicting
    a. whether a person will graduate from college.
    b. a person's high school grades.
    c. a person's choice of occupation.
    d. how well a person performs in his or her chosen occupation.

    ANS: B   DIF: Moderate   REF: 288   OBJ: 9.7

97. Which statement is true?
    a. During adolescence, IQ scores become more predictable but creativity seems to wax and wane.
    b. During adolescence, creativity becomes more predictable but IQ scores seem to wax and wane.
    c. During adolescence, both IQ scores and creativity become more predictable.
    d. During adolescence, both IQ scores and creativity seem to wax and wane.

    ANS: A   DIF: Moderate   REF: 288   OBJ: 9.7

98. The phrase, "I really want to be the best," illustrates the key element of _____ that exemplifies the behavior of many child prodigies.
    a. specific talent
    b. supportive environment
    c. motivation
    d. ideational fluency

    ANS: C   DIF: Easy   REF: 288   OBJ: 9.8

99. Which parenting practice is best associated with the development of creativity?
    a. Firm hand with lots of training
    b. Start slow and build firmness quickly
    c. Enroll child in gifted classes even if he or she has no clear talent
    d. Allowing children the freedom to explore and opportunities to experiment

    ANS: D   DIF: Easy   REF: s   OBJ: 9.8

100. What lesson about parenting and the development of creativity is a main theme of the movie *Shine*?
    a. The loss of a mother is negatively associated with the development of creativity.
    b. Abusive parenting can negatively impact the expression of creativity.
    c. The younger the parent, the less likely a child will express creativity.
    d. Adopted children appear to "inherit" creativity.

    ANS: B   DIF: Moderate   REF: 289   OBJ: 9.8

101. On average, _____ tend to have the highest IQs.
    a. manual laborers
    c. technical workers
    b. blue collar workers
    d. white collar workers

    ANS: C   DIF: Moderate   REF: 290   OBJ: 9.9

102. As a general pattern, _____ tend to have the lowest IQs.
    a. manual laborers
    c. technical workers
    b. professional workers
    d. white collar workers

    ANS: A   DIF: Moderate   REF: 290   OBJ: 9.9
    KEY: WWW

103. A large-scale study on intelligence, income, and occupational prestige by Judge, Klinger, and Simon (2010) found that
    a. general intelligence was not significantly related to either income or occupational prestige.
    b. general intelligence was significantly related to income but not occupational prestige.
    c. general intelligence was significantly related to occupational prestige but not income.
    d. general intelligence was significantly related to both income and occupational prestige.

    ANS: D   DIF: Moderate   REF: 290   OBJ: 9.9

104. To what extent does a person's IQ predict his or her degree of occupational success (productivity)?
    a. Not at all (r = .00)
    c. Fairly well (r = +.30 to .50)
    b. Only very weakly (r = +.5 to .15)
    d. Extremely well (r = +.90 to 1.0)

    ANS: C   DIF: Moderate   REF: 290   OBJ: 9.9

105. Research on IQ and diabetes indicates that the reason individuals with higher IQs may live longer is because they are
    a. better able to monitor and treat their illness.
    b. genetically superior.
    c. able to pay for better car.
    d. more likely to be males, and males tend to live longer than females.

    ANS: A   DIF: Moderate   REF: 291   OBJ: 9.9

106. The best way to describe the relationship of IQs between ages 11 and 61 is
    a. unrelated.
    c. relatively stable.
    b. inversely related.
    d. virtually identical.

    ANS: C   DIF: Easy   REF: 291   OBJ: 9.10

563

107. Which statement best describes Kaufman's (2001) findings on the pattern of IQ change from young adulthood though old age generated by cross-sectional studies?
    a. IQ scores peak in young adulthood (age 20-30) and decline steadily through middle age (40-50) and old age (80-90).
    b. IQ scores rise gradually until middle age (age 40-50) then decline slowly until old age (around 80) when the decline accelerates.
    c. IQ scores remain fairly constant across the lifespan.
    d. IQ scores increase gradually between young adulthood (age 20-30) and old age (80-90).

    ANS: B   DIF: Difficult   REF: 260   OBJ: 9.10

108. Schaie's sequential study of stability of intellectual abilities showed that
    a. both cohort and age affect intellectual performance.
    b. cohort, but not age, affects intellectual performance.
    c. age, but not cohort, affects intellectual performance.
    d. neither cohort nor age affects intellectual performance.

    ANS: A   DIF: Easy   REF: 292   OBJ: 9.10

109. Research on changes in intellectual abilities during adulthood indicates that
    a. fluid and crystallized intelligence decline at the same rate.
    b. fluid intelligence declines earlier and more quickly than crystallized intelligence.
    c. crystallized intelligence declines earlier and more quickly than fluid intelligence.
    d. crystallized and fluid intelligence fluctuate up and down throughout the entire lifespan.

    ANS: B   DIF: Moderate   REF: 292   OBJ: 9.10

110. Longitudinal research on IQ change during adulthood indicates that
    a. crystallized intelligence peaks in young adulthood and then declines steadily.
    b. both fluid and crystallized and fluid intelligence peak in middle adulthood and then decline steadily.
    c. crystallized intelligence peaks and then declines, while fluid intelligence remains steady into middle-old adulthood.
    d. fluid intelligence peaks and then declines, while crystallized intelligence remains steady into middle-old adulthood.

    ANS: D   DIF: Moderate   REF: 292   OBJ: 9.10

111. Which type of test is most apt to put an older adult at a disadvantage?
    a. Test of general knowledge   c. Vocabulary test
    b. "Speeded" (timed) test   d. Test on arithmetic operations

    ANS: B   DIF: Easy   REF: 292   OBJ: 9.10

112. Which is the best characterization of intellectual functioning in adulthood?
    a. The time in history in which someone is born does not impact his or her intellect.
    b. Remaining cognitively active does little to stem the natural loss of intellectual skills associated with aging.
    c. Early education levels have little impact on adult levels of intelligence.
    d. Declines are not universal.

    ANS: D   DIF: Moderate   REF: 293   OBJ: 9.10

113. Which of the following can we conclude about intellectual functioning across the lifespan?
    a. Preference for familiar items and tasks is associated with higher levels of intellectual performance.
    b. Intellectual functioning is not affected by practice or familiarity.
    c. The speed with which someone processes information is related to intellectual performance.
    d. Age-related declines in intellectual ability are universal in nature.

    ANS: C   DIF: Moderate   REF: s   OBJ: 9.9
    KEY: WWW

114. Terminal drop is best associated with
    a. poor health.   c. poverty.
    b. automatization.   d. cultural bias.

    ANS: A   DIF: Easy   REF: 293   OBJ: 9.10

115. Terminal drop is the name given to
    a. a low score on an IQ test brought about by the child not feeling well on the day of the test.
    b. a rapid decline in the mental abilities of elderly people a few years prior to dying.
    c. placing an underachieving child in a special education class.
    d. a gifted student dropping out of high school and remaining underemployed during his or her adult life.

    ANS: B   DIF: Easy   REF: 293   OBJ: 9.10

116. Research would predict that _____ would show the largest intellectual declines in the coming years.
    a. 68-year-old Jay, who is married and leading an active social life,
    b. 69-year-old May, who lives alone and is socially inactive,
    c. 70-year-old Kay, who is married but socially inactive,
    d. 71-year-old Fay, who is lives alone but is socially active,

    ANS: B   DIF: Easy   REF: 293   OBJ: 9.10

117. What saying is most applicable to describing intellectual functioning in later life?
    a. Only the good die young.   c. Use it or lose it.
    b. You can't teach an old dog new tricks. d. Absence makes the heart grow fonder.

    ANS: C   DIF: Moderate   REF: 293   OBJ: 9.10

118. Which is the best definition of wisdom?
    a. Expert knowledge in the fundamental pragmatics of life
    b. Superb habituation speed
    c. Scoring at least two standard deviations above the norm on an IQ test
    d. The ability to generate many novel but potentially impractical answers

    ANS: A   DIF: Easy   REF: 293   OBJ: 9.11

119. Research on wisdom suggests that
    a. most adults are considered to possess wisdom.
    b. only adults with expertise or experience display wisdom.
    c. personality and intelligence have little to do with wisdom.
    d. age predicts wisdom.

    ANS: B   DIF: Moderate   REF: s   OBJ: 9.11
    KEY: WWW

120. A study on the development of wisdom in young and elderly women by Staudinger, Smith, and Baltes (2001) found that
    a. wisdom is quite common in old age.
    b. expertise is a better predictor of wisdom than age.
    c. age predicts wisdom.
    d. life experiences have little to do with the expression of wisdom.

    ANS: B   DIF: Moderate   REF: s   OBJ: 9.11

121. The fact that the brain can be restructured in response to training exemplifies the concept of
    a. terminal drop.   c. the secular trend.
    b. neuroplacticity.   d. psychometrics.

    ANS: B   DIF: Moderate   REF: 294   OBJ: 9.11

122. Peak levels of creativity tend to occur EARLIEST in individuals who are in the
    a. sciences.   c. mathematics.
    b. humanities.   d. arts.

    ANS: D   DIF: Moderate   REF: 295-296   OBJ: 9.12

123. Creative achievement requires
    a. only enthusiasm.   c. both enthusiasm and experience.
    b. only experience.   d. neither enthusiasm nor experience.

    ANS: C   DIF: Easy   REF: 296   OBJ: 9.12

124. Concerning creativity, ideation is to elaboration as
    a. doing is to seeing.   c. complex is to simple.
    b. generating is to executing. d. arts are to sciences.

    ANS: B   DIF: Difficult   REF: 296   OBJ: 9.12

125. Research on aging and creativity has shown that older individuals are _____ than younger adults.
    a. less original and less productive with creative ideas
    b. as original and less productive with creative ideas
    c. original but more productive with creative ideas
    d. as productive but less original with creative ideas

    ANS: B   DIF: Moderate   REF: 296   OBJ: 9.12

126. Which best describes the Flynn effect?
    a. Changes in genes underlie changes in intellect.
    b. Most psychologists now accept the theory of "general mental ability."
    c. Average IQ scores in the United States have risen dramatically over the past decades.
    d. Studies of adopted children have demonstrated a significant difference in IQ scores between infant males and infant females.

    ANS: C   DIF: Moderate   REF: 297   OBJ: 9.13

127. The fact that adults born in the 1980s have higher adult IQs than adults born in the 1950s illustrates the _____ effect.
    a. cumulative-deficit   c. intellectual disability
    b. Flynn   d. terminal drop

    ANS: B   DIF: Moderate   REF: 297   OBJ: 9.13
    KEY: WWW

128. Which has NOT been used to explain the Flynn effect?
    a. Better nutrition   c. Better education
    b. Smaller family size   d. Smaller gene pools

    ANS: D   DIF: Easy   REF: 297   OBJ: 9.13

129. Which of the following is the strongest piece of evidence showing that genetic factors influence intelligence (as measured by IQ tests)?
    a. Identical twins reared apart are more alike than fraternal twins reared together.
    b. Fraternal twins reared together are more alike than identical twins reared apart.
    c. Fraternal twins reared together are more alike than fraternal twins reared apart.
    d. Identical twins reared apart are more alike than identical twins reared together.

    ANS: A   DIF: Moderate   REF: 297   OBJ: 9.13

130. How many of the following four home situations (father is absent from family, mother has poor mental health, family has two or less children, head of household is unemployed) represent possible risk factors for negatively impacting a child's IQ score?
    a. 1   c. 3
    b. 2   d. 4

    ANS: C   DIF: Difficult   REF: 298   OBJ: 9.13

567

131. A researcher is using a measure in which both the emotional and verbal responsiveness of a parent and the provision of appropriate play materials are being assessed. Given this description, the researcher appears to be using the
a. Wechsler Intelligence Scale for Children.
b. Stanford-Binet IQ Test.
c. Bayley Scales of Infant Development.
d. HOME inventory.

ANS: D   DIF: Moderate   REF: 298   OBJ: 9.13

132. Which "home environment" factor seems to be most important for the intellectual development of a child?
a. Having several older siblings
b. Having several younger siblings
c. A permissive parenting style
d. Parental involvement with the child

ANS: D   DIF: Moderate   REF: s   OBJ: 9.13

133. Which best describes the impact of genetics and environment on a child's IQ?
a. At age two, maternal IQ best predicts the IQ of a child; by age four, the impact of the quality of the home environment becomes as good a predictor as maternal IQ.
b. At age two, the quality of the home environment best predicts the IQ of a child; by age four, maternal IQ becomes as good a predictor as the quality of the home environment.
c. At age two, paternal IQ best predicts the IQ of a child; by age four, the impact of the quality of the home environment becomes as good a predictor as paternal IQ.
d. At age two, of the quality of the home environment best predicts the IQ of a child; by age four, paternal IQ becomes as good a predictor as the quality of the home environment.

ANS: A   DIF: Difficult   REF: 298-299   OBJ: 9.13

134. Child poverty involves
a. only low family income.
b. only a lack of meeting a child's needs.
c. both low family income and a lack of meeting a child's needs.
d. neither low family income nor a lack of meeting a child's needs.

ANS: C   DIF: Easy   REF: 300   OBJ: 9.13

135. Studies on _____ have shown that being in an impoverished environment has a direct impact on brain development.
a. rats
b. infants
c. toddlers with Down syndrome
d. older adults

ANS: A   DIF: Easy   REF: 300   OBJ: 9.13

136. Scarr and Weinberg's research on social class and IQ showed that
   a. children from disadvantaged homes could raise their IQs if adopted into middle-class homes with intelligent adoptive parents.
   b. children from disadvantaged homes continue to show significant deficits in IQ even after being adopted into middle-class homes with intelligent adoptive parents.
   c. children from poor economic conditions do not differ significantly in IQ from children from average or above average economic conditions.
   d. improving the economic conditions of the home has no significant impact on children's IQs because IQ is so strongly affected by genes.

   ANS: A   DIF: Moderate   REF: 300   OBJ: 9.13

137. Research on race, ethnicity, and intelligence has shown that
   a. you cannot predict an individual's IQ on the basis of their race or ethnic status.
   b. the gap between the IQ scores of European and African-American children has increased in the past few decades.
   c. different subcultures tend to show the same profile of mental abilities.
   d. Asian Americans tend to score lower on IQ tests than Hispanic Americans.

   ANS: A   DIF: Moderate   REF: 300   OBJ: 9.13

138. The fact that IQ tests are more appropriate for Caucasian middle-class children than low-income African-American children provide an example of a(n) _____ bias in testing.
   a. genetic   c. cultural
   b. creativity   d. ideation

   ANS: C   DIF: Easy   REF: 300   OBJ: 9.12

139. A culture fair test is best defined as one that
   a. completely eliminates cultural bias from testing.
   b. can be administered to children from more than one culture.
   c. includes questions that are equally familiar or unfamiliar to children from all cultures.
   d. includes questions about all cultures.

   ANS: C   DIF: Difficult   REF: s   OBJ: 9.12

140. What has been shown to increase the IQ scores of disadvantaged children from minority racial and ethnic groups?
   a. Giving a test with only hard items
   b. Having an unfamiliar examiner
   c. Telling the child that the exam was not going to be scored
   d. Making sure they associate the test with "white" culture

   ANS: C   DIF: Moderate   REF: 301   OBJ: 9.12

141. The concept of stereotypic threat is most often used to explain the lower IQ scores found in
   a. African Americans.   c. women.
   b. the elderly.   d. infants and toddlers.

   ANS: A   DIF: Moderate   REF: 301   OBJ: 9.13
   KEY: WWW

569

142. Which statement concerning racial and ethnic differences in IQ is FALSE?
a. The fear of "stereotype threat" (i.e., being judged on qualities associated with negative stereotypes) can help explain why African Americans score lower on IQ tests.
b. Stereotype threat appears to account for about 80 points of the gap between majority and non-majority students.
c. Mentors tend to increase the level of stereotype threat in members of minority groups.
d. Positive stereotypes about a group may increase test performance of that group.

ANS: B   DIF: Moderate   REF: s   OBJ: 9.13

143. Research on genetics and intelligence test scores has shown that
a. genetic factors can help partially explain between-group variation but not within-group variation.
b. genetic factors can help partially explain within-group variation but not between-group variation.
c. genetic factors can help partially explain between-group variation and within-group variation.
d. genetic factors cannot help partially explain neither between-group variation or within-group variation.

ANS: A   DIF: Difficult   REF: 302   OBJ: 9.13

144. Which environmental change is most likely to positively impact an African-American child's IQ score?
a. Having them reside in an understimulating home environment
b. Exposing them to a "culture of tests and the school"
c. Telling them to ignore the impact of poverty
d. Offering more developmental programs in high school

ANS: B   DIF: Easy   REF: 302   OBJ: 9.13

145. Mental retardation (intellectual disability) is defined as
a. significantly below-average IQ alone.
b. significant deficits in adaptive behavior alone.
c. significantly below-average IQ and deficits in adaptive behavior.
d. significantly below-average IQ and deficits in adaptive behavior and above-average skills in at least one academic area.

ANS: C   DIF: Moderate   REF: 303   OBJ: 9.14

146. Eighteen-year-old Becker is accurately classified as being mildly intellectually disabled. Given this diagnosis, it is most likely that he
a. is able to live and work independently and has no academic limitations.
b. is able to live and work independently but has some academic limitations.
c. needs constant supervision in order to work.
d. is completely dependent on others for care.

ANS: B   DIF: Difficult   REF: 303   OBJ: 9.14

147. A _____ disabled child will show major delays in all areas of development.
    a. mildly
    c. severely
    b. moderately
    d. profoundly

ANS: D   DIF: Easy   REF: 303   OBJ: 9.14

148. Organic retardation is the term given to retardation caused by
    a. heredity, disease, or injury.
    c. lack of intellectual stimulation.
    b. lack of schooling.
    d. poor nutrition.

ANS: A   DIF: Moderate   REF: 303   OBJ: 9.14

149. Reba has been accurately diagnosed as being affected by organic retardation. Which statement about Reba would ALWAYS be true?
    a. Reba's retardation is due to some identifiable biological cause.
    b. Reba's level of retardation would be either severe or profound.
    c. Reba was raised in an understimulating environment.
    d. Reba has three 21st chromosomes.

ANS: A   DIF: Moderate   REF: 303   OBJ: 9.14

150. Which statement about the classification of intellectual disabilities is true?
    a. About 10% of school-age children are classified as having an intellectual disability.
    b. The rate of children diagnosed with mild intellectual disabilities has increased dramatically in the past few decades.
    c. Parents seldom negatively react to a child's disability.
    d. Children with intellectual disabilities often have associated impairments like cerebral palsy or a sensory disorder.

ANS: D   DIF: Moderate   REF: 304   OBJ: 9.14

151. A group of English individuals with intellectual disabilities who participated in a long-term study are referred to as the
    a. Camberwell Cohort.
    c. Gang of Six.
    b. Termites.
    d. Flynn Family.

ANS: A   DIF: Moderate   REF: 304   OBJ: 9.14
KEY: WWW

152. It was found that when they were in their 40s, _____ of the Camberwell Cohort lived with their families.
    a. 25%
    c. 75%
    b. 50%
    d. 100%

ANS: A   DIF: Difficult   REF: 304   OBJ: 9.14

153. Results from the Camberwell Cohort study indicated that for adults diagnosed with intellectual disabilities in early life, the
    a. majority of symptoms disappeared by adolescence.
    b. original diagnosis had been change by middle age.
    c. overall quality of their lives was lower than that of non-impaired peers.
    d. level of impact on their lives was unrelated to the severity of the disability.

    ANS: C   DIF: Moderate   REF: 304   OBJ: 9.14

154. Using today's standards, how would Wendy be accurately classified as a "gifted" child?
    a. She only needs an IQ score of at least 160.
    b. She only needs to perform in the top 50% of her group on a given task.
    c. She needs a high IQ score and some special abilities.
    d. She needs a high IQ score or some special abilities.

    ANS: C   DIF: Moderate   REF: 304   OBJ: 9.14

155. The primary way gifted children can be identified at an early age is by their
    a. advanced language skills.
    b. good social interaction skills.
    c. high level of motor activity.
    d. lack of motivation to act due to a fear of perfectionism.

    ANS: A   DIF: Moderate   REF: s   OBJ: 9.14

156. Researchers using the Characteristics of Giftedness Scale found that gifted children could be distinguished from average children in a number of ways including all of the following EXCEPT their
    a. extensive vocabularies.   c. excellent sense of humor.
    b. lack of concern about perfection.   d. strong ability with puzzles.

    ANS: B   DIF: Moderate   REF: 305   OBJ: 9.14

157. Which of the following accurately summarizes Terman's famous longitudinal study of findings regarding gifted children (i.e., the "Termites")?
    a. Gifted children are often emotionally immature and experience more frequent physical problems.
    b. Gifted children are not as well adjusted as their age-mates.
    c. Gifted children are well adjusted and morally mature.
    d. Gifted children are well adjusted but physically frail.

    ANS: C   DIF: Moderate   REF: 305   OBJ: 9.14

158. Which best described the average of Terman's "Termites" when they reached adulthood?
    a. Healthy, happy, productive   c. Unhealthy, happy, productive
    b. Healthy, unhappy, productive   d. Healthy, happy, unproductive

    ANS: A   DIF: Easy   REF: 304   OBJ: 9.14

572

159. Which type of theorist would be most likely to describe intellectual development in terms of qualitative changes in thought with age (e.g., transformation from a caterpillar to a butterfly)?
a. A Piagetian
b. A Vygotskyian
c. An information-processor
d. A psychometrician

ANS: A   DIF: Easy   REF: 306   OBJ: 9.15

TRUE/FALSE

1. The "g" in Spearman's two-factor theory of intelligence stands for genius.

ANS: F   DIF: Moderate   REF: 277   OBJ: 9.1

2. Crystallized intelligence is the ability to use one's mind actively to solve novel problems.

ANS: F   DIF: Moderate   REF: 277   OBJ: 9.1
KEY: WWW

3. IQ = CA/MA*100.

ANS: F   DIF: Moderate   REF: 278   OBJ: 9.1

4. If a set of data is normally distributed the number of individuals scoring low, moderate, and high is identical.

ANS: F   DIF: Moderate   REF: 278   OBJ: 9.1

5. Gardner's list of multiple intelligences included both musical intelligence and artistic intelligence.

ANS: F   DIF: Moderate   REF: 279   OBJ: 9.2

6. Sternberg's practical component defines intelligence differently depending on the sociocultural context in which it is displayed.

ANS: T   DIF: Moderate   REF: 281   OBJ: 9.2

7. According to Sternberg, an individual high in successful intelligence is strong in practical, creative, and analytical areas.

ANS: T   DIF: Moderate   REF: 281   OBJ: 9.2
KEY: WWW

8. Convergent thinking involves finding the one "best answer" to a problem.

ANS: T   DIF: Moderate   REF: 282   OBJ: 9.3

9. Ideational fluency is measured by the shear number of different answers an individual can generate.

ANS: T   DIF: Difficult   REF: 282   OBJ: 9.3

573

10. The Bayley DQ score does a good job of predicting later school grades.

    ANS: F   DIF: Moderate   REF: 284   OBJ: 9.4

11. Children whose IQ scores fluctuate tend to come from unstable home environments.

    ANS: T   DIF: Moderate   REF: 285   OBJ: 9.5

12. IQ scores in high school are very good predictors of college grades.

    ANS: F   DIF: Moderate   REF: 258   OBJ: 9.7
    KEY: WWW

13. The average IQ of workers increases as the prestige of the occupation increases.

    ANS: T   DIF: Easy   REF: 280   OBJ: 9.9

14. Most adults suffer drastic declines in mental abilities and IQ between age 40 and 50.

    ANS: F   DIF: Moderate   REF: 291-292   OBJ: 9.10

15. Very few older adults develop wisdom.

    ANS: T   DIF: Moderate   REF: 293-295   OBJ: 9.11

16. In the field of psychology, as in many fields, creative production tends to peak in the mid 50s.

    ANS: F   DIF: Moderate   REF: 295-296   OBJ: 9.12

17. The Flynn effect states that racial differences in IQ scores are likely due to genetic differences.

    ANS: F   DIF: Moderate   REF: 297   OBJ: 9.13
    KEY: WWW

18. A stimulating home environment is one of the best predictors of a child having a high IQ.

    ANS: T   DIF: Easy   REF: 297-298   OBJ: 9.12

19. Organic-based intellectual disabilities may be the result of a genetic disorder or maternal alcohol consumption.

    ANS: T   DIF: Moderate   REF: 303   OBJ: 9.14

20. Gifted children tend to be significantly less well-adjusted than children of average intelligence.

    ANS: F   DIF: Moderate   REF: 304-305   OBJ: 9.13
    KEY: WWW

COMPLETION

1. According to Horn and Cattell, _____ intelligence involves the use of knowledge acquired through life experience.

   ANS: crystallized

   DIF: Moderate   REF: 277   OBJ: 9.1

2. According to Horn and Cattell, _____ intelligence is the ability to use your active mind to solve novel problems.

   ANS: fluid

   DIF: Moderate   REF: 277   OBJ: 9.1   KEY: WWW

3. The formula for calculating an IQ score is _____ x 100.

   ANS: MA/CA

   DIF: Moderate   REF: 278   OBJ: 9.1

4. The bell-shaped symmetrical spread of scores associated with the Stanford-Binet Scale is called a _____ distribution.

   ANS: normal

   DIF: Moderate   REF: 278   OBJ: 9.1

5. Gardner would describe a person with a great understanding of his or her own inner feelings as having a high level of _____ intelligence.

   ANS: intrapersonal

   DIF: Difficult   REF: 279   OBJ: 9.2   KEY: WWW

6. Gardner would describe a person with great social skills and sensitivity as having a high level of _____ intelligence.

   ANS: interpersonal

   DIF: Difficult   REF: 279   OBJ: 9.2

7. An individual who is otherwise mentally retarded yet displays exceptional ability in one area is classified as having _____ syndrome.

   ANS: savant

   DIF: Moderate   REF: 279   OBJ: 9.2

8. Stenberg's _____ component focuses on the information-processing skills that are assessed by traditional intelligence tests.

ANS: analytic

DIF: Moderate   REF: 281   OBJ: 9.2

9. Sternberg has recently begun to focus on the aspect of intellect that allows someone to succeed in life using the term _____ intelligence.

ANS: successful

DIF: Easy   REF: 281   OBJ: 9.2

10. _____ thinking involves generating a variety of solutions when there is no one correct answer to a problem.

ANS: Divergent

DIF: Moderate   REF: 282   OBJ: 9.3   KEY: WWW

11. _____ thinking involves generating the single best answer to a problem.

ANS: Convergent

DIF: Moderate   REF: 282   OBJ: 9.3

12. The Bayley Scales of Infant Development test generates a _____ quotient score.

ANS: developmental

DIF: Moderate   REF: 284   OBJ: 9.4

13. The fact that negative environmental effects can accumulate over time and can result in losses in IQ is called the _____ hypothesis.

ANS: cumulative-deficit

DIF: Difficult   REF: 285   OBJ: 9.5   KEY: WWW

14. The rapid decline in intellectual abilities that occurs in the years preceding death is referred to as the _____ drop.

ANS: terminal

DIF: Moderate   REF: 293   OBJ: 9.10

576

15. The highest level of thought defined as a constellation of rich factual knowledge about life combined with procedural knowledge that permits one to offer exceptional insight or judgment about complex matters is referred to as _____.

   ANS: wisdom

   DIF: Moderate   REF: 293   OBJ: 9.11

16. A phenomenon called the _____ effect is concerned with the fact that the average IQ of children appears to climb about three to four points each decade.

   ANS: Flynn

   DIF: Moderate   REF: 297   OBJ: 9.13

17. A test question that is appropriate for one ethnic group but inappropriate for another is said to contribute to _____ bias in testing.

   ANS: culture

   DIF: Easy   REF: 293   OBJ: 9.13

18. IQ test performance of African-American children may be negatively impacted by the fear that they will be judged to have qualities associated with negative stereotypes of African Americans in a process called stereotype _____.

   ANS: threat

   DIF: Moderate   REF: 301   OBJ: 9.13

19. What was for decades referred to as mental retardation is now referred to as intellectual _____.

   ANS: disability

   DIF: Moderate   REF: 303   OBJ: 9.14   KEY: WWW

20. _____ involves having either a high IQ or showing some special ability in some area valued by a society.

   ANS: giftedness

   DIF: Easy   REF: 304   OBJ: 9.14

ESSAY

1. What is the psychometric approach to intelligence, and how do the Spearman and Cattell & Horn models reflect this approach?

   ANS: Answer not provided   REF: 277-278   OBJ: 9.1

2. How do the Stanford-Binet, Wechsler Scales, and the Bayley Scales of Infant Development differ in the way each reports a person's level of intelligence?

ANS: Answer not provided   REF: 278 & 283-284   OBJ: 9.1-9.4

3. To what extent are IQ scores stable during childhood? What factors influence whether IQ scores stay the same or change?

ANS: Answer not provided   REF: 285   OBJ: 9.5

4. How would you go about fostering creativity in a teenager?

ANS: Answer not provided   REF: 288-289   OBJ: 9.7

5. How is IQ related to occupational success and health in adulthood?

ANS: Answer not provided   REF: 290-291   OBJ: 9.9

6. What factors contribute to the development of wisdom and creativity in adulthood?

ANS: Answer not provided   REF: 293- 296   OBJ: 9.11-2.12

7. What is the Flynn effect and how can it be used to support of refute the impact of genes and the environment on intelligence?

ANS: Answer not provided   REF: 297-299   OBJ: 9.12

8. Describe Howard Gardner's conceptualization of intelligence.

ANS: Answer not provided   REF: 279   OBJ: 9.2   KEY: WWW

9. Describe the three components of Sternberg's triarchic theory of intelligence. Then discuss the fourth element (a type of intelligence) that he added in recent years.

ANS: Answer not provided   REF: 270-281   OBJ: 9.2   KEY: WWW

10. How are giftedness and mental retardation (intellectual disability) defined? What is that predicted outcome for a child identified in either of these categories?

ANS: Answer not provided   REF: 303-305   OBJ: 9.12   KEY: WWW

CHAPTER 10
LANGUAGE AND EDUCATION

MULTIPLE CHOICE

1. Which best defines a language?
   a. Limited number of signals producing infinite number of messages
   b. Unlimited number of signals producing infinite number of messages
   c. Limited number of signals producing finite number of messages
   d. Unlimited number of signals producing finite number of messages

   ANS: A   DIF: Moderate   REF: 312   OBJ: 10.1

2. All forms of language are
   a. spoken.
   b. based on some agreed-upon set of rules.
   c. inherited.
   d. gesture-based.

   ANS: B   DIF: Difficult   REF: 312   OBJ: 10.1

3. The basic units of sound in a given language are called
   a. phonemes.
   b. pragmatics.
   c. semantics.
   d. morphemes.

   ANS: A   DIF: Moderate   REF: 312   OBJ: 10.1

4. How many of the following ("d," "da," "dada," "daddy") are phonemes?
   a. 1
   b. 2
   c. 3
   d. 4

   ANS: A   DIF: Moderate   REF: 312   OBJ: 10.1

5. _____ are the basic units of meaning in a language
   a. Phonemes
   b. Syntax
   c. Morphemes
   d. Intonation

   ANS: C   DIF: Moderate   REF: 312   OBJ: 10.1

6. Which word consists of three morphemes?
   a. Cat
   b. Volcano
   c. Previewing
   d. Breakfast

   ANS: C   DIF: Difficult   REF: 312-313   OBJ: 10.1

7. How many morphemes are there in the word football?
   a. 1
   b. 2
   c. 3
   d. 4

   ANS: B   DIF: Difficult   REF: 312-313   OBJ: 10.1
   KEY: WWW

579

8. The systematic rules for forming sentences is referred to as
   a. phonology.
   b. prosody.
   c. syntax.
   d. pragmatics.

   ANS: C   DIF: Moderate   REF: 313   OBJ: 10.1

9. The sentence, "I the text read Chapter 10 in" violates the English rules of
   a. syntax.
   b. pragmatics.
   c. joint attention.
   d. morphology.

   ANS: A   DIF: Moderate   REF: 313   OBJ: 10.1

10. Shakespeare turned in a paper in his English composition class. The teacher returned it with a note that he needs to work on sentence structure (i.e., the order in which words are placed in a sentence). To which aspect of language does this comment refer?
    a. Phonology
    b. Morphology
    c. Prosody
    d. Syntax

    ANS: D   DIF: Moderate   REF: 313   OBJ: 10.1
    KEY: WWW

11. When someone says, "It's a matter of semantics," they are referring to the _____ of a sentence.
    a. context
    b. meaning
    c. length
    d. syllables

    ANS: B   DIF: Easy   REF: 313   OBJ: 10.1

12. When Jasmine says, "That song makes me blue." Her friend Rice says, "You don't look like a different color to me." Rice's failure to understand that in certain context the word "blue" in English means depressed illustrates a lack of _____ understanding.
    a. morpheme
    b. syntactic
    c. prosody
    d. semantic

    ANS: D   DIF: Difficult   REF: 313   OBJ: 10.1

13. Frances brings home a math assignment from kindergarten and shows it to her Mom, who says, "Wow, Frances, that assignment looks really rough!" Frances runs her hand over the paper and says, "No, Mommy, it's not rough; it's smooth!" Which aspect of language is causing Frances and her Mommy to have some communication difficulties?
    a. Semantics
    b. Pragmatics
    c. Phonology
    d. Syntax

    ANS: A   DIF: Difficult   REF: 313   OBJ: 10.1
    KEY: WWW

14. Which linguistic concept is best defined as an understanding of the rules concerning the appropriate use of language in different social context?
    a. Prosody
    b. Pragmatics
    c. Holophrasing
    d. Syntax

    ANS: B   DIF: Easy   REF: 313   OBJ: 10.1

15. When four-year-old Methuselah sees an elderly gentleman enter a store, he screams, "Mommy, look at that old man who looks like he should be dead!" The fact that Methuselah does not yet realize that such statements are socially inappropriate indicates that he lacks a complete understanding of the _____ of language.
    a. semantics
    b. syntax
    c. prosody
    d. pragmatics

    ANS: D   DIF: Difficult   REF: 313   OBJ: 10.1

16. Prosody involves _____ sounds are produced.
    a. when
    b. where
    c. how
    d. why

    ANS: C   DIF: Easy   REF: 313   OBJ: 10.1

17. Nina's mom has been warning her about the danger of playing with her balloon near a burning candle. Suddenly, the balloon hits the flame and explodes. Nina's mom looks at her and says, "I hope that you are happy," but because of the tone of her voice, her mom is really saying, "See, I told you to watch out!" This use of tone to change the meaning of a sentence provides a good example of the concept of
    a. word segmentation.
    b. syntactic bootstrapping.
    c. overregulation.
    d. prosody.

    ANS: D   DIF: Difficult   REF: 313   OBJ: 10.1

18. Which aspect of speech involves the melody, intonation, or timing of a word production?
    a. Semantics
    b. Prosody
    c. Syntax
    d. Morphology

    ANS: B   DIF: Easy   REF: 313   OBJ: 10.1
    KEY: WWW

19. The fact that eight-month-old Robin recognizes that the sentence, "There is a bird in the tree" has seven distinct words indicates that she understands
    a. intonation.
    b. overextension.
    c. word segmentation.
    d. holophrases.

    ANS: C   DIF: Difficult   REF: 313   OBJ: 10.1

20. Word segmentation is best defined as the number of
    a. letters in a word.
    b. distinct sounds in a word.
    c. distinct words in a sentence.
    d. sentences in a paragraph.

    ANS: C   DIF: Moderate   REF: 313   OBJ: 10.1

21. A "coo" is best defined as a _____ sound.
    a. vowel-like
    b. consonant-plus-vowel
    c. meaningful
    d. crying

    ANS: A   DIF: Easy   REF: 314   OBJ: 10.1

22. Most infants begin cooing about 6-8 _____ after birth.
    a. hours
    b. days
    c. weeks
    d. months

    ANS: C   DIF: Easy   REF: 314   OBJ: 10.1
    KEY: WWW

23. Six-week-old Beck is lying in his crib and making a melodic sound that might be described as an "ooooh." Beck is best thought of as currently
    a. babbling.
    b. using pragmatics.
    c. cooing.
    d. holophrasing.

    ANS: C   DIF: Difficult   REF: 314   OBJ: 10.1

24. Most infants begin babbling about 3-4 _____ after birth.
    a. hours
    b. days
    c. weeks
    d. months

    ANS: D   DIF: Easy   REF: 314   OBJ: 10.1

25. A "babble" is best defined as a _____ sound.
    a. vowel-like
    b. consonant-plus-vowel
    c. meaningful
    d. crying

    ANS: B   DIF: Moderate   REF: 314   OBJ: 10.1
    KEY: WWW

26. Six-month-old Emir is sitting in his car seat and repeatedly saying "na na na na na." Emir is best described as
    a. babbling.
    b. using pragmatics.
    c. cooing.
    d. holophrasing.

    ANS: A   DIF: Moderate   REF: 314   OBJ: 10.1

27. Which statement is true?
    a. At five months of age, deaf and hearing children from all cultures make similar sounds.
    b. At five months of age, deaf and hearing children produce very different sounds.
    c. At five months of age, children from different cultures produce very different sounds.
    d. At five months of age, deaf children produce no sounds while hearing children produce many sounds.

    ANS: A   DIF: Moderate   REF: 314   OBJ: 10.1

28. In most one-year-olds,
    a. language comprehension typically precedes language production.
    b. language production typically precedes language comprehension.
    c. language comprehension and language production occur simultaneously.
    d. neither language comprehension nor language production is readily apparent.

    ANS: A   DIF: Moderate   REF: 314   OBJ: 10.1

29. One-year-old Van Damn's ability to learn the meaning of words has been greatly enhanced by the fact that his dad, Claude, often points and repeatedly names objects that are around Van Damn. Claude's teaching style best reflects the process of
    a. intonation.
    c. joint attention.
    b. vocabulary spurt.
    d. decontextualized language.

    ANS: C   DIF: Moderate   REF: 314   OBJ: 10.1

30. Concerning language development, joint attention is best defined as occurring when
    a. a baby and parent view an object together.
    b. a parent directs a child's gaze to an object and names the object for the child.
    c. two infants repeat the same nonsense word.
    d. the same word is used to describe several unrelated objects.

    ANS: B   DIF: Moderate   REF: 314   OBJ: 10.1

31. When using syntactic bootstrapping, a child
    a. uses a word's placement in a sentence to help determine its meaning.
    b. generates a one-word utterance that has the meaning of a full sentence.
    c. uses a grammar rule in an inappropriate manner (e.g., uses the "-ed" which means past tense on a word like "run" to create the word "runned").
    d. is able to immediately connect a word in one language to its counterpart in a second language.

    ANS: A   DIF: Moderate   REF: 314   OBJ: 10.1

32. Nadine's father says, "Look at that ferret with that man." She has never before heard the term "ferret," but because of where the term occurred in her dad's statement, she is sure that it refers the little furry animal that the man has on a leash. Nadine's ability to ascertain the meaning of the word "ferret" was accomplished using
    a. overextension.
    c. telegraphic speech.
    b. syntactic bootstrapping.
    d. emergent literacy.

    ANS: B   DIF: Difficult   REF: 314   OBJ: 10.1

33. Which is the typical order of linguistic attainment (from earliest to latest)?
    a. Coo, then babble, then word, then holophrase
    b. Babble, then coo, then word, then holophrase
    c. Coo, then babble, then holophrase, then word
    d. Babble, then coo, then holophrase, then word

    ANS: A   DIF: Moderate   REF: 314   OBJ: 10.1
    KEY: WWW

34. In a holophrase,
    a. a single word conveys the meaning of an entire sentence.
    b. the same word is used for many objects in an environment.
    c. an infant makes vocalizations consisting only of vowel sounds.
    d. a vocalization is produced, but it has no meaning.

    ANS: A   DIF: Easy   REF: 314   OBJ: 10.1

35. Joel reaches up to Daddy with waving outstretched arms and says "Up!" meaning "Daddy, pick me up!" This is an example of
   a. underextension.
   b. echolalia.
   c. a holophrase.
   d. babbling.

   ANS: C   DIF: Moderate   REF: 314   OBJ: 10.1

36. Nelson (1973) found that the majority of words found in the vocabularies of one-year-olds were
   a. verbs concerning actions of people who were familiar to the child.
   b. verbs concerning actions of people who were unfamiliar to the child.
   c. nouns representing objects or people who were unfamiliar to the child.
   d. nouns representing objects or people who were familiar to the child.

   ANS: D   DIF: Easy   REF: 314-315   OBJ: 10.1

37. Eighteen-month-old Gavin has just learned 10 new words in the past week. This brings his total vocabulary to 30 words. Gavin is best described as
   a. babbling.
   b. experiencing a vocabulary spurt.
   c. overextending.
   d. acquiring metalinguistic awareness.

   ANS: B   DIF: Moderate   REF: 315   OBJ: 10.1

38. Toddlers substantially increase their vocabulary when they
   a. have an older sibling to whom they can listen.
   b. turn one year of age.
   c. attend preschool.
   d. realize that everything has a name.

   ANS: D   DIF: Moderate   REF: 315   OBJ: 10.1

39. Overextension occurs when a person
   a. uses the same word to describe too wide a range of objects.
   b. initially learns all the letters of the alphabet.
   c. cannot understand the relationship between the sound for a word and the object it represents.
   d. uses many words to describe a single object.

   ANS: A   DIF: Easy   REF: 315   OBJ: 10.1

40. Two-year-old Tonka calls every four-wheeled vehicle he sees "truck." This is an example of
   a. overextension.
   b. overregularization.
   c. telegraphic speech.
   d. social speech.

   ANS: A   DIF: Moderate   REF: 315   OBJ: 10.1

41. Underextension occurs when a child uses a
   a. term from a nonnative language.
   b. sign instead of a spoken word.
   c. word too narrowly.
   d. verb in the place of a noun.

   ANS: C   DIF: Easy   REF: 315   OBJ: 10.1

584

42. Reserving the use of the word "puppy" to refer only to the dog at home and not other dogs is an example of
   a. babbling.
   b. functional grammar.
   c. underextension.
   d. overextension.

   ANS: C   DIF: Moderate   REF: 315   OBJ: 10.1
   KEY: WWW

43. Though 18-month-old Saturn knows the word "car," she only uses it when referring to her mother's sedan (i.e., she does not use it to describe any other vehicle). Saturn's linguistic limitation is best described as involving
   a. underextension.
   b. overregularization.
   c. telegraphic speech.
   d. overextension.

   ANS: A   DIF: Moderate   REF: 315   OBJ: 10.1

44. Underextension is most likely the result of a toddler's limited
   a. vocabulary size.
   b. joint attention.
   c. phonetic ability.
   d. pragmatic skills.

   ANS: A   DIF: Moderate   REF: 316   OBJ: 10.1

45. A vocabulary dominated by phrases or words like _____ would indicate that a child is using an expressive style of language acquisition.
   a. "kitty, horsy, puppy"
   b. "stop, go, now"
   c. "elevator, escalator, navigator"
   d. "I like cake, watch TV, I am two"

   ANS: D   DIF: Difficult   REF: 316   OBJ: 10.1

46. When a person speaks using several critical content words but does not actually use full sentences, he or she is said to be engaging in
   a. underextension.
   b. telegraphic speech.
   c. babbling.
   d. joint attention.

   ANS: B   DIF: Moderate   REF: 316   OBJ: 10.1
   KEY: WWW

47. Which is the best example of telegraphic speech?
   a. "Baabaa"
   b. "Bottle"
   c. "Want bottle"
   d. "I would like you to hand me the bottle"

   ANS: C   DIF: Moderate   REF: 316   OBJ: 10.1

48. Functional grammar emphasizes the _____ relations between words.
   a. semantic
   b. morphological
   c. phonological
   d. intonation

   ANS: A   DIF: Moderate   REF: 316   OBJ: 10.1

585

49. Logan has just realized that the phrase "daddy run" can mean both "daddy is going for a run" and "can I go for a run with daddy." This realization best illustrates the acquisition of
   a. overregulation.
   b. functional grammar.
   c. metalinguistic awareness.
   d. child-directed speech.

   ANS: B   DIF: Difficult   REF: 316   OBJ: 10.1

50. Applying language rules to cases in which the rule is not appropriate defines the concept of
   a. joint attention.
   b. overregularization.
   c. telegraphic speech.
   d. holophrasing.

   ANS: B   DIF: Moderate   REF: 316-317   OBJ: 10.1

51. Dumbo and his Dad are at the zoo. "Look at those huge foots!" exclaims Dumbo, as they watch an elephant in its cage. Dumbo's error in speech best demonstrates
   a. overregularization.
   b. telegraphic speech.
   c. overextension.
   d. holophrasing.

   ANS: A   DIF: Difficult   REF: 316-317   OBJ: 10.1

52. Rachel stubs her toe and says "Ouch! I hurted myself!" This is an example of
   a. animism.
   b. metacognition.
   c. overregularization.
   d. overextension.

   ANS: C   DIF: Moderate   REF: 316-317   OBJ: 10.1
   KEY: WWW

53. Transformation grammar is best associated with rules of
   a. phonology.
   b. semantics.
   c. morphology.
   d. syntax.

   ANS: D   DIF: Moderate   REF: 317   OBJ: 10.1

54. John has just developed the ability to convert a declarative sentence (e.g., "I like pizza") into both a question (e.g., "Do I like eating pizza?") and an imperative (e.g., "I must eat pizza!"). This would indicate that he now is aware of
   a. overregulation.
   b. functional grammar.
   c. overextension.
   d. transformation grammar.

   ANS: D   DIF: Moderate   REF: 317   OBJ: 10.1

55. Changes in language use during preschool and early elementary school years typically include
   a. decreased use of decontextualized language.
   b. decreased vocabulary size.
   c. increased babbling.
   d. increased use of transformational grammar rules.

   ANS: D   DIF: Moderate   REF: 317   OBJ: 10.1

56. Which question demonstrates the correct placement of the auxiliary verb?
   a. "How pig?"
   b. "How big pig?"
   c. "How can the pig oink?"
   d. "How big the pig is?"

   ANS: C   DIF: Easy   REF: 317   OBJ: 10.1

586

57. The typical first-grader would begin school with a vocabulary of around _____ words.
   a. 500
   b. 1,000
   c. 5,000
   d. 10,000

   ANS: D   DIF: Moderate   REF: 317   OBJ: 10.1

58. Metalinguistic awareness is best defined as
   a. vocabulary size.
   b. rules for appropriately using language in social settings.
   c. knowledge of language as a system.
   d. an innate system for understanding language.

   ANS: C   DIF: Easy   REF: 317   OBJ: 10.1

59. Which is the best example of metalinguistic awareness?
   a. Being able to pronounce all the phonemes in a language
   b. Becoming less egocentric and then becoming better able to understand the meaning of selfishness
   c. Confusing a "w" with an "m" and reading "wow" as "mom"
   d. Using the term "truck" when referring to all wheeled vehicles (e.g., trucks, cars, motorcycles)

   ANS: B   DIF: Difficult   REF: 317   OBJ: 10.1

60. Due to a slight hearing loss, 90-year-old Tiger has begun to have trouble differentiating some English sounds. For example, the last time he was golfing, his partner said "nice putt," but Tiger thought he said "nice butt." This difficulty is best thought of as a deficiency in
   a. morphology.
   b. phonology.
   c. syntax.
   d. intonation.

   ANS: B   DIF: Moderate   REF: 317-318   OBJ: 10.1

61. Older adults experience all of the following changes in language EXCEPT
   a. they use less complex sentences than younger adults do.
   b. they show refinements in the pragmatic use of language.
   c. their knowledge of semantics increases.
   d. their knowledge of grammar decreases.

   ANS: D   DIF: Moderate   REF: 317-318   OBJ: 10.1

62. The increasing "tip-of-the-tongue" experience in older age is most likely the result of the
   a. inability to retrieve a word stored in memory.
   b. permanent loss of a word from memory.
   c. reduced speed of access to items in sensory memory.
   d. lack of ability to encode new words into memory.

   ANS: A   DIF: Moderate   REF: 317-318   OBJ: 10.1

63. Concerning language, Broca's area is to Wenicke's area as
   a. visual is to auditory.
   b. production is to comprehension.
   c. syntax is to semantics.
   d. left hemisphere is to right hemisphere.

   ANS: B   DIF: Difficult   REF: 318   OBJ: 10.2

64. As a neurobiologist, Dr. Proctor would be most likely to utilize _____ as an assessment tool.
    a. MMPIs
    b. ERPs
    c. APGARs
    d. MIDs

    ANS: B   DIF: Moderate   REF: 318   OBJ: 10.2

65. Researchers have shown that individuals who are better able to learn new words show more connectivity between their left and right
    a. supramarginal gyrus.
    b. pons.
    c. adrenal medulla.
    d. reticular formation.

    ANS: A   DIF: Difficult   REF: 318   OBJ: 10.2

66. The main role of the arcuate fasciculus is to help produce
    a. memories.
    b. mathematical analysis.
    c. achievement motivation.
    d. speech.

    ANS: D   DIF: Moderate   REF: 318   OBJ: 10.2

67. Which is a type of language disorder?
    a. Aphasia
    b. Apoptosis
    c. Dysphoria
    d. Anoxia

    ANS: A   DIF: Moderate   REF: 318   OBJ: 10.2

68. Carter has been diagnosed with aphasia. What symptom is he most likely exhibiting?
    a. Difficulty in maintaining his balance
    b. Difficulty in retrieving an autobiographical memory
    c. Difficulty in repeating a sentence he just heard
    d. Difficulty in scoring above average on an IQ test

    ANS: C   DIF: Moderate   REF: 318   OBJ: 10.2

69. What is the best summary of implications of neurobiological research on language?
    a. There is no doubt that language acquisition is impacted solely by heredity factors.
    b. There is no doubt that language acquisition is impacted by both heredity and environmental factors.
    c. There is no doubt that language acquisition is impacted solely by environmental factors.
    d. There is no doubt that the factors which underlie language acquisition cannot be identified.

    ANS: B   DIF: Easy   REF: 318   OBJ: 10.2

70. Tyler argues that language is best explained in terms of a baby imitating the speech of her parents and being reinforced by parents for speaking words properly. These arguments best fit with the _____ perspective on language acquisition.
    a. constructivist
    b. learning
    c. humanist
    d. cognitive

    ANS: B   DIF: Moderate   REF: 319   OBJ: 10.2

71. Which best reflects the nurture-based research on language acquisition?
    a. Children only learn words that are directly spoken to them.
    b. Reinforcing a word does not increase the odds that a word will be learned.
    c. Frequent caregiver conversation involving questions encourages language development in children.
    d. Aphasia may be related to damage of arcuate fasciculus fibers.

    ANS: C   DIF: Moderate   REF: 319   OBJ: 10.2

72. Learning theory does the poorest job of explaining the _____ aspect of language development.
    a. morphology   c. semantics
    b. phonology   d. syntax

    ANS: D   DIF: Difficult   REF: 319   OBJ: 10.2

73. Which statement concerning language acquisition is true?
    a. Imitation alone can account for the learning of grammatical rules.
    b. Reinforcement alone can account for the learning of grammatical rules.
    c. Imitation and reinforcement together can account for the learning of grammatical rules.
    d. Imitation and reinforcement together cannot account for the learning of grammatical rules.

    ANS: D   DIF: Difficult   REF: 319   OBJ: 10.2

74. With regard to language learning, nativists believe that
    a. language is learned as a result of differential parental reinforcement.
    b. children learn language by listening, observing, and imitating.
    c. children are biologically programmed for language acquisition.
    d. the social environment plays the most critical role in language learning.

    ANS: C   DIF: Moderate   REF: 319   OBJ: 10.2

75. Universal grammar is best described as
    a. a list of the manner in which all words should be pronounced.
    b. the biological factor that limits the specific language (e.g., English, French) a newborn will acquire.
    c. the belief that there are an unlimited number of possibilities for forming language.
    d. a system of common rules and properties for learning any of the world's languages.

    ANS: D   DIF: Easy   REF: 319   OBJ: 10.2

76. The fact that humans have a unique genetic capacity to learn language is best associated with the concept of
    a. metalinguistic awareness.   c. mastery motivation.
    b. syntactic bootstrapping.   d. universal grammar.

    ANS: D   DIF: Moderate   REF: 319   OBJ: 10.2

589

77. If you believe in a language acquisition device, then you believe that
    a. language is acquired mostly though the process of modeling.
    b. infants have an inborn brain mechanism for processing language.
    c. parental reinforcement can explain most of language acquisition.
    d. the most difficult part of language acquisition involves grasping the rules of language.

    ANS: B   DIF: Moderate   REF: 319-320   OBJ: 10.2

78. Which of the following claims does Chomsky make regarding language acquisition?
    a. Humans have an inborn knowledge of all components of language.
    b. Humans have an inborn mechanism for sifting through the language they hear and generating rules for that language.
    c. Humans simply imitate the sounds they hear.
    d. Humans must be exposed to language at a developmentally appropriate time in order for language to develop.

    ANS: B   DIF: Difficult   REF: 319-320   OBJ: 10.2
    KEY: WWW

79. Chomsky asserts that humans have an inborn mechanism for mastering language. He calls this the
    a. executive grammar governor.   c. language acquisition device.
    b. inborn language processor.   d. programmed language center.

    ANS: C   DIF: Moderate   REF: 319-320   OBJ: 10.2

80. Which statement about the language acquisition device is FALSE?
    a. It is activated by exposure to language.
    b. It determines the language an infant speaks.
    c. It involves specific areas of the brain.
    d. It helps a child learn the specific language to which he or she is exposed.

    ANS: B   DIF: Moderate   REF: 319-320   OBJ: 10.2

81. From the nativist perspective, the language "learnability factor" states that children tend to acquire an incredibly complex communication system
    a. slowly and without formal instruction.
    b. slowly and only through formal instruction.
    c. rapidly and without formal instruction.
    d. rapidly and only through formal instruction.

    ANS: C   DIF: Moderate   REF: 320   OBJ: 10.2

82. Which finding would be most difficult to explain from the nativist perspective of language acquisition?
    a. The human brain contains areas that appear to be specifically designed to process language.
    b. Children progress through the same sequence in acquiring language skills and at roughly the same ages.
    c. Children exhibit remarkable cultural differences in early language learning.
    d. Overregularization and other characteristics of early language appear to be universal phenomena.

    ANS: C   DIF: Difficult   REF: 319-320   OBJ: 10.2

83. Research on the mastery of American Sign Language in Deaf students seems to support the rule,
    a. "the earlier, the better."
    b. "hearing and speaking are unrelated variables."
    c. "starting late is the way to go."
    d. "parents can't sign, kids can't sign."

    ANS: A   DIF: Moderate   REF: 320   OBJ: 10.2

84. In which areas does there appear to be a sensitive period?
    a. Only first spoken language
    b. Only spoken second language
    c. Only signed language
    d. First spoken, second spoken, and signed languages

    ANS: D   DIF: Easy   REF: 320-321   OBJ: 10.2

85. Research on language acquisition among Deaf children has shown that
    a. Deaf infants "babble" in sign language in the same manner as hearing infants "babble" in spoken language.
    b. the sequence of language acquisition between Deaf children learning sign and hearing children learning spoken language are quite different.
    c. while hearing parents speak in child-directed speech, Deaf parents do not sign in a child-directed manner.
    d. the language areas of the brain developed in Deaf children exposed to sign language are in the opposite hemisphere of hearing children exposed to speech.

    ANS: A   DIF: Difficult   REF: 321   OBJ: 10.2

86. Which of the following is evidence for a critical period for language acquisition?
    a. Children denied access to language often have difficulty mastering language skills in later life.
    b. Deaf children who never hear language can learn to speak.
    c. Adults are more likely to acquire multiple languages than are children.
    d. Children do not acquire large vocabularies until they learn to read.

    ANS: A   DIF: Moderate   REF: 320-321   OBJ: 10.2

87. The FOXP2 gene has been shown to be connected with
    a. the development of aphasia:
    b. motor skills necessary from speech .
    c. significant hearing impairments.
    d. a malfunctioning language acquisition device.

    ANS: B   DIF: Difficult   REF: 320   OBJ: 10.2

88. Which type of theorist would be most likely to view language development as a combination of nature and nurture factors?
    a. Learning   c. Interactionist
    b. Cognitive   d. Nativist

    ANS: C   DIF: Easy   REF: 322   OBJ: 10.2
    KEY: WWW

89. When describing his ideas on language acquisition, Harlan says, "I believe that humans have a natural biological predisposition toward language and that the environment that the child is raised in also impacts the development of language skills." Given this description, Harlan appears to hold a(n) _____ perspective concerning the acquisition of language.
    a. nativist   c. learning
    b. interactionist   d. psychodynamic

    ANS: B   DIF: Moderate   REF: 322   OBJ: 10.2

90. The interactionist perspective concerning language acquisition is most like the position taken by
    a. Piaget.   c. Chomsky.
    b. Bandura.   d. Skinner.

    ANS: A   DIF: Moderate   REF: 322   OBJ: 10.2

91. Child-directed speech is best defined as
    a. a type of speech adults use with small children.
    b. a child's first words.
    c. a type of speech children use with adults.
    d. speech directed from one child to another.

    ANS: A   DIF: Moderate   REF: 322   OBJ: 10.2

92. When talking to their two-year-old, Steve and Eve typically use short, simple sentences, lots of repetition, and high-pitched voices. This sort of speech is known as
    a. abbreviated speech.   c. child-directed speech.
    b. caretaker speech.   d. telegraphic speech.

    ANS: C   DIF: Moderate   REF: 322   OBJ: 10.2

93. When Daisy is talking to her infant son, Duke, she tends to use a more high-pitched voice, slow speech, and short simple sentences. Daisy's speech would best be described as
   a. telegraphic.
   b. holophrastic.
   c. child-directed.
   d. underextended.

   ANS: C   DIF: Moderate   REF: 322   OBJ: 10.2
   KEY: WWW

94. Young infants appear to pay more attention to speech characterized by
   a. low-pitch sounds and nonvaried intonation.
   b. low-pitch sounds and varied intonation.
   c. high-pitch sounds and nonvaried intonation.
   d. high-pitch sounds and varied intonation.

   ANS: D   DIF: Moderate   REF: 322   OBJ: 10.2

95. Catherine Snow and associates' study of Dutch-speaking children who watched a great deal of German television demonstrated that
   a. it is easy to acquire a second language via television.
   b. to learn a language, children must be actively involved with the language.
   c. German is significantly easier to learn than Dutch.
   d. bilingualism is inherited.

   ANS: B   DIF: Moderate   REF: 322   OBJ: 10.2

96. In speech, expansion is best defined as responses involving
   a. greater intonation.
   b. significant overregularization.
   c. more grammatically complete expressions.
   d. nontransformational grammar.

   ANS: C   DIF: Moderate   REF: 323   OBJ: 10.2

97. When her toddler holds her cup up and says, "Milk," her mother says, "You're ready for more milk." The mother's response is best described as an example of
   a. expansion.
   b. holophrastic speech.
   c. child-directed speech.
   d. babbling.

   ANS: A   DIF: Moderate   REF: 323   OBJ: 10.2

98. The intrinsic drive to be successful in one's environment defines
   a. mastery motivation.
   b. external motivation.
   c. learned helplessness.
   d. metalinguistic awareness.

   ANS: A   DIF: Motivation   REF: 323   OBJ: 10.3
   KEY: WWW

99. Which is the best example of mastery motivation?
    a. Jerry's innate ability to understand phonemes
    b. Kramer's innate drive to succeed
    c. George's parents' rewards for his success in school
    d. Elaine's extremely large vocabulary

    ANS: B   DIF: Motivation   REF: 323   OBJ: 10.3

100. Mastery motivation tends to be found in children whose parents
    a. avoid sensory stimulation and teach the child that most events are due to fate or luck.
    b. provide sensory stimulation and teach the child that most events are due to fate or luck.
    c. avoid sensory stimulation but provide the opportunity for the child to see that children can control their environment.
    d. provide sensory stimulation and the opportunity for the child to see that children can control their environment

    ANS: D   DIF: Motivation   REF: 323-324   OBJ: 10.3

101. Which best summarizes Elkind's opinion on products like the "Baby Einstein" DVD and the "Baby Mozart" CD?
    a. Best idea ever.
    b. I have no opinion.
    c. Be careful as it may result in children with less self-initiation and intrinsic motivation.
    d. Great for teaching motivation, terrible at teaching information.

    ANS: C   DIF: Moderate   REF: 324   OBJ: 10.4

102. Research has shown that children in preschools with very strong academic orientations tend to be less _____ by the end of their kindergarten year.
    a. anxious   c. negative toward schooling
    b. creative   d. intelligent

    ANS: B   DIF: Difficult   REF: 324   OBJ: 10.4

103. Which group seems to gain the most benefit from being enrolled in quality preschool programs?
    a. Deaf children   c. Male children
    b. Gifted children   d. Disadvantaged children

    ANS: D   DIF: Moderate   REF: 324   OBJ: 10.4

594

104. Preschool programs that emphasize _____ appear to be of the most benefit to children, especially those from disadvantaged families.
    a. play but not academic skill-building
    b. academic skill-building but not play
    c. academic skill-building and play
    d. overregularization and academic skill-building

    ANS: C   DIF: Moderate   REF: 324   OBJ: 10.4
    KEY: WWW

105. Individuals with high levels of achievement tend to attribute their success to _____ causes.
    a. internal and unstable   c. external and unstable
    b. internal and stable   d. external and stable

    ANS: B   DIF: Moderate   REF: 326   OBJ: 10.5

106. Individuals with high levels of mastery orientation _____ challenges and _____ in the face of failure.
    a. thrive on; quit   c. thrive on; persist
    b. avoid; quit   d. avoid; persist

    ANS: C   DIF: Moderate   REF: 326   OBJ: 10.5

107. Belmont has a high degree of mastery orientation. On his first psychology test, he scores 52 out of 100 (an "F"). What is his most likely reaction?
    a. He blames himself for being stupid.
    b. He blames himself for not studying.
    c. He blames the instructor for writing such a hard test.
    d. He doesn't care about his level of performance.

    ANS: C   DIF: Difficult   REF: 326   OBJ: 10.5

108. Erin has a high level of mastery orientation. Given this fact, her most likely response to failing a test would be to
    a. quit.
    b. blame her self.
    c. believe that trying harder on the next test will lead to failure.
    d. believe that trying harder on the next test will lead to success.

    ANS: D   DIF: Moderate   REF: 326   OBJ: 10.5
    KEY: WWW

109. Jeff is a low achiever. After doing well on an exam, he is LEAST likely to say
    a. "Boy, did I get lucky!"   c. "I really studied hard for that."
    b. "That was an easy test."   d. "I knew I was smart enough!"

    ANS: D   DIF: Moderate   REF: 326   OBJ: 10.5

110. When attempting to learn to play football, Farve has great difficulty in throwing the odd-shaped ball. After several bad passes, he decides that he will never be good at football and gives up. Farve's behavior provides an excellent example of
    a. a helpless orientation.
    b. high mastery motivation.
    c. overregulation.
    d. an external motivation.

    ANS: A   DIF: Moderate   REF: 326   OBJ: 10.5

111. The tendency to avoid challenges is best associated with having a _____ orientation.
    a. mastery
    b. helpless
    c. social-learning-theory
    d. contextual

    ANS: B   DIF: Easy   REF: 326   OBJ: 10.5

112. If you believe in mastery goals, then you believe that
    a. effort does not matter.
    b. you can learn to get better at a task.
    c. most abilities are inherited.
    d. superficial processing is the key to success.

    ANS: B   DIF: Moderate   REF: 326   OBJ: 10.5

113. Which statement would indicate that Elvis has adopted mastery goals concerning playing the guitar?
    a. "The key is to play better than my friend Costello."
    b. "If I can't learn to play, then I am a loser."
    c. "If I practice, I will get better."
    d. "Music is an innate talent."

    ANS: C   DIF: Moderate   REF: 326   OBJ: 10.5

114. The key motivation for someone with a strong sense of performance goals is to
    a. significantly improve his or her performance.
    b. process information as deeply as possible.
    c. feel shame when successful.
    d. be seen as smart and not dumb.

    ANS: D   DIF: Difficult   REF: 326   OBJ: 10.5
    KEY: WWW

115. Giada's statement that she is trying to prove that she is a good cook, not that she can improve her cooking, reflects a _____ goals orientation.
    a. mastery
    b. learning
    c. performance
    d. integration

    ANS: C   DIF: Moderate   REF: 326   OBJ: 10.5

596

116. Maria has made a performance goal decision concerning her ability to play tennis. What is the most likely impact of this decision?
   a. She will try to prove that she can play tennis.
   b. She will feel little anxiety if she fails at tennis.
   c. She will not care how others play, but rather focus only on increasing her ability.
   d. She will avoid playing tennis.

   ANS: A   DIF: Moderate   REF: 326   OBJ: 10.5

117. When a student values a subject,
   a. neither motivation nor achievement levels tend to be higher
   b. both motivation and achievement levels tend to be higher
   c. motivation level, but not achievement level tends to be higher
   d. achievement level, but not motivation level tends to be higher

   ANS: B   DIF: Moderate   REF: 327   OBJ: 10.5

118. If Rachel wants to help her son Ray develop a mastery motivation orientation she should
   a. de-emphasize the importance of self-reliance.
   b. encourage him to do things well.
   c. try to not offer guidance.
   d. praise him lavishly for his accomplishments even if the performance is actually very poor.

   ANS: B   DIF: Moderate   REF: 327   OBJ: 10.5
   KEY: WWW

119. Angelina doesn't seem to even want to try to do well in her high school math class. If her mom Jolie wants to help her change her self-defeating pattern of behavior, Jolie should
   a. provide the most cognitively stimulating home environment that she can.
   b. tell Angelina her failures thus far have just been due to bad luck.
   c. offer her a bribe if her scores go up.
   d. continually nag her about her grades.

   ANS: A   DIF: Moderate   REF: 327   OBJ: 10.5

120. Economist Roland Fryer Jr. attempted to determine whether _____ could be used to raise students' standardized test scores.
   a. monetary rewards   c. more highly trained teachers
   b. new school facilities   d. cognitive-enhancing medications

   ANS: A   DIF: Easy   REF: 327   OBJ: 10.5

121. Based on recent research, which strategy should a school district employ if it wants to have the best chance of raising student's standardized test scores?
   a. Pay students $100 dollars for every A they get in their academic classes
   b. Pay students $50 for not missing any school
   c. Pay student $5 for every book they read and on which they subsequently then pass a quiz
   d. Pay students nothing; show them statistics on how much more money graduates make than nongraduates

   ANS: C   DIF: Moderate   REF: 327   OBJ: 10.5

122. An effective method for a school to positively influence motivation is to
   a. stress competition concerning class grades.
   b. discourage parental involvement, making children respond on their own.
   c. emphasize intrinsic motivation techniques.
   d. avoid adopting learning goals.

   ANS: C   DIF: Moderate   REF: 327-328   OBJ: 10.5

123. "Low ability" students with a mastery goal
   a. persist, but only when they succeed.
   b. persist and show major frustration when they fail.
   c. persist and show little frustration despite failure.
   d. do not persist, regardless of success or failure.

   ANS: C   DIF: Moderate   REF: 328-329   OBJ: 10.5

124. The idea that the letters in printed words represent the sounds in spoken words in a systematic way is referred to as the _____ principle.
   a. decontextualized   c. morphological
   b. alphabetic   d. expansion

   ANS: B   DIF: Easy   REF: 329   OBJ: 10.6

125. During the _____ phase of reading, a child is first able to "read" something that he or she memorized during a previous reading session.
   a. prealphabetic   c. full alphabetic
   b. partial alphabetic   d. full phonological awareness

   ANS: A   DIF: Difficult   REF: 329   OBJ: 10.6
   KEY: WWW

126. Brandy has just begun to learn to read. At this point, she knows that the letter with one line and two bumps is the "B." She also knows that this letter corresponds to the "b" sound, and it is the first letter of her name. While Brandy has this knowledge, she is not yet able to connect all written words with their sounds. Brandy is best classified as being in the _____ phase of reading development.
   a. prealphabetic   c. full alphabetic
   b. partial alphabetic   d. phonological awareness

   ANS: B   DIF: Difficult   REF: 329   OBJ: 10.6

127. Phonological awareness allows a child to
   a. apply a sound to an object.
   b. segment spoken words into sounds.
   c. understand the meaning of words.
   d. realize that some letters are commonly grouped together (e.g., "ed").

   ANS: B   DIF: Moderate   REF: 329   OBJ: 10.6

128. Hamid has just acquired the ability to "sound out" a word. This means that when he sees the word "bend" for the first time, he is able to decode it as "b" plus "e" plus "n" plus "d" and say "bend." Hamid's newfound ability indicates that he has acquired _____ awareness.
a. semantic
b. syntactical
c. morphological
d. phonological

ANS: D   DIF: Difficult   REF: 329   OBJ: 10.6

129. When a child is able to realize that some letter combinations (e.g., "br," "st," "ed") need to be perceived as a single unit versus several individual units, he or she is said to be in the _____ phase of reading.
a. pre-alphabetic
b. consolidated alphabetic
c. partial alphabetic
d. full alphabetic

ANS: B   DIF: Difficult   REF: 329   OBJ: 10.6

130. Emergent literacy is best described as involving
a. the acquisition of a second language in later life.
b. all non-verbal language skills acquired by deaf children.
c. critical developmental precursors of actual reading skills.
d. any language skill acquired after a child has learned to read.

ANS: C   DIF: Moderate   REF: 330   OBJ: 10.6

131. Exposure to rhyming stories is most likely to enhance the _____ aspect of emergent literacy.
a. phonological awareness
b. babbling
c. telegraphic speech
d. decontextualized language

ANS: A   DIF: Moderate   REF: 330   OBJ: 10.6

132. Unskilled readers tend to _____ more than skilled readers.
a. rely on phonological cues
b. make sure their eyes "hit" all words
c. use context to help identify words
d. connect letters and sounds

ANS: C   DIF: Difficult   REF: 330   OBJ: 10.6

133. Mystique sees the sentence, "I saw a dog," but reads the sentence as, "I was a god." This indicates that Mystique is best classified as
a. ignoring joint attention cues.
b. lacking mastery motivation.
c. engaging in child-directed speech.
d. being dyslexic.

ANS: D   DIF: Moderate   REF: 330   OBJ: 10.6

134. Individuals with dyslexia
a. show deficiencies in every reading area except phonological awareness.
b. are best classified as having a speech disorder.
c. devote so much effort to decoding words that recall for the words is compromised.
d. tend to outgrow the problem in adulthood even without intervention.

ANS: C   DIF: Moderate   REF: 330-331   OBJ: 10.6

135. Which approach to reading would support the advice to, "Just look at the words before and after that word, and you should be able to figure out the meaning of the word?"
   a. Phonetic approach
   b. Code-oriented approach
   c. Whole-language approach
   d. Alphabetic principle approach

   ANS: C   DIF: Moderate   REF: 331   OBJ: 10.6

136. Research on reading programs has shown that the most effective programs
   a. are phonics-only programs.
   b. are whole language-only programs.
   c. emphasize phonics but do include some whole language instruction.
   d. emphasize whole language but do include some phonics instruction.

   ANS: C   DIF: Moderate   REF: 331-332   OBJ: 10.6

137. Which appears to have the LEAST impact on a school's effectiveness?
   a. Reduced class size from 36 to 24
   b. Tutoring students in the early grades
   c. An effective discipline program
   d. A strong emphasis on academics

   ANS: A   DIF: Moderate   REF: 332   OBJ: 10.7

138. The most effective way to improve school effectiveness is to
   a. have year-round school.
   b. add money to the budget but do not directly target academic instruction issues.
   c. modestly reduce the student-faculty ratio.
   d. encourage parents to purchase books and intellectually stimulating toys for their children.

   ANS: D   DIF: Moderate   REF: 333   OBJ: 10.7

139. Which statement concerning ability grouping is FALSE?
   a. In ability grouping, students of similar academic talents are placed together into work groups.
   b. In general, ability grouping has no clear advantage over mixed-ability grouping.
   c. High-ability students tend to benefit more from ability grouping.
   d. Using ability grouping appears to significantly increase a school's effectiveness.

   ANS: D   DIF: Moderate   REF: 332   OBJ: 10.7

140. School integration
   a. is illegal.
   b. significantly decreases white prejudice toward black students.
   c. has eliminated discrimination against minority students.
   d. leads to small increases in achievement and self-esteem in Caucasian and African-American students.

   ANS: D   DIF: Difficult   REF: 334   OBJ: 10.7

600

141. "Inclusion" refers to
    a. placing physically handicapped youngsters in special classrooms housed within the public schools.
    b. the provision of public education services to mentally handicapped youngsters from birth to age 26.
    c. placing handicapped children into regular education classes for at least a portion of their educational programming.
    d. creating segregated classrooms based on ability grouping.

    ANS: C   DIF: Difficult   REF: 334-335   OBJ: 10.7

142. Cooperative learning techniques have resulted in all of the following EXCEPT a(n)
    a. more positive attitude toward mathematics than when traditional instruction is used.
    b. greater acceptance of minority students by non-minority peers.
    c. enhanced self-esteem for members of the cooperative learning team.
    d. slight decline in actual level of achievement in mathematics.

    ANS: D   DIF: Difficult   REF: 335   OBJ: 10.7

143. Which have been shown to be the best predictors of effectiveness of schools?
    a. Small classes, an academic focus, and grouping by ability level
    b. High expectations for success, rewarding good work, and a high funding base
    c. Task-oriented atmosphere, strong emphasis on academics, and effective discipline
    d. Mixed-ability grouping, high expectations for success, and small classes

    ANS: A   DIF: Moderate   REF: 333   OBJ: 10.7

144. The concept of appropriately matching an environment with a person's characteristics is called
    a. overregulation.   c. mastery orientation.
    b. goodness-of-fit.   d. joint attention.

    ANS: B   DIF: Easy   REF: 334-335   OBJ: 10.7

145. Reasons for declining achievement motivation during adolescence include all of the following EXCEPT
    a. great stability in physical development.
    b. poor person-environment fit.
    c. increasingly negative feedback from teachers regarding ability.
    d. increased importance of peer acceptance.

    ANS: A   DIF: Moderate   REF: 336-338   OBJ: 10.8

146. The decline in achievement during adolescence is likely the result of individuals at this age
   a. viewing strengths and weaknesses more realistically and a loss in expectancies of success.
   b. viewing strengths and weaknesses more unrealistically and a loss in expectancies of success.
   c. viewing strengths and weaknesses more realistically and a gain in expectancies of success.
   d. viewing strengths and weaknesses more unrealistically and a gain in expectancies of success.

   ANS: A   DIF: Difficult   REF: 337   OBJ: 10.8

147. Which family characteristic is NOT associated with lower achievement?
   a. Growing up in a single-parent family
   b. Being a member of minority group
   c. Having an uneducated mother
   d. Having a parent who uses consistent discipline

   ANS: D   DIF: Easy   REF: 337   OBJ: 10.8

148. Lower academic performance in African-American teens has been linked to
   a. negative peer pressure.   c. overinvolved parents.
   b. an attempt to reject cultural identity.   d. too extreme a valuation on academics.

   ANS: A   DIF: Moderate   REF: 337   OBJ: 10.8

149. Research on the transition from elementary school into the next level of education has shown that
   a. when adolescents make a change is more important than the characteristics of their new school.
   b. transition at grade six is much easier than transition at grade eight.
   c. the less degree of control that students feel following the transition the greater their academic motivation.
   d. supportive teachers in the new school are actually detrimental to academic motivation.

   ANS: A   DIF: Moderate   REF: 338   OBJ: 10.8

150. Research has shown that _____ had the largest percentage of students scoring in the top 10 percent on math and science tests.
   a. Japan
   b. the United States
   c. Brazil
   d. Singapore

   ANS: D   DIF: Easy   REF: 338   OBJ: 10.9

151. When compared to American students, Asian students appear to have higher levels of academic achievement. Which of the following is NOT one of the proposed reasons for this advantage?
   a. Asian students spend more time being educated.
   b. Asian student are assigned and complete more homework.
   c. Asian parents tend to have a "hands-off" attitude concerning their children's education.
   d. Asian peers value academic achievement.

   ANS: D   DIF: Moderate   REF: 338-340   OBJ: 10.9

602

152. Cross-cultural research results suggest that if you want to improve academic performance, teachers need to
   a. engage in more discourse (conversation) with students about their answers.
   b. move through class material more quickly.
   c. assign less homework.
   d. prevent parents from becoming actively involved in setting high achievement goals.

   ANS: A   DIF: Moderate   REF: 339-340   OBJ: 10.8

153. Ronald is a typical teenager attempting to balance high school and a 20-hour-a-week job at a fast-food restaurant. Research has shown that Ronald is most likely to _____ than his non-working classmates.
   a. have a lower average GPA
   b. be engaged in school
   c. be closer to his parents
   d. have more varied future vocational prospects

   ANS: A   DIF: Moderate   REF: 340   OBJ: 10.10

154. Loretta is a high school junior looking for a 20-hour-per-week job during the school year. What type of employment would be the LEAST detrimental to her academic and psychological well-being?
   a. Janitorial work that she can perform overnight
   b. Fast-food restaurant cashier
   c. Accounting work in which she will be required to learn new math skills
   d. Lawn-service work (e.g., lawn-mowing)

   ANS: D   DIF: Moderate   REF: 340-341   OBJ: 10.10

155. Statistically, _____ students have the lowest high school graduation rate in the United States.
   a. Caucasian
   b. Hispanic
   c. Asian-American
   d. African-American

   ANS: B   DIF: Easy   REF: 341   OBJ: 10.10

156. Which best describes achievement motivation during adulthood?
   a. Achievement motivation is steady from middle to old age for both females and males.
   b. The loss of motivation is an inevitable part of the aging process (especially in those over age 70).
   c. For both females and males, achievement motivation increases steadily from young adulthood to middle age.
   d. Achievement motivation is more affected by work and family context than by the process of aging.

   ANS: D   DIF: Moderate   REF: 341-342   OBJ: 10.11

157. Literacy is defined as the ability to use
    a. printed information to function in society.
    b. verbal speech to function in school.
    c. gestures to communicate ideas to another person.
    d. written language to demonstrate one's intelligence.

    ANS: A   DIF: Moderate   REF: 342   OBJ: 10.12

158. Research on adult education has shown that
    a. literacy programs for adults tend to be highly successful.
    b. older adult college students are more likely to be motivated by external expectations than traditional students.
    c. adult men tend to return to the classroom for personal enrichment reasons.
    d. returning adult students often put more effort into learning material because they want or need to use the information.

    ANS: D   DIF: Moderate   REF: 343-344   OBJ: 10.12
    KEY: WWW

159. Which statement about adult literacy in the United States is true?
    a. About 95 percent of U.S. adults are literate.
    b. Programs to raise adult literacy tend to be very effective.
    c. Lower levels of literacy are related to living in poverty.
    d. The U.S. has no large pockets of illiterate adults.

    ANS: C   DIF: Moderate   REF: 342   OBJ: 10.12

TRUE/FALSE

1. Phonemes are the basic units of meaning that exist in a language.

    ANS: F   DIF: Moderate   REF: 312   OBJ: 10.1

2. The focus on semantics is on the meaning of words.

    ANS: T   DIF: Moderate   REF: 313   OBJ: 10.1
    KEY: WWW

3. Changing the pitch of a sentence to change the meaning from actual to sarcastic is an example of prosody.

    ANS: T   DIF: Moderate   REF: 313   OBJ: 10.1

4. Babies "coo" before they "babble."

    ANS: T   DIF: Easy   REF: 314   OBJ: 10.1

5. A holophrase always contains at least two words.

    ANS: F   DIF: Moderate   REF: 314   OBJ: 10.1
    KEY: WWW

604

6. Underextension occurs when a person uses a word too narrowly (i.e., for a specific example versus the entire category).

   ANS: T   DIF: Moderate   REF: 315   OBJ: 10.1
   KEY: WWW

7. "Go school" is an example of telegraphic speech.

   ANS: T   DIF: Moderate   REF: 316   OBJ: 10.1

8. The acquisition of metalinguisitc awareness tends to result in more difficulty in defining abstract terms.

   ANS: F   DIF: Moderate   REF: 317   OBJ: 10.1

9. Individuals with aphasia can neither hear nor speak.

   ANS: F   DIF: Moderate   REF: 318   OBJ: 10.2
   KEY: WWW

10. Chomsky proposed that humans are born with a common set of rules and properties for learning any language in the world.

    ANS: T   DIF: Moderate   REF: 319-320   OBJ: 10.2

11. The earlier one is exposed to a language (including sign language), the faster and more effectively it tends to be learned.

    ANS: T   DIF: Easy   REF: 320   OBJ: 10.2

12. Child-directed speech is characterized by long sentences spoken in a monotone with no repetition of ideas.

    ANS: F   DIF: Easy   REF: 322   OBJ: 10.3
    KEY: WWW

13. The most effective preschool programs emphasize academic skill-building and de-emphasize play.

    ANS: F   DIF: Moderate   REF: 324   OBJ: 10.5

14. Performance goals emphasize proving one's ability versus improving one's ability.

    ANS: T   DIF: Moderate   REF: 326   OBJ: 10.5

15. During the partial alphabetic phase of reading, children first are able to read a word that they have previously memorized.

    ANS: F   DIF: Difficult   REF: 329   OBJ: 10.6

16. Acquiring phonological awareness allows a child to segment a spoken word into sounds or phonemes.

    ANS: T   DIF: Moderate   REF: 329   OBJ: 10.6

17. Ability grouping has been shown to be a highly effective technique for improving academic performance for most school-age children.

    ANS: F   DIF: Moderate   REF: 332   OBJ: 10.7
    KEY: WWW

18. Management of student discipline appears to have little impact on school effectiveness.

    ANS: F   DIF: Moderate   REF: 333-334   OBJ: 10.7

19. Negative peer pressure many negatively impact the academic performance of African-American adolescents.

    ANS: T   DIF: Easy   REF: 337   OBJ: 10.8

20. Programs designed to raise older-adult levels of literacy are rarely successful.

    ANS: T   DIF: Moderate   REF: 342   OBJ: 10.12

COMPLETION

1. _____ are the basic units of sound that change the meaning of a word (e.g., /b/ versus /p/).

    ANS: Phonemes

    DIF: Moderate   REF: 312   OBJ: 10.1

2. The rules for forming sentences from words are referred to as the rules of _____.

    ANS: syntax

    DIF: Moderate   REF: 313   OBJ: 10.1

3. A vowel-like sound such as "ooooh" is best classified as a _____ sound.

    ANS: coo

    DIF: Easy   REF: 314   OBJ: 10.1

4. _____ bootstrapping occurs when an individual uses the cue of word placement within a sentence to help determine the meaning of the word.

    ANS: Syntactic

    DIF: Difficult   REF: 314   OBJ: 10.1

5. When a child uses a word too broadly, he or she is committing an error of _____.

ANS: overextension

DIF: Moderate   REF: 315   OBJ: 10.1

6. When a child uses a word too narrowly, he or she is committing an error of _____.

ANS: underextension

DIF: Moderate   REF: 315   OBJ: 10.1   KEY: WWW

7. _____ speech is characterized by two- to three-word sentences that contain critical content words, but omit "frill" words.

ANS: Telegraphic

DIF: Moderate   REF: 316   OBJ: 10.1

8. A child who understands the idea of past tense, but says words like "wanted," is engaging in _____.

ANS: overregularization

DIF: Moderate   REF: 317   OBJ: 10.1   KEY: WWW

9. Damage to the arcuate fasciculus fibers connecting Broca's and Wernicke's areas can result in the language disorder known as _____.

ANS: aphasia

DIF: Moderate   REF: 318   OBJ: 10.2

10. Chomsky proposed the existence of a LAD or _____ device that allows children to master language with greater ease.

ANS: language acquisition

DIF: Moderate   REF: 319   OBJ: 10.2   KEY: WWW

11. After a child says, "Daddy goed," her mother responds, "Yes, daddy went to the store." The communication strategy being used by mom is called _____.

ANS: expansion

DIF: Difficult   REF: 323   OBJ: 10.2

12. Children with a high level of _____ orientation are intrinsically motivated and tend to thrive on challenges, believing that their efforts will eventually pay off.

ANS: mastery

DIF: Moderate   REF: 326   OBJ: 10.5

13. A child who has adopted _____ or learning goals aims to learn new things improve his or her ability.

   ANS: mastery

   DIF: Moderate   REF: 326   OBJ: 10.5   KEY: WWW

14. A child who has adopted _____ goals aims to prove his or her ability rather than to improve this ability.

   ANS: performance

   DIF: Moderate   REF: 326   OBJ: 10.5

15. During the partial _____ phase of reading, children first learn the shapes and sounds of letters.

   ANS: alphabetic

   DIF: Moderate   REF: 329   OBJ: 10.6

16. The developmental precursors of reading skills in children are referred to as _____ literacy.

   ANS: emergent

   DIF: Moderate   REF: 330   OBJ: 10.6

17. The reading disorder in which the word "saw" is read as "was" is called _____.

   ANS: dyslexia

   DIF: Moderate   REF: 330   OBJ: 10.6

18. Placing students into groups on the basis of their talents is referred to as _____ grouping.

   ANS: ability

   DIF: Moderate   REF: 332   OBJ: 10.7   KEY: WWW

19. The educational practice of mainstreaming is now referred to as _____.

   ANS: inclusion

   DIF: Difficult   REF: 334   OBJ: 10.7

20. _____ is defined as the ability to use printed information to function in society, achieve goals, and develop one's potential.

ANS: Literacy

DIF: Moderate   REF: 342   OBJ: 10.12

ESSAY

1. Describe the linguistic concepts of phonemes, syntax, semantics, pragmatics, prosody, and word segmentation.

ANS: Answer not provided   REF: 312-313   OBJ: 10.1

2. How does language development progress from cooing until the production of holophrases?

ANS: Answer not provided   REF: 314   OBJ: 10.1

3. How do neurobiologists, learning theorists, nature-oriented theorists, and interactionists explain the acquisition of language?

ANS: Answer not provided   REF: 318-322   OBJ: 10.2

4. What are the characteristics of child-directed speech, and how does its use enhance or inhibit the acquisition of language?

ANS: Answer not provided   REF: 322-323   OBJ: 10.2

5. What are the advantages and disadvantages of preschool education programs and media enhancement materials like "Baby Einstein?" What would be the ideal characteristics of a quality preschool program?

ANS: Answer not provided   REF: 324-325   OBJ: 10.4

6. Describe the key processes involved in learning to read (including the alphabetic principle and emergent literacy)? How can schools best promote effective reading?

ANS: Answer not provided   REF: 329-332   OBJ: 10.6

7. How does level of achievement change during adolescence and adulthood? What factors lead to declines in achievement? What factors lead to increases in achievement?

ANS: Answer not provided   REF: 336-338 & 341-342   OBJ: 10.8 & 10.1

8. How do overextension, underextension, overregularization, and telegraphic speech limit a child's language abilities?

   ANS: Answer not provided   REF: 315-316   OBJ: 10.1   KEY: WWW

9. How does experience impact language? Be sure to directly address language development in the deaf, the acquisition of a second language, and the idea of a critical period in language acquisition.

   ANS: Answer not provided   REF: 320-321   OBJ: 10.2   KEY: WWW

10. How are mastery orientation, the helpless orientation, mastery/learning goals, and performance goals related?

   ANS: Answer not provided   REF: 326-327   OBJ: 10.5   KEY: WWW

MULTIPLE CHOICE

1. _____ is defined as an organized combination of an individual's unique attributes, motives, values, and behaviors.
   a. Sociability
   b. Generativity
   c. Personality
   d. Integrity

   ANS: C   DIF: Moderate   REF: 348   OBJ: 11.1

2. Introversion is best classified as a
   a. narrative identity.
   b. self-esteem.
   c. dispositional trait.
   d. characteristic adaptation.

   ANS: C   DIF: Easy   REF: 348   OBJ: 11.1

3. The most accurate description of a dispositional trait is that it is
   a. a unique life event.
   b. a situation-specific way of acting.
   c. the cultural in which we live.
   d. a relatively enduring dimension of personality.

   ANS: D   DIF: Moderate   REF: 348   OBJ: 11.1

4. Characteristic adaptations are _____ ways of adapting to one's environment.
   a. situation-specific and changeable
   b. situation-specific and unchangeable
   c. unrelated to situation and changeable
   d. unrelated to situation and unchangeable

   ANS: A   DIF: Moderate   REF: 348   OBJ: 11.1

5. Around the holidays, Holly feels motivated to change her ways and become a more generous individual. This goal is best characterized as a
   a. narrative identity.
   b. self-esteem.
   c. dispositional trait.
   d. characteristic adaptation.

   ANS: D   DIF: Moderate   REF: 348   OBJ: 11.1

6. The personality principle of _____ concerns situation-specific ways in which people adapt to their roles.
   a. narrative identities
   b. self-esteems
   c. dispositional traits
   d. characteristic adaptations

   ANS: D   DIF: Moderate   REF: 348   OBJ: 11.1
   KEY: WWW

7. Which concept is best associated with an individual's unique "life story"?
   a. Dispositional trait
   b. Characteristic adaptation
   c. Narrative identity
   d. Temperament

   ANS: C   DIF: Moderate   REF: 348   OBJ: 11.1

8. Which of Tela's statements best exemplifies a narrative identity?
   a. "I like who I am."
   b. "Whenever I go to a party, I have to remember not to drink too much."
   c. "I am introverted."
   d. "Given my past failures in school, graduating from college will make my life meaningful."

   ANS: D   DIF: Difficult   REF: 348   OBJ: 11.1

9. According to researchers McAdams and Pals, we all share the same
   a. human nature.
   b. self-concept.
   c. characteristics adaptations.
   d. narrative identities.

   ANS: A   DIF: Moderate   REF: 348   OBJ: 11.1

10. Self-concept is best defined as
    a. positive or negative perceptions of your unique attributes.
    b. the ability to recognize one's self in a mirror.
    c. an overall evaluation of your self-worth.
    d. the goodness-of-fit between self and environment.

    ANS: A   DIF: Moderate   REF: 348   OBJ: 11.1

11. Fonzie's statement, "I am a fairly competent motorcycle rider," provides a good example of his
    a. self-concept.
    b. self-esteem.
    c. self-recognition.
    d. ideal self.

    ANS: A   DIF: Moderate   REF: 348   OBJ: 11.1

12. An overall evaluation of your own self-worth best defines your
    a. self-recognition.
    b. self-concept.
    c. self-efficacy.
    d. self-esteem.

    ANS: D   DIF: Moderate   REF: 348   OBJ: 11.1

13. Which statement best exemplifies the concept of self-esteem?
    a. "I am white, 52 years old, and live in Wisconsin."
    b. "All in all, I am a worthy individual."
    c. "Women find me highly physically attractive."
    d. "I can recognize my own voice when I hear it on tape."

    ANS: B   DIF: Moderate   REF: 348   OBJ: 11.1

14. Which is best described as the overall sense of who you are?
    a. Identity
    b. Self-efficacy
    c. Looking-glass self
    d. Temperament

    ANS: A   DIF: Easy   REF: 348   OBJ: 11.1
    KEY: WWW

15. Your identity consists of
    a. your characteristic adaptations, self-esteem, but not your self-concept.
    b. your self-concept, self-esteem, but not your characteristic adaptations.
    c. your characteristic adaptations, self-concept, but not your self-esteem.
    d. your characteristic self-perceptions, self-esteem, and self-concept.

    ANS: D   DIF: Easy   REF: 348   OBJ: 11.1

16. Who would be most likely to argue that the vast majority of personality is formed between birth and age six?
    a. Fred, who is a psychoanalytic theorist
    b. Barney, who is a psychometric theorist
    c. Wilma, who is a social learning theorist
    d. Betty, who is a behavioral theorist

    ANS: A   DIF: Easy   REF: 349   OBJ: 11.2

17. In comparing the views of Freud and Erikson with regard to personality development, it is most accurate to say that Erikson placed more emphasis on _____ than did Freud.
    a. the impact of early life experiences
    b. social influences on the development of the rational ego
    c. the impact of harsh parenting practices
    d. sexual urges

    ANS: B   DIF: Moderate   REF: 349   OBJ: 11.2

18. Both Freud and Erikson believed that
    a. a person's personality is primarily genetically determined.
    b. there are four stages in the development of personality.
    c. while personality develops gradually over the first 15 to 20 years of life, people change very little throughout the years of adulthood.
    d. people in every culture progress through stages of personality development.

    ANS: D   DIF: Moderate   REF: 349   OBJ: 11.2

19. The psychometric approach to personality has led researchers to believe that personality
    a. is best thought of in terms of a set of dispositional traits.
    b. develops through a series of stages.
    c. cannot be measured.
    d. is not affected by biological factors.

    ANS: A   DIF: Moderate   REF: 349   OBJ: 11.2

20. Oscar is conducting a factor analysis on a set of personality traits; this means that he is most likely attempting to
    a. assess the degree of difficulty for each trait.
    b. determine which items tap into similar traits.
    c. Identify the age-group for which the traits are most appropriate.
    d. create a test of intelligence.

    ANS: B   DIF: Difficult   REF: 349   OBJ: 11.2

21. Albright is a self-described "Big Five" advocate when it comes to personality. Given this self-description, Albright would be best described as a _____ theorist.
    a. social learning   c. trait
    b. psychodynamic   d. classical conditioning

    ANS: C   DIF: Moderate   REF: 349   OBJ: 11.2
    KEY: WWW

22. Which is NOT one of Big Five traits?
    a. Openness to experience   c. Extraversion
    b. Conscientiousness   d. Inferiority

    ANS: D   DIF: Moderate   REF: 349-350   OBJ: 11.2

23. The key characteristics of someone with the personality dimension of high agreeableness would be
    a. open to fantasy and interested in variety.
    b. hostile and anxious.
    c. trustworthy and compliant.
    d. a high achiever and a person with self-discipline.

    ANS: C   DIF: Difficult   REF: 349-350   OBJ: 11.2

24. Cleo has received a high score on the conscientiousness scale of a personality test. This indicates that she would most likely be
    a. curious and interested in a variety of experiences.
    b. extremely outgoing.
    c. emotional, unstable, and hostile.
    d. well-organized and highly self-disciplined.

    ANS: D   DIF: Difficult   REF: 349-350   OBJ: 11.2
    KEY: WWW

25. Rave is a blast at parties. She seems to love the spotlight and craves excitement. A psychometric theorist would most likely describe Rave as being
    a. conscientious.   c. agreeable.
    b. extraverted.   d. neurotic.

    ANS: B   DIF: Moderate   REF: 349-350   OBJ: 11.2

614

26. The key characteristics of someone scoring high on the personality dimension of neuroticism would be
   a. open to fantasy and interested in variety.
   b. hostile and anxious.
   c. trustworthy and compliant.
   d. a high achiever and a person with self-discipline.

   ANS: B   DIF: Difficult   REF: 349-350   OBJ: 11.2

27. Which word can be used as a mnemonic cue for recalling the Big Five traits that is based on the first letter in each trait?
   a. OCEAN   c. LINKS
   b. HOMES   d. PSYCH

   ANS: A   DIF: Easy   REF: 349-350   OBJ: 11.2

28. The Big Five traits
   a. are expressed only in individuals in Western societies.
   b. are genetically influenced.
   c. emerge late in life.
   d. are not considered to be dispositional traits.

   ANS: B   DIF: Moderate   REF: 349   OBJ: 11.2

29. Who is accurately associated with the social learning perspective of personality?
   a. Skinner   c. Freud
   b. Erikson   d. Mischel

   ANS: D   DIF: Difficult   REF: 349   OBJ: 11.2

30. The social learning perspective assumes that
   a. there are universal stages in the development of personality.
   b. personality is best described in terms of trait dimensions.
   c. personality traits have a strong genetic basis.
   d. personality development is highly influenced by environmental experience.

   ANS: D   DIF: Moderate   REF: 349   OBJ: 11.2
   KEY: WWW

31. Vicki was reserved as a baby, shy as a child, and shy as an adult. Social learning theorists would say that Vicki
   a. was genetically predisposed to be shy.
   b. is a product of environments that consistently fostered the same personality trait.
   c. was unable to resolve psychosocial crises in positive ways.
   d. identified with her shy mother and drove her id to adopt this as a permanent personality characteristic.

   ANS: B   DIF: Moderate   REF: 349   OBJ: 11.2

32. Social learning theorists argue that
    a. personality does not change with age.
    b. personality always changes with age.
    c. personality can change with age if individuals experience different environments.
    d. personality can change with age if individuals experience changes to their genes due to exposure to chemicals or radiation.

    ANS: C   DIF: Easy   REF: 349   OBJ: 11.2

33. With regard to personality development, what belief is shared by Albert Bandura and Erik Erikson?
    a. There are universal, age-related changes in personality development.
    b. Biological factors are critical in the development of personality.
    c. Humans are best described in terms of five critical core personality traits.
    d. Personality has the potential to change during adulthood.

    ANS: D   DIF: Difficult   REF: 349   OBJ: 11.2

34. When Carmello is playing basketball, he is very aggressive. When he is playing at his house with his young daughter, he is very passive. These situations best exemplify the concept of
    a. same context, different personality.   c. different context, same personality.
    b. different context, different personality.   d. same context, same personality.

    ANS: B   DIF: Difficult   REF: 349   OBJ: 11.2

35. The average newborn appears to have
    a. no sense of self.   c. self-recognition but not self-awareness.
    b. self-awareness but not self-recognition.   d. both self-awareness and self-recognition.

    ANS: A   DIF: Moderate   REF: 351   OBJ: 11.3

36. Nine-month-old Elmer sees a rabbit in the yard. He then looks at his father, Fudd, and tries to direct Fudd's focus toward the bunny by pointing at the hopping rabbit. Elmer's behavior illustrates the process of _____ as an indicator of an emerging self-awareness.
    a. joint attention   c. temperament
    b. industry   d. behavioral inhibition

    ANS: A   DIF: Moderate   REF: 351   OBJ: 11.3

37. When Bao looks in a mirror and remarks, "Hey, that's me!" she is demonstrating
    a. self-esteem.   c. self-recognition.
    b. self-efficacy.   d. a sense of categorical self.

    ANS: C   DIF: Moderate   REF: 351   OBJ: 11.3

38. Krusty's mother paints his face like a clown for Halloween and holds him up to look at himself in the mirror. Krusty laughs, and rubs his hands all over his own cheeks making a mess of the paint job! Given his behavior, the YOUNGEST you should expect Jimmy to be is
   a. 6 months.
   b. 12 months.
   c. 18 months.
   d. 2 years.

   ANS: C   DIF: Difficult   REF: 351   OBJ: 11.3

39. Which of the following utterances clearly demonstrates that an infant has developed a categorical sense of self?
   a. "My car"
   b. "I big girl"
   c. "Pick me up"
   d. "Daddy's book"

   ANS: B   DIF: Moderate   REF: 351   OBJ: 11.3
   KEY: WWW

40. When talking to his grandmother on the phone, Riley says, "I am four years old, I am a boy, and I have red hair." This statement best illustrates the concept of
   a. a looking-glass self.
   b. self-esteem.
   c. diffusion status.
   d. categorical self.

   ANS: D   DIF: Moderate   REF: 351   OBJ: 11.3

41. The fact that mentally retarded children are slower at developing self-awareness illustrates the role of _____ in the process of the acquisition of self.
   a. genetics
   b. cognitive development
   c. social experience
   d. temperament

   ANS: B   DIF: Easy   REF: 351-352   OBJ: 11.3

42. Which of the following accomplishments is typically the LAST to occur?
   a. Recognition of self-image in the mirror
   b. Engaging in joint attention with an adult
   c. Recognition of self as physically distinct from others
   d. The influence of social feedback on the sense of self

   ANS: D   DIF: Moderate   REF: 351-352   OBJ: 11.3

43. Temperament is best described as
   a. a genetically based tendency to respond in a predictable way that is first seen in early infancy.
   b. a genetically based tendency to respond in a predictable way that is first seen in late infancy.
   c. a social experience based tendency to respond in a predictable way that is first seen in early infancy.
   d. a social experience based tendency to respond in a predictable way that is first seen in later infancy.

   ANS: A   DIF: Moderate   REF: 352   OBJ: 11.4

44. How does the concept of an infant as a "blank slate" fit with the concept of infant temperament?
    a. They are incompatible notions
    b. They are the identical concept
    c. They are similar and complimentary concepts
    d. They are unrelated as one is based on psychometric theory and the other on psychoanalytic theory

    ANS: A   DIF: Moderate   REF: 352   OBJ: 11.4

45. Easy temperament is characterized by
    a. dysphoria and fear of new experience.
    b. happiness and fear of new experience.
    c. dysphoria and openness to new experience.
    d. happiness and openness to new experience.

    ANS: D   DIF: Moderate   REF: 352   OBJ: 11.4

46. Three-month-old Gerber is eating strained peas for the very first time. Despite the fact that this is a new experience, Gerber appears quite happy with her meal. With regard to temperament, Gerber is best classified as
    a. easy.   c. slow-to-warm-up.
    b. difficult.   d. resistant.

    ANS: A   DIF: Moderate   REF: 352   OBJ: 11.4

47. Difficult temperament is characterized by
    a. low irritability and negative reactions to change in routine.
    b. high irritability and negative reactions to change in routine.
    c. low irritability and positive reactions to change in routine.
    d. high irritability and positive reactions to change in routine.

    ANS: B   DIF: Moderate   REF: 352   OBJ: 11.4

48. Infant Marisa cries and throws tantrums when she doesn't get her way. Moreover, she becomes very upset when her parents attempt to change her diaper. With regard to temperament, Marisa is best classified as
    a. easy.   c. slow-to-warm-up.
    b. difficult.   d. secure.

    ANS: B   DIF: Easy   REF: 352   OBJ: 11.4

49. Slow-to-warm-up temperament is characterized by
    a. relative inactivity and mild reactions to change in routine.
    b. relative inactivity and intense reactions to change in routine.
    c. high levels of activity and mild reactions to change in routine.
    d. high levels of activity and intense reactions to change in routine.

    ANS: A   DIF: Moderate   REF: 352   OBJ: 11.4

50. While she does not scream when her parents attempt to cuddle with her, Inga does tend to look away and demonstrate some discomfort with this activity. With regard to temperament, Inga is best classified as
    a. easy.
    b. difficult.
    c. slow-to-warm-up.
    d. secure.

    ANS: C   DIF: Moderate   REF: 352   OBJ: 11.4

51. One-year-old Barker has some trouble dealing with new situations. In addition, he tends to be relatively inactive and moody. With regard to temperament, Barker is best classified as
    a. easy.
    b. difficult.
    c. slow-to-warm-up.
    d. secure.

    ANS: C   DIF: Easy   REF: 352   OBJ: 11.4
    KEY: WWW

52. In Thomas and Chess's longitudinal study of temperament, the largest percent of infants were
    a. classified as easy.
    b. classified as difficult.
    c. classified as slow-to-warm-up.
    d. unclassifiable.

    ANS: A   DIF: Moderate   REF: 352   OBJ: 11.4

53. Children who are behaviorally inhibited are
    a. high in extraversion and openness to new experience.
    b. low in emotionality and extraversion.
    c. high in neuroticism and low in extraversion.
    d. low in sociability and neuroticism.

    ANS: C   DIF: Difficult   REF: 352   OBJ: 11.4

54. While normally calm, 10-year-old Gretta becomes very shy and highly distressed when she is in an unfamiliar setting with people she does not know. Gretta would best be categorized as
    a. extraverted.
    b. conscientious.
    c. open to new experiences.
    d. behaviorally inhibited.

    ANS: D   DIF: Moderate   REF: 352   OBJ: 11.4

55. Which best illustrates the actions of a behaviorally inhibited individual?
    a. Being extremely fearful in a room full of strangers
    b. Being the talkative kid who "won't shut up"
    c. Being the smartest kid in the class
    d. Being wild at the beach and quite in home

    ANS: A   DIF: Moderate   REF: 352-353   OBJ: 11.4

56. Research by Kagan and his colleagues concluded that behavioral inhibition is _____ rooted.
    a. biologically
    b. socially
    c. subconsciously
    d. cognitively

    ANS: A   DIF: Moderate   REF: 353   OBJ: 11.4

619

57. The tendency to actively approach a new situation in a positive way is referred to as
    a. surgency.
    b. negative affectivity.
    c. behavioral inhibition.
    d. neuroticism.

    ANS: A   DIF: Moderate   REF: 353   OBJ: 11.4

58. Which statement would indicate that an individual has a high level of surgency?
    a. "Paying attention to boring people is hard."
    b. "I am always excited, in a good way, to meet people."
    c. "Meeting people makes me nervous."
    d. "I hate people."

    ANS: B   DIF: Moderate   REF: 353   OBJ: 11.4

59. One-year-old Markus loves interacting with his peers. A developmental theorist would most likely describe Markus as being high on the _____ dimension of temperament.
    a. slow-to-warm-up
    b. effortful control
    c. negative affectivity
    d. surgency

    ANS: D   DIF: Moderate   REF: 353   OBJ: 11.4
    KEY: WWW

60. A person high in negative affectivity would most likely be described as
    a. psychotic.
    b. affable.
    c. irritable.
    d. energetic.

    ANS: C   DIF: Moderate   REF: 353   OBJ: 11.4

61. When asked to describe his sister Maggie, Jake says, "It's like she is afraid all of the time." If accurate, this statement indicates that Maggie would likely score high on a measure of
    a. extraversion.
    b. conscientiousness.
    c. effortful control.
    d. negative affectivity.

    ANS: D   DIF: Moderate   REF: 353   OBJ: 11.4

62. The temperament dimension of _____ is defined as the tendency to be sad or easily frustrated.
    a. surgency
    b. negative affectivity
    c. behavioral inhibition
    d. extraversion

    ANS: B   DIF: Moderate   REF: 353   OBJ: 11.4
    KEY: WWW

63. The temperament dimension of _____ control is defined as the tendency to sustain attention.
    a. behavioral inhibition
    b. negative affectivity
    c. effortful control
    d. surgency

    ANS: C   DIF: Easy   REF: 353   OBJ: 11.4

64. Which behavior would indicate that Manny has a high level of effortful control?
    a. He is very easily frustrated
    b. He can quickly shift his attention from one topic to another
    c. He makes friends very easily
    d. He likes taking on new challenges

    ANS: B   DIF: Easy   REF: 353   OBJ: 11.4

65. Research on early temperament and later development suggests that
    a. temperament and personality are developmentally unrelated concepts.
    b. there is a meaningful relationship between early childhood temperament and later adult personality.
    c. behavioral inhibitions in early life are related to extraversion in later life.
    d. "easy" children may turn out to be maladjusted adults, but "difficult" children are certain to do so.

    ANS: B   DIF: Easy   REF: 353   OBJ: 11.4

66. Goodness-of-fit is best defined as
    a. the extent to which the child's temperament is compatible with the social world to which the child must adapt.
    b. a child's ability to distinguish himself from his environment.
    c. the amount of impact genetic factors has on the development of personality.
    d. the extent to which a child develops an attachment to a caregiver.

    ANS: A   DIF: Moderate   REF: 353   OBJ: 11.4

67. In most settings, an easy temperament is associated with more positive adaptation. However, in times of famine, infants with "difficult" temperaments in the Masai tribe have been known to outlive babies with "easy" temperaments. This finding is used to illustrate the important effect that _____ has on developmental outcome.
    a. goodness-of-fit   c. self-esteem
    b. parenting style   d. life review

    ANS: A   DIF: Difficult   REF: 353   OBJ: 11.4

68. The fact that parents who are taught to interpret and respond more effectively to their child's cues can produce calmer infants who cry less best illustrates the concept of
    a. slow-to-warm-up temperament.   c. individualistic culture.
    b. goodness-of-fit.   d. big-fish-little-pond effect.

    ANS: B   DIF: Moderate   REF: 353   OBJ: 11.4

69. The self-concept of most preschoolers is based on _____ traits.
    a. psychological   c. physical
    b. temperamental   d. surgency

    ANS: C   DIF: Moderate   REF: 354   OBJ: 11.5
    KEY: WWW

621

70. As a typical three-year-old, when asked about his self-concept, Talisker's answer would most likely be,
   a. "I am smart."   c. "I am small."
   b. "I am funny."   d. "I am excitable."

   ANS: C   DIF: Moderate   REF: 354   OBJ: 11.5

71. A significant change in self-description that appears at about age eight is a shift from descriptions focusing on
   a. physical characteristics to descriptions focusing on social qualities.
   b. inner qualities to descriptions focusing on action statements.
   c. subjective to objective self-evaluations.
   d. action statements to physical characteristics.

   ANS: A   DIF: Moderate   REF: 354   OBJ: 11.5

72. While Ginger has always thought of herself as the best dancer in the world, she has just begun to notice that some of the other kids in her class are better than she. This realization indicates that Ginger has begun to engage in
   a. behavioral inhibition.   c. disengagement.
   b. social comparison.   d. joint attention.

   ANS: B   DIF: Moderate   REF: 354-355   OBJ: 11.5

73. Which statement about the self-conception of typically preschoolers is FALSE?
   a. They tend to see themselves as "the greatest" at doing things.
   b. They may be devastated if they are outdone by a member of the opposite sex.
   c. They are very poor at making comparisons between their skill level and the skill level of others.
   d. They tend to not include aspects of physical and cognitive competence in their assessment of self-esteem.

   ANS: D   DIF: Difficult   REF: 354-355   OBJ: 11.5

74. Harter's self-perception research with older children indicated that self-esteem
   a. emerges as a single entity and remains unchanged after this.
   b. is unidimensional, consisting of a global sense of self.
   c. becomes less realistic as children enter adolescence.
   d. is multidimensional, consisting of several distinct domains.

   ANS: D   DIF: Moderate   REF: 355   OBJ: 11.5

75. Ideal self is best defined as what a person
   a. is like.   c. senses they should be like.
   b. is not.   d. sees in others.

   ANS: C   DIF: Moderate   REF: 355-356   OBJ: 11.5

76. When considering himself, Shaggy thinks, "While I am not any of these things, I should be smarter, less afraid, and good at detective work." These thoughts best represent Shaggy's
a. ideal self.
b. temperament.
c. self-recognition.
d. joint attention.

ANS: A   DIF: Easy   REF: 355-356   OBJ: 11.5

77. Children who are high in self-esteem have parents who
a. have few rules and generally let children decide for themselves what is best.
b. make decisions for their children so they are not burdened with making choices.
c. have a "warm" and democratic parenting style.
d. do not discipline their children.

ANS: C   DIF: Moderate   REF: 356   OBJ: 11.5

78. Damon (1994) and others complaint against American educators and parents is that many tend to
a. underestimate the significance of self-esteem.
b. provide children with an inflated sense of self-worth.
c. underestimate the importance of telling children how great they are (even if it is false praise).
d. provide feedback that is too harsh.

ANS: B   DIF: Easy   REF: 356   OBJ: 11.6

79. Which statement between temperament and later personality is FALSE?
a. Well-adjusted three-year-olds tend to be well-adjusted adults
b. Highly emotional and difficult to control three-year-olds tend to be impulsive teens
c. Behavioral inhibition in preschool is predictive of low extraversion in middle childhood
d. An infant's high ability to exhibit effortful control predicts a lack of conscientiousness in later life

ANS: D   DIF: Moderate   REF: 356   OBJ: 11.6

80. At what age does personality tend to fully "gel" (i.e., begin to predict adult personality)?
a. Infancy
b. Elementary school years
c. Late adolescence
d. Middle adulthood

ANS: B   DIF: Moderate   REF: 356   OBJ: 11.6

81. Rose is 16 years old and her sister Blossom is nine. In terms of their self-perceptions, research would suggest that
a. Rose's self-description is more likely to be based on physical attributes than Blossom's.
b. Rose's self-portrait would be less abstract than Blossom's.
c. Rose would be more self-aware than Blossom.
d. Rose would have a less differentiated self than Blossom.

ANS: C   DIF: Moderate   REF: 357   OBJ: 11.7

82. During adolescence, self-descriptions become LESS
    a. self-aware.
    b. differentiated.
    c. coherent.
    d. concrete.

    ANS: D   DIF: Moderate   REF: 357   OBJ: 11.7

83. Who is most likely to experience a decrease in self-esteem in early adolescence?
    a. A white female
    b. A Latino female
    c. A white male
    d. A Latino male

    ANS: A   DIF: Moderate   REF: 357   OBJ: 11.7

84. Marsh and Kit-Tai Hua's 2003 study on the "big-fish-little-pond effect" found that a student's academic self-concept is less positive when students are
    a. gifted.
    b. mentally retarded.
    c. in a school with a lot of high achievers.
    d. in a school with a lot of low achievers.

    ANS: C   DIF: Easy   REF: 357-358   OBJ: 11.7

85. Research on the big-fish-little-pond effect suggests that
    a. gifted children are at risk for low self-concept.
    b. placing children with learning disabilities in a regular education room may negatively impact their self-esteem.
    c. male athletes tend to have high academic self-esteem.
    d. students from larger high schools tend to have the highest self-esteem.

    ANS: B   DIF: Moderate   REF: 357-358   OBJ: 11.7
    KEY: WWW

86. Which question best exemplifies the identity and role confusion conflict?
    a. What kind of moral and religious values do I have?
    b. Has my life been worthwhile?
    c. Am I the fastest runner in my class?
    d. Have I produced something that will outlive me?

    ANS: A   DIF: Moderate   REF: 358   OBJ: 11.7

87. Harrison believes that Erikson's theory of personality development is very accurate. Thus, Harrison would most likely believe that his 17-year-old son, Ford, would currently be experiencing the psychosocial conflict involving
    a. trust versus mistrust.
    b. identity and role confusion.
    c. initiative versus guilt.
    d. generativity versus stagnation.

    ANS: B   DIF: Moderate   REF: 358   OBJ: 11.7

88. The period of experimenting with different roles that is so common during adolescence is referred to as the _____ period.
    a. foreclosure
    b. joint attention
    c. moratorium
    d. temperament

    ANS: C   DIF: Moderate   REF: 358   OBJ: 11.7

89. Fidel is a college student who is currently experiencing a moratorium period. This means that he is most likely
   a. depressed.
   b. highly focused on a specific major.
   c. experiencing a crisis of trust.
   d. relatively free of responsibilities.

   ANS: D   DIF: Moderate   REF: 358   OBJ: 11.7

90. According to James Marcia, adolescent identity can be classified into one of four statuses that are based on the key issues of
   a. crisis and commitment.
   b. commitment and conscientiousness.
   c. conscientiousness and comparison.
   d. comparison and crisis.

   ANS: A   DIF: Moderate   REF: 358-359   OBJ: 11.8

91. The _____ identity status would best be described as "no conflict, no crisis, and no clue."
   a. foreclosure
   b. moratorium
   c. identity achievement
   d. diffusion

   ANS: D   DIF: Moderate   REF: 359   OBJ: 11.8

92. Which best represents "identity diffusion status"?
   a. Gee plans to be a teacher because his parents and siblings are all teachers.
   b. Bea doesn't really know what she wants to be when she "grows up" and couldn't care less about even exploring the possibilities.
   c. Dee has taken a battery of interest inventories and is exploring different majors at the university, thinking about possibilities for her future career.
   d. Lee has talked with career counselors, his parents, peers, and instructors, and has determined that he is best suited for a career in teaching. He is now doing his student teaching.

   ANS: B   DIF: Moderate   REF: 359   OBJ: 11.8

93. The _____ identity status would best be described as "I haven't really thought about it, but my parents think…"
   a. foreclosure
   b. moratorium
   c. identity achievement
   d. diffusion

   ANS: A   DIF: Moderate   REF: 359   OBJ: 11.8

94. Gaga's mother and father are both professional singers, as are her two older sisters. Gaga is in college, enrolled in a music curriculum. When asked about her career goals, she states, "I'll be a singer, of course. Everyone in my family is a singer. I've never thought of being anything else." Gaga 's identity status is best described in terms of
   a. foreclosure.
   b. moratorium.
   c. identity achievement.
   d. diffusion.

   ANS: A   DIF: Difficult   REF: 359   OBJ: 11.8

95. Hoffman is planning to enter the family's plastics business as soon as he graduates from high school. His parents have a job for him in their shop, and they expect that Hoffman will eventually run the business. Hoffman has never questioned this career goal. According to Erikson, Hoffman's identity status is best described as
   a. identity diffusion.
   b. identity achievement.
   c. moratorium status.
   d. identity foreclosure.

   ANS: D   DIF: Difficult   REF: 359   OBJ: 11.8
   KEY: WWW

96. The _____ identity status would best be described as "very active exploration of options."
   a. foreclosure
   b. moratorium
   c. identity achievement
   d. diffusion

   ANS: B   DIF: Easy   REF: 359   OBJ: 11.8

97. Bo has always considered a career in professional baseball as his best career option. Lately, he has begun to question this choice. In fact, he has been actively trying other sports (football, soccer) to see if they may be more of what he wants in life. James Marcia would say that Bo is currently experiencing _____ status concerning his career goals.
   a. diffusion
   b. moratorium
   c. foreclosure
   d. identity achievement

   ANS: B   DIF: Moderate   REF: 359   OBJ: 11.8

98. The _____ identity status would best be described as "crisis resolved and direction in life set."
   a. foreclosure
   b. moratorium
   c. identity achievement
   d. diffusion

   ANS: C   DIF: Moderate   REF: 359   OBJ: 11.8
   KEY: WWW

99. After months of consideration, college sophomore Burrhus has just come to the conclusion that a career in psychology is the right thing for him. As a result, he has just switched to a psychology major and has signed up for several psychology courses for the next semester. Concerning his career plans, Burrhus appears to be in the _____ status stage.
   a. foreclosure
   b. moratorium
   c. identity achievement
   d. diffusion

   ANS: C   DIF: Difficult   REF: 359   OBJ: 11.8

100. Which statement regarding the achievement of identity status is FALSE?
   a. The rate of identify achievement differs across domains of identity.
   b. By age 20, most individuals have reached complete identity achievement status.
   c. Some reliable sex differences in identity achievement have been observed.
   d. The actual process of identity achievement is sometimes different than the theory proposed by Marcia.

   ANS: B   DIF: Moderate   REF: 359   OBJ: 11.8

101. The reliable sex difference concerning identity achievement during adolescence is that
    a. males tend to attach more emphasis on aspects of identity involving interpersonal relationships.
    b. females tend to attach more emphasis on aspects of identity involving career identity.
    c. males tend to attach a greater emphasis on aspects of identity involving sexuality.
    d. females tend to attach a greater emphasis on aspects of identity involving balancing family and career goals.

    ANS: D   DIF: Moderate   REF: 359-360   OBJ: 11.8

102. If you were to assess the domain identity status of 100 typical high school juniors concerning occupational choice, gender-role attitudes, religious beliefs, and political ideologies, you should expect to find
    a. the same level of status in all for domains.
    b. the highest status on gender roles and the lowest on religious beliefs.
    c. the highest status on political ideologies and the lowest on occupational choice.
    d. different levels of status in most of the domains.

    ANS: D   DIF: Moderate   REF: 360   OBJ: 11.8

103. Using a life-story approach, McLean and Pratt (2006) found that the more the sophisticated the "meaning making" in an adolescent's life narrative, the
    a. more likely he or she would be depressed.
    b. less likely he or she would be in a state of foreclosure.
    c. more likely he or she would become pregnant.
    d. less likely he or she would have close friends.

    ANS: B   DIF: Difficult   REF: 360   OBJ: 11.8

104. The sense of personal identification with an ethnic group and its cultural values and traditions is referred to as one's ethnic
    a. identity.   c. foreclosure.
    b. moratorium.   d. comparison.

    ANS: A   DIF: Easy   REF: 361   OBJ: 11.8

105. Who is most likely to have just begun to demonstrate that she notices the difference in the faces of individuals from different racial backgrounds?
    a. 3-minute-old Ash   c. 3-month-old Jessie
    b. 3-day-old Pikachu   d. 3-year-old Meowth

    ANS: C   DIF: Moderate   REF: 361   OBJ: 11.8

106. The process of developing an ethnic identity is
    a. very similar to developing other forms of identity.
    b. quite distinct from forming other identities since ethnicity is not chosen.
    c. easier than the process of forming other types of identities.
    d. completed earlier than the formation of other identities.

    ANS: A   DIF: Easy   REF: 361   OBJ: 11.8

107. A positive sense of ethnic identity
   a. is seldom found in African-American adolescents.
   b. can protect an adolescent from damaging effects of racial or ethnic discrimination.
   c. tends to be completed by elementary school (especially in children growing up in homogenous environments with few interactions with other ethnic groups).
   d. has little to do with parental behavior.

   ANS: B   DIF: Moderate   REF: 361   OBJ: 11.8

108. The main development trend concerning vocational identity in late adolescence is that
   a. for the first time in life, individuals actively explore vocational possibilities.
   b. one's sex comes first into consideration when thinking about career options.
   c. choices become more realistic.
   d. the match between personality and occupation is seen more and more as irrelevant.

   ANS: C   DIF: Moderate   REF: 361-362   OBJ: 11.8

109. Which statement concerning vocational development in adolescence is true?
   a. The fit between one's self-concept, personality, and occupation is unimportant.
   b. Chance events seldom impact career decisions.
   c. Minority status may lead one to lower or compromise one's career plans.
   d. In women, holding traditional gender-role attitudes tends to lead to higher vocational aspirations.

   ANS: C   DIF: Moderate   REF: 362   OBJ: 11.8

110. What cognitive skill acquisition is best associated with adolescents who are able to effectively resolve identity issues?
   a. Object permanence   c. Postconventional thinking
   b. Memory rehearsal   d. Formal operational thought

   ANS: D   DIF: Moderate   REF: 362   OBJ: 11.8

111. College attendance appears to provide the _____ that Erikson believed was essential to identity formation.
   a. imaginary audience   c. dispositional traits
   b. sense of despair   d. moratorium period

   ANS: D   DIF: Easy   REF: 363   OBJ: 11.8

112. Self-esteem rating tends to be highest in people in their
   a. teens.   c. 60s.
   b. 30s.   d. 90s.

   ANS: C   DIF: Moderate   REF: 363   OBJ: 11.9

628

113. Which statement concerning self-esteem development is true?
    a. Most older adults suffer from a poor sense of self-image.
    b. Older individuals may retain a high sense of self-image by reducing the ideal-real self gap.
    c. The average level of self-esteem at age 60 is half of that at age 16.
    d. Males show higher levels of self-esteem across all developmental age levels.

    ANS: B   DIF: Moderate   REF: 363-364   OBJ: 11.9

114. What is the developmental relationship between ideal self, present self, and future self?
    a. The three aspects of self are most similar in the teenage years.
    b. The three aspects of self are most similar in the young adult years.
    c. The three aspects of self are most similar in the middle-aged years.
    d. The three aspects of self are most similar in the elderly adult years.

    ANS: D   DIF: Moderate   REF: 363-364   OBJ: 11.9

115. When contemplating their self-esteem, older individuals tend to compare themselves to
    a. young, healthy individuals.   c. older, healthy individuals.
    b. young, but unhealthy individuals.   d. older and unhealthy individuals.

    ANS: D   DIF: Moderate   REF: 364   OBJ: 11.9
    KEY: WWW

116. Negative stereotypes concerning aging
    a. do more harm than good.
    b. are seldom held by older adults.
    c. need to be combated at the individual, not societal, level.
    d. can protect the elderly from the effects of age discrimination.

    ANS: A   DIF: Moderate   REF: 365   OBJ: 11.9

117. Holding a negative image (stereotype) of aging
    a. may reduce the risk of cardiovascular events in adulthood.
    b. can lead to physically slower behavior in older adulthood.
    c. tends to lead to improvements in memory in old age as people know they need to try harder .
    d. does not appear to have any measurable impact on adult physical or mental status.

    ANS: B   DIF: Moderate   REF: 365   OBJ: 11.9

118. People living in individualistic cultures tend to define themselves as
    a. individuals, and put the good of society ahead of their own good.
    b. individuals, and put their own good ahead of that of society.
    c. group members, and put the good of society ahead of their own good.
    d. group members, and put their own good ahead of that of society.

    ANS: B   DIF: Easy   REF: 365   OBJ: 11.9

119. Parents living in an individualistic culture tend to socialize children to be
    a. self-reliant.   c. interdependent.
    b. modesty.   d. in social harmony.

    ANS: A   DIF: Moderate   REF: 365   OBJ: 11.9
    KEY: WWW

120. Which statement indicates that Jade adheres to a collectivist culture philosophy?
    a. "It is important to be independent and self-reliant."
    b. "It's my way or the highway."
    c. "It's not about me, it's about my people."
    d. "The needs of the one outweigh the needs of the whole."

    ANS: C   DIF: Moderate   REF: 365   OBJ: 11.9

121. One impact of living in an individualistic versus a collectivist culture is that
    a. people in collectivist cultures tend to talk more about their unique qualities.
    b. people in collectivist cultures tend describe their behavior in terms of specific
       different contexts (e.g.. home, work).
    c. people in individualistic cultures tend to view their personality as "quite variable"
       across different settings.
    d. people in individualistic cultures tend to view their ability as "below average."

    ANS: B   DIF: Moderate   REF: 365-367   OBJ: 11.9

122. Cultural differences in self-description lead
    a. American mothers to tell more stories to their children in which the emphasis is on
       some family experience.
    b. Chinese mother to tell children stories in which the child is the "star."
    c. American children to talk more about their preferences and feelings.
    d. Chinese children talk more about individual freedom and characteristics.

    ANS: C   DIF: Moderate   REF: 367   OBJ: 11.9

123. Research on individuals from collectivist cultures challenge the Western assumption that
    a. a person cannot develop normally without placing the needs of society before their
       own.
    b. women are superior to men.
    c. a person cannot develop normally without individuating one's self from others.
    d. the elderly are superior to youth.

    ANS: C   DIF: Moderate   REF: 367   OBJ: 11.9

124. Which is true regarding personality during adulthood?
    a. There is little stability of personality traits between young and old adulthood.
    b. Broad personality dimensions, such as extroversion and neuroticism, are fairly
       stable across adulthood.
    c. An introverted young adult will most likely become an extraverted older adult.
    d. Personality traits cannot be measured in older adults.

    ANS: B   DIF: Moderate   REF: 367-368   OBJ: 11.9

630

125. Research has indicated that as individuals move from adolescence to middle age, they would be most likely to experience a modest increase in
   a. neuroticism.
   b. extraversion.
   c. openness to new experience.
   d. conscientiousness.

   ANS: D   DIF: Difficult   REF: 368   OBJ: 11.9

126. With regard to personality development during adulthood, which is true?
   a. There is generally more change in personality between adolescence and middle age than there is between middle age and old age.
   b. There are virtually no changes in personality beyond adolescence.
   c. The historical context in which people grow up appears to have little influence on personality development.
   d. Most people undergo highly significant personality changes as they progress from middle age to old age.

   ANS: A   DIF: Moderate   REF: 369   OBJ: 11.9

127. Which has NOT been proposed as a key factor in explaining why personality is so stable across the lifespan?
   a. Heredity
   b. Lasting effects of childhood
   c. Biological factors like diseases
   d. The tendency of environments to remain stable

   ANS: C   DIF: Easy   REF: 369   OBJ: 11.9
   KEY: WWW

128. Which is likely to contribute most to change in personality across the lifespan?
   a. Consistent environments
   b. Genetic inheritance
   c. Long-lasting childhood experiences
   d. Poor person-environment fit

   ANS: D   DIF: Easy   REF: 369   OBJ: 11.9

129. Five-month-old Ruby is beginning to recognize that her mother, Opal, does not tend to come to feed her when she is hungry. According to Erikson, Ruby is currently involved in a psychosocial crisis of
   a. industry versus inferiority.
   b. autonomy versus shame and doubt.
   c. integrity versus despair.
   d. trust versus mistrust.

   ANS: D   DIF: Moderate   REF: 370   OBJ: 11.10

130. Children's initial recognition of themselves as physically separate from others corresponds with Erikson's _____ psychosocial stage?
   a. trust versus mistrust
   b. autonomy versus shame and doubt
   c. initiative versus guilt
   d. industry versus inferiority

   ANS: A   DIF: Moderate   REF: 370   OBJ: 11.10
   KEY: WWW

131. Three-year-old Anthony has just begun to throw tantrums when he does not get his way. Erikson would argue that this initial assertion of his will demonstrates that Anthony is in the _____ stage of development.
a. generativity versus stagnation
c. initiative versus guilt
b. autonomy versus shame and doubt
d. industry versus inferiority

ANS: B   DIF: Moderate   REF: 370   OBJ: 11.10

132. Kristi's mother finds four-year-old Kristi in the kitchen, mixing up a muffin mix and making a marvelous mess! Kristi announces, "Surprise! I'm making dinner!" Kristi's mother squelches her desire to yell at Kristi and with great control says, "Oh, how nice! Can I help?" She responds in this way because she has been studying Erik Erikson's theory in her psychology class and she knows that Kristi's behavior is typical of a child in the stage of
a. autonomy versus shame and doubt.
c. initiative versus guilt.
b. intimacy versus isolation.
d. trust versus mistrust.

ANS: C   DIF: Difficult   REF: 370   OBJ: 11.10

133. Mia has just become concerned with how she compares to her peers. For example, she wants to know if she can kick a soccer ball farther or read better than her friends. Mia is in which of Erikson's psychosocial stages?
a. Autonomy versus shame and doubt
c. Industry versus inferiority
b. Initiative versus guilt
d. Identity versus role confusion

ANS: C   DIF: Moderate   REF: 370   OBJ: 11.10

134. Twenty-five-year-old Clint has gained enough confidence that he has decided to commit himself to a shared life with his girlfriend. Erikson would suggest that this indicates that Clint is most likely dealing with the conflict of
a. integrity versus despair.
c. intimacy versus isolation.
b. identity versus role confusion.
d. generativity versus stagnation.

ANS: C   DIF: Easy   REF: 370   OBJ: 11.10

135. Research investigating Erikson's claim that identity paves the way for the establishment of intimate relationships has revealed that
a. there is no relationship between identity and intimacy.
b. the acquisition of a well-formed identity does appear to facilitate intimacy in relationships equally well for both men and women.
c. the acquisition of a well-formed identity does appear to facilitate intimacy in relationships, but the impact may vary somewhat by sex and gender.
d. we can truly love another even though we do not "know ourselves."

ANS: C   DIF: Moderate   REF: 370   OBJ: 11.10

136. According to Erikson, psychologically healthy middle-aged adults are most likely to
    a. begin to be concerned about how their abilities compare with their age peers.
    b. be concerned with death and dying.
    c. develop a deep concern with making a contribution to society and passing on something of value to younger generations.
    d. focus on the establishment of intimate relationships with others.

    ANS: C   DIF: Moderate   REF: 371   OBJ: 11.10

137. Forty-year-old Zelda is proud of the tutoring she is doing at school with kids who have learning problems and feels that she is doing something positive for future generations. It is most likely that Zelda is in Erikson's stage of
    a. integrity versus despair.   c. intimacy versus isolation.
    b. identity versus role confusion.   d. generativity versus stagnation.

    ANS: D   DIF: Moderate   REF: 371   OBJ: 11.10
    KEY: WWW

138. Karin's children are all in college. She works as a legal secretary, and most of what she earns goes toward paying her children's college tuition. Her own children lead busy lives, with friends and school activities occupying most of their time, so Karin volunteers one evening each week at the Boys' Home, reading bedtime stories to the young delinquents there. Karin is best classified as fitting into Erikson's stage of
    a. intimacy versus isolation.   c. integrity versus despair.
    b. generativity versus stagnation.   d. identity versus role confusion.

    ANS: B   DIF: Moderate   REF: 371   OBJ: 11.10

139. Erikson would argue that 80-year-old Mable is most likely confronting the psychosocial issue of
    a. identity versus role confusion.   c. industry versus inferiority.
    b. autonomy versus self-doubt.   d. integrity versus despair.

    ANS: D   DIF: Moderate   REF: 371   OBJ: 11.10

140. The phrase, "If only I had my life to live over again I would…" is best associated with Erikson's _____ psychosocial stage of development.
    a. integrity versus despair   c. intimacy versus isolation
    b. identity versus role confusion   d. initiative versus guilt

    ANS: A   DIF: Moderate   REF: 371-372   OBJ: 11.10

141. Which event is best associated with Erikson's integrity versus despair stage of development?
    a. Committing to a long-term relationship c. Comparing yourself to your peers
    b. Having your first child   d. Life review

    ANS: D   DIF: Moderate   REF: 371-372   OBJ: 11.10

142. Which best summarizes the research on the "midlife crisis"?
   a. Most males experience a significant midlife crisis, but few females have such an experience.
   b. Most females experience a significant midlife crisis, but few males have such an experience.
   c. Most middle-aged people experience a significant midlife crisis.
   d. Most middle-aged people experience some questioning of self during midlife, but few experience a true midlife crisis.

   ANS: D   DIF: Moderate   REF: 372   OBJ: 11.10

143. Which statement concerning career issues is FALSE?
   a. Gender-role expectations have little impact on one's career.
   b. Personality factors can influence vocational development in adulthood.
   c. Mentors can be of great assistance in launching a career.
   d. An individual's work experience can change one's personality.

   ANS: A   DIF: Moderate   REF: 372-373   OBJ: 11.11

144. Research on women's vocation development has found that
   a. women are more likely than men to transfer to a new work location.
   b. giving birth can negatively impact a woman's earning potential.
   c. women who make it to the top of their career ladder tend to be in long-term marriages and have one to two children.
   d. when you control for the tendency for women to step out of the workplace more often, women earn about 20% more than men.

   ANS: B   DIF: Moderate   REF: 373   OBJ: 11.11

145. The idea of remaining effective by developing ways to get around the need for other skills than the ones you already possess best fits with the _____ component of the selective optimization with compensation theory.
   a. selective   c. compensation
   b. optimization   d. integrity

   ANS: C   DIF: Moderate   REF: 373-374   OBJ: 11.11

146. Sixty-year-old Irene has been a secretary for 30 years. Despite her advancing age, her typing skills remain excellent. This is in most part due to the fact that Irene continues to practice her typing every day. The Baltes' would suggest that the process of _____ is most responsible for Irene's continued high level of performance.
   a. selective   c. compensation
   b. optimization   d. stagnation

   ANS: B   DIF: Moderate   REF: 373-374   OBJ: 11.11

147. When 50-year-old Mustafa says, "I need to decide which work goals are more important and then develop skills to meet these goals," he is speaking about the process of
   a. optimization.   c. generativity.
   b. compensation.   d. selection.

   ANS: D   DIF: Moderate   REF: 373-374   OBJ: 11.11

148. Sal has decided that his wife and he should sit down and begin talking about how their financial status when they retire in a few years. This indicates that Sal is in the _____ phase of retirement.
    a. honeymoon
    b. reorientation
    c. preretirement
    d. disenchantment

ANS: C   DIF: Easy   REF: 375   OBJ: 11.11

149. According to Ashley's model, a month or so after retirement, most workers are in the _____ phase.
    a. honeymoon
    b. reorientation
    c. preretirement
    d. disenchantment

ANS: A   DIF: Easy   REF: 375   OBJ: 11.11
KEY: WWW

150. About one year after she retired, Betty Joe suddenly became very unhappy and expressed the opinion that she now had nothing to do in her life. Atchley would argue that Betty Joe appears have entered the _____ phase of retirement.
    a. honeymoon
    b. reorientation
    c. midlife
    d. disenchantment

ANS: D   DIF: Easy   REF: 375   OBJ: 11.11

151. Yumi has just entered the phase of retirement best described as "realistic and satisfying." This would indicate that she is in the _____ phase of retirement.
    a. honeymoon
    b. reorientation
    c. midlife
    d. disenchantment

ANS: B   DIF: Moderate   REF: 375   OBJ: 11.11

152. For Britta, the novelty of retirement has begun to wear off and she suddenly finds herself feeling quite unhappy. This indicates that Britta has entered the _____ phase of retirement.
    a. honeymoon
    b. reorientation
    c. midlife
    d. disenchantment

ANS: D   DIF: Easy   REF: 375   OBJ: 11.11

153. Which factor is associated with a NEGATIVE retirement experience?
    a. Involuntary retirement
    b. Good physical health
    c. Being married
    d. Having strong financial resources

ANS: A   DIF: Easy   REF: 375-376   OBJ: 11.11

154. The debate concerning successful aging in old age involves the _____ debate.
    a. nature-nurture
    b. continuity-discontinuity
    c. activity-disengagement
    d. foreclosure-diffusion

ANS: C   DIF: Easy   REF: 377   OBJ: 11.12
KEY: WWW

155. Mickelson is about to retire. In preparation, he has begun to take up golf as a way to fill some of the time he would normally have been at work. Mickelson's response best fits with the _____ theory concerning successful aging.
a. temperament
b. activity
c. disengagement
d. stagnation

ANS: B   DIF: Moderate   REF: 377   OBJ: 11.12

156. As she nears her 100th birthday, Kijana, though remaining happy, has begun to become much less involved with her church and other social groups. Ruth's reaction to aging best fits with the _____ theory concerning successful aging.
a. honeymoon
b. activity
c. disengagement
d. generativity

ANS: C   DIF: Moderate   REF: 377   OBJ: 11.12

157. Research on successful aging has found
a. more support for activity theory.
b. more support for disengagement theory.
c. little support for either activity or disengagement theory.
d. identical levels of support for activity and disengagement theory.

ANS: A   DIF: Easy   REF: 377   OBJ: 11.12

158. What is the best advice concerning successful aging?
a. Elderly people need to keep active and engaged.
b. Elderly people need to be allowed to disengage.
c. Elderly people should be encouraged to find a good fit between their personality, preferences, and the environment in which they live.
d. Successful aging in the elderly is virtually impossible to find.

ANS: C   DIF: Easy   REF: 377   OBJ: 11.12

TRUE/FALSE

1. Dispositional traits are also referred to as "life stories."

ANS: F   DIF: Easy   REF: 348   OBJ: 11.1

2. Self-esteem refers an overall evaluation of your worth.

ANS: T   DIF: Easy   REF: 348   OBJ: 11.1

3. Erikson and Freud both view adult personality as being primarily determined byexperiences during infancy and early childhood.

ANS: F   DIF: Moderate   REF: 349   OBJ: 11.2

4. According to the psychometric approach, personality can be characterized as a set of distinct traits on which people differ.

ANS: T   DIF: Moderate   REF: 349   OBJ: 11.2

5. Big Five traits include neuroticism, extraversion, and conscientiousness.

   ANS: T   DIF: Moderate   REF: 349-350   OBJ: 11.2
   KEY: WWW

6. When a child says, "That's me" when looking in a mirror, she is illustrating a looking-glass self.

   ANS: F   DIF: Moderate   REF: 351   OBJ: 11.3

7. Babies with difficult temperaments tend to be very passive and seldom cry.

   ANS: F   DIF: Moderate   REF: 352   OBJ: 11.4

8. Behavioral inhibition is the tendency to be shy and restrained.

   ANS: T   DIF: Moderate   REF: 352   OBJ: 11.4
   KEY: WWW

9. The ability to focus and shift one's attention is called effortful control.

   ANS: T   DIF: Moderate   REF: 353   OBJ: 11.4

10. The "ideal self" is who we wish others would be.

    ANS: F   DIF: Moderate   REF: 355   OBJ: 11.5

11. Personality is thought to "gel" during infancy.

    ANS: F   DIF: Moderate   REF: 356   OBJ: 11.6

12. Most adolescents experience a dip in self-esteem that tends to rebound in later adolescence.

    ANS: T   DIF: Moderate   REF: 357-358   OBJ: 11.7

13. Foreclosure status is characterized by no crisis and no commitment.

    ANS: F   DIF: Moderate   REF: 359   OBJ: 11.7
    KEY: WWW

14. The identity moratorium status is characterized by active exploration of identity and possible crisis.

    ANS: T   DIF: Moderate   REF: 359   OBJ: 11.8

15. The main developmental trend in vocational choice during the adolescent years involves decreasing realism.

    ANS: F   DIF: Moderate   REF: 362   OBJ: 11.8

16. Older individuals tend to adjust their ideal selves to be more in line with their real selves.

    ANS: T   DIF: Moderate   REF: 363-364   OBJ: 11.9
    KEY: WWW

17. In collectivist societies, the individual comes before the collective group.

    ANS: F   DIF: Moderate   REF: 365   OBJ: 11.9

18. Big Five personality traits tend to change dramatically following adolescence.

    ANS: F   DIF: Moderate   REF: 367-369   OBJ: 11.9

19. Erikson's psychosocial crisis of generativity versus stagnation concerns a person's life review typically conducted in very old age.

    ANS: F   DIF: Moderate   REF: 371   OBJ: 11.10

20. Successful aging in later life requires engagement in society.

    ANS: F   DIF: Moderate   REF: 377   OBJ: 11.12
    KEY: WWW

COMPLETION

1. The situational-specific ways in which people adapt to their roles is referred to as _____ adaptations.

    ANS: characteristic

    DIF: Difficult   REF: 348   OBJ: 11.1

2. Unique life stories that we construct about our past and future are called narrative _____.

    ANS: identities

    DIF: Moderate   REF: 348   OBJ: 11.1   KEY: WWW

3. McCrae and Costa developed the _____ trait theory of personality.

    ANS: Big Five

    DIF: Moderate   REF: 349   OBJ: 11.2

4. When a child classifies himself into social groups based on age and sex, he is forming a _____ self.

    ANS: categorical

    DIF: Moderate   REF: 351   OBJ: 11.2   KEY: WWW

5. Thomas and Chess characterized infants who were even-tempered and happy as having an _____ temperament.

    ANS: easy

    DIF: Moderate   REF: 352   OBJ: 11.4

6. Thomas and Chess characterized infants who were highly irritable and irregular in habit as having a _____ temperament.

    ANS: difficult

    DIF: Moderate   REF: 352   OBJ: 11.4   KEY: WWW

7. The tendency to be extremely shy or distressed in response to unfamiliar situations is called behavioral _____.

    ANS: inhibition

    DIF: Moderate   REF: 352   OBJ: 11.4

8. _____ affectivity is the tendency for an individual to be easily frustrated, sad, or irritable.

    ANS: Negativity

    DIF: Difficult   REF: 353   OBJ: 11.4

9. The extent to which an environment matches a child's needs is referred to as the _____ of fit.

    ANS: goodness

    DIF: Easy   REF: 353   OBJ: 11.4

10. _____ identity status is characterized by no commitment made and no crisis experienced.

    ANS: Diffusion

    DIF: Difficult   REF: 359   OBJ: 11.8

11. _____ identity status is characterized by both commitment made and crisis experienced.

    ANS: Identity achievement

    DIF: Difficult   REF: 359   OBJ: 11.8   KEY: WWW

12. People in _____ cultures define themselves in terms of group membership and place great emphasis on group goals.

    ANS: collectivist

    DIF: Moderate   REF: 365   OBJ: 11.9

13. Erikson's first psychosocial stage involves a crisis of trust versus _____.

ANS: mistrust

DIF: Easy   REF: 370   OBJ: 11.10

14. Erikson characterized adolescence as involving a crisis of _____ versus role confusion.

ANS: identity

DIF: Moderate   REF: 370   OBJ: 11.10

15. The final of Erikson's psychosocial stages involves the crisis of integrity versus _____.

ANS: despair

DIF: Moderate   REF: 371   OBJ: 11.10   KEY: WWW

16. According to Erikson, most middle-aged people are dealing with a crisis of _____ versus stagnation.

ANS: generativity

DIF: Moderate   REF: 371   OBJ: 11.10

17. Levinson is best associated with his belief in a _____ crisis.

ANS: midlife

DIF: Moderate   REF: 372   OBJ: 11.10

18. Many researchers have suggested that the best strategy for coping with aging involves selective _____ with compensation.

ANS: optimization

DIF: Difficult   REF: 373-374   OBJ: 11.11

19. Atchley referred to the retirement period characterized by a relish for one's newfound freedom as being the _____ phase of retirement.

ANS: honeymoon

DIF: Difficult   REF: 375   OBJ: 11.11

20. _____ theory argues that successful aging involves a withdrawal from society.

ANS: Disengagement

DIF: Moderate   REF: 377   OBJ: 11.12

ESSAY

1. How does the development of self proceed from birth though age three?

   ANS: Answer not provided   REF: 351-352   OBJ: 11.3

2. What is self-esteem, and how does it change across the lifespan? What factors influence self-esteem in positive or negative directions?

   ANS: Answer not provided   REF: 355-356 & 357-358   OBJ: 11.5 & 11.7

3. Describe Marcia's model of identity achievement by discussing the development of a hypothetical child/adolescent and their search for a religious identity.

   ANS: Answer not provided   REF: 358-360   OBJ: 11.8

4. In what way might one's culture and ethnic identity impact self-concept?

   ANS: Answer not provided   REF: 361 & 365-367   OBJ: 11.8 & 11.9

5. Discuss the issues of real and ideal self in adulthood. How does the gap between these two concepts tend to change between young and older adulthood?

   ANS: Answer not provided   REF: 363-365   OBJ: 11.9

6. Describe Erikson's eight psychosocial stages.

   ANS: Answer not provided   REF: 370-372   OBJ: 11.10

7. What have researchers found concerning selective optimization with compensation in aging workers? How do older individuals react to retirement?

   ANS: Answer not provided   REF: 373-378   OBJ: 11.11

8. In what ways does Erikson's view of personality development differ from Freud's view?

   ANS: Answer not provided   REF: 349   OBJ: 11.2   KEY: WWW

9. How would a psychometric theorist use the concept of the "Big Five" to describe personality?

   ANS: Answer not provided   REF: 349-350   OBJ: 11.2   KEY: WWW

10. How are the concepts of behavioral inhibition, easy, difficult, and slow-to-warm-up, related to temperament?

    ANS: Answer not provided   REF: 352-353   OBJ: 11.3   KEY: WWW

MULTIPLE CHOICE

1. _____ includes all behavioral characteristics that a society considers appropriate for men or women.
   a. Biological sex
   b. Genetic sex
   c. Hormonal sex
   d. Gender

   ANS: D   DIF: Easy   REF: 382   OBJ: 12.1

2. In the hypothetical country of Whoville, only females are allowed to cook roast beast. This best exemplifies a _____ difference.
   a. gender
   b. biological sex
   c. psychosomatic
   d. prenatal

   ANS: A   DIF: Easy   REF: 382   OBJ: 12.1

3. Which is the most common chromosome pattern for a female?
   a. XX
   b. XY
   c. YY
   d. XO

   ANS: A   DIF: Easy   REF: 382   OBJ: 12.1

4. Which is the most common chromosome pattern for a male?
   a. XX
   b. XY
   c. YY
   d. XO

   ANS: B   DIF: Easy   REF: 382   OBJ: 12.1
   KEY: WWW

5. Each society generally has a set of expectations regarding the behaviors and traits that are considered appropriate for males as compared to females. These sets of expectations are
   a. gender roles.
   b. gender-role stereotypes.
   c. gender types.
   d. gender identities.

   ANS: A   DIF: Moderate   REF: 382   OBJ: 12.1

6. In the hypothetical country called Ozland, females drive trucks and males drive cars. This indicates that Ozland has
   a. androgyny.
   b. joint attention.
   c. gender roles.
   d. behavioral inhibition.

   ANS: C   DIF: Moderate   REF: 382   OBJ: 12.1

7. The key element of gender-role norms is that within a society, they are viewed as
   a. stereotypes.
   b. desirable characteristics.
   c. genetically-based.
   d. destructive.

   ANS: B   DIF: Moderate   REF: 382   OBJ: 12.1

8. While Charlotte is growing up, she is socialized into believing that a woman should stay home and take care of the children while men go off to work and "bring home the bacon." This message best reflects a
   a. gender-role stereotype.
   b. gender type.
   c. gender identity.
   d. gender-role norm.

   ANS: D   DIF: Difficult   REF: 382   OBJ: 12.1
   KEY: WWW

9. The defining element of gender-role stereotypes is that they are
   a. uncommon.
   b. largely inaccurate.
   c. genetically-based.
   d. highly desirable traits.

   ANS: B   DIF: Moderate   REF: 382   OBJ: 12.1

10. Mr. and Mrs. Hill have two children, Jack and Jill. They make no bones about telling Jack that he should be an engineer, since men are good at math, and that Jill should be a nurse, since women are good at taking care of other people. Given the fact that male-female differences in math and nurturing are questionable, the Hill's message best reflects a(n)
    a. Electra complex.
    b. gender-role stereotype.
    c. sexual orientation.
    d. sex difference.

    ANS: B   DIF: Difficult   REF: 382   OBJ: 12.1

11. Overgeneralizations about attributes for each sex are called
    a. sex differences.
    b. androgyny.
    c. gender-role norms.
    d. gender-role stereotypes.

    ANS: D   DIF: Easy   REF: 382   OBJ: 12.1
    KEY: WWW

12. Agency is to communality as
    a. masculine is to feminine.
    b. sex is to gender.
    c. heterosexual is to homosexual.
    d. attitude is to behavior.

    ANS: A   DIF: Difficult   REF: 383   OBJ: 12.1

13. Which is the best example of a communality role in American society?
    a. Telling off a bad waiter
    b. Working on a project by one's self
    c. Caring for a sick child
    d. Winning a tennis tournament

    ANS: C   DIF: Moderate   REF: 383   OBJ: 12.1

14. Communality roles are designed to prepare someone to be
    a. aggressive.
    b. independent.
    c. connected to others.
    d. achievement oriented.

    ANS: C   DIF: Moderate   REF: 383   OBJ: 12.1

15. A brain "hardwired" for _____ would always show a high level of sensitivity toward others.
    a. communality
    b. agency
    c. systemize
    d. gender identity

    ANS: A   DIF: Moderate   REF: 383   OBJ: 12.1

16. "Agency" is defined as the
   a. central aspect of the masculine gender role.
   b. acquisition of one's sexual orientation.
   c. confusion felt when one encounters a gender-role stereotype.
   d. desire for a sexual relationship with a parent.

   ANS: A   DIF: Moderate   REF: 383   OBJ: 12.1

17. The goal of the gender role aspect called "agency" is to prepare a person for
   a. the acquisition of sexist language.   c. developing a "nurturing side."
   b. individual achievement.   d. the onset of sexual urges in puberty .

   ANS: B   DIF: Moderate   REF: 383   OBJ: 12.1

18. Which is the best example of an agency aspect of gender?
   a. Emotionality   c. Connectedness to others
   b. Dominance   d. Linguistic skills

   ANS: B   DIF: Moderate   REF: 383   OBJ: 12.1
   KEY: WWW

19. Baron-Cohen claims that a man's tendency to systemize is the result of
   a. gender training.   c. the androgyny shift.
   b. a double standard.   d. having a male brain.

   ANS: D   DIF: Difficult   REF: 383   OBJ: 12.1

20. Which trait is best associated with the tendency to systemize?
   a. Exploration of how things work   c. Depression over academic failure
   b. Worry about how others treat you   d. Hoy over having lots of friends

   ANS: A   DIF: Moderate   REF: 383   OBJ: 12.1

21. Research on gender-role stereotypes has shown that in the United States during the past few
   decades, gender-role stereotypes have
   a. remained the same as in the past.   c. become even stronger.
   b. virtually disappeared.   d. changed slightly.

   ANS: D   DIF: Easy   REF: 383   OBJ: 12.1

22. Concerning gender stereotypes in the 1990s vs. today,
   a. more males now view themselves as having no communality traits.
   b. more women now view themselves as having more agentic traits.
   c. more boys who reject communality traits are developing homosexual or bisexual
      orientations.
   d. more girls who reject agentic traits are experiencing teen pregnancy.

   ANS: B   DIF: Moderate   REF: 383   OBJ: 12.1

23. The gender similarity hypothesis proposes that males and females are similar on
   a. all psychological variables.   c. most physical variables.
   b. most psychological variables.   d. all physical variables.

   ANS: B   DIF: Moderate   REF: 384   OBJ: 12.2

645

24. If Kirsten believes in the saying, "Boys and girls are more alike than different," she is clearly a fan of
    a. psychodynamic theory.
    b. a double standard.
    c. the gender similarity hypothesis.
    d. gender segregation.

    ANS: C   DIF: Easy   REF: 384   OBJ: 12.2

25. The best summary concerning differences in verbal abilities is that
    a. males appear to have a large advantage.
    b. males appear to have a small advantage.
    c. females appear to have a small advantage.
    d. females appear to have a large advantage.

    ANS: C   DIF: Moderate   REF: 384   OBJ: 12.2

26. Males out-perform females on tests of mental rotation
    a. only until about 10 years of age.
    b. only during adolescence.
    c. only during adulthood.
    d. throughout the lifespan.

    ANS: D   DIF: Moderate   REF: 384   OBJ: 12.2

27. Research on gender differences in math ability has shown that
    a. males have superior computational skills.
    b. females obtain slightly higher grades in math classes.
    c. males score higher on math tests in all countries.
    d. females express more negative attitudes about math.

    ANS: B   DIF: Moderate   REF: 384   OBJ: 12.2

28. Which is true regarding common gender stereotypes?
    a. There is solid research evidence that females generally have better visual/spatial skills than males.
    b. There is consistent research support for the fact that males are more aggressive than females.
    c. Females are more vulnerable to diseases and disorders than males.
    d. There are no gender stereotypes that are consistently supported by research.

    ANS: B   DIF: Moderate   REF: 384   OBJ: 12.2

29. With regard to actual differences between males and females, research has consistently found that, on average,
    a. females have poorer memory skills.
    b. females are more physically aggressive.
    c. males perform better on verbal tasks.
    d. males are more physically active.

    ANS: D   DIF: Moderate   REF: 384   OBJ: 12.2

30. The statement, "Girls are more _____," has received the most empirical research support.
    a. vulnerable to prenatal disorders
    b. empathic
    c. likely to develop antisocial behaviors
    d. likely to use a computer

    ANS: B   DIF: Moderate   REF: 384   OBJ: 12.2

31. Research on gender differences suggests that girls are
    a. more compliant than boys in all situations.
    b. more demanding than boys.
    c. more compliant than boys with authority figures but not with peers.
    d. more likely than boys to engage in risky behavior.

    ANS: C   DIF: Difficult   REF: 384   OBJ: 12.2

32. Which of the following tends to be found at higher levels in males?
    a. Anxiety   c. Being tactful
    b. Empathy   d. Confidence in use of computers

    ANS: D   DIF: Easy   REF: 385   OBJ: 12.2
    KEY: WWW

33. If American children Nicholas (a boy) and Alexandra (a girl) are typical of other members of
    their sex, then you would predict that
    a. Nicholas would likely be more cooperative.
    b. Alexandra would show more interest in caring for an infant.
    c. Nicholas would be more cautious.
    d. Alexandra would be more likely to be learning disabled.

    ANS: B   DIF: Moderate   REF: 384   OBJ: 12.2

34. What is the best conclusion about psychological differences between the sexes?
    a. Males and females are far more similar than different.
    b. Gender stereotypes that are not supported by research can have no effect on actual
       behavioral or psychological differences between males and females.
    c. Most gender-role stereotypes have been eliminated in our society.
    d. When differences are found between males and females, it means that nearly all
       members of one gender perform better or worse than nearly all members of the
       other gender.

    ANS: A   DIF: Moderate   REF: 385   OBJ: 12.2

35. If we identified 100 typical males and 100 typical females and assessed them across a variety
    of psychological attributes, chances are that about _____ of the observed differences could be
    attributed to whether the person was male or female.
    a. 0%   c. 25%
    b. 5%   d. 50%

    ANS: B   DIF: Moderate   REF: 385   OBJ: 12.2

36. The social-role hypothesis predicts that
    a. once formed, gender differences cannot be changed.
    b. men and women adopt different roles in society because they differ in basic traits
       and abilities.
    c. gender differences vary from culture to culture depending on the roles men and
       women hold in each society.
    d. gender differences are fairly universal because they originate in biological
       differences.

    ANS: C   DIF: Easy   REF: 385   OBJ: 12.3

647

37. Eagly's social-role hypothesis argues that gender-role stereotypes
   a. result from biological differences between males and females.
   b. are driven by the social context in which males and females find themselves.
   c. are seldom unfounded.
   d. tend to be more negatively biased against males.

   ANS: B   DIF: Moderate   REF: 385   OBJ: 12.3

38. If you believe in the social-role hypothesis, then you would be most likely to argue that the most effective way to change the stereotype of men as dominant would be to
   a. reduce the average amount of testosterone in the male body.
   b. tell men that it is okay to display their "feminine side."
   c. ban the use of the terms masculine and feminine.
   d. put women in charge of every major business.

   ANS: D   DIF: Difficult   REF: 385   OBJ: 12.2

39. Which statement concerning sex differences is true?
   a. Although actual psychological gender differences are small, they make a major difference in a society.
   b. Although actual psychological gender differences are large, they make little difference in a society.
   c. Actual gender psychological differences are small, and they make little difference in a society.
   d. Actual gender psychological differences are large, and they make a major difference in a society.

   ANS: A   DIF: Moderate   REF: 385   OBJ: 12.3

40. If asked to list the top occupations held by women in the U.S., you should avoid saying,
   a. "secretary."   c. "doctor."
   b. "teacher."   d. "cashier."

   ANS: C   DIF: Easy   REF: 386   OBJ: 12.3

41. Shawn and Dawn are a typical U.S. couple. What makes them a little unusual is that Dawn works outside the home while Shawn is a stay-at-home dad. Research has indicated that Shawn and Dawn most likely
   a. divide their at-home labor responsibilities along traditional lines.
   b. divide their at-home labor responsibilities along gender-neutral lines.
   c. divide their at-home labor responsibilities in direct opposition traditional lines.
   d. do not divide their at-home labor responsibilities.

   ANS: A   DIF: Moderate   REF: 386   OBJ: 12.3

42. Non-anatomical differences between newborn females and males are best described as
   a. small yet consistent.   c. large yet inconsistent
   b. large and consistent.   d. small and inconsistent

   ANS: D   DIF: Easy   REF: 386   OBJ: 12.3

43. Adults are asked to interact with an unknown infant. Half of the adults are told that the infant is "Steve" and the other half are told that the infant is "Stacy." What are you likely to observe of these interactions?
   a. At such a young age, there are not likely to be any differences in how adults treat the infant in the two conditions.
   b. Adults will treat the infant similarly until it begins to act in stereotypical ways, and then there will be differences in the adults' reactions to the infant.
   c. Adults will be able to detect the real biological sex of the infant, regardless of whether they are told the infant is "Steve" or "Stacy."
   d. Adults are likely to rate "Steve" as strong and brave and "Stacy" as soft and cuddly.

   ANS: D   DIF: Moderate   REF: 386   OBJ: 12.4

44. At what age do infants first appear to demonstrate cross-modal associations concerning gender information by looking longer at a female face when a female voice is heard vs. when a male voice is heard?
   a. 1 hour   c. 1 month
   b. 1 week   d. 1 year

   ANS: D   DIF: Difficult   REF: 386   OBJ: 12.4

45. The initial awareness that you are either a boy or girl is referred to as
   a. gender identity.   c. gender intensification.
   b. gender segregation.   d. gender stability.

   ANS: A   DIF: Easy   REF: 387   OBJ: 12.4

46. For the first time in her life, little Glenda looks at her mom and says, "Glenda is a girl." This statement indicates that Glenda has just achieved
   a. gender intensification.   c. gender identity.
   b. gender segregation.   d. gender stability.

   ANS: C   DIF: Moderate   REF: 387   OBJ: 12.4

47. Most children clearly demonstrate basic gender identity by
   a. 1 to 1½ years of age.   c. 3½ to 4 years of age.
   b. 2½ to 3 years of age.   d. 5 to 6 years of age.

   ANS: B   DIF: Difficult   REF: 387   OBJ: 12.4

48. The process by which children become aware of the fact that they are either male or female and that there are different cultural expectations concerning the pattern of behavior for the two sexes is called
   a. androgenizing.   c. sexual orienting.
   b. gender-role stereotyping.   d. gender typing.

   ANS: D   DIF: Moderate   REF: 387   OBJ: 12.5

49. Through her mother's efforts, Olive has just come to realize that she is a girl and has also begun to acquire behaviors expected of girls. This process is best classified as
   a. gender typing.
   b. androgenizing.
   c. sexual orienting.
   d. the double standard.

   ANS: A   DIF: Moderate   REF: 387   OBJ: 12.5

50. Children appear to learn gender stereotypes
   a. at about the time they understand that they cannot change their sex.
   b. during the first few months after birth.
   c. around the point that they become aware of their basic gender identities.
   d. around the end of the elementary school years.

   ANS: C   DIF: Moderate   REF: 387-388   OBJ: 12.5

51. Which statement concerning toddlers' understanding of gender roles is true?
   a. Females appear to understand gender-based activities much earlier than males.
   b. Males appear to understand gender-based activities much earlier than females.
   c. Females and males appear to understand gender-based activities at the same age.
   d. Neither males nor female toddlers show any understanding of gender-based activities.

   ANS: C   DIF: Diffficult   REF: 388   OBJ: 12.5

52. Who would a typical 5-year-old in the U.S. believe to be most competent at their job?
   a. A female construction worker
   b. A male nurse
   c. A female secretary
   d. A male stay-at-home dad

   ANS: C   DIF: Moderate   REF: 388   OBJ: 12.5

53. With regard to children's views of gender stereotypes, research has indicated that
   a. 9-year-olds are more bothered than 5-year-olds when kids engage in activities that violate gender-role stereotypes.
   b. 5-year-olds are more upset by violations of gender-role stereotypes than are 9-year-olds.
   c. concern about violations of gender stereotypes is very high throughout childhood (age four through nine).
   d. concern about violations of gender stereotypes is nonexistent until the teenage years.

   ANS: B   DIF: Moderate   REF: 388   OBJ: 12.5

54. When asked if it is OK for a boy to play with dolls, Geoffery says, "Absolutely not, it's a rule that only girls can play with dolls." Based on research on gender roles and stereotypes, what age is Geoffery's most likely age?
   a. 3
   b. 6
   c. 8
   d. 11

   ANS: B   DIF: Difficult   REF: 388   OBJ: 12.5

650

55. What effect does the establishment of a firm sense of gender identity tend to have on children?
    a. They develop more rigid rules concerning appropriate "boy" and "girl" behavior.
    b. They develop more flexible rules concerning appropriate "boy" and "girl" behavior.
    c. They abandon all rules concerning appropriate "boy" and "girl" behavior.
    d. They initially identify rules concerning appropriate "boy" and "girl" behavior.

    ANS: B   DIF: Difficult   REF: 389   OBJ: 12.5

56. The establishment of a preference for same-sexed friendships is first apparent by around age
    a. 12 months.   c. 48 months.
    b. 30 months.   d. 60 months.

    ANS: B   DIF: Moderate   REF: 389   OBJ: 12.5

57. Spanky, Alfalfa, and the rest of the boys in the first-grade class have decided that from now on boys will only play with boys and never with girls. This decision provides a nice example of the concept of
    a. gender stereotyping.   c. gender segregation.
    b. gender typing.   d. gender stability.

    ANS: C   DIF: Moderate   REF: 389   OBJ: 12.5

58. Which best illustrates gender segregation?
    a. The fact that boys are better at spatial abilities than girls.
    b. Seeing one group consisting of all girls playing at one end of a gym and an all-boy group playing at the other end.
    c. The fact that girls are more emotional than boys.
    d. Seeing a sign that says both boys and girls can try out for the dance team.

    ANS: B   DIF: Moderate   REF: 389   OBJ: 12.5

59. Which best illustrates the concept of gender segregation?
    a. A "girls only" scout troop
    b. The statement "I am a boy and I will always be a boy"
    c. The belief that males are more aggressive
    d. The initial realization of the existence of two sexes (males and females)

    ANS: A   DIF: Moderate   REF: 389   OBJ: 12.5
    KEY: WWW

60. It was proposed that young children initially segregate themselves into same-sex peer groups because
    a. their play styles are different from one another, making it difficult for the two groups to play together.
    b. the physical differences between boys and girls make it unlikely that they could find common interests.
    c. biological predispositions lead children to interact with others who are most like them.
    d. children are reinforced for playing with opposite-sex children by adults.

    ANS: A   DIF: Moderate   REF: 389   OBJ: 12.5

651

61. Five-year-old Penny draws clear lines between what types of games boys and girls should play and makes every effort to avoid playing with boys like her neighbor Pee Wee. Research has shown that preschoolers with attitudes like Penny tend to be
    a. aggressive.
    b. shy.
    c. rejected by peers.
    d. well adjusted.

    ANS: D   DIF: Moderate   REF: 389   OBJ: 12.5

62. In the U.S., which 8-year-old would be most likely to be ridiculed and teased by his or her classmates?
    a. A male who identifies himself as masculine.
    b. A female who identifies herself as feminine.
    c. A male who identifies himself as a "sissy."
    d. A female who identifies herself as a "tomboy."

    ANS: C   DIF: Moderate   REF: 389   OBJ: 12.5

63. Which two groups view violations of gender roles most negatively?
    a. Young elementary school-aged children and adolescents
    b. Preschoolers and elementary school-aged children
    c. Middle-school-aged children and adolescents
    d. Preschoolers and adults

    ANS: A   DIF: Moderate   REF: 390   OBJ: 12.6

64. Based on research by Stoddart and Turiel, which two people would you expect to hold the most negative attitudes concerning the violation of gender roles (e.g., a boy wearing nail polish)?
    a. A 5-year-old and a 7-year-old
    b. A 5-year-old and a 13-year-old
    c. A 7-year-old and a 9-year-old
    d. A 9-year-old and a 13-year-old

    ANS: B   DIF: Difficult   REF: 390   OBJ: 12.6
    KEY: WWW

65. In general, young adolescents
    a. view gender-role violations as a sign of psychological abnormality.
    b. are more accepting of peers' cross-sex interests than they are likely to be as adults.
    c. make less negative judgments of peers who violate traditional gender roles than do those in middle childhood.
    d. show significantly fewer sex difference on tests of cognitive abilities.

    ANS: A   DIF: Moderate   REF: 390   OBJ: 12.6

66. Gender intensification involves an increased
    a. desire to be viewed as androgynous.
    b. intolerance of any deviation from proscribed gender roles.
    c. drive to have sex with one's parent.
    d. experimentation with sexual orientation.

    ANS: B   DIF: Moderate   REF: 390   OBJ: 12.6

67. An example of gender intensification would involve
    a. boys noticing that some girls like romance.
    b. a boy asserting his masculinity among his peers.
    c. a girl acting like a "tomboy."
    d. a boy acting like a "sissy."

    ANS: B   DIF: Moderate   REF: 390   OBJ: 12.6

68. Gender intensification appears to be driven by
    a. the desire to have sex with one's parent.
    b. prenatal hormones and social experiences in infancy.
    c. the need to experiment with one's gender role.
    d. hormonal changes at puberty and peer pressure to conform to gender roles.

    ANS: D   DIF: Moderate   REF: 390   OBJ: 12.6

69. According to Money and Ehrhardt's biosocial theory of gender-role development,
    a. Freud was correct when he said that "biology is destiny."
    b. children begin acting like boys or girls once they acquire gender identity and constancy.
    c. several critical biological events set the stage for different social reactions to males and females.
    d. pubertal hormones alone account for gender-role development.

    ANS: C   DIF: Moderate   REF: 391   OBJ: 12.7

70. Biosocial theory views the sex chromosome pattern of an infant (e.g., XX) as
    a. irrelevant to gender-role development.
    b. a starting point for biological differentiation of the sexes.
    c. the determinant one's gender.
    d. the after effect of gender-identification.

    ANS: B   DIF: Moderate   REF: 391   OBJ: 12.7

71. With regard to biological differentiation of the sexes, which is FALSE?
    a. It is possible for a male (XY) fetus to develop a female internal reproductive system.
    b. The male hormone testosterone affects the development of the brain and nervous system.
    c. External genitalia are fully differentiated by the fourth week after conception.
    d. Hormones influence the development of the testes and ovaries.

    ANS: C   DIF: Difficult   REF: 391   OBJ: 12.7

653

72. A baby with an XY chromosome pattern
    a. can only develop the internal and external sex system of a male.
    b. can develop the internal system of a male or female, but can only develop the external genitalia of a male.
    c. can develop the external system of a male or female, but can only develop the internal reproductive system of a male.
    d. can develop the internal or external sex and reproductive system of either sex .

    ANS: D   DIF: Moderate   REF: 391   OBJ: 12.7
    KEY: WWW

73. Which biological event directly results in the growth of a penis in a male fetus?
    a. Receiving a Y chromosome at conception
    b. Secretion of testosterone by the testes
    c. Absence of the release of female hormones
    d. The presence of a gene on the X chromosome

    ANS: B   DIF: Difficult   REF: 391   OBJ: 12.7

74. Which statement concerning the development of genitalia and internal reproductive structures is true?
    a. A fertilized egg can acquire the anatomical and physiological features of either sex.
    b. Only an XY chromosome fetus can develop a penis.
    c. Only an XY chromosome fetus can develop testes.
    d. While both XY and XX chromosome fetuses can develop a penis, only the XX chromosome fetus can develop the internal reproductive system of a female.

    ANS: A   DIF: Moderate   REF: 391   OBJ: 12.7

75. Money and Ehrhardt's biosocial theory of gender typing suggests all of the following EXCEPT
    a. gender-role development is strongly influenced by socialization.
    b. there are critical periods for the establishment of gender identity.
    c. early biological developments influence how parents label and treat a child at birth.
    d. fetal chromosomal differences (e.g., XX versus XY) are the most important factors in determining gender-role behavior.

    ANS: D   DIF: Difficult   REF: 391   OBJ: 12.7

76. Androgenized females are girls who
    a. have been exposed prenatally to male hormones.
    b. are born with only a single X sex-chromosome.
    c. fail to develop any external genitalia.
    d. are best characterized as "excessively feminine."

    ANS: A   DIF: Moderate   REF: 392   OBJ: 12.7

77. Some individuals inherit an XX chromosome pattern but are exposed prenatally to drugs that are converted to male hormones once in the body. These individuals are likely to
   a. physically resemble females but behaviorally act like males.
   b. look and act no differently as a result of this prenatal exposure.
   c. have masculinized genitalia at birth but lose this appearance at puberty and become indistinguishable from others.
   d. have masculinized genitalia and behave in more "masculine ways."

   ANS: D   DIF: Moderate   REF: 392   OBJ: 12.7

78. _____ females have external genitalia that resemble those of a boy.
   a. Androgynous   c. Androgenized
   b. Gender typed   d. Gender consistent

   ANS: C   DIF: Easy   REF: 392   OBJ: 12.7
   KEY: WWW

79. What is the most likely behavioral outcome of exposing a female rhesus monkey to testosterone during its prenatal time of development?
   a. It will be unable to become pregnant.
   b. It will show significant improvements in spatial skills.
   c. It will attempt to sexually "mount" male partners when it reaches sexual maturity.
   d. It will show significant declines in aggressive behavior.

   ANS: C   DIF: Moderate   REF: 392   OBJ: 12.7

80. What evidence did Money and Ehrhardt use as the basis for concluding that there is a critical period for the establishment of gender identity?
   a. Hormones must be released prenatally to have any impact on behavior.
   b. Sex reassignment can be successfully done when a child has achieved gender identity, but not once a child has achieved gender stability.
   c. Sex reassignment before 18 months of age causes few adjustment problems, while reassignment after 3 years of age is very difficult.
   d. Sex reassignment while still in the preoperational stage of development causes few adjustment problems, while reassignment once concrete operational thought has begun is very difficult.

   ANS: C   DIF: Moderate   REF: 393   OBJ: 12.7

81. What "lesson" was learned through the life and death of Money's sex-reassignment patient Bruce/Brenda/David?
   a. Life as a female is much easier than life as a male
   b. Gender identity may not be as pliable as once thought
   c. Reassigning sex prior to age 2 has little impact on later self-conceptions of gender
   d. Any surgical procedure may result in potentially deadly medical complications

   ANS: B   DIF: Difficult   REF: 394   OBJ: 12.7

82. Research on individuals from the Dominican Republic who are raised as girls (due to the ambiguous genitalia) but become males following puberty has challenged the Money and Ehrhardt argument that
    a. genes play a key role in gender development.
    b. reconstructive surgery and sex reassignment always result in gender dysfunction.
    c. males have superior spatial and math skills.
    d. socialization during the first three years of life is critical.

    ANS: D   DIF: Difficult   REF: 394   OBJ: 12.7

83. From the time they are born, twins Johnny (a boy) and Joannie (a girl) are treated differently. For example, whenever Johnny plays with a truck, his parents praise his behavior. Whenever Joannie shows an interest in a doll, her parents praise her actions. A social learning theorist would likely argue that this _____ will likely lead to distinct gender roles for Johnny and Joannie.
    a. observational learning   c. systemizing
    b. parental identification   d. differential reinforcement

    ANS: D   DIF: Moderate   REF: 393   OBJ: 12.7

84. A social learning theorist would use the concept of _____ to explain how a child watching her mother engage in feminine activities would directly lead the child to acquire a feminine gender identity.
    a. observational learning   c. differential reinforcement
    b. androgyny shift   d. agency

    ANS: A   DIF: Moderate   REF: 393   OBJ: 12.7

85. Research by Morrongiello and Hogg (2004) found that when asked to imagine their children misbehaving in some dangerous way (e.g., bicycling fast down a hill), moms reported that they felt _____ toward their sons and _____ toward their daughters.
    a. indifference; sadness   c. sadness; indifference
    b. anger; disappointment   d. disappointment; anger

    ANS: B   DIF: Difficult   REF: 393   OBJ: 12.7

86. Research by Morrongiello and Hogg (2004) found that when asked to prevent future risky behavior in a child who had misbehaved in some dangerous way (e.g., bicycling fast down a hill), moms reported that they would
    a. set more rules for both boys and girls.
    b. not intervene with the boys but would set more rules with girls.
    c. not intervene with the girls but would set more rules with boys.
    d. not intervene with either boys or girls as risky behavior was "in their blood."

    ANS: B   DIF: Difficult   REF: 393   OBJ: 12.7
    KEY: WWW

87. In families where parents show clear patterns of differential reinforcement concerning sex-appropriate behavior, children tend to
    a. be androgynous.
    b. develop strong sex-appropriate toy preferences.
    c. seldom label themselves as a boy or girl.
    d. develop few gender-role stereotypes.

    ANS: B   DIF: Moderate   REF: 393   OBJ: 12.7

88. Research on reinforcement of sex-appropriate behavior indicates that
    a. fathers are more likely than mothers to discourage youngsters for playing with gender-inappropriate toys.
    b. peers are more critical of cross-sex behavior in the infant years than in later childhood.
    c. while impacting gender-role attitudes, parental reinforcement appears not to impact children's behavior on sex-related tasks (e.g., mathematics).
    d. differential reinforcement of sex-appropriate behavior typically begins when a child reaches kindergarten.

    ANS: A   DIF: Moderate   REF: 393   OBJ: 12.7

89. Which would best fit with the theory that differential treatment by parents negatively influences math skills in a child through the creation of self-fulfilling prophecy?
    a. Math-talented parents tend to encourage their children to do well in math.
    b. Math-untalented parents tend to discourage their children from doing well in math.
    c. Parents attribute their daughter's math success to luck and not ability so the daughter becomes convinced that she is not good at math but rather gets lucky on math tests sometimes.
    d. Son's math performance is not good (and his parents tell him so), but he decides to take more math to challenge himself.

    ANS: C   DIF: Difficult   REF: 393 & 395   OBJ: 12.7

90. Audrey grows up in a family in which her father provides at-home daycare and her mother is a construction worker. A social learning theorist would be most likely to explain Audrey's unusual attitudes (i.e., she loves trucks and hates dolls) in terms of
    a. the Electra complex.
    b. observational learning.
    c. a double standard.
    d. gender segregation.

    ANS: B   DIF: Moderate   REF: 393 & 395   OBJ: 12.7
    KEY: WWW

91. Which type of theorist would be most likely to argue that watching videos in which males are rewarded for sexual violence would directly lead to them engaging in violent sex acts in order to be manly?
    a. A psychodynamic theorist
    b. A biosocial theorist
    c. A social learning theorist
    d. A humanist

    ANS: C   DIF: Moderate   REF: 393 & 395   OBJ: 12.7
    KEY: WWW

92. Five-year-old Emeril loves watching cooking shows on television. Emeril's dad is very concerned that by watching these shows, Emeril will become feminine. Which type of theorist would be most likely to agree with Emeril's dad's concern over the impact of television on gender-role development?
    a. A psychodynamic theorist
    b. A biosocial theorist
    c. A social learning theorist
    d. A humanist

    ANS: C   DIF: Moderate   REF: 393 & 395   OBJ: 12.7

93. Research on gender portrayals in of characters in picture and elementary school books found that
    a. age-old sexist portrayals of men and women are now virtually nonexistent.
    b. in most picture books, mothers are absent from families.
    c. female characters are often still portrayed as passive and helpless.
    d. male characters tend to promote non-violent solutions to problems.

    ANS: C   DIF: Easy   REF: 395   OBJ: 12.7

94. In which type of media outlet would you expect to find the strongest portrayal of traditional gender stereotypes (i.e., the aggressive male and the victimized female)?
    a. Television
    b. Picture books
    c. Video games
    d. Elementary textbooks

    ANS: C   DIF: Easy   REF: 395   OBJ: 12.7

95. With regard to gender-role development, social learning theorists have been criticized for
    a. portraying children as passive participants in the developmental process.
    b. overemphasizing the role of biological factors.
    c. placing too little emphasis on the role of differential reinforcement.
    d. denying the role that the media (e.g., television) play in promoting gender typing.

    ANS: A   DIF: Moderate   REF: 395   OBJ: 12.7

96. According to Kohlberg's cognitive-developmental theory of gender typing, gender-role development
    a. is driven by hormonal changes.
    b. is highly dependent on the successful mastery of the Oedipus or Electra complex.
    c. depends on stage like changes in thinking.
    d. first begins as children enter puberty.

    ANS: C   DIF: Easy   REF: 396   OBJ: 12.7

97. A major theme of Kohlberg's cognitive-developmental theory of gender typing involves a child engaging in.
    a. resolution of the Oedipal complex.
    b. an androgyny shift.
    c. repression.
    d. self-socialization.

    ANS: D   DIF: Moderate   REF: 396   OBJ: 12.7

658

98. "I am a boy. Therefore I want to do the things boys do." This statement is reflective of which theoretical perspective regarding gender-role development?
   a. Biosocial theory
   b. Cognitive-developmental theory
   c. Psychoanalytic theory
   d. Social-learning theory

   ANS: B   DIF: Difficult   REF: 396   OBJ: 12.7

99. For Kohlberg, the outcome of the three childhood stages of gender development is the acquisition of gender
   a. moratorium.
   b. flexibility.
   c. androgyny.
   d. constancy.

   ANS: D   DIF: Moderate   REF: 396   OBJ: 12.7

100. According to cognitive-developmental theory, the initial phase of gender identity is established around age 2 or 3, when a child
   a. realizes that boys and girls do different things.
   b. first begins to use the terms "boy" and "girl."
   c. first begins to be treated differently by their parents.
   d. recognizes that they are a male or female.

   ANS: D   DIF: Moderate   REF: 396   OBJ: 12.7

101. Which statement indicates that a child is in Kohlberg's initial basic gender identity stage of development?
   a. "Girls do housework."
   b. "If you wear a dress, you are a girl."
   c. "I am a girl."
   d. "Some girls are pretty."

   ANS: C   DIF: Difficult   REF: 396   OBJ: 12.7

102. Whose statement indicates an understanding of gender stability?
   a. Tom, who says "Once a boy always a boy."
   b. Dick, who says, "Boys should always play rough."
   c. Harry who says, "My dad is a boy."
   d. Sally, who says, "I do girl things."

   ANS: A   DIF: Difficult   REF: 396   OBJ: 12.7

103. Gender stability is defined as understanding that
   a. there are two genders.
   b. gender is stable across situations.
   c. gender impacts what one should like and do.
   d. gender is stable across time.

   ANS: D   DIF: Easy   REF: 396   OBJ: 12.7

104. RuPaul has just come to realize that when a boy dresses like a girl, he does not actually become a girl. In cognitive-developmental theory, RuPaul appears to have just acquired
   a. basic gender identity.
   b. gender consistency.
   c. gender stability.
   d. gender segregation.

   ANS: B   DIF: Moderate   REF: 396   OBJ: 12.7

105. According to the cognitive-developmental perspective of gender typing, which is the most mature understanding?
    a. Understanding that some things are "boy things" and others are "girl things"
    b. Understanding how to correctly label one's self as male or female
    c. Understanding that gender is stable across situations
    d. Understanding that gender is stable across time

    ANS: C   DIF: Difficult   REF: 396   OBJ: 12.7
    KEY: WWW

106. The Piagetian stage of _____ appears to be most directly linked to the acquisition of gender consistency.
    a. concrete-operational thought   c. object permanence
    b. sensorimotor thought   d. formal-operational thought

    ANS: A   DIF: Moderate   REF: 396   OBJ: 12.7

107. The most common criticism of Kohlberg's cognitive-developmental explanation of gender typing is that
    a. children often acquire gender-typed behaviors and preferences before they acquire gender stability and consistency.
    b. his proposed sex differences in the rate at which boys acquire gender versus girls remains unsupported.
    c. there is no evidence that the development of cognitive skills is related to the acquisition of gender typing.
    d. it places too much emphasis on hormonal factors.

    ANS: A   DIF: Moderate   REF: 396   OBJ: 12.7

108. Martin and Halverson's gender schema model suggests that
    a. children learn gender roles solely as a result of parental reinforcement of sex-appropriate behaviors.
    b. children are intrinsically interested in learning about objects or activities that fit their own-sex schemas.
    c. inaccurate gender stereotypes are easily changed.
    d. children are passive participants in gender-role development.

    ANS: B   DIF: Moderate   REF: 396   OBJ: 12.7

109. A major difference between Kohlberg's cognitive-developmental theory and Martin and Halverson's gender-schema theory is that gender typing in the gender-schema theory
    a. does not begin to develop until after children have developed gender stability and gender consistency.
    b. begins as soon as children acquire gender identity at around 2 to 3 years of age.
    c. develops via passive exposure to external models of gender-typed behaviors.
    d. is unrelated to cognitive development.

    ANS: B   DIF: Difficult   REF: 396   OBJ: 12.7

110. Gender schemata
   a. typically begin to develop during puberty.
   b. involve behaviors, not expectations.
   c. are unaffected by social experience.
   d. influence what people pay attention to and remember regarding gender.

   ANS: D   DIF: Moderate   REF: 396   OBJ: 12.7

111. The basic premise of gender-schema theory is that children actively seek objects and/or activities that
   a. satisfy their biological drive for sex.
   b. match their own-sex schemata.
   c. they like, even if those activities are at odds with their self-concept concerning sex and gender.
   d. are valued by their parents.

   ANS: B   DIF: Moderate   REF: 396-397   OBJ: 12.7
   KEY: WWW

112. Which is the best example of an in-group-out-group gender schema?
   a. Black children are more athletic than white children.
   b. Having sex with mom is a bad idea.
   c. Boys can fight, but girls should play nice.
   d. If you are a girl, you will grow up to be a woman.

   ANS: C   DIF: Moderate   REF: 397   OBJ: 12.7

113. Four-year-old Austin believes that only girls can be nurses. At his next check-up, he happens to be seen by a male nurse. According to gender-schema theory, if a week later you were to ask Austin if boys can be nurses, his answer would most likely be
   a. "No."   c. "Yes, but only for little kids."
   b. "Yes, boys can be nurses."   d. "Yes, but only if their wife is a doctor."

   ANS: A   DIF: Difficult   REF: 397   OBJ: 12.7

114. According to gender-schema theory, if 4-year-old Ginny (who classifies herself as a girl) believes that jumping rope is a "girl thing" and playing football is a "boy thing," then she would most likely
   a. talk a lot about football, but would not play football.
   b. think that jumping rope is for her (even if she has never done it in the past).
   c. argue that boys should be made to jump rope.
   d. try playing football to make sure that it is not for her.

   ANS: B   DIF: Difficult   REF: 397   OBJ: 12.7

115. If Zsa Zsa argues that gender schemas are the key to gender acquisition, she is best characterized as a taking a _____ perspective.
   a. biosocial   c. social learning
   b. psychodynamic   d. cognitive

   ANS: D   DIF: Moderate   REF: 397   OBJ: 12.7

116. On which of the following point do most theories of gender-role development agree?
    a. Biological forces are the most important determinant of gender-role development.
    b. Children identify with their same-sex parent in order to resolve painful feelings of family conflict.
    c. Gender roles that children develop depend on an interaction between biological factors and what their society offers in terms of gender models.
    d. Gender roles depend on acquiring a certain level of cognitive development.

    ANS: C   DIF: Moderate   REF: 397-398   OBJ: 12.7

117. In general, gender roles
    a. are more differentiated during adolescence than they are among newlyweds.
    b. become more traditional and differentiated in a married couple following the birth of a child.
    c. tend to remain constant across the adult years.
    d. are more pronounced for couples when both partners are working.

    ANS: B   DIF: Moderate   REF: 398-399   OBJ: 12.8

118. Which statement concerning gender roles in adulthood is FALSE?
    a. In families where both parents work, the division of housework is 50-50.
    b. Men and women tend to develop more similar gender roles after their children have "left the nest."
    c. Marriage often leads to the development of more distinct gender roles.
    d. Gender role differences between men and women tend to decrease in older age.

    ANS: A   DIF: Moderate   REF: 399   OBJ: 12.8

119. Androgyny refers to individuals who are
    a. high in masculine traits and low in feminine traits.
    b. high in masculine traits and high in feminine traits.
    c. low in masculine traits and low in feminine traits.
    d. low in masculine traits and high in feminine traits.

    ANS: B   DIF: Easy   REF: 399   OBJ: 12.9

120. An androgynous person would have a _____ agentic score and a _____ communal score.
    a. low; low   c. high, low
    b. low; high   d. high; high

    ANS: D   DIF: Moderate   REF: 399   OBJ: 12.9
    KEY: WWW

121. On a personality test, Burt scores very low on both the agentic and communal scales. As such, he is best classified as
    a. masculine.   c. androgynous.
    b. feminine.   d. undifferentiated.

    ANS: D   DIF: Difficult   REF: 399   OBJ: 12.9

662

122. How would you demonstrate androgyny?
    a. Be both assertive and compassionate.
    b. Be both compassionate and understanding.
    c. Be both understanding and affectionate.
    d. Be both affectionate and compassionate.

    ANS: A   DIF: Moderate   REF: 399   OBJ: 12.9

123. Most college students believe that the ideal person has a(n) _____ gender type.
    a. masculine   c. androgynous
    b. feminine   d. undifferentiated

    ANS: C   DIF: Moderate   REF: 399   OBJ: 12.9

124. Sarah is an 8-year-old female who displays many male traits. What is the most likely peer reaction to Sarah?
    a. Envy   c. Rejection
    b. Delight   d. Empathy

    ANS: C   DIF: Moderate   REF: 399   OBJ: 12.9

125. The theory that becoming parents pressures males to be more "masculine" and females to be more "feminine" is referred to as the
    a. androgyny shift.   c. parental imperative.
    b. double standard.   d. gender segregation.

    ANS: C   DIF: Moderate   REF: 400   OBJ: 12.9

126. Gutmann's hypothesis regarding the "parental imperative" suggests that
    a. most women in our society feel they must have children.
    b. most males and females in our society feel they must have children.
    c. becoming parents pressures males to be more "masculine" and females to be more "feminine."
    d. becoming parents pressures young men and women to take on non-traditional gender roles.

    ANS: C   DIF: Moderate   REF: 400   OBJ: 12.9
    KEY: WWW

127. Prior to the birth of their first child, Ward and June have very strong gender-role orientation. Ward, the father, is extremely masculine while June, the mother, is extremely feminine. According to the "parental imperative," what would you expect to happen to Ward and June's gender roles following the birth of their first son, Wally?
    a. Both June and Ward will become more feminine.
    b. June will become more masculine and Ward more feminine.
    c. Both June and Ward will become more masculine.
    d. There will be little change in their gender roles.

    ANS: D   DIF: Difficult   REF: 400   OBJ: 12.9

663

128. According to the concept of androgyny shift,
   a. preschoolers believe that they can change sexes (e.g., a boy can grow up to be a mommy).
   b. during midlife, people begin to adopt some of the gender traits associated with the opposite sex.
   c. shifting from masculine to feminine or feminine to masculine will result in a change in sexual orientation.
   d. becoming less masculine and less feminine will lead to a significant improvement in mental health.

   ANS: B   DIF: Moderate   REF: 400   OBJ: 12.9

129. When he became a grandfather, Lorne retained his masculine traits but also became more nurturing and learned to cook. This best exemplifies the concept of
   a. gender segregation.   c. androgyny shift.
   b. parental imperative.   d. double standard.

   ANS: C   DIF: Moderate   REF: 400   OBJ: 12.9

130. Observations of infants and infant sexuality suggest all of the following EXCEPT
   a. they appear to derive pleasure from oral stimulation.
   b. their genitals are sensitive to stimulation.
   c. they actively seek sexual contact with other infants.
   d. they undergo what appear to be orgasms.

   ANS: C   DIF: Moderate   REF: 401-402   OBJ: 12.10

131. Which of the following is true regarding children's knowledge of sex and reproduction?
   a. Children's level of understanding is linked to their cognitive development.
   b. Children tend to rely on adult explanations for reproduction, rather than constructing their own form of understanding.
   c. By age 4, most children know that intercourse is the key process in reproduction.
   d. Understanding of the role of the egg and sperm in reproduction typically occurs around age 7.

   ANS: A   DIF: Moderate   REF: 402   OBJ: 12.11

132. According to Freud, during the school-age years, children who all been previously sexually active enter a latency period in which they repress their sexuality. Research has demonstrated that this conceptualization is
   a. right on.
   b. off target, as children younger than school age have been shown to have no interest in sexual activity.
   c. off target, as children's early sexual activity appears to continue during the school-age years.
   d. off target as the main change in sexual behavior in school age is an increase is public sexual activity.

   ANS: C   DIF: Moderate   REF: 402   OBJ: 12.11

133. Research supports all of the following EXCEPT
    a. adrenal gland activity around age 10 appears to be linked to the first sexual attraction.
    b. attitudes concerning sexual behavior vary between cultures.
    c. the first sexual attraction tends to occur prior to the maturation of the sex organs.
    d. sexual behavior in puberty is best conceptualized as being solely driven by hormones.

    ANS: D   DIF: Moderate   REF: 402-403   OBJ: 12.11

134. Research on children who are victims of sexual abuse has indicated that
    a. over 75% of victims become clinically depressed.
    b. some victims can experience symptoms of posttraumatic stress disorder.
    c. the best way to characterize the impact is using the idea of a single concept referred to as "sexual abuse syndrome" or "SAS."
    d. over 75% of victims engage in "sexualized behaviors," including public masturbation and extreme promiscuity.

    ANS: B   DIF: Moderate   REF: 403   OBJ: 12.12

135. How many of the following (flashbacks to the traumatizing events, feelings of helplessness, feelings of extreme euphoria) are characteristic of an individual experiencing posttraumatic stress disorder?
    a. 0   c. 2
    b. 1   d. 3

    ANS: C   DIF: Moderate   REF: 403   OBJ: 12.12

136. The impact of sexual abuse appears to be most severe when the abuse was a
    a. one-time event involving a stranger.
    b. one-time event involving a close relative.
    c. frequent, long-term event involving a stranger.
    d. frequent, long-term event involving a close relative.

    ANS: D   DIF: Moderate   REF: 403   OBJ: 12.12

137. Which statement concerning the establishment of one's sexual orientation is true?
    a. The process of accepting one's sexuality as homosexual is as stressful as accepting one's sexual identity as heterosexual.
    b. Most homosexual individuals "come out" shortly after their initial awareness of their sexual orientation.
    c. Homosexual experimentation is fairly common during adolescence.
    d. The majority of gay men are effeminate and the majority of lesbians are masculine.

    ANS: C   DIF: Easy   REF: 404   OBJ: 12.13

665

138. Twin studies on sexual orientation show that
  a. genes are much more influential than environmental factors in determining sexual orientation.
  b. sexual orientation is determined almost completely by environmental factors.
  c. a genetic link cannot be established because not enough twins will participate in this kind of research.
  d. genetic and environmental influences appear about equally responsible for sexual orientation.

  ANS: D   DIF: Moderate   REF: 404   OBJ: 12.13

139. Research on sexual orientation indicates that
  a. the majority of lesbian and bisexual relationships last less than one month.
  b. consistent, strong cross-sex interests in late childhood may predict later homosexual or bisexual orientation.
  c. most gay children have gay parents.
  d. a defect on the short arm of the Y chromosome appears to be the cause of homosexuality in males.

  ANS: B   DIF: Moderate   REF: 404   OBJ: 12.13
  KEY: WWW

140. One promising theory is that _____ influences during prenatal development are responsible for determining your sexual orientation.
  a. toxic   c. drug
  b. viral   d. hormonal

  ANS: D   DIF: Moderate   REF: 405   OBJ: 12.13

141. Most teens in the U.S. believe that
  a. sex, both in the context of a committed relationship and in casual relationships, is acceptable.
  b. sex, in the context of a committed relationship is acceptable, but casual sex is much less acceptable.
  c. casual sex is acceptable, but sex in the context of a committed relationship is much less acceptable.
  d. neither causal sex nor sex in the context of a committed relationship are acceptable.

  ANS: B   DIF: Moderate   REF: 405-406   OBJ: 12.14

142. Which best illustrates the underlying premise of the double standard?
  a. What's OK for him is not OK for her.   c. Men are smart, women are dumb.
  b. I want to only play with girls, not   d. Male but feminine equals gay.
     boys.

  ANS: A   DIF: Easy   REF: 406   OBJ: 12.14
  KEY: WWW

143. When discussing sex with his buddies, Hef says, "The key is to understand that normal guys want and need sex, whereas girls who want sex are immoral and corrupt." Hef's comments best exemplify the concept of
    a. the double standard.
    b. gender segregation .
    c. the androgyny shift.
    d. gender intensification.

    ANS: A   DIF: Moderate   REF: 406   OBJ: 12.14

144. Research on 12th-graders indicates that
    a. significantly more males than females are sexually active (i.e., have had at least one sexual encounter).
    b. significantly more females than males are sexually active (i.e., have had at least one sexual encounter).
    c. both males and females tend to be sexually active (i.e., have had at least one sexual encounter) and are so at similar rates.
    d. neither males nor females are sexually active.

    ANS: C   DIF: Moderate   REF: 406   OBJ: 12.14

145. Which statement concerning current teen sexuality is the United States is true?
    a. The sexual double standard is as strong as ever.
    b. Early sexual involvement is more common in teens whose parents became parents later in life.
    c. Teens tend to view oral sex as significantly less "intimate" than did their parents' generation.
    d. Teenage males are more likely than females to view their first sexual intercourse experience as "disappointing."

    ANS: C   DIF: Moderate   REF: 406-407   OBJ: 12.14

146. A 2007 study of college students found that about _____ agreed that they "had sex" when they engaged in oral-genital stimulation.
    a. 20%
    b. 40%
    c. 80%
    d. 100%

    ANS: A   DIF: Moderate   REF: 406   OBJ: 12.14

147. Research on 16-year-old sexual abstainers, low risk-takers, and high risk-takers found that
    a. abstaining was most common in teens with unwed mothers.
    b. high-risk teens looked more mature at earlier ages than teens from the other groups.
    c. low-risk teens were most likely to be involved in romantic relationships.
    d. there was no relationship between behaviors exhibited between ages 9 and 12 and later sexual activity.

    ANS: C   DIF: Difficult   REF: 407   OBJ: 12.14

148. How many of the following (high levels of adventuresomeness, low levels of impulse control, high levels of alcohol consumption) have been shown to increase the likelihood of a teenager engaging in risky sexual behavior?

a. 0
b. 1
c. 2
d. 3

ANS: D   DIF: Moderate   REF: 407   OBJ: 12.14

149. Which statement concerning condom use is true?

a. Adolescent females report less condom use than adolescent males.
b. Condom use increases from mid to late adolescence.
c. Condom use has decreased during the past few decades.
d. About two-thirds of teens use condoms each time they engage in sexual intercourse.

ANS: A   DIF: Moderate   REF: 407   OBJ: 12.14

150. Which statement concerning sexual activity and adulthood is true?

a. There has been a significant increase in incidence of sexually transmitted diseases in middle-aged Americans.
b. Middle-aged women are more likely than middle-aged men to use frequency of intercourse as the key indicator of sexual satisfaction.
c. Men ages 75-85 are less likely to be sexually active than their female age peers.
d. The book *HIV Wisdom for Older Woman* was designed to educate grandmothers in how to talk to grandchildren about sexually transmitted diseases.

ANS: A   DIF: Moderate   REF: 409-410   OBJ: 12.15

151. Regarding sexuality during old age,

a. men peak sexually in their 40s while women peak sexually in their 60s.
b. the majority of old women lose interest in sex entirely.
c. sexual activity is most common when a person is married (versus divorced).
d. only a very small minority (less than 5%) of people over age 70 continue to engage in sexual intercourse.

ANS: C   DIF: Moderate   REF: 409-410   OBJ: 12.15

152. Women

a. tend to have a shorter sexual refractory period than men.
b. show increases in the speed of sexual arousal in older age.
c. lose the physiological capacity to have sex before men.
d. who have experienced menopause show a steep decline in interest in sexual activity.

ANS: A   DIF: Moderate   REF: 410   OBJ: 12.15

153. Which appears to contribute most to the lack of sexual activity among old women?
   a. A physiological incapacity to engage in intercourse
   b. Lack of a partner
   c. Negative social attitudes toward sex during old age
   d. Sexual activity seen as "dirty"

   ANS: B   DIF: Moderate   REF: 410-411   OBJ: 12.15
   KEY: WWW

154. What childhood behavior did the authors of the text use as an analogy for the decline in sexual activity in old age?
   a. Going to the circus   c. Eating candy
   b. Swinging on a swing   d. Riding a bike

   ANS: D   DIF: Easy   REF: 411   OBJ: 12.15

TRUE/FALSE

1. Gender-role norms are societal expectations about what males and females should be like.

   ANS: T   DIF: Moderate   REF: 382   OBJ: 12.1

2. Agency is a feminine gender orientation that emphasizes connectedness to others.

   ANS: F   DIF: Moderate   REF: 383   OBJ: 12.1
   KEY: WWW

3. Males are more developmentally vulnerable to prenatal stressors.

   ANS: T   DIF: Easy   REF: 384   OBJ: 12.2

4. The social-role hypothesis argues that there are no gender stereotypes.

   ANS: F   DIF: Moderate   REF: 385   OBJ: 12.3

5. The acquisition of a gender identity is typically complete by age one.

   ANS: F   DIF: Easy   REF: 387   OBJ: 12.4

6. Third-graders are likely to be more concerned and troubled by violations of traditional gender-role standards than are first-grade youngsters.

   ANS: F   DIF: Moderate   REF: 388   OBJ: 12.5

7. Gender segregation results in children having peer groups that consist of both male and female friends.

   ANS: F   DIF: Easy   REF: 389   OBJ: 12.6
   KEY: WWW

8. Gender intensification appears to be magnified by hormonal release during puberty.

   ANS: T   DIF: Moderate   REF: 390   OBJ: 12.6

9. Fertilized eggs (both XX and XY) have the potential to acquire the anatomical and physical features of either sex.

   ANS: T   DIF: Moderate   REF: 391   OBJ: 12.7
   KEY: WWW

10. Androgenized females may undergo surgery to alter their genitalia.

    ANS: T   DIF: Moderate   REF: 392   OBJ: 12.7

11. Observational learning is best associated with the social-learning theory of gender acquisition.

    ANS: T   DIF: Easy   REF: 393 & 395   OBJ: 12.7

12. Parents may perpetuate gender-role stereotypes through differential reinforcement of their children's behavior.

    ANS: T   DIF: Moderate   REF: 393   OBJ: 12.7

13. Gender stability involves understanding that gender is stable across situations.

    ANS: F   DIF: Moderate   REF: 396   OBJ: 12.7

14. According to gender-schema theory, children have a strong preference for learning about objects and activities that fit their own-sex schema.

    ANS: T   DIF: Moderate   REF: 396-397   OBJ: 12.7

15. An androgynous person has neither masculine nor feminine characteristics.

    ANS: F   DIF: Moderate   REF: 399   OBJ: 12.9

16. The parental imperative involves adopting the gender role of a person of the opposite sex.

    ANS: F   DIF: Moderate   REF: 400   OBJ: 12.9
    KEY: WWW

17. Most children who are abused will develop "child abuse syndrome."

    ANS: F   DIF: Easy   REF: 403   OBJ: 12.12

18. Being raised by a gay parent significantly increases the likelihood of a child becoming gay.

    ANS: F   DIF: Moderate   REF: 404-405   OBJ: 12.13

19. In the United States, the double standard is on the decline.

ANS: T   DIF: Moderate   REF: 406   OBJ: 12.14
KEY: WWW

20. Prevailing social attitudes that view sexual activity in old age as ridiculous contribute to reduced sexual activity in older individuals.

ANS: F   DIF: Moderate   REF: 411   OBJ: 12.15

COMPLETION

1. Gender _____ are overgeneralized and highly inaccurate beliefs about what males and females are like.

ANS: stereotypes

DIF: Moderate   REF: 382   OBJ: 12.1

2. The _____ (or communion) aspect of the feminine gender role involves an orientation that emphasizes connectedness to others.

ANS: communality

DIF: Difficult   REF: 383   OBJ: 12.1

3. The _____ aspect of the masculine gender role involves an orientation that emphasizes action and achievement.

ANS: agency

DIF: Difficult   REF: 383   OBJ: 12.1   KEY: WWW

4. Baron-Cohen suggests that the male focus on achievement stems from the brain's tendency to _____ (analyze or explore) how things work.

ANS: systemize

DIF: Difficult   REF: 383   OBJ: 12.1

5. According to the gender _____ hypothesis, females and males are similar on most but not all psychological variables.

ANS: similarities

DIF: Easy   REF: 384   OBJ: 12.2

671

6. According to the _____ hypothesis, the different roles the sexes play in society create many gender-role stereotypes.

   ANS: social-role

   DIF: Moderate   REF: 385   OBJ: 12.3

7. The initial awareness that you are a boy or a girl is defined as gender _____.

   ANS: identity

   DIF: Moderate   REF: 387   OBJ: 12.4

8. The process in which children acquire awareness of biological males and females and the patterns of behavior that their culture views as appropriate for each sex is called gender _____.

   ANS: typing

   DIF: Moderate   REF: 387   OBJ: 12.5

9. When boys and girls separate themselves into same-sex only groups, they are demonstrating gender _____.

   ANS: segregation

   DIF: Moderate   REF: 389   OBJ: 12.5

10. Gender _____ tends to occur around puberty, when hormonal changes magnify intolerance to deviation from gender-role expectations.

    ANS: intensification

    DIF: Moderate   REF: 390   OBJ: 12.6   KEY: WWW

11. Girls who are born with masculinized genitalia due to exposure to excess levels of androgens are technically referred to as _____ females.

    ANS: androgenized

    DIF: Easy   REF: 392   OBJ: 12.7

12. When a mother uses one form of reinforcement with her daughters and another form with her sons, she is engaging in _____ reinforcement.

    ANS: differential

    DIF: Difficult   REF: 393   OBJ: 12.7

13. Kohlberg's approach of gender is best classified as a _____ developmental theory.

    ANS: cognitive

    DIF: Moderate   REF: 396   OBJ: 12.7

14. A child with gender _____ understands that gender is stable over time, but does not understand that gender is stable across situations.

    ANS: stability

    DIF: Difficult   REF: 396   OBJ: 12.7   KEY: WWW

15. A child who has just acquired gender _____ understands that gender is stable over time and across situations.

    ANS: consistency

    DIF: Difficult   REF: 396   OBJ: 12.7

16. A gender _____ is an organized set of beliefs and expectations about males and females that impacts what types of information an individual will attend to and remember.

    ANS: schema

    DIF: Moderate   REF: 396   OBJ: 12.7

17. Psychological _____ is the term used when referring to individuals with high levels of masculine and feminine traits.

    ANS: androgyny

    DIF: Moderate   REF: 399   OBJ: 12.9

18. Gutmann suggested that parents tend to adopt different roles when raising children, in a process he called the parental _____.

    ANS: imperative

    DIF: Difficult   REF: 400   OBJ: 12.9

19. Middle-aged individuals may undergo an _____ shift in which they begin to adopt some of the gender stereotypes associated with the opposite sex.

    ANS: androgyny

    DIF: Difficult   REF: 400   OBJ: 12.9   KEY: WWW

20. The argument that some sexual behaviors are appropriate for males but not females is known as the _____ standard.

ANS: double

DIF: Easy   REF: 406   OBJ: 12.14

ESSAY

1. How are the issues of gender norms, gender stereotypes, masculinity, femininity, communality, and agency interrelated?

ANS: Answer not provided   REF: 382-383   OBJ: 12.1

2. What is the gender similarity hypothesis and what evidence is used to support this position (provide at least five examples)?

ANS: Answer not provided   REF: 384-385   OBJ: 12.2

3. How does the need to adhere to gender roles change between preschool and late adolescence, and how is gender segregation impacted by this change?

ANS: Answer not provided   REF: 387-390   OBJ: 12.5 & 12.6

4. How does biosocial theory attempt to explain gender-role development, and how are androgenized females used to illustrate the key points of this approach?

ANS: Answer not provided   REF: 391-394   OBJ: 12.7

5. Compare and contrast cognitive-developmental theory and gender schema theory in their attempt to describe the acquisition of gender roles.

ANS: Answer not provided   REF: 396-398   OBJ: 12.7

6. Describe why an infant could be considered a sexual being. How does this conceptualization carry over into the school-age years?

ANS: Answer not provided   REF: 401-403   OBJ: 12.10 & 12.11

7. What is the typical developmental pattern of sexual behavior from adolescence through old age?

ANS: Answer not provided   REF: 406-411   OBJ: 12.14 & 12.15

8. How would a social-learning theorist describe the acquisition of gender roles?

ANS: Answer not provided   REF: 393 & 395   OBJ: 12.7   KEY: WWW

9. What are the parental imperative and the androgyny shift, and how are they used to describe possible changes in gender roles in adulthood?

ANS: Answer not provided   REF: 400-401   OBJ: 12.9   KEY: WWW

10. What factor(s) appear responsible for determining a person's sexual orientation?

ANS: Answer not provided   REF: 404-405   OBJ: 12.13   KEY: WWW

675

MULTIPLE CHOICE

1. John Gibbs, author of *Moral Development and Reality*, experienced a significant moral dilemma as a child at
   a. home, where he saw his mother abused by his father.
   b. camp, where he saw a mildly retarded man tormented by campers.
   c. school, where he was pressured into picking on an overweight classmate.
   d. church, where he struggled to understand how good church-going people could say mean things about others.

   ANS: B   DIF: Easy   REF: 415-416   OBJ: 13.1

2. Social cognition is best defined as
   a. memories for interesting life events.
   b. knowing who gets along with whom.
   c. thinking about the thoughts, feelings, motives, and behaviors of one's self and others.
   d. being aware of current "codes" for dressing and dating.

   ANS: C   DIF: Moderate   REF: 416   OBJ: 13.1

3. The "false belief" task is used to assess
   a. the difference between a sensorimotor and a preoperational thinker.
   b. the understanding that people may hold incorrect personal beliefs that influence their behaviors.
   c. a person's level of religiosity.
   d. how a person would reason about a moral.

   ANS: B   DIF: Moderate   REF: 416-417   OBJ: 13.1
   KEY: WWW

4. Having a theory of mind indicates that an individual
   a. understands the physiological workings of the brain.
   b. can draw inferences.
   c. understands that mental states exist and guide behavior.
   d. can reason about abstract concepts.

   ANS: C   DIF: Moderate   REF: 417   OBJ: 13.1

5. Zola puts her toys away in the toy chest and goes to eat dinner. Her brother, unbeknownst to her, decides to take all of her toys and put them under his bed. As a child who has a theory of mind, when Zola returns after dinner, she will
   a. look for her toys in the toy chest.
   b. look for her toys where her brother has hidden them.
   c. not remember anything about her toys.
   d. try to think of where her brother likes to hide things.

   ANS: A   DIF: Difficult   REF: 417   OBJ: 13.1

6. While watching her friend Veronica picking out a dress, Betty thinks to herself, "I know that Veronica really likes to look nice and impress the boys. I bet she will pick out a very sexy outfit." Betty's thoughts indicate that she possesses
   a. postconventional moral thought.   c. joint attention.
   b. a morality of justice.   d. a theory of mind.

   ANS: D   DIF: Moderate   REF: 417   OBJ: 13.1

7. Bubba is a football linebacker attempting to guess what play the opposing quarterback will call. He thinks to himself, "I know that QB really likes to pass the ball to score because when he does, the newspapers always write articles about him. Thus, I bet he'll pass the ball on the next play." Bubba's thoughts indicate that he possesses
   a. postconventional moral thought.   c. joint attention.
   b. a morality of justice.   d. a theory of mind.

   ANS: D   DIF: Moderate   REF: 417   OBJ: 13.1
   KEY: WWW

8. In a study using the false belief task with four-year-olds of average intelligence, four-year-olds with Down syndrome, and slightly older children with autism, Baron-Cohen found that
   a. only the average intelligence children passed the task.
   b. both the average intelligence children and the children with Down syndrome passed the task.
   c. both the average intelligence children and the children with autism passed the task.
   d. all three groups of children passed the task.

   ANS: B   DIF: Difficult   REF: 417   OBJ: 13.1

9. Why do autistic children have difficulty passing the false belief task?
   a. They lack the general intelligence.
   b. They lack the linguistic skills.
   c. They lack a theory of mind.
   d. They engage in too many stereotyped movements.

   ANS: C   DIF: Moderate   REF: 417   OBJ: 13.1

10. At or before nine months of age, most children begin to _____. This activity is one of the earliest milestones in developing a theory of mind.
    a. talk
    b. show prosocial behavior
    c. engage in joint attention
    d. demonstrate the ability to recognize themselves in a mirror

    ANS: C   DIF: Moderate   REF: 417   OBJ: 13.1

11. One-year-old Andy notices a rag doll sitting in the corner. He is very excited and begins to point at the doll in the hopes that his mother, Ann, will notice. Suddenly, Ann notices the doll and the two look at the rag doll together. At this point, this mutual experience represents
    a. joint attention.   c. classical conditioning.
    b. sympathy.   d. prosocial behavior.

    ANS: A   DIF: Moderate   REF: 417   OBJ: 13.1

678

12. How many of the following (understanding that others people have intentions, engaging in pretend play, imitation of others) are skills underlying having a theory of mind?
a. 0   c. 2
b. 1   d. 3

ANS: D   DIF: Moderate   REF: 417   OBJ: 13.1

13. Which linguistic skills provide solid evidence that a child is developing a theory of mind?
a. Producing a first word
b. Cooing
c. Producing a first grammatically correct sentence
d. Saying, "I whistle because I am happy"

ANS: D   DIF: Easy   REF: 417   OBJ: 13.1

14. The ability to explain one's behavior as being driven by what one wants is the basis of _____ psychology.
a. classical conditioning   c. operant conditioning
b. physiological   d. desire

ANS: D   DIF: Easy   REF: 418   OBJ: 13.1

15. Little Debbie, who is two years old, loves cupcakes and hates fruit pie. She has observed that her mother hates cupcakes and loves fruit pies. If Debbie were handed a plate with a piece of pie and a different plate with a cupcake, and was asked to give one to her mother, Debbie would most likely
a. hand mom the pie.   c. hand mom both plates.
b. hand mom the cupcake.   d. keep both plates for herself.

ANS: A   DIF: Difficult   REF: 418   OBJ: 13.1

16. Someone with a belief-desire psychology understands that
a. people do not always hold accurate beliefs, but these beliefs still influence behavior.
b. beliefs accurately reflect what we desire.
c. desires shape our behavior.
d. people develop accurate beliefs based on interactions with others.

ANS: A   DIF: Difficult   REF: 418   OBJ: 13.1

17. Understanding belief-desire psychology means understanding
a. that most people are driven to obey laws.
b. that some beliefs that influence behavior are not accurate.
c. that wants and desires are a poor motivation for a behavior.
d. the pain others feel when they make tough decisions.

ANS: B   DIF: Moderate   REF: 418   OBJ: 13.1
KEY: WWW

18. Which of the following is NOT necessary for attaining a theory of mind?
    a. Some language skills
    b. Symbolic thinking skills
    c. Experience interacting with other people
    d. Being human

    ANS: D   DIF: Easy   REF: 418-419   OBJ: 13.1

19. Which neurological component has been implicated in the development of a theory of mind?
    a. Mirror neurons
    b. Glial cells
    c. Tympanic membrane cells
    d. Substantia nigra cells

    ANS: A   DIF: Moderate   REF: 419   OBJ: 13.1
    KEY: WWW

20. Mirror neurons are activated when a person
    a. is performing an action and sees someone else performing the same action.
    b. says what someone else is thinking.
    c. engages in an activity witnessed the previous day.
    d. sees and speaks a word at the same time.

    ANS: A   DIF: Moderate   REF: 419-420   OBJ: 13.1

21. Difference in mirror neuron activity in the right temporoparietal area of the brain may explain the lack of theory of mind that characterizes children with
    a. ADHD.
    b. Down syndrome.
    c. PKU.
    d. autism.

    ANS: D   DIF: Difficult   REF: 419   OBJ: 13.1

22. Davis was born Deaf to Deaf parents who signed to him at an early age. How would this be most likely to affect his acquisition of a theory of mind?
    a. He would show slightly slower development than that of a sensory-normal child.
    b. He would show a similar development as that of a Down syndrome child.
    c. He would show a similar development as that of an autistic child.
    d. He would show similar development to that of a sensory-normal child.

    ANS: D   DIF: Difficult   REF: 420   OBJ: 13.1

23. The key factor in determining whether being born Deaf will result in a delay in the acquisition of a theory of mind appears to be
    a. how well parents are able to communicate with the child.
    b. whether the deafness was the result of fetal alcohol syndrome or rubella.
    c. the number of mirror neurons the child has in their cochlea.
    d. the use of signing by parents (which almost always results in a delay).

    ANS: A   DIF: Moderate   REF: 420   OBJ: 13.1
    KEY: WWW

24. What is the most effective way a parent can help instill theory of mind skills in his or her child?
    a. Utilize coercive discipline.
    b. Encourage the child to think about how others may feel.
    c. Discourage empathy.
    d. Avoid engaging in joint attention.

    ANS: B   DIF: Moderate   REF: 420   OBJ: 13.1

25. Peruvian children among the Junin Quechua people who live in a culture in which adults rarely talk about thoughts and beliefs
    a. have difficulty understanding that a belief can be false.
    b. acquire language at an earlier age.
    c. show higher levels of intentional lying.
    d. master the theory of mind at a younger age.

    ANS: A   DIF: Moderate   REF: 420   OBJ: 13.1

26. How would a typical four-year-old most likely describe his sister?
    a. "She is kind of is moody."   c. "She is a good friend."
    b. "She eats corn flakes."   d. "Everyone says she's smart."

    ANS: B   DIF: Moderate   REF: 420   OBJ: 13.2

27. Which is the most developmentally advanced description of a friend?
    a. "He is a good dancer."
    b. "He has a cool car and rides around a lot."
    c. "He buys me ice cream because he's generous."
    d. "He is big, hairy, and smells like a really rotten egg."

    ANS: C   DIF: Moderate   REF: 420-421   OBJ: 13.2

28. Which is the LEAST developmentally advanced description of a friend?
    a. "He has a big head and blue eyes."
    b. "He is pretty good at math."
    c. "He is so smart that everyone likes him."
    d. "He sometimes is nice and other times is mean."

    ANS: A   DIF: Moderate   REF: 420-421   OBJ: 13.2
    KEY: WWW

29. What important advance in social cognition generally occurs at age 11 or 12?
    a. Children begin to describe others in terms of the activities they engage in.
    b. Children begin to describe others in terms of inner psychological traits and characteristics.
    c. Children begin to attempt to explain why people do what they do.
    d. Children begin to focus heavily on others' physical appearance in their descriptions of them.

    ANS: C   DIF: Moderate   REF: 421   OBJ: 13.2

30. Which best describes the initial perceptions of others made by young children?
    a. Psychology and specific
    b. Psychology and global
    c. Physical and specific
    d. Physical and global

    ANS: D   DIF: Difficult   REF: 420-421   OBJ: 13.2

31. Which provides the best example of a social perspective-taking skill?
    a. Understanding that the person across the table has beliefs in direct opposition to yours.
    b. Believing that your position on an issue is the most accurate.
    c. Realizing that an object hidden in one place may have been moved to another place.
    d. Deciding that the most moral decisions are ones in which you personally benefit.

    ANS: A   DIF: Easy   REF: 421   OBJ: 13.2

32. In order to engage in role-taking, children must outgrow what Piaget called _____ thought.
    a. egocentric
    b. reversible
    c. abstract
    d. hypothetical-deductive reasoning

    ANS: A   DIF: Easy   REF: 421   OBJ: 13.2

33. Studies on perspective-taking indicate that it is not until a child attains concrete operational thinking that he or she is able to
    a. form a theory of mind.
    b. attain a belief-desire psychology.
    c. mentally "juggle" several perspectives of others.
    d. appreciate that two people can have different points of view, even with access to the same information.

    ANS: D   DIF: Moderate   REF: 421   OBJ: 13.2
    KEY: WWW

34. Georgia sees her friend Bill running down the street. Without warning, Bill falls flat on his face. While Georgia finds this funny, she does not laugh because she knows that Bill does not find this funny. In not laughing, Georgia is demonstrating
    a. egocentrism.
    b. role-taking skills.
    c. morality of justice.
    d. prosocial behavior.

    ANS: B   DIF: Moderate   REF: 421   OBJ: 13.2

35. Which of the following is true regarding the development of role-taking skills?
    a. It is not until at least age 20 that people are able to include a mental perspective of some "generalized other."
    b. By age four years, most children understand that parents may not think the way they do.
    c. Concrete-operational thinkers are capable of simultaneously considering several different points of view.
    d. The ability to consider a situation from a number of different points of view increases the quality of one's social relationships.

    ANS: D   DIF: Moderate   REF: 421-422   OBJ: 13.2

682

36. Studies on perspective-taking indicate that it is not until a child attains formal operational thinking that he or she is able to
    a. form a theory of mind.
    b. attain a belief-desire psychology.
    c. mentally "juggle" several perspectives of others.
    d. appreciate that two people can have different points of view, even with access to the same information.

    ANS: C   DIF: Moderate   REF: 421-422   OBJ: 13.2

37. The best description of the development of social cognitive skills during adulthood is,
    a. "if you use it, you will lose it."
    b. "a time of steady decline."
    c. "more gains than losses."
    d. "a dramatic shift from postconventional to conventional."

    ANS: C   DIF: Moderate   REF: 422   OBJ: 13.2

38. Which of the following had NOT been used to explain the fact that social cognitive skills tend to hold up better than non-social cognitive skills in later life?
    a. The fact that the brain cortex responsible for social cognition skills ages slower than brain areas supporting non-social cognitive skills
    b. The fact that social skills are practiced (exercised) everyday
    c. The fact that older adults tend to have more strongly held beliefs about people when making social-cognitive decisions
    d. The fact that older adults reject the use of "rules of thumb" in social cognitive decision-making

    ANS: D   DIF: Difficult   REF: 422-423   OBJ: 13.2

39. Adults who maintain their social cognitive abilities into old age tend to have all of the following characteristics EXCEPT they are
    a. in a meaningful relationship (e.g., parent, grandparent).
    b. well-educated.
    c. in good physical health.
    d. socially isolated.

    ANS: D   DIF: Moderate   REF: 422-423   OBJ: 13.2
    KEY: WWW

40. Which is NOT part of the text definition of morality?
    a. Distinguishing right from wrong
    b. Acting on the distinction between right and wrong
    c. Experiencing pride when doing right and shame when doing wrong
    d. Knowing what is right and wrong without having to perform the act

    ANS: D   DIF: Moderate   REF: 423-424   OBJ: 13.3

41. Which of the following is an example of the affective component of morality?
    a. Knowing that you made the right decision in a difficult situation
    b. Feeling good about giving money to charity
    c. Taking some food from the cafeteria without paying for it
    d. Jumping up and down in joy after you win the lottery

    ANS: B   DIF: Moderate   REF: 424   OBJ: 13.3

42. The self-statement, "I do not steal because it is wrong," is best exemplifies the _____
    component of morality.
    a. affective   c. cognitive
    b. behavioral   d. emotional

    ANS: C   DIF: Moderate   REF: 424   OBJ: 13.3

43. The actual act of stealing a car provides a good example of the _____ component of morality.
    a. affective   c. cognitive
    b. behavioral   d. emotional

    ANS: B   DIF: Easy   REF: 424   OBJ: 13.3
    KEY: WWW

44. Michelle wanted a "Beanie Baby" stuffed animal but didn't have the money to buy one. One
    day she was in a store at the mall, and when she thought no one was looking, she slipped a
    Beanie Baby into her bag and left without paying for it. Later, when she was playing with it,
    she found she wasn't enjoying herself very much, and she felt bad that she had stolen the toy.
    Taking the Beanie Baby from the store represents the _____ component of morality, while the
    fact that she felt bad represents the _____ component of morality.
    a. affective; cognitive   c. cognitive; affective
    b. behavioral; affective   d. behavioral; cognitive

    ANS: B   DIF: Moderate   REF: 424   OBJ: 13.3

45. The affect aspect of morality focuses on what a person
    a. thinks.   c. knows.
    b. does.   d. feels.

    ANS: D   DIF: Moderate   REF: 424   OBJ: 13.4

46. How many of the following (shame, guilt, anxiety, fear of being caught) would be considered
    emotions related to moral affect?
    a. 1   c. 3
    b. 2   d. 4

    ANS: D   DIF: Easy   REF: 424   OBJ: 13.4

47. Empathy refers to
    a. vicariously experiencing another's feelings.
    b. reading minds.
    c. being able to resist temptation.
    d. knowing that someone holds a false belief.

    ANS: A   DIF: Moderate   REF: 424   OBJ: 13.4

684

48. Who is experiencing an empathic response?
    a. Lily, who is depressed because she lost her job
    b. Daisy, who feels bad that she did not give money to a street person
    c. Rose, who cries as she watches a news documentary featuring a very distraught mother talking about a son she lost to AIDS
    d. Fern, who is excited about going on her first date

    ANS: C   DIF: Difficult   REF: 424   OBJ: 13.4

49. An example of empathy would be
    a. escaping pain.
    b. sensing that you are about to get a phone call.
    c. being afraid for the hero in a movie who is in danger.
    d. looking forward to watching the villain in a movie die.

    ANS: C   DIF: Moderate   REF: 424   OBJ: 13.4
    KEY: WWW

50. Prosocial behavior is defined as
    a. any act that makes a person feel better.
    b. a positive social act reflecting a concern for others.
    c. an act intended to do good, but that actually results in harm to the person at whom the act is aimed.
    d. the vicarious experiencing of another person's emotions.

    ANS: B   DIF: Moderate   REF: 424   OBJ: 13.4

51. Which of the following best exemplifies prosocial behavior?
    a. Doing chores to earn allowance
    b. Driving no faster than the speed limit
    c. Getting homework done on time
    d. Stopping to help a stranger change a flat tire

    ANS: D   DIF: Easy   REF: 424   OBJ: 13.4

52. According to Freud, a moral conscience is formed during the _____ stage, with the emergence of the _____.
    a. phallic; superego   c. genital; superego
    b. phallic; ego   d. latency; Oedipus complex

    ANS: A   DIF: Moderate   REF: 424   OBJ: 13.4

53. Jessica feels guilty after taking pocket change from her father's dresser drawer. According to Freud, this emotional response best indicates that Jessica
    a. is in the oral stage of development.
    b. is sexually attracted to her father.
    c. has successfully resolved an emotional conflict over her love for her father.
    d. has no superego.

    ANS: C   DIF: Difficult   REF: 424   OBJ: 13.4

685

54. Freud suggested that females have weaker superegos than males because they
    a. lack an id.
    b. over identify with their fathers.
    c. rely on a morality of care perspective.
    d. do not experience any fear of castration.

    ANS: D   DIF: Moderate   REF: 424   OBJ: 13.4
    KEY: WWW

55. Which of Freud's assertions has been upheld by research?
    a. Females have weaker superegos than males.
    b. Complete moral maturity is achieved by age six or seven.
    c. Emotions play a critical role in moral development.
    d. Threatening, punitive parents produce children who are more morally strong than parents who are warm and affectionate.

    ANS: C   DIF: Moderate   REF: 424-425   OBJ: 13.4

56. Which theoretical perspective tends to focus the most attention on the development of moral reasoning?
    a. Psychoanalytic
    b. Social learning
    c. Classical conditioning
    d. Cognitive developmental

    ANS: D   DIF: Moderate   REF: 425   OBJ: 13.5

57. Moral reasoning is best defined as the
    a. act of helping or hurting.
    b. thought process used to determine if an act is right or wrong.
    c. emotion(s) felt following a positive or negative act.
    d. unconscious drive to fulfill one's id-driven need.

    ANS: B   DIF: Easy   REF: 425   OBJ: 13.5

58. After paying for his groceries, Linnie went to his car and loaded the bags into his trunk. On the bottom of the grocery cart, Linnie found a case of beer and realized that he hadn't been charged for it. Linnie popped it into his trunk and when he got home, he told his roommate what had happened. Linnie then said, "Oh, well, it's a big store and they can do without the money. It's really not my fault. The cashier should have spotted it and rung it up." Linnie's mental consideration best illustrates the _____ component of morality.
    a. psychomotor
    b. cognitive
    c. behavioral
    d. affective

    ANS: B   DIF: Moderate   REF: 425   OBJ: 13.5

59. When both individuals in a relationship engage in an equal amount of give and take while conversing, they are demonstrating
    a. power assertion.
    b. sympathy.
    c. reciprocity.
    d. induction.

    ANS: C   DIF: Easy   REF: 425   OBJ: 13.5

60. Which best exemplifies reciprocity?
    a. Caring deeply for an injured friend
    b. Two people agreeing that they each give the same amount to a relationship
    c. Deciding that the morality of justice is superior to the morality of care
    d. When a parent tells a child to clean her room and she does it

    ANS: B   DIF: Moderate   REF: 425   OBJ: 13.5

61. Cognitive developmental theorists tend to view moral reasoning as involving
    a. the progression through an invariant sequence of ways of thinking.
    b. a set of behaviors acquired through observation.
    c. a battle between id, ego, and superego.
    d. a genetic predisposition toward helping that is based on the evolutionary need to survive.

    ANS: A   DIF: Moderate   REF: 425   OBJ: 13.5

62. According to Piaget, during the premoral period children,
    a. first form their superego.
    b. cannot be considered moral beings.
    c. believe in an unbreakable set of moral rules.
    d. think only about how their actions affect society.

    ANS: B   DIF: Moderate   REF: 425   OBJ: 13.5

63. As a typical four-year-old, Michael would most likely be at the _____ of moral development.
    a. heteronomous morality stage   c. autonomous morality stage
    b. conventional level   d. premorality period

    ANS: D   DIF: Moderate   REF: 425   OBJ: 13.5

64. Concerning morality, heteronomous means
    a. without conscience.   c. same as the opposite-sex parent.
    b. under the rule of another.   d. self-centered.

    ANS: B   DIF: Moderate   REF: 425   OBJ: 13.5

65. Martha is at home by herself. While flipping through channels, she sees a show on "real-life" teens who live together in a house and get into lots of sexual situations. Martha really wants to watch the show but remembers that her mom's rule is that she can never watch that type of program. Because of her mom's rule, Martha turns the channel and checks out a show on home improvement. Given these actions, Martha appears to be at Piaget's _____ of moral development.
    a. heteronomous morality stage   c. autonomous morality stage
    b. conventional level   d. premorality period

    ANS: A   DIF: Difficult   REF: 425   OBJ: 13.5

687

66. Which of the following people would be most likely just to have begun to understand that, if a group of people realize a rule is bad, they can change the rule so that a behavior that used to be seen as bad is now ok?
    a. Mary, who is at the heteronomous morality stage
    b. Larry, who is at the postconventional level
    c. Garry, who is at the autonomous morality stage
    d. Terri, who is in the premorality period

    ANS: C   DIF: Moderate   REF: 425   OBJ: 13.5

67. Howie has just seen one brother break an expensive glass while showing off his juggling skills to his girlfriend and another brother break three of the same types of glasses while trying to help his grandmother move. According to Piaget, if Howie thought that the brother who broke the single glass was more wrong, Howie is most likely in the _____ of moral development.
    a. heteronomous morality stage   c. autonomous morality stage
    b. postconventional level   d. premorality period

    ANS: C   DIF: Difficult   REF: 425   OBJ: 13.5

68. Individuals at Piaget's _____ of moral development have first begun to make moral judgments on the basis of someone's intent versus the actual outcome of their behavior.
    a. heteronomous morality stage   c. autonomous morality stage
    b. postconventional level   d. premorality period

    ANS: C   DIF: Moderate   REF: 425   OBJ: 13.5
    KEY: WWW

69. Kohlberg's approach to moral reasoning was most directly influenced by the work of
    a. Skinner.   c. Bandura.
    b. Freud.   d. Piaget.

    ANS: D   DIF: Easy   REF: 425   OBJ: 13.5

70. Kohlberg's cognitive developmental theory of moral development claims that
    a. regression from a higher to a lower stage of moral reasoning is quite common.
    b. through an exploration of moral dilemmas, it is possible to teach someone to skip over the lower stages of moral development.
    c. the sequence of stages one goes through may vary from one culture to another.
    d. a person's stage of moral development is determined by the person's thoughts, rather than his or her actions.

    ANS: D   DIF: Moderate   REF: 425-426   OBJ: 13.5

71. What did Kohlberg use to assess moral reasoning?
    a. Reactions to written moral dilemmas
    b. Parental descriptions of their children's moral decision-making
    c. A modified version of the Minnesota Multiphasic Personality Inventory
    d. Naturalistic observation of people in real-life settings

    ANS: A   DIF: Easy   REF: 425-426   OBJ: 13.5

72. Macy really wants the cool new jacket she has just seen in the store, but she does not have enough money to buy it. For a second, she thinks about stealing the jacket but decides that while stealing is not wrong, she might get punished if she is caught. Macy's moral reasoning appears to be at Kohlberg's _____ level.
    a. preconventional
    b. conventional
    c. postconventional
    d. unconventional

    ANS: A   DIF: Moderate   REF: 426   OBJ: 13.5

73. Which statement provides the best example of the morality of instrumental hedonism?
    a. Doing evil is fun.
    b. Wrong is always wrong.
    c. I steal for you, you steal for me.
    d. The law determines right from wrong.

    ANS: C   DIF: Difficult   REF: 426   OBJ: 13.5

74. Which of the following would Kohlberg consider the LEAST sophisticated stage of moral thinking?
    a. Authority and social order-maintaining morality
    b. Morality of contract, individual rights, and democratically accepted law
    c. Morality of individual principles of conscience
    d. Instrumental hedonism

    ANS: D   DIF: Moderate   REF: 426   OBJ: 13.5
    KEY: WWW

75. At what level of moral development are the rules and standards of society internalized and held as one's own?
    a. Preconventional
    b. Conventional
    c. Postconventional
    d. Unconventional

    ANS: B   DIF: Easy   REF: 426   OBJ: 13.5
    KEY: WWW

76. An individual who is at Kohlberg's conventional level of moral development is most likely to
    a. do anything to avoid being punished.
    b. do something nice for someone so that the individual will be rewarded in return.
    c. ignore the intent of an act and focus on its impact.
    d. behave in ways that earn the approval and avoid the disapproval of others.

    ANS: D   DIF: Difficult   REF: 426   OBJ: 13.5

77. Mahatma bases all of his moral decisions on a simple rule: "Always follow the rules set by a legitimate authority." Mahatma would best be placed at the _____ level of moral reasoning.
    a. unconventional
    b. preconventional
    c. conventional
    d. postconventional

    ANS: C   DIF: Moderate   REF: 426   OBJ: 13.5

78. Which statement reflects Kohlberg's conventional morality?
    a. Do your own thing.
    b. It's me against the world.
    c. Rules are made to be broken.
    d. Buckle up, it's the law.

    ANS: D   DIF: Difficult   REF: 426   OBJ: 13.5

79. While trying to help his mother bake cookies, Amos accidentally breaks a bowl. His mom's comment, "That's OK, I know that you were just trying to be a good boy and help me out," indicates that she is operating at the _____ level of moral reasoning.
    a. preconventional
    b. conventional
    c. postconventional
    d. unconventional

    ANS: B   DIF: Difficult   REF: 426   OBJ: 13.5

80. _____ morality transcends the perspective of specific groups and attempts to encompass the perspective of all people.
    a. Preconventional
    b. Conventional
    c. Postconventional
    d. Amoral

    ANS: C   DIF: Easy   REF: 426   OBJ: 13.5

81. Which statement is the best example of postconventional moral reasoning?
    a. While it may be legally wrong, it is morally right.
    b. Depending on what I get out of the deal, it may be right.
    c. My intent is to be nice.
    d. Rules are not meant to be broken.

    ANS: A   DIF: Moderate   REF: 426   OBJ: 13.5

82. Max refuses to pay his income tax because he believes that the government uses taxes for poor purposes. Most notably, he is opposed to the use of tax funds to support war efforts, because he doesn't believe that violence is an acceptable way to solve problems. He is willing to go to jail for his belief. Max is best classified as being in Kohlberg's _____ level of moral development.
    a. premoral
    b. preconventional
    c. conventional
    d. postconventional

    ANS: D   DIF: Difficult   REF: 426   OBJ: 13.5
    KEY: WWW

83. When considering whether or not to steal a car, Fairlane thinks, "Stealing is good for the owner who will be able to collect insurance but bad for the insurance company because it has to pay. On the other hand, stealing provides a useful service for the police on the street because it gives them something to do, but it's bad for police at the station because if I am caught, they will have a lot of paperwork to complete." Fairlane's multiple perspective approach is best classified as being at the _____ level of moral development.
    a. premoral
    b. preconventional
    c. conventional
    d. postconventional

    ANS: D   DIF: Difficult   REF: 426   OBJ: 13.5

84. Kohlberg's highest stage of moral reasoning involves
    a. authority and social order-maintaining morality.
    b. morality of contract, individual rights, and democratically accepted law.
    c. morality of individual principles of conscience.
    d. instrumental hedonism.

    ANS: C   DIF: Moderate   REF: 426   OBJ: 13.5

690

85. When asked what she thinks of mercy killing in which a doctor gave a terminally ill individual a lethal injection, Indira says, "While some may see this as illegal, helping end someone's suffering is always justified." This statement indicates that on this issue, Indira is at the _____ stage of moral development.
   a. authority and social order-maintaining morality
   b. morality of contract, individual rights, and democratically accepted law
   c. good boy or nice girl
   d. instrumental hedonism

   ANS: B   DIF: Difficult   REF: 426   OBJ: 13.5

86. Regarding Kohlberg's theory of moral development, which cognitive skill is particularly instrumental in promoting movement from one level of moral development to the next?
   a. The development of perspective-taking abilities
   b. Emergence of the object permanence concept
   c. The development of a theory of mind
   d. The development of conservation skills

   ANS: A   DIF: Moderate   REF: 427   OBJ: 13.5

87. The social learning perspective on moral development holds that morality is
   a. a generalized personality trait.
   b. a situation-specific behavior.
   c. driven by physiological motives.
   d. determined more by level of reasoning than by actual behavior.

   ANS: B   DIF: Easy   REF: 428   OBJ: 13.6

88. Mr. Mitchell's son Dennis is a menace. Dennis is cruel to animals and often shoplifts. In attempting to explain Dennis's morals, Mr. Mitchell says, "I think that his moral habits were learned by watching bad television shows." Mr. Mitchell's comments are best associated with the _____ view concerning moral behavior.
   a. psychodynamic   c. social learning theory
   b. Piagetian   d. cognitive developmental

   ANS: C   DIF: Moderate   REF: 428   OBJ: 13.6

89. Winston sees his brother steal a pack of gum from the drug store and get away with it. The next time Winston goes to the drug store, he steals a pack of gum. According to the _____ perspective on moral development, Winston's behavior is the result of _____.
   a. psychoanalytic; observational learning
   b. cognitive developmental; an underdeveloped superego
   c. social learning; observational learning
   d. psychoanalytic; a weak ego

   ANS: C   DIF: Moderate   REF: 428   OBJ: 13.6

691

90. For Bandura, _____ is the key mechanism that monitors and evaluates one's actions and produces moral actions.
    a. self-esteem
    b. self-recognition
    c. self-categorization
    d. self-regulation

    ANS: D   DIF: Easy   REF: 428   OBJ: 13.6

91. Moral disengagement
    a. tends to only be found in individuals with conduct disorders.
    b. allows a person to justify his or her own immoral behavior.
    c. is a basic component of the theory of mind.
    d. is found exclusively in premoral thinkers.

    ANS: B   DIF: Moderate   REF: 428   OBJ: 13.6

92. Ira has just stolen a purse from a woman on the subway. He then says to himself, "If that woman really wanted her purse, she would have held it closer to her body." This statement provides a good example of
    a. morality of justice.
    b. moral disengagement .
    c. autonomous morality.
    d. empathy.

    ANS: B   DIF: Difficult   REF: 428   OBJ: 13.6

93. Evolutionary theorists have argued that it is in our genetic self-interest to be altruistic because
    a. it perfectly matches the premise of survival of the fittest.
    b. helping our kin may allow our genes to be passed along.
    c. the more we help, the better spouse we will attain.
    d. chromosome 13 has been found to have a specific "helping gene."

    ANS: B   DIF: Moderate   REF: 428-429   OBJ: 13.7

94. Evolutionary-based research on altruism has demonstrated that
    a. only humans show any example of helping behavior.
    b. altruism does not begin to emerge until puberty.
    c. we abandon immature forms of moral thinking as we develop.
    d. humans may have a genetic make-up that predisposes them to behave both antisocially and prosocially.

    ANS: D   DIF: Moderate   REF: 428-429   OBJ: 13.7

95. When considering why college student Waldo just cheated on his exam, which theorist would be most focused on whether Waldo lived with relatives who he had observed cheating?
    a. Bandura
    b. Freud
    c. Piaget
    d. Kohlberg

    ANS: A   DIF: Moderate   REF: 428-429   OBJ: 13.7
    KEY: WWW

96. An amoral person
    a. only does good things.
    b. lacks any sense of morality.
    c. is pure evil.
    d. is overly concerned about rules and laws when making moral decisions.

    ANS: B   DIF: Easy   REF: 430   OBJ: 13.8

97. Who would most likely NOT be held accountable for his or her actions because he or she is incapable of evaluating their behavior as "right" or "wrong"?
    a. Donnie, who is amoral
    b. Connie, who displays heteronomous morality
    c. Lonnie, who is preconventional
    d. Bonnie, who displays autonomous morality

    ANS: A   DIF: Moderate   REF: 430   OBJ: 13.8

98. Children as young as _____ have been shown to display visible signs of distress when they violate some standard of behavior.
    a. newborns   c. four years old
    b. two years old   d. six years old

    ANS: B   DIF: Difficult   REF: 430   OBJ: 13.8

99. Which family situation is associated with the best form of moral development in young children?
    a. Mutually responsive orientation   c. Induction
    b. Power assertion   d. Coercive family environment

    ANS: A   DIF: Moderate   REF: 430   OBJ: 13.8

100. Which would be the WORST advice for a parent trying to foster moral development in a toddler?
    a. Discuss the toddler's behavior openly with them
    b. Express your feelings
    c. Do not evaluate a child's actions in terms of good of bad
    d. Establish a positive and cooperative relationship with the child

    ANS: C   DIF: Moderate   REF: 430   OBJ: 13.8

101. How do newborns demonstrate a sense of empathy?
    a. They become distressed when other infants cry.
    b. They look at objects that their parents are looking at.
    c. They prefer to be held by other children versus an adult.
    d. They pass the false belief task.

    ANS: A   DIF: Moderate   REF: 430   OBJ: 13.8

102. When two-year-old Simoné sees her friend start to cry when his ice cream cone falls to the ground, she walks over and hands him her cone. In performing this act, Simoné is demonstrating
   a. amoral behavior.
   b. postconventional morality.
   c. spirituality.
   d. empathy.

   ANS: D   DIF: Easy   REF: 431   OBJ: 13.8

103. What did Kohlberg's research reveal about the moral thinking of five-year-olds?
   a. It demonstrated that they were amoral.
   b. It demonstrated that they were premoral.
   c. It demonstrated that they were conventional thinkers.
   d. Nothing, as Kohlberg never studied young children.

   ANS: D   DIF: Difficult   REF: 432   OBJ: 13.9

104. Concerning the development of morality,
   a. both Kohlberg and Piaget overestimated children's levels of moral thinking.
   b. Kohlberg overestimated children's levels of moral thinking, and Piaget underestimated children's levels of moral thinking.
   c. Kohlberg underestimated children's levels of moral thinking, and Piaget overestimated children's levels of moral thinking.
   d. both Kohlberg and Piaget underestimated children's levels of moral thinking.

   ANS: D   DIF: Moderate   REF: 432   OBJ: 13.9

105. Nelson (1980) presented three-year-olds with a story in which a character throws a ball to a playmate, and in which the motive of the thrower and consequence of the act were manipulated. The results of this study showed that three-year-olds _____ when judging the act.
   a. disregarded both intent and consequence
   b. disregarded intent and but considered consequence
   c. disregarded consequence but considered intent
   d. considered both intent and consequence

   ANS: D   DIF: Difficult   REF: 432   OBJ: 13.9

106. Based on the research of Jean Piaget, whom would you expect to have a basis for moral reasoning based on the rule, "All violations will be handled swiftly and harshly—there will be no exceptions."
   a. 4-year-old Molly
   b. 8-year-old Dolly
   c. 12-year-old Polly
   d. 16-year-old Holly

   ANS: B   DIF: Difficult   REF: 432-433   OBJ: 13.9

107. According to researcher Elliot Turiel, "moral rules"
   a. focus on the welfare and basic rights for all individuals.
   b. cannot be violated.
   c. are situation specific.
   d. cannot be defined.

   ANS: A   DIF: Easy   REF: 432-433   OBJ: 13.9
   KEY: WWW

694

108. Turiel made a distinction between "moral" rules and "social-conventional" rules. Which best exemplifies the concept of a moral rule?
   a. Don't run in the halls.
   b. Don't take things that don't belong to you.
   c. Don't chew gum in school.
   d. Don't sneak snacks into the movie theater.

   ANS: B   DIF: Difficult   REF: 432-433   OBJ: 13.9

109. Which is the best example of a moral rule?
   a. You should take turns talking when at a dinner party.
   b. Everyone has the right to vote.
   c. There is no crying at a baseball game.
   d. You cannot bring candy into a movie theater.

   ANS: B   DIF: Moderate   REF: 433   OBJ: 13.9

110. A standard of appropriate behavior that has been determined by social consensus and that applies to a specific social situation is called a
   a. moral rule.   c. social-conventional rule.
   b. postconventional law.   d. preconventional law.

   ANS: C   DIF: Moderate   REF: 433   OBJ: 13.9

111. Not sitting in your assigned seat in school is best classified as a
   a. moral rule.   c. social-conventional rule.
   b. type of empathy.   d. mutually responsive orientation.

   ANS: C   DIF: Difficult   REF: 433   OBJ: 13.9

112. Children who have attained theory of mind
   a. are more in tune with the feelings of others.
   b. still cannot pass the false belief task.
   c. have also attained the highest level of moral thinking proposed by Kohlberg.
   d. do not let the intent of an act influence how they feel about what was done.

   ANS: A   DIF: Moderate   REF: 433   OBJ: 13.9

113. Every time his daughter Luci swears (something he does not like), Lou walks away from her (pays her no attention). This strategy provides a good example of the _____ parental approach.
   a. power assertion   c. love withdrawal
   b. induction   d. empathy

   ANS: C   DIF: Moderate   REF: 433   OBJ: 13.10

114. The purpose of _____ is to create anxiety by threatening a loss of reinforcement.
   a. power assertion   c. love withdrawal
   b. induction   d. empathy

   ANS: C   DIF: Moderate   REF: 433   OBJ: 13.10

115. Ned tells his son Flanders, "For hitting your brother, you need to be disciplined so get ready for a spanking." Ned's parenting approach to moral development best matches with the parenting style referred to as

a. power assertion. c. love withdrawal.
b. induction. d. empathy.

ANS: A DIF: Easy REF: 433 OBJ: 13.10

116. Which is the best example of a power assertion form of discipline?

a. Telling a child that you hate him
b. Taking away a child's television privileges
c. Telling a child that a child who gets hit feels bad
d. Taking away parental love from a child

ANS: B DIF: Moderate REF: 433 OBJ: 13.10

117. Harvey practically killed his pet hamster when he popped him in the tub for a bubble bath. His parents take an inductive approach in responding to this situation by

a. giving the hamster away so Harvey can't do any more damage.
b. spanking Harvey for doing the wrong thing.
c. explaining to Harvey that hamsters don't like baths and can get sick or die from getting too wet.
d. telling Harvey he's a very mean little boy and they are very disappointed in him.

ANS: C DIF: Difficult REF: 433 OBJ: 13.10

118. The statement, "Tell a child that hitting is wrong because you can hurt the people" best fits with the _____ parental approach for fostering moral development.

a. power assertion c. love withdrawal
b. induction d. amoral

ANS: B DIF: Moderate REF: 433 OBJ: 13.10
KEY: WWW

119. In summarizing the best parenting approach for fostering moral growth in children, Hoffman (2000) suggests a "blend of _____."

a. no inductions, some power assertions, and over-the-top affection
b. half power assertion and half affection
c. half inductions and half power assertions
d. frequent inductions, occasional power assertions, and a lot of affection

ANS: D DIF: Moderate REF: 434 OBJ: 13.10

120. Proactive parenting strategies are designed to _____ misbehavior.

a. promote c. predict
b. prevent d. produce

ANS: B DIF: Easy REF: 434 OBJ: 13.10

121. The fact that a fearful child may become more anxious when disciplined than a fearless child best demonstrates how the factor of _____ can impact moral development.
    a. vicarious consequences
    b. temperament
    c. observational learning
    d. unconscious desires

    ANS: B   DIF: Moderate   REF: 435   OBJ: 13.10

122. Throughout adolescence, there is a decrease in _____ moral reasoning and an increase in _____ moral reasoning.
    a. conventional; postconventional
    b. preconventional; conventional
    c. conventional; preconventional
    d. rule-based; social-conventional

    ANS: B   DIF: Moderate   REF: 435-436   OBJ: 13.11

123. Juvenile delinquency is best defined as
    a. law breaking by a minor.
    b. felon commitment by a young adult.
    c. irritating, but not illegal, behavior by an adolescence.
    d. a lack of intellect in the 'tween years.

    ANS: A   DIF: Easy   REF: 436   OBJ: 13.10

124. Which is an act of juvenile delinquency?
    a. A 25-year-old speeding in a car
    b. A 15-year-old in a drive-by shooting
    c. A 10-year-old failing a math test
    d. A 5-year-old not being put into kindergarten

    ANS: B   DIF: Easy   REF: 436   OBJ: 13.10

125. Persistently violating the rights of peers through fighting or bullying would most accurately lead to a diagnosis of _____ in a teenager.
    a. conduct disorder
    b. schizophrenia
    c. aphasia
    d. dysphoria

    ANS: A   DIF: Easy   REF: 436   OBJ: 13.10

126. Research on antisocial behavior has shown that
    a. most antisocial teens grow up to be antisocial adults.
    b. juvenile delinquents are more likely than other peers to be conventional thinkers.
    c. early-onset aggressive children tend to not display significant antisocial behavior until early adulthood.
    d. aggressive youth tend to show less empathy.

    ANS: D   DIF: Moderate   REF: 436   OBJ: 13.11

127. According to Dodge's social information-processing model, the main thing wrong with teenagers who commit violent, antisocial acts is
    a. their genetic makeup.
    b. the coercive family environments in which they were raised.
    c. the way they interpret and process social cues.
    d. the culture in which they live.

    ANS: C   DIF: Easy   REF: 437   OBJ: 13.11
    KEY: WWW

128. According to Dodge's social information-processing model, an aggressive teenager who is run into in the hallway will likely
    a. assume that the event was intentional.
    b. set a goal of soothing relationships with the person who hit him.
    c. consider a wide range of options for dealing with the situation.
    d. focus on the potential negative outcomes if he decides to pound the person who ran into him.

    ANS: A   DIF: Moderate.   REF: 437   OBJ: 13.11

129. Highly aggressive youth tend to
    a. belong to groups in which bullying is seen as a punishable offense.
    b. consider many reactions (including passive ones) before acting aggressively.
    c. be highly accepted by most of their age peers.
    d. believe that their aggressive acts will produce positive consequences.

    ANS: D   DIF: Moderate   REF: 437   OBJ: 13.11

130. Julius is currently trying to determine exactly why his best friend Caesar just slapped him in the face. According to Dodge's social information-processing model, Julius is engaging in
    a. interpretation of cues.   c. response search.
    b. clarification of goals.   d. behavioral enactment.

    ANS: A   DIF: Moderate   REF: 437   OBJ: 13.11

131. Tyra is weighing the personal advantages and disadvantages of retaliating with violence against her friend Banks, who just called her a "fat pig." According to Dodge's social information-processing model, Tyra is engaging in
    a. encoding of cues.   c. behavioral enactment.
    b. response decision.   d. clarification of goals.

    ANS: B   DIF: Moderate   REF: 437   OBJ: 13.11

132. Which decision is a highly aggressive youth most likely to make when a classmate runs into her in the hallway?
    a. The conclusion that violent actions lead to bad consequences
    b. Deciding to set a goal of becomes friends with the classmate
    c. The assumption that the classmate's intent was to hurt her
    d. Assuming that the incident was an accident

    ANS: C   DIF: Moderate   REF: 437   OBJ: 13.11

133. When considering social cognitive causes of aggression, concern over a person's levels of impulsivity best reflect the extent to which the problem is due to _____ one thinks.
    a. how
    b. what
    c. whether
    d. where

    ANS: C   DIF: Difficult   REF: 438   OBJ: 13.11

134. Coercive family environments refer to situations where family members
    a. eventually gain complete control over their children.
    b. are locked in power struggles.
    c. use discussion to try to persuade others to adopt their position.
    d. establish a power hierarchy that allows them to solve problems swiftly and smoothly.

    ANS: B   DIF: Easy   REF: 438   OBJ: 13.11

135. According to Patterson's model of development, antisocial behavior
    a. first occurs when children fall in with a bad crowd when they are teens.
    b. begins with poor parental discipline.
    c. is the result of a genetic predisposition to act aggressively.
    d. starts when children begin to imitate antisocial behaviors they see depicted in the media (e.g., television, movies).

    ANS: B   DIF: Moderate   REF: 438   OBJ: 13.11

136. Which statement concerning the role of genetics in determining aggression is true?
    a. Behavioral geneticists suggest that 90 percent of aggression can be accounted for by genetics.
    b. The fact that males can only have a limited number of children contributes significantly to their evolutionary-based levels of aggression.
    c. Children who inherit a predisposition toward aggression may evoke aggressive reactions from their parents.
    d. Having parents and children who are both genetically predisposed toward aggression tends to result in a paradox effect, which results in little aggression by either child or parent.

    ANS: C   DIF: Difficult   REF: 438-439   OBJ: 13.11

137. Which statement concerning violence and culture is true?
    a. Japanese children are more likely to react angrily to interpersonal conflicts than American children.
    b. Cultural contexts do not "breed" aggression.
    c. The United States is a relatively violent country.
    d. Hispanic children raised with traditional Hispanic cultural values engage in more antisocial behavior than those acculturated into American society.

    ANS: C   DIF: Easy   REF: 439   OBJ: 13.11

138. Rates of aggression and violence tend to be highest in
    a. lower socioeconomic highly transient neighborhoods.
    b. middle socioeconomic highly transient neighborhoods.
    c. lower socioeconomic non-transient neighborhoods.
    d. middle socioeconomic non-transient neighborhoods.

    ANS: A   DIF: Moderate   REF: 439   OBJ: 13.11

139. Bullying
    a. it typically aimed at individuals who are most prepared to defend themselves.
    b. is a one-time event.
    c. is seldom reinforced by other bullies.
    d. can involve harm via words or actions.

    ANS: D   DIF: Easy   REF: 439   OBJ: 13.11

140. How many of the following factors (inconsistent parenting, affiliation with prosocial peers, academic failure) increase the risk of a child being aggressive?
    a. 0   c. 2
    b. 1   d. 3

    ANS: C   DIF: Moderate   REF: 439   OBJ: 13.11

141. The goal of the Fast Track Program was to reduce a child's risk of becoming aggressive through
    a. exposure to non-violent forms of media (e.g., television shows, movies).
    b. academic success.
    c. participation in athletics.
    d. teaching social information-processing and social skills.

    ANS: D   DIF: Moderate   REF: 439   OBJ: 13.11

142. Regarding moral development in adulthood, which is true?
    a. Moral development in older males progresses at a faster rate than in older females.
    b. Moral reasoning deteriorates significantly in old age.
    c. The majority of older adults are preconventional thinkers.
    d. Postconventional thinking emerges only during adulthood.

    ANS: D   DIF: Moderate   REF: 441   OBJ: 13.12

143. Critics have charged that Kohlberg's theory is biased against people living in
    a. Western cultures and people who are politically liberal.
    b. non-Western cultures and people who are politically liberal.
    c. Western cultures and people who are politically conservative.
    d. non-Western cultures and people who are politically conservative.

    ANS: D   DIF: Moderate   REF: 441   OBJ: 13.13

700

144. According to Kohlberg, moral development
   a. occurs in a universal manner.
   b. is determined by genes.
   c. cannot be accurately studied in older adults.
   d. is shaped by the social context in which someone is raised.

   ANS: D   DIF: Easy   REF: 441-442   OBJ: 13.13

145. Kohlberg's _____ of moral reasoning is best associated with Gilligan's morality of care.
   a. stage 2 – instrumental hedonism
   b. stage 3 – "good boy" or "good girl"
   c. stage 4 – authority and social order-maintaining morality
   d. stage 5 – morality of contract, individual rights, and democratically accepted laws

   ANS: B   DIF: Difficult   REF: 442   OBJ: 13.13

146. The fact that Meg exhibits great responsibility toward her mother Lois and brother Stewie rather than focusing on herself indicates that she is exhibiting what Gillian referred to as a morality of
   a. truth.   c. care.
   b. justice.   d. nurturance.

   ANS: C   DIF: Moderate   REF: 442   OBJ: 13.13

147. Which statement best exemplifies the morality of justice?
   a. "I follow the letter of the law."
   b. "Being a good father is my only desire."
   c. "Always consider the impact of an act on all of humanity."
   d. "You help me, and I help you."

   ANS: A   DIF: Moderate   REF: 442   OBJ: 13.13

148. Which question best reflects the "morality of justice"?
   a. Does the act break a law?
   b. Will my act make someone feel bad?
   c. Should a person in my situation act this way?
   d. How would my parents react if they knew I was doing this?

   ANS: A   DIF: Moderate   REF: 442   OBJ: 13.13
   KEY: WWW

149. Research on gender differences in moral thinking has shown that
   a. females and males clearly think differently about moral dilemmas.
   b. men and women both use care- and justice-based reasoning.
   c. there is clear evidence that estrogen levels in females "bias" their brains to act in a more moral manner.
   d. males are significantly better at resisting temptation to do wrong.

   ANS: B   DIF: Moderate   REF: 442-443   OBJ: 13.13

701

150. Kohlberg's model of moral development has been characterized as placing too great an emphasis on
a. genes.
b. moral reasoning.
c. peers.
d. unconscious motivation.

ANS: B   DIF: Moderate   REF: 443   OBJ: 13.13

151. According to Haidt's evolutionary theory, humans have evolved as a species in which
a. quick moral intuitions are common and critical.
b. females are better at suppressing amoral tendencies than males.
c. moral decision-making is based solely on situational context.
d. most moral decision-making involves long, deliberative reasoning.

ANS: A   DIF: Moderate   REF: 443   OBJ: 13.13

152. The key premise of dual-process models of morality is that both _____ inform moral decisions.
a. deliberate thought and emotions/intuition
b. genes and neurotransmitters
c. peers and parents
d. conscious and unconscious desires

ANS: A   DIF: Moderate   REF: 443   OBJ: 13.13

153. Religiosity is defined as
a. sharing the beliefs but not participating in the practices of an organized religion.
b. participating in the practices of but not sharing the beliefs of an organized religion.
c. both sharing the beliefs and participating in the practices of an organized religion.
d. neither sharing the beliefs nor participating in the practices of an organized religion.

ANS: C   DIF: Easy   REF: 444   OBJ: 13.13

154. Spirituality is defined as the search for
a. the ultimate meaning of life, always tied to religion.
b. the ultimate meaning of life, not always tied to religion.
c. God, always tied to religion.
d. God, not always tied to religion.

ANS: B   DIF: Moderate   REF: 444   OBJ: 13.12

155. Concerning the developmental pattern of religiosity and spirituality,
a. religiosity is strongest in middle age.
b. levels of spirituality are lower than religiosity throughout adulthood.
c. spirituality declines significantly in old age (particularly among women).
d. adolescents tend to be neither spiritual nor show religiosity.

ANS: B   DIF: Moderate   REF: 445   OBJ: 13.13

156. Research has shown that
   a. highly spiritual people tend to be not open to new experiences.
   b. highly religious adults tend to not be involved in their religious community.
   c. highly spiritual people tend to be involved in activities that allow them to express their creativity.
   d. highly religious people tend to have poorer mental and physical health.

   ANS: C   DIF: Easy   REF: 445   OBJ: 13.13

TRUE/FALSE

1. The false belief task is designed to assess the understanding that others can hold incorrect beliefs that can influence their behavior.

   ANS: T   DIF: Moderate   REF: 416-417   OBJ: 13.1

2. Desire psychology has been seen in children as young as six months of age.

   ANS: F   DIF: Moderate   REF: 418   OBJ: 13.1

3. Mirror neurons are activated when someone views his or her reflection in a pane of glass.

   ANS: F   DIF: Moderate   REF: 419-420   OBJ: 13.1

4. Young children's initial attempts at self-description tend to focus on physical attributes.

   ANS: T   DIF: Moderate   REF: 420   OBJ: 13.2
   KEY: WWW

5. The affective component of morality concerns the feelings surrounding right or wrong actions.

   ANS: T   DIF: Moderate   REF: 424   OBJ: 13.3

6. Research has demonstrated that males have stronger superegos than females.

   ANS: F   DIF: Moderate   REF: 424   OBJ: 13.4

7. A child in the stage of autonomous morality has the ability to consider the intent of someone's actions when determining the morality of an act.

   ANS: T   DIF: Moderate   REF: 425   OBJ: 13.5

8. Piaget stated that premoral thinkers cannot be considered moral beings.

   ANS: T   DIF: Moderate   REF: 425   OBJ: 13.5
   KEY: WWW

9. "Good boy" or "good girl" morality is found in the conventional level of morality.

   ANS: T   DIF: Moderate   REF: 426   OBJ: 13.5
   KEY: WWW

10. Individuals at the postconventional level of moral reasoning view right and wrong in terms of existing societal laws.

   ANS: F   DIF: Moderate   REF: 426   OBJ: 13.5

11. Social learning theory claims that morality is highly situation specific.

   ANS: T   DIF: Moderate   REF: 428   OBJ: 13.6

12. An individual acting at the highest moral level is said to be "amoral."

   ANS: F   DIF: Moderate   REF: 430   OBJ: 13.8

13. A social-conventional rule often involves rules of proper social etiquette.

   ANS: T   DIF: Easy   REF: 433   OBJ: 13.9

14. Spanking is an excellent example of a form of induction discipline.

   ANS: F   DIF: Moderate   REF: 433   OBJ: 13.10

15. The majority of adolescents have achieved Kohlberg's conventional level of moral reasoning.

   ANS: T   DIF: Moderate   REF: 435-436   OBJ: 13.11

16. According to Dodge's model, antisocial adolescents process information differently than other adolescents.

   ANS: T   DIF: Moderate   REF: 437   OBJ: 13.11

17. Aggressive youths tend to evaluate the consequences of aggression far more negatively than their non-violent peers.

   ANS: F   DIF: Moderate   REF: 437   OBJ: 13.11
   KEY: WWW

18. By middle age, most adults have progressed to Kohlberg's postconventional level of moral reasoning.

   ANS: F   DIF: Moderate   REF: 441   OBJ: 13.12

19. Some critics have argued that Kohlberg's model is biased against people from collectivist societies.

   ANS: T   DIF: Moderate   REF: 441   OBJ: 13.13
   KEY: WWW

20. A key aspect of spirituality is a quest for ultimate meaning.

   ANS: T   DIF: Moderate   REF: 444   OBJ: 13.14

1. Two key aspects of _____ psychology concern understanding that people's desires guide their behavior and that two people can hold different beliefs.

   ANS: belief-desire

   DIF: Easy   REF: 418   OBJ: 13.1

2. The _____ component of morality consists of the feelings associated with right or wrong actions.

   ANS: affective

   DIF: Moderate   REF: 424   OBJ: 13.3

3. _____ is defined as vicariously experiencing the feelings of another person.

   ANS: Empathy

   DIF: Easy   REF: 424   OBJ: 13.3   KEY: WWW

4. Piaget proposed that preschool children were in the _____ period of moral development.

   ANS: premoral

   DIF: Moderate   REF: 425   OBJ: 13.5   KEY: WWW

5. According to Piaget, a child who has just come to believe that rules handed down by parents are viewed as sacred and unalterable has just entered the _____ morality stage.

   ANS: heteronomous

   DIF: Difficult   REF: 425   OBJ: 13.5

6. The punishment-and-obedience orientation stage is found at Kohlberg's _____ level of moral reasoning.

   ANS: preconventional

   DIF: Moderate   REF: 426   OBJ: 13.5

7. The authority and social order-maintaining morality stage is found at Kohlberg's _____ level of moral reasoning.

   ANS: conventional

   DIF: Moderate   REF: 426   OBJ: 13.5   KEY: WWW

8. Thinking at Kohlberg's _____ level of moral reasoning can be based on a set of abstract universal principles applicable to all individuals.

ANS: postconventional

DIF: Moderate   REF: 426   OBJ: 13.5

9. The mechanism of moral _____ allows an individual to engage in an immoral behavior, yet avoid self-condemnation.

ANS: disengagement

DIF: Difficult   REF: 428   OBJ: 13.6

10. As they lack any sense of morality, infants are often classified as _____.

ANS: amoral

DIF: Moderate   REF: 430   OBJ: 13.8

11. When a child and parent show close, affectionate, and positive interactions, they are said to have a _____ responsive orientation.

ANS: mutually

DIF: Difficult   REF: 430   OBJ: 13.8

12. Spanking is an excellent example of the power _____ form of discipline.

ANS: assertion

DIF: Moderate   REF: 433   OBJ: 13.10

13. The disciplinary technique of _____ is characterized by explaining to a child why a behavior is wrong and emphasizing how negative behavior affects other people.

ANS: induction

DIF: Moderate   REF: 433   OBJ: 13.10   KEY: WWW

14. The love _____ discipline technique is often designed to create anxiety by threatening the loss of reinforcement from parents.

ANS: withdrawal

DIF: Moderate   REF: 433   OBJ: 13.10

15. Law breaking by a minor is referred to juvenile _____.

ANS: delinquency

DIF: Easy   REF: 436   OBJ: 13.11

706

16. Patterson suggested that children who are raised in families characterized by power struggles, threats, and violence should be classified as being in a _____ family environment.

ANS: coercive

DIF: Moderate   REF: 438   OBJ: 13.11

17. The act of repeatedly inflicting harm on weak and defenseless peers is called _____.

ANS: bullying

DIF: Moderate   REF: 439   OBJ: 13.11

18. According to Gilligan's original model, females are socialized to display a feminine, "morality of _____."

ANS: care

DIF: Moderate   REF: 442   OBJ: 13.13

19. According to Gilligan's original model, males are socialized to display a masculine, "morality of _____."

ANS: justice

DIF: Moderate   REF: 442   OBJ: 13.13   KEY: WWW

20. Religiousness or _____ involves sharing the beliefs and participating in the practices of an organized religion.

ANS: religiosity

DIF: Easy   REF: 444   OBJ: 13.14

ESSAY

1. What is the theory of mind and how is the false belief task used to assess this concept?

ANS: Answer not provided   REF: 416-418   OBJ: 13.1

2. How is psychoanalytic theory related to the affective component of moral development?

ANS: Answer not provided   REF: 424-425   OBJ: 13.4

3. Dr. Cairns must decide whether or not to give a lethal dose of narcotics to a dying patient who is in a great deal of pain. What sorts of things would Dr. Cairns consider in making his decision at each of Kohlberg's six stages of moral development?

ANS: Answer not provided   REF: 425-428   OBJ: 13.5

4. How would a social learning theorist describe moral socialization and the acquisition of moral behavior?

ANS: Answer not provided   REF: 428   OBJ: 13.6

5. How might Dodge's social information-processing model be used to explain the behavior of teenagers who shoot their classmates?

ANS: Answer not provided   REF: 437-438   OBJ: 13.11

6. What roles do family and cultural environments play in the development of prosocial and aggressive behaviors?

ANS: Answer not provided   REF: 430 & 435-440
OBJ: 13.8-13.10-13.11

7. What is the nature of the debate between the moral reasoning perspectives of Kohlberg and Gilligan? Who is right?

ANS: Answer not provided   REF: 442-443   OBJ: 13.13

8. What are the fundamental differences between the preconventional, conventional, and postconventional levels of moral reasoning?

ANS: Answer not provided   REF: 425-428   OBJ: 13.5   KEY: WWW

9. Describe Piaget's view of moral development.

ANS: Answer not provided   REF: 425   OBJ: 13.5   KEY: WWW

10. Differentiate between the concepts of religiosity and spirituality. Then discuss how each develops between the teenage years through old age.

ANS: Answer not provided   REF: 443-446   OBJ: 13.14   KEY: WWW

MULTIPLE CHOICE

1. Freud's opinions on social relationships were clear; the most important first bond was between an infant and his or her
   a. father.
   b. mother.
   c. sibling(s).
   d. peers.

   ANS: B   DIF: Moderate   REF: 450   OBJ: 14.1

2. Which theory did the text identify as today's most influential theory of parent-child and other close relationships?
   a. Social learning theory
   b. Humanistic theory
   c. Attachment theory
   d. Cognitive developmental

   ANS: C   DIF: Moderate   REF: 450   OBJ: 14.2

3. Which two theorists are best associated with attachment theory?
   a. Craik and Lockhart
   b. Freud and Erikson
   c. Piaget and Kohlberg
   d. Bowlby and Ainsworth

   ANS: D   DIF: Easy   REF: 450   OBJ: 14.2

4. An attachment is best defined as a strong affectional tie that binds a person to a(n)
   a. intimate companion.
   b. peer.
   c. friend.
   d. acquaintance.

   ANS: A   DIF: Moderate   REF: 450   OBJ: 14.2

5. Attachments
   a. occur exclusively in infancy.
   b. are expressed behaviorally in the same manner across the lifespan.
   c. serve the same function in infancy, adolescence, and old age.
   d. are, throughout the lifespan, aimed at individuals from whom we derive a sense of security.

   ANS: D   DIF: Moderate   REF: 450   OBJ: 14.2

6. Which best reflects the ethological perspective regarding parent/child attachments?
   a. Attachments form automatically as a result of biological programming.
   b. Human infants and caregivers have biological tendencies to form attachments.
   c. The key to forming close attachments lies in the principles of conditioning and reinforcement.
   d. Learning plays no significant role in the process of developing parent/child attachments.

   ANS: B   DIF: Moderate   REF: 450-451   OBJ: 14.2

7. Imprinting refers to
   a. an innate tendency to follow moving objects.
   b. the ability of parents to instill their values into their children.
   c. severing ties from a social convoy.
   d. becoming attached to whomever provides oral gratification.

   ANS: A   DIF: Easy   REF: 451   OBJ: 14.2

8. Based on research on imprinting, a newly hatched duck is most likely to innately become attached to
   a. its biological mother, even if the mother is not present.
   b. its biological mother, but only if she remains perfectly still.
   c. a human, but only if that person moves around.
   d. a human, but only if that person stays perfectly still.

   ANS: C   DIF: Moderate   REF: 451   OBJ: 14.2
   KEY: WWW

9. Bowlby argued that in humans, imprinting
   a. is solely due to an infant responding to the sight, sound, and touch of a caregiver.
   b. is solely due to a caregiver's biologically driven response to an infant's signals.
   c. is due to a combination of interactions between the infant and caregiver.
   d. is impossible (as it is only found in lesser species).

   ANS: C   DIF: Moderate   REF: 451   OBJ: 14.2

10. _____ has been referred to as the "love hormone" due to its potential role in attachments.
    a. Oxytocin   c. Adrenaline
    b. Testosterone   d. Estrogen

    ANS: A   DIF: Difficult   REF: 451   OBJ: 14.2

11. How does oxytocin appear to impact relationships?
    a. Excess levels are associated with uncontrolled aggression.
    b. It primes us to affiliate with others.
    c. If released by mothers shortly after birth, it will result in the infant failing to imprint/bond with the mother.
    d. Adults with similar levels (whether high or low) make the best romantic partners.

    ANS: B   DIF: Difficult   REF: 452   OBJ: 14.2

12. The ethological perspective asserts that the sensitive period for human attachment relationships typically lasts for just the first three _____ after birth.
    a. hours   c. months
    b. days   d. years

    ANS: D   DIF: Moderate   REF: 451   OBJ: 14.2

13. Bonding is
    a. an alternative term used for an attachment.
    b. a biologically-based connection between infant and parent.
    c. the result of skin-to-skin contact between infant and caregiver.
    d. absolutely essential for later development.

    ANS: B   DIF: Moderate   REF: 451   OBJ: 14.2

14. Who is most likely to be experiencing bonding?
    a. Five-hour-old Derek and his mother Bo, who are cuddling.
    b. Five-month-old Demi, who is watching her son Moore take his first step.
    c. Five-year-old Scarlett, who is playing catch with her new adoptive dad Johansson.
    d. Fifteen-year-old Penelope, who is on a first date with a boy that she really likes named Cruz.

    ANS: A   DIF: Difficult   REF: 451   OBJ: 14.2

15. Internal working models
    a. are formed during a critical period when an infant first sees a moving object.
    b. are constructed through early interactions with caregivers and influence future social relationships.
    c. depend largely on the broad cultural context in which they are formed.
    d. develop during the first few hours and days following birth.

    ANS: B   DIF: Difficult   REF: 451   OBJ: 14.2
    KEY: WWW

16. As a securely attached infant, Janeway is most likely to hold an internal working model that she is
    a. lovable.   c. amoral.
    b. unreliable.   d. part of a clique.

    ANS: A   DIF: Easy   REF: 451   OBJ: 14.2

17. Why are internal working models important in the attachment process?
    a. They are one of the few known genetic components of attachments.
    b. They are the only anti-conformity element of an attachment.
    c. They are the key behavioral component of attachments.
    d. They are a key mechanism that allows early experience to impact later behavior.

    ANS: D   DIF: Moderate   REF: 451   OBJ: 14.2

18. A peer is best defined as someone of
    a. the same chronological age.   c. the same ethnic or racial group.
    b. equal social status.   d. greater social importance.

    ANS: B   DIF: Moderate   REF: 452   OBJ: 14.2

711

19. How many of the following dyads (a father and his son, two kindergarten classmates, a preteen girl and her track coach) represent peer relationships?
   a. 0   c. 2
   b. 1   d. 3

   ANS: B   DIF: Moderate   REF: 452   OBJ: 14.2

20. Sullivan used the term _____ to describe close childhood friendships.
   a. bonding mates   c. chumships
   b. peers   d. confidants

   ANS: C   DIF: Easy   REF: 453   OBJ: 14.2

21. Which is the best example of a chumship?
   a. Seventy-year-olds Kate and Nate, who have been happily married for 40 years.
   b. Forty-somethings Bill and Jill, who are really enjoying their first date.
   c. Five-year-old Mary, who is on a great camping trip with her dad Larry.
   d. Third-graders Ray and Jay, who are best friends.

   ANS: D   DIF: Moderate   REF: 453   OBJ: 14.2

22. Which would be considered the most advanced emotion for an infant to exhibit?
   a. Fear   c. Guilt
   b. Interest   d. Sadness

   ANS: C   DIF: Moderate   REF: 453   OBJ: 14.4

23. Self-conscious emotions require
   a. postformal operational thought.   c. self-awareness.
   b. postconventional thought.   d. self-efficacy.

   ANS: C   DIF: Moderate   REF: 454   OBJ: 14.4

24. If they are all normally developing children, who would be most likely to have just begun to display self-conscious emotions?
   a. Bob, who is 2 months old   c. Carol, who is 24 months old
   b. Ted, who is 18 months old   d. Alice, who is 4 years old

   ANS: B   DIF: Moderate   REF: 454   OBJ: 14.4
   KEY: WWW

25. Two-year-old Babs is asked by her mother to sing a song in front of her relatives. For the first time in her life, Babs experiences the emotion of embarrassment. Developmentalists refer to this type of emotion as a(n) _____ emotion.
   a. amoral   c. imprinting
   b. primary   d. self-conscious

   ANS: D   DIF: Moderate   REF: 454   OBJ: 14.4

26. Research on emotional development indicates that when interacting with moms, infant's display
    a. a limited number of positive emotions, which they change at a very slow rate.
    b. a wide range of emotions (positive and negative), which they change at a very slow rate.
    c. a limited number of positive emotions, which they change at a rapid rate.
    d. a wide range of emotions (positive and negative), which they change at a rapid rate.

    ANS: D   DIF: Moderate   REF: 454   OBJ: 14.4

27. When a child has begun to monitor the reaction of someone else in order to decide how to react to an ambiguous situation, he or she is demonstrating
    a. self-awareness.   c. imprinting.
    b. chumship.   d. social referencing.

    ANS: D   DIF: Moderate   REF: 454   OBJ: 14.4

28. Tabitha is at the zoo with her dad, Darwin. How could Tabitha demonstrate social referencing?
    a. She could refer to the tiger as a "big kitty."
    b. She could watch her dad's hesitation at touching the snake and recoil her hand when a snake is handed to her.
    c. She could pick up an ant and tell her dad that if the ant were bigger, it could be in the zoo.
    d. She could find it funny when she feeds the goat her ice cream cone.

    ANS: B   DIF: Moderate   REF: 454   OBJ: 14.4

29. _____ is best defined as the process of initiating, maintaining, and altering emotions.
    a. Power assertion   c. Joint attention
    b. Emotion regulation   d. Empathy

    ANS: B   DIF: Easy   REF: 454-455   OBJ: 14.4

30. Two-month-old Holmes has learned that whenever he is around his mother, Katie, it is best not to show any fear because she does not react well when confronted by a fearful child. Holmes' behavior best illustrates the concept of
    a. chumship.   c. imprinting.
    b. emotion regulation.   d. separation anxiety.

    ANS: B   DIF: Moderate   REF: 454-455   OBJ: 14.4

31. In order to calm herself after she hears a loud noise, Tanya keeps repeating, "Dad says noises are funny." This behavior best illustrates the concept of
    a. imprinting.   c. emotion regulation.
    b. separation anxiety.   d. conformity.

    ANS: C   DIF: Moderate   REF: 454-455   OBJ: 14.4
    KEY: WWW

32. During infancy, caregivers
    a. can be the source of comfort and overstimulation.
    b. can be the source of comfort but not overstimulation.
    c. can be the source of overstimulation but not comfort.
    d. are neither a source of comfort nor overstimulation.

    ANS: A   DIF: Easy   REF: 455   OBJ: 14.4

33. A game of peek-a-boo between a mother and her infant daughter best exemplifies the concept of
    a. imprinting.   c. false belief.
    b. synchronized routine.   d. induction.

    ANS: B   DIF: Moderate   REF: 456   OBJ: 14.5

34. Which is the best example of a synchronized routine?
    a. A baby and a mother who are taking turns sticking out their tongues at each other
    b. A ducking following around a mother hen
    c. Dealing with the deaths of a social convoy of relatives as you age
    d. Two best friends watching a hockey game together

    ANS: A   DIF: Moderate   REF: 456   OBJ: 14.5
    KEY: WWW

35. The most likely outcome of an infant and parent who are in synchrony is a(n) _____ infant attachment.
    a. secure   c. insecure resistant
    b. insecure avoidant   d. undifferentiated

    ANS: A   DIF: Moderate   REF: 456   OBJ: 14.5

36. It is most accurate to say that a parent's attachment relationship with his or her child
    a. becomes firmly established before the child is born.
    b. is formed during the few hours immediately following the child's birth.
    c. will be seriously impaired if there are no opportunities for prolonged and immediate contact following the child's birth.
    d. builds gradually over a period of many months.

    ANS: D   DIF: Easy   REF: 456-457   OBJ: 14.5

37. At what age do infants typically first begin to express a preference for one familiar person over another?
    a. 2-6 weeks old   c. 7-8 months old
    b. 2-3 months old   d. 11-12 months or older

    ANS: B   DIF: Moderate   REF: 456   OBJ: 14.5

38. Displaying _____ would indicate the LEAST advanced social-cognitive abilities.
   a. goal-corrected partnership
   b. undiscriminating social responsiveness
   c. active proximity-seeking/true attachment
   d. discriminating social responsiveness

   ANS: B   DIF: Difficult   REF: 456-457   OBJ: 14.5
   KEY: WWW

39. Amanda shows a clear interest in listening to voices of humans but shows no particular preference for one person over another. Amanda is best classified as being in the _____ phase.
   a. goal-corrected partnership
   b. undiscriminating social responsiveness
   c. active proximity-seeking/true attachment
   d. discriminating social responsiveness

   ANS: B   DIF: Difficult   REF: 456   OBJ: 14.5

40. Displaying _____ would indicate the most advanced social-cognitive abilities.
   a. goal-corrected partnership
   b. undiscriminating social responsiveness
   c. active proximity-seeking/true attachment
   d. discriminating social responsiveness

   ANS: A   DIF: Moderate   REF: 457   OBJ: 14.5

41. Sven has just realized that before his daddy goes to work in the morning, he first eats breakfast in the kitchen. As a result of this realization, he now goes to the kitchen as soon as he hears his dad get up so that he can be near dad. This behavior best exemplifies
   a. goal-corrected partnership.
   b. undiscriminating social responsiveness.
   c. active proximity-seeking/true attachment.
   d. discriminating social responsiveness.

   ANS: A   DIF: Difficult   REF: 457   OBJ: 14.5

42. Which behavior best exemplifies a goal-correct partnership?
   a. An infant who knows that when mommy puts on her shoes she goes out running; so when the infant sees mommy put on her shoes, she follows her and plans to go with her
   b. An infant who cries whenever mommy leaves
   c. An infant who smiles broadly whenever she sees her mommy enter a room
   d. An infant who, when at the store, gets excited when anyone (family or stranger) picks up a toy that she finds interesting

   ANS: A   DIF: Difficult   REF: 457   OBJ: 14.5

43. Separation anxiety is best associated with the emotion of
   a. trust.
   b. euphoria.
   c. indigence.
   d. fear.

   ANS: D   DIF: Easy   REF: 457   OBJ: 14.5

715

44. Separation anxiety
    a. only occurs as a result of unresponsive parenting.
    b. is an important sign of attachment.
    c. occurs mainly in children who attend preschool.
    d. is a sign of an unhealthy attachment.

    ANS: B   DIF: Moderate   REF: 457   OBJ: 14.5

45. Separation anxiety generally appears
    a. at the time when infants begin to prefer human to nonhuman stimuli.
    b. at the time when infants begin to express a preference for familiar people.
    c. when the child forms his or her first genuine attachment.
    d. toward the end of the preoperational period.

    ANS: C   DIF: Moderate   REF: 457   OBJ: 14.5
    KEY: WWW

46. A college student becomes homesick during her first semester on campus. This response is
    most related to
    a. stranger anxiety.   c. separation anxiety.
    b. resistant attachment.   d. avoidant attachment.

    ANS: C   DIF: Moderate   REF: 457   OBJ: 14.5

47. _____ anxiety peaks first and is followed by _____ anxiety.
    a. Stranger; separation   c. Goal; separation
    b. Separation; stranger   d. Relationship; social

    ANS: B   DIF: Moderate   REF: 457   OBJ: 14.5

48. Two-year-old Floss is going to the dentist for the first time. She is sitting on her dad's lap
    when she first sees the dentist dressed in a long white coat. Floss reacts by turning and
    hugging her dad while she begins sobbing. Floss's reaction is best explained as involving
    _____ anxiety.
    a. stranger   c. goal
    b. separation   d. relationship

    ANS: A   DIF: Moderate   REF: 457   OBJ: 14.5

49. Regarding stranger anxiety, which is FALSE?
    a. Stranger anxiety is less likely to occur when mom is close by.
    b. Children are most wary of strangers when they are encountered in familiar
       surroundings.
    c. Stranger anxiety is lessened when the caregiver responds positively to the stranger.
    d. Stranger anxiety is affected by the appearance of the stranger.

    ANS: B   DIF: Difficult   REF: 456   OBJ: 14.5

716

50. According to Ainsworth, an attachment figure is best defined as serving as a(n) _____ for an attached child.
    a. secure base
    b. id replacement
    c. chum
    d. conscience

    ANS: A   DIF: Easy   REF: 457   OBJ: 14.5

51. Which research technique is best associated with the study of the quality of an attachment?
    a. Habituation paradigm
    b. Dichotomous listening task
    c. Incidental learning paradigm
    d. Strange situation procedure

    ANS: D   DIF: Easy   REF: 457   OBJ: 14.6

52. Greg and his infant daughter Dharma recently participated in a research study at the local college campus. Greg's simplified description of the study is "dad and baby together, baby by itself, someone else with baby, and then dad back with baby." Based on this description, you would be correct in assuming that Greg had participated in a studying using the _____ procedure.
    a. habituation
    b. dichotomous listening
    c. incidental learning
    d. strange situation

    ANS: D   DIF: Moderate   REF: 457   OBJ: 14.6

53. Most infants develop a(n) _____ attachment relationship with their caregiver(s).
    a. secure
    b. disorganized-disoriented
    c. resistant
    d. avoidant

    ANS: A   DIF: Easy   REF: 457-458   OBJ: 14.6

54. In which type of attachment does a child use a caregiver as a base, becomes somewhat upset when separated from the caregiver, and is fairly outgoing with a stranger if the caregiver is present?
    a. Secure
    b. Disorganized-disoriented
    c. Resistant
    d. Avoidant

    ANS: A   DIF: Moderate   REF: 457-458   OBJ: 14.6
    KEY: WWW

55. Pam loves to play with other children. As she plays in the sandbox at the park, she frequently climbs out to run over to her mommy, gives her a hug, and then runs back to the sandbox. When her mother walks a short distance away to get a drink at a fountain, Pam begins to cry and runs after her. After they both get a drink, they head back toward the sandbox, with Pam running ahead to join the other children in play. Pam's attachment relationship with her mother is best described as
    a. secure.
    b. resistant.
    c. avoidant.
    d. disorganized-disoriented.

    ANS: A   DIF: Difficult   REF: 457-458   OBJ: 14.6

56. Which best exemplifies the concept of proximity maintenance with a secure attachment?
    a. Becoming distressed when not near mommy
    b. Attempting to keep track of mommy's location
    c. Exploring away from mommy when she is present
    d. Moving toward mommy if comfort is needed

    ANS: B   DIF: Difficult   REF: 458   OBJ: 14.6

57. In which type of attachment does a child show clear distress when the caregiver to whom he is attached leaves, but ambivalence when the caregiver returns?
    a. Secure   c. Resistant
    b. Disorganized-disoriented   d. Avoidant

    ANS: C   DIF: Moderate   REF: 458   OBJ: 14.6

58. Kono takes her one-year-old son, Chin Ho, to visit an infant-toddler program that he will soon join. Chin Ho appears very anxious and is unwilling to explore and play with toys, even though Kono is close by. When Kono leaves the room, Chin Ho becomes extremely upset and remains that way all the time his mother is gone. When Kono returns, Chin Ho stays close to his mother, but makes it clear he does not want her to touch him or pick him up. He appears angry with Kono. This best demonstrates which sort of attachment relationship?
    a. Disorganized   c. Avoidant
    b. Resistant   d. Secure

    ANS: B   DIF: Moderate   REF: 458   OBJ: 14.6
    KEY: WWW

59. When Billie takes her son, Joel, to the park one day, he demands to be held and does not want to get down to play on the equipment. When another young mother comes over and strikes up a conversation with Billie, Joel hides his head in his mother's skirt, and refuses to play with the other woman's child. Eventually, Billie leaves Joel with the other woman briefly so she can buy drinks for all of them at the concession stand. Joel screams and cries, and is inconsolable. Joel's attachment relationship with his mother is best characterized as
    a. secure.   c. avoidant.
    b. resistant.   d. disorganized-disoriented.

    ANS: B   DIF: Moderate   REF: 458   OBJ: 14.6

60. A(n) _____ attachment is characterized by a lack of interest in exploring, little distress when separated from the attached caregiver, and lack of contact when the caregiver returns from separation.
    a. secure   c. resistant
    b. disorganized-disoriented   d. avoidant

    ANS: D   DIF: Easy   REF: 458   OBJ: 14.6

61. Frieda (18 months) and her mother are visiting at a friend's house. Although there are lots of toys to play with, Frieda seems disinterested. When Frieda's mother and her friend go to the kitchen for tea, Frieda appears undisturbed. Twenty minutes later, her mother emerges from the kitchen and tries to pick Frieda up. Frieda is unresponsive and wants to get down. When put down, Frieda ignores her mother and wanders around. This best demonstrates a(n) _____ attachment relationship between Frieda and her mom.
   a. disorganized-disoriented
   b. resistant
   c. avoidant
   d. secure

   ANS: C   DIF: Moderate   REF: 458   OBJ: 14.6

62. When disorganized-disoriented infants are reunited with their parent, they tend to
   a. not remember prior experiences.
   b. act dazed or seek attention (but move away if attention appears to be on its way).
   c. always scream in terror.
   d. sleep to escape the situation.

   ANS: B   DIF: Moderate   REF: 458   OBJ: 14.6

63. Odin is attached to his dad, Thor. The most interesting feature is Odin's seeming confusion about whether to approach or avoid his dad. Odin also seems unable to handle the negative emotions he feels following separation from Thor. Given this description, Odin is best classified as having a(n) _____ attachment with Thor.
   a. disorganized-disoriented
   b. resistant
   c. avoidant
   d. secure

   ANS: A   DIF: Moderate   REF: 458   OBJ: 14.6

64. Which infant attachment type is most highly associated with later emotional problems?
   a. Resistant
   b. Avoidant
   c. Reliant
   d. Disorganized-disoriented

   ANS: D   DIF: Moderate   REF: 458   OBJ: 14.6

65. Freud believed that the attachment relationship between parent and child occurs as a result of
   a. conditioning and reinforcement.
   b. an innate tendency to engage in proximity-seeking behaviors.
   c. advances in the infant's cognition that enable the child to discriminate between familiar and unfamiliar companions.
   d. early feeding experiences.

   ANS: D   DIF: Moderate   REF: 459   OBJ: 14.6
   KEY: WWW

66. Babita believes that her nursing relationship with her baby is absolutely essential to her child's well-being, and that it will have a powerful impact on her overall relationship with her child. Based on this outlook, Babita's views with regard to the attachment process are most similar to those of
   a. Harlow.
   b. Bandura.
   c. Freud.
   d. Ainsworth.

   ANS: C   DIF: Moderate   REF: 459   OBJ: 14.6

67. Harlow and Zimmerman's classic research regarding Freud's views of feeding practices and the attachment process indicated that
  a. Freud was correct in assuming that the feeding process plays the central role in establishing parent/child attachments.
  b. breast feeding is far superior to bottle feeding with regard to promoting parent/child attachments.
  c. contact with a soft, cuddly caregiver is more important than specific feeding practices with regard to the establishment of parent/child attachments.
  d. attachments are biologically programmed, therefore feeding becomes irrelevant in the attachment process.

  ANS: C   DIF: Moderate   REF: 459   OBJ: 14.6

68. Harlow and Zimmerman's classic research on feeding and attachment utilized _____ as research participants.
  a. rats   c. pigeons
  b. monkeys   d. humans

  ANS: B   DIF: Easy   REF: 459   OBJ: 14.6

69. Contact comfort is pleasurable _____ sensations.
  a. auditory   c. olfactory
  b. visual   d. tactile

  ANS: D   DIF: Moderate   REF: 459   OBJ: 14.6

70. While researching attachment behavior, Professor Plumb notes that infants are most likely to securely attach to caregivers who wear soft and "cuddly" sweaters and who hold the infants a lot while they are wearing these sweaters. This discovery best fits with research demonstrating the importance of
  a. a social convoy.   c. imprinting.
  b. contact comfort.   d. chumship.

  ANS: B   DIF: Moderate   REF: 459   OBJ: 14.6

71. Lisa is a very high-strung, active mom. Her baby, Marie, is very laid back and calm. When Lisa bounces Marie on her knee, tickles her, and talks to her in a loud and excited voice, Marie turns away. Lisa turns Marie back toward her, bounces her more rigorously, and continues to talk and sing more loudly than before. Based on this pattern of behavior, it is most likely that Marie will develop a(n) _____ to her mother.
  a. avoidant attachment   c. resistant attachment
  b. secure attachment   d. Oedipal complex

  ANS: A   DIF: Difficult   REF: 459   OBJ: 14.6

72. Which type of infant attachment is best associated with having a mother who is abusing drugs?
  a. Disorganized-disoriented   c. Avoidant
  b. Resistant   d. Secure

  ANS: A   DIF: Moderate   REF: 459   OBJ: 14.6

73. As Winston has been a victim of physical abuse as an infant, he has the greatest chance of developing a(n) _____ attachment style.
   a. disorganized-disoriented
   b. resistant
   c. avoidant
   d. secure

   ANS: A   DIF: Difficult   REF: 459   OBJ: 14.6

74. The Piagetian term _____ is used to describe the cognitive skill of appreciating a person even when that person is removed from one's view.
   a. preoperational thought
   b. person permanence
   c. synchronized routine
   d. active proximity

   ANS: B   DIF: Easy   REF: 460   OBJ: 14.6

75. A sensitive parent can do _____ to convert a "difficult" baby into an infant who can regulate emotions and who is socially competent.
   a. nothing
   b. a little
   c. a fair amount
   d. a lot

   ANS: D   DIF: Easy   REF: 460   OBJ: 14.6

76. German parents tend to encourage _____ in their children while Japanese parents encourage _____.
   a. dependence; independence
   b. independence; dependence
   c. violence; passivity
   d. passivity; violence

   ANS: B   DIF: Easy   REF: 460   OBJ: 14.6

77. Which statement concerning the role of culture on infant attachment is true?
   a. Attachment styles are universal and unaffected by culture.
   b. In collectivist cultures, infants are more likely to develop autonomous behaviors.
   c. Most infants raised in individualistic cultures are insecurely attached to their primary caregiver.
   d. A secure attachment is best defined by cultural standards that can vary from country to country.

   ANS: D   DIF: Moderate   REF: 460   OBJ: 14.6

78. Which saying was used to summarize research on infants raised in deprived institutional settings?
   a. An apple does not fall far from the tree.
   b. Beauty is in the eye of the beholder.
   c. Experience is overrated.
   d. It is better to have loved and lost than never to have loved at all.

   ANS: D   DIF: Difficult   REF: 461   OBJ: 14.7

721

79. Research on infants raised in deprived institutions in Romania found that
    a. early experiences had little impact on later development.
    b. a lack of physical contact can lead to significant delays in cognitive, physical, and socioemotional development.
    c. the longer a child is in the deprived environment, the less the negative impact of the experience (as the child will acclimate to the deprivation).
    d. the impact of the deprivation is directly related to the biological parents' level of intellect (i.e., IQ).

    ANS: B   DIF: Easy   REF: 461   OBJ: 14.7

80. Yara spent the first 12 months of her life in an environment best described as "extremely deprived." What characteristic would you LEAST expect to see in Yara at age five?
    a. Significant likelihood of schizophrenia   c. Mild cognitive retardation
    b. Emotional withdrawal   d. Delayed motor skills

    ANS: A   DIF: Difficult   REF: 461   OBJ: 14.7

81. Romanian orphans who had experienced the longest duration of early deprivation were most likely to show indiscriminate friendliness and difficulty in reciprocal social interactions that characterize _____ attachment.
    a. avoidant   c. disinhibited
    b. resistant   d. disorganized

    ANS: C   DIF: Moderate   REF: 461   OBJ: 14.7

82. Studies of infants raised in deprived orphanages for the first eight or more months of their lives indicate that
    a. a lack of a biological mother during the first year of life leads to significant and lasting developmental delays.
    b. male infants are more at risk for a lack of early life stimulation.
    c. children who are deprived of intellectual stimulation during the first six months of life often display long-term negative impact on their cognitive skills.
    d. being surrounded by infant peers can make up for the lack of stimulation by adults.

    ANS: C   DIF: Moderate   REF: 461-462   OBJ: 14.7
    KEY: WWW

83. What is the best way to prevent the negative impacts typically found in infants raised in institutions?
    a. Better physical care
    b. Improved sensory stimulation
    c. A stable team of caregivers
    d. Ensuring that each child has a designated "mother figure"

    ANS: C   DIF: Moderate   REF: 462   OBJ: 14.7

84. According to a 2006 National Institute of Child Health and Human Development study, the most critical summary of daycare is that
    a. whether or not a child was in daycare was the best predictor of the establishment of attachment type.
    b. infants from disadvantaged environments tend not to benefit from a stimulating daycare experience.
    c. quality of care matters.
    d. children in daycare typically fail to thrive.

    ANS: C   DIF: Easy   REF: 462   OBJ: 14.7

85. Which does NOT belong on a list of characteristics of a quality daycare?
    a. High rate of staff turnover (to expose children to more people)
    b. Responsive caregivers
    c. Age-appropriate stimulation activities
    d. Child-to-caregiver ratio of about 3:1 for infants

    ANS: A   DIF: Easy   REF: 462-463   OBJ: 14.7

86. As an infant, Molly was securely attached to her mother and her father, and this attachment has not changed. When she enters preschool, she is most likely to
    a. strenuously resist separating from her parents.
    b. cling to her teacher in her parents' absence.
    c. be curious and willing to explore her environment.
    d. be socially immature.

    ANS: C   DIF: Moderate   REF: 463   OBJ: 14.7

87. Longitudinal research on the long-term effects of having been securely attached as an infant indicates that
    a. a secure attachment in infancy predicted the quality of peer relationships in elementary school.
    b. an insecure attachment in infancy predicted the quality of one's marriage.
    c. a secure attachment in adolescence predicted the quality of life review near death.
    d. an insecure attachment in adolescence predicted college grades.

    ANS: A   DIF: Moderate   REF: 463   OBJ: 14.7

88. Regarding attachment, which is true?
    a. A secure attachment to one's father can compensate for a poor attachment relationship with one's mother.
    b. The quality of attachments in childhood does not predict later social competence.
    c. Insecurely attached infants are doomed to problems for the rest of their lives.
    d. Life events do not impact an attachment style once it has been formed.

    ANS: A   DIF: Moderate   REF: 463   OBJ: 14.7

89. Which best summarizes the effects of parent-child attachments on later development?
    a. Insecurely attached infants have life-long emotional problems, even if the attachment style improves after infancy.
    b. A secure relationship with one's father cannot compensate for an insecure mother-child attachment relationship.
    c. A secure attachment may become insecure as a result of major stresses in the family, such as divorce or a mother returning to work.
    d. An infant who is securely attached to its mother at age one appears to make that child "invulnerable to later socioemotional" difficulties.

    ANS: C   DIF: Moderate   REF: 463   OBJ: 14.7
    KEY: WWW

90. Research on infants raised on Israeli kibbutzim where they spend a great deal of time being cared for in groups has shown that children as young as _____ can first   begin to show true attachments to other children.
    a. 5 days old   c. 1 year old
    b. 1 month old   d. 5 years old

    ANS: C   DIF: Moderate   REF: 464   OBJ: 14.7

91. According to Bowlby, the key change in parent/child attachments during childhood involves
    a. more socialize efforts by the child and less by the parent.
    b. the child's abandonment of the notion of the parent as a safe haven when frightened.
    c. a more goal-directed partnership.
    d. a reduction in the child attempting to negotiate when ritualistic events (e.g., reading a book) occur.

    ANS: C   DIF: Moderate   REF: 464-465   OBJ: 14.8

92. Which is the most common peer network play behavior for a six-year-old boy?
    a. Playing by himself   c. Playing with a group of other boys
    b. Playing with one other boy   d. Playing with a group of girls

    ANS: C   DIF: Moderate   REF: 465   OBJ: 14.8

93. During the play years, age two to five, play behavior becomes
    a. more social and more imaginative.   c. less social and more imaginative.
    b. more social and less imaginative.   d. less social and less imaginative.

    ANS: A   DIF: Moderate   REF: 465   OBJ: 14.9

94. _____ play is characterized by aimless activities (e.g. pacing) and/or idly standing by.
    a. Unoccupied   c. Onlooker
    b. Solitary   d. Parallel

    ANS: A   DIF: Moderate   REF: 465   OBJ: 14.9

95. Five-year-old Otto is watching a group of children who are playing with Lego blocks. Occasionally, he says things like "that's a neat car" or "want some blocks?" However, he does not sit down and play with the Legos himself. This best demonstrates which form of play?
   a. Unoccupied
   b. Cooperative
   c. Onlooker
   d. Solitary

   ANS: C   DIF: Difficult   REF: 465   OBJ: 14.9

96. Thomas is on the floor and highly engaged with the toy train engine that he is pushing around the track by himself. Thomas is most accurately said to be engaged in _____ play.
   a. unoccupied
   b. solitary
   c. onlooker
   d. associative

   ANS: B   DIF: Easy   REF: 465   OBJ: 14.9

97. Addy and Kit are both playing with dolls in the doll corner. They are dressing and undressing the dolls, and pretending to feed them dinner. However, Addy and Kit do not talk to one another or involve each other in their play. This best demonstrates which type of play?
   a. Associative
   b. Cooperative
   c. Solitary
   d. Parallel

   ANS: D   DIF: Moderate   REF: 465   OBJ: 14.9

98. Which is the primary distinction between associative and cooperative play?
   a. Cooperative play involves activities directed toward a common goal and associative play does not.
   b. Cooperative play involves sharing the same materials while associative play does not.
   c. Cooperative play involves interaction between playmates while associative play does not.
   d. Cooperative play emerges during the concrete-operational period while associative play emerges during preoperational thought.

   ANS: A   DIF: Difficult   REF: 465   OBJ: 14.9

99. Benny and June are playing school. Benny is the teacher and June is the student. After a while, they decide they need a principal and some more students, so they ask Johnny and Winona to join them. This activity best demonstrates the concept of _____ play.
   a. associative
   b. cooperative
   c. functional
   d. parallel

   ANS: B   DIF: Difficult   REF: 465   OBJ: 14.9
   KEY: WWW

100. One-year-old Tiffany looks in a cup and sees that it is empty. She then lifts the cup to her lips, tips it toward her mouth, and smiles as if she is drinking something she likes. Tiffany's behavior is best categorized as _____ play.
   a. onlooker
   b. parallel
   c. pretend
   d. cooperative

   ANS: C   DIF: Moderate   REF: 465   OBJ: 14.9

101. In order to demonstrate pretend play. a child must
    a. possess language.
    b. have the ability to construct a mental representation of an event.
    c. have reached the concrete-operational stage of thinking.
    d. prefer parallel to associative play.

    ANS: B   DIF: Moderate   REF: 465-466   OBJ: 14.9

102. Which is the best example of social pretend play?
    a. Using a stick to represent a gun
    b. Using some dolls to act out a tea party
    c. Using a soccer ball to play soccer
    d. Using a smile when you act out eating a candy bar that is not there

    ANS: B   DIF: Moderate   REF: 466   OBJ: 14.9

103. How would the social pretend play of a Korean preschooler and a U.S. preschooler most likely vary?
    a. Due to cultural differences, a Korean preschooler would be unlikely to have begun to engage in social pretend play
    b. Due to cultural differences, a U.S. preschooler would be unlikely to have begun to engage in social pretend play
    c. Due to cultural differences, the Korean child's play will more likely focus on family roles while the U.S. child will focus on superhero play
    d. Due to cultural differences, the U.S. child's play will more likely focus on family roles while the Korean child will focus on superhero play

    ANS: C   DIF: Moderate   REF: 466   OBJ: 14.9

104. Piaget believed that in order for a child to engage in cooperative play with others in games that involved rules, he or she must have reached the _____ stage of thought.
    a. sensorimotor   c. concrete-operational
    b. preoperational   d. formal operations

    ANS: C   DIF: Moderate   REF: 466   OBJ: 14.9

105. In 19th-century America, childhood play was seen as
    a. essential.   c. frivolous.
    b. satanic.   d. mind-building.

    ANS: C   DIF: Easy   REF: 466   OBJ: 14.9

106. Which is true with regard to the effects of play on development?
    a. Preschoolers who engage in considerable amounts of social pretend play tend to be more popular and more socially mature than those who do not.
    b. Play contributes significantly to physical and social development, but has little impact on the development of cognitive skills.
    c. While engagement in pretend play tends to stimulate creative thought processes, it tends to interfere with the development of logical thought.
    d. Play contributes to the emotional development of preschoolers by helping children work through unresolved conflicts, but it detracts from children's intellectual development by keeping them from engaging in more productive academic tasks.

    ANS: A   DIF: Moderate   REF: 467   OBJ: 14.9

107. Sociometric techniques are specifically used to measure
    a. cognitive maturity.   c. who is liked or disliked in a group.
    b. intelligence.   d. psychomotor activity levels.

    ANS: C   DIF: Easy   REF: 467   OBJ: 14.10

108. Which question would you be most likely to find on a sociometric assessment?
    a. What is the capital of Wisconsin?   c. Do you feel good about yourself?
    b. What is the square root of 9?   d. Which classmate do you hate?

    ANS: D   DIF: Moderate   REF: 467   OBJ: 14.10
    KEY: WWW

109. Molly's classmates rarely choose her as a work- or playmate, yet she is not disliked by most of her peers. She tends to be shy and quiet, and on those rare occasions that someone does ask her to play, Molly often says no and walks away. According to categories of sociometric status, Molly is best classified as
    a. neglected.   c. antisocial.
    b. rejected.   d. controversial.

    ANS: A   DIF: Moderate   REF: 467   OBJ: 14.10

110. On a sociometric measure, an "average" child will be
    a. liked by most and disliked by few.
    b. liked by few and disliked by most.
    c. rated in the middle on both liked and disliked scales.
    d. rated in the high on both liked and disliked scales.

    ANS: C   DIF: Moderate   REF: 467   OBJ: 14.10

111. When commenting on a rejected child, peers would be most likely to say,
    a. "no comment."
    b. "he's okay most of the time."
    c. "I hate that kid."
    d. "I don't even know who you are talking about."

    ANS: C   DIF: Easy   REF: 467   OBJ: 14.10

112. Sterling is both well liked by many of his peers and hated by others. The kids who like him focus on his leadership skills, while those who hate him focus on the fact that he likes to start fights. According to categories of sociometric status, Sterling is best classified as
a. neglected.
b. rejected.
c. antisocial.
d. controversial.

ANS: D   DIF: Moderate   REF: 467   OBJ: 14.10

113. A "popular child" is one who is
a. liked by half and rejected by half.
b. liked by most and rejected by few.
c. liked by a few more than he or she is rejected by.
d. equally liked and disliked.

ANS: B   DIF: Easy   REF: 467   OBJ: 14.10

114. Which of the following is NOT associated with "popularity" in childhood?
a. Being physically attractive
b. Being intelligent
c. Being socially competent
d. Being unassertive

ANS: D   DIF: Easy   REF: 467   OBJ: 14.10

115. Reggie has both leadership qualities and is an aggressive bully. Given this mix of characteristics, he is most likely to be rated as _____ by his peers.
a. controversial
b. rejected
c. neglected
d. average

ANS: A   DIF: Moderate   REF: 467   OBJ: 14.10

116. Which of the following is FALSE with regard to rejected children?
a. A child who is rejected by peers one year will probably again be rejected the next, especially if the rejection is due to aggression.
b. Rejected children are at risk for becoming juvenile delinquents.
c. Rejection by peers during the childhood years is unlikely to have long-term effects on behavior.
d. Rejected children tend to enter new situations expecting to be disliked.

ANS: C   DIF: Moderate   REF: 467   OBJ: 14.10

117. Which statement concerning childhood friendships is FALSE?
a. Many unpopular children have at least one reciprocal friend.
b. Having a friend increases the odds of being happy.
c. Having a chum is detrimental to the development of a friendship.
d. True friends are not considered attachment figures.

ANS: C   DIF: Difficult   REF: 467   OBJ: 14.10

118. Adolescents who have secure attachments with their parents have
a. higher levels of self-esteem.
b. more behavioral problems.
c. lower levels of social competence.
d. poorer emotional adjustment.

ANS: A   DIF: Moderate   REF: 469   OBJ: 14.11

119. Which best exemplifies co-rumination?
    a. Talking to a friend excessively about your thoughts of suicide
    b. Living in the same household with your parents and at least one other relative
    c. Hanging out at the mall with a small group of acquaintances
    d. Falling in love with two people at the same time

    ANS: A   DIF: Moderate   REF: 470   OBJ: 14.11

120. One of the biggest disadvantages of engaging in co-rumination is that it
    a. tends to lead to illegal behavior.
    b. often results in a child "hanging out with the wrong crowd."
    c. can increase the negative effects one's anxiety.
    d. reinforces the idea that not talking about a problem is the best way to deal with your troubles.

    ANS: C   DIF: Moderate   REF: 470   OBJ: 14.11

121. According to Dumpy (1963), the typical developmental sequence of events in the adolescent peer group is
    a. isolated unisex cliques, interaction between unisex cliques, heterosexual cliques, fully developed crowds.
    b. heterosexual crowds, isolated unisex cliques, interaction between unisex cliques, groups of couples.
    c. isolated heterosexual cliques, interaction between heterosexual crowds, unisex cliques, groups of couples.
    d. isolated unisex groups, heterosexual crowds, interaction between heterosexual groups, groups of cliques.

    ANS: A   DIF: Difficult   REF: 470   OBJ: 14.12

122. Which statement is true?
    a. Cliques and crowds are unrelated.
    b. Crowds are homosexual and cliques are heterosexual.
    c. Crowds are a collection of cliques.
    d. Cliques consist of a heterosexual crowd and a homosexual crowd.

    ANS: C   DIF: Moderate   REF: 470   OBJ: 14.12
    KEY: WWW

123. Heather hangs with a group of four other girls who, just like her, all wear the trendiest fashions. According to Dunphy (1963), this group is best classified as a
    a. population.   c. confidant.
    b. crowd.   d. clique.

    ANS: D   DIF: Moderate   REF: 470   OBJ: 14.12

729

124. In Mary Jane's high school, there is one large group of kids who are called the "stoners." The stoners are a large group of males and females who are a little different from other groups of kids in the class (e.g., the "goths") in that they hold a very casual attitude concerning drug use. The stoners are best classified as a
   a. chumship.
   b. clique.
   c. crowd.
   d. dyad.

   ANS: C   DIF: Moderate   REF: 470   OBJ: 14.12

125. A _____ must consist of both male and female members.
   a. chumship
   b. clique
   c. crowd
   d. dyad

   ANS: C   DIF: Moderate   REF: 470   OBJ: 14.12
   KEY: WWW

126. During adolescence,
   a. peer influences are typically negative.
   b. those with friends are more likely to engage in delinquent behavior.
   c. crowd affiliation has implications for social identity.
   d. crowd membership is best predicted by personality factors.

   ANS: C   DIF: Moderate   REF: 470-471   OBJ: 14.12

127. During adolescence, early dating relationships tend to be more _____ when compared to dating in later adolescence.
   a. short-lived
   b. sexual
   c. formal
   d. romantic

   ANS: A   DIF: Moderate   REF: 471-472   OBJ: 14.12

128. To Doug and Carrie, dating involves a sense of long-term commitment and high levels of emotional intimacy. Given this description, this relationship appears to be in Brown's _____ dating phase.
   a. initiation
   b. status
   c. affection
   d. bonding

   ANS: D   DIF: Moderate   REF: 472   OBJ: 14.12

129. When Latrell is on his date, his main focus is on coming to see himself as a person who is capable of relating to the opposite sex in a romantic way. Given this description, Latrell appears to be in Brown's _____ dating phase.
   a. initiation
   b. status
   c. affection
   d. bonding

   ANS: A   DIF: Moderate   REF: 472   OBJ: 14.12

130. To Van, the most important aspect of his current romantic relationship is the fact that he is dating the head cheerleader, which means that the group he hangs out with now seems to be much "cooler" than it used to be. This description indicates that Van is best classified as being in Brown's _____ phase of dating.
   a. initiation
   b. status
   c. affection
   d. bonding

   ANS: B   DIF: Difficult   REF: 472   OBJ: 14.12
   KEY: WWW

131. During the _____ phase of dating, the relationship becomes the focus and romantic relationships become more personal.
   a. initiation
   b. status
   c. affection
   d. bonding

   ANS: C   DIF: Easy   REF: 472   OBJ: 14.12

132. The array of significant individuals who serve as sources of social support is called the social
   a. convoy.
   b. status.
   c. situation.
   d. cognition.

   ANS: A   DIF: Easy   REF: 472   OBJ: 14.13

133. Aunts and uncles who know and support you across your lifetime are best classified as part of your social
   a. convoy.
   b. clique.
   c. crowd.
   d. chumship.

   ANS: A   DIF: Moderate   REF: 472   OBJ: 14.13
   KEY: WWW

134. In what ways do the social networks of younger and older adults differ?
   a. Middle-aged adults have more close friends than younger adults do.
   b. Old people feel more need to receive social stimulation.
   c. Younger adults have broader social networks than middle-aged adults.
   d. Older adults interact more frequently with acquaintances.

   ANS: C   DIF: Moderate   REF: 472-473   OBJ: 14.13

135. According to socioemotional selectivity theory,
   a. teenagers are biologically programmed to be more conforming.
   b. most older adults will conduct a life review.
   c. the older we get, the more important it becomes to acquire knowledge.
   d. shrinking social networks in adulthood are by choice.

   ANS: D   DIF: Moderate   REF: 473   OBJ: 14.13

136. As an individual who subscribes to socioemotional selectivity theory, Darlene is most likely to believe that
    a. social networks in adulthood serve no useful purpose.
    b. older adults seek interactions that are emotionally meaningful.
    c. older adults experience significantly more negative emotions than young adults.
    d. having fewer friends in older adulthood is a sign of potential psychosis.

    ANS: B   DIF: Moderate   REF: 473   OBJ: 14.13

137. When discussing her life, 60-year-old Erica says, "I am quite happy the way I am and I see no need to go out and make new friends." This statement best with the basic premise of _____ theory.
    a. socioemotional selectivity   c. activity
    b. social learning   d. gender typing

    ANS: A   DIF: Moderate   REF: 473   OBJ: 14.13

138. Which statement concerning emotional lives is true?
    a. Older adults have more depressed emotional lives than young adults.
    b. Negative emotions are less common in older adults than in younger adults.
    c. Younger adults experience longer-lasting periods of positive emotions.
    d. No differences exist in the typical emotional lives of young versus older age adults.

    ANS: B   DIF: Moderate   REF: 473   OBJ: 14.13

139. The process of paying more attention to and remembering more positive information than negative information is referred to as the _____ effect.
    a. contact comfort   c. positivity
    b. equity   d. synchronized

    ANS: C   DIF: Easy   REF: 473   OBJ: 14.13

140. Seventy-year-old Heidi had a doctor appointment in the morning. At the appointment, her physician told Heidi that her blood pressure was "pretty high," her bone density was "scary," and her cholesterol level was "fine." When Heidi's husband asks her how the appointment, Heidi says, "the doctors said that I was fine." This comment illustrates the concept of
    a. a positivity effect.   c. generativity.
    b. chumship.   d. co-rumination.

    ANS: A   DIF: Moderate   REF: 473   OBJ: 14.13

141. Results from evolutionary theorist research on mate selection indicates that when comparing women and men,
    a. males place more emphasis on physical attractiveness.
    b. males place more emphasis on a potential mate's resources.
    c. females place more emphasis on selecting a passive mate.
    d. females place more emphasis on race/ethnicity.

    ANS: A   DIF: Moderate   REF: 474   OBJ: 14.14

142. The notion that potential romantic partnerships begin with both individuals looking for external similarities in their partner (e.g., race, education, socioeconomic status), then eventually looking for similarity of inner qualities (e.g., values, beliefs) and if both comparative phases are successful, the relationship may continue best fits with the _____ theory of mate selection.
    a. psychoanalytic
    b. triangular
    c. social-learning
    d. filter

    ANS: D   DIF: Moderate   REF: 474   OBJ: 14.14

143. If someone says that the key to mate selection is homogamy, that person is saying that the most important determinant of success is
    a. sex.
    b. similarity.
    c. security.
    d. self-efficacy.

    ANS: B   DIF: Moderate   REF: 474   OBJ: 14.14

144. The saying, "_____" best illustrates the mate selection concept of homogamy.
    a. you can't teach an old dog new tricks
    b. opposites attract
    c. beauty is only skin deep
    d. birds of a feather flock together

    ANS: D   DIF: Easy   REF: 474   OBJ: 14.14

145. Which should NOT be included on a list of the three key components of the triangular theory love?
    a. Passion
    b. Intimacy
    c. Aptitude
    d. Decision/commitment

    ANS: C   DIF: Easy   REF: 474   OBJ: 14.14
    KEY: WWW

146. When Amanda describes her romantic partner, she says, "the only thing that we have going for us is raw sexual attraction." Sternberg would argue that this relationship is based solely on
    a. passion.
    b. intimacy.
    c. aptitude.
    d. decision/commitment.

    ANS: A   DIF: Easy   REF: 474   OBJ: 14.14

147. When Tom is describing his relationship with Gisele, he says, "It's got everything: sexual attraction, trust and respect, and we know that we are both in it for the long haul." This description indicates that their relationship is most accurately described as involving _____ love.
    a. consummate
    b. fatuous
    c. infatuation
    d. companionate

    ANS: A   DIF: Moderate   REF: 474-475   OBJ: 14.14

733

148. Companionate love is best characterized by
   a. high levels of intimacy, commitment, and passion.
   b. high levels of intimacy and commitment, but low levels of passion.
   c. high levels of commitment and passion, but low levels of intimacy.
   d. high levels of passion, but low levels of intimacy and passion.

   ANS: B   DIF: Moderate   REF: 474-475   OBJ: 14.14

149. When asked to describe herself, Hazel says, "I like people, but they don't seem to like me. I would really like to meet someone I could be close to." This attitude best fits with the _____ model of self.
   a. secure   c. preoccupied
   b. dismissing   d. fearful

   ANS: C   DIF: Difficult   REF: 475   OBJ: 14.15

150. When asked to describe himself, Dewayne says, "I don't need people, I don't need relationships, I am fine on my own." This attitude best fits with the _____ model of self.
   a. secure   c. preoccupied
   b. dismissing   d. fearful

   ANS: B   DIF: Difficult   REF: 475-476   OBJ: 14.15
   KEY: WWW

151. When asked to describe himself, Goober says, "I really don't like myself. I really don't like other people. On the other hand, it would be nice to meet someone but I don't really know how to do that." This attitude best fits with the _____ model of self.
   a. secure   c. preoccupied
   b. dismissing   d. fearful

   ANS: D   DIF: Difficult   REF: 475-476   OBJ: 14.15

152. In a pioneering study on adult love relationships, Hazan and Shaver found that most adults have a(n) _____ attachment style.
   a. avoidant   c. disorganized
   b. resistant   d. secure

   ANS: D   DIF: Moderate   REF: 476   OBJ: 14.15

153. Which best describes results from research on adults' internal working models of self?
   a. Early attachment styles have little bearing on love relationships.
   b. Internal working models predict the capacity for exploration in adulthood.
   c. There appears to be little intergenerational transmission of attachment styles.
   d. Internal working models are not subject to revision.

   ANS: B   DIF: Moderate   REF: 476   OBJ: 14.15

154. Which is FALSE?
   a. For elderly individuals, "old friends are the best friends."
   b. The quality of an adult's social relationships is closely related to a sense of well-being.
   c. Older people are relatively unconcerned with equity issues in friendships.
   d. For most married people, spouses are the most important confidant.

   ANS: C   DIF: Moderate   REF: 477   OBJ: 14.15

155. An elderly adult is likely to be most uncomfortable and distressed if he or she is
   a. the overbenefited person in a relationship.
   b. the underbenefited person in a relationship.
   c. in a highly equitable relationship.
   d. in a confidant relationship.

   ANS: A   DIF: Moderate   REF: 477   OBJ: 14.15

156. How many of the following (your husband, your sister, your coworker) could be a confidant?
   a. 0   c. 2
   b. 1   d. 3

   ANS: D   DIF: Easy   REF: 478   OBJ: 14.16

157. Which statement concerning relationships in old age is true?
   a. Social supports impact psychological but not physical health.
   b. Relationships with a spouse can undermine emotional well-being.
   c. Being involved with others wears the body down faster than living in isolation.
   d. Efforts to reduce loneliness in socially isolated elderly adults have not been shown to have any positive impact.

   ANS: B   DIF: Moderate   REF: 478   OBJ: 14.16

TRUE/FALSE

1. An attachment is a strong affectional tie that binds a person to an intimate companion.

   ANS: T   DIF: Easy   REF: 450   OBJ: 14.2

2. Human infants imprint to mothers during the first hours after birth as long as they are in close proximity (i.e., the same room).

   ANS: F   DIF: Moderate   REF: 451   OBJ: 14.2

3. A peer is defined as a social equal.

   ANS: T   DIF: Easy   REF: 452   OBJ: 14.3

4. A chumship is best described as a close adult friendship.

   ANS: F   DIF: Moderate   REF: 453   OBJ: 14.3

5. Embarrassment is a good example of a self-conscious emotion.

ANS: T   DIF: Moderate   REF: 453-454   OBJ: 14.4
KEY: WWW

6. A key characteristic of synchronized routines involves taking turns in response to each other's leads.

ANS: T   DIF: Moderate   REF: 456   OBJ: 14.5

7. Bowlby suggested that the first phase of attachment formation involves active proximity-seeking.

ANS: F   DIF: Difficult   REF: 456-457   OBJ: 14.5
KEY: WWW

8. Separation anxiety generally appears before stranger anxiety.

ANS: T   DIF: Moderate   REF: 457   OBJ: 14.5

9. A resistant attachment is characterized by a great deal of infant anxiety and ambivalence to the attached caregiver.

ANS: T   DIF: Difficult   REF: 458   OBJ: 14.6

10. An avoidant attachment is characterized by an infant who seems uninterested in exploration and who shows little distress when separated from the caregiver to whom it is attached.

ANS: T   DIF: Moderate   REF: 458   OBJ: 14.6
KEY: WWW

11. Infants who are socially deprived over a long time period can easily recover from any negative effects of this deprivation once they are given attention.

ANS: F   DIF: Easy   REF: 461-462   OBJ: 14.7

12. Onlooker play involves active interest and talking but no direct participation with another child.

ANS: T   DIF: Difficult   REF: 465   OBJ: 14.9

13. Sociometric techniques are typically used to assess infant-caregiver attachment.

ANS: F   DIF: Moderate   REF: 467   OBJ: 14.10
KEY: WWW

14. Controversial children are both liked and disliked by many children.

ANS: T   DIF: Easy   REF: 467   OBJ: 14.10

15. Adolescent friendships are characterized by increasing intimacy and self-disclosure.

ANS: T   DIF: Moderate   REF: 469-470   OBJ: 14.11

16. Social networks tend to proceed from crowds in late childhood to unisexual cliques in later adolescence.

ANS: T   DIF: Moderate   REF: 470   OBJ: 14.12

17. The bonding phase of adolescent romantic relationships is characterized by a focus on one's self.

ANS: F   DIF: Moderate   REF: 472   OBJ: 14.12

18. According to the socioemotional selectivity theory, social networks tend to expand dramatically between young and older adulthood.

ANS: F   DIF: Moderate   REF: 473   OBJ: 14.13
KEY: WWW

19. The commitment component of love is characterized by warmth, caring, and respect.

ANS: F   DIF: Moderate   REF: 474   OBJ: 14.14

20. Adults with dismissing styles of attachment have a negative view of both self and others.

ANS: F   DIF: Difficult   REF: 475   OBJ: 14.15

COMPLETION

1. _____ is an innate form of learning in which an animal will follow a moving object.

ANS: Imprinting

DIF: Moderate   REF: 451   OBJ: 14.2

2. Infants appear to construct a cognitive representation of themselves that is referred to as an _____ working model.

ANS: internal

DIF: Difficult   REF: 451   OBJ: 14.2   KEY: WWW

3. Emotional _____ is the process by which you initiate, maintain, and alter emotional responses.

ANS: regulation

DIF: Moderate   REF: 455   OBJ: 14.4

4. Two-year-old Rona becomes very upset when approached by an unfamiliar person. This common reaction is called _____ anxiety.

ANS: stranger

DIF: Moderate   REF: 457   OBJ: 14.5

5. One-year-old Burt becomes very upset whenever his mommy leaves the room. This common reaction is called _____ anxiety.

ANS: separation

DIF: Moderate   REF: 457   OBJ: 14.5   KEY: WWW

6. Most infants are classified as having a _____ attachment to their caregiver.

ANS: secure

DIF: Easy   REF: 457-458   OBJ: 14.6   KEY: WWW

7. The _____ style of attachment is most commonly seen in infants who have been physically abused or maltreated.

ANS: disorganized-disoriented

DIF: Difficult   REF: 459   OBJ: 14.6

8. Romanian orphans who had long-term exposure to a severely deprived environment often developed _____ attachments characterized by indiscriminate friendliness, lack of wariness of strangers, and difficulty in participating in reciprocal social interactions.

ANS: disinhibited

DIF: Difficult   REF: 461   OBJ: 14.7

9. During _____ play, children play next to each other and do the same thing, yet do not interact with each other.

ANS: parallel

DIF: Difficult   REF: 465   OBJ: 14.9

10. A child engaged in _____ play uses an object or themselves to stand for something or someone else.

ANS: pretend

DIF: Difficult   REF: 465   OBJ: 14.9

11. On sociometric measures, _____ individuals are liked by most and rarely disliked.

    ANS: popular

    DIF: Difficult   REF: 467   OBJ: 14.10

12. On sociometric measures, _____ individuals are neither liked nor disliked.

    ANS: neglected

    DIF: Difficult   REF: 467   OBJ: 14.10   KEY: WWW

13. When teenagers spend an excessive amount of time discussing personal problems with a friend they are engaging in _____.

    ANS: co-rumination

    DIF: Moderate   REF: 470   OBJ: 14.11

14. A _____ is generated by the merging of several heterosexual cliques.

    ANS: crowd

    DIF: Moderate   REF: 470   OBJ: 14.12

15. Dunphy used the term _____ when referring to small, same-sex friendship groups formed in late childhood.

    ANS: clique

    DIF: Moderate   REF: 470   OBJ: 14.12   KEY: WWW

16. Individuals in Brown's _____ phase of adolescent romantic relationships first begin to focus on the relationship rather than their self or peer-group acceptance.

    ANS: affection

    DIF: Difficult   REF: 472   OBJ: 14.12

17. A social support group that follows an individual across their lifetime is referred to as a social _____.

    ANS: convoy

    DIF: Moderate   REF: 472   OBJ: 14.13

18. Socioemotional _____ theory explains the shrinking social networks in aging adults as involving a choice designed to meet their emotional needs.

    ANS: selectivity

    DIF: Moderate   REF: 473   OBJ: 14.13

19. According the triangular theory of love, _____ love is characterized by high levels of passion, intimacy, and commitment.

ANS: companionate

DIF: Moderate   REF: 475   OBJ: 14.14

20. Adults with a _____ working model resemble infants with disorganized-disoriented attachments in that they need social relationships but lack a coherent strategy for meeting their attachment needs.

ANS: fearful

DIF: Difficult   REF: 475   OBJ: 14.15

ESSAY

1. How do Bowlby and Ainsworth integrate psychoanalytic, cognitive, and ethological concepts into their theory of attachment?

ANS: Answer not provided   REF: 450-452   OBJ: 14.2

2. Discuss the phases involved in attachment formation in infancy.

ANS: Answer not provided   REF: 456-457   OBJ: 14.5

3. What are the basic categories of peer acceptance and popularity? How does peer acceptance influence behavior?

ANS: Answer not provided   REF: 467-468   OBJ: 14.10

4. How do social networks change during adolescence?

ANS: Answer not provided   REF: 470-471   OBJ: 14.12

5. Discuss Brown's phases of romantic relationships in adolescence.

ANS: Answer not provided   REF: 472   OBJ: 14.12

6. Describe Sternberg's triangular theory of love.

ANS: Answer not provided   REF: 474-475   OBJ: 14.11

7. How do attachment styles and internal working models influence behavior in adulthood?

ANS: Answer not provided   REF: 475-476   OBJ: 14.15

8. Describe early emotional development from the display of primary emotions, to the expression of self-conscious emotions, to the act of self-referencing.

ANS: Answer not provided   REF: 453-455   OBJ: 14.4   KEY: WWW

740

9. How do the four basic types of attachment differ?

   ANS: Answer not provided   REF: 457-459   OBJ: 14.6   KEY: WWW

10. Describe Parten's types of play.

    ANS: Answer not provided   REF: 465   OBJ: 14.9   KEY: WWW

MULTIPLE CHOICE

1. Which statement concerning Michelle and Barack Obama is true?
   a. Barack was born in Illinois.
   b. Barack and Michelle were married when both were still teenagers.
   c. Michelle was Barack's mentor in law school.
   d. When Barack and Michelle moved into the White House, Barack's mother- and father-in-law joined them.

   ANS: C   DIF: Moderate   REF: 483   OBJ: 15.1

2. The family systems approach to understanding families suggests that
   a. the larger the family network, the lower the quality of interaction between parent and child.
   b. the mother is the central influence on a child's development.
   c. every relationship within the system has an impact on every other individual in the system.
   d. families function in a similar manner from one culture to the next.

   ANS: C   DIF: Moderate   REF: 484   OBJ: 15.1

3. Before the family systems perspective, the major focus of developmentalists who studied the family was on _____ relationships.
   a. father-mother   c. infant-peer
   b. peer-parent   d. mother-infant

   ANS: D   DIF: Easy   REF: 484   OBJ: 15.1

4. The nuclear family consists of
   a. the siblings in a family.
   b. mother, father, and one or more children.
   c. grandparents, parents, and offspring.
   d. one's family "tree."

   ANS: B   DIF: Easy   REF: 484   OBJ: 15.1

5. Which is the best example of a "nuclear" family?
   a. Anthony, who is a single parent of Julius
   b. Anthony and Cleo, who have a child named Julius
   c. Cleo, who lives by herself
   d. Anthony and Cleo, who are married but without children

   ANS: B   DIF: Moderate   REF: 484   OBJ: 15.1
   KEY: WWW

6. The minimum number of members required in a nuclear family is
   a. 1.   c. 3.
   b. 2.   d. 4.

   ANS: C   DIF: Moderate   REF: 484   OBJ: 15.1

7. Which is the best example of a reciprocal influence within a nuclear family?
   a. Kindergartner Alice playing with her favorite doll
   b. Baby Alice smiling and her dad, Mel, who upon seeing the smile, gives her some candy
   c. Single parent Mel thinking about having another child
   d. Teenager Alice talking to her best friend, Flo

   ANS: B   DIF: Moderate   REF: 484   OBJ: 15.1

8. When both parents act as a single team when childrearing, _____ is taking place.
   a. coparenting   c. a blended family
   b. an extended family   d. autonomy

   ANS: A   DIF: Easy   REF: 485   OBJ: 15.1

9. Which best exemplifies the concept of coparenting?
   a. When singles Joe and Josephine decide that they will have a baby together
   b. When daughter Ella and her mother Elsa decide to complete a school project together
   c. When parents Edwin and Edwina agree to not spank their children
   d. When father Max and his father Ax decide that they will both speak to Max's daughter and Axe's grandson Dax about his drug use

   ANS: C   DIF: Moderate   REF: 485   OBJ: 15.1

10. Which is the best example of an extended family household?
    a. A mother and father, their children, and the grandparents who live with them
    b. Mother, father, and their 12 children
    c. A large group of orphans residing in the same room
    d. A single man and his roommate

    ANS: A   DIF: Moderate   REF: 485   OBJ: 15.1

11. Madison lives with her dad, mother, grandmother, aunt, and older brother, Austin. Madison's family is best termed a(n) ___ family household.
    a. dysfunctional   c. reconstituted
    b. nuclear   d. extended

    ANS: D   DIF: Moderate   REF: 485   OBJ: 15.1

12. Which is a commonly cited advantage of the extended family household?
    a. Fewer mouths to feed
    b. Provides for shared responsibility for raising children
    c. Ensures more income for family
    d. Provides safe environment for gay/lesbian couple to raise a family

    ANS: B   DIF: Moderate   REF: 485   OBJ: 15.1

744

13. The conceptualization of a "family as a system" best matches the _____ approach to psychology.
   a. bioecological
   b. classical conditioning
   c. psychodynamic
   d. Gestalt

ANS: A   DIF: Moderate   REF: 485   OBJ: 15.1

14. The concept of a family life cycle
   a. rejects the notion of stages of development.
   b. emphasizes the role of the id and ego in decision-making.
   c. suggests that the nuclear family is the ideal family system.
   d. highlights systematic role changes that occur within family relationships from marriage to death.

ANS: D   DIF: Moderate   REF: 485-486   OBJ: 15.2

15. According to the family lifecycle approach, the initial stage of the family cycle involves a
   a. preschool boy and girl being socialized into the role of a father or mother.
   b. dating couple.
   c. married couple without children.
   d. married couple that have just had their first child (the childbearing family).

ANS: C   DIF: Difficult   REF: 485-486   OBJ: 15.2
KEY: WWW

16. How do most modern theorists react to the notion of sequential phases of a traditional family life cycle?
   a. They are highly supportive.
   b. They support the idea, but only in nuclear families.
   c. They support the idea, but only in extended families.
   d. They question the idea and embrace the view of individuals and families following a wider variety of life cycles.

ANS: D   DIF: Moderate   REF: 486   OBJ: 15.2

17. The concept of linked lives involves the notion that development as an individual is _____ that of other family members.
   a. intertwined with
   b. independent from
   c. inversely related to
   d. identical to

ANS: A   DIF: Moderate   REF: 486   OBJ: 15.2

18. Which of the following changes in the nature of the American family is true?
   a. Family size (number of offspring) is on the rise.
   b. The number of working moms is declining.
   c. The age of marriage has been delayed.
   d. There has been a decrease in the number of children living in poverty.

ANS: C   DIF: Moderate   REF: 486-487   OBJ: 15.2

19. U.S. Census Bureau data indicates that compared with the recent past, there are currently fewer
   a. single adults.
   b. single-parent families.
   c. remarriages.
   d. caregivers for aging adults.

   ANS: D   DIF: Moderate   REF: 486-487   OBJ: 15.2

20. Morticia and Gomez are getting married. It is a first marriage for both of them. Based on recent research (including U.S. census data), which is true?
   a. Morticia and Gomez are most likely younger than their parents were when they got married.
   b. There is a 60% probability that Morticia and Gomez will get divorced.
   c. Morticia is more likely than her mother was to work outside of the home.
   d. Morticia and Gomez are likely to have more children than their parents did.

   ANS: C   DIF: Moderate   REF: 486-487   OBJ: 15.2

21. A "reconstituted" family must contain
   a. a widow.
   b. a step-parent.
   c. at least three generations residing in the same household.
   d. a step-brother or step-sister.

   ANS: B   DIF: Moderate   REF: 487   OBJ: 15.2

22. Jayme and Joshua live with their mom and her new husband and their new baby. Jayme and Joshua's family is best termed a(n) ___ family.
   a. beanpole
   b. reconstituted
   c. extended
   d. single-parent

   ANS: B   DIF: Moderate   REF: 487   OBJ: 15.2

23. When compared to recent past generations in the United States, children today are more likely to
   a. have multiple siblings.
   b. live in a multigenerational household.
   c. have a stay-at-home mom.
   d. reside in a two-parent headed household.

   ANS: B   DIF: Moderate   REF: 487   OBJ: 15.2
   KEY: WWW

24. Concerning modern trends in family life,
   a. today's two wage-earner families are financially worse off that families with one wage earner.
   b. most adults now view marriage as an unimportant institution.
   c. more children today have relationships with their grandparents than in generations past.
   d. the nuclear family continues to be the dominant family type in the United States.

   ANS: C   DIF: Easy   REF: 486-487   OBJ: 15.2

25. Which is true with regard to the nature of early parent-child interactions?
   a. As the result of genetic factors, fathers have been shown to be incapable of sensitive parenting.
   b. Mothers are far more sensitive to infants' cues during feeding.
   c. Fathers are more likely to engage in "playful interactions" (e.g., tickling, bouncing) with their children.
   d. Fathers are significantly less effective at feeding infants.

   ANS: C   DIF: Moderate   REF: 489   OBJ: 15.3
   KEY: WWW

26. Mothers _____ than fathers.
   a. spend more time with children   c. devote less time to caregiving
   b. devote more time to play   d. are qualitatively better parents

   ANS: A   DIF: Easy   REF: 488   OBJ: 15.3

27. Fathers are most likely to adopt a "motherlike" caregiver role if they
   a. are the primary caregiver.   c. hold traditional gender values.
   b. work outside the home.   d. are in a blended family.

   ANS: A   DIF: Moderate   REF: 489   OBJ: 15.3

28. Fathers
   a. are less likely to challenge children during play than mothers.
   b. who are supportive contribute to better cognitive, social, and emotional development in their children
   c. who are unmarried tend to be very involved parents
   d. tend to avoid engaging in playful behavior with their children

   ANS: B   DIF: Easy   REF: 489   OBJ: 15.3

29. Which is true according to research on parent-child attachments?
   a. Parental responsiveness to an infant does not appear to be a determinant of the type of attachment formed by the infant.
   b. It is not possible for an infant to attach securely to its father unless it first establishes a secure attachment with its mother.
   c. Infants who are securely attached to both parents are more socially competent than those who are securely attached only to mother.
   d. Attachment to mother predicts later social competence, while attachment to father does not.

   ANS: C   DIF: Moderate   REF: 489   OBJ: 15.3

30. The fact that through their interactions with each other, spouses may influence the behavior of a child, even when the child does not experience these interactions, underlies the concept of
   a. caregiver burden.   c. autonomy.
   b. indirect effects.   d. spillover effects.

   ANS: B   DIF: Moderate   REF: 489   OBJ: 15.3

31. While Gao never shouts at his wife, Fumi, when their young daughter Kim is present, the shouting does make Kim upset as it sometimes results in Fumi being verbally aggressive with her daughter. This description demonstrates the
    a. impact of indirect effects within a family system.
    b. power of hereditary factors in determining behavior.
    c. main flaw in the family systems approach.
    d. role of classical conditioning in the development of social cognitive abilities.

    ANS: A   DIF: Difficult   REF: 489   OBJ: 15.3

32. The extent to which a parent is supportive, sensitive, and willing to provide affection and praise is referred to as the _____ dimension of childrearing.
    a. acceptance-responsiveness   c. demandingness-control
    b. responsiveness-demandingness   d. control-acceptance

    ANS: A   DIF: Moderate   REF: 490   OBJ: 15.4

33. Seika's attitude towards parenting is best described as "a lot of praise, a lot of affection, and feedback for negative behavior that is designed to teach but not belittle." This description indicates that Seika is best classified as being high on the _____ dimension of childrearing.
    a. acceptance-responsiveness   c. demandingness-control
    b. responsiveness-demandingness   d. control-acceptance

    ANS: A   DIF: Difficult   REF: 490   OBJ: 15.4

34. The amount of influence of decisions that lie with the parent versus the child is referred to as the _____ dimension of childrearing.
    a. acceptance-responsiveness   c. demandingness-control
    b. responsiveness-demandingness   d. control-acceptance

    ANS: C   DIF: Moderate   REF: 490   OBJ: 15.4
    KEY: WWW

35. Gorden's parenting style is summarized with the statement, "It's my way or the highway." This description indicates that Gorden is best classified as being high on the _____ dimension of childrearing.
    a. acceptance-responsiveness   c. demandingness-control
    b. responsiveness-demandingness   d. control-acceptance

    ANS: C   DIF: Difficult   REF: 490   OBJ: 15.4

36. The authoritarian parenting approach is characterized by _____ acceptance-responsiveness and _____ demandingness-control.
    a. high; high   c. low; high
    b. high; low   d. low; low

    ANS: C   DIF: Moderate   REF: 490   OBJ: 15.4

37. Julie wants special permission to stay out on a date past her normal curfew. Her parents, who are authoritarian parents, are most likely to respond
    a. "Why should we let you do this?"
    b. "No!"
    c. "I guess you'll have to make that choice and suffer the consequences."
    d. "It doesn't matter to us what you do."

    ANS: B   DIF: Difficult   REF: 490   OBJ: 15.4

38. A parent with a _____ style would most likely to give a child a severe spanking for disobedience.
    a. neglectful   c. authoritarian
    b. authoritative   d. permissive

    ANS: C   DIF: Difficult   REF: 490   OBJ: 15.4

39. The _____ parenting approach involves high acceptance-responsiveness and high demandingness-control.
    a. authoritative   c. neglectful
    b. authoritarian   d. permissive

    ANS: A   DIF: Moderate   REF: 490   OBJ: 15.4

40. Dolph's parents have very clear rules about what is okay to do and what is not. They are very careful to enforce the rules. However, they are willing to listen to Dolph's side of the story and are careful to explain why the rules are important. They even consider changing rules that don't seem to be working well. Dolph's parents are best described as having which sort of childrearing pattern?
    a. Neglectful   c. Authoritarian
    b. Authoritative   d. Permissive

    ANS: B   DIF: Difficult   REF: 490   OBJ: 15.4

41. Sixteen-year-old Becky wants to go on a weekend camping trip with a group of her friends (some of whom are male). She brings up the idea with her parents. As they tend to be authoritative parents, their most likely response is to say,
    a. "Absolutely not. Case closed."
    b. "Do as you please. It's your life!"
    c. "Let's sit down and discsuss this. We're not sure if this is a good idea, but we'd like to hear your views. Then we'll come to some sort of agreement."
    d. "We don't approve, but if you insist..."

    ANS: C   DIF: Difficult   REF: 490   OBJ: 15.4
    KEY: WWW

42. The permissive parenting approach is characterized by _____ acceptance-responsiveness and _____ demandingness-control.
    a. high; high   c. low; high
    b. high; low   d. low; low

    ANS: B   DIF: Moderate   REF: 490   OBJ: 15.4
    KEY: WWW

43. When asked to describe her parenting style, Mercedes says, "I can sum it up in a single word: indulgent!" This description indicates that Mercedes is best classified as being a(n) _____ parent.
    a. authoritarian
    b. authoritative
    c. moderate
    d. permissive

    ANS: D   DIF: Moderate   REF: 490   OBJ: 15.4

44. As a permissive parent, Mr. Twister is most likely to tell his temper tantrum-throwing son,
    a. "One more word, and you are going to get a whipping."
    b. "We need to talk about these outbursts."
    c. "That's right, you go ahead and let out any of those bad feelings and don't worry if you break something in the process."
    d. "While I know you are upset and maybe you are right, we do have rules of conduct and outbursts like this will not be tolerated."

    ANS: C   DIF: Difficult   REF: 490   OBJ: 15.4

45. The neglectful parenting approach is characterized by _____ acceptance-responsiveness and _____ demandingness-control.
    a. high; high
    b. high; low
    c. low; low
    d. low; high

    ANS: D   DIF: Moderate   REF: 490   OBJ: 15.4

46. Mallory works two different jobs to make ends meet and, as a result, she is so wrapped up in her own problems that she has little time to devote to her children. They basically do whatever they want and Mallory seems not to care. Which style of child rearing does this reflect?
    a. Authoritative
    b. Authoritarian
    c. Permissive
    d. Neglectful

    ANS: D   DIF: Moderate   REF: 490   OBJ: 15.4

47. Riff is a member of a teenage gang. He's doing drugs and is into petty crime. On the rare days he shows up at school, he invariably ends up in a fight and leaves early. Riff's behavior is most typical of children raised by parents who are
    a. authoritative.
    b. authoritarian.
    c. permissive.
    d. neglectful.

    ANS: D   DIF: Difficult   REF: 490-491   OBJ: 15.4
    KEY: WWW

48. Kitty and David want their children to grow up to be self-reliant, cooperative, and achievement-oriented. Based on research by Baumrind, Kitty and David should
    a. tell their children that school is really not that important.
    b. set firm limits and enforce them consistently.
    c. place few restrictions on their children's behavior.
    d. severely punish the children if they receive a bad grade.

    ANS: B   DIF: Difficult   REF: 490-491   OBJ: 15.4

49. Which parenting style is best associated with children who are unhappy, relatively aimless, and unpleasant to be around?
   a. Permissive
   b. Neglectful
   c. Authoritarian
   d. Authoritative

   ANS: C   DIF: Moderate   REF: 490-491   OBJ: 15.4

50. Hostile, antisocial youngsters who abuse drugs tend to have parents who have parenting styles that are
   a. high in acceptance and high in control.
   b. high in acceptance and low in control.
   c. low in acceptance and low in control.
   d. low in acceptance and high in control.

   ANS: C   DIF: Moderate   REF: 490-491   OBJ: 15.4

51. A parenting style based on _____ is most likely to be associated with positive child outcomes.
   a. love and limits
   b. love and no limits
   c. indulgence and sensitivity
   d. indulgence and insensitivity

   ANS: A   DIF: Easy   REF: 491   OBJ: 15.4
   KEY: WWW

52. Which statement concerning parenting styles and culture is true?
   a. Parents in collectivist cultures stress the importance of childhood autonomy.
   b. Native-American parents feel that it is the place of a parent to force children to do what they feel is right.
   c. African-American children view coercive parenting as a sign of care and not hostility.
   d. The more a child views spanking as a normal cultural behavior, the more emotional upsetting it is for them to get a spanking.

   ANS: C   DIF: Difficult   REF: 492   OBJ: 15.4

53. Compared to middle- and upper-class parents, lower-class parents tend to
   a. place less value on obedience to authority.
   b. show more warmth and affection to their children.
   c. spend more time reasoning with their children.
   d. be more restrictive and stress obedience.

   ANS: D   DIF: Moderate   REF: 491   OBJ: 15.4

54. Explanations on socioeconomic differences in parenting have focused on all of the following except
   a. genetic differences.
   b. stress associated with being poor.
   c. fewer resources to invest in their children.
   d. heavy reliance on an authoritative parenting style.

   ANS: A   DIF: Difficult   REF: 491 & 493   OBJ: 15.4

55. How many of the following (noise pollution, unsafe conditions, family instability) can negatively contribute to a child's development?
a. 0
c. 2
b. 1
d. 3

ANS: D   DIF: Easy   REF: 491 & 493   OBJ: 15.4

56. Gates is a highly-paid Chief Operating Officer of a major software firm. How is his position most likely to impact how he raises his son Bill?
a. He will emphasize the importance of obedience to authority.
b. He will become significantly more authoritarian.
c. He will downplay the importance of education.
d. He will attempt to foster initiative and creativity skills.

ANS: D   DIF: Moderate   REF: 493   OBJ: 15.4

57. The basic premise of the parent effects model is that
a. parents cause the behavior of their children
b. children cause the behavior of their parents
c. parents influence children and children influence parents
d. parents' genes have more impact than parents' interaction style

ANS: A   DIF: Moderate   REF: 493   OBJ: 15.5

58. The _____ family systems model would be most accepting of the notion, "It's always mommy's fault!"
a. social learning model
c. transactional model
b. indirect effects model
d. parents effects model

ANS: D   DIF: Moderate   REF: 493   OBJ: 15.5

59. In terms of the cause and effect of a child's behavior, the parent effects model tends to view the influence
a. as a one-way street.
c. as a random occurrence.
b. as a two-way street.
d. as genetic.

ANS: A   DIF: Easy   REF: 493   OBJ: 15.5

60. According to a child effects model,
a. children influence their parents through variables such as their age and personality.
b. parents are most influential in the parent-child relationship.
c. parents are responsible for how children turn out.
d. children's behaviors are almost all due to innate genetic factors.

ANS: A   DIF: Easy   REF: 493   OBJ: 15.5

61. The fact that infants elicit more sensitive care from adults than teens is best explained by
a. the parent effects model.
c. the child effects model.
b. caregiver burden.
d. permissive parenting.

ANS: C   DIF: Moderate   REF: 493   OBJ: 15.5
KEY: WWW

62. Which family systems model would be most accepting of the notion, "My kid's behaviors made me act that way!"
    a. Social learning model
    b. Child effects model
    c. Parent effects model
    d. Indirect effects model

    ANS: B   DIF: Moderate   REF: 493   OBJ: 15.5

63. Rudy just turned 17 and has begun to hang with a bad crowd and engage in antisocial behaviors (e.g., drug use). His parents react by taking away his cell phone and treating him in a less supportive manner. Which family systems model is best exemplified by Rudy's parent's reaction?
    a. Social learning
    b. Parent effects
    c. Indirect effect
    d. Child effects

    ANS: D   DIF: Moderate   REF: 493   OBJ: 15.4

64. According to the transactional model of family influence, children's antisocial behaviors are due
    a. to a combination of the child's genetic predisposition and parent-child interactions.
    b. solely to genetic predisposition in the child.
    c. to parent-child social interactions.
    d. to cultural factors beyond the scope of the child or parent.

    ANS: A   DIF: Easy   REF: 493-494   OBJ: 15.5

65. When attempting to explain why his son is so violent, Cedrick says, "He seems to have a natural tendency toward violence, and my spanking him has just made the situation worse." Cedrick's explanation best exemplifies the _____ model of family influence.
    a. parent effects
    b. child effects
    c. transactional
    d. indirect

    ANS: C   DIF: Moderate   REF: 493-494   OBJ: 15.5

66. Which family systems model would be most accepting of the notion, "The combination of an aggressive parent and a noncompliant child is the worst possible world!"
    a. Permissive parenting model
    b. Child effects model
    c. Transactional model
    d. Parents effects model

    ANS: C   DIF: Moderate   REF: 493-494   OBJ: 15.5

67. The arrival of a new baby in the family is most likely to
    a. be a joyous occasion for all.
    b. promote feelings of resentment and dependency behaviors in existing firstborn children.
    c. result in parents overcompensating by paying more attention to older siblings than the newborn.
    d. enhance an older sibling's feelings of competence and self-reliance.

    ANS: B   DIF: Moderate   REF: 494   OBJ: 15.6

68. Paul and Mary have a toddler, Peter, and are expecting a new baby. What is the best advice for assisting Paul and Mary in helping Peter to adjust?
    a. Make sure he knows he is their favorite.
    b. Let him have special privileges such as staying up late and eating whatever he wants.
    c. Encourage him to help take care of the new baby after it's born.
    d. Send him to stay with his grandparents for a few weeks while they get settled with the new baby.

    ANS: C   DIF: Moderate REF: 494   OBJ: 15.6

69. Sibling rivalry is typically characterized by
    a. resentment and jealousy.   c. forgiving and empathy.
    b. love and limits.   d. violence and psychosis.

    ANS: A   DIF: Easy   REF: 494   OBJ: 15.6
    KEY: WWW

70. What is the evolutionary-based explanation for sibling rivalry?
    a. Competition for the limited parental resources
    b. Natural sexual tension between close relatives
    c. A kinship-violence gene
    d. There is none, as evolutionary theorists reject the notion of sibling rivalry

    ANS: A   DIF: Moderate REF: 494   OBJ: 15.6

71. Regarding sibling rivalry relationships,
    a. if parents get along, brothers and sisters are less likely to get along.
    b. conflicts between siblings is abnormal.
    c. conflict tends to decrease when siblings begin spending more time away from home.
    d. the more extreme and destructive the rivalry, the less likely the negative impact on development.

    ANS: C   DIF: Easy   REF: 494   OBJ: 15.6

72. Which statement concerning sibling influences is true?
    a. Brothers tend to confide in each other more than sisters.
    b. The use of siblings as babysitters is found in only a few societies (e.g., United States).
    c. Having a large number of siblings can negatively impact cognitive development.
    d. Siblings are unable to have any indirect impact on another sibling's development.

    ANS: C   DIF: Moderate REF: 495   OBJ: 15.6

73. Cross-cultural research has shown that children as young as _____ years old can be involved in meaningful care for younger siblings.
    a. 2   c. 8
    b. 5   d. 11

    ANS: B   DIF: Difficult REF: 495   OBJ: 15.6

74. Which is true regarding parent-adolescent relationships?
    a. Interactions in childhood have no impact on an adolescent's relationship with his or her parents.
    b. The conflict level between teens and parents has grown dramatically during the past few decades.
    c. The best way to describe the typical parent-child relationship from the teen years through middle age is a roller coaster of big highs and great lows.
    d. Most adolescents respect their parents.

    ANS: A   DIF: Moderate   REF: 496   OBJ: 15.7

75. Autonomy is best defined as
    a. the capacity to make independent decisions.
    b. a high dependence on the ideas of others.
    c. the ability to sense and react to the emotional states of others.
    d. a strong sense of belonging to a larger group (collective).

    ANS: A   DIF: Moderate   REF: 496   OBJ: 15.7
    KEY: WWW

76. Wong's comment, "I can do it myself," indicates a strong sense of
    a. autonomy.
    b. filial responsibility.
    c. coparenting.
    d. collectivism.

    ANS: A   DIF: Moderate   REF: 496   OBJ: 15.7

77. Results from cross-cultural studies have shown that
    a. Mexican-American adolescents are more likely than European-American adolescents to believe that they should disagree with their parents.
    b. Japanese teens are socialized to be highly autonomous.
    c. Chinese-American teens expect more freedom to date at younger ages than do European-American teens.
    d. in collectivist Asian cultures, parents tend to impose a great number of rules.

    ANS: D   DIF: Moderate   REF: 497   OBJ: 15.7

78. If Fay and Ray want their adolescent daughter Kay to "make it" as an independent adult, they should
    a. exert strong control over Kay's behavior during the adolescent years.
    b. distance themselves from Kay, to weaken their attachment relationship.
    c. let Kay make her own choices and withhold their own opinions, because they won't be around to help their child forever.
    d. gradually relinquish power and control so that Kay gains experience in making wise choices.

    ANS: D   DIF: Moderate   REF: 497   OBJ: 15.7

79. Which parenting style is most likely to promote psychological autonomy in adolescents?
    a. Authoritative
    b. Authoritarian
    c. Permissive
    d. Neglecting

    ANS: A   DIF: Moderate   REF: 497   OBJ: 15.7

80. In the United States, approximately _____ of adults marry at some point in their lives.
    a. 60%
    b. 70%
    c. 80%
    d. 90%

    ANS: D   DIF: Easy   REF: 497   OBJ: 15.8

81. In general, marital satisfaction tends to
    a. increase steadily over the first two to three years of marriage.
    b. decrease somewhat over the first year of marriage.
    c. remain stable for most couples until the "seven-year itch."
    d. decrease drastically within six months of the wedding.

    ANS: B   DIF: Moderate   REF: 497-498   OBJ: 15.8

82. Heidi and Spencer are nearing their first wedding anniversary. It is most likely that
    a. they are engaging in less sexual intercourse than when they first married.
    b. they are talking a lot more than when they were first married.
    c. they are divorced.
    d. they spend more time with each other now than ever before.

    ANS: A   DIF: Moderate   REF: 498   OBJ: 15.8

83. Research on the "escalating conflict" view of marital satisfaction has shown that
    a. marriages tend to crumble due to the build up of negative feelings that accumulate over the years.
    b. an early negative reaction concerning a marriage will likely continue to be seen at about the same level throughout the marriage.
    c. most divorces are due to a midlife crisis occurring about 14 years into a marriage.
    d. divorce is less likely in couples who hold an overly romantic view of their marriage at its start.

    ANS: B   DIF: Difficult   REF: 498   OBJ: 15.8

84. Donald and Daisy have just become first-time parents. If they are like more couples in this situation, you would expect that they
    a. have taken on the gender role of the opposite sex (e.g., Donald has become more feminine).
    b. have a lot more time to devote to each other.
    c. are feeling little joy concerning the birth of their baby.
    d. have added new roles that complicate their lives.

    ANS: D   DIF: Easy   REF: 498   OBJ: 15.8

85. As children are added to the family, marital satisfaction tends to
    a. increase for mothers and fathers, but more so for fathers.
    b. increase for mothers and fathers, but more so for mothers.
    c. decrease for mothers and fathers, but more so for fathers.
    d. decrease for mothers and fathers, but more so for mothers

    ANS: D   DIF: Moderate   REF: 498   OBJ: 15.8

86. Which would make parenthood especially difficult for a first-time parent?
    a. Having a difficult baby
    b. Having a supportive spouse
    c. Having grown up in a warm and accepting family
    d. Having good general coping skills

    ANS: A   DIF: Moderate   REF: 498   OBJ: 15.8
    KEY: WWW

87. Which parental characteristics are most highly associated with effective coping to the addition of a child to a family?
    a. Realistic expectation about children and good overall mental health
    b. Authoritarian style and ambivalence toward the child
    c. Low socioeconomic level and newly married
    d. Low sense of filial responsibility and high levels of marital satisfaction

    ANS: A   DIF: Moderate   REF: 499   OBJ: 15.8

88. The best predictor of successful adaptation of a new couple to the arrival of a new baby is
    a. in-law support.   c. support of siblings.
    b. the support of other children.   d. partner support.

    ANS: D   DIF: Easy   REF: 499   OBJ: 15.8

89. Jada and Will are a typical American couple expecting their second child. Once the baby arrives, it is most likely that
    a. Jada and Will will become more satisfied with their marriage.
    b. Will will become more involved in caring for the children.
    c. the stress level in the family will lessen, as the two children will keep each other company.
    d. Jada and Will will experience a sharp decline in their overall level of marital satisfaction.

    ANS: B   DIF: Moderate   REF: 499   OBJ: 15.8

90. Which statement concerning the childrearing family is true?
    a. Conflicts between parents and children tend to decrease between childhood and adolescence.
    b. The stress of caring for a toddler tends to be greater than caring for an infant.
    c. Parents with teens tend to be less likely to question their own life path.
    d. Parents of teens tend to be unaffected when the teenager is having personal problems.

    ANS: B   DIF: Moderate   REF: 499   OBJ: 15.8

91. When interviewed about the impact of parenthood on their lives, most parents emphasize the
   a. positive contributions that parenthood made to their personal development.
   b. positive contributions that parenthood made to their marital satisfaction.
   c. negative contributions that parenthood had on their personal development.
   d. negative contributions that parenthood had on their marital satisfaction.

   ANS: A   DIF: Easy   REF: 500   OBJ: 15.8

92. The idea of an "empty nest" is best associated with the concept of the
   a. end of menopause when childbearing is no longer possible.
   b. feeling of a "new life" experienced following divorce.
   c. launching of the last child from the family home.
   d. death of a life-long spouse.

   ANS: C   DIF: Easy   REF: 500   OBJ: 15.8

93. How is marital satisfaction typically associated with the entry of the first child into a family and the exit of the last child from the family?
   a. Both events are characterized by a slight increase in marital satisfaction.
   b. The entry is characterized by a slight increase and the launching with a slight decrease in marital satisfaction.
   c. The entry is characterized by a slight decrease and the launching with a slight increase in marital satisfaction.
   d. Both events are characterized by a slight decrease in marital satisfaction.

   ANS: C   DIF: Moderate   REF: 500   OBJ: 15.8

94. George and Martha have just "emptied their nest" by dropping their youngest son off at college. It is most likely that
   a. Martha will become depressed.
   b. George will spend less time with Martha now that there are no children to keep him at home.
   c. Martha will feel like the marriage has become more equitable.
   d. Martha and George will become distant from one another without the children to bring them together.

   ANS: C   DIF: Moderate   REF: 500   OBJ: 15.8

95. Erikson would argue that the positive feeling of self associated with the empty nest in middle age indicates a successful attainment of a sense of
   a. generativity.   c. wisdom.
   b. integrity.   d. initiative.

   ANS: A   DIF: Moderate   REF: 500   OBJ: 15.8

96. "Refilling" (adult children returning to the nest) is most likely to occur as the result of
   a. teenage pregnancy.   c. passionate love.
   b. unemployment.   d. an authoritative parenting style.

   ANS: B   DIF: Moderate   REF: 500   OBJ: 15.8

97. How are the "empty nest" and "refilling" related?
   a. They refer to the same concept.
   b. Empty nest precedes refilling.
   c. Refilling precedes the empty nest.
   d. Refilling causes the empty nest.

   ANS: B   DIF: Moderate   REF: 500   OBJ: 15.8

98. Aladdin and Jasmine are about to experience a "boomerang effect" with their children. How should they prepare?
   a. Get ready for a major fight about autonomy and about how teens are adults and should be treated like adults and given their freedom.
   b. Pack the car because their last child is heading off to college.
   c. Sit back and smile because their adult children are in the process of paying them back financially for all the children received from Aladdin and Jasmine while they were growing up.
   d. Make up the spare room because one of their children is about to move back home.

   ANS: D   DIF: Difficult   REF: 500   OBJ: 15.8

99. Which grandparenting style was created in a large part by the increasing geographical difference between grandparents and grandchildren?
   a. Remote
   b. Companionate
   c. Involved
   d. Permissive

   ANS: A   DIF: Moderate   REF: 500-501   OBJ: 15.9

100. _____ grandparenting style is best characterized as "emotionally distant."
   a. Remote
   b. Companionate
   c. Involved
   d. Permissive

   ANS: A   DIF: Easy   REF: 500-501   OBJ: 15.9

101. As a "remote" grandparent, Lilo _____ her grandson Stitch.
   a. enjoys being a part-time parent for
   b. seldom sees
   c. goes to lots of activities with
   d. lives with

   ANS: B   DIF: Moderate   REF: 500-501   OBJ: 15.9

102. Recent research has shown that the _____ grandparenting style is the most common in the United States.
   a. remote
   b. companionate
   c. involved
   d. permissive

   ANS: B   DIF: Easy   REF: 500-501   OBJ: 15.9
   KEY: WWW

103. The most common form of grandparenting in the United States appears to be one where there is
    a. little contact between grandparent and grandchild, largely due to geographical distance.
    b. frequent contact between grandparent and grandchild, with the grandparent often assuming a parental role.
    c. frequent contact between grandparent and grandchild, with the primary goal being enjoyment of one another.
    d. infrequent contact between grandparent and grandchild, but when together the grandparents tend to meddle in the way the child is being reared.

    ANS: C   DIF: Moderate   REF: 500-501   OBJ: 15.9

104. Grandpa Sylvester loves spending time going to professional wrestling events with his grandson Elmer. He comments that the best part is that he can have fun without worrying about parenting responsibilities. Sylvester is best described as having a _____ style.
    a. remote   c. involved
    b. companionate   d. permissive

    ANS: B   DIF: Moderate   REF: 500-501   OBJ: 15.9

105. The involved grandparent would be best characterized as
    a. fun.   c. harmful.
    b. detached.   d. parentlike.

    ANS: D   DIF: Moderate   REF: 500-501   OBJ: 15.9

106. Due to his level of involvement, Butch might best be considered a substitute parent for his grandson Patrick. This indicates that Butch has a _____ grandparenting style.
    a. remote   c. involved
    b. companionate   d. watch dog

    ANS: C   DIF: Moderate   REF: 501   OBJ: 15.9

107. In the United States, most grandparents prefer a role that is
    a. high in enjoyment and high in responsibility.
    b. high in enjoyment and low in responsibility.
    c. low in enjoyment and high in responsibility.
    d. low in enjoyment and low in responsibility.

    ANS: B   DIF: Moderate   REF: 501   OBJ: 15.9

108. Why have grandparents been referred to as "the family national guard"?
    a. They are a voluntary group.
    b. They can help families in crisis.
    c. They tend to perform tough tasks with little positive emotional reward.
    d. They are diminishing in our society.

    ANS: B   DIF: Moderate   REF: 501   OBJ: 15.9

109. The most likely negative outcome of being an involved grandparent is
    a. guilt over lack of interaction with grandkids.
    b. lack of money due to overspending.
    c. depression over the responsibility of having a grandchild move into their home.
    d. remorse over not having had more children and more grandkids.

    ANS: C   DIF: Moderate   REF: 501   OBJ: 15.9

110. All else being equal, who is likely to feel most satisfied with their marriage?
    a. Julie and Jim, who just got married
    b. Jane and Jake, who just had their first child
    c. Jessica and John, who have two young children
    d. Janet and Jack, whose children are in high school

    ANS: A   DIF: Moderate   REF: 501   OBJ: 15.10

111. Which tends to increase in older married couples?
    a. Passion   c. Conflicts
    b. Affection   d. Venting

    ANS: B   DIF: Difficult   REF: 501   OBJ: 15.10

112. Marital satisfaction tends to be highest in middle-aged couples
    a. with "opposite" traits.
    b. whose early marriage satisfaction was very low.
    c. where there is a perceived inequity of effort concerning the marriage.
    d. in which both husband and wife have pleasant personality characteristics.

    ANS: D   DIF: Moderate   REF: 501   OBJ: 15.10

113. Which event ends the traditional family life cycle?
    a. Death of the last child
    b. Retirement
    c. Widowhood
    d. Death of the only remaining member of a family

    ANS: C   DIF: Moderate   REF: 502   OBJ: 15.10

114. In the United States, at age 65, the largest group consists of
    a. married men living with their wives.
    b. married women living with their husbands.
    c. unmarried men living alone.
    d. unmarried women living alone.

    ANS: A   DIF: Difficult   REF: 502   OBJ: 15.10

115. Which best describes sibling relationships over the adulthood years?
    a. Sibling rivalry disappears once the children are on their own.
    b. Most siblings share intimate problems frequently across the years.
    c. Siblings often grow emotionally closer from middle age to old age.
    d. Significant life events like the death of a parent can bring close siblings together and push rival siblings apart.

    ANS: D   DIF: Difficult   REF: 502   OBJ: 15.10

116. Research on adult sibling relationships has shown that they
    a. spend a great deal of time discussing intimate issues.
    b. are negatively impacted if parents "played favorites" with one of the siblings.
    c. are not there to support each other.
    d. display virtually no competition as they build their lives.

    ANS: B   DIF: Moderate   REF: 502   OBJ: 15.10

117. Which statement concerning child-parent relationships in older age is true?
    a. Aging fathers tend to be closer to their sons than aging mothers are to their daughters.
    b. Most older parents would prefer to live with their children not near their children.
    c. Hispanic and African-American elders enjoy more supportive relationships with their children than European-American elders.
    d. Relationships between the generations are seldom affectionate.

    ANS: C   DIF: Difficult   REF: 502-503   OBJ: 15.10

118. The switch from parent as caregiver to child as caregiver best describes
    a. the spillover effect.   c. role reversal.
    b. authoritarian parenting.   d. a modified extended family.

    ANS: C   DIF: Moderate   REF: 503   OBJ: 15.10
    KEY: WWW

119. Though Wilma is Pebbles's mother, due to a chronic illness, Pebbles now has to take almost total care for her aging mother. Pebbles's situation provides a great example of
    a. a blended family.   c. role reversal.
    b. authoritarian parenting.   d. the empty nest.

    ANS: C   DIF: Moderate   REF: 503   OBJ: 15.10

120. The "middle generation squeeze" refers to
    a. young grandparents who must simultaneously care for their own and their children's children.
    b. middle-aged adults who find themselves simultaneously caring for both younger and older generations.
    c. children of divorce who must split their time between living with both mother and father.
    d. children who are the middle-born in a large family.

    ANS: B   DIF: Moderate   REF: 503   OBJ: 15.10

121. Which concept is also known as "the sandwich generation"?
    a. The blended family
    b. The spillover effect
    c. The middle generation squeeze
    d. The indirect effect

    ANS: C   DIF: Easy   REF: 503   OBJ: 15.10

122. In the United States, who is typically the first in line to care for an elderly individual?
    a. A spouse
    b. A son
    c. A daughter-in-law
    d. A third party

    ANS: A   DIF: Moderate   REF: 503   OBJ: 15.10

123. In many Asian collectivist cultures, who is typically the first in line to care for an elderly individual?
    a. A son-in-law
    b. A son
    c. A daughter-in-law
    d. A third party

    ANS: C   DIF: Moderate   REF: 503   OBJ: 15.10
    KEY: WWW

124. The psychological distress associated with providing assistance for someone with a cognitive or physical impairment is called
    a. the midlife crisis.
    b. caregiver burden.
    c. the modified extended family.
    d. the spillover effect.

    ANS: B   DIF: Easy   REF: 503   OBJ: 15.10

125. Who is most likely to experience the greatest amount of caregiver burden?
    a. Inga, who is married and cares for her 90-year-old mother, who is paralyzed and really wants Inga's assistance
    b. Uma, who cares for both of her 80-year-old parents living next door
    c. Ida, who is single and cares for her 85-year-old mother who is suffering from dementia and does not want any help
    d. Ushi, who is single and has put her 70-year-old father in a nursing home following a stroke

    ANS: C   DIF: Moderate   REF: 504   OBJ: 15.10

126. Whose care is most likely to lead to caregiver burden if they are taken in by an adult child?
    a. 80-year-old Vick, who has cancer but can get around pretty well
    b. 80-year-old Nick, whose dementia makes her disruptive and who engages in socially inappropriate behavior
    c. 80-year-old Dick, who has no legs
    d. 80-year-old Mick, who is wealthier than the daughter who will be taking her in

    ANS: B   DIF: Moderate   REF: 504   OBJ: 15.10
    KEY: WWW

127. Will and Grace are a romantically involved but unmarried couple living together. They are best categorized as
a. cohabitating.
b. a modified extended family.
c. a reconstituted family.
d. empty nesters.

ANS: A   DIF: Moderate   REF: 505   OBJ: 15.11

128. How many of the following (convenience, trail marriage, alternative to marriage) are reasons for cohabitation?
a. 0
b. 1
c. 2
d. 3

ANS: D   DIF: Easy   REF: 505   OBJ: 15.11

129. Couples who engage in cohabitation before marriage tend to
a. experience greater satisfaction in the marriage relationship than those who do not live together before marriage.
b. have less eventual marital problems if their partner has had multiple cohabitation experiences.
c. be more likely to divorce that first-time married couples once they are married.
d. be more religious and more committed to marriage than those who do not live together before marriage.

ANS: C   DIF: Moderate   REF: 505   OBJ: 15.11

130. In general, adults who never marry tend to be
a. at an advantage in old age due to their lack of family supports.
b. happier than singles that have been divorced.
c. socially maladjusted.
d. very lonely.

ANS: B   DIF: Easy   REF: 505   OBJ: 15.11

131. Married couples who voluntarily remain "childfree"
a. generally experience greater marital satisfaction than couples with children during the childrearing years.
b. tend to be less satisfied with their lives in middle age and old age than couples whose children have grown and gone.
c. tend to have higher levels of depression than couples with children.
d. typically feel like failures for never having children.

ANS: A   DIF: Moderate   REF: 505   OBJ: 15.11

132. The "spillover effect" occurs when
a. a person's sexual orientation impacts his or her job status.
b. an adult child has to care for an elderly parent or grandparent.
c. work life affects home life and vice versa.
d. two divorced families remarry to form one large family.

ANS: C   DIF: Easy   REF: 505   OBJ: 15.11
KEY: WWW

764

133. Little Debbie's comment, "When my mom has a good day at work, we always get a great dessert after dinner" indicates that Debbie's family is
   a. experiencing spillover effects.
   c. experiencing a transactional effect.
   b. a reconstituted family.
   d. is promoting autonomy.

   ANS: A   DIF: Moderate   REF: 505   OBJ: 15.11

134. What factor decreases the likelihood that living in a dual-career family will be a positive experience for a child?
   a. A higher level of income
   b. Increased father involvement with the family
   c. A happy mother
   d. A lack of quality time spent with children

   ANS: D   DIF: Easy   REF: 505   OBJ: 15.11

135. _____ couples are most likely to experience societal discrimination including the inability to make life-or-death decisions concerning their partner.
   a. Blended family
   c. Middle generation squeeze
   b. Gay or lesbian
   d. Nuclear family

   ANS: B   DIF: Easy   REF: 506   OBJ: 15.11

136. In general, gay and lesbian couples
   a. have less satisfying relationships than married heterosexuals.
   b. assign traditional roles of "wife" to one partner and the role of "husband" to the other.
   c. tend to have more egalitarian relationships than married heterosexuals.
   d. follow a very different pattern of stages of relationship development than heterosexual couples.

   ANS: C   DIF: Moderate   REF: 506   OBJ: 15.11

137. Research on lesbian mothers has shown that, when compared to heterosexual parents, they are
   a. less likely to hit.
   b. more likely to engage in imaginative play.
   c. less likely to raise well-adjusted children.
   d. more likely to raise children with bisexual or homosexual orientations.

   ANS: A   DIF: Moderate   REF: 506-507   OBJ: 15.11

138. The highest risk for divorce occurs in couples who
   a. postponed having children for five or more years following marriage.
   b. are young and have been married for about seven years.
   c. married in their mid 30s.
   d. never had children.

   ANS: B   DIF: Moderate   REF: 507   OBJ: 15.12

139. Fergie and Andrew just got divorced. It is most likely that, early on, Fergie (custodial mother) will be more _____ and Andrew (non-custodial father) will be more _____ with the children.
    a. warm and loving; cold and distant
    b. permissive; highly controlling
    c. impatient; indulgent
    d. cold and distant; inconsistent

    ANS: C   DIF: Moderate   REF: 507   OBJ: 15.12

140. In the United States, divorce is
    a. typically initiated by the husband.
    b. no longer seen as a right taken by people who do not feel personally fulfilled in their marriage (as it was in the 20th century).
    c. typically the result of lack of communication, emotional fulfillment, or compatibility.
    d. legally required to list one of the spouses as being "at fault."

    ANS: C   DIF: Moderate   REF: 507   OBJ: 15.12

141. After a divorce,
    a. the rate of depression for the divorced spouses is lower than for couples remaining in a marriage.
    b. the wife is typically named as the primary caregiver of the children.
    c. finding a new relationship has little impact on adjustment.
    d. the husband tends to face greater financial problems than the wife.

    ANS: B   DIF: Moderate   REF: 507   OBJ: 15.12

142. Which statement about the impact of divorce on child development is true?
    a. In response to divorce, most custodial mothers become more sensitive and responsive to their children's needs.
    b. Children who display negative behaviors as the result of the divorce tend to exhibit such behaviors only in the home and show few negative effects in the school setting.
    c. Adolescents whose parents divorce are less likely to perceive relationships with their fathers as close and caring.
    d. Adults from divorced families are less likely than those from intact families to divorce.

    ANS: C   DIF: Moderate   REF: 508   OBJ: 15.12

143. Which of the following factors was identified as reducing the negative effects of divorce?
    a. Inadequate financial support
    b. Increased conflict between parents
    c. Poor parenting by the noncustodial parent
    d. Increased levels of social supports

    ANS: D   DIF: Easy   REF: 508   OBJ: 15.12
    KEY: WWW

144. Research has shown that _____ is most likely to facilitate a positive adjustment to divorce.
   a. a lack of contact with the custodial parent
   b. having the custodial parent change jobs or move to a new city
   c. a child who is intelligent and has good coping skills
   d. not requiring the noncustodial parent to pay child support

   ANS: C   DIF: Easy   REF: 508   OBJ: 15.12

145. Which statement concerning reconstituted families is true?
   a. Difficulties are more likely if both parents bring children into the family
   b. The first few years in the new family tend to be the time of least conflict
   c. Boys tend to resent step-fathers more than girls resent step-mothers
   d. Children in blended reconstituted families are less likely to show antisocial behaviors than children from intact two-parent families

   ANS: A   DIF: Moderate   REF: 508-509   OBJ: 15.13

146. Which statement concerning remarriage is true?
   a. The rate of divorce among remarried couples is near 25%.
   b. The impact on children is worsened if both parents bring children into the reconstituted family.
   c. Boys tend to have a harder time adjusting to being in a reconstituted marriage.
   d. Within a year of the remarriage, children in reconstituted families show no psychological or behavioral differences from children in intact first-marriage families.

   ANS: B   DIF: Moderate   REF: 509   OBJ: 15.13

147. In the United States, about _____ of every 1,000 children are victims of substantial maltreatment.
   a. 11   c. 110
   b. 44   d. 440

   ANS: D   DIF: Moderate   REF: 509   OBJ: 15.13

148. In the United States, the most common form of mistreatment involves
   a. physical abuse.   c. psychological abuse.
   b. sexual abuse.   d. neglect.

   ANS: D   DIF: Easy   REF: 509   OBJ: 15.13

149. _____ abuse is the most common form of family violence worldwide.
   a. Spouse (or partner)   c. Child
   b. Sibling   d. Elderly

   ANS: A   DIF: Moderate   REF: 510   OBJ: 15.13

150. Which combination has the highest risk for abuse?
   a. Powerless mom and disabled child   c. Powerless mom and non-disabled child
   b. Powerful mom and disabled child   d. Powerful mom and non-disabled child

   ANS: A   DIF: Moderate   REF: 510-513   OBJ: 15.13

151. Statistically speaking, who is at greatest risk for abusing their child?
    a. Ralph, a young, employed male with two children.
    b. Rene, a young, unemployed single women with four children.
    c. Ron, a middle-aged, poor, single father of one.
    d. Ruby, a middle-aged, married, working mother of five.

    ANS: B   DIF: Moderate   REF: 510   OBJ: 15.13

152. Most parents who abuse their children
    a. never witnessed or experienced violence when they were children.
    b. have an inflated sense of self-esteem.
    c. have inaccurate expectations concerning child development.
    d. are older fathers.

    ANS: C   DIF: Moderate   REF: 510-511   OBJ: 15.13
    KEY: WWW

153. As a child, Chester was physically abused by his mother. He has now begun to physically abuse his daughter. His behavior best exemplifies
    a. spillover effects.
    b. intergenerational transmission of parenting.
    c. an extended family household.
    d. middle generation squeeze.

    ANS: B   DIF: Moderate   REF: 510   OBJ: 15.13

154. How might the epigenetic model describe the transmission of parenting across generations?
    a. Harsh treatment in childhood may trigger the expression of a gene for aggressive parenting in later life.
    b. A child who sees his mother hit by his dad learns to hit his wife.
    c. Despite never experiencing violence, due to a recessive gene effect, a mother being abusing her son.
    d. A violent child grows up to be a passive parent.

    ANS: A   DIF: Difficult   REF: 511   OBJ: 15.13

155. Which is the best example of a macroenvironmental contributor to child abuse?
    a. Many abusers are former abuse victims.
    b. Abuse is higher in transient and poor neighborhoods.
    c. The fact that difficult children are at risk for abuse.
    d. A society that promotes physical punishment tends to have higher incidences of abuse.

    ANS: D   DIF: Difficult   REF: 512   OBJ: 15.13

156. Children who are victims of physical mistreatment
    a. tend to show behavioral impacts (e.g., aggression toward peers) and intellectual impacts (e.g., lower IQs).
    b. tend to show behavioral impacts (e.g., aggression toward peers) but no intellectual impacts (e.g., lower IQs).
    c. tend to show intellectual impacts (e.g., lower IQs) but no behavioral impacts (e.g., aggression toward peers).
    d. seldom show behavioral impacts (e.g., aggression toward peers) or intellectual impacts (e.g., lower IQs).

    ANS: A   DIF: Moderate   REF: 512   OBJ: 15.13

157. Victims of child abuse tend to
    a. display great empathy for others.
    b. have higher rates of depression.
    c. be insensitive to anger cues in others.
    d. try to protect other individuals who are crying.

    ANS: B   DIF: Moderate   REF: 512   OBJ: 15.13

158. It appears that _____ can protect a child from the impact of abuse.
    a. only genetic factors   c. both genetic and environmental factors
    b. only environmental factors   d. nothing

    ANS: C   DIF: Moderate   REF: 512-513   OBJ: 15.13

TRUE/FALSE

1. A nuclear family consists of a least three generations.

    ANS: F   DIF: Moderate   REF: 484   OBJ: 15.1

2. Modern couples in the United States are having fewer children.

    ANS: T   DIF: Easy   REF: 486   OBJ: 15.2

3. As compared to past decades, there are fewer caregivers for aging adults.

    ANS: T   DIF: Moderate   REF: 487   OBJ: 15.2
    KEY: WWW

4. When it comes to childcare, men and women are more similar than different.

    ANS: T   DIF: Easy   REF: 488   OBJ: 15.3

5. An authoritative parenting style involves many rules and few explanations.

    ANS: F   DIF: Moderate   REF: 490   OBJ: 15.4

6. A neglecting parent has high demands but is not involved in children's lives.

ANS: F   DIF: Moderate REF: 490   OBJ: 15.4
KEY: WWW

7. According to the child effects model, parents alone impact children's behavior.

ANS: F   DIF: Moderate REF: 493   OBJ: 15.5
KEY: WWW

8. According to the transactional model, parents alone impact children's behavior.

ANS: F   DIF: Moderate REF: 493-494 OBJ: 15.5

9. Sibling rivalry is normal.

ANS: T   DIF: Moderate REF: 494   OBJ: 15.6

10. Achieving autonomy during adolescence involves establishing an identity that matches one's parents.

ANS: F   DIF: Moderate REF: 496   OBJ: 15.7

11. Marital satisfaction tends to rise dramatically in the years following the honeymoon.

ANS: F   DIF: Easy   REF: 498   OBJ: 15.8
KEY: WWW

12. The birth of the first child tends to result in an increase in marital satisfaction.

ANS: F   DIF: Moderate REF: 498   OBJ: 15.8

13. The launching of the last child tends to result in an increase in marital satisfaction.

ANS: T   DIF: Easy   REF: 500   OBJ: 15.8

14. The most common grandparenting style is the "involved" style.

ANS: F   DIF: Moderate REF: 500-501 OBJ: 15.9

15. The family life cycle ends with widowhood.

ANS: T   DIF: Easy   REF: 502   OBJ: 15.10

16. Couples who marry after engaging in cohabitation prior to marriage tend to be less likely to divorce.

ANS: F   DIF: Moderate REF: 505   OBJ: 15.11

17. Homosexual couples are likely to have more egalitarian relationships than heterosexual couples.

   ANS: T   DIF: Moderate   REF: 506-507   OBJ: 15.11

18. Good parenting by the noncustodial parent can positively influence a child's adjustment to divorce.

   ANS: T   DIF: Easy   REF: 506   OBJ: 15.11

19. Most children who are maltreated are victims of neglect, not physical or sexual abuse.

   ANS: T   DIF: Moderate   REF: 509-510   OBJ: 15.12
   KEY: WWW

20. Adults who physically abuse children tend to have very accurate expectations concerning the behavior of children at different ages.

   ANS: F   DIF: Easy   REF: 510-511   OBJ: 15.13

COMPLETION

1. According to the _____ theory, a family is like a whole body consisting of interrelated parts (people) that affect each other as well as the family as a whole.

   ANS: family system

   DIF: Difficult   REF: 484   OBJ: 15.1

2. A _____ family consists entirely of two parents and their biological children.

   ANS: nuclear

   DIF: Moderate   REF: 484   OBJ: 15.1

3. Since Beth lives in a household with her parents, siblings, and aunt, and a grandparent, she is best described as in an _____ family household

   ANS: extended

   DIF: Moderate   REF: 485   OBJ: 15.1

4. When two divorced people, each with a child, remarry, they create a blended or _____ family.

   ANS: reconstituted

   DIF: Moderate   REF: 487   OBJ: 15.2

5. The fact that one parent can influence a child's development through interactions with the other parent provides exemplifies an _____ effect on behavior.

ANS: indirect

DIF: Difficult   REF: 489   OBJ: 15.2   KEY: WWW

6. The _____ dimension of childrearing refers to the extent to which parents are supportive and sensitive to the needs of their children and are willing to provide affection and praise.

ANS: acceptance-responsiveness

DIF: Difficult   REF: 480   OBJ: 15.4

7. The _____ parenting style is characterized by low levels of parental acceptance-responsiveness and low levels of parental demandingness-control.

ANS: neglectful

DIF: Moderate   REF: 480   OBJ: 15.4

8. The _____ parenting style is characterized by high levels of parental acceptance-responsiveness and high levels of parental demandingness-control.

ANS: authoritative

DIF: Moderate   REF: 480   OBJ: 15.4   KEY: WWW

9. According to the _____ effects model, a child's behavior is determined exclusively by the actions of their parent.

ANS: parent

DIF: Moderate   REF: 493   OBJ: 15.5

10. According to the _____ model, a child's behavior is determined by both the actions of a parent and the child's characteristics (including genetically-based responses).

ANS: transactional

DIF: Moderate   REF: 493   OBJ: 15.5

11. The natural jealousy and resentment seen between brothers and sisters is called _____.

ANS: sibling rivalry

DIF: Moderate   REF: 494   OBJ: 15.6

12. _____ is defined as the ability to make independent decisions and to manage one's life without being overly dependent on others.

ANS: Autonomy

DIF: Moderate   REF: 496   OBJ: 15.7   KEY: WWW

13. The departure of the last child from a family creates a situation referred to as the _____.

ANS: empty nest

DIF: Moderate   REF: 500   OBJ: 15.8

14. _____ grandparenting is the most common grandparenting style and is characterized by frequent visits and shared activities with grandchildren.

ANS: Companionate

DIF: Difficult   REF: 500   OBJ: 15.9

15. The sandwich generation is also referred to as the _____ squeeze.

ANS: middle generation

DIF: Difficult   REF: 503   OBJ: 15.10   KEY: WWW

16. A middle-aged person caring for their demented parent is likely to experience _____ burden.

ANS: caregiver

DIF: Easy   REF: 503   OBJ: 15.10

17. A romantically involved couple that lives together, but is not married, is said to be engaged in _____.

ANS: cohabitation

DIF: Easy   REF: 505   OBJ: 15.11   KEY: WWW

18. When events in the workplace impact events in the home, and vice versa, a _____ effect has occurred.

ANS: spillover

DIF: Moderate   REF: 505   OBJ: 15.11

19. The broad term used to categorize harmful behaviors aimed at children including abuse and neglect is child _____.

ANS: maltreatment

DIF: Moderate   REF: 509-510   OBJ: 15.13

773

20. The passing down of parenting styles from grandparent to parent to child exemplifies the phenomenon of _____ of parenting.

ANS: intergenerational transmission

DIF: Difficult   REF: 510   OBJ: 15.13

ESSAY

1. Describe the basics of family systems theory.

ANS: Answer not provided   REF: 484-485   OBJ: 15.1

2. How do parenting styles influence children's development? In general, which style works best? Why?

ANS: Answer not provided   REF: 490   OBJ: 15.4

3. How does marital satisfaction change over the course of a marriage? What factors influence marital satisfaction?

ANS: Answer not provided   REF: 497-499   OBJ: 15.8

4. Describe the role of sibling relations and rivalries from childhood through adulthood.

ANS: Answer not provided   REF: 494-495 & 502   OBJ: 15.6 & 15.10

5. What are the issues associated with the middle generation squeeze? How can the associated problem of caregiver burden be reduced?

ANS: Answer not provided   REF: 503-504   OBJ: 15.10

6. What are the advantages and disadvantages of being single, being a childless couple, being a dual-career family, and being in a gay/lesbian family?

ANS: Answer not provided   REF: 504-507   OBJ: 15.11

7. What factors contribute to child abuse? How can knowledge of these factors impact our ability to reduce abuse?

ANS: Answer not provided   REF: 509-513   OBJ: 15.13

8. Compare and contrast the parent effects, child effects, and transactional effects models of family influence.

ANS: Answer not provided   REF: 493-494   OBJ: 15.5   KEY: WWW

774

9. What are the characteristics, advantages, and disadvantages of the three major grandparenting styles?

   ANS: Answer not provided   REF: 500-501   OBJ: 15.9   KEY: WWW

10. What are potential advantages and disadvantages for children and parents who experience divorce?

   ANS: Answer not provided   REF: 507-509   OBJ: 15.12   KEY: WWW

MULTIPLE CHOICE

1. All of the following are criteria that have been used for identifying psychologically abnormal behavior EXCEPT
   a. behavior must be statistically outside of the normal range.
   b. behavior must be present prior to young adulthood.
   c. behavior must interfere with personal and social adaptation.
   d. behavior must cause personal distress.

   ANS: B   DIF: Easy   REF: 518   OBJ: 16.1
   KEY: WWW

2. When commenting on his patient's compulsive behavior, Dr. Hernandez says, "He is not just a little compulsive, his level of behavior is as severe as I have ever seen." Dr. Hernandez's comment best illustrates the criteria of _____ in defining abnormal behavior.
   a. social norms   c. statistical deviance
   b. personal distress   d. joint attention

   ANS: C   DIF: Moderate   REF: 518   OBJ: 16.1

3. When describing the voices that he hears in his head, Bell says, "They really don't bother me, but they did cost me my job as a telephone operator as I kept giving out numbers to the voices rather than the callers." Bell's situation illustrates the criteria of _____ in defining abnormal behavior.
   a. maladaptiveness   c. statistical deviance
   b. personal distress   d. joint attention

   ANS: A   DIF: Moderate   REF: 518   OBJ: 16.1

4. When describing his problem, John says, "I know that my fear of spiders is not that unusual and that I still have my job as an exterminator, but this fear is mentally killing me!" John's comments illustrate the criteria of _____ in defining abnormal behavior.
   a. maladaptiveness   c. statistical deviance
   b. personal distress   d. joint attention

   ANS: B   DIF: Moderate   REF: 518   OBJ: 16.1

5. The "DSM" in DSM-IV refers to the
   a. Diagnostic and Statistical Manual of Mental Disorders
   b. Doctor's Scientific/Psychological Medical Guide
   c. Diagram of Severe Mental Illnesses
   d. Direct Services Method of Psychological Intervention

   ANS: A   DIF: Easy   REF: 518   OBJ: 16.1

6. It has been proposed that in the DMS-V, discussion on the concept of autism
   a. will be removed from the text.
   b. be discussed as a single category of "autism spectrum disorders" rather than a list that includes numerous subcategories.
   c. will be replaced with a broader category referred to as "conduct disorders of autistic type" and will drop references to linguistic problems.
   d. will remain unchanged.

   ANS: B   DIF: Moderate   REF: 518   OBJ: 16.1

7. If drafters of the DMS-5 have their way, the term "_____" will be replaced with the term "intellectual disability."
   a. learning disability   c. cognitive disability
   b. multiple personality   d. mental retardation

   ANS: D   DIF: Easy   REF: 518   OBJ: 16.1

8. With regard to depressive disorders, the DSM-IV
   a. defines major depression by the presence of a group of symptoms consistently evident for a period of time.
   b. recommends the use of MAO inhibitors as a treatment.
   c. includes affective symptoms like sad moods in the definition of depression but excludes behavioral symptoms like sleep disturbance.
   d. recognizes that some people may suffer from major depression with as few as one or two symptoms.

   ANS: A   DIF: Moderate   REF: 518-519   OBJ: 16.1

9. To be accurately diagnosed with major depressive disorder, you would have to display at least five symptoms from a nine-symptom list. That nine-item list includes all of the following except
   a. significant weight loss or weight gain.
   b. insomnia or too much sleeping.
   c. feelings of worthlessness or extreme guilt.
   d. auditory or visual hallucinations.

   ANS: D   DIF: Moderate   REF: 518-519   OBJ: 16.1

10. Forty-year-old Alfred has been accurately diagnosed with major depressive disorder. This means that you would be most likely to expect him to
    a. be hyperactive.   c. be more decisive in decision-making.
    b. show great interest in usual activities. d. have recurrent thoughts of death.

    ANS: D   DIF: Moderate   REF: 518-519   OBJ: 16.1

11. Which characteristic would not be found on an accurate list of symptoms of major depression?
    a. Significant weight loss   c. Excessive sleep
    b. Decreased ability to concentrate   d. Feelings of extreme shyness

    ANS: D   DIF: Difficult   REF: 518-519   OBJ: 16.1
    KEY: WWW

778

12. Which major depressive disorder criteria will likely be dropped in the DSM-5?
    a. Psychomotor agitation or sluggishness
    b. Recurrent suicidal thoughts
    c. Should not better be described as reaction to bereavement
    d. Not due the direct result of a substance abuse

    ANS: C   DIF: Moderate   REF: 519   OBJ: 16.1

13. How are cultural considerations handled in the DSM-IV section on depression?
    a. It has separate diagnostic criteria to be used in each of the industrialized nations.
    b. It indicates that Asians are more likely to report somatic ailments than psychological ailments.
    c. It notes that in many cultures the preferred treatment of exorcism is "spiritual cleansing."
    d. Cultural and developmental variations are identified as irrelevant to diagnosis and treatment.

    ANS: B   DIF: Difficult   REF: 519   OBJ: 16.1

14. Your psychology professor asks you to list at least five somatic symptoms. Which of the following should be on your accurate list?
    a. Loss of appetite   c. Shame
    b. Paranoia   d. Lack of conscience

    ANS: A   DIF: Moderate   REF: 519   OBJ: 16.1

15. Developmental psychopathologists focus on
    a. developing therapies for treatment of psychological disorders.
    b. disorders of infancy and early childhood.
    c. studying the origins and the path of maladaptive behaviors.
    d. trying to establish genetic contributions to maladaptive behavior.

    ANS: C   DIF: Easy   REF: 519   OBJ: 16.2

16. As developmental psychologists, Rutter and Sroufe (2000) argue that psychological disorders are best
    a. described in terms of a disease.
    b. conceptualized as a pattern of adaptation that unfolds over time.
    c. thought to be defects lying within the person.
    d. understood without knowledge concerning the individual's personal characteristics, history, or developmental status as these factors bias the diagnosis.

    ANS: B   DIF: Difficult   REF: 519   OBJ: 16.2

17. Which statement best describes an element of the developmental pathways model?
    a. Different developmental pathways can lead to the same outcome.
    b. Change is only possible during one specific point of development.
    c. A particular pathway can lead only in one direction.
    d. The line between normal and abnormal behavior is clear and absolute.

    ANS: A   DIF: Moderate   REF: 519-520   OBJ: 16.2

18. According to the developmental pathways model,
    a. psychological disorders are best characterized as diseases.
    b. once a person's behavior deviates from the normal path, it will not return to normal.
    c. normal genes and normal environments tend to push development along a normal course.
    d. with age, individuals whose early development is maladaptive will almost always show deviation back to the norm.

    ANS: C   DIF: Moderate   REF: 519-520   OBJ: 16.2

19. Vanna takes a lifespan neurodevelopmental view concerning depression. As such, she would be most interested in
    a. parental modeling.   c. social norms.
    b. the developing brain.   d. repressed memories.

    ANS: B   DIF: Easy   REF: 520   OBJ: 16.1

20. Social norms are best defined as
    a. the tendency to go against what others are doing.
    b. cross-cultural expectations for behavior that are devoid of social context.
    c. genetic-based programming that results in the expression of specific behaviors.
    d. expectations of how to behave in a given social context.

    ANS: D   DIF: Easy   REF: 520   OBJ: 16.2
    KEY: WWW

21. In the fictitious country of Rosieland, all married men are expected to wear pink hats when attending any soccer match. Within this culture, this expectation is best described as a(n)
    a. form of imprinting.   c. non-normative event.
    b. social norm.   d. type of psychopathology.

    ANS: B   DIF: Moderate   REF: 520   OBJ: 16.2

22. The fact that depressed children in Thailand are less likely to engage in "acting out" behavior, because the Thai culture places great emphasis on internalizing problems, best illustrates the concept of _____ norms.
    a. test   c. gender
    b. social   d. age

    ANS: B   DIF: Moderate   REF: 520   OBJ: 16.2

23. An age norm is best defined as
    a. societal expectations for the behavior of all people in a particular social context.
    b. expectations regarding behavior that is appropriate or inappropriate at a given age.
    c. expectations for how to behave at a party.
    d. cross-cultural expectations for behavior that are not tied to age.

    ANS: B   DIF: Easy   REF: 520   OBJ: 16.2

24. The question, "Is it appropriate for a 2-year-old to suck his thumb, but inappropriate for a 42-year-old to engage in the same behavior?" underlies the issue of
    a. imprinting.
    b. comorbidity.
    c. generativity.
    d. age norms.

    ANS: D   DIF: Moderate   REF: 520   OBJ: 16.2

25. In the diathesis-stress model, the term diathesis refers to a(n)
    a. genetic or personality-based predisposition toward vulnerability.
    b. state of calm.
    c. anxiety-producing environmental event.
    d. social norm.

    ANS: A   DIF: Moderate   REF: 521   OBJ: 16.3

26. If research indicated that having an extra 22nd chromosome and being very jolly made an individual at risk for developing schizophrenia, then for schizophrenia the extra 22nd chromosome and a jolly personality would exemplify a
    a. somatic symptom.
    b. recessive trait.
    c. diathesis.
    d. social norm.

    ANS: C   DIF: Difficult   REF: 521   OBJ: 16.1

27. According to the diathesis-stress model, psychopathology results when
    a. a stressful event triggers an already existing vulnerability or predisposition.
    b. the id develops.
    c. a gene that is programmed to activate at a certain point during the lifespan "turns on" without any trigger.
    d. a mentally healthy person takes a psychoactive drug.

    ANS: A   DIF: Moderate   REF: 521   OBJ: 16.3

28. According to the diathesis-stress model, _____ should be the most likely to show the most extreme levels of a psychological disorder.
    a. Bert, who is highly resilient and in an extremely stressful environment
    b. Ernie, who is highly resilient and in a very low-stress environment
    c. Grover, who is highly vulnerable and in an extremely stressful environment
    d. Fozzie, who is highly vulnerable and in a very low-stress environment

    ANS: C   DIF: Moderate   REF: 521   OBJ: 16.3
    KEY: WWW

29. According to the diathesis-stress model, if 100% of individuals with a genetic predisposition to a disorder actually display symptoms of the disorder, regardless of their environmental experiences, this indicates that the behavior is
    a. strongly related to diathesis.
    b. strongly related to stress.
    c. strongly related to both diathesis and stress.
    d. neither related to diathesis nor stress.

    ANS: A   DIF: Moderate   REF: 521-522   OBJ: 16.3

30. If the diathesis for a psychological disorder is strong, then
   a. personality or genetic predisposition will play a significant role in whether it is expressed.
   b. the behavior will not occur until midlife.
   c. it is more common in females than males.
   d. the environment can shape the cause but not the course of the disorder.

   ANS: A   DIF: Moderate   REF: 521-522   OBJ: 16.3

31. Doc Oc adheres to the diathesis-stress position when it comes to explaining the development of psychological disorders. As such, he would predict that if stress is the sole contributor to depression, than in a group of 100 individuals all carrying the same "at-risk gene" for depression who live in a stress-free world, _____ would develop depression.
   a. 0
   b. 25
   c. 50
   d. 100

   ANS: A   DIF: Difficult   REF: 521-522   OBJ: 16.3

32. Suppose two people experience the same stressful events, and as a result of the experience, one person develops an affective disorder while the second person shows no ill effects. The diathesis-stress model would most likely explain this by saying that the
   a. person who developed the disorder was older than the other person.
   b. disordered person must be female and the other person male.
   c. two people had different predispositions for the disorder and had likelyexperienced different levels of stress during past encounters with similar stimuli.
   d. person who developed the disorder had a gene that guaranteed the disorder would develop at some point (even without any stress).

   ANS: C   DIF: Difficult   REF: 521-522   OBJ: 16.3

33. An imbalance in _____ appears to play a role in the acquisition of major depressive disorder.
   a. serotonin levels
   b. sensorimotor and concrete-operational thinking
   c. beta-amyloids
   d. corpus callosum activity

   ANS: A   DIF: Moderate   REF: 522   OBJ: 16.1

34. According to the diathesis-stress model, the death of a loved one
   a. would have no impact on the development of major depression.
   b. is typically not enough to trigger major depression.
   c. typically triggers major depression.
   d. virtually always triggers the development of major depression.

   ANS: B   DIF: Moderate   REF: 521   OBJ: 16.1

35. Diathesis is to stress as
   a. gene is to the environment.
   b. externalized is to internalized.
   c. cultural is to individual.
   d. cause is to effect.

   ANS: A   DIF: Difficult   REF: 521-522   OBJ: 16.1

36. Research using the diathesis-stress model indicates that
    a. genes cannot predispose some people to depression but can influence the extent to which an individual experiences stressful life events.
    b. genes predispose some people to depression but cannot influence the extent to which an individual experiences stressful life events.
    c. genes predispose some people to depression and influence the extent to which an individual experiences stressful life events.
    d. genes cannot predispose people to depression nor influence their experiences to stressful life events.

    ANS: C   DIF: Moderate   REF: 521-522   OBJ: 16.1

37. According to Kanner's original description, _____ is not a defining feature of autism.
    a. abnormal social development
    b. impaired language and communicative skill development
    c. repetitive, stereotyped behavior
    d. moderate to severe mental retardation

    ANS: D   DIF: Moderate   REF: 522-523   OBJ: 16.4
    KEY: WWW

38. Augie has been correctly diagnosed with autism. As such, you should expect that Augie will be most likely to
    a. show great empathy.
    b. exhibit a superb ability to read the emotions of others.
    c. have a great desire to make eye contact with peers.
    d. find social contact to be aversive.

    ANS: D   DIF: Moderate   REF: 522-523   OBJ: 16.4

39. Tom has noticed that his 2-year-old son, Jerry, often repeats phrases that he has heard on television. Interestingly, these are the only vocalizations that Jerry makes. A psychologist would be most likely to classify Jerry's deviant language behavior as
    a. underextension.   c. echolalia.
    b. private speech.   d. overregularization.

    ANS: C   DIF: Moderate   REF: 523   OBJ: 16.4

40. Echolalia is best described as
    a. parroting what someone else is saying.   c. saying socially inappropriate things.
    b. not speaking at all.   d. a lack of organized speech.

    ANS: A   DIF: Easy   REF: 523   OBJ: 16.4

41. Which would indicate that a child is reversing pronouns?
    a. Encountering a very smelly stranger and saying "I stink" rather than "you stink"
    b. Correcting a stranger by saying, "My name is Ed not Edward"
    c. Mixing up the concept of pet by referring to a "dog" using the word "cat"
    d. Confusing when something happened by saying "I goed" instead of "I will go"

    ANS: A   DIF: Difficult   REF: 523   OBJ: 16.4

42. You enter a room and see an average-looking child wildly flapping his arms repetitively for no apparent reason. You then notice that this child becomes extremely agitated when an adult pulls a shade on a window down just a few inches. As a knowledgeable psychology student, you would rightly surmise that this child
    a. has Down syndrome.
    b. suffers from autism.
    c. has muscular dystrophy.
    d. is suffering from rubella.

    ANS: B   DIF: Moderate   REF: 523   OBJ: 16.4

43. Which is the best example of a stereotyped repetitive behavior?
    a. Never speaking
    b. Rocking back and forth continuously
    c. Being depressed all of the time
    d. Getting mad while you are taking a test

    ANS: B   DIF: Easy   REF: 523   OBJ: 16.4

44. Why is autism referred to as a "spectrum" of disorders?
    a. It can occur at any time of the lifespan.
    b. It includes a wide variety of conditions.
    c. It impacts speech, behavior, and social skills.
    d. It is related to other anxiety and mood disorders.

    ANS: B   DIF: Easy   REF: 523   OBJ: 16.4

45. Under which DSM-IV category would you find autism spectrum disorders?
    a. Personality disorders
    b. Dissociative disorders
    c. Adjustment disorders
    d. Pervasive developmental disorders

    ANS: D   DIF: Moderate   REF: 523   OBJ: 16.4

46. On the DSM-IV, Asperger syndrome would be found under the label "_____ disorders."
    a. personality
    b. autism spectrum
    c. somatoform
    d. anxiety

    ANS: B   DIF: Moderate   REF: 523   OBJ: 16.4

47. Winne has good verbal skills and is highly intelligent, but has social relationship skills typical of an autistic child. Given this description, Winnie is most likely to be diagnosed with _____ syndrome.
    a. Turner
    b. Down
    c. Kleinfelter
    d. Asperger

    ANS: D   DIF: Moderate   REF: 523   OBJ: 16.4

48. Rex is a teenager who characterized by his peers as a "little professor" who knows and talks a lot about one topic, dinosaurs. Given this description, Rex would most likely have _____ syndrome.
    a. Turner
    b. Down
    c. Kleinfelter
    d. Asperger

    ANS: D   DIF: Moderate   REF: 523   OBJ: 16.4
    KEY: WWW

49. Which statement concerning the incidence of autism is true?
    a. The rates of autism have declined in recent years.
    b. Autism affects about 1 out of every 10 children.
    c. The rate of autism is higher in males.
    d. Most autistics with normal levels of intelligence are female.

    ANS: C   DIF: Moderate   REF: 523   OBJ: 16.4

50. A now retracted article by Wakefield and others claimed that autism is caused by
    a. baby formula fortified with iron.
    b. lead poisoning.
    c. the MMR vaccine.
    d. excessive infantile exposure to television and computer screens.

    ANS: C   DIF: Easy   REF: 523-524   OBJ: 16.4

51. What key evidence has emerged to disprove the myth that thimerosal (a mercury-based preservative) is responsible for autism?
    a. Historically, no children with autism ever came into direct contact with thimerosal.
    b. The incidence of autism has climbed after thimerosal was removed from the MMR vaccine.
    c. As the amount of thimerosal in baby food has increased, the incidence of autism has decreased.
    d. The incidence of autism has decreased significantly, but only in females who are immune the impact of thimerosal.

    ANS: B   DIF: Moderate   REF: 523-524   OBJ: 16.4
    KEY: WWW

52. The most likely reason for the increase in the number of children diagnosed with autism spectrum disorders is that
    a. in the 1990s, autism was removed from the U.S. list of disabilities eligible for special education services.
    b. the rise has corresponded with the significant increase in the number of infants born with HIV.
    c. in the 1990s, Asperger syndrome was removed from the DSM-IV.
    d. there is now a broader definition for what used to be just autism.

    ANS: D   DIF: Easy   REF: 524   OBJ: 16.4

53. What behavior would an infant display that would lead a competent doctor to accurately suspect the child is suffering from autistic disorder?
    a. Failure to respond to human voices
    b. Excessive levels of joint attention
    c. Showing a clear preference for human over nonhuman stimuli
    d. An obsession with playing peek-a-boo and other social games

    ANS: A   DIF: Moderate   REF: 524   OBJ: 16.4

54. Which statement concerning the intellectual abilities of autistic individuals is most accurate?
    a. The vast majority of autistics are mildly to severely mentally retarded.
    b. Autistic individuals tend to score lower higher on nonverbal than verbal measures of intelligence.
    c. More than half of children with autism score above 71 on IQ tests.
    d. The description of some individuals with autism as "savants" with special abilities in a given area (e.g., quickly calculating the days of the week corresponding to dates on a calendar) is a myth.

    ANS: C   DIF: Moderate   REF: 524   OBJ: 16.4

55. The social impairment that defines autism is now viewed as being
    a. qualitatively and quantitatively different than from typical social behavior.
    b. qualitatively rather than quantitatively different from typical social behavior.
    c. quantitatively rather than qualitatively different from typical social behavior.
    d. qualitatively and quantitatively similar to that of typical social behavior.

    ANS: C   DIF: Difficult   REF: 524   OBJ: 16.4

56. All of the following are currently legitimate suspected causes of autism except
    a. a lack of executive functions.   c. genetic defect.
    b. cold, rigid parenting.   d. lack of a theory of mind.

    ANS: B   DIF: Moderate   REF: 524-525   OBJ: 16.4

57. Concerning genetic explanations of autism,
    a. at this point there is no evidence of any genetic basis of the disorder.
    b. there is clear evidence that autism is solely due to the presence of a third 21st chromosome.
    c. the genes involved appear to cause a rapid deceleration of head and brain development over the course of the first three years after birth.
    d. many genes have been implicated including some that appear to have been copied too many times.

    ANS: D   DIF: Difficult   REF: 524-525   OBJ: 16.4

58. Which brain areas have been implicated as a possible cause of the behavioral problems found in individuals with autism?
    a. The amygdala and frontal cortex   c. The hippocampus and parietal cortex
    b. The hypothalamus and temporal cortex   d. The thalamus and the occipital cortex

    ANS: A   DIF: Moderate   REF: 525   OBJ: 16.4

59. The mirror neuron simulation hypothesis is best associated with the disorder of
    a. autism.   c. depression.
    b. schizophrenia.   d. attention deficit disorder.

    ANS: A   DIF: Easy   REF: 525   OBJ: 16.4
    KEY: WWW

60. Mirror neurons
    a. allow us to relate the feelings of others to our own experiences.
    b. generate multiple copies of themselves, and each copy leads to an increase in dopamine levels.
    c. are very fragile, and when they "die," they produce excessive levels of neuritic plaque.
    d. only fire when they are stimulated by other mirror neurons.

    ANS: A   DIF: Moderate   REF: 525   OBJ: 16.4

61. Executive functions are thought to take place in the _____ cortex of the brain.
    a. occipital   c. prefrontal
    b. temporal   d. parietal

    ANS: C   DIF: Moderate   REF: 525   OBJ: 16.4

62. According to the executive dysfunction hypothesis, autistic behavior is the result of a brain that is
    a. too small.
    b. unable to plan and change one's course of actions.
    c. lacking Broca's area.
    d. overrun with mirror neurons.

    ANS: B   DIF: Moderate   REF: 525   OBJ: 16.4

63. Baron-Cohen has recently suggested that the extreme _____ hypothesis may explain the cause of Asperger syndrome.
    a. theory-of-mind   c. central coherence
    b. executive dysfunction   d. male brain

    ANS: D   DIF: Difficult   REF: 525-526   OBJ: 16.4
    KEY: WWW

64. According to the extreme male brain theory of autism, the key problem with individuals with autism is that they
    a. lack empathy and do not attempt to keep the world orderly.
    b. lack empathy and try too hard to keep the world orderly.
    c. are too empathetic and do not attempt to keep the world orderly.
    d. are too empathetic and try too hard to keep the world orderly.

    ANS: B   DIF: Moderate   REF: 525-526   OBJ: 16.4

65. Recent research has shown that the nasal administration of _____ appears to improve social information and understanding in high-functioning individuals with autism.
    a. beta-amyloid   c. antihistamines
    b. thimerosal   d. oxytocin

    ANS: D   DIF: Difficult   REF: 525   OBJ: 16.4

66. Which statement concerning the long-term prognosis for autistic children is true?
    a. Most can be improved significantly through drug treatment.
    b. Most autistics achieve a normal level of functioning when they reach adulthood.
    c. The best interventions involve intensive and highly structured behavioral and educational programs aimed at young children.
    d. Intensive behavior modification programs have been shown to increase levels of aggressiveness and self-stimulation.

    ANS: C   DIF: Moderate   REF: 525-527   OBJ: 16.4

67. Ivar Lovaas conducted pioneering research on children with autism in which he was able to use _____ to significantly improve their language and social skills.
    a. psychoactive medications   c. reinforcement principles
    b. psychoanalysis   d. mirror therapy

    ANS: C   DIF: Moderate   REF: 526   OBJ: 16.4

68. The major criticism of Lovaas's research findings on autism was that his research
    a. was not a true experiment because participants were not randomly assigned to treatment and control groups.
    b. used physical pain as an unethical form of punishment.
    c. can never be replicated because the drugs he administered to the children are now illegal.
    d. was sexist as he only studied males with autism.

    ANS: A   DIF: Moderate   REF: 527   OBJ: 16.4

69. The most accurate statement concerning the use of behavioral and cognitive interventions with children with autism is that they
    a. are virtually worthless at changing behaviors.
    b. can lead to significant gains, especially in young children who do not have severe intellectual disabilities.
    c. can lead to significant gains, especially in older children who do have significant intellectual disabilities.
    d. typically lead to significant improvements in all children, regardless of their age or level of intellect.

    ANS: B   DIF: Moderate   REF: 527   OBJ: 16.4

70. Which is true regarding depression in infancy?
    a. Infants do not exhibit depression-like symptoms.
    b. Infants experience the same cognitions that are common among adults (e.g., feelings of low self-esteem, worthlessness, hopelessness).
    c. Infants who display depression-like symptoms are those who are most securely attached to their caregivers.
    d. Infants sometimes display depression-like symptoms and states.

    ANS: D   DIF: Moderate   REF: 527   OBJ: 16.5

71. Depression-like symptoms are most likely to be seen in infants who
    a. show no somatic reactions.
    b. have experienced perinatal complications.
    c. are mentally retarded.
    d. show a disorganized pattern of attachment.

    ANS: D   DIF: Moderate   REF: 527   OBJ: 16.5

72. Failure to thrive in otherwise healthy infants is usually
    a. attributed to perinatal complications.
    b. so severe that it cannot be undone.
    c. the result of having unaffectionate or depressed caregivers.
    d. misdiagnosed as autism.

    ANS: C   DIF: Moderate   REF: 527-528   OBJ: 16.5
    KEY: WWW

73. Despite having been born of normal weight, 1-year-old Trevor's weight has not increased as expected. In addition, he is showing depression-like responses. Given these symptoms, Trevor is best diagnosed with
    a. autism.   c. Down syndrome.
    b. failure to thrive.   d. agoraphobia.

    ANS: B   DIF: Easy   REF: 528   OBJ: 16.5

74. Internalizing is to externalizing as
    a. being inhibited is to acting out.   c. undercontrolled is to overcontrolled.
    b. aggression is to depression.   d. hyperactive is to inactive.

    ANS: A   DIF: Difficult   REF: 528   OBJ: 16.6

75. The defining element of an externalizing problem involves
    a. hallucinations.   c. acting out.
    b. delusions.   d. phobias.

    ANS: C   DIF: Moderate   REF: 528   OBJ: 16.6
    KEY: WWW

76. Who is displaying an externalizing problem?
    a. Darrin, who is worrying about his psychology exam
    b. Samantha, who is depressed
    c. Tabitha, who punches other children on the playground
    d. Stevens, who is extremely shy

    ANS: C   DIF: Moderate   REF: 528   OBJ: 16.6

77. Which statement best describes an internalizing problem?
    a. More disruptive to self than others   c. Difficult to control one's actions
    b. Almost always illegal   d. Violation of social expectations

    ANS: A   DIF: Moderate   REF: 528   OBJ: 16.6

78. Which of the following is an example of an internalizing disorder?
   a. Constantly interrupting the activities of others
   b. Constantly worrying about whether you are performing adequately
   c. Loudly refusing to follow the rules established for the classroom
   d. Hitting other children

   ANS: B   DIF: Difficult   REF: 528   OBJ: 16.6

79. Internalizing problems are
   a. actions that violate social expectations.
   b. particularly disruptive to people who come in contact with the child.
   c. easier to directly observe than externalizing disorders.
   d. more prevalent among girls than boys.

   ANS: D   DIF: Moderate   REF: 529   OBJ: 16.6

80. How many of the following (having a clinically depressed father, living in a disturbed family environment, residing in a stressful environment) would the diathesis-stress model consider as risk factors for a child exhibiting a psychological disorder?
   a. 0   c. 2
   b. 1   d. 3

   ANS: D   DIF: Moderate   REF: 529   OBJ: 16.6

81. A study on the impact of living through Hurricane Katrina on children in New Orleans found that the event resulted in a significant increase in the number of children with symptoms of
   a. attention deficit-hyperactivity disorder.   c. paranoid schizophrenia.
   b. posttraumatic stress syndrome.   d. dissociative identity disorder.

   ANS: B   DIF: Difficult   REF: 530   OBJ: 16.6

82. Hurricane Katrina appeared to have the greatest negative psychological impact on children who
   a. were born within 1 year after the event.
   b. had experienced previous traumas in their life.
   c. lived closest to the levees that gave way.
   d. lived in single-parent-headed households.

   ANS: B   DIF: Difficult   REF: 530   OBJ: 16.6

83. Caspi and colleagues found that inhibited, uncontrolled children who were shy, anxious, and easily upset at age 3 were most likely to be diagnosed as _____ at age 21.
   a. ADHD   c. with depression
   b. with an anxiety disorder   d. autistic

   ANS: C   DIF: Difficult   REF: 529   OBJ: 16.8

84. The fact that children with behavioral disorders are unlikely to exhibit these disorders as adults best illustrates the concept of developmental
   a. continuity.   c. comorbidity.
   b. discontinuity.   d. rigidity.

   ANS: B   DIF: Moderate   REF: 529   OBJ: 16.8

85. The fact that children with anxiety problems are likely to exhibit similar disorders as adults best illustrates the concept of developmental
   a. continuity.
   b. discontinuity.
   c. comorbidity.
   d. rigidity.

   ANS: A   DIF: Moderate   REF: 529   OBJ: 16.8
   KEY: WWW

86. Which statement best summarizes the pattern of developmental disorders from childhood to adolescence?
   a. Both continuity and discontinuity
   b. Only continuity
   c. Only discontinuity
   d. Neither continuity nor discontinuity

   ANS: A   DIF: Moderate   REF: 529 & 531   OBJ: 16.6

87. Protective factors
   a. work against strong social support systems.
   b. do not develop until the teenage years.
   c. help children from becoming maladjusted in the face of risk.
   d. are especially apparent in autistic children.

   ANS: C   DIF: Easy   REF: 531   OBJ: 16.8

88. Depression is most rare in
   a. childhood.
   b. adolescence.
   c. young adulthood.
   d. middle adulthood.

   ANS: A   DIF: Moderate   REF: 531   OBJ: 16.6

89. By definition, all individuals who are classified with comorbidity
   a. are extremely close to death.
   b. possess two psychological conditions at the same time.
   c. have been negatively impacted by both genetic and environmental factors.
   d. cannot control their impulses.

   ANS: B   DIF: Moderate   REF: 531   OBJ: 16.6

90. Conrad has just seen a clinical psychologist who has told him that he is both depressed and has an anxiety disorder. This indicates that Conrad would accurately be described as
   a. being highly externalizing.
   b. having ADHD.
   c. exemplifying comorbidity.
   d. showing somatic symptoms.

   ANS: C   DIF: Moderate   REF: 531   OBJ: 16.6

91. Depressed preschool-aged children
   a. display the same behavioral and cognitive symptoms as do depressed adults.
   b. are most often extremely aggressive.
   c. usually mask their depression such that it is nearly impossible to detect that they are feeling sad.
   d. are less likely than adults to display cognitive symptoms of depression such as hopelessness.

   ANS: D   DIF: Difficult   REF: 531   OBJ: 16.7

92. Children as young as age _____ are capable of attempting suicide.
    a. 2
    b. 5
    c. 8
    d. 11

ANS: A   DIF: Moderate   REF: 531   OBJ: 16.7

93. Children who have a depressive disorder
    a. differ from adolescents and adults with depression, because children never attempt suicide while the older age groups often do.
    b. are easy to identify because they frequently talk about their negative feelings.
    c. often have problems with depression as adolescents and adults.
    d. seldom respond well to any form of psychotherapy.

ANS: C   DIF: Moderate   REF: 531   OBJ: 16.7

94. Research has shown that _____ treatments tend to be the most effective when treating depression in children.
    a. psychoanalytic
    b. drug
    c. parental intervention
    d. cognitive behavioral

ANS: D   DIF: Moderate   REF: 531-532   OBJ: 16.7

95. As a cognitive behavioral therapist, Niles's main goal in treating a child with depression would be to
    a. remove all repressed memories.
    b. strengthen the child's id.
    c. change the child's distorted thinking.
    d. teach parents to punish sadness and reward happiness.

ANS: C   DIF: Moderate   REF: 531-532   OBJ: 16.7
KEY: WWW

96. Many antidepressant drugs like Prozac are selective _____ reuptake inhibitors.
    a. serotonin
    b. dopamine
    c. GABA
    d. norepinephrine

ANS: A   DIF: Moderate   REF: 532   OBJ: 16.7

97. In 2004, the United States government issued a warning concerning the use of some antidepressant drugs and the possible increased risk of _____ in adolescence.
    a. pregnancy
    b. birth defects
    c. suicide
    d. addiction

ANS: C   DIF: Easy   REF: 532   OBJ: 16.7

98. After reading G. Stanley Hall's groundbreaking book called *Adolescence* (1904), a parent would be most likely to believe that the teen years
    a. were highly traumatic.
    b. did not exist as a separate time of life from adulthood.
    c. was a time of life without stress or care.
    d. was a time when young people were cognitively superior to their parents.

ANS: A   DIF: Moderate   REF: 533   OBJ: 16.8

99. G. Stanley Hall referred to adolescence as a time of
   a. unbridled sex and violence.
   b. cognitive explosion.
   c. emotional storm and stress.
   d. a great buzzing, booming confusion.

   ANS: C   DIF: Moderate   REF: 533   OBJ: 16.8
   KEY: WWW

100. Which is true with regard to psychological "health" during adolescence?
   a. Most adolescents suffer at some point from some sort of significant psychological disturbance.
   b. Few adolescents who are psychologically disturbed were maladjusted before they reached puberty.
   c. Adolescence is a time of heightened vulnerability for some forms of psychological disorders.
   d. Adolescents are far more likely than adults to experience some sort of psychological disturbance.

   ANS: C   DIF: Easy   REF: 533   OBJ: 16.8

101. When compared with the rate in adolescence, the estimated diagnosable rate of psychological disorders in childhood is
   a. significantly lower.
   b. almost identical.
   c. slightly higher.
   d. significantly higher.

   ANS: A   DIF: Moderate   REF: 533   OBJ: 16.8

102. Which statement concerning adolescence is true?
   a. Most adolescents cope remarkably well with the challenges of this period of life.
   b. Most adolescents experience serious psychopathology during this period of life.
   c. Few adolescents engage in delinquent or risky behavior during this period of life.
   d. Adolescents have little difficulty with self-regulatory behaviors.

   ANS: A   DIF: Moderate   REF: 533   OBJ: 16.8

103. Anorexia nervosa literally means "nervous loss of _____."
   a. mind
   b. appetite
   c. control
   d. weight

   ANS: B   DIF: Moderate   REF: 533   OBJ: 16.9

104. The American Psychiatric Association defines anorexia nervosa as the refusal to maintain a weight that is at least _____ of what is expected for one's height and age.
   a. 95%
   b. 85%
   c. 75%
   d. 65%

   ANS: B   DIF: Difficult   REF: 533   OBJ: 16.9

105. At age 18, Marie is 5'9" and weighs about 75 pounds. She thinks of herself as being fat, and she is desperately afraid she will become overweight. Marie most likely suffers from
   a. anorexia nervosa.
   b. bulimia nervosa.
   c. Turner syndrome.
   d. Asperger syndrome.

   ANS: A   DIF: Moderate   REF: 533   OBJ: 16.9

106. Gwen has been diagnosed with bulimia nervosa. Which of the following characteristics would she be least likely to possess?
    a. A tendency to consume huge quantities of foods in a single sitting
    b. The use of laxatives or self-vomiting to purge food
    c. A refusal to maintain body weight in spite of being in an emaciated state
    d. A feeling of being fat

    ANS: C   DIF: Difficult   REF: 533   OBJ: 16.9
    KEY: WWW

107. Denise is about average in height and weight, and is often dieting. From time to time, however, she sits down and eats huge quantities of food all at once, after which, she makes herself vomit. Denise suffers from
    a. anorexia nervosa.   c. Turner syndrome.
    b. bulimia nervosa.   d. Asperger syndrome.

    ANS: B   DIF: Moderate   REF: 533   OBJ: 16.9

108. Anorexia nervosa is more common in
    a. females than males.
    b. African Americans than European Americans.
    c. unindustrialized than industrialized nations.
    d. third-graders than ninth-graders.

    ANS: A   DIF: Easy   REF: 533-534   OBJ: 16.9

109. When television was introduced to the island of Fiji,
    a. normally thin girls developed the strong desire to gain weight.
    b. normally thin boys developed the strong desire to gain weight.
    c. girls who had seen a plump body as a status symbol developed the strong desire to lose weight.
    d. boys who had seen a plump body as a status symbol developed the strong desire to lose weight.

    ANS: C   DIF: Moderate   REF: 534   OBJ: 16.9

110. Why does adolescence appear to be a prime time for the development of eating disorders in females?
    a. It is the first time that girls receive media images promoting thinness.
    b. It takes someone at the formal operational stage of thinking to develop the obsessive food-related behaviors seen in anorexia and bulimia.
    c. The gene that controls eating does not "turn-on" until that time of life.
    d. The normal weight gain in puberty is viewed as problematic.

    ANS: D   DIF: Moderate   REF: 534   OBJ: 16.9

111. Which is the best example of a diathesis for anorexia?
    a. The media's portrayal of women
    b. A gene that controls appetite
    c. Peer pressure to be thin
    d. Parental statements like, "Boys don't date fat girls"

    ANS: B   DIF: Difficult   REF: 534   OBJ: 16.9

112. Anorexia is best explained as being
    a. solely due to the images seen in the media.
    b. a genetic defect that impacts metabolic rate.
    c. the result of media images interacting with family pressures.
    d. a genetic predisposition interacting with environmental pressures.

    ANS: D   DIF: Easy   REF: 534   OBJ: 16.9
    KEY: WWW

113. The main initial focus of the Maudsley approach to treating anorexia is on
    a. eliminating the notion that anorexia is a psychological problem.
    b. encouraging weight gain.
    c. removing harmful media image from television and movies.
    d. teaching anorexics about the dangers of using laxatives and purgatives.

    ANS: B   DIF: Moderate   REF: 535   OBJ: 16.9

114. Abbey is a strong supporter of the Maudsley approach to treating anorexia. Thus, when
    considering the role of parents in the treatment process, she would be most likely to suggest
    that the parents
    a. need to accept blame for the problem before therapy can be effective.
    b. stay out of the way and let the psychotherapists do their job unimpeded.
    c. must be a critical part of the treatment team with the goal of facilitating weight
       gain.
    d. should go on diets in support of their child.

    ANS: C   DIF: Moderate   REF: 535   OBJ: 16.9

115. The two biggest reasons for the difficulty often seen in treating anorexic individuals involves
    ineffective drugs and
    a. strong resistance to admitting they have a problem.
    b. families who are resistant to changing the behavior of their children.
    c. problems in properly diagnosing the disorder.
    d. a common metabolic reaction in which the body craves excessive amounts of
       calories.

    ANS: A   DIF: Moderate   REF: 535   OBJ: 16.9

116. According to the DSM-IV, a key distinction between substance abuse and substance
    dependence is that
    a. dependence involves illegal drugs.
    b. abuse involves those under 18 and dependence involves those over 18.
    c. dependence involves continued use in spite of significant problems (inability to
       quit).
    d. abuse is a physical disorder and dependence is a psychological disorder.

    ANS: C   DIF: Moderate   REF: 535   OBJ: 16.10

117. The one drug that young teens use more often than older teens is
    a. inhalants.   c. marijuana.
    b. alcohol.   d. codeine.

    ANS: A   DIF: Moderate   REF: 535-536   OBJ: 16.10

118. What would qualify 17-year-old Daniels as a binge-drinker?
   a. Consuming at least 3 different types of alcohol in on sitting
   b. Consuming alcohol for 5 days in a row
   c. Consuming alcohol with at least 3 peers present
   d. Consuming more than 5 drinks in a row in a single drinking session

   ANS: D   DIF: Easy   REF: 536   OBJ: 16.10

119. The initial step in the cascade model of substance abuse involves
   a. exposure to harsh parenting.
   b. development of conduct problems.
   c. being a child who is at risk due to a difficult temperament.
   d. being born into a family environment characterized by poverty and substance abuse.

   ANS: C   DIF: Difficult   REF: 536   OBJ: 16.10

120. The final step in the cascade model of substance abuse involves
   a. having a parent who abuses drugs.
   b. being in a deviant peer group in which one is reinforced for drug use.
   c. peer rejection at school.
   d. frustrated parents giving up trying to monitor or supervise the behavior of a deviant child.

   ANS: B   DIF: Difficult   REF: 536   OBJ: 16.10

121. According to the cascade model of substance abuse, intervention
   a. is only possible when peer mentors are involved.
   b. can only occur once a child or adolescent has reached the final step.
   c. is impossible, although reduction of use is possible.
   d. can occur during each step.

   ANS: D   DIF: Difficult   REF: 536   OBJ: 16.10

122. The biggest complaint against the cascade model of substance abuse is that it
   a. is too Freudian.
   b. explains abuse in adults but not in teens.
   c. needs to place greater emphasis on the role of genetic factors.
   d. does not consider contextual factors.

   ANS: C   DIF: Moderate   REF: 536   OBJ: 16.10

123. Who would be at greatest risk for developing depression?
   a. An early maturing adolescent female who is in a stressful relationship with peers
   b. An early maturing adolescent male who is in a stressful relationship with peers
   c. A late maturing adolescent female who is in a stressful relationship with peers
   d. A late maturing adolescent male who is in a stressful relationship with peers

   ANS: A   DIF: Moderate   REF: 537   OBJ: 16.1

124. Who provides the best example of ruminative coping?
    a. Pam, who just cannot stop thinking about how depressed she feels
    b. Jim, who has become addicted to the antidepressants he is taking
    c. Angela, who is relying heavily on the advice of coworkers as she works through her anger issues
    d. Dwight, who refuses to acknowledge the fact that he has ADHD

    ANS: A   DIF: Difficult   REF: 537   OBJ: 16.11

125. Unproductively dwelling on one's problems is referred to as
    a. role reversal.   c. ruminative coping.
    b. echolalia.   d. comorbidity.

    ANS: C   DIF: Easy   REF: 537   OBJ: 16.11

126. In the United States, suicide is the _____ leading cause of death in adolescence.
    a. first   c. third
    b. second   d. fourth

    ANS: C   DIF: Moderate   REF: 537   OBJ: 16.11

127. According to statistics, who is most likely to commit suicide?
    a. George, an 18-year-old black male   c. Andrew, a 45-year-old white male
    b. Washington, an 80-year-old white   d. Jackson, a 25-year-old black male
       male

    ANS: B   DIF: Moderate   REF: 537-538   OBJ: 16.11

128. Which of the following is true with regard to adolescent suicide?
    a. More males than females attempt and are successful at committing suicide.
    b. More females than males attempt and are successful at committing suicide.
    c. More males attempt suicide, but more females are successful at committing suicide.
    d. More females attempt suicide, but more males are successful at committing suicide.

    ANS: D   DIF: Moderate   REF: 537-538   OBJ: 16.11

129. Which is not one of the four key risk factors in teenage suicide?
    a. Family pathology   c. Stressful life events
    b. Access to firearms   d. Late maturation

    ANS: D   DIF: Moderate   REF: 538   OBJ: 16.11

130. According to statistics, what characteristic puts a teenage at the greatest risk for committing suicide?
    a. A homosexual orientation   c. Being a victim of physical abuse
    b. A history of behavioral problems d. Living in poverty

    ANS: B   DIF: Moderate   REF: 538   OBJ: 16.11

131. Which type of disorder is most likely to increase between young adulthood and old age?
    a. Antisocial personality
    b. Major depression
    c. Cognitive impairments
    d. Schizophrenia

    ANS: C   DIF: Moderate   REF: 539   OBJ: 16.12
    KEY: WWW

132. Why is depression difficult to diagnose in older adults?
    a. Many of the diagnostic symptoms are similar to normal losses associated with aging.
    b. Normal cognitive loss associated with aging makes it hard for older people to answer questions about their mental state.
    c. There are no diagnostic criteria for diagnosing depression in the elderly.
    d. As nearly all older depressed individuals commit suicide, there are few depressed individuals left to diagnose.

    ANS: A   DIF: Moderate   REF: 540   OBJ: 16.12

133. Who is most likely to be diagnosed with depression?
    a. Mork, a 25-year-old male
    b. Mindy, a 30-year-old female
    c. Robin, a 75-year-old male
    d. Pam, a 90-year-old female

    ANS: B   DIF: Difficult   REF: 539-540   OBJ: 16.12

134. Which statement concerning psychopathology in adulthood is true?
    a. Treatments for depression in adulthood are highly ineffective.
    b. The elderly are highly likely to be overdiagnosed with depression.
    c. Depression symptoms in older adulthood are so different from young adulthood that different DSM criteria are used in its detection.
    d. A major challenge in treating older individuals with depression is getting them to seek treatment.

    ANS: D   DIF: Moderate   REF: 540   OBJ: 16.12

135. Dementia is the technical term for
    a. insanity.
    b. senility.
    c. incontinence.
    d. seniority.

    ANS: B   DIF: Easy   REF: 540   OBJ: 16.13

136. Dementia is best defined as
    a. a sudden loss of memory and intelligence.
    b. an inevitable, normal change in the brain with age.
    c. a progressive loss of neural functioning.
    d. a one-time period of significant disorientation.

    ANS: C   DIF: Moderate   REF: 540   OBJ: 16.13

137. What is the most common form of dementia?
    a. Down syndrome
    b. Parkinson's disease
    c. Alzheimer's disease
    d. Vascular dementia

    ANS: C   DIF: Easy   REF: 541   OBJ: 16.13

798

138. Dr. Quincy is about to conduct an autopsy on an individual he suspects has died due to complications of Alzheimer's disease. Which findings would verify his suspicion?
   a. Neurofibrillary tangles
   b. Occipital lobe degeneration
   c. A severely damaged brain stem
   d. An excessively large corpus callosum

   ANS: A   DIF: Moderate   REF: 541   OBJ: 16.13

139. What brain change is best associated with Alzheimer's disease?
   a. Senile plaque
   b. Excessive quantities of the metal mercury
   c. Neurofibrillary bundles surrounding alpha-amyloid
   d. Excessive levels of the neurotransmitter dopamine

   ANS: A   DIF: Moderate   REF: 541   OBJ: 16.13
   KEY: WWW

140. Beta-amyloids are found
   a. in large quantity in individuals with vascular dementia.
   b. only in clinically depressed individuals.
   c. at the core of senile plaques.
   d. to contribute significantly to the development of anorexia nervosa.

   ANS: C   DIF: Moderate   REF: 541   OBJ: 16.13

141. Alzheimer's disease is best described as
   a. progressive and curable.
   b. progressive and incurable.
   c. nonprogressive and curable.
   d. nonprogressive and incurable.

   ANS: B   DIF: Easy   REF: 541   OBJ: 16.13

142. The first sign of Alzheimer's disease is typically
   a. trouble remembering recently learned verbal material.
   b. a loss of language skills.
   c. personality changes.
   d. difficulty on recognition tasks.

   ANS: A   DIF: Moderate   REF: 541   OBJ: 16.13

143. A gene segment on the _____ chromosome has been implicated as a likely cause of late-onset Alzheimer's disease.
   a. 9th
   b. 14th
   c. 19th
   d. 24th

   ANS: C   DIF: Moderate   REF: 542   OBJ: 16.13

144. How does the ApoE4 gene appear to contribute to the development of Alzheimer's disease?
   a. Through an increased buildup of beta-amyloid
   b. By decreasing blood flow to the prefrontal lobe
   c. Through the creation of new synapses within the brain
   d. By making the brain more susceptible to damage from a blow to the head

   ANS: A   DIF: Moderate   REF: 542   OBJ: 16.13

145. How many of the following (head injuries in adulthood, low blood pressure, exposure to lead) increase the risk of Alzheimer's disease?
   a. 0
   b. 1
   c. 2
   d. 3

   ANS: B   DIF: Moderate   REF: 542   OBJ: 16.13

146. The extra "brain power" that individuals can sometimes rely on when disease begins to take a toll on their brain functioning is referred to as
   a. cognitive reserve.
   b. mirroring neurons.
   c. ruminative coping.
   d. reversed roles.

   ANS: A   DIF: Easy   REF: 542   OBJ: 16.13

147. What young adult behavior would have the least positive impact on one's cognitive reserve in adulthood?
   a. Being a marathon runner
   b. Obtaining a PhD
   c. Being very active in social organizations
   d. Cutting back on using one's mental skills to solve nonessential problems

   ANS: D   DIF: Easy   REF: 543   OBJ: 16.13

148. Drugs like Aricept and Namenda that are currently used to treat Alzheimer's disease tend to
   a. have little measureable impact on behavioral or cognitive abilities.
   b. positively impact cognitive functioning and reduce behavioral problems but do not slow the progression of the disease.
   c. positively impact behavioral problems but have little impact on cognitive functioning.
   d. positively impact cognitive functioning, reduce behavioral problems and   slow the progression of the disease.

   ANS: D   DIF: Moderate   REF: 543   OBJ: 16.13

149. Current treatments being investigated for Alzheimer's disease include
   a. antioxidants like vitamin E and C.
   b. injections of Leva-dopa to replace levels of dopamine in the brain.
   c. use of stimulants like methylphenidate.
   d. drugs to enhance the production of beta-amyloids.

   ANS: A   DIF: Moderate   REF: 543   OBJ: 16.13

150. What is the second most common type of dementia?
   a. Down syndrome
   b. Parkinson's disease
   c. Alzheimer's disease
   d. vascular dementia

   ANS: D   DIF: Moderate   REF: 543   OBJ: 16.14

151. It appears as if the same lifestyle factors that contribute to the development of _____ also increase the risk for vascular dementia.
    a. Asperger syndrome
    b. cerebrovascualr disease
    c. respiratory failure
    d. ADHD

    ANS: B   DIF: Moderate   REF: 543   OBJ: 16.14
    KEY: WWW

152. Vascular dementia
    a. is a slowly progressive deterioration of memory and thinking skills.
    b. results from a series of small strokes, each adding rather quickly to the observed deterioration.
    c. has a very powerful genetic basis.
    d. results from taking medications or having a poor diet and can be reversed when these problems are corrected.

    ANS: B   DIF: Moderate   REF: 543   OBJ: 16.14

153. A key difference between Alzheimer's disease and vascular dementia is that vascular dementia is more strongly
    a. influenced by genetic factors.
    b. influenced by lifestyle choices.
    c. associated with dementia.
    d. associated with delirium.

    ANS: B   DIF: Difficult   REF: 543   OBJ: 16.14

154. Delirium is best defined as
    a. another term for dementia.
    b. incurable.
    c. a reversible state of confusion and disorientation.
    d. a normal part of the aging process.

    ANS: C   DIF: Moderate   REF: 543   OBJ: 16.14

155. Which of the following is the most easily reversible condition?
    a. Dementia
    b. Alzheimer's disease
    c. Delirium
    d. Vascular dementia

    ANS: C   DIF: Easy   REF: 543   OBJ: 16.14
    KEY: WWW

156. Due to their mental slowness, elderly adults who are _____ are frequently misdiagnosed with delirium.
    a. depressed
    b. mentally retarded
    c. autistic
    d. ADHD

    ANS: A   DIF: Moderate   REF: 543   OBJ: 16.14

157. It is _____ to distinguish among irreversible dementias, reversible dementias, and delirium.
    a. unimportant
    b. impossible
    c. easy
    d. critical

    ANS: D   DIF: Easy   REF: 543   OBJ: 16.14

158. The diagnosis for Alzheimer's disease should be made
    a. at the first sign of memory loss.
    b. when an individual first begins to experience hallucinations and delusions.
    c. only after their blood test shows elevated levels of dopamine.
    d. only after all other causes are ruled out.

    ANS: D   DIF: Moderate   REF: 543   OBJ: 16.14

TRUE/FALSE

1. Statistical deviance from the norm, maladaptive, and personal distress are three critical elements for determining if a behavior is abnormal.

    ANS: T   DIF: Easy   REF: 528   OBJ: 16.1

2. Attempted suicide is a DSM-IV criteria for major depressive disorder.

    ANS: F   DIF: Moderate   REF: 528-529   OBJ: 16.12
    KEY: WWW

3. According to the diathesis-stress model, psychopathology is due solely to genetic factors.

    ANS: F   DIF: Moderate   REF: 521   OBJ: 16.3

4. In general, autistic children are very intelligent but they simply cannot interact socially in a normal fashion.

    ANS: F   DIF: Moderate   REF: 522-524   OBJ: 16.4

5. There is clear evidence that MMR vaccinations cause autism.

    ANS: F   DIF: Moderate   REF: 523-524   OBJ: 16.4

6. Asperger syndrome is a type of autism spectrum disorder.

    ANS: T   DIF: Moderate   REF: 523   OBJ: 16.4
    KEY: WWW

7. The executive function theory suggests that autism occurs as the result of a hyperactive prefrontal lobe.

    ANS: F   DIF: Moderate   REF: 525   OBJ: 16.4

8. Babies can and do experience depression-like states and symptoms.

    ANS: T   DIF: Moderate   REF: 527   OBJ: 16.5

9. Hitting is a good example of an internalizing problem.

    ANS: F   DIF: Moderate   REF: 528   OBJ: 16.6

10. Experiencing Hurricane Katrina increased the incidence of symptoms of posttraumatic stress disorder in New Orleans' children.

    ANS: T   DIF: Difficult   REF: 530   OBJ: 16.6

11. Children as young as two or three years are capable of attempting suicide.

    ANS: T   DIF: Moderate .   REF: 531   OBJ: 16.7

12. Comorbidity is characterized by having a single, extremely damaging form of mental illness.

    ANS: F   DIF: Moderate   REF: 531   OBJ: 16.7
    KEY: WWW

13. Although drugs like Prozac can improve symptoms of depression, cognitive-behavioral therapies have been found to be of little to no success.

    ANS: F   DIF: Moderate   REF: 531-532   OBJ: 16.6

14. A defining feature of anorexia nervosa is a binge-purge syndrome pattern.

    ANS: F   DIF: Moderate   REF: 533   OBJ: 16.9
    KEY: WWW

15. The cascade model of substance abuse suggests that one factor (e.g., exposure to harsh parenting) can influence the next (e.g., the development of aggressive behavioral problems).

    ANS: T   DIF: Moderate   REF: 536   OBJ: 16.10

16. Females are more likely to commit suicide than males.

    ANS: F   DIF: Moderate   REF: 538   OBJ: 16.11

17. Adult females are more likely to be diagnosed with depression than adult males.

    ANS: T   DIF: Moderate   REF: 539-540   OBJ: 16.12

18. Becoming senile is a normal part of the aging process.

    ANS: F   DIF: Moderate   REF: 540   OBJ: 16.13

19. The brain of an individual with Alzheimer's disease will show excessive amounts of beta-amyloids and neurofibrillary tangles.

    ANS: T   DIF: Moderate   REF: 541   OBJ: 16.13

20. Delirium is an often reversible condition involving a disturbance of consciousness.

    ANS: T   DIF: Moderate   REF: 543   OBJ: 16.14
    KEY: WWW

COMPLETION

1. The current American Psychiatric Association text used to diagnose psychological disorders is known by the abbreviation _____.

   ANS: DSM-IV

   DIF: Moderate   REF: 518   OBJ: 16.1

2. Fatigue, insomnia, sluggishness, feelings of extreme guilt, and recurrent death thoughts are all diagnostic criteria for major _____ disorder.

   ANS: depressive

   DIF: Easy   REF: 518   OBJ: 16.1

3. Bodily symptoms like loss of appetite and disruption of normal sleep patterns are also referred to as _____ symptoms.

   ANS: somatic

   DIF: Moderate   REF: 519   OBJ: 16.1

4. Expectations on how one is to act in a particular cultural context are called _____ norms.

   ANS: social

   DIF: Moderate   REF: 520   OBJ: 16.2

5. The _____-stress model views the cause of psychological disorders in terms of an interaction between genetic and environmental factors.

   ANS: diathesis

   DIF: Difficult   REF: 521   OBJ: 16.3

6. Deviant social development, deviant language and communicative skills, and repetitive, stereotyped behavior were Kanner's diagnostic criteria for _____.

   ANS: autism

   DIF: Moderate   REF: 522-523   OBJ: 16.4   KEY: WWW

7. _____ syndrome is a type of autism spectrum disorder in which a child has normal intelligence and good verbal skills, but lacks social skills.

   ANS: Asperger

   DIF: Moderate   REF: 523   OBJ: 16.4

8. During the first six months after being born, Kyle was in an abusive environment and as a result of this experience, he failed to gain any weight during that time. This potentially life-threatening condition is referred to as failure to _____.

ANS: thrive

DIF: Moderate   REF: 528   OBJ: 16.5

9. _____ problems are also called undercontrolled disorders and involve acting out.

ANS: Externalizing

DIF: Moderate   REF: 528   OBJ: 16.6

10. Overcontrolled disorders involving inner distress are referred to as _____ problems.

ANS: internalizing

DIF: Moderate   REF: 528   OBJ: 16.6   KEY: WWW

11. The simultaneous existence of two or more mental health conditions in the same person is called _____.

ANS: comorbidity

DIF: Moderate   REF: 531   OBJ: 16.7   KEY: WWW

12. Selective reuptake inhibitors like Prozac are most likely to be used to treat people diagnosed with _____.

ANS: depression

DIF: Difficult   REF: 532   OBJ: 16.7

13. G. Stanley Hall famously referred to adolescence as a time of _____ and stress.

ANS: storm

DIF: Moderate   REF: 533   OBJ: 16.8

14. _____ nervosa literally means "nervous loss of appetite."

ANS: Anorexia

DIF: Easy   REF: 533   OBJ: 16.9

15. _____ nervosa is an eating disorder also known as "binge-purge syndrome."

ANS: Bulimia

DIF: Easy   REF: 533   OBJ: 16.9   KEY: WWW

16. _____ coping involves unproductive dwelling on a problem that often makes the problem worse.

ANS: Ruminative

DIF: Difficult REF: 537 OBJ: 16.11

17. _____ is the technical term for senility.

ANS: Dementia

DIF: Moderate REF: 540 OBJ: 16.13

18. _____ disease is characterized by a buildup of beta-amyloids and neurofibrillary tangles.

ANS: Alzheimer's

DIF: Easy REF: 541 OBJ: 16.13 KEY: WWW

19. _____ dementia is characterized by a series of strokes and is also known as multi-infarct dementia.

ANS: Vascular

DIF: Moderate REF: 543 OBJ: 16.14

20. _____ refers to a reversible disturbance of consciousness characterized by wandering attention, confusion, and hallucinations.

ANS: Delirium

DIF: Moderate REF: 543 OBJ: 16.14

ESSAY

1. How does the diathesis-stress model account for psychopathology?

ANS: Answer not provided REF: 521-522 OBJ: 16.3

2. Your neighbor has just learned that her little boy has autism. Describe the symptoms, cause, and treatment of this disorder.

ANS: Answer not provided REF: 522-527 OBJ: 16.4

3. Why is the conceptualization of adolescence as a time of storm and stress inaccurate?

ANS: Answer not provided REF: 533 OBJ: 16.8

4. How does the cascade model of substance abuse envision the development of drug problems? What are the implications of adopting this approach to intervening with an individual with a developing drug problem?

   ANS: Answer not provided   REF: 536   OBJ: 16.10

5. How does the expression of depression vary across the lifespan? How does age influence the treatment of depression?

   ANS: Answer not provided   REF: 527-528 & 531-532 & 537
   OBJ: 16.5 & 16.7 & 16.11

6. What is the relationship between depression and suicide rate? How are age and sex related to the rate of suicide attempt and success?

   ANS: Answer not provided   REF: 537-538   OBJ: 16.11

7. Differentiate between dementia and delirium? Why is the distinction so important?

   ANS: Answer not provided   REF: 540-543   OBJ: 16.13 & 16.4

8. What is the criterion for psychological abnormality? How is the DSM-IV used in this process, and how might the next edition of the text (DSM-V) be altered to reflect new thinking in the field?

   ANS: Answer not provided   REF: 518-519   OBJ: 16.1   KEY: WWW

9. How are internalizing problems different from externalizing problems? Provide specific examples.

   ANS: Answer not provided   REF: 528-529   OBJ: 16.6   KEY: WWW

10. Compare and contrast anorexia nervosa and bulimia nervosa. Be sure to discuss symptoms, causes, and treatment.

    ANS: Answer not provided   REF: 533-535   OBJ: 16.9   KEY: WWW

MULTIPLE CHOICE

1. It is most accurate to say that biological death
    a. is a single event with a clear-cut end point.
    b. occurs when a person stops breathing.
    c. is a process consisting of multiple events and the line between life and death is blurry.
    d. officially occurs when the heart stops beating.

    ANS: C   DIF: Moderate   REF: 548   OBJ: 17.1

2. A Harvard group definition of biological death includes the criteria of
    a. failure to move for 1 hour and failure to breathe for 3 minutes after removal from ventilator.
    b. only eye response is reflexive eye blink.
    c. heart-beat rate of 0 per minute for 10 consecutive minutes.
    d. lack of electrical activity throughout entire brain and spinal cord.

    ANS: A   DIF: Moderate   REF: 548   OBJ: 17.1

3. Total brain death includes all of the following components except
    a. the person is totally unresponsive to stimuli (including a lack of pain).
    b. there is a lack of reflexes.
    c. there is a failure to breathe for 36 hours.
    d. there is no electrical activity in the cortex of the brain.

    ANS: C   DIF: Moderate   REF: 548   OBJ: 17.1
    KEY: WWW

4. Total brain death involves
    a. irreversible loss in only the higher centers of the cerebral cortex.
    b. reversible loss in only the lower centers of the brain.
    c. irreversible loss in both the higher and lower centers of the brain.
    d. reversible loss in both the higher and lower centers of the brain.

    ANS: C   DIF: Easy   REF: 548   OBJ: 17.1

5. Comas are most likely to be reversible when the coma is due to
    a. massive external head trauma.   c. heart failure.
    b. an abnormally low body temperature.   d. HIV/AIDS.

    ANS: B   DIF: Difficult   REF: 548   OBJ: 17.1

6. Despite being in an irreversible coma, Karen Ann Quinlan was not considered to be totally brain dead because
   a. it was likely that she would regain consciousness at some time in the future.
   b. she continued to show significant activity in her cerebral cortex.
   c. her condition was due to an environmental accident (drug use) not a natural biological process (e.g., cancer).
   d. she continued to breathe even after being taken off of a respirator.

   ANS: D   DIF: Moderate   REF: 548   OBJ: 17.1

7. What did Karen Ann Quinlan and Terri Schaivo have in common?
   a. Their situations demonstrated that there is only one legitimate definition of death.
   b. They both demonstrated that once machines used to keep an individual alive are terminated, death is swift.
   c. Their situations were the bases for two of the most famous right-to-life cases in the past few decades.
   d. They both regained consciousness and lived normal lives after having been in comas for over 10 years.

   ANS: C   DIF: Moderate   REF: 548-549   OBJ: 17.1

8. Owens and colleagues (2006) conducted research on a young woman who had been in a vegetative state for 5 months. When she was asked to imagine visiting rooms of her house, she
   a. awakened from the vegetative state.
   b. remained in the state, but spoke aloud stating which rooms she was visiting.
   c. had a brain that responded in the same manner as a healthy brain would respond.
   d. showed no measurable neurological reaction to the stimulation.

   ANS: C   DIF: Moderate   REF: 549   OBJ: 17.1

9. Euthanasia is best defined as "_____" death.
   a. quick   c. painless
   b. good   d. natural

   ANS: B   DIF: Moderate   REF: 549   OBJ: 17.1

10. Active euthanasia is also called
    a. mercy killing.   c. physician-assisted suicide.
    b. assisted suicide.   d. passive euthanasia.

    ANS: A   DIF: Moderate   REF: 549   OBJ: 17.1

11. Who is engaging in active euthanasia?
    a. Adam, who is withholding pain-killing drugs
    b. Sandler, who is removing a feed-tube from a patient who cannot feed him/herself
    c. Will, who is injecting a terminally ill patient with a lethal dose of drugs
    d. Farrell, who is removing a respirator from a patient who is totally brain dead

    ANS: C   DIF: Easy   REF: 549   OBJ: 17.1

12. How many of the following (active euthanasia, passive euthanasia, physician-assisted suicide) result in a terminally ill individual dying of natural causes?
    a. 0
    b. 1
    c. 2
    d. 3

    ANS: B   DIF: Moderate   REF: 549   OBJ: 17.1

13. Which of the following is an example of passive euthanasia?
    a. Giving a terminally ill patient a lethal dose of drugs
    b. Permitting a terminally ill patient to give him/herself a lethal dose of drugs
    c. Removing a patient who is brain dead and in an irreversible coma from a respirator
    d. Smothering a terminally ill patient to death at his request

    ANS: C   DIF: Easy   REF: 549   OBJ: 17.1

14. Deanna is dying of cancer and her feeding tube was just removed by a nurse. If the goal of this action would be to have her eventually die, it is best considered
    a. passive euthanasia.
    b. active euthanasia.
    c. physician-assisted suicide.
    d. self-inflicted suicide.

    ANS: A   DIF: Difficult   REF: 549   OBJ: 17.1

15. Which of the following is an example of assisted suicide?
    a. Instructing a terminally ill patient on what household chemicals to mix together to create a deadly gas
    b. Injecting someone with a lethal dose of a drug that he or she is already taking
    c. Withholding medical treatment for a chronic disorder
    d. Removing someone from a respirator when brain activity is nonexistent

    ANS: A   DIF: Difficult   REF: 549   OBJ: 17.1

16. Some doctors will prescribe painkillers or sleeping pills for terminally ill patients, knowing that the patient may very well deliberately take a lethal overdose. This is an example of
    a. active euthanasia.
    b. passive euthanasia.
    c. fratricide.
    d. assisted suicide.

    ANS: D   DIF: Difficult   REF: 549   OBJ: 17.1
    KEY: WWW

17. In the United States, there is overwhelming support among members of the general public for
    a. passive euthanasia.
    b. assisted suicide.
    c. active euthanasia.
    d. no overwhelming support exists for any of these above mentioned concepts.

    ANS: A   DIF: Moderate   REF: 549   OBJ: 17.1

18. Vaughn says, "I believe that everyone has the right to tell other people what they want done in the case they get hurt badly. For example, if I am ever in an accident and go into a coma, I do not want anyone hooking me up to any machines to keep me alive. That's why I have a piece of paper that says that they cannot do that to me!" This statement indicates that Vaughn is a strong proponent of
   a. assisted suicide.
   b. physician-assisted suicide.
   c. active euthanasia.
   d. living wills.

   ANS: D   DIF: Moderate   REF: 549-550   OBJ: 17.1

19. The main purpose of a living will is to
   a. make provisions for the division of property among loved ones after one's own death.
   b. specify how much medical care you wish to receive if you become terminally ill.
   c. appoint guardians to care for all living minor offspring upon one's death.
   d. make active euthanasia legal for one's self.

   ANS: B   DIF: Moderate   REF: 549-550   OBJ: 17.1
   KEY: WWW

20. _____ was the first state to legalize physician-assisted suicide.
   a. California
   b. Massachusetts
   c. Oregon
   d. Florida

   ANS: C   DIF: Moderate   REF: 550   OBJ: 17.1

21. As a right-to-life advocate, Ophelia is most likely to state that,
   a. "Everyone has the right to decide they should die."
   b. "Cutting short a life under any circumstance, even if it is requested, is murder."
   c. "People against active euthanasia are idiots."
   d. "I plan to do everything I can to legalize physician-assisted suicide."

   ANS: B   DIF: Difficult   REF: 550   OBJ: 17.1

22. Compared to modern people in the United States, Europeans in the Middle Ages were more likely to
   a. fear death.
   b. go off and die alone.
   c. care for their dying relatives at home.
   d. die in a medical setting.

   ANS: C   DIF: Moderate   REF: 550   OBJ: 17.1

23. Olga is a right-to-die activist. As such, she is most likely to agree with the statement,
   a. death needs to be seen as a medical failure.
   b. the hospice movement is a move in the wrong direction.
   c. death needs to be experienced and shared within the family.
   d. it is the quantity of life that matters, not the quality of life.

   ANS: C   DIF: Difficult   REF: 550   OBJ: 17.1

24. Cross-cultural research on death-hastening practices in the frail elderly has shown that practices include all of the following except
    a. depriving them of food..
    b. stabbing upon request.
    c. driving them from their home.
    d. injecting them with poison made from local plants.

    ANS: D   DIF: Difficult   REF: 551   OBJ: 17.1

25. In which culture would you expect the loudest celebration following someone's death?
    a. Irish   c. Japanese
    b. Jewish   d. Puerto Rican

    ANS: A   DIF: Easy   REF: 551   OBJ: 17.1

26. _____ families often engage in shivah in which the dead are mourned immediately, at 1-month, and at 1-year.
    a. Irish   c. Japanese
    b. Jewish   d. Puerto Rican

    ANS: A   DIF: Moderate   REF: 551   OBJ: 17.1

27. Which is the best definition of average life expectancy to birth?
    a. The average number of years the average newborn in a population will live.
    b. The maximum number of years the average newborn in a population will live.
    c. The average number of years a member of an entire species can live.
    d. The maximum number of years a member of an entire species can live.

    ANS: A   DIF: Moderate   REF: 551   OBJ: 17.2

28. In the United States, the average life expectancy to birth is currently about _____ years.
    a. 72   c. 84
    b. 78   d. 90

    ANS: B   DIF: Difficult   REF: 551   OBJ: 17.2

29. Which is true with regard to life expectancies in the United States today?
    a. Life expectancy for all people, regardless of race and gender, is very similar.
    b. Males are generally expected to outlive females, by about five years.
    c. Hormonal difference may account for sex differences in life expectancy.
    d. Life expectancy is based on biological factors and does not vary by socioeconomic level (e.g., poverty versus wealth).

    ANS: C   DIF: Moderate   REF: 551   OBJ: 17.2

30. Based on statistics, which United States resident would you expect to have the longest lifespan?
    a. Lenny, an African-American male   c. Larry, a European-American male
    b. Lacy, an African-American female   d. Lucy, a European-American female

    ANS: D   DIF: Moderate   REF: 552   OBJ: 17.2

31. Based on statistics, which United States resident would you expect to have the shortest lifespan?
   a. Tyler, an African-American male   c. Taylor, an European-American male
   b. Tonya, an African-American female   d. Teri, an European-American female

   ANS: A   DIF: Moderate   REF: 552   OBJ: 17.2
   KEY: WWW

32. Statistically, an individual born in _____ would have the shortest life expectancy.
   a. Sweden   c. China
   b. Japan   d. Zambia

   ANS: D   DIF: Easy   REF: 552   OBJ: 17.2

33. In the United States, an eight-year-old child would be most likely to die
   a. from a terminal illness.   c. as the result of a car accident.
   b. from some congenital abnormalities.   d. from child abuse.

   ANS: C   DIF: Moderate   REF: 552   OBJ: 17.2

34. You see an obituary in the local newspaper for a 15-year-old. If you live in the United States, what would be the more likely cause of the individual's death?
   a. Heart disease   c. Homicide
   b. Cardiovascular   d. Cancer

   ANS: C   DIF: Easy   REF: 552   OBJ: 17.2
   KEY: WWW

35. Jen's 70-year-old Uncle Ben who lives in the United States just died. As a knowledgeable individual, Jen would realize statistically, the most likely cause of his death was
   a. heart disease.   c. cancer .
   b. suicide.   d. cerebrovascular disease.

   ANS: A   DIF: Difficult   REF: 552   OBJ: 17.2

36. According to the programmed theories, aging and death are
   a. more psychological events than physical events.
   b. too complicated to study.
   c. under genetic control.
   d. the result of a gradual buildup of damage to cells and organs.

   ANS: C   DIF: Moderate   REF: 553   OBJ: 17.3

37. The _____ theory of aging emphasizes the haphazard processes causing errors in cells to accumulate and organ systems to deteriorate.
   a. programmed theories   c. telomeres theory
   b. damage theories   d. the Hayflick Limit theory

   ANS: B   DIF: Moderate   REF: 554   OBJ: 17.3

814

38. Concerning theories of aging, programmed is to damage as
    a. systematic is to haphazard.
    c. average life span is to maximum lifespan.
    b. environmental is to genetic.
    d. active is to passive.

    ANS: A   DIF: Difficult   REF: 553-554   OBJ: 17.3

39. Maximum life span is best defined as the _____ number of years that a member of a species lives.
    a. median
    c. minimum
    b. average
    d. ceiling

    ANS: D   DIF: Moderate   REF: 553   OBJ: 17.3

40. The maximum lifespan of a human is closest to _____ years.
    a. 102
    c. 122
    b. 112
    d. 132

    ANS: C   DIF: Moderate   REF: 553   OBJ: 17.3
    KEY: WWW

41. For humans, which number is closest to 120?
    a. Number of years in maximum lifespan
    b. Number of cells in the body that contain telomeres
    c. Number of years in median life expectancy
    d. Number of times a cell can divide

    ANS: A   DIF: Moderate   REF: 553   OBJ: 17.3

42. The fact that the maximum lifespan of a mouse is around 3½ years, while the maximum lifespan for a dog and a Galapagos tortoise are about 20 years and 150 years, respectively, indicates that
    a. species-wide genes likely play a role in longevity.
    b. size is unrelated to longevity.
    c. longevity is highly related to intelligence.
    d. the slower you go the longer you live.

    ANS: A   DIF: Moderate   REF: 553   OBJ: 17.3

43. During the past few centuries,
    a. both average life expectancy and maximum lifespan have increased dramatically.
    b. average life expectancy has increased dramatically, while maximum lifespan has increased only a little.
    c. maximum lifespan has increased dramatically, while average life expectancy has increased only a little.
    d. both average life expectancy and maximum lifespan have decreased dramatically.

    ANS: B   DIF: Difficult   REF: 553   OBJ: 17.3

815

44. Your child has just been diagnosed with progeria. What outcome should you expect?
    a. Death due to a lack of blood clotting within a year
    b. A normal life except for the inability to reproduce
    c. Death by the teen years as the result of premature aging
    d. A normal life except for severe to moderate communication and linguistic deficiencies

    ANS: C   DIF: Moderate   REF: 553   OBJ: 17.3

45. Progeria is best associated with
    a. extended lifespan.   c. severe mental retardation.
    b. accelerated aging.   d. irreversible comas.

    ANS: B   DIF: Easy   REF: 553   OBJ: 17.3
    KEY: WWW

46. Despite being only 12 years old, Chris shows many signs of advanced aging. His skin is wrinkled, his face looks like that of an old man, and he is suffering from heart failure. Given these characteristics, it is most likely that Chris is suffering from
    a. sickle-cell disease.   c. progeria.
    b. Klinefelter syndrome.   d. Turner syndrome.

    ANS: C   DIF: Moderate   REF: 553   OBJ: 17.3

47. The Hayflick limit refers to
    a. how much infection the immune system can handle.
    b. a person's average life expectancy.
    c. the number of times a cell can divide/double itself.
    d. the amount of time the hypothalamus can function before it malfunctions.

    ANS: C   DIF: Moderate   REF: 554   OBJ: 17.3

48. The average human cell appears to have the capacity to divide about
    a. 5 times, plus or minus 2.   c. 1,000 times, plus or minus 50.
    b. 50 times, plus or minus 10.   d. 5,000,000 times, plus or minus 10,000.

    ANS: B   DIF: Moderate   REF: 554   OBJ: 17.3

49. When describing aging, Dr. Dog says, "It is almost as if we are all born with a biological death clock that starts cells dividing at conception and later stops the cells so we die." Dr. Dog's comments fit best with
    a. the Hayflick limit.
    b. free radical theory.
    c. the damage theory of aging.
    d. the concept of average life expectancy at birth.

    ANS: A   DIF: Moderate   REF: 554   OBJ: 17.3

816

50. \The Hayflick limit is most related to the
    a. onset of progeria.
    b. creation of free radicals.
    c. average life expectancy at birth for an individual.
    d. maximum life span per species.

    ANS: D   DIF: Difficult   REF: 554   OBJ: 17.3

51. The stretch of DNA that forms the tip of a chromosome is called the
    a. telomere.   c. nucleus.
    b. free radical.   d. autosome.

    ANS: A   DIF: Easy   REF: 554   OBJ: 17.3

52. Research on cellular contributions to aging suggests that
    a. cells may be limited in how often they can divide because telomeres do not appear
       to replicate.
    b. cells cannot make connections with other cells after the developmental period, and
       the lack of communication among cells leads to death.
    c. cells can only divide once; after this, they slowly degenerate over the years.
    d. there are no limits on cell life; without environmental wear and tear, we could live
       indefinitely.

    ANS: A   DIF: Moderate   REF: 554   OBJ: 17.3

53. How are telomeres related to the Hayflick limit?
    a. A child born with more than two telomeres will double his or her limit.
    b. The fact that telomeres do not replicate appears to create the limit.
    c. Telomeres create the free radicals that work against the Hayflick limit.
    d. Telomeres have no direct relationship to the Hayflick limit.

    ANS: B   DIF: Moderate   REF: 554   OBJ: 17.3

54. The notion of the hypothalamus serving as an "aging clock" for the body best fits with the
    _____ theory of aging.
    a. programmed   c. antioxidant
    b. free radical   d. damage

    ANS: A   DIF: Moderate   REF: 554   OBJ: 17.3

55. _____ theories of aging argue that in early development cells replicate faithfully, but in later
    life, this fidelity is lost and cells become increasingly likely to undergo problematic
    replication.
    a. Programmed   c. Progeria
    b. Telomere   d. Damage

    ANS: D   DIF: Moderate   REF: 554   OBJ: 17.3

56. Damage theories of aging suggest that
    a. aging is the result of cells that are biologically programmed to divide a limited number of times.
    b. death results from an accumulation of defects in cells and organs over time.
    c. hormone levels in the brain are systematically altered in old age, and this results in aging and death.
    d. autoimmune reactions damage normal body cells, leading to aging and death.

    ANS: B   DIF: Moderate   REF: 554   OBJ: 17.3
    KEY: WWW

57. Free radical theory is best categorized as a _____ theory of aging.
    a. programmed   c. mutation
    b. hormonal   d. damage

    ANS: D   DIF: Moderate   REF: 554   OBJ: 17.3

58. One toxic byproduct of normal metabolic processing within a cell is called a(n)
    a. hormone.   c. antioxidant.
    b. free radical.   d. telomere.

    ANS: B   DIF: Difficult   REF: 554   OBJ: 17.3

59. How do "free radicals" damage the body and result in aging?
    a. They have a "free electron" that is chemically unstable and can damage a cell's DNA.
    b. They tend to create elevated levels of testosterone within the body, and this damages the reproductive system.
    c. They generate large numbers of telomeres that attack and destroy brain cells.
    d. They produce excess levels of the neurotransmitter GABA that is associated with age-related disorders like Alzheimer's disease.

    ANS: A   DIF: Moderate   REF: 554   OBJ: 17.3

60. Free radicals are byproducts of
    a. the metabolism of oxygen.   c. the suppression of Hayflick's limit.
    b. a diet high in vitamin E.   d. telomere division.

    ANS: A   DIF: Moderate   REF: 554   OBJ: 17.3
    KEY: WWW

61. Sixty-year-old Njia says, "I'll prove to you that free radicals can impact the body. Just look at this!" If Njia knows what she is talking about, she will most likely show you
    a. a report on high levels of vitamin E in her blood stream.
    b. a medical chart indicating excessive levels of oxygen in her lungs.
    c. a darkened "age spot" on her arm.
    d. a doctor's report indicating the level o the neurotransmitter GABA is extremely high within her brain.

    ANS: C   DIF: Moderate   REF: 554   OBJ: 17.3

818

62. How many of the following (the Hayflick limit, systematic changes in the immune system, normal changes in the activity of certain genes as we age) are linked to the damage theory approach to aging?
   a. 0
   b. 1
   c. 2
   d. 3

   ANS: A   DIF: Difficult   REF: 554   OBJ: 17.3

63. Which is the best summary concerning theories of aging?
   a. Damage theories are vastly superior
   b. Programmed theories are vastly superior
   c. A combination of damage and programmed theories is the best explanation
   d. A rejection of both damage and programmed theories is the best explanation

   ANS: C   DIF: Easy   REF: 554-555   OBJ: 17.3

64. The sentences, "Toxic waste products accumulate because genes shut off. Genes shut off because toxic waste products build up," were used to make the point that aging is
   a. best explained by biological factors.
   b. best explained by environmental factors.
   c. best explained by a combination of biological and environmental factors.
   d. unexplainable.

   ANS: C   DIF: Moderate   REF: 555   OBJ: 17.3

65. The most likely change in aging that will take place in the near future is a significant
   a. increase in maximum lifespan.
   b. increase in average age of death.
   c. decrease in average age of death.
   d. decrease in maximum lifespan.

   ANS: B   DIF: Easy   REF: 555   OBJ: 17.4

66. One concern over attempting to stop the aging process by controlling the shortening of telomeres is that the process may increase the risk of
   a. blood-related disorders.
   b. respiratory failure.
   c. heart disease.
   d. cancer.

   ANS: D   DIF: Difficult   REF: 555   OBJ: 17.4

67. How do antioxidants appear to increase longevity?
   a. They repair damaged done by the division of telomeres.
   b. They greatly increase the quantity of telomeres in the body.
   c. They inhibit free radical activity in the body.
   d. They greatly increase the quantity of free radicals in the body.

   ANS: C   DIF: Moderate   REF: 555   OBJ: 17.4

68. When Charlene visits her doctor, she is told that one way to slow the aging process is by the consumption of antioxidants. As a knowledgeable individual, Charlene would realize that she needs to consume more
   a. red meat.
   b. vitamin E.
   c. iron supplements.
   d. calcium.

   ANS: B   DIF: Moderate   REF: 555   OBJ: 17.4

69. Which is the best advice concerning the connection between vitamin E and longevity?
   a. Avoid vitamin E at all costs
   b. One dose a month is ideal
   c. Moderate doses seem ideal
   d. The more the better

   ANS: C   DIF: Moderate   REF: 555   OBJ: 17.4

70. Which technique has been shown to be most successful at extending life in laboratory animals?
   a. Severe calorie restriction
   b. Manipulation of a gene on the 21st chromosome
   c. Hormone replacement therapy
   d. Injections of free radicals

   ANS: A   DIF: Moderate   REF: 555   OBJ: 17.4

71. Which dietary suggestion has been shown to successfully and significantly extend the life of some animals?
   a. A diet high in free radicals
   b. An antioxidant-free diet
   c. Severe caloric restriction
   d. Ingesting large quantities of vitamins C and E

   ANS: C   DIF: Moderate   REF: 555   OBJ: 17.4
   KEY: WWW

72. In order to effectively alter the maximum lifespan in rats and primates, researchers have used dietary restrictions of about _____ below normal caloric intake.
   a. 5-10%
   b. 10-20%
   c. 20-30%
   d. 30-40%

   ANS: D   DIF: Moderate   REF: 555   OBJ: 17.4

73. Severely restricting one's diet appears to impact aging by doing all of the following except
   a. reducing the number of free radicals.
   b. altering gene activity.
   c. triggering hormones that slow the metabolism.
   d. eliminating telomeres from the ends of chromosomes.

   ANS: D   DIF: Moderate   REF: 555   OBJ: 17.4

74. How did the 1,800 calorie-a-day diet impact individuals in the Biosphere II?
   a. They showed permanent improvement in several physiological indicators.
   b. They showed improvement in several physiological indicators that disappeared when they resumed their normal diets.
   c. They showed permanent declines in several physiological indicators.
   d. They showed declines in several physiological indicators that disappeared when they resumed their normal diets.

   ANS: B   DIF: Moderate   REF: 555   OBJ: 17.4

75. The notion of "stages of dying" is best associated with
    a. Freud.
    b. Kübler-Ross.
    c. Hayflick.
    d. Parkes.

    ANS: B   DIF: Easy   REF: 557   OBJ: 17.5

76. Kübler-Ross suggested that upon initially being told that they are going to die, most people's response in one of
    a. denial.
    b. anger.
    c. bargaining.
    d. depression.

    ANS: A   DIF: Moderate   REF: 557   OBJ: 17.5

77. Denial is a defense mechanism in which
    a. anxiety-producing thoughts are forced into conscious awareness.
    b. anxiety-producing thoughts are isolated from conscious awareness.
    c. pleasurable thoughts are forced into conscious awareness.
    d. pleasurable thoughts are isolated from conscious awareness.

    ANS: B   DIF: Moderate   REF: 557   OBJ: 17.5

78. Despite the fact that Davis knows his friend Alice is dying of cancer, the next time they meet, Davis says, "Don't worry about it, we all know that you are going to be fine." According to Kübler-Ross, Davis's statement exemplifies the dying-related coping device of
    a. denial.
    b. anger.
    c. bargaining.
    d. depression.

    ANS: A   DIF: Moderate   REF: 557   OBJ: 17.5
    KEY: WWW

79. When the doctor tells him that he is dying of cancer, Harley refuses to believe the doctor and insists that the laboratory results must be inaccurate. Harley is likely in the _____ stage of dying.
    a. denial
    b. anger
    c. bargaining
    d. depression

    ANS: A   DIF: Moderate   REF: 557   OBJ: 17.5

80. In Kübler-Ross's original model, the reaction of denial and isolation is followed by the reaction of
    a. acceptance.
    b. anger.
    c. bargaining.
    d. depression.

    ANS: B   DIF: Easy   REF: 557   OBJ: 17.5

81. Frieda has been told she is going to die due to an inoperable brain tumor. Her children are young, and she cannot stand the thought of leaving them behind. All day long, she thinks over and over again, "I hate those doctors for not finding this sooner." Frieda appears to be in the _____ stage of dying.
    a. denial
    b. bargaining
    c. anger
    d. depression

    ANS: C   DIF: Moderate   REF: 557   OBJ: 17.5

821

82. Sylvia has terminal cancer. After years of very irregular church attendance, Sylvia begins to go to church every Sunday. She asks of God, "Please let me live to see my daughter graduate from college. I'll be a good Christian. I'll mend my ways. Just let me live..." This description indicates that Sylvia is in the _____ stage of dying.
    a. anger
    b. bargaining
    c. denial
    d. depression

    ANS: B   DIF: Moderate   REF: 557   OBJ: 17.5

83. A hope for less pain, more time, or provisions for children are most common during the _____ stage of dying.
    a. isolation
    b. denial
    c. bargaining
    d. acceptance

    ANS: C   DIF: Moderate   REF: 557   OBJ: 17.5

84. Kübler-Ross's depression stage of dying is characterized by a sense of
    a. anger.
    b. hopelessness.
    c. calm.
    d. exultation.

    ANS: B   DIF: Easy   REF: 557   OBJ: 17.5

85. In her original model, Kübler-Ross's last stage of dying involved
    a. anguish over unfinished business that must be left behind.
    b. depression and feelings of hopelessness.
    c. anger and resentment directed toward those who will go on living.
    d. peaceful acceptance of the inevitable.

    ANS: D   DIF: Moderate   REF: 557   OBJ: 17.5
    KEY: WWW

86. Kübler-Ross viewed the _____ stage of development as characterized by a feeling that, "the pain is gone," "the struggle is over," and "a time of rest before the journey."
    a. bargaining
    b. isolation
    c. acceptance
    d. depression

    ANS: C   DIF: Moderate   REF: 557   OBJ: 17.5

87. According to Kübler-Ross, a sense of _____ permeates through all five stages of the dying process.
    a. resentment
    b. uncertainty
    c. hope
    d. fear

    ANS: C   DIF: Moderate   REF: 557   OBJ: 17.5

88. With regard to Kübler-Ross's theory, subsequent research on death and dying has
    a. provided substantial support for her theory.
    b. found that anger is not a typical reaction to death.
    c. determined that the dying process does not unfold in the manner she suggested.
    d. found that her theory holds in the United States, but not in other cultures.

    ANS: C   DIF: Moderate   REF: 558   OBJ: 17.5

822

89. The major problem with the Kübler-Ross model of dying is that
   a. there are specific stages, but she had them in the incorrect order.
   b. the dying process is simply not stage-like.
   c. there appears to be several stages in the process she has missed.
   d. the emotional responses she describes largely don't occur.

   ANS: B   DIF: Moderate   REF: 558   OBJ: 17.5

90. Shneidman's work in the area of death and dying suggests that
   a. it is more normal to remain depressed than to reach acceptance toward the end of the dying process.
   b. there is a distinct sequence of stages that people pass through with regard to the acceptance of death.
   c. dying people experience myriad emotional responses, with many unpredictable ups and downs.
   d. the cause of death has little impact on one's reaction to the dying process.

   ANS: C   DIF: Moderate   REF: 558   OBJ: 17.5

91. All of the following are valid criticisms of Kübler-Ross's theory of dying, except
   a. there is no standard order to the stages of dying.
   b. it does not describe any of the emotions experienced by people facing death.
   c. it does not really take the course of the illness into account.
   d. it does not account for how individual differences in personality affect reactions to death.

   ANS: B   DIF: Moderate   REF: 558   OBJ: 17.5
   KEY: WWW

92. _____ is defined as a state of loss.
   a. Grief   c. Mourning
   b. Bereavement   d. Internment

   ANS: B   DIF: Difficult   REF: 558   OBJ: 17.6

93. Grief is best defined as
   a. the emotional response to loss.
   b. culturally accepted ways of displaying one's reactions to loss.
   c. a decision concerning how to deal with the corpse.
   d. a status of being without.

   ANS: A   DIF: Moderate   REF: 558   OBJ: 17.6

94. _____ is defined as a "culturally prescribed way of reacting to death."
   a. Bereavement   c. Anticipatory grief
   b. Grieving   d. Mourning

   ANS: D   DIF: Easy   REF: 558   OBJ: 17.6
   KEY: WWW

95. Nine-year-old Sarah died from cancer. Her teacher and her classmates made black armbands to wear for a month following her death. Due to the fact that in Sarah's culture the wearing of black is common following a death, wearing the armbands best illustrates the concept of
   a. bargaining.
   b. depression.
   c. grief.
   d. mourning.

   ANS: D   DIF: Difficult   REF: 558   OBJ: 17.6

96. Anticipatory grief involves grieving
   a. without the expression of emotions.
   b. that violates cultural standards.
   c. before death occurs.
   d. in stages.

   ANS: C   DIF: Easy   REF: 558   OBJ: 17.6

97. Clint has just found out that his friend Eastwood is terminally ill. This has made him feel sad and lonely at the thought of living life without his pal. Clint's feelings best represent the concept of
   a. bargaining.
   b. anticipatory grief.
   c. denial and isolation.
   d. maturational grief.

   ANS: B   DIF: Moderate   REF: 558   OBJ: 17.6

98. The Parkes/Bowlby model of bereavement suggests that
   a. a grieving adult is much like an infant who is experiencing separation anxiety.
   b. there is a series of clear-cut stages one passes through in mourning one's loss.
   c. grief that lasts much longer than six months is maladaptive.
   d. longing to have the loved one return becomes most intense about one year following death.

   ANS: A   DIF: Moderate   REF: 558   OBJ: 17.6

99. Lawrence just found out that his best friend was killed in a car accident. Lawrence's emotional state would best be described as one of shock, and he feels like his emotions will burst out of him at any moment. Parkes/Bowlby would most likely describe his grief state in terms of
   a. reorganization.
   b. numbness.
   c. yearning.
   d. disorganization/despair.

   ANS: B   DIF: Moderate   REF: 558-559   OBJ: 17.6

100. The sense of separation anxiety described in the Parkes/Bowlby attachment model of bereavement is most closely associated with the _____ reaction.
   a. reorganization
   b. numbness
   c. yearning
   d. disorganization/despair

   ANS: C   DIF: Difficult   REF: 559   OBJ: 17.6

101. After her husband dies, Hannah finds herself unable to sleep and very preoccupied with thoughts of her husband and the events surrounding his death. Hannah is best described as experiencing what Parkes/Bowlby referred to as
   a. yearning.
   b. numbness.
   c. reorganization.
   d. disorganization and despair.

   ANS: A   DIF: Moderate   REF: 559   OBJ: 17.6
   KEY: WWW

102. According to the Parkes/Bowlby model of bereavement, the feelings of apathy and defeat felt in response to knowing that you will never be reunited with the deceased are most likely to initially occur during the _____ stage of bereavement.
   a. yearning
   b. numbness
   c. reorganization
   d. disorganization and despair

   ANS: D   DIF: Moderate   REF: 559   OBJ: 17.6

103. Allen's wife died almost one year ago. For a long period, he experienced overwhelming emotional turmoil. In the past few weeks, however, he seems to have pulled himself together and started to make the transition into being a widower. According to the Parkes/Bowlby model, Allen is best classified as now being in a state of
   a. yearning.
   b. numbness.
   c. reorganization.
   d. disorganization and despair.

   ANS: C   DIF: Moderate   REF: 559   OBJ: 17.6

104. Research on the Parkes/Bowlby model demonstrated that _____ was the strongest reaction 24-month after the time of loss.
   a. depression
   b. disbelief
   c. anger
   d. acceptance

   ANS: D   DIF: Difficult   REF: 559   OBJ: 17.6

105. According to the dual-process model, the bereaved
   a. is typically both happy and sad.
   b. oscillates between coping and taking a break from coping.
   c. experiences physical stress but not emotional stress.
   d. can be in a state of acceptance and denial at the same time.

   ANS: B   DIF: Moderate   REF: 560   OBJ: 17.6

106. While dealing with his wife's death, Chuck says, "I will deal with the financial issues this week, probably cry next week, and then tackle the issues of dealing with her parents the following week." This statement provides a great example of the _____ model of coping.
   a. complicated
   b. assisted
   c. dual-process
   d. engagement

   ANS: C   DIF: Moderate   REF: 560   OBJ: 17.6

107. Which best exemplifies loss-oriented coping?
   a. Needing to reconcile oneself with the loss following the death of a spouse
   b. Starting to date following the death of a spouse
   c. Taking over the checking account following the death of a spouse
   d. Learning to cook following the death of a spouse

   ANS: A   DIF: Difficult   REF: 560   OBJ: 17.6

108. After her husband died, Talat focused a great deal of her attention on learning how to take care of the garden, a task formerly performed by her deceased husband. Her actions represent _____ coping.
   a. anticipatory   c. complicated
   b. restoration-oriented   d. loss-oriented

   ANS: B   DIF: Difficult   REF: 560   OBJ: 17.6

109. When dealing with a bereaved individual who is depressed or irritable, the typical pattern of response is that, early we
   a. sympathize, and later we grow weary.
   b. sympathize, and later we continue with sympathy.
   c. are unsympathetic, and later we grow weary.
   d. are unsympathetic, and later we sympathize.

   ANS: A   DIF: Moderate   REF: 560   OBJ: 17.6

110. What can we conclude regarding an infant's experience of death?
   a. Infants who have developed an understanding of here vs. all gone may show some of the same reactions that adults do in response to loss of an attachment figure.
   b. Most infants understand that death means that life processes stop, but they believe that it can be undone or reversed.
   c. Infants are biologically programmed to show grief responses to the loss of a caretaker, regardless of the age of the infant.
   d. Infants who show separation protest and depression-like symptoms have clearly demonstrated that they have an accurate cognitive understanding of death.

   ANS: A   DIF: Moderate   REF: 560-561   OBJ: 17.7

111. Bowlby suggested that the order of infant bereavement is
   a. protest to despair to detachment.   c. despair to protest to detachment.
   b. protest to detachment to despair.   d. despair to detachment to protest.

   ANS: A   DIF: Difficult   REF: 561   OBJ: 17.7

112. Three months after her mother died, 13-month-old Jessica, who initially searched everywhere for her mom and then appeared very sad, has now taken a renewed interest in playing with her toys and interaction with new people. Bowlby would suggest that Jessica is in the _____ phase of bereavement.
   a. protest   c. despair
   b. detachment   d. complicated

   ANS: B   DIF: Difficult   REF: 561   OBJ: 17.7

113. When the family dog dies at home, Timmy does not understand how this could happen. He doesn't see any marks on the dog, and without any physical signs, Cory doesn't believe the dog could actually be dead. This suggests that Cory does not understand the _____ of death.
    a. finality
    b. irreversibility
    c. universality
    d. biological causality

    ANS: D   DIF: Difficult   REF: 561   OBJ: 17.8

114. Amber was not that upset at her grandfather's funeral because, as she puts it, "It's okay. We can see him when he gets better tomorrow." Amber's statement indicates that she lacks an understanding of both the _____ aspects of death.
    a. finality and irreversibility
    b. irreversibility and universality
    c. universality and biological causality
    d. biological causality and finality

    ANS: A   DIF: Moderate   REF: 561   OBJ: 17.8
    KEY: WWW

115. Whose statement indicates that they understand the universality of death?
    a. James, who says, "My grandpa died and never came back."
    b. West, who says, "You can die from cancer that is inside of you."
    c. Artie, who says, "Everything that lives dies."
    d. Gorden, who says, "Machines cannot die."

    ANS: C   DIF: Moderate   REF: 561   OBJ: 17.8

116. Which statement represents an understanding of the most cognitively challenging aspect of death?
    a. "You cannot come back from the dead."
    b. "Once dead, always dead."
    c. "Everyone eventually dies."
    d. "You can die because of something inside of you that you cannot see."

    ANS: D   DIF: Difficult   REF: 561-562   OBJ: 17.8

117. The only thing that Gabe understands about death is that if it stops moving and thinking it's dead. This indicates an understanding of
    a. finality.
    b. irreversibility.
    c. universality.
    d. biological causality.

    ANS: A   DIF: Moderate   REF: 561   OBJ: 17.8

118. The phrase "once dead, always dead" best matches the death concept of
    a. finality.
    b. irreversibility.
    c. continuing bonds.
    d. biological causality.

    ANS: B   DIF: Easy   REF: 561   OBJ: 17.8

119. As a typical 7-year-old, Masterson has likely understands the basics of every death concept except
    a. finality.
    b. irreversibility.
    c. continuing bonds.
    d. biological causality.

    ANS: D   DIF: Moderate   REF: 561-562   OBJ: 17.8

827

120. Telling a young child that death is like "going to sleep" is
    a. a good way to protect him or her from the brutality of death.
    b. a good way to help him or her understand that death happens to everyone.
    c. likely to contribute to his or her misconception that death is a temporary state.
    d. likely to lead to a more mature conception of why people die.

    ANS: C   DIF: Moderate   REF: 563   OBJ: 17.8

121. Research on young children with terminal illnesses shows that they
    a. usually know that they are going to die.
    b. should not be told the details about their illness or that they are going to die.
    c. do not have any idea that their illness will result in death.
    d. continue to focus on what will happen to them as adults.

    ANS: A   DIF: Moderate   REF: 563   OBJ: 17.9
    KEY: WWW

122. Preschool-aged children who are dying are most likely to
    a. stop engaging in normal activities with their peers.
    b. behaviorally act out their frustrations regarding the illness through violent pretend play.
    c. talk a great deal about their feelings regarding death.
    d. give away their belongings.

    ANS: B   DIF: Moderate   REF: 563   OBJ: 17.9

123. Which of the following is NOT a common reaction of young children who experience the death of a parent?
    a. Asking lots of questions
    b. Striking out at the surviving parent
    c. Denying the loss
    d. Exhibiting more emotional than behavioral reactions

    ANS: D   DIF: Moderate   REF: 563-564   OBJ: 17.9

124. Twelve-year-old Harry and his four-year-old brother Potter recently experienced the death of their mother. How are their reactions to this loss most likely to differ?
    a. Potter is less likely to throw temper tantrums.
    b. Potter is less likely to manifest toileting difficulties.
    c. Harry is more likely to show disturbances in his eating behavior.
    d. Harry is more likely to be able to find comfort by imaging his deceased parents.

    ANS: D   DIF: Difficult   REF: 564   OBJ: 17.9

828

125. Which of the following is true regarding the difference between young children's and adolescent's understanding of death?
    a. Adolescents are more likely than younger children to think about the possibility of an afterlife.
    b. Adolescents are less likely than younger children to think about the abstract meaning of death.
    c. Adolescents are less likely than younger children to say that death was the result of cessation of biological processes.
    d. Adolescents are more likely than younger children to view death as just a biological ending of life.

    ANS: A   DIF: Moderate   REF: 564   OBJ: 17.10

126. Adolescents who are dying are likely to be concerned with their appearance (e.g., loss of weight, loss of hair). This is most likely because
    a. they are in denial about their illness and are trying to focus on other things.
    b. they have a strong desire to continue to be dependent on parents and peers.
    c. concern over appearance is a common theme among adolescents.
    d. they are probably unaware that they are dying.

    ANS: C   DIF: Moderate   REF: 564   OBJ: 17.10

127. Although their grief process is similar to that of adults, adolescents are
    a. more likely to be concerned that their reaction is abnormal.
    b. less likely to express their grief in terms of ailments.
    c. more likely to show almost no reaction to the death of a close friend.
    d. less likely to bottle up their feelings.

    ANS: A   DIF: Moderate   REF: 565   OBJ: 17.10

128. Research on widowers and widows has indicated that a common cognitive grief reaction is
    a. overindulgence in alcohol.   c. impaired memory.
    b. loss of appetite.   d. sleep disturbances.

    ANS: C   DIF: Easy   REF: 566   OBJ: 17.11

129. Research on adults who have lost a spouse tend to show _____ disruptions in cognitive, emotional, physical, and interpersonal functioning.
    a. no   c. modest
    b. insignificant   d. overwhelming

    ANS: C   DIF: Moderate   REF: 566   OBJ: 17.11

130. Following the death of her husband, Lionel, Latisha shows a consistent pattern of low levels of distress. Latisha's reactions best fit the _____ pattern of widowhood.
    a. common   c. resilient
    b. chronic   d. depressed

    ANS: C   DIF: Moderate   REF: 566   OBJ: 17.11

131. According to a model of widow/widower reactions developed by Bonanno and colleagues, _____ grief is characterized by heightened grief that continues to linger following the death of a spouse.
   a. common
   b. chronic
   c. resilient
   d. improved

   ANS: B   DIF: Difficult   REF: 566   OBJ: 17.11
   KEY: WWW

132. A _____ pattern of grief is characterized by heightened and then diminishing distress after the loss.
   a. common
   b. chronic
   c. resilient
   d. depressed-improved

   ANS: A   DIF: Difficult   REF: 566   OBJ: 17.11

133. The best predictor for depression four years after the death of a spouse is having
   a. cohabitated prior to the death of the spouse.
   b. the spouse have died from a long, chronic ailment.
   c. been depressed prior to the death of the spouse .
   d. failed to actively engage in grief work.

   ANS: C   DIF: Early   REF: 566   OBJ: 17.11

134. _____ grief is not fully recognized by others and is generally harder to cope with than other forms of grief.
   a. Anticipatory
   b. Disenfranchised
   c. Chronic
   d. Finality

   ANS: B   DIF: Moderate   REF: 567   OBJ: 17.11

135. In the United States, who would be least likely to experience disenfranchised grief?
   a. A female whose ex-husband just died
   b. A gay male whose partner just died
   c. A teenager male whose girlfriend was killer by a drunk driver
   d. A women who just miscarried her fetus

   ANS: C   DIF: Difficult   REF: 567   OBJ: 17.11

136. Which best describes complicated grief?
   a. Grieving for multiple deaths at the same time
   b. An unusually prolonged or intense pattern of grief
   c. Grieving for someone you did not particularly care for
   d. Death of a partner from AIDS when you were the individual who infected him or her

   ANS: B   DIF: Moderate   REF: 567   OBJ: 17.11

137. Despite the fact that her son died 10 years ago, Helena has such an intense yearning to have him back alive that she is unable to keep a job. This description indicates that Helena is best classified as experiencing _____ grief.
   a. complicated
   b. disenfranchised
   c. palliative
   d. anticipatory

   ANS: A   DIF: Moderate   REF: 567   OBJ: 17.11

138. Which of the following is true regarding the loss of a child?
   a. Parents tend to become overly concerned about the surviving siblings and tend to offer them too much support.
   b. The younger the child is at the time of death, the more difficult it is for parents to cope with the loss.
   c. The inability to make sense of the loss increases the intensity of the grief.
   d. Marital strain following the loss is higher in couples who had a good relationship prior to the death versus those who had shaky marriages prior to the death.

   ANS: C   DIF: Moderate   REF: 567-568   OBJ: 17.11

139. Why is death of a grandchild considered a "double whammy" for grandparents?
   a. They feel guilt about the loss of a grandchild and helpless to protect their adult child from pain.
   b. They tend to bear the major financial responsibility for the burial and for assisting their adult children with their bills.
   c. The death of the grandchild and age of their adult children remind them of the short time they have left on earth.
   d. It represents both a social and personal loss.

   ANS: A   DIF: Moderate   REF: 568   OBJ: 17.11

140. Research suggests that for an adult, the loss of a parent is
   a. more difficult to deal with for women than for men.
   b. upsetting, but in some ways expected and therefore tends to be easier to deal with than the death of a child or of a spouse.
   c. typically the most difficult type of loss with which to cope.
   d. characterized by anger but not guilt.

   ANS: B   DIF: Moderate   REF: 568   OBJ: 17.11

141. According to the grief-work perspective, in order to cope with death a bereaved individual must
   a. move toward a detachment from the deceased.
   b. avoid directly confronting loss.
   c. take some responsibility for the death of the loved one.
   d. avoid experiencing painful emotions.

   ANS: A   DIF: Moderate   REF: 568   OBJ: 17.12
   KEY: WWW

142. The grief-work perspective grew out of _____ theory.
    a. cognitive-behavioral
    b. classical conditioning
    c. psychoanalytic
    d. social-learning

    ANS: C   DIF: Moderate   REF: 568   OBJ: 17.12

143. An individual taking a strong _____ perspective would be most likely to suggest that in order to cope with the death of a husband, a wife must confront their loss and detach from her husband.
    a. grief-work
    b. disenfranchised grief
    c. anticipatory grief
    d. damage theory

    ANS: A   DIF: Moderate   REF: 568   OBJ: 17.12

144. Javier's wife died five years ago. He still daily sets a place at the table for his wife, and breaks into tears when he must sit down, once again, without his wife beside him at the table. According to the grief work perspective, Javier's grief reaction is best termed _____ grief.
    a. normal
    b. chronic
    c. distorted
    d. inhibition

    ANS: B   DIF: Difficult   REF: 568   OBJ: 17.12

145. What research support has been generated concerning the grief-work perspective?
    a. A great deal of support that grief is very similar across cultures.
    b. A great deal of support for the assumption that bereaved individuals must confront their loss and experience painful emotions in order to cope successfully with the loss.
    c. A great deal of support for the fact that grief tends to be delayed.
    d. Support for the hypothesis that too much ruminating may backfire and actually prolong psychological distress rather than to relieve it.

    ANS: D   DIF: Moderate   REF: 569   OBJ: 17.12

146. Which is the best example of a continuing bond?
    a. An inheritance
    b. A bond a child has with the remaining parent after the death of the other parent
    c. A reminisce of the deceased
    d. A bond parents share with each other after the death of a child

    ANS: C   DIF: Moderate   REF: 569   OBJ: 17.12

147. Even though Carly's husband Freddie died four years ago, she continues to feel his presence and works hard at her job to "make him proud." Carly's behavior best exemplifies the concept of
    a. disenfranchised grief.
    b. palliative care.
    c. anticipatory grief.
    d. continuing bonds.

    ANS: D   DIF: Moderate   REF: 569   OBJ: 17.12

148. Research has shown that continuing bonds are most helpful when they
   a. are between a mother and a child.
   b. are internal memories of the deceased that provide a base for becoming independent.
   c. contain illusions reflecting a continuing effort to reunite with the deceased.
   d. occur in Western cultures like the United States and not in Eastern cultures like China.

   ANS: B   DIF: Difficult   REF: 569   OBJ: 17.12

149. Which attachment style is associated with coping well with the death of a loved one?
   a. Avoidant   c. Resistant
   b. Secure   d. Disorganized

   ANS: B   DIF: Easy   REF: 570   OBJ: 17.12

150. People who have the most difficult time coping with the death of a loved one have
   a. high self-esteem and are highly optimistic.
   b. low self-esteem and are highly optimistic.
   c. high self-esteem and are highly neurotic.
   d. low self-esteem and are highly neurotic.

   ANS: D   DIF: Moderate   REF: 570   OBJ: 17.12

151. Grieving would likely be greatest if the deceased was
   a. very close and the death was seen as "senseless."
   b. very close and the death was expected (as in a terminal illness).
   c. not very close and the death was seen as "senseless."
   d. not very close and the death was expected (as in a terminal illness).

   ANS: A   DIF: Easy   REF: 570   OBJ: 17.12

152. How many of the following (good parenting by the living parent, strong support from siblings, having people willing to talk to about feelings) would positively influence the response of a child to the death of a parent?
   a. 0   c. 2
   b. 1   d. 3

   ANS: D   DIF: Easy   REF: 570   OBJ: 17.12

153. The basic philosophy of a hospice is best summarized as one of
   a. "active euthanasia."   c. "caring."
   b. "curing."   d. "institutionalization of death."

   ANS: C   DIF: Moderate   REF: 571   OBJ: 17.13

154. Palliative care is best summarized as involving
   a. direct attempts to cure disease.
   b. meeting the physical, psychological, and social needs of someone with an incurable illness.
   c. hospitals but not hospices.
   d. recognizing that the dying and their family members are experts (i.e., they know what they want and need).

   ANS: B   DIF: Moderate   REF: 572   OBJ: 17.13

155. A major difference between hospice care and hospital care for dying individuals is that
   a. pain control is emphasized more in the hospital setting.
   b. prolonging life is emphasized more in the hospice care setting.
   c. the presence of family members is more strongly encouraged in the hospital setting.
   d. a more homelike setting of care is emphasized in the hospice care setting.

   ANS: D   DIF: Moderate   REF: 572   OBJ: 17.13

156. Research has shown that when compared to those in conventional hospital care, dying individuals in hospices tend to
   a. have far fewer visitors.
   b. spend more time in pain.
   c. undergo fewer medical interventions..
   d. receive less medical care aimed at their emotional needs.

   ANS: C   DIF: Easy   REF: 572   OBJ: 17.13

157. Which statement concerning bereavement programs is true?
   a. Most bereaved individuals need psychological interventions to help them cope.
   b. A past history of depression does not increase the risk of depression in a bereaved individual.
   c. Family therapy can help bereaved parents and children communicate more openly.
   d. Support groups are effective for those dealing with the death of a spouse, but ineffective for those dealing with the death of a child.

   ANS: C   DIF: Easy   REF: 572-573   OBJ: 17.13

158. Which is a key theme of the modern lifespan perspective on development?
   a. Development is solely continuous across the lifespan.
   b. Development proceeds in multiple directions.
   c. Humans become less diverse as they age.
   d. We are passive in our own development.

   ANS: B   DIF: Easy   REF: 573-574   OBJ: 17.14

TRUE/FALSE

1. One aspect of the definition for total brain death is total unresponsiveness to stimuli.

   ANS: T   DIF: Moderate   REF: 548   OBJ: 17.1

834

2. Passive euthanasia results in instantaneous death.

    ANS: F   DIF: Moderate   REF: 549   OBJ: 17.1

3. In the United States, the leading cause of death among children age 1-4 years involves unintentional injuries.

    ANS: T   DIF: Moderate   REF: 552   OBJ: 17.2

4. In the United States, cancer is the leading cause of death of adults over age 65.

    ANS: F   DIF: Moderate   REF: 552   OBJ: 17.2
    KEY: WWW

5. Programmed theories of aging stress the impact of systematic genetic processes.

    ANS: T   DIF: Moderate   REF: 553   OBJ: 17.3
    KEY: WWW

6. Damage theories of aging stress the impact of haphazard errors in cells.

    ANS: T   DIF: Moderate   REF: 554   OBJ: 17.3

7. Telomeres typically do not replicate.

    ANS: T   DIF: Moderate   REF: 554   OBJ: 17.3

8. Antioxidants increase the number of free radicals in the body.

    ANS: F   DIF: Moderate   REF: 554   OBJ: 17.3

9. Severe caloric restriction is one of the most successful life-extension techniques in primates.

    ANS: T   DIF: Moderate   REF: 555   OBJ: 17.4

10. Kübler-Ross's denial stage of dying is characterized by severe depression.

    ANS: F   DIF: Moderate   REF: 557   OBJ: 17.5
    KEY: WWW

11. The cultural prescribed way of responding to death is called mourning.

    ANS: T   DIF: Moderate   REF: 558   OBJ: 17.6

12. Parkes and Bowlby claimed that yearning while bereaved is a sign of separation anxiety.

    ANS: T   DIF: Moderate   REF: 559   OBJ: 17.6

13. Children tend to understand the death concept of biological causality long before they understand the concept of finality.

    ANS: F   DIF: Difficult   REF: 561-562   OBJ: 17.8

14. Parents who use the analogy of "sleep" when describing death to children tend to have children with advanced understanding of death and death topics.

ANS: F   DIF: Moderate   REF: 563   OBJ: 17.8

15. The most common adjustment reaction to death of a spouse involves a resilient pattern.

ANS: T   DIF: Difficult   REF: 566   OBJ: 17.11

16. The death of a young child has been found to be much more difficult for parents to bear than the death of an adult child.

ANS: F   DIF: Moderate   REF: 567-568   OBJ: 17.11
KEY: WWW

17. Recent research has generated little support for the grief-work perspective.

ANS: T   DIF: Moderate   REF: 568-570   OBJ: 17.12

18. Hospice programs emphasize the importance of death care taking place in a hospital setting.

ANS: F   DIF: Easy   REF: 571-572   OBJ: 17.13
KEY: WWW

COMPLETION

1. The Harvard group defined biological death as involving _____ brain death.

ANS: total

DIF: Moderate   REF: 548   OBJ: 17.1

2. A legal document that specifically outlines the types of medical procedures that can be applied if a person becomes terminally ill is called a _____ will.

ANS: living

DIF: Moderate   REF: 549-550   OBJ: 17.1

3. _____ theories of aging emphasize systematic genetic control of aging.

ANS: Programmed

DIF: Moderate   REF: 553   OBJ: 17.3   KEY: WWW

4. _____ theories of aging emphasize haphazard cellular processes that result in errors and contribute to aging.

ANS: Damage

DIF: Moderate   REF: 553   OBJ: 17.3

5. _____ lifespan is the ceiling number of years a member of a species can live.

   ANS: Maximum

   DIF: Moderate   REF: 553   OBJ: 17.3   KEY: WWW

6. _____ is a genetic disorder that results in extremely rapid aging of the body.

   ANS: Progeria

   DIF: Moderate   REF: 553   OBJ: 17.3

7. The fact that a human cell can only divide about 50 times (plus or minus 10) is referred to as the _____ limit.

   ANS: Hayflick

   DIF: Moderate   REF: 554   OBJ: 17.3

8. The DNA section at the tip of a chromosome that does not replicate is called the _____.

   ANS: telomere

   DIF: Moderate   REF: 554   OBJ: 17.3

9. Toxic byproducts of the metabolism of oxidation of a cell are called _____ radicals.

   ANS: free

   DIF: Moderate   REF: 554   OBJ: 17.3

10. Kübler-Ross's first stage of dying of dying was called _____ and isolation.

    ANS: denial

    DIF: Moderate   REF: 557   OBJ: 17.5

11. Kübler-Ross's original final stage of dying was _____.

    ANS: acceptance

    DIF: Moderate   REF: 557   OBJ: 17.5   KEY: WWW

12. _____ is defined as the emotional reaction to death.

    ANS: Grief

    DIF: Moderate   REF: 558   OBJ: 17.6

13. _____ grief occurs before a terminally ill individual dies.

   ANS: Anticipatory

   DIF: Moderate   REF: 558   OBJ: 17.6   KEY: WWW

14. According to the Parkes/Bowlby model, the initial reaction to bereavement is that of _____.

   ANS: numbness

   DIF: Difficult   REF: 558-559   OBJ: 17.6

15. According to the _____ -process model, bereaved individual oscillates between coping with the emotional blow of a loss and coping with practical challenges of living.

   ANS: dual

   DIF: Moderate   REF: 560   OBJ: 17.6

16. The term _____ is used to discuss the fact that death is inevitable and happens to all living beings.

   ANS: universality

   DIF: Difficult   REF: 561   OBJ: 17.8

17. _____ grief occurs when the relationship between the deceased and bereaved is not fully recognized or appreciated by others (e.g., death of an ex-wife).

   ANS: Disenfranchised

   DIF: Difficult   REF: 567   OBJ: 17.11

18. According to the _____ perspective, the only adaptive way to cope with death is to detach from the deceased.

   ANS: grief work

   DIF: Moderate   REF: 568-569   OBJ: 17.12

19. Bowlby suggested that bereaved individuals often maintain attachments to the deceased indefinitely through _____ bonds.

   ANS: continuing

   DIF: Difficult   REF: 569   OBJ: 17.12

20. _____ programs, which are part of the palliative care movement, emphasize "caring" over "curing" when dealing with dying individuals.

ANS: Hospice

DIF: Easy   REF: 571-572   OBJ: 17.13   KEY: WWW

ESSAY

1. How do programmed theories of aging differ from damage theories of aging? Be sure to use specific examples to illustrate the difference.

ANS: Answer not provided   REF: 553-555   OBJ: 17.3

2. What are Kübler-Ross's stages of dying? How has research supported this model?

ANS: Answer not provided   REF: 557-558   OBJ: 17.5   KEY: WWW

3. How does the understanding of death change between infancy and adolescence?

ANS: Answer not provided   REF: 560-561 & 561-563 & 564-565
OBJ: 17.7 & 17.8 & 17.10

4. Tony is a terminally ill child. Tina is a child whose mother has just died. Describe the processes that each is going through.

ANS: Answer not provided   REF: 563-564   OBJ: 17.9

5. In general, which is harder to deal with, the death of a parent, spouse, or child? What determines how difficult a particular death will be for someone to cope with?

ANS: Answer not provided   REF: 565-568   OBJ: 17.11

6. What is the grief work perspective? In what ways has it come under serious attack by numerous researchers?

ANS: Answer not provided   REF: 568-571   OBJ: 17.12

7. In your job as a counselor, you must meet with a family in the hospital as they are confronted with the news that their son has been in a terrible car accident. He is on life support and not expected to live. They are interested in the hospice option but are really unfamiliar with how it works and whether there is any benefit to the terminally ill individual or the family. Please enlighten them.

ANS: Answer not provided   REF: 571-573   OBJ: 17.13

8. What is the biological definition of death? What are the social meanings of death?

ANS: Answer not provided   REF: 548-549 & 550-551
OBJ: 17.1   KEY: WWW

9. Compare and contrast passive euthanasia, active euthanasia, and assisted suicide.

ANS: Answer not provided   REF: 549-550   OBJ: 17.1   KEY: WWW

10. How do the Parkes/Bowlby and dual-process models describe the process of bereavement?

ANS: Answer not provided   REF: 558-560   OBJ: 17.6   KEY: WWW